Month-By-Month

GARDENING
IN THE
MID-ATLANTIC

Delaware • Maryland • Virginia • Washington, D.C.

Viette, André.
  Month-by-month gardening in the Mid-Atlantic / André and Mark Viette with Jacqueline Hériteau.
    p. cm.
  Includes bibliographical references and index.
  ISBN 1-59186-048-2
  1. Gardening--Middle Atlantic States. I. Viette, Mark. II. Hériteau, Jacqueline. III. title.

SB453.2.M527V54 2004
635'.0974--dc22   2004004081

Published by Cool Springs Press, a Division of Thomas Nelson, Inc.,
P.O. Box 141000, Nashville, Tennessee 37214

First printing 2004

Printed in the United States of America
10 9 8 7 6 5 4 3 2 1

Managing Editor: Cindy Kershner
Designer: James Duncan Creative
Horticulture Editor: Troy Marden
Illustrator: Bill Kersey, Kersey Graphics
Production Artist: S.E. Anderson

On the cover: Clematis, photo by André Viette

Visit the Thomas Nelson website at www.ThomasNelson.com

Month-By-Month

GARDENING IN THE MID-ATLANTIC

Delaware • Maryland • Virginia • Washington, D.C.

ANDRÉ & MARK VIETTE
WITH JACQUELINE HÉRITEAU

COOL SPRINGS PRESS
A Division of Thomas Nelson Publishers
Since 1798

www.thomasnelson.com

Dedication

I dedicate this book to my mother and father, Jessie and Martin Viette, who instilled in me strong family values, a good work ethic, and a deep love of plants.

Acknowledgements

I want to thank the many people who have touched my life and made me a better person. Especially my wife, Claire, who has been by my side throughout my career and has given me such wonderful children—Mark, Scott, Holly, and Heather. And my son Mark, who works with me daily in the nursery, shares teaching duties with me at Blue Ridge Community College, and has been such an important part of the "In The Garden" radio programs. It has been a wonderful partnership. And my father, a great plantsman, who passed on to me his keen knowledge of plants and their culture. I also wish to thank the many fine professors at Cornell University who helped mold my scientific mind. Rachel Carson changed my approach to the way we use our planet when I met her when I was just 24 years old. And I wish to recognize all my fellow members, past and present, of the New York Hortus Club, members who through the years have represented the finest in horticulture from New York City, New York, Connecticut, and New Jersey. And finally, my very good friend and fellow author, Jacqueline Hériteau. Jacqui is a knowledgeable gardener and author of many distinguished books in the field of gardening. She is fabulous to work with and has the organization and work ethic to get things done.

André Viette
Fishersville, Virginia
February 20, 2004

Contents

Contents

Introduction

The Benefits of a Month-By-Month Gardening Schedule

If you had all the time in the world and were willing to use it to remember and record every move you and nature made in the garden all year long, it would look a lot like this book. The chapters that follow cover the eleven major categories of garden plants, starting with Annuals and ending with Water Gardening—everybody's new love.

When we do what we do in our gardens during the year dictated the month-by-month prompts each chapter offers you. This is our collective garden log, a way of hanging out over the back fence to answer your questions as they come up throughout the year. It's the next best thing to having a decades-old garden log of your own.

The month-by-month prompts are easy to work with because they always are presented under the same "do this now" headings: **Planning, Planting, Care, Pruning, Watering, Fertilizing,** and **Pests.**

In Chapter 2, Bulbs, Corms, Rhizomes, and Tubers, for example, the June pages include prompts for the Care of summer-flowering bulbs and Planning

for the all-important fall planting season. Planning in the June pages for Trees offers information about trees in containers, and, under Care, you're reminded to check the mulch around your newly planted trees.

The color tints you'll notice as you browse the book are there to set key information apart from basic how-to and do-this-now prompts. Flag information you want to come back to with a sticky note.

GARDEN DESIGN AND HEALTH

Answers to questions about where a plant will do the most for your garden depend on its season of bloom, height, color, and its preferences for light, soil, pH, and water. Our suggestions for the role of each category of plant in garden design appear in the introduction and in the Planning sections and sidebars in each plant chapter.

The most basic questions about plant culture are answered in broad, general terms on the following pages—**Climate, Light, Soil Preparation and**

Improvement, Planting, Watering, Staking, Mulches, and Fertilizing. You will find information specific to each category of plant in the introductions to each of the eleven plant chapters.

Keep a garden log. As you go through the month-by-month entries in this book, use them to begin a garden log that is your own.

Your monthly observations can be a tremendous asset when it comes to garden design. We forget so quickly the color and plant combinations we admired at flower shows and in public gardens. By the time we start studying the new garden catalogs, past seasons have a way of blurring at the edges. We forget the expected wonders the plants create season by season. The charm of fluffy *Clematis tangutica* seedheads entangled with gilded **fennel** flower heads is a lovely memory—and useful information—saved in a garden log.

A record of the microclimates in your garden teaches useful lessons you can use year after year. Your written record of when you divide a perennial is a better guide than memory when slower

Introduction

Did You Know?

About Plant Names

Botanical plant names—which are in Latin, the language of science when the first herbals were written—tell you a lot about a plant.

A plant tag that reads *Picea abies* forma *pendula* is saying this is a **Weeping Norway Spruce:** *Picea,* **spruce**, the genus, or overall group; *abies* a species or category of spruce that came from Norway; *pendula* says this variety is pendulous, or weeping. Names between single quotes, like *Spiraea japonica* 'Anthony Waterer' **(pink spiraea)** indicate the plant is a named, or cultivated, variety, a "cultivar."

Don't get too hung up on cultivar names; new names turn up every season. 'Gold Flame' is the cultivar name for a **pink spiraea** whose foliage is a fiery gold in spring and turns red, copper, and orange in the fall. If your local gardening center doesn't have it, ask for a golden-leaved **pink spiraea,** and your garden supplier should be able to tell you some choices.

flower production is suggesting it may be time to divide again.

A reliable record of where you placed plants and their names answers questions that come up the next year and years later. On the simplest level, you know where to look for the name of a species, or a variety that a friend is eager to try, or one you never want to plant again.

Last year's log, well kept, can also tell you where to look for the **tulips** you planted 10 to 12 inches deep to outwit the moles and voles. If they don't come up, you know it's the wrong species to plant that deep, and being able to look up the name in your garden log means you needn't repeat the mistake.

Knowing where to find out who sold you very good or very bad plants is also a very good idea.

To get you started on your own garden log, we've included garden log prompts in the Planning sections of Chapter 1, Annuals.

GOOD GARDENING PRACTICES

Here in the Mid-Atlantic we are blessed with a climate neither too cold nor too hot for almost all favorite garden plants. **Pansies** bloom in the winter and some **narcissus** as early as February. Spring comes with lavish displays of flowering bulbs, trees, and shrubs. Summer is hot and stormy, but with September rains wilted plants freshen, fall bulbs bloom, and October is a dazzle of leaf and berry color as **Virginia creeper, maples, oaks, barberries, cotoneasters,** and **hollies** respond to the cold.

Garden design. This wonderful climate has produced exceptional gardeners and gardens, many of them now open to the public (see Appendix). Look to these superb display gardens to learn what you can grow, what's new, and what good garden design looks like.

Winterthur Museum and Gardens in Winterthur, Delaware, is a textbook on formal planting. Lilypons Water Gardens in Buckeystown, Maryland, showcases water gardens. Ladew Topiary Gardens in Maryland is the finest example of topiary training in North America. To see what our forebears' home gardens looked like, visit the Colonial Williamsburg Restoration in the Tidewater area of Virginia and Jefferson's Monticello in Central Virginia. Dumbarton Oaks, in the District of Columbia, is famous for its garden rooms, and both the U.S. Botanic Garden on the Mall, and the U.S. National Arboretum have superb plant collections.

The American Horticultural Society, which is headquartered on a beautiful

Introduction

historic farm in Alexandria, offers membership to interested gardeners, and can also put you in touch with local garden groups and plant societies, which are matchless sources of information. They can tell you, for example, which of Mid-Atlantic's climate zones apply to you.

CLIMATE

To help gardeners choose plants that will do well in their gardens, the USDA developed the Plant Hardiness Zone Map published in 1990. It assigns numbered zones to regions according to their average lowest winter temperature. The zone data on plant tags and in mail-order catalogs and garden literature indicate the region in which you can expect the plant to survive winter.

Virginia, Maryland, and Delaware share the warmest climate in the Northeast/Mid-Atlantic Region, with Zones 6, 7, and 8 temperatures. To locate your hardiness zone, study the USDA Plant Hardiness Zone Map for your region located in this chapter. Most of the Mid-Atlantic is in Zone 7. If you are right on the coast of Delaware, Maryland, or Virginia, your garden is in Zone 7B. Winters there are warmer by 5 to 10 degrees Fahrenheit than they are in Zone 7A, which includes 10 to 20 miles inland and the northern reaches of Delaware.

The coldest regions of the Mid-Atlantic are in the mountains, which are rated Zone 6B (0 to -5 degrees Fahrenheit). The area around Harrisonburg on the West Virginia border is in Zone 6A (-5 to -10 degrees Fahrenheit).

Our hot spots are in the Tidewater and Piedmont (French for "foot of the mountain") areas of southern Virginia, Zone 8 (15 to 10 degrees Fahrenheit).

For most of us, winter lasts about four months. Summer's high heat comes in mid-June and stays until mid-September, punctuated by afternoon thunderstorms and an extended drought in August. A 3-inch mulch helps to keep the ground cool around plant roots during this time. When a plant slows down in high heat, don't try to force growth by fertilizing or pruning. Shutting down is the plant's way of protecting itself.

The first frost date of the year in and around DC and Northern Virginia is October 19; October 16 in Culpepper; November 13 in Richmond; October 28 in Williamsburg. The last frost of the year in Williamsburg is about April 14; in Culpepper, April 17; in Richmond, May 4; in DC it is March 25.

Microclimates and Planting Dates. While the USDA zone map is a guide to what is likely to succeed in your yard, it isn't the last word about what or when you can plant. Spring and fall are the best planting seasons, and summer is okay for container-grown plants. But your community has a variety of spots that become warmer or cooler, sooner or later, than the prevailing climate.

Cold sinks, so valleys and low spots are cooler than high ground. High hills and hillocks are colder than the zone indicates. Slopes facing north are colder than those facing south. Cities are 5 to 10 degrees warmer than the 'burbs and the country. Inland locations have greater fluctuations with early fall and late spring than the buffered maritime climates, and they have harder freezes.

Bodies of water modify temperatures. The shore is warmer in winter than 10 to 20 miles inland. In spring the shore is colder by 10 degrees or more because the ocean holds on to winter cold. In summer the shore is cooler because the ocean takes time to warm up. These same changes of zone occur around coastal bays, rivers, lakes, and even large ponds.

In addition, every garden is home to microclimates—spots warmer or cooler than the prevailing temperatures. A south-facing wall can warm a corner. Shade cools it. White and reflective surfaces increase light and heat. A windbreak, a vine-covered pergola, a large tree, or a high hedge moderates summer heat and winter chill.

Introduction

You can take advantage of these microclimates to try plants that, by the book, aren't right for your climate. However, when it comes to flowering trees and big shrubs, stay with those recommended for your zone. Late frosts can devastate the flower buds on a **camellia** that isn't hardy in your zone even though the foliage and the plant make it. All these factors affect plant selection.

You can outwit the climate by choosing varieties that peak "early," "mid-season," or "late." Where the growing season is short, plant early varieties. When you want late season bloom, select late varieties. To enjoy a long season, plant all three varieties.

Another way to outwit a short growing season is to start seeds indoors early—in late winter for spring crops and in late summer for fall crops. Or you can start seeds early outdoors in a cold frame or a hot bed (see November, Chapter 3, Herbs & Vegetables) or in the open garden under "hot caps," cloches, tenting, and other solar collectors. One popular plant protector surrounds each plant with a wall of water held in a ring of plastic tubes. These solar collectors tend to heat up under the sun, so you must remember to vent them on hot days. The same is true of cold frames and hot beds. Tenting and other plant

Did You Know?

Light Needs of Plants

Full sun means at least six hours of direct, full sun. **Part sun** calls for four to six hours of direct sun, or dappled light all day. **Shade** can be two to three hours of direct sun a day, or bright dappled shade all day, for example, the shade from a tall tree.

Flowers, herbs, and vegetables need six hours of direct sun unless they are described as shade plants. In Zones 8 and 7, protection at noon—a trellis, the dappled shade of tall trees—may be needed. Plants growing in humusy moist soil and mulched 2 to 3 inches deep can stand more heat and sun. In Zone 6 with its cooler temperatures, plants growing in full sun may be able to stand the cold better.

protectors also keep insects and small pests away in the early stages of plant growth.

Two weeks after the date of the last annual frost, it generally is safe to transplant seedlings to the open garden. The outside temperature should have reached at least 55 degrees Fahrenheit during the day. The soil will still be cool. Transplanting too early leaves seedlings sulking. Tell your garden log when the first and last frosts occurred in your yard—that will be a better guide than any generalization experts offer.

Specific information on when to plant appears throughout the individual plant chapters.

LIGHT

Unless noted as flowering in shade, plants require six hours of direct sun to bloom well. Shade for plants means bright, not deep shade; examples are filtered light under a tall tree and all-day dappled shade under a tree with open branching.

If you are in warm Zones 7 and 8, you'll find that early morning sun is more beneficial than hot late afternoon sun for shade plants. In the Tidewater and the warmest spots in Zone 7, Washington, DC, for example, shade-tolerant varieties benefit from protection at noon. The shade provided by lathing, a tall hedge, or a vine arbor will keep a shade plant safe. The plants can stand more noon sun when they are growing in humusy moist soil and when you maintain a 3-inch layer of mulch over the roots in summer.

SOIL PREPARATION AND IMPROVEMENT

The best garden is one you can maintain without more effort than you have time to give. It begins with well prepared good garden soil and sound garden practices.

The ideal garden soil has good drainage, lots of water-holding humus, and is loose enough so you can dig in it with your fingers. We evaluate garden soil in terms of its structure or composition, its pH, and its fertility.

Soil structure. There are two main types of soil here. Soil may be sandy in the Tidewater, along the coasts of Maryland and Delaware, and all along the Atlantic. There's a layer of hardpan under some sandy soils. Sandy soils are easy to dig and drain well, which is essential for many plants.

If your garden is in the mountains, the soil may be rocky. In the Shenandoah Valley of Virginia, limestone rock and clay soils partner not far from shale-like soil. Soil that is sandy or rocky doesn't retain water or the nutrients dissolved in the water. Dry plants desiccate and starve, and, we now believe, change some starches into sugars that insects find tasty.

As the land rises on the Coastal Plain, the soil still tends to be sandy, but moving inland and westward, clay appears and eventually dominates. Clay soils are rich in nutrients, but the very fine particles may stick together, resulting in poor drainage and aeration and making it more difficult for roots to develop. If clay goes dry, summer rain and water irrigation runs off. That means tender rootlets are unable to penetrate the soil around them, and the plant's growth is checked.

Humus, the spongy remains of decomposed leaves, peat moss, and other organics, holds moisture and nutrients. It is the great modifier of rocky, sandy, and clay soils, but it's not a permanent fix. As plants grow, they deplete the organic content of the soil, and it loses its capacity to hold moisture and nutrients.

Soil pH. A plant's access to nutrients also depends on the soil's "potential of hydrogen," its relative acidity or alkalinity or pH. Soil of pH 7.0 is neutral; pH 4 is very, very acid; pH 8 is very alkaline. Most garden plants do best in soil whose pH is in a range between 5.5 and 6.5. Most herbaceous flowers and vegetables do well when the pH is between 6.0 and 7.0. For shrubs and trees the pH ranges far and wide.

Soil-testing kits for analyzing the pH of your soil are available at garden cen-

ters and from mail-order suppliers, as is everything you need to adjust the pH. To raise the pH of soils whose pH is too low, mix in 5 to 10 pounds of limestone per 100 square feet of garden bed. To lower pH that is too high, apply elemental fertilizer sulfur (water-soluble garden sulfur) at the rate of 5 to 10 pounds per 100 square feet. Other acidifiers are aluminum sulfate and iron sulfate; they act faster but do not last as long in the soil.

Fertilizing. Plants empty their larder of nutrients every season. To help plants to be all they can be, you must fertilize at planting time and at least once yearly in subsequent years.

The fertilizers we recommend are organic and release their nutrients slowly during the season, so we get solid stocky plants with loads of gorgeous foliage and flowers.

A sound **annual soil maintenance** program for an established garden includes:

• Checking and adjusting the soil pH in late winter.

• Fertilizing and adding Rich Earth™ humate in late winter—late February, early March—before growth begins, and fertilizing again in late summer or early fall.

• Watering slowly and deeply as needed.

Introduction

• Replenishing the mulch cover after spring fertilization and before summer heat.

STARTING A RAISED BED

A raised bed, either a low berm or one surrounded by stones, bricks, or other material, is the best start a plant can have and an excellent solution to a site with poor drainage. You can start a raised bed in the spring, summer, or early fall. It takes three to four weeks from start to planting. When you start a raised bed governs when you can plant. We favor late summer or early fall.

1 Use a garden hose to outline the bed. Island beds are the easiest to work since you can get at the middle from either side. Long, slow, gentle curves are easy to maintain and pleasant to look at.

2 Thoroughly water the turf covering the area to get the roots activated.

3 Spray the entire area with RoundUp® Weed and Grass Killer, following the instructions on the label. It takes about two weeks to completely die. As an alternative, you can remove the turf—the top layer of growth and its roots—but that's hard work.

4 Cover the area with enough of the garden soil you can find that is freest of weeds to raise the soil level about 12 to 16 inches above ground.

5 The next step is to determine the pH of the soil and amend it as needed to reach a pH between 6.0 and 7.0 following the procedures described in Soil pH above.

6 Cover the bed with 3 to 4 inches of humus, enough so that one quarter of the content of the soil is organic matter. The humus can be decomposed bark, compost, partially decomposed leaves or seaweed, sphagnum peat moss, black peat humus, decomposed animal manures, or other decomposed organic material.

7 Next, for each 10-foot by 10-foot area, (100 square feet) add the following—available at most garden centers.

A new garden in full sun:

Plant-tone 5-3-3—5 to 10 pounds
Rock phosphate—5 to 10 pounds
Green sand—5 to 10 pounds
Clay soils only—gypsum 5 to 10 pounds
Osmocote® 8-month—2 pounds

A new garden in shade:

Holly-tone 4-6-4—4 to 7 pounds
Superphosphate—3 to 5 pounds
Green sand—5 to 10 pounds
Clay soils only—gypsum 5 to 10 pounds

Osmocote® 8-month—2 pounds

A new bed for bulbs in full sun:

Bulb-tone—5 to 10 pounds
Rock phosphate—5 to 10 pounds
Green sand—5 to 10 pounds
Clay soils only—gypsum 5 to 10 pounds
Osmocote® 8-month—2 pounds

A new bed for roses:

Rose-tone or Plant-tone—5 to 10 pounds
Rock phosphate—5 to 10 pounds
Green sand—5 to 10 pounds
Clay soils only—gypsum 5 to 10 pounds
Osmocote® 8-month—2 pounds

8 Next, with a rear-tine rototiller, which you can rent from a garden center, mix all this deeply and thoroughly. The bed should now be so soft you can dig in it with your bare hands.

9 When you are ready to plant, rake the bed smooth and discard rocks, lumps, and bumps.

10 Finally, pack and tamp the edge of the bed into a long, gradual slope and cover it with mulch to keep the soil from eroding. Or, frame the bed with low retaining walls of stone or painted cement blocks, 2-by-2 red cedar or pressure treated wood, or railroad ties.

Introduction

Note: Before planting in a new flower bed that has not been raised, mix into the existing soil the same proportion of supplements (except for the garden soil), and follow the same procedures as for a raised bed. If the area you are planting measures only 10 square feet, combine one-tenth of the amount of each supplement given for a raised bed of 100 square feet. If you have leftovers, they keep.

UNDERSTANDING FERTILIZERS

Whatever your climate, for unchecked growth and satisfying bloom, your plants need a continuous supply of nutrients. When to fertilize depends on the type of fertilizer you are using.

Timing. Generally speaking, the time for the first application is before growth begins in spring, and the last application is as growth slows toward the end of the growing season.

The end of the growing season in Zones 6 and 7 falls some time between early September and early October. In Zone 8, Richmond and the Tidewater areas of Virginia, the time for the last fertilization is between the end of September and mid-October.

If you are using **organic blends**, such as Holly-tone or Plant-tone, then you will need to fertilize the first time a few weeks before growth is due to begin in spring, and then again toward the end of the growing season. Some plants, roses for example, need more.

If you are using only **water-soluble chemical fertilizers**, such as 5-10-10, which are immediately available to the plants, then you will need to fertilize every four to six weeks from beginning to end of the growing season.

If you are using **time- or controlled-release chemical fertilizers**, such as Osmocote® or Sierra®, then you will need to fertilize just before the plants start to grow and then repeat according to the formulation inscribed on the fertilizer container.

Fertilizer contents. To be all they can be, plants need the three primary plant nutrients—nitrogen for foliar growth, phosphorus for healthy roots and flower development, and potassium to maintain vigor—as well as a number of secondary and trace elements.

Fertilizers are made in formulations for plants that do best in either a low pH or a normal pH. Where soils are acid and the pH recommended for the plants is between 6.0 and 7.0, we recommend balancing the acidity by using a non-acid slow-release fertilizer blend such as Plant-tone. In soils whose pH is above 7.0, or up in the alkaline range, we suggest balancing the alkalinity by using Holly-tone or other fertilizer formulated for acid-loving plants.

Organic Fertilizers. The organic fertilizer blends many horticulturists now favor may take up to four weeks before bacterial activity starts to make the nutrients available to the plants. Nutrients are then continually released over a three- to four-month period or longer. Water-soluble organic fertilizers that are immediately available to the plant can be found in both starter solutions and in products for foliar feeding for a quick pick-up if plants show signs of nutrient deficiencies. Garden centers carry soluble organics such as fish emulsion, liquid seaweed, the compost teas that are becoming popular, and manure teas made by steeping dehydrated manure.

Natural organic fertilizers have a positive effect on soil microorganisms and beneficial earthworms. In their presence, soil structure and aeration are improved. The organics break down gradually, depending on the amount of moisture in the soil, on the temperature, and on the microbial activity. Nutrients become available over an extended period of time, which decreases fertilizer run-off.

There are many organic fertilizer blends on the market, and each has its own rate of application. Fairly typical are the granular products Holly-tone and Plant-tone. They are sprinkled over the soil surface four to six weeks before growth is due to begin in spring, and then again toward the end of the

Introduction

growing season. They're easy to apply; just use your fingers to scratch handfuls of it about a quarter inch deep into the soil surface.

For Holly-tone 4-6-4, in a new bed apply ten pounds per 100 square feet; for an established bed, apply five pounds per 100 square feet. For Plant-tone 5-3-3, for a new bed apply ten pounds per 100 square feet; for an established bed apply five pounds per 100 square feet.

Supplemental organic fertilization. In addition to the two annual applications of organic fertilizers, we recommend four supplemental feedings.

Rich Earth™ humate is a mined product, a 100 percent natural rich humate soil which supplies humic, ulmic, and fulvic acids containing over seventy trace minerals. It aerates the soil, improves water retention, conditions the soil, and enhances root development. Apply at the rate of 1 pound per 100 square feet of garden area.

Rock phosphate is a pure mined phosphate rock containing 32 percent total phosphate which has been washed free of clay impurities. Phosphates help a good root system to develop and promote luxuriant flowering. Apply at the rate of 10 pounds per 100 square feet when planting.

Greensand, also known as glau-conite, is a mined, mineral-rich, ancient sea deposit that is an all-natural source of potash. Thirty-two or more micro ingredients are contained in greensand. It helps to loosen heavy clay soil. It also binds sandy soil for a better structure. It increases the water holding capacity of soils and is considered an excellent soil conditioner. It promotes plant vigor, disease resistance, and good color in fruit. Apply 5 to 10 pounds per 100 square feet of garden area.

Gypsum is a hydrated calcium sulfate that replaces sodium in alkaline soils with calcium and improves the drainage, aeration, and structure of heavier soils. It is an effective ammonia-conserving agent when applied to manured soils and other rapidly decomposing organic matter. It does not affect the soil pH. Apply at the rate of 5 to 10 pounds per 100 square feet in moderately clay soil; 10 pounds per 100 square feet in heavy clay soil.

Chemical Fertilizers. Granular chemical fertilizers, known as "complete fertilizers," are made up of the three essential plant nutrients—nitrogen (N), phosphorus (P), and potassium (K) in balanced proportions. Numerals on the bags, like 5-10-5, 10-10-10, and their variations, refer to the proportions of each essential element present in that mix. If you use only this type of fertilizer, make the year's first application just before the plants begin to grow in spring, and continue every four to six weeks until the growing season ends in your area.

If you use water-soluble fertilizers, they must be applied every two weeks, beginning two weeks before growth starts in spring and ending two weeks before the growing season is over. You would also add it to the water used as a starter solution at planting time, and for foliar feeding for plants showing signs of nutrient deficiency.

Slow-, Controlled-, or Time-Release Chemical Fertilizers. The complete chemical fertilizers have been packaged by scientists so they act like tiny time pills, releasing their nutrients over a specified period. The pellets are formulated to deliver nutrients at a slow, steady rate.

Examples are Osmocote® and Sierra® controlled-release fertilizers, which come in three to four month, eight to nine month, and twelve to fourteen month formulations. A similar product is Scott's controlled-release Agriform fertilizer tablets, which can last up to two years.

PLANTING PROCEDURES

Our planting season begins in early spring as soon as cold and moisture have left the earth. To test, make a

Introduction

Did You Know?

Water Conservation Tips

• Water early in the morning, not when the sun is blazing because then you lose water to evaporation. Watering during the day reduces water loss by the plant due to transpiration, and that can be a good thing when the weather is very hot and plants are wilting.

• Mulch your gardens.

• Shut the hose off when moving between gardens.

• Turn the hose off at the faucet when you finish watering.

• Water deeply; when the water has penetrated to a depth of 6 to 8 inches, that's enough.

• Install rain barrels under drain pipes, and cover them with mosquito netting.

"snowball" of soil—if it is so wet it won't easily crumble, the soil is still too wet for planting.

When you are planting in a new raised bed with improved, fluffed-up soil, digging a generous hole is easy. You can do it with your bare hands. Digging a big hole in a new spot, and even in an established garden, can be tough.

Each chapter gives specific information about planting the plants in that chapter. Here are some general recommendations:

1 Make the planting hole big. For trees and shrubs, make the hole up to three times as wide and twice as deep as the rootball. For perennials and annuals make the hole twice as wide and twice as deep as the rootball. Plant bulbs at depths specified for their type on a base of improved soil.

2 Backfill the hole with soil amended as described in Raised Beds above.

For trees and shrubs, tamp the soil in the hole down very firmly to create a base for the rootball that will place the top of the container soil or ball an inch or two above the surrounding soil to compensate for settling.

For perennials and annuals, tamp the soil in the hole down to create a base for the rootball that will place the crown of the plant about an inch above the level of the earth around.

3 Free the plant from matted roots. When it's possible, unwind roots that may be circling the rootball. If you can't untangle them, make four shallow vertical slashes in the root mass. Cut off the matted roots on the bottom. Dip the rootball in a bucket containing starter solution, which can be purchased at your garden center.

4 Set the plant in the hole. Half-fill the hole with amended soil, and tamp it down firmly. Then fill the hole all the way to the top with improved soil, and tamp it firmly again.

5 Shape the soil around the stem or the crown into a rim creating a wide saucer. The saucer is really important for shrubs and trees, less so for perennials and annuals.

6 Mulch the area starting a few inches from the trunk or crown.

WATERING

From late winter on, there's usually enough rain to keep gardens growing through June. Summer storms drench our gardens in July, but the unrelenting summer heat in Zones 7 and 8 often causes perennials and annuals to wilt at midday and some to stop growing. Late July and August is drought season here, and you will probably need to

15

Introduction

water two or three times a month before the fall rains arrive in September. One of the most important preparations for winter is a deep and thorough watering before the soil freezes; if the sky doesn't provide the rain, you must.

Overhead watering is fine as long as you water deeply. There's less waste if you water before the sun reaches the garden in the early morning or late afternoon or evening. In hot dry periods, daytime watering lowers leaf temperatures and reduces stress and plant water loss to transpiration. Evening watering is okay since dew naturally wets foliage every clear night anyway.

When watering, arrange to provide slow, gentle, deep watering. The ideal is to put down 1½ inches of water at each session. To measure, set an empty 1-pound coffee tin to catch the water, and record in your garden log the time it takes your sprinkler to deliver 1½ inches.

Electrically-timed mechanical watering systems tend to ignore the weather and water too often and shallowly; however, they can do a good job if they are set up with the correct low-gallon nozzles and are timed to run long enough to water gently and deeply every week or ten days.

MULCHING

We recommend applying mulch 2 to 3 inches deep around annuals and perennials and 3 to 4 inches deep around trees and shrubs. That is enough to keep weeds out, to minimize the loss of soil moisture, and to maintain soil temperatures. Mulch that's 5 inches deep or more keeps the ground so wet that the roots lack oxygen, and it also keeps the soil frozen late into spring.

Start the mulch 2 to 3 inches from the plant's central stem or trunk. Piling mulch right up against the plant can rot it. Deep mulch also makes a cozy home for field mice.

Organic mulch does more than just maintain soil moisture and temperatures. As it decomposes on the underside, organic mulch replenishes the soil's supply of humus. You can mulch with almost any healthy organic material available—seaweed or chopped leaves for example—as long as it is at least partially decomposed. The commercial mulches we recommend include cypress mulch, pine needles, fir, hardwood, and shredded pine bark.

As mulch decomposes—whether it's spread over or mixed into the soil—it has only a very slight effect on pH.

Mulch Maintenance. Keep a 2- to 3-inch layer of mulch on beds and around plants starting 2 to 3 inches from the central stem and covering an area that is wider than the plant's diameter.

Top off the mulch cover after the **late winter/early spring** fertilization. Check and replenish the mulch before **the high heat of summer** to keep the roots cool in summer. Maintain your mulch **in fall** to delay the freezing of the ground and to keep moisture available for roots that will continue to grow until the earth grows cold.

The need for additional **winter mulch** depends on the severity of your climate, and on the exposure of the beds. In the Mid-Atlantic, winter mulch can save plants that are borderline hardy from temperatures that are especially severe.

Apply winter mulch only after the ground has frozen hard, and remove it when you first spot signs of active growth in the plants. As a winter mulch we recommend airy organics like straw, pine needles, and pine boughs. Tent the plants so thinly you can still see some of the plant and the soil through the mulch. For coastal dwellers, marsh hay and salt hay from the shore are excellent winter mulches as they are weed-free, and they can be saved, covered, in a pile from year to year.

Introduction

STAKING

Flowers. Growing in improved soil and fertilized with organic fertilizers, only a few of the tallest flowers should need staking. Tall, weak growth can be caused by force-feeding with non-organic fertilizers and by over-fertilization.

Set a wood, bamboo, or metal stake close to the young plant's stem. As it leafs out, it will hide the stake. Use soft green wool, raffia, or cotton string, and tie the main stem loosely to the stake.

Trees. Staking a tree isn't necessary unless the stem or trunk shows a tendency to lean over or to grow at an angle—and it should not need the stake for more than a year or so. In cold regions, a burlap windbreak is helpful to young shrubs and trees for their first winter.

WEEDING AND GROOMING

Weeding. Remove weeds to eliminate competition, to keep the air moving in the garden, and to avoid the pests and diseases inherent to some. A radical approach is to put down a weed barrier, such as landscape fabric; it lets in water and air but inhibits weeds. Hide it under a layer of mulch.

Even with a weed barrier you'll likely have some of the little pests to deal with. Weeds start up in spring and come into their own in mid-summer, along with drought and high heat. Before renewing or applying a summer mulch, rake the weeds up. If you get the little green heads before they're an inch high you won't have to hoe them when they are 8 inches high. If they get ahead of you, don't pull big weeds from bone-dry soil in a drought. Water the garden first, and then gently free the weeds and their roots. If you let weeds flourish and go to seed, they'll haunt you for years.

Grooming. To be at their best, plants need grooming, and that's true of water garden plants as well those grown in soil. In early spring, clear the gardens of last year's dead foliage, and prune to promote health and growth and to shape plants for beauty's sake. In summer, deadhead and shear spent blooms to encourage flowering this year and next.

Looking back on years of gardening, the moments that stand out in memory are the quiet times spent grooming the garden. Clipping boxwoods in the cool early morning, birds calling; strolling the flower beds at sunset checking for spent blooms that need deadheading; weeding in summer; raking leaves on smoky autumn days, Canada geese calling overhead. These homely garden chores lift us out of our everyday lives and into the life of the garden and a promise of beauty that nourishes the soul.

KEEPING YOUR GARDEN HEALTHY

The first defense against plant problems is to follow healthy garden practices. There's a huge bonus . . . lower maintenance. Here are some approaches that prevent difficulties—

- Introduce plant diversity into your garden and your neighborhood.

- Give cultivars of native plants a place in your design.

- Buy only healthy plants that are pest and disease resistant.

- Limit your choices to plants that thrive in your climate and your soil; these best withstand insect attacks and diseases to which the species may be susceptible, and they survive the normal droughts.

- Rotate crops of annual flowers, vegetables, and herbs.

- Clear out and destroy infested and diseased plants.

- Keep the garden free of weeds that are carriers of insects and diseases.

Introduction

• When you can, buy from the nearest reliable full service garden center or nursery, and ask for field grown or container stock that has proven successful in your area.

• Avoid plants identified as invasive.

Give Back to the Earth. Nourish the earth—and the earth will nourish your garden. Compost amends the soil. It can be used as a mulch, or it can be spread over the soil to a depth of 2 or 3 inches and dug or rototilled in. A handful of compost scratched into the soil around plants during the growing season is beneficial.

Some counties in the Mid-Atlantic give away wood chip mulches, and others are marketing composted waste. Northern Virginia's LeafGRO is effective and modestly priced.

You can, of course, make your own. Instructions appear in the October section of Chapter 9, Trees, the month we have lots of dry brown leaves, an important ingredient in compost.

Healthy leaves, weeds, grass clippings, vegetable garden debris, and vegetable or fruit peels are all excellent for composting. Don't compost fruit in bear country because it attracts them. Don't compost fish or meat, which attracts neighborhood pets. Don't compost garden debris that is diseased or harbors insects.

PESTS AND DISEASES

Bears. Where bears may be a problem, they may come to bird and hummingbird feeders. They harvest berries and sometimes your pets. If there are bear sightings near you, take in bird feeders and other attractions.

Birds. Our feathered friends are beautiful, lovable, inspiring, and useful in that they eat insects, some good and some bad. They also eat berries and fruit, your kind as well as theirs; seeds you give them and seeds you don't; and sunflowers.

Deer. Deer are the most destructive of all wild creatures that visit our gardens. If deer are a problem in your area, avoid plants they particularly like, build fences, and use deterrents. New repellents for deer come on the market every season, but at this writing we know of none that has proven to be a permanent deterrent; the best solution is to regularly change the deterrents you use so the deer don't become accustomed to the smell.

Rabbits, woodchucks, raccoons, and other rodents. Other four-footed mammals can cause destruction in your garden too. Again, if they're a problem in your garden, the key is to avoid their favorite plants and to block them from plants you want to protect.

In the Appendix under Pests, Diseases, and Controls, there is more information about coping with mammal and insect pests and the diseases that can afflict your garden.

Integrated Pest Management. Known as IPM, integrated pest management is an environmentally friendly approach to dealing with the pests that bug your plants.

The goal of IPM is to try to handle problems by taking into account the environment in which the problem occurs. To disrupt the environment as little as possible, we try to encourage and we also release certain predatory "beneficial" insects that are natural enemies of the destructive insects. We also employ some physical barriers, such as row covers, to keep plants safe.

Beneficial insects. The first line of defense in IPM is to encourage beneficial insects and to use biological controls, rather than poisons—pesticides—to control the others.

There are two groups of beneficials, the predators and the parasites. The most familiar predators are praying mantids, lady beetles, green lacewings, and spiders. They hunt and feed on the others. The parasites are primarily various tiny wasps that hatch inside other insects and . . . you can imagine!

Introduction

Several mail-order houses (see Mail-Order Sources in the Appendix) offer batches of the beneficial insects with instructions on releasing them. Successfully established in your garden, the beneficials help control the bad guys. To keep beneficials with you season after season, you must not use broad spectrum insecticides. Not using insecticides is "integrated pest management."

Horticultural oil sprays. If you need more control than the beneficials provide, look into horticultural oils. Sprayed on infected plants, these dense oils smother insects and their eggs. Some are based on petroleum and others on vegetables such as cottonseed and soybeans. They're environmentally okay. Applied in early spring before the buds break, they control the undesirables and have a limited effect on the beneficials. Sprayed on in summer they control whiteflies, mealybugs, scale, spider mites, and aphids.

Botanical pesticides and insecticidal soaps. Safer as far as the beneficials are concerned, some of these are derived from plants. From *Pyrethrum,* a daisy-like flower, manufacturers extract an insecticidal chemical. The tropical neem tree provides a very effective insecticide that is also a fungicide; it even can help with Japanese beetles. (The main control for Japanese beetles is to treat the soil with milky disease spores in late summer. It harms the larvae. To be effective, the treatment must be repeated the following year.) Insecticidal soaps are milder than the sprays—they are effective when they come into contact with the insects.

For a great deal of detail about insect pests and common plant diseases turn to the section on Pests, Diseases, and Controls in the Appendix.

Welcome to Gardening in the Mid-Atlantic

What André Viette, Mark Viette, and I have put down here is an overview of the rhythm of the year in a Mid-Atlantic garden. **A truly beautiful garden is a very healthy garden. The gardening practices we recommend in the following chapters emphasize health over remedy.** Our approach is easy on the environment. Happily, what is good for the environment is very good for the garden and for you, and not just in a grand save-the-planet design. Good garden practices make healthy gardens, and that means lower maintenance, plus dollar savings, which equals happy gardeners.

Welcome to the wonderful world of gardening in Delaware, Maryland, Virginia, and the District of Columbia!

Jacqueline Hériteau

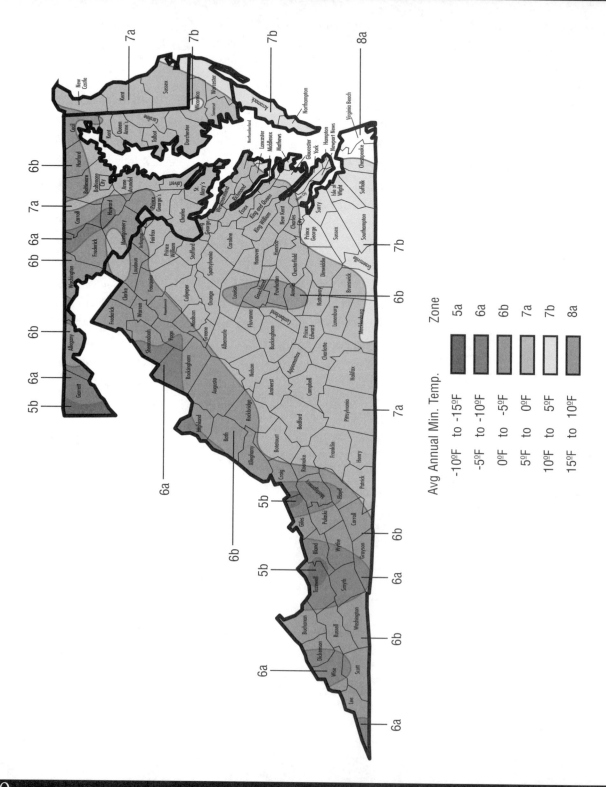

Avg Annual Min. Temp.	Zone
-10ºF to -15ºF	5a
-5ºF to -10ºF	6a
0ºF to -5ºF	6b
5ºF to 0ºF	7a
10ºF to 5ºF	7b
15ºF to 10ºF	8a

CHAPTER ONE

Annuals & Biennials

Annuals, biennials, tender perennials, and tropicals last just one season, but they're a delight to grow and dear to every gardener's heart.

Annuals, biennials, tender perennials, and tropicals last just one season, but they're a delight to grow and dear to every gardener's heart.

A hurry-up attitude and lavish, long-season blooms make the annuals just about indispensable. All in this group are one-year plants, but they are not all "true" annuals. Some are biennials, some are short-lived perennials, some are cold-tender perennials, and some are tropicals. That is to say, expect to replant them every year, but don't expect them to behave exactly alike.

True annuals. The botanist's "true" annual develops from seed, grows up and blooms, sets seed, and dies in one year. **Zinnias, sunflowers,** and **marigolds** are "true" annuals. Some true annuals **appear** to be perennial because they reseed themselves and come back year after year. **Love-in-a-mist** (*Nigella*), **larkspur,** and **four o'clocks** are among those that self-sow. The self-sown "volunteers" come into bloom at about the same time as seeds you sow in the garden.

Biennials bloom the second year after planting, not the first year, and they don't come back unless they are self-sowers. To have blooms every year, you must sow seeds or plant new plants every year. There are a few exceptions to the rule—like the **forget-me-not** species *Myosotis sylvatica*, which blooms from seed in just six weeks. Some biennials belong to genera that include annual and perennial species; for example, there's a perennial **forget-me-not,** *Myosotis scorpioides* (*M. palustris*). To know what to expect you must read the seed packet.

Short-lived perennials act like biennials and disappear after the second year. Examples are fragrant **sweet William** and furry-leaved **silver sage,** which raises a superb flower spike in late spring. These all must be replanted every year.

Cold-tender perennials, like **geraniums, coleus, pentas, impatiens, lantana,** and **sweet potato vine,** can't survive our winters, so they're handled like annuals. But, being perennial, they can live on for years. Several are worth potting up and bringing indoors for the winter. (See September, Care.)

Tropicals and semi-tropicals, like the gorgeous **glory bush,** *Tibouchina urvilleana,* and lovely **bougainvillea,** are perennial in very warm climates. You can buy these as container-grown plants already blooming in late spring. They're great container plants and fillers for empty spots. They winter well in a greenhouse—are so-so as houseplants. (**Canna, dahlias,** and other popular bulb flowers grown as annuals are mentioned in Chapter 2, Bulbs, Corms, Rhizomes, and Tubers.)

USES OF ANNUALS

Colorful Fillers. Summer-flowering annuals are the plants to use when you need to fill gaps in perennial beds after the spring flowers go by—**zinnias** and **marigolds** are prime examples. Seedlings of taller annuals help mask the oh-so-slow ripening of spring-flowering bulbs—**sweet William, pinks, rocket larkspur,** and **garden balsam.** Almost all annuals can be used to fill the wide open spaces in new beds of perennials and shrubs. Annuals are a kitchen garden's best friend because they make it a popular destination.

Hedges and screening. Some annuals grow big enough to use as a temporary hedge—giant ('Climax') **marigolds**

and **burning bush,** (*Bassia scoparia* forma (sic) *trichophylla*) for example. Annual vines (see Vines and Ground Covers) will envelop porches, poles, tree stumps, and garden eyesores for you in a matter of weeks.

Annuals as bedding plants. Bedding plants are flowers used in sequence to carpet large areas—for example, an early spring display of **pansies,** replaced as soon as they have peaked by upright **bedding petunias.** The lavish summer-long bloom of **marigolds** makes them excellent bedding plants.

Edging plants. Low-growing **sweet alyssum, wax begonias,** and **ageratum** are among many first-rate edging plants. They're often used to create ribbons of color spelling out municipal and business names and logos.

Baskets and planters. The cascading annuals are ideal for baskets and planters; they have a small root system that allows you to jam a whole lot in to a modest space. **Cascade petunias** are the stars. Close seconds are tiny, bright-as-sunshine **creeping zinnias,** *Sanvitalia procumbens*, a true annual, and the tender perennials *Scaevola aemula, Sutura cordata* 'Snowflake', and **sweet potato vine.** Spills of **ivy** and **balcony geraniums, helichrysym,** and **variegated vinca** (which often perennializes here) lend grace to flowery compositions.

Cutting flowers. Cut-and-come-again annuals are among the best cutting flowers. To have masses of blooms for bouquets, plant **zinnias, snapdragons,** and **China asters.** Give them a bed of their own in an out of the way place. Or plant them in the kitchen garden— they'll make it beautiful!

Children's gardens. Annuals are a child's best garden friend. Quick popper-uppers like **zinnias** and **sunflowers** satisfy a youngster's need for early results. Seeing buried seeds grow, watching butterflies and bees seeking nectar, and sharing flowers and a garden's endless surprises gives children proud stories to tell.

SEQUENCE OF BLOOM

Keeping color in the garden all season long requires that you know the sequence in which plants in the annuals group bloom. Some species come in varieties that bloom either early, mid-season, or late. Garden literature, seed packets, and our annuals list tell you when each species peaks—spring, summer, or fall.

Choose cool-weather species like velvet, sweet-scented **wallflowers, pot marigolds,** cheery **primroses,** and **pansies** for the **spring garden.** To keep the **summer garden** blooming, make a series of sowings of heat-tolerant annuals like **marigolds** and **zinnias.** Late

summer bloomers like **cosmos** (we love 'Sonata White'), **snapdragons,** and **China asters** will keep the *fall garden* bright. **Impatiens** are the favorite summer and fall flower for semi-shade. Plant **pansies** and **ornamental cabbages** and **kale** to take the garden through fall and winter and into spring.

To have a garden that's interesting in and out of bloom, include annuals with colorful foliage. They're the long-distance runners. **Dusty Miller,** *Senecio cineraria* 'Silver Dust', and 'Cirrus' stay silver. **Variegated geraniums** and kaleidoscopic **coleus** grow and glow until mid-autumn.

STARTING ANNUALS AND BIENNIALS FROM SEED

For bedding displays and effective garden design, you will need enough seeds or seedlings of annuals to plant them in groups of five, seven, ten, or more; the smaller the plant, the more you will need. Seedlings of the most popular annuals are readily available. Growing your own plants from seeds is a savings and allows you a much more interesting plant selection. You can save on seed costs, and avoid lots of leftover seeds, by sharing seed packets with friends.

You'll find annuals and biennials are easy to grow outdoors from seed. They

Did You Know?

Outstanding Self-Sowers

- **Annual Phlox,** *Phlox drummondii*
- **Bachelor's-button, Cornflower,** *Centaurea cyanus*
- **Spider Flower,** *Cleome hasslerana*
- **Corn Poppy, Field Poppy,** *Papaver rhoeas*
- **Cosmos,** *Cosmos bipinnatus*
- **Dahlberg Daisy,** *Dyssodia tenuiloba*
- **Flossflower,** *Ageratum houstonianum*
- **Flowering Tobacco,** *Nicotiana* species and cultivars
- **Larkspur,** *Consolida ambigua* (syn. *Delphinium ajacis*)
- **Love-in-a-mist, Fennel Flower,** *Nigella damascena*
- **Annual Rose Mallow,** *Lavatera trimestris*
- **Rose Moss, Sun Plant,** *Portulaca grandiflora*
- **Spurred Snapdragon, Toadflax,** *Linaria maroccana* 'Fairy Bouquet'

Outstanding for Fall Color

- **Annual Aster, China Aster,** *Callistephus chinensis*
- **Wax Begonia,** *Begonia* Semperflorens-Cultorum
- **Burning Bush, Red Summer Cypress,** *Bassia scoparia* forma(sic) *trichophylla* 'Childsii'
- **Coleus, Painted Nettle,** *Coleus blumei, C. pumilus*
- **Cosmos,** *Cosmos bipinnatus*
- **Dahlia,** *Dahlia* x *hybrida* Unwin Hybrids
- **Flowering Kale and Cabbage,** *Brassica oleracea* Acephala Group
- **Impatiens, Busy Lizzy,** *Impatiens wallerana*
- **Lysimachia,** *Lysimachia congestifolia* 'Eco Dark Stain'
- **Ornamental Pepper,** *Capsicum annuum* var. *annuum*
- **Pot Marigold,** *Calendula officinalis*
- **Mealycup Sage,** *Salvia farinacea*
- **Spider Flower,** *Cleome hasslerana*
- **Sweet Alyssum,** *Lobularia maritima*
- **Yellow Sage,** *Lantana camara*

Outstanding for Cutting

- **Annual Clary Sage,** *Salvia viridis* (syn. *horminum*)
- **Annual Phlox,** *Phlox drummondii*
- **Blue Lace Flower,** *Trachymene coerulea*
- **China Aster, Annual Aster,** *Callistephus chinensis*
- **Cosmos 'Sonata White',** *Cosmos bipinnatus*
- **Cockscomb,** *Celosia cristata*
- **Globe Amaranth,** *Gomphrena globosa*
- **Heliotrope,** *Heliotropum arborescens*
- **Marigold,** *Tagetes*
- **Mealycup Sage,** *Salvia farinacea*
- **Mexican Sunflower,** *Tithonia rotundifolia*
- **Orange Cosmos,** *Cosmos sulphureus*
- **Statice,** *Limonium sinuatum*
- **Snapdragon,** *Antirrhinum majus*
- **Sunflower,** *Helianthus annuus*
- **Zinnia,** *Zinnia elegans*

also may be started indoors ahead of the outdoor planting season, as described in January, Planting.

When to sow seeds depends on how long the seeds take to germinate—some need twice as much time as others—and on how cold hardy the seedlings are, how much cold they can stand. Seed packets label the seeds "hardy," "half-hardy," or "tender," and most packets suggest when and where to sow the seeds in the garden, and whether and when they can be started indoors to get a head start on the growing season.

Hardy. The seedlings of hardy annuals and biennials can take some frost. These do well sown in early spring, even before the last frost. Seed packets indicate that some can even be sown in fall after freezing temperatures have come.

Did You Know?

Outstanding for Drying

- **Bells of Ireland,** *Moluccella laevis*
- **Everlasting,** *Helipterum* species
- **Foxtail, Italian Millet,** *Setaria italica*
- **Globe Amaranth,** *Gomphrena globosa*
- **Honesty, Silver Dollar,** *Lunaria annua*
- **Kiss-me-over-the-garden-gate,** *Polygonum orientale*
- **Love-in-a-mist,** *Nigella damascena*
- **Our Lady's Bedstraw,** *Galium verum*
- **Paper Moon,** *Scabiosa stellata* 'Drumstick'

- **Pearly Everlasting,** *Anaphalis margaritacea*
- **Salvia 'Blue Bedder',** *Salvia farinacea*
- **Sea Lavender,** *Limonium bonduelli, L. suworowii* (syn. *Psylliostachys suworowii*)
- **Strawflowers,** *Helichrysum bracteatum*
- **Tall Crested Cockscomb,** *Celosia argentea* var. *cristata*
- **White Sage, Silver Sage,** *Salvia argentea*
- **Zinnia,** *Zinnia*

Outstanding for Edging

- **Bedding Begonia, Wax Begonia,** *Begonia* Semperflorens-Cultorum hybrids
- **Bluewings,** *Torenia fournieri*
- **Edging Lobelia,** *Lobelia erinus*
- **Flossflower,** *Ageratum houstonianum*
- **French Marigold,** *Tagetes patula* varieties
- **Impatiens, Busy Lizzy,** *Impatiens wallerana*
- **Nasturtium,** *Tropaeolum majus*
- **Pansy, Ladies-delight,** *Viola* x *wittrockiana*

- **Petunia,** *Petunia* x *hybrida*
- **Rocket Candytuft,** *Iberis amara*
- **Rose Moss, Sun Plant,** *Portulaca grandiflora*
- **Signet Marigold,** *Tagetes tenuifolia* (syn. *signata*) varieties
- **Snapdragon, Dwarf,** *Antirrhinum* hybrids
- **Sweet Alyssum,** *Lobularia maritima*
- **Zinnia, Peter Pan Series, Dwarf** *Zinnia* **Varieties**

Half-hardy. These seedlings are harmed by frost, but they tolerate cool, wet weather and cold soil. Most of the popular annuals are half-hardy (sometimes called semi-hardy). You would sow these seeds outdoors a couple of weeks after the last frost.

Tender. The seeds of tender annuals grow fastest and do best when they are sown outdoors after the air and the soil have warmed.

Sowing the seeds. The planting depth for seeds is usually given on the seed packet. The rule of thumb is to sow seeds at a depth about three times the seed's diameter, not its length.

Always sow seeds in moist soil, and always water them well after planting. If you can plant shortly after a rain and before the next one is expected, you won't have to water before and after.

Larger seeds are sown in "hills," groups of four to six, or three to five, equidistant from each other. Flowers for edging paths or the fronts of flower beds are usually sown in "drills," dribbled at spaced intervals along a shallow furrow. An easy way to make the furrow is to drag the edge of a rake or a hoe handle along the planting line.

Preparing the soil. Annuals and biennials depend on modest root systems to produce masses of flowers and foliage. So they need soil that is well supplied with nutrients all season long, as well as sustained moisture, especially the first several weeks in the garden.

Annuals & Biennials

In the general Introduction to our book, we've given the step-by-step process for preparing and fertilizing a new garden bed. That includes adjusting the soil pH. Most annuals do best with a pH between 6.0 and 7.0.

Transplanting annuals. The time to transplant most hardy annuals is after the air temperature has reached 55 degrees Fahrenheit during the day. The others will do best planted after the soil has warmed too. Transplanting too early just leaves seedlings sulking and yellowing. Before planting seedlings—your own, or seedlings from the garden center—it's a good idea to let them "harden-off" or acclimate a bit in a sheltered location protected from direct sun and wind.

Apply a 2-inch layer of mulch after planting.

CARE

Annuals flourish when they have regular attention.

1 Thin sown seedlings to space the plants as recommended on the seed packet.

2 Shortly after seedlings reach a height of 2 or 3 inches, pinch out the tips of cascading plants and those that have one, two, or three central stems, like **cleome** and **snapdragons.** Pinching out the tips encourages branching. Throughout the growing season, keep pinching out the tips of **petunias**, other cascading container plants, and young branching annuals.

3 Run weed patrol as the garden grows. Some self-sowers are so productive they become weeds—**love-in-a-mist** comes to mind. Root out the extras just as you would weeds.

4 Remove fading blooms consistently to prevent seedheads. Plants developing seeds generally stop or slow blooming. This exercise is called "deadheading," and it keeps the plants looking their best.

5 Snip off stems of plants crowding others, as **nasturtiums** often will.

WATERING

Seeds and seedlings need rain or watering not only before and right after planting, they also need enough water their first two or three weeks to maintain soil moisture. If spring turns dry, or if you see signs of wilting, water your seedlings deeply. In periods of drought, water deeply every week or ten days. Or when you see signs of wilting.

Specific directions of slow, deep watering are given in the general Introduction to the book.

FERTILIZING

In the Introduction to the book, we give detailed information about improving soil with organic matter and slow-release fertilizers. Make the effort to improve your soil, and it will carry your annuals through one growing season with little additional fertilization. If the annuals seem to slow after a first flush of bloom, they may benefit from a modest additional fertilization with a water-soluble organic fertilizer, such as seaweed or fish emulsion.

For established annual beds, we recommend that every year in late winter or early spring you recheck the pH, amend it if needed, and dig in organic fertilizers that release their nutrients over eight to nine months.

PESTS

When controlling pests, practice integrated pest management (IPM), which encourages the good guys to survive. It's a common sense approach that focuses on establishing and maintaining healthy plants and understanding pests in the garden. For common pest and disease controls, see the section on Pests, Diseases, and Controls in the Appendix.

Annuals & Biennials

Common Name (*Botanical Name*)	Type	Light	Bloom Time	Height (Inches)
Alyssum, Sweet (*Lobularia maritima*)	Annual	Sun, part sun	Summer	4 to 8
Bachelor's-button (*Centaurea cyanus*)	Annual	Sun, part sun	Summer	12 to 30
Begonia, Wax/ Fibrous Begonia (*Begonia* Semperflorens-Cultorum hybrids	Tender perennial	Part sun to shade	Late spring to early fall	6 to 12
Black-eyed Susan (*Rudbeckia hirta*)	Perennial or short-lived perennial	Sun	Summer	24 to 30
Blanket Flower (*Gaillardia pulchella*)	Annual	Sun	Summer	24 to 30
Busy Lizzie (*Impatiens* hybrids)	Tender perennial	Part shade, shade	Late spring to fall	8 to 24
California Poppy (*Eschscholzia californica*)	Annual	Sun	Spring through summer	8 to 12
Candytuft, Globe (*Iberis umbellata*)	Annual	Sun	Spring	8
Cockscomb (*Celosia cristata*)	Tender perennial	Sun	Summer through fall	6 to 12
Coleus (*Solenostemon scutellarioides*)	Tender perennial	Part shade	Late spring to early fall	8 to 20
Corn Poppy (*Papaver rhoeas*)	Annual	Sun	Summer	18
Cosmos (*Cosmos bipinnatus*)	Annual	Sun	Summer to fall	24 to 60
Dusty Miller (*Senecio cineraria*)	Annual	Sun	Spring, summer, fall	12
Floss Flower (*Ageratum houstonianum*)	Annual	Sun, part shade	Summer	6 to 24
Forget-me-not (*Myosotis sylvantica*)	Biennial or short-lived perennial	Sun	Spring	7 to 12
Four-o'-clock (*Mirabilis jalapa*)	Tender perennial	Sun, part shade	Mid-summer to fall	10 to 18
Geranium (*Pelargonium* x *hortorum*)	Tender perennial	Sun, part shade	Summer	8 to 14
Globe Amaranth (*Gomphrena globosa*)	Annual	Sun	Late spring to early fall	8 to 30
Heliotrope (*Heliotropium arborescens*)	Tender perennial	Sun, part shade	Summer to fall	15 (dwarf) to 48
Johnny-jump-up (*Viola tricolor*)	Annual, biennial, short-lived perennial	Sun, part shade	Spring and fall	8
Larkspur (*Consolida ambigua*)	Annual that self sows	Sun, part shade	Spring	18 to 36
Licorice Plant (*Helichrysum petiolare*)	Tender perennial	Sun	Spring through fall	16 to 18

Annuals & Biennials

Common Name (*Botanical Name*)	Type	Light	Bloom Time	Height (Inches)
Love-in-a-mist (*Nigella damascena*)	Annual	Sun	Spring	12 to 18
Marigold (*Tagetes* sp.)	Annual	Sun	Summer, fall	8 to 36
Mexican Sunflower (*Tithonia rotundifolia*)	Annual	Sun	Summer to fall	36 to 60
Moss Rose (*Portulaca grandiflora*)	Annual	Sun	Summer to early fall	4 to 8
Nasturtium (*Tropaeolum majus*)	Annual	Sun	Summer and fall	Creeps 8 to 12 feet
New Guinea Impatiens (*Impatiens* hybrid)	Tender perennial	Part sun	Summer	12 to 24
Ornamental Cabbage and Kale (*Brassica oleracea*)	Biennial grown as an annual	Sun	Fall to spring	8 to 14
Pansy (*Viola* x *wittrockiana*)	Annual	Sun, part shade	Fall, winter, spring	4 to 8
Petunia (*Petunia* x *hybrida*)	Tender perennial or warm-weather annual	Sun	Spring through summer	6 to 18
Phlox, Annual (*Phlox drummondii*)	Annual	Sun	Summer	To 18
Pot Marigold (*Calendula officinalis*)	Annual	Sun, part shade	Spring	18 to 25 dwarf, 12
Red Salvia (*Salvia splendens*)	Tender perennial	Sun	Summer to early fall	7 to 24
Snapdragon (*Antirrhinum majus*)	Tender perennial	Sun, part shade	Spring, summer to late fall	6 to 36
Spider Flower (*Cleome hasslerana*)	Annual	Sun	Summer through fall	3 to 5 feet
Sunflower (*Helianthus annuus*)	Annual	Sun	Summer	2 to 12 feet
Sweet William (*Dianthus barbatus*)	Biennial or short-lived perennial	Sun	Late summer	6 to 12
Tobacco Flower (*Nicotiana alata*)	Annual or short-lived perennial	Part shade	Summer to mid-fall	To 5 feet
Transvaal Daisy, Gerbera (*Gerbera jamesonii*)	Tender perennial	Sun	Summer	12 to 24
Verbena (*Verbena* x *hybrida*)	Tender perennial	Sun	Summer	10 to 20
Vinca, Pink/Madagascar Periwinkle (*Catharanthus roseus*)	Tender perennial	Sun, part shade	Summer	4 to 18
Wishbone Flower (*Torenia fournieri*)	Annual	Part shade, shade	Summer through fall	8
Zinnia, Tall (*Zinnia elegans*)	Annual	Sun	Summer to fall	To 36

PLANNING

Use pages torn from the many garden catalogs to create your own album of annuals. It is a real help in planning your garden. Put a sticky note by each plant reminding yourself where you think it would fit in your garden and why you pulled the page. Organize the plants according to their season of bloom. When considering flowers prone to powdery mildew, like **zinnias**, **verbena**, and **annual phlox,** choose disease-resistant varieties.

An album made up of catalog pages showing garden equipment and accessories you like is another useful reference and helps locate better pricing for expensive items.

Seed packets tell you whether the seeds can be started early indoors, and when. The introduction to this chapter explains how the "hardy," "half-hardy," and "tender" tags on packets relate to the seed's planting time. Seed packets tell you that speedy germinators, like **zinnias,** can be started indoors just four to six weeks before planting time but are often sown outdoors here. Slow annuals, like **petunias,** can be started indoors as many fifteen weeks before the weather will be warm enough to put them outdoors. For

Zone 8, that would be soon now. Get together the things you will need for the project.

Garden log. Make a record of the catalogs that provide the most useful information. Note the dates you placed your catalog order. Record the dates you started seeds indoors, and their progress.

PLANTING

Starting seeds indoors. This is a two-part project. First you sow the seeds and encourage them to germinate; then you transplant the seedlings and grow them into sturdy plants ready for their date with the garden.

Equipment. Commercial seed starting kits include strips of planting pockets, water-tight flats to hold them, and plastic covers to keep the soil moist while the seeds germinate.

You can improvise. For planting pockets and flats, use baking tins or porous cardboard egg cartons set on cookie tins. For a cover, tent the containers with clear plastic, the type used to insulate windows. Seeds that transplant with difficulty (the packet will tell you) you had best grow in individual peat pots.

Use a sterile **seed starting** mix for plants that will be moved outdoors in four to eight weeks. Use a commercial **potting mix** for plants that will be indoors eight to ten weeks. Soak clay and peat pots thoroughly before filling them.

Sowing the seeds. Moisten the planting medium in its bag so that it's moist but not so wet you can squeeze water out of it, and then scoop it into the containers. Seed packets tell you whether the seeds need to germinate in dark or with light. Sprinkle seeds whose packets say they need light to germinate over the growing medium, but don't cover them. Sow seeds that germinate in the dark in planting holes made with a pencil or a pointed stick—1/4 inch deep for medium-size seeds and 1 inch deep for large seeds.

To plant a flat, make shallow furrows in the potting medium, drop in the seeds, and cover them with the soil. Mix very fine seeds half and half with sand, sprinkle them from a salt shaker, and cover them with a dusting of the starter mix.

Provide each planting pocket, or row, with a label identifying the seeds. Popsicle sticks sized to fit under the cover are a fine substitute for commercial row markers. **Write the names on the labels with a waterproof marker.**

Germination. Cover the flats for the week or two needed for germination. Moderate (ambient) light is enough at this stage. The annuals labeled "hardy" do not need bottom heat to germinate, and do best in a cool room or basement. Others germinate most rapidly with bottom heat, and in air temperatures of 65 to 70 degrees Fahrenheit. Heat mats are offered by catalogs and available at garden centers. A heating pad on Low will do the job; protect it from moisture with plastic film.

Check your flats daily. When most of the seeds have germinated, remove the covers, and move the flats to good light on a sill or in a light garden.

Water flats of seedlings from the bottom, or just mist the seedlings. Air the room often. Cool nights are beneficial. Seedlings that will be growing indoors for six weeks need good light to thrive.

An installation of two 4-foot fluorescent lights burning fourteen to sixteen hours a day is especially helpful if you plan to start a lot of your own seedlings indoors.

CARE

Change the water in which cuttings taken last fall are rooting and add two or three

Did You Know?

Easy to Start Indoors

- **Ageratum,** 8 to 10 weeks
- **Cosmos,** 4 to 6 weeks
- **Celosia,** 5 to 6 weeks
- **China Aster,** 6 to 10 weeks
- **Cleome,** 6 to 10 weeks
- **Flowering Tobacco,** 9 to 11 weeks
- **Mallow,** *Lavatera trimestris* 6 to 8 weeks
- **Marigolds,** dwarf, 8 to 10 weeks
- **Marigolds,** tall, 5 to 6 weeks
- **Petunia,** 11 to 15 weeks
- **Portulaca,** 10 to 12 weeks
- **Salvia,** 8 to 10 weeks
- **Snapdragon,** dwarf, 12 to 14 weeks
- **Snapdragon,** tall, 6 to 10 weeks
- **Verbena,** 8 to 10 weeks
- **Zinnias,** dwarf, 6 to 8 weeks
- **Zinnias,** tall 4 to 6 weeks

pieces of charcoal, the kind that keeps the water in fish tanks clear.

PRUNING

Pinch back leggy cuttings and plants.

WATERING

Maintain moisture in pots of annuals and tropicals wintering indoors.

FERTILIZING

We gain almost a whole hour of extra daylight this month, so plants are starting to grow again. Add a half-strength dose of houseplant fertilizer to the water

for cuttings, plants, and tropicals stored indoors for winter that are showing new growth.

PESTS

Damping off is a threat to seedlings. It's a fungal disease that attacks the seedlings at the base of their stems. It rots the stems so the plants fall over.

A sterile growing medium and good drainage help avoid the condition. The fungicide Thiram (Arasan) is a good preventative against damping off.

PLANNING

As you finalize your catalog orders and buying plans, make sure there is a suitable place and space in your plan for each plant chosen. Heights and widths appear on the catalog pages in your album, on seed packets, and in our charts. Tall plants go to the back, mid-height in the middle, and shorties up front. The width measurement tells you how many of each type will fill the space.

Ordering seeds. Check your buying plans against your inventory of seeds that were left over or saved from last year and the cuttings and potted plants brought indoors last fall. List what you have, will order by mail, will buy at a garden center, and what you will have to go looking for. Seeds of the fragrant **petunias, 'Celebrity White', 'Ultra White',** and **'Apollo',** for example, may take time to locate.

That done, you are ready to write up mail-orders and prepare shopping lists for later purchases at garden centers. Many mail-order houses now offer seedlings as well as seeds.

Garden log. Note design ideas picked up at flower shows and in visits to other gardens. Record the progress of the seeds started indoors.

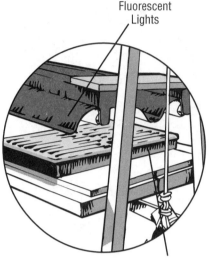

Fluorescent Lights

Seed-Starter Tray in 10x20" Flat Tray

 PLANTING

Indoors. Zones 6 and 7: Start seeds for **ageratum, alyssum, China asters, geraniums, nicotiana, pansies, petunias, annual phlox, snapdragons,** and **stock.** (See Planting, January.) Zone 8 weather may encourage starting the hardiest of these outdoors late this month.

Sowing annuals outdoors. Most annuals sown outdoors come into bloom soonest when the seeds are sown where they are to flower. Seeds germinate most satisfactorily in moist, fluffy soil. If you can plant shortly after a rain and before the next one is expected, you won't have to water. If not, water well both before and after sowing the seeds.

The planting depth for seeds is usually given on the seed packet. The rule of thumb is to sow seeds at a depth about three times the seed's diameter, not its length.

The easy way to sow fine seeds evenly is to "broadcast" them, that is, sprinkle them over the bed. When the seedlings are up, thin them to the distance suggested by seed packets, or so that they are at least 3 to 5 inches apart.

Larger seeds are sown in "hills," groups of four to six, or three to five, equidistant from each other. Flowers for edging paths or the front of a flower bed are usually sown in "drills," dribbled at spaced intervals along a shallow furrow. An easy way to make the furrow is to drag the edge of a rake or a hoe handle along the planting line.

CARE

When the seedlings started earlier indoors become crowded, transplant each to an individual 3- to 4-inch pot filled with a good potting mix.

When the seedlings started earlier indoors become crowded, transplant each to an individual 3- to 4-inch pot filled with a good potting mix.

Seedlings that will be growing indoors for six weeks need good light to thrive. At this stage, an installation of grow lights burned fourteen to sixteen hours a day is especially helpful. If you plan to start a lot of your own seedlings indoors, it would be worth your while to invest in a light table.

Begin repotting plants brought indoors last fall, and pot up the strongest cuttings. (See March, New Plants from Stem Cuttings.) Continue to fertilize them.

If you planted a cover crop in your garden in the fall, (see October, Planting) turn it under now.

Did You Know?

Annuals for Colorful Foliage

- **Alternanthera,** *Alternanthera* cvs.
- **Beefsteak Plant,** *Acalypha wilkesiana*
- **Burning Bush,** *Bassia scoparia* forma(sic) *trichophylla*
- **Coleus,** *Coleus* x *hybridus*
- **Coppertone Mallow,** *Hibiscus acetosella*
- **Dusty Miller,** *Senecio cineraria* 'Silver Dust' and 'Cirrus'
- **Jacob's Coat,** *Acalypha wilkesiana*
- **Joseph's Coat,** *Amaranthus tricolor* 'Joseph's-coat'
- **New Guinea Impatiens,** *Impatiens hawkeri* hybrids
- **Polka Dot Plant,** *Hypoestes phyllostachya*
- **Snow on the Mountain,** *Euphorbia marginata*
- **Variegated Impatiens,** *Impatiens wallerana* variety
- **Variegated Wax Begonia,** *Begonia* Semperflorens Cultorum Hybrids
- **Variegated Zonal Geranium,** *Pelargonium* 'Ben Franklin'

 PRUNING

Pull out, and discard **ornamental cabbages** and **kale.** Deadhead the **pansies.**

 WATERING

Water pots of transplanted seedlings as the soil becomes dry to the touch.

 FERTILIZING

Do not fertilize transplanted seedlings until the appearance of two or three new leaves tells you the root system is growing again.

Every two weeks fertilize all the seedlings that will remain indoors another six weeks or more with a houseplant fertilizer at half strength.

 PESTS

Seedlings suffering from poor drainage, lack of air, and crowding are vulnerable to the fungus called "damping off," which rots stems near the soil surface. Discard affected plants, reduce watering, and increase light and fresh air. If the problem persists, mist the seedlings with a fungicide, such as Thiram (Arasan.)

MARCH
Annuals & Biennials

 PLANNING

Take advantage of sales this month of fertilizers and other soil additives. But be cautious—these may be leftovers. If the price is a steal, make sure the bag is whole.

Go out to your garden, and reserve the space meant for the plants you've ordered. Take along a set of row markers on which you have written the names of the plants you will be setting out.

- In gardens of perennials and shrubs: outline each bay meant for annuals with a stick, and plant a row marker indicating the flower that goes there.

- In cutting and kitchen gardens: plant a row marker at the end of each row, indicating the vegetable or flower that goes there.

- In a garden for annuals: outline the bays, and press a row marker into the ground to designate which plant belongs where.

Garden log. Record the date of the last frost and when you planted what in your garden. Record the dates of any really good early plant sales. Chronicle the progress of seeds started indoors and your impression of the growing mediums used because you may want to try a different brand next time. Record the arrival of seedlings ordered from catalogs and their condition on arrival.

PLANTING

You can begin prepping your garden beds as soon as winter moisture has left the soil. A new bed needs the careful soil preparation described in the Introduction to the book. An established bed for annuals also needs attention every year, as do areas reserved for annuals in gardens of perennials and shrubs.

The first step is to clean up the remains of last year's annuals. Take this debris to the trash. Don't compost it because there's a good chance organisms you don't want to encourage have developed over the winter.

Shortly **before the last frost**, gardeners can begin sowing seeds and planting seedlings of **hardy** annuals in garden beds, hanging baskets, window boxes, and large containers set in a sheltered spot. The fragrant **sweet pea variety 'Sugar 'n Spice'** is recommended for baskets.

Shortly **after the last frost,** you can sow seeds and plant seedlings of **semi-hardy** annuals. You can plant fragrant **sweet peas** outdoors now; these climbers need support—strings, brambles, obelisks. Soak or nick the seeds before planting.

In Zone 8 the last frost should occur sometime toward the end of March. In March the soil usually is still wet and cold, so it's not likely you'll need to water before or after sowing the seeds. Sow seeds of fast-growing annuals among the spring-flowering bulbs; as they grow up they'll mask the bulbs' yellowing foliage.

For detailed how-to instructions on sowing seeds and planting seedlings, turn to Planting, April.

Repot **geraniums, lantana, mandevilla** saved from last year. Plant **pansies.**

CARE

Look over the cuttings and plants you brought indoors last year, and discard poor performers.

PRUNING

Pinch out the growing tips of seedlings that are becoming leggy.

Deadhead the **pansies** planted last fall to encourage blooming.

WATERING

Continue watering indoor seedlings.

FERTILIZING

Every other time you water annuals wintering indoors, include fertilizer at half strength.

To assure the lavish production annuals are capable of, before planting each year André checks the pH of the garden soil and adjusts it to between 6.0 and 7.0. You can learn how to do this in the Introduction to the book. Then André works into the top 6 to 8 inches of the soil a generous helping of nutrients (except for **nasturtiums**). An organic fertilizer will carry the plants through the whole growing season.

When working the soil, disturb as little as possible the area where self-sowers like **cleome** and **nigella** grew last year and where you had planted seeds of hardy biennials. Even if there's no sign of growth, the seeds are there and will germinate and develop soonest if undisturbed.

Did You Know?

New Plants from Stem Cuttings

Cuttings and potted-up plants brought indoors last fall can provide you with new plants for your garden. Here's how you can multiply your holdings:

Geraniums. Cut off the top 4 inches of a sturdy, healthy stem just below a leaf node. Remove the leaves from the bottom 2 inches. Let the cuttings dry for a few hours or overnight. Then put them in a solution that is a gallon of water to which you have added $\frac{1}{2}$ to 1 teaspoon of bleach, and set them in a sunny window. When they have grown a full set of roots—usually a matter of three or four weeks—transplant your cuttings to 3- to 4-inch pots filled with a gritty potting mix or non-clumping kitty litter. Or, root the cuttings in a rooting mixture. Grow your cuttings in a south-facing window.

You can also get cuttings to root by dipping the ends lightly in a rooting hormone and standing them in damp vermiculite or sand tented with plastic film. When the cuttings have developed enough roots to resist a slight tug, they're ready to transplant.

Coleus and wax begonias. Cut off the top 6 inches of a leafy stem just below a leaf node. Remove the leaves from the bottom 3 inches, then place the cutting in water containing a few drops of bleach, and set it in a semi-sunny window to root. When it has grown roots, transplant it into an all-purpose potting mix. Grow it in an east or west facing sunny window.

PESTS

Spider mites can be a problem with indoor seedlings. See the section on Pests, Diseases, and Controls in the Appendix.

PLANNING

Take the list of the annuals you are planning to purchase as seedlings to the garden centers and compare prices, sizes, and quality,

Garden log. Record the annuals that are coming into bloom as a prompt for plant combinations to try next year.

Record each and every planting date, and record how seeds and seedlings planted outdoors are doing.

PLANTING

When you plant your baskets and container gardens, be sure to include annuals with a graceful drooping habit, like **variegated vinca, sweet potato vine,** and **cascade petunias.** Don't overplant! Leave space for second and third plantings of **petunia** seedlings. **Petunias** tend to play out in August, even when deadheaded regularly; adding **petunias** at three week intervals will keep the containers in full flower until early fall. The **'Surfinia'** and **'Wave' petunias** have more staying power than others.

Before filling moss-lined baskets with soil, patch or replace the moss so the earth won't dribble out. You'll find bags of moss at garden centers and florists. Fill your pots, windowboxes, and planters with commercial bagged potting mix that includes slow-release fertilizers and moisturizing polymers that will save you time watering.

Prepare containers too big to empty for planting by mixing slow-release fertilizer and 2 inches of compost into the top 6 inches of the soil.

In Zone 7 the last frost comes toward the end of this month. Zone 7 gardeners can sow seeds and plant seedlings of hardy annuals a little before that date, and of semi-hardy annuals a little after it.

When night temperatures are steady at 55 degrees Fahrenheit, you can put out seeds and seedlings of tender annuals and perennials

If the **icicle pansies** planted last fall look meager, give them a few weeks to grow out, and then fill the bed with fresh **pansy** seedlings, or with **primroses.**

To hide the yellowing leaves of your **spring-flowering bulbs,** plant big container-grown hardy biennials; **sweet William** and tall **snapdragons** are excellent possibilities.

Quick and easy transplanting instructions:

1 To prepare seedlings started indoors for life in the garden, harden them off for five or six days in a sheltered spot out of the wind and direct sun. The soil they are growing in will dry more quickly outdoors, so check it often and water as needed. Seedlings fresh from a greenhouse also benefit from a few days in a sheltered spot before being planted in the open garden.

2 When you bring home more flats of seedlings than you have time to plant (we always do), water them well, and place them out of direct sun until you are ready to transplant. Check the soil moisture daily, especially flats whose soil is hidden by foliage. A six-pack's tiny planting pockets can dry out in just hours on a hot, windy day, and you won't know it until the leaves collapse. That check in growth isn't a good thing!

3 When you head for the garden to transplant your seedlings, take along a pail of water to which you have added starter solution or a dose of manure tea or liquid seaweed. If you followed the March suggestions to prepare beds for planting, you will not need additional fertilizer now.

4 Make planting holes with the end of your trowel for as many seedlings as you will be putting in the area. Remove an equal number of seedlings from their containers; use shears to cut apart those that have grown together.

5 Before setting a seedling in its hole, gently unwind roots circling the rootball, and cut off those matted at the bottom. Set the seedlings upright in their planting holes, starting with the hole farthest from you. Add a half cupful of water from the pail to each planting hole.

6 When the water has drained, fill the holes with soil, and firm the soil around each seedling. The seedlings should be set in tightly enough so they resist a gentle tug. Pinch out the central stem and branch tips of the seedlings to encourage branching and more surfaces where flowers can develop.

7 Water the area with a sprinkler for half an hour or so. Apply a 2-inch layer of mulch all around, starting 3 inches from the crown.

Did You Know?

Outstanding Annuals for Baskets

- **Bacopa,** *Sutera cordata* 'Snowflake'
- **Basket Begonia,** *Begonia* x *tuberhybrida* Pendula Group
- **Black-eyed Susan Vine,** *Thunbergia alata*
- **Cascade Petunia,** *Petunia* x *hybrida*
- **Cigar Flower,** *Cuphea ignea*
- **Creeping Zinnia,** *Sanvitalia procumbens*
- **Edging Lobelia,** *Lobelia erinus*
- **Fanflower,** *Scaevola aemula*
- **Impatiens, Busy Lizzy,** *Impatiens wallerana*
- **Ivy-leaf** and **Balcon Geraniums,** *Pelargonium peltatum*
- **Lady's-eardrops,** *Fuchsia* x *hybrida*
- **Nasturtium,** *Tropaeolum majus*
- **Painted Nettle,** *Coleus blumei*
- **Rose Moss,** *Portulaca grandiflora*
- **Sapphire Flower,** *Browallia speciosa*
- **Tall Nasturtium,** *Tropaeolum majus*
- **Trailing Coleus 'Trailing Rose',** *Coleus rehnelthianus*
- **Verbena,** *Verbena* x *hybrida*
- **Water Hyssop,** *Bacopa caroliniana*
- **Yellow Sage,** *Lantana camara*

 ## CARE

Transplant seedlings outgrowing their containers to larger pots.

 ## PRUNING

Deadhead **pansies**, **primroses**, and other early spring annuals.

Pinch out the growing tips of plants that have become leggy.

 ## WATERING

Seeds and seedlings in the garden need rain often enough during the next two or three weeks to maintain soil moisture. If spring turns dry, or if you see signs of wilting, water your seedlings deeply. Specific directions of deep watering are given in the general Introduction to the book.

 ## FERTILIZING

Continue to fertilize seedlings of the tender perennials and annuals that will remain indoors until the air temperature reaches 55 degrees Fahrenheit at night.

 ## PESTS

Spider mites can be a problem for indoor seedlings. For controls check the section on Pests, Diseases, and Controls in the Appendix.

PLANNING

On cold, rainy days, cruise the garden centers searching for seedlings to fill gaps left by spring-flowering bulbs and other seedlings for late summer bloom.

Look for places in the garden where you could tuck in a few annuals that are fragrant at night and for flowers that will reflect moonlight—white, pale yellow, or pink. Seedlings of white **annual stock** are very fragrant late in the day.

Garden log. As spring gardens peak, visit public and private gardens looking for inspiration. Record the names of annuals and plant combinations you wish were blooming in your own garden right now.

Note when night temperatures reached a steady 55 degrees Fahrenheit . . . what you planted when, what is blooming.

Evaluate your spring garden and your responses to it.

 PLANTING

In Zone 6 and where the last frost may come in mid-May, wait to plant seeds and seedlings of **hardy annuals** until a little before that date, and of **semi-hardy** annuals a little after it.

When night temperatures reach 55 degrees Fahrenheit and above, you can sow seeds of tender annuals outdoors and set out seedlings of tender perennials grown indoors. The tropicals are safe outdoors now, too.

Where spring bulbs have gone by, make successive sowings of **zinnias** and **annual phlox.**

Sow late-blooming annuals and biennials for next year's display—either indoors, outdoors in a cold frame (see November, Herbs & Vegetables), or in an out-of-the-way place in the garden.

When the **pansies** and **primroses** fade, replace them with edging **lobelia** and follow with long-season low edgers like **wax begonias, dwarf snapdragons, dwarf marigolds,** and **dwarf zinnias.** Little **sweet alyssum** is a full-sun edger that will perfume evenings in late summer.

 CARE

Thin self-sown and other seedlings to 2 to 3 inches apart.

If plants in hanging baskets and containers become crowded, remove the least vigorous seedlings.

 PRUNING

Deadhead **pansies** and **primroses,** and shear **lobelia** to prolong the flowering cycle.

Monitor and pinch out the tips of branching annuals that develop one or more strong central stems. Continue to pinch them back until the stems are 6 inches long. Tall **snapdragons, salvia, stock, petunias,** and other cascading plants are among those that benefit from persistent pinching.

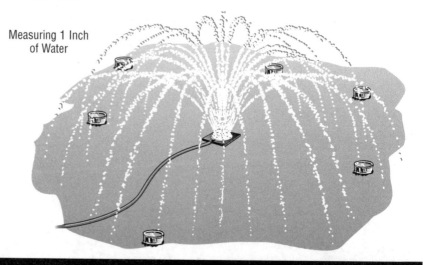

Measuring 1 Inch of Water

Weeding. Weeds aren't always ugly, but they always take up water and soil nutrients. They appear plentifully now, and by mid-summer the big roots are hard to pull. A permanent mulch, close planting, and planting through a porous black plastic film keep them down.

Get weeds gone early. Less than an inch high, you can rake them up. When they're 6 inches high, you'll need a hoe to cut them down. After that—well, the worst thing for a newly established garden is to have weeds flower and set seed there or nearby. They'll haunt you for years to come.

Don't pull big weeds from bone-dry soil—they're more tenacious than they are in moist soil, and the upheaval of the soil can cost moisture. Water the garden first, then tug the weeds out gently but firmly to get the roots up. Shake the soil back into the garden, and compost the weeds.

 # WATERING

Unless the garden is moist from recent rain, before every planting gently and slowly water long enough to lay down 1 to 1½ inches. Use an empty coffee tin to measure. After planting, water the area for half an hour more.

Did You Know?

Outstanding for Fragrance

- **Four-o'clock,** *Mirabilis jalapa*
- **Evening Stock,** *Matthiola tricuspidata*, *M. bicornis* 'Starlight Sensation'
- **Heliotrope,** *Heliotropium arborescens*
- **Large White Petunia,** *Petunia axillaris*, *P.* F2 hybrids
- **Mignonette,** *Reseda odorata*
- **Nicotiana hybrids,** *N.* x *sanderae*
- **Sweet Alyssum,** *Lobularia maritima* 'Sweet White'
- **Sweet Pea,** *Lathyrus odoratus* 'Cupani', 'Old Spice', 'Old-Fashioned Scented Mixed'
- **Wallflower,** *Cheiranthus cheirii*
- **Wild Sweet William,** *Phlox drummondii*
- **Woodland Tobacco,** *Nicotiana sylvestris*

Maintain the moisture in newly planted seeds and seedlings. Unchecked growth is essential to the development of root systems strong enough to bloom and withstand summer heat. If you do not have a good soaking rain every week to ten days, water planted beds gently and slowly long enough to lay down 1 or 2 inches.

This month begin bi-weekly checks of the moisture in plant containers; check the moisture level in small pots and hanging baskets every day or two.

 # FERTILIZING

Begin a regular fertilizing program for hanging baskets and container plants. They'll benefit from bi-weekly applications of a soluble fertilizer or manure tea at half strength.

PESTS

Be on guard against aphids, spider mites, whiteflies, and, in rainy weather, snails and slugs. For controls, see the section on Pests, Diseases, and Controls in the Appendix.

JUNE
Annuals & Biennials

 PLANNING

Visit public gardens, and check out the follow-on plants used to replace spring bulbs.

Garden log. Record the dates of especially worthwhile plant sales held as spring ends.

Continue to record and date the development of this year's plantings.

It is far enough into the season now to evaluate the performance of transplants of rooted cuttings and plants saved from last year—**geraniums, coleus, impatiens, wax begonias,** and others—and decide whether this is something you want to do again in the fall. Was saving the **mandevilla** and **bougainvillea** worth the effort? Did saving plants save money?

 PLANTING

Remove the last of the spring flowers, and replace them with seeds or seedlings of annuals that will bloom until frosts—blue and white **salvia, China asters, cosmos,** and **'Silver Cup' mallow** (*Lavatera trimestris*) whose showy pink blooms light up the late garden. Sow seeds for a final succession planting of **zinnias** for cutting.

Make space in baskets and containers for fresh **petunia** seedlings. They'll keep color there after earlier plantings play out.

Use seedlings to fill gaps opening up in flower beds as spring-flowering bulbs die away.

Volunteers of self-sown **snapdragons, French marigolds, cosmos,** and other annuals pop up every year, and they make good fillers. **Petunias** often volunteer, but they're so slow to bloom they're only worth transplanting where months of growing weather lie ahead.

 CARE

To keep roots cool and weeds down, mulch flower beds 2 inches deep starting 3 inches from the crown of each flower. André uses fine grade hammermill bark and also recommends pine and hardwood bark, West Coast fir bark, cedar bark, and cypress. Coconut hulls are pretty, but they aren't best where mold is a problem. Compost and leaf mold (decomposed leaves) are beneficial mulches, but weeds and roots grow into them, and they decompose quickly in heat.

Staking. The tallest flowers benefit from staking—tall **snapdragons** and **zinnias, 'Climax' marigolds,** and **woodland tobacco.** Set the stakes within 2 to 3 inches of the stems. Choose stakes as tall as the plants are likely to grow. Tie the main stems loosely to the stakes with soft green wool, raffia, or cotton string.

 PRUNING

Continue weed patrol. Root out prolific self-sowers like **love-in-a-mist** just as you would weeds.

Continue to pinch out the tips of the **petunias** and other cascading plants and branching annuals.

Snip off at ground level the stems of plants crowding others, as **nasturtiums** often will, and cut back the outer stems of perennials that are crowding annuals planted among them.

 WATERING

Check the moisture in plant containers, hanging baskets, and windowboxes daily or every other day. On hot, windy days even large containers may need more frequent watering. Terracotta containers dry out especially quickly.

Check the moisture in plant containers, hanging baskets, and window boxes daily or every other day. On hot, windy days even large containers may need more frequent watering.

Did You Know?

Deadheading/Harvesting

Removing fading blooms stops plants from developing seeds and stimulates the production of flowers. It's called "deadheading." If your garden is small, you can enjoy pinching out dying blossoms. A big garden is something else: starting in June, André goes through his six acres of gardens with hand-held shears and deadheads spent flowers. It takes him about an hour to do the whole garden.

"Pinching out" is the quick and easy way to deadhead flowers on slender stems. Place your thumbnail and forefinger back of the bracts—the small scale-like leaves behind the petals—and squeeze the flower head off. To deadhead stems too thick to pinch out, use small pointed pruning shears made especially for the purpose.

Shearing may help plants attacked by mildew; take them down to the ground. Diseased foliage goes into the garbage—not into the compost pile. The new foliage may grow in clean.

Harvesting most annuals has the same effect as deadheading. Cut the stems of **zinnias** and **cosmos** just above a pair of leaves, which is where the next set of flowering stems will develop.

Maintain moisture in new plantings of seeds and seedlings. Annuals have shallow roots, and to grow they need sustained moisture. Water wilting plants at noon or in late afternoon.

FERTILIZING

Add enough compost or potting soil to plant containers to maintain the level where it was when you first planted them. Continue to fertilize with a half dose of houseplant fertilizer or weak manure tea every two weeks.

Annuals that have been blooming benefit from a sidedressing of compost, or a foliar feeding of liquid fish emulsion, liquid seaweed, manure, or compost tea.

PESTS

Avoid over-watering in hot muggy weather because it encourages mildew. If powdery mildew appears, as it often does on ordinary varieties of **zinnias** and **annual phlox,** remove severely infected plants, thinning the bed to allow air all around. Check the plantings often, and take spent flowers, fallen petals, and leaves to the trash. Don't compost them. Spray the plant with André's remedy: a combination of 1 tablespoon of baking soda, and 1 tablespoon of ultra-fine horticultural oil in a gallon of water.

JULY
Annuals & Biennials

 PLANNING

Before your vacation, arrange to have the container plantings watered. Ease the chore by grouping the containers in a semi-shaded spot and providing each with a saucer. Investigate automatic watering systems.

Garden log. Note when dry spells begin and how long they last.

Weary of deadheading? Make a note to try annuals that self-clean next year—for example, **narrowleaf zinnias, wax begonias, impatiens, ageratum, pentas, New Guinea impatiens, spider flower.**

 PLANTING

Starting now until early August, seeds of hardy fall-flowering annuals can be started—**pansies**, **sweet alyssum**, **calendula** (try the newcomer '**Pink Surprise**'), **ornamental cabbage,** and **kale.** Biennials to start now include **foxgloves, money plant,** and **sweet William.**

In the warm Mid-Atlantic, **cleome, cosmos, sunflowers, zinnias,** and **marigolds** sown now may have time to bloom.

 CARE

Remove crowded plants and poor performers from baskets and window boxes. If there is space and time, replant with fresh seedlings.

Monitor staked annuals, and tie the main stems and branches higher up.

 PRUNING

Continue to deadhead. Pull out unwanted self-sowers. Snip off leggy **petunia** stems with only a few buds at the tips. Pinch off spiky **coleus** flowers, and cut back ungainly stems. Shear small-flowered plants such as **annual coreopsis** and **dwarf cosmos** to encourage a new round of flowers.

 WATERING

Ageratum and other annuals that brown out in high heat will revive in the cool moist weather of early fall. For now, water but don't fertilize.

Water your compost pile when you water the garden, and turn it weekly.

Flower beds and new plants thrive with two to three hours of gentle rain every ten days to two weeks. At this point in summer André usually waters twice a month with hose-fed brass impulse sprinklers that deliver two gallons a minute. He runs them for twelve hours in each spot.

Overhead watering should not cause problems as long as you water deeply and the foliage dries between sessions. Watering early in the morning saves water loss to evaporation. Daytime watering lowers leaf temperatures and reduces stress, but evening watering is all right if you can't do it earlier.

Where mildew is a problem, water with soaker hoses to avoid wetting the foliage.

 FERTILIZING

Plants that are blooming vigorously may benefit from a side dressing of a handful of compost. Or, with a hose end sprayer, apply diluted solutions of fish emulsion, liquid seaweed, manure, or compost tea to the foliage.

Continue to fertilize container plants every two weeks with a half-strength dose of liquid fertilizer.

Top the soil in containers with a layer of compost.

 PESTS

In hot, airless corners, aphids, spider mites, and whiteflies are a threat. Spraying with a neem-based product helps.

If you see powdery mildew, remove the infected plants, and thin the bed to provide more air. Remove spent flowers, fallen petals, and leaves, and take them to the trash.

For other controls, see the section on Pests, Diseases, and Controls in the Appendix.

Did You Know?

Harvesting and Drying Flowers

As flowers used in potpourris and dried bouquets come into bloom, harvest the best specimens. Summer's dry heat speeds the process.

When harvesting for **potpourris**, pick the flower heads in a dry, hot moment of the day. Spread the petals over paper towels on screens. Set the screens to dry in a warm, airy, dry place.

For **dried bouquets**, harvest large, moist flowers like **zinnias** when the blooms are fully open. Single varieties are better for drying than doubles. Harvest dryish flowers like the **everlastings** and **salvia** just before the buds open. Cut fresh, healthy stems 12 to 14 inches long, and strip away all the lower leaves to prepare them for drying.

- **Air drying.** Tie the stems together in small, loose bunches, then enclose the heads in paper bags as they shed. Label the bags. Hang the bunches upside down for two to ten days, or until very dry, in a warm, airy, dark place. Direct sunlight fades the colors.

- **Silica gel.** Use this light, grainy gel to dry delicate, moist flowers like **cosmos.** Spread 2 or 3 inches of gel in a large box. Wire the flower stems, lay them on the gel, and cover them with more silica gel. In twenty-four hours check a flower; if it is dry, remove the others from the gel, and leave them on top of it for another day. Then store them layered in tissue in air-tight, labeled boxes to which you have added a few table-spoons of silica gel. If gel clings to the petals, pour a little clean sand over them to remove them.

With use, the gel's blue crystals turn pink. To restore it for later use, spread the gel over cookie sheets covered with paper towels and heat in a conventional oven on low, thirty minutes for a 1-pound can. The gel turns light blue when it is ready to use again. The gel gets hot, so cool it in the oven five to ten minutes, and then store it in air-tight containers.

- **Oven-drying.** Dryish flowers dry well in a conventional oven on a low setting. A microwave oven at half-power can dry flowers in minutes. Dry a test flower for each batch to learn the length of time the others will need. Support the flower with a paper towel before drying it. The outside petals dry sooner than those inside.

To avoid over-drying in either type of oven, check progress often through the oven window.

AUGUST
Annuals & Biennials

 PLANNING

Begin preparing places to plant the fall seedlings started earlier.

Garden log. Note how the annuals, in public, private, and your own gardens, are reacting to August drought. Those that are doing well are the ones you want to try next year.

 PLANTING

Early this month you can start seeds of **pansies, calendula, flowering cabbage, kale,** and other fall annuals. Toward the end of the month, you'll find their seedlings at garden centers.

If you can find fresh **petunia** seedlings, add a final round to hanging baskets and windowboxes.

In our warmest regions there's still time to sow **snapdragons, calendula,** and **stock.**

 CARE

Do not let weeds mature!! They're drifting into your garden right now looking for a start.

Check the mulch. It decomposes rapidly in high heat and humidity.

Mid-month check the staking annuals. If needed, install taller stakes.

 PRUNING

Continue to deadhead and harvest flowers. The late summer annuals provide some of the year's loveliest bouquets. Our favorite bouquets include airy **cosmos** with spikes of **blue salvia,** mid-size **dahlias,** and stems of **basil** and **mint** for their sweet spicy aroma.

Attics and garages are hot and dry in August, perfect for air-drying **statice, blue salvia,** and others recommended in our July list.

Cut all older **petunia** stems back by two-thirds, and fertilize the plants.

 WATERING

You will probably have to water this month. If you can, water in the early morning. Water slowly and well, as described in July. Where mildew is a threat, water the soil rather than the plants. In extreme heat, shower the garden at noon to lower the temperature and provide the plants with immediate relief.

Containers will have filled up with roots by now—so they need more frequent watering than earlier when plenty of moist soil surrounded the roots.

Water your compost pile when you water the garden. Turn it often.

 FERTILIZING

The mulch you applied is decomposing and providing fresh organic elements, and the organic fertilizers added to the soil last spring are still making nutrients available.

But the self-sowing annuals that will give you next year's crop can use a little help. Rake a compost or a slow-release fertilizer into the soil under the parent plants. The seeds will do best if they fall into a 1- or 2-inch layer of humusy soil. When the seedheads begin to swell and dry, gather a few and scatter the seeds over the soil. Or, wait until the seedheads are dry and seeds are loose inside, and then shake the flower heads vigorously over the soil.

PESTS

Aphid and spider mites love warm weather. Plants infested by spider mites have a faded, stippled look. Blow them away with a strong spray from the hose; rogue out badly infested plants. If the damage is considerable, consider a non-toxic spray.

If mildew is a problem, spray with André's remedy: 1 tablespoon baking soda, 1 tablespoon of ultra-fine horticultural oil mixed well in a gallon of water. When mildew persists, clear the bed, rake out the remains of the plants, and dispose of them in the trash—do not compost.

For other controls, see the section on Pests, Diseases, and Controls in Appendix.

Did You Know?

Harvesting and Drying Seeds

Harvesting seeds can give you great pleasure. To be sure you get the plant you expect from the seeds collected, harvest only seeds of *species*. Seeds of hybrids do not reliably repeat the qualities that are special; some or all may revert to the original species.

Harvesting. Harvest seeds that are ripe but not so ripe the seedheads drop or spew seeds to the ground. Ripe seeds are usually dark. When the vegetative envelopes swelling at the base of spent flowers begin to yellow and dry up, you can begin to harvest. Place the open end of a paper bag under a seedhead, and snip it into the bag.

Drying seeds. Spread seedheads and seeds on screens (try second-hand shops) lined with newspaper, and set them to dry in a warm, dry room until the seed envelopes are crackling dry, about five days. Separate the seeds from the chaff by rubbing the seedheads between your palms over a bowl. Gently blow away the chaff. Spread the seeds out to dry for another ten days.

Pour the seeds into glass jars, and cap them tightly. Check in a few days; if moisture has appeared inside the glass, air dry the seeds another few days. Store them in jars or small freezer bags. Label and date each one. Put a small mesh bag filled with flour into each container to absorb moisture. André stores seeds in the fridge.

SEPTEMBER

PLANNING

Right now, as you begin to plant the bulbs that will be the first to flower next spring, start to look for seeds of annuals you'd like to see coming up when the bulbs fade.

Garden log. Visit public and neighboring gardens, and keep notes on attractive combinations of fall bedding plants.

Note when the annuals in each of your gardens finished, when you removed them, which fall flowers you are replacing them with, and how they are performing.

Note where you have sown biennials and hardy annuals so you will know to leave the soil undisturbed when preparing the garden beds next spring.

PLANTING

Where frosts are early, begin to clear away played-out annuals. *Petunia integrifolia* and "supertunias" in the **Wave** series withstand some frost so let them bloom on, along with the hardy **snapdragons** and **geraniums.**

Replace the soil in windowboxes and containers you plan to replant for fall. The growing medium needn't include water-holding polymers. It does need a four-month supply of slow-release fertilizer. Replant with seedlings of hardy annuals, such as **pansies, violas, flowering cabbage** and **kale, calendula.** For its cascading foliage, plant **variegated myrtle,** which may winter over.

CARE

During dry spells, maintain soil moisture where you are encouraging self-sowers—**cleome, sweet alyssum, love-in-a-mist.**

Keep the compost pile moist, and turn it often.

When nighttime temperatures plunge towards 55 degrees Fahrenheit, move tender perennials and tropicals indoors.

Tropicals like **mandevilla** and **bougainvillea** thrive in a greenhouse and indoors in a sunny place. They may survive in a semi-dormant state in a frost-free garage, garden shed, or basement if you keep the soil damp. Move them when the soil is almost dry.

Several **tender perennials** make happy houseplants. **Impatiens** (African violet potting mix; semi-sun), **pentas,** and **browallia** do well indoors.

By September **coleus** plants are usually too big to bring in. We keep **coleus** by growing bouquets of cuttings in water. Here's how: Cut a dozen or more stems 12 to 14 inches long from the most beautiful **coleus** plants. Make the cut just below a node. Strip the leaves from the bottom 6 inches, and arrange the stems in clean water containing six drops of a liquid fertilizer. Place the cuttings in a cool room in good light. Change the water every month, and add a few drops of liquid fertilizer. Pinch out flower spikes as they appear.

Geraniums can come indoors, too. Choose well-branched plants, hose them down gently, and repot them in clean clay pots filled with slightly gritty potting soil. Indoors, **geraniums** do best in a cool room in full sun.

Another way to keep **geraniums** is by rooting cuttings. Cut 4-inch stems just below a node. Dip the cut ends lightly in rooting hormone, and stand them in damp vermiculite or sand. Tent them with plastic film, and keep the film in place until the stems have developed enough roots to resist a slight tug. Then transplant the rooted cuttings to individual pots.

Wax **begonias** and **impatiens** make excellent houseplants and bloom all winter. Dig up healthy plants, rinse them, and pot the roots in a potting mix. Grow them in a sunny window.

 # PRUNING

Thin the late blooming annuals planted earlier.

Harvest **impatiens** stems with half-opened buds for fillers for bouquets. A branch of one of the giant **marigolds** makes a bouquet all by itself.

Continue to deadhead and harvest late summer bloomers. Deadhead the **pansies.**

Attics and garages are still hot and dry, perfect for air drying **statice** and **blue salvia,** as described in our July list.

At this season, weeds are sowing seeds everywhere. Rake up weeds and their seedlings!

 ## Did You Know?

Making a Geranium Tree Standard

A **geranium** (or a **lantana** or **rosemary** for that matter) with a strong central stem is easy to train as a tree standard. Repot it in gritty potting soil. Tie the central stem firmly to a straight, sturdy stake. Bring the plant indoors to a sunny window in a cool room. Turn it at least once a month so all sides get equal sun.

- In January or February when new growth begins, remove all the branches and leaves except those growing at the top of the central stem. Pinch out the tips of those branches to begin to shape the top into a globe.

- In May repot the plant, and move it outdoors for the summer.

- In coming years continue to prune, shape, repot, and stake the plant. Winter it indoors, and summer it outdoors.

- When the central stem reaches 4 feet, allow the plant to bush out at the top. Continue to pinch the branch tips to encourage it to bush out in the shape of a globe.

 # WATERING

If you run into a dry spell, thoroughly water annuals sown recently.

 # FERTILIZING

Apply a light foliar feeding to **snapdragons** and other annuals that bloom until frosts.

PESTS

Protect plantings you plan to bring indoors for the winter against whiteflies and spider mites by applying an insecticide. Occasional showers, fresh air, and applications of insecticidal soap should keep problems away.

For other controls, see the section on Pests, Diseases, and Controls in the Appendix.

OCTOBER

 ## PLANNING

As the beds empty, their shapes emerge. This is an especially good time to make changes in the shapes and sizes of existing beds. Use a garden hose to outline potential changes and live with them a few days before you start to dig.

Planning a new bed for annuals? Start one now when you have time to grow a winter cover crop to improve the soil.

Early fall is ideal for dividing and moving most perennials. If you'd like to make more space for annuals next year in beds combining perennials and annuals, make the moves now.

Garden log. Record the date of the first **light frost,** the one that blackened the tips of the **impatiens** leaves. And record the date of the first **hard frost.**

Note the bedding plants used to replace faded summer annuals in public gardens.

Note the planting of a cover crop and its progress.

 ## PLANTING

Once you've had freezing weather, scratch up the soil, add fertilizer, and sow seeds of spring-blooming hardy annuals and perennials that germinate in cool temperatures—**foxglove, money plant, stock, larkspur, calendula,** and **sweet alyssum.** (Note: **sweet alyssum** often self-sows.) Mark the beds so you'll remember not to disturb the seedlings next spring.

Cover crop. A cover crop is a planting of a fast-growing grass or legume that is sown in an empty bed or row to keep weeds out and which is turned under after it grows. Called "green manure," it provides the soil with organic matter that enhances soil structure, adds nutrients, increases microbial activity, and helps to break up compacted areas. According to *Wyman's Gardening Encyclopedia,* three successive sowings of cover crops have been known to turn barren soil into rich, productive loam.

In the Mid-Atlantic, cover crops sown for spring are **clover, alfalfa,** and **lespedeza;** for summer, **millet, sorghum,** and **supan; winter rye** and **winter wheat** grow when temperatures are barely above freezing.

Planting a cover crop is simple enough. Till a quick-acting fertilizer into the soil, then broadcast the seeds over the bed. Make sure the soil stays moist until the seeds have sprouted. Rake, dig, or till in your cover crop before the plants go to seed, and at least ten days before planting the garden.

 ## CARE

Pull up, and compost frost-blacked **marigolds, impatiens,** and the tender annuals still out in the garden and in containers.

Turn the compost pile.

 ## PRUNING

Continue to deadhead the **pansies, calendula,** and any other flowers blooming in the garden.

 ## WATERING

If the weather turns dry, water the seedlings planted in late summer and early fall, the **pansies,** the areas around the self-sowing annuals, and the cover crop if you planted one.

As the beds empty, their shapes emerge. This is an especially good time to make changes in the shapes and sizes of existing beds.

# FERTILIZING

Apply a light foliar feeding to **snapdragons** and other annuals that bloom until frosts.

# PESTS

Keep an eye out for whiteflies and spider mites on the plants brought indoors for winter. If occasional showers and applications of insecticidal soap don't keep them away, apply an insecticide.

For other controls, see the section on Pests, Diseases, and Controls in the Appendix.

Did You Know?

About Flowering Cabbages and Kales

The leaves of these fabulous **cabbages** and **kales** are streaked, splotched, and edged red, purple, and cream. As the temperature drops, the colors grow more vibrant. They're the garden's last chance at beautiful fall color, a perfect replacement for fading garden mums. If you didn't sow seed last spring or early summer, you can buy good-sized plants at most garden centers.

Ornamental cabbage is a real cabbage that looks like a huge rose edged with red, pink, or cream. One of the most beautiful is **'Color Up Hybrid'**, which is almost 12 inches in diameter, brilliantly splotched and streaked over 80 percent of the head.

Flowering kale, Peacock hybrid, is spectacular. Just 12 inches tall, it has feathery leaves that are extravagantly serrated or notched and make a remarkable display in red or white.

Like kitchen cabbages, the ornamentals are cool-season plants. They stay beautiful all fall and through mild winters into spring when they send up seedheads. Keep the flower heads pinched out, and the plants stay in shape longer.

The **flowering cabbages** and **kales** thrive in deeply-dug, well-drained, fertile soil that holds moisture.

NOVEMBER
Annuals & Biennials

PLANNING

If you have planted the spring-flowering bulbs, the areas they occupy will be fresh in your mind. This is a good time to go through old garden catalogs looking for annuals you might plant next spring to hide the ripening foliage of those bulbs after they bloom.

Borrow from the public library garden books and videos that can teach you more about using annuals in garden design. Graham Rice's books, *Discovering Annuals* and *The Sweet Pea Book* (Timber Press) are a joy. One of Britain's most respected garden authorities, Graham now lives in America. The individual entries are a pleasure to read, and will inspire ideas for next year's gardens. The photography is superb.

Garden log. Record frost dates, and bring your garden log up to date.

If you don't have a garden log, this might be a moment when you have time to start one.

Computer or paper diary? A computer log is easy to adjust, change, improve. If you are computer literate and have a digital camera and photographer's software, you could include images with plant entries.

Writing in a diary takes time, but you may be more open to inspiration and pleasant memories. Holding a written diary in your hand can be a richer experience than looking something up on the computer.

Whichever way you go, a kept-up garden log provides answers to many questions you ask yourself every year. A record of the effect of the weather on your annuals can be really helpful. USDA and American Horticultural Society Climate maps zone our country into areas according to extremes of cold and heat. But in every yard there are microclimates, areas that are more or less exposed or sheltered. That changes what happens to annuals as well as to perennials.

Entries that remind you how various plants performed are invaluable when ordering seeds for the new season. Thoughts about plant and color combinations are worth keeping. You think you will remember, but when you start studying the year's new garden catalogs, the past season has a way of blurring at the edges.

PLANTING

In **frost-free** areas you can still transplant cold hardy annuals.

CARE

This is a good time to empty, clean, and store hanging baskets, windowboxes, and other containers.

Stack wire baskets, and hang them from a rafter in a garage or basement. Before putting plastic and terracotta containers away for the season, clean them in soapy water with a stiff brush or a scrub pad. Rinse them, then dip them in a solution of half a cup of bleach to 3 gallons of water. Rinse them again in clean water, and store them upside down. Find a storage place for terracotta pots out of the weather because they tend to crack when they are left outside.

Take the soil from hanging baskets, small and medium pots, planters, and windowboxes, and spread it over your compost pile. If you do not use your windowboxes for holiday displays, turn them upside down.

PRUNING

Remove dead annuals from the garden.

Deadhead plants you brought indoors for the winter.

Keep an eye out for whiteflies and spider mites on the plants brought indoors for winter. If occasional showers and applications of insecticidal soap don't keep them away, apply an insecticide.

 # WATERING

If you hit a dry spell, water your plantings.

Maintain soil moisture in plants you brought indoors for the winter.

Water the compost pile, and turn it weekly.

 # FERTILIZING

Do not fertilize the plants you brought indoors until they show signs of new growth in January.

 # PESTS

Keep an eye out for whiteflies and spider mites on the plants brought indoors for winter. If occasional showers and applications of insecticidal soap don't keep them away, apply an insecticide.

For other controls, see the section on Pests, Diseases, and Controls in the Appendix.

Did You Know?

Growing Scent-Leaf Geraniums

The scent-leaf geraniums you see at florist shops and garden centers are aromatic tender perennials that make great room fresheners. Happy indoors in the winter and outdoors in the summer, they have only modest blooms. But brush against the foliage, and the room fills with potent scents of nutmeg, mint, rose, or lemon. They're so potent that they're used fresh to flavor sweets and dried in potpourris. The varieties with the strongest aroma have small white or pale pink blossoms.

Lemon geranium (*Pelargonium crispum*) is the species to grow for leaves to use in finger bowls. Small and crinkly, the leaves have a lemony scent. The flowers are two-toned pink. Recommended are '**Prince Rupert**', '**Mable Grey**', and '**Lemon Fancy**'.

Rose geranium (*P. graveolens*) is the one to choose for gift giving. Grown commercially for its sweet-scented essential oils, it is the most popular of the scented geraniums. The foliage is green-gray, and the flowers are rose-lavender with a dark purple blotch in the middle of the upper petal.

Apple geranium (*P. odoratissimum* 'Gray Lady Plymouth') is the plant to choose if you love variegated foliage. It has small, velvety, sweetly scented, ruffled leaves and bears white flowers.

Peppermint geranium, woolly geranium (*P. tomentosum*) is the plant to choose if you like the smell of peppermint. It has large, soft, fuzzy, grape-like leaves and bears tiny purple-veined white flowers.

DECEMBER
Annuals & Biennials

 PLANNING

Go back to last year's garden log, and check your album of catalog pages of garden accessories. Order for the gardeners on your holiday list, and do family and friends a favor by telling them about tools and accessories you'd enjoy receiving.

Evaluate the progress of the tender perennials you brought indoors in the fall. Presented in a cache-pot or a vase, some might make holiday gifts. If the plants lack light, invest in a light garden. Cuttings root well there, and in late winter and early spring a light garden promotes growth in seeds started indoors.

If you know now which seeds you intend to start indoors in February, use spare moments to make row markers for them.

Organize a seed-saver file. Organize your supply of seeds—those purchased that weren't used, and the seeds gathered in your garden. Nicely packaged, they make nifty stocking stuffers.

One of the most convenient ways we have found to file and store seeds is in a spiral binder equipped with clear plastic sleeves. Place each variety of seed in its own small freezer bag. Mark the date on the bag, and store each bag inside its own sleeve in the binder. Slide a catalog image of the seed, and any comments you have, into each sleeve.

André stores seeds in small plastic bags in a refrigerator. Seeds are generally considered viable for three to five years after they have been gathered, though it may be that with each passing year fewer seeds will germinate.

Garden log. Record the progress of the cuttings of, or potted up, tender perennials you brought in earlier in the fall. Note especially whether there's enough light indoors for all you brought in—sunny sills, a picture window, or a Florida room—and whether you are enjoying them, or finding they take too much space and are too much work.

 PLANTING

Transplant well-rooted cuttings of the plants you brought in the fall.

 CARE

Indoors. Cuttings of **geraniums**, **coleus**, **impatiens**, and **wax begonias** growing in water should have masses of hair-like rootlets by now. Discard any that aren't rooting. If the water is growing murky, change it, and add a few small pieces of charcoal to keep it pure. André recommends adding $\frac{1}{2}$ teaspoon of bleach per gallon of water.

Outdoors. After cycles of freezing followed by thaws, check the **pansies, flowering cabbages,** and **kales** for signs of heaving—and heel them back in place.

 PRUNING

Indoors. Pinch out the tips of the **wax begonias** and **geraniums** you brought indoors as they get leggy.

Outdoors. Check the progress of spring-flowering seedlings growing in the open garden, and water them if December is dry.

 WATERING

Maintain the soil moisture in pots of tender perennials growing indoors.

 FERTILIZING

There is no fertilizing at this time.

 PESTS

Continue to check for whiteflies and spider mites on the plants wintering indoors. Misting, fresh air, occasional showers, and applications of insecticidal soap should keep them healthy.

CHAPTER TWO

Bulbs, Corms, Rhizomes, & Tubers

Bulbs, corms, rhizomes, and tubers are a whole different category from annuals and perennials. Although each category has specific qualities, what bulbs, corms, rhizomes, and tubers have in common with each other is a bulbous type of root.

Asked when a bulb is a bulb and not a corm or a rhizome or a tuberous something, Dr. August A. de Hertog, horticulturist with the University of North Carolina famed for his work with tulips, responded by saying, "Plant materials with underground storage organs can all correctly be called 'bulbs.' But the agreed-upon technical name for bulbous and tuberous plants is 'ornamental geophyte.'"

The term was coined by Danish plant geographer Christian Raunkiaer back in 1933, but was ignored until the early eighties. Now it is turning up in professional literature shortened to "geophytes." De Hertogh predicts it will be the name our children and our children's children will know.

What bulb breeders have in common is a desire to add annually to the already overwhelming variety of showier, hardier, and more disease-resistant varieties. In the future we can expect to be tempted by more fragrant varieties, a red **narcissus** (pink is where we are at this writing), and a truly black **tulip.**

What geophytes have in common is that they are all large storage organs ready to produce a plant—like seeds, but on a much larger scale. For now, André, Mark, and I refer to the group as a whole as bulbs; our children can take it from there.

PLANNING

You can count on bulb flowers to bloom the first year planted, like annuals. Under the right circumstances, you can expect them to come back year after year, like perennials. What you need to be aware of when combining bulb flowers with annuals and perennials is that if you hope to have them perennialize you must allow the foliage to ripen at least six weeks after blooming before removing it. You also need to be aware that good drainage, one of the benefits from improving your soil as we recommend, is essential to bulbs.

There are bulb flowers that bloom in every season. In spring **daffodils** and **bluebells** spread carpets of color in our woodlands. The perfume of the majestic **lilies** haunts summer gardens in late afternoon. **Autumn crocus** comes up when the leaves start to fall, and perfumed **paper-white narcissus** and **hyacinths, golden daffodils,** cheery **amaryllis,** and a host of others can be brought into bloom in your home all winter long.

Spring-flowering bulbs, the year's earliest show, are planted the preceding fall. They all tolerate our winter cold and summer heat with the possible exception of the **alliums**, which may not do well in the warmest reaches of Zone 8. Many come back year after year and multiply if protected from creatures that think of them as food.

The group's only drawback is that the foliage must be allowed to "ripen" (yuk!) for many weeks after the blooms fade. The larger bulbs, like **tulips** and **daffodils**, take forever, so plan to place them where the growth of summer-flowering bulbs, perennials, annuals, and/or shrubs will screen the fading foliage.

Bulbs, Corms, Rhizomes, & Tubers

Did You Know?

Which Is What?

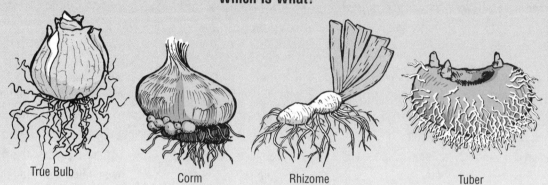

True Bulb   Corm   Rhizome   Tuber

- "True" **bulbs** are onion-like and have pointed tops and flattish bottoms that develop roots quite modest compared to the system of the same size perennial. Examples are **daffodils, tulips, Dutch iris,** and **hyacinths.** Stored within the bulb are the stem, the flower bud, and layers that are compressed leaves. Plant bulbs flat end down.

Some bulbs, like onions, are protected by a papery cover called a "tunic." **Lilies** and some other true bulbs have no protective cover; they are easily damaged and dry out quickly, so handle with care!

- **Corms** are roundish storage units that have flattish bottoms and a top that has one or more growing tips. This group includes **crocus, gladiolus, crocosmia,** and **freesia.** Plant these with the flattish part down.

- **Rhizomes** are fleshy lengths of thick, modified stem. They have lumpy tops and flattish bottoms from which the roots emerge. Examples are **cannas** and **waterlilies**. **Bearded irises**, which grow from a knobbly rhizome, André groups with perennials. Lay rhizomes horizontally on the soil with the bottom down and the top even with the soil surface.

- **Tubers** are swollen rounded stems with "eyes," or growth buds, here and there. Think old potato. The eyes will grow roots or shoots, depending on their position in the soil. Examples are **dahlias, caladiums,** and **lotus.** Lay these horizontally under 2 or 3 inches of soil, or at whatever depth the supplier recommends.

Summer-flowering bulbs begin to grow after the nights turn warm—mid- and late June. Early and late varieties bring color to mixed borders and container gardens when they need it most, mid- and late summer.

The summer-flowering bulbs whose winter hardiness rating is north of Zone 6 may be planted in mid-fall or mid-spring and need no special protection in winter. Those that are at the upper edge of their cold tolerance in Zone 6 are safer planted in mid-fall if they're provided with winter mulch. Examples are **crocosmia** and **wood sorrel,** *Oxalis adenophylla.*

Summer-flowering bulbs rated winter-hardy only as far north as Zone 8, **canna, colocasia,** and the perfumed **tuberose,** are best planted in mid-fall in our region. In Zone 8 they may be safe wintering in the ground protected by a light winter mulch. In Zones 6 and 7, in autumn, lift, clean, and store the bulbs for winters indoors in a cool, dry place. Most need cool storage temperatures—between 35 to 50 degrees for bulbs such as **canna, dahlias,** and **tigridia.** Others can be stored at room temperatures—**caladiums** and **colocasia** for example.

Bulbs not rated winter-hardy in regions colder than Zone 8, like the showy **caladiums,** are grown here as annuals—wintered indoors at temperatures in the 70s. Since they can't be planted in the garden until it's warm enough for tomato seedlings, plan to set out started plants, either your own home-grown or purchased plants.

Few summer-flowering bulbs have trouble with hot summers in Zone 8. Some lilies do better in our regions than others, so ask your garden center for recommendations.

Fall flowering bulbs are planted in summer for fall blooming. If you haven't grown these beautiful late bloomers, try a few this fall. **Colchicum, fall crocus,** and **winter daffodil** open showy blooms just above-ground in early fall, then in spring large glossy leaves rise and, after many weeks, disappear for the summer. The beautiful **resurrection lily,** *Lycoris squamigera,* produces exotic, fragrant, trumpet-shaped blooms from bulbs planted in August.

Bulbs for winter bloom **indoors,** except for a few very early varieties of **daffodils** that flower in the garden in warm years in November. In early fall, plan to pot up spring-flowering bulbs—we recommend **tulips, daffodils,** and perfumed **hyacinths**—which can be forced into early bloom in winter (see September). A few tropical bulb flowers can also be forced into bloom in winter, notably **amaryllis** (*Hippeastrum*) and perfumed **paperwhites** (see November).

PLANTING AND MULCHING

Light. **Crocus, daffodils, bluebells (squill, scilla),** and the lovely **wood hyacinth** bloom in partial shade, as do some of the smaller bulbs. But most big bulb flowers do their best in full sun, and need at least six hours of sun daily to come into flower a second year. The farther south the garden, the less sun is necessary for top performance. Bulbs that thrive in full sun or light shade in New England will do better in partial sun or semi-shade in hot Zone 8. Sudden summer heat shuts down plant production just as next season's flowers are forming.

Soil for Bulbs. The garden and container soil in which bulbs do best is light and very well drained. Repeat, **very** well drained. Ideally, a raised bed on a slope. There are always exceptions to the rule; a few summer-bloomers tolerate moist spots—**canna, Dutch iris, summer snowflake, crinum, rain lily,** and **spider lily.**

The pH range most bulbs prefer is 6.0 to 7.0. There are exceptions to that rule, too. The most popular **lilies** prefer a somewhat acid soil (see About Lilies, February). For step-by-step instructions on creating a raised bed and adjusting soil pH, turn to the section on Soil Preparation and Improvement in the Introduction to the book.

When you are planting bulbs in an existing bed, the soil needs the same careful preparation as for a raised bed. Outline the area, then cover it with 3 to 4 inches of humus, enough so that one quarter of the content of the soil from the hole will be organic matter. The humus can be decomposed bark, compost, partially decomposed leaves or seaweed, sphagnum peat moss, black peat humus, decomposed animal manures, or other decomposed organic material. Adding humus is particularly important if your soil has a high clay content.

Did You Know?

Dangerous Daffs

Fresh-cut **daffodils** exude a substance toxic to other flowers sharing the vase, especially **tulips**. Soak the dangerous daffs alone overnight to dissipate the toxic substance. In the morning rinse the stems in fresh water, then arrange with other flowers in vase.

Mix the humus into the soil as you dig it out of the hole, along with:

For every 100 square feet:

  Bulb-tone: 5 to 10 pounds
  Rock phosphate: 5 to 10 pounds
  Green sand: 5 to 10 pounds
  Clay soils only: gypsum 5 to
      10 pounds
  Osmocote® 8-month: 2 pounds

Planting. About bulb planters—they work well only if the soil has been well prepared. We recommend **the Dutch method of planting bulbs,** which is to use a spading fork to dig a generous hole or a bed, remove the soil and mix it thoroughly with the soil amendments above. Then, return 2 or 3 inches of improved soil to the hole, tamp it down, and plant the bulbs on top at the depth recommended.

We've explained the planting depth and spacing for the various bulb sizes in the Planting section of the October pages. When you aren't sure of the planting depth, set the bulbs at a depth that is about three times the height of the bulb itself.

Set **true bulbs** so the pointed tips are upright; set **corms** and **tubers** with the roots facing down. Set **rhizomes** horizontally in the soil with the roots down.

If voles, chipmunks, and squirrels are in the habit of transplanting, or eating, your bulbs, plant them with a deterrent such as VoleBloc™ or PermaTill®. It's easy. Line the planting hole or bed with 2 inches of either product. Set the bulbs on top, and fill in around them with VoleBloc or PermaTill leaving just the bulb tip exposed. Cover with an inch of VoleBloc of PermaTill, then fill the rest of the hole with a mix of 30 percent VoleBloc or PermaTill and improved soil from the hole. Mulch with 2 inches of pine needles, oak leaves, composted wood chips, or shredded bark.

Mulch. Most bulbs do not tolerate wet feet, especially when their blooming period is over. Two or 3 inches of a light mulch is all you need to give the garden a nice finish, keep weeds down, retain soil moisture, and moderate soil temperature. Never cover bulbs with more than 2 or 3 inches of mulch.

Winter mulch provides protection for bulbs whose cold hardiness is marginal in your area. For winter mulch, André recommends airy organics such as straw, pine needles, and pine boughs. For coastal dwellers, marsh hay or salt hay from the shore are excellent winter mulches.

PERENNIALIZING AND MULTIPLYING YOUR BULBS

Most hardy flowering bulbs planted in the garden will perennialize. Growers identify the spring-flowering bulbs likely to come back year after year. Most do. The **tulips** most likely to perennialize are **Darwin hybrids** and the little **species tulips.**

Bulbs, Corms, Rhizomes, & Tubers

Did You Know?

Tulipology

A Persian symbol of love and a major inspiration for artists, a potful of tulips in bloom makes a perfect holiday gift for lovers. Tulips have a romantic history.

The tulip was brought to Europe in the mid-1500s from the court gardens of Suleiman the Magnificent in Constantinople. The species probably was *Tulipa gesneriana*, an ancestor of most modern hybrids. It had more in common with our little **species tulips** than with the spectacular modern hybrids. Species tulips are tulips as they evolved in nature, the original tulips from which all modern hybrids were developed. A few decades after their arrival in Europe, tulips were being grown in Holland.

The magic wrought on the Suleiman's bulbs by the Dutch growers so captivated people that speculation on the price of bulbs became a hazard to Europe's financial health. Laws had to be introduced to limit the prices. A single tulip was considered a suitable dowry for a bride, and in France a brewery was once exchanged for one **tulip** bulb. The market collapsed in 1637 ruining speculators, but 200 years later, one bulb of a rare type could still command a price of 650 pounds. Even today, a high price for a new variety is not all that unusual.

Tulips for Cutting

These tulips together make beautiful bouquets, and they are all readily available.

'Duke of Wellington', big, pure white

'Temple of Beauty', lily-shaped pink/orange

'Marilyn', white with rose-red streaks

'Ballerina', fragrant yellow/red/orange

'Fancy Frills', fringed rose/white

'Queen of the Night', deep purple-maroon

'Aleppo', fringed raspberry/rose/apricot.

Smaller bulbs and naturalized **daffodils** don't need deadheading, but deadheading the larger bulbs helps them to store up the energy needed for a fine flower show the following year. Even more important than deadheading is allowing the foliage of the large bulb flowers six to seven weeks to ripen (yellow) before removing it. **Tulip** foliage may be cut when it is yellow halfway down. The foliage of the smaller bulbs tends to disappear on its own.

Once small bulb flowers are established in a garden, they send up clumps of grass-like foliage—in spring for bulbs that flower in fall, and in late summer for bulbs that bloom in spring. Those grassy clumps aren't weeds! If you happen to dig up small bulbs when you are planting in the area, just push them back into the soil, and they likely will survive.

Some spring flowering bulbs, notably **daffodils** and **hyacinths**, forced into bloom indoors and replanted in the garden, are likely to perennialize.

Dividing bulbs is a way to multiply your holdings, and, in some species, it improves their performance.

True bulbs growing well produce offsets that in three to four years may crowd the planting and cause the flowers to diminish. The best time to divide bulbs is after the foliage has withered.

Bulbs, Corms, Rhizomes & Tubers

It's easy. Use a spading fork to dig and lift the bulbs, gently pull them apart or leave the clump intact, and replant. Bulblets (baby bulbs) need years to mature enough to bloom, so plant these in an out-of-the-way place.

You don't have to divide **daffodils** to keep them gorgeous . . . just fertilize them. **Lilies**, on the other hand, André recommends moving or dividing every four years.

You may divide rhizomes and tubers either before the growing cycle begins (easier since there is no foliage to contend with) or when it is over. Just cut the rhizome or tuber into sections that each contain at least one growth bud or eye. Tuberous roots, such as **dahlias,** do best when separated before growth begins.

Transplanting. Dutch growers tell us the best place for spring-flowering bulbs is in the ground. Lifted and stored, which once was recommended, they are susceptible to fungus and disease. But growers do recommend lifting and storing bulbs that can't survive winters in your garden.

Spring-flowering bulbs can be transplanted successfully in spring, summer, or fall. You can move daffodils in bloom. Or wait until the flowers have faded, then cut off the flower heads, leaving the green leaves. Dig the plants with care so as not to damage the roots, and move the bulbs to the desired location. Allow the foliage to ripen naturally, just as it would have in its original spot. You can also dig the bulbs in summer or very early fall, but after the foliage dies they're not easy to locate, and digging blind you may damage the bulbs. So before the foliage fades, mark the positions of bulbs you want to move.

Summer-flowering bulbs that are hardy enough to be left in the ground in Zone 6 (-10 F winter lows) or Zone 7 (0 F winter lows) may be transplanted either in fall after the foliage has yellowed, or in spring just as growth begins.

Fall-flowering bulbs may be moved after the blooms fade. Those whose foliage comes up in spring, like the fall-blooming crocus, can be moved then.

Winter-flowering bulbs that have been forced into bloom indoors are weakened. **Tulips** and the smaller bulb flowers are best discarded. However, if you keep forced **daffodils** and **hyacinths** in a sunny window, water and fertilize them while the foliage ripens and dies down, then plant them in the garden in the fall, they probably will eventually bloom in their outdoor locations.

WATERING

It's not necessary to water the soil after planting bulbs, but the rootball of bulb flowers purchased as container-grown plants do need watering.

Provide **spring-flowering bulbs** with ample moisture from the moment the tips first break ground and all during the season of active growth. Once the foliage disappears, the bulbs are dormant and excess watering can be detrimental. Underground automatic sprinkling systems spell death to most bulbs unless adjusted to water deeply and only when moisture is needed—not every day, not every other day, not even every third day.

Summer-flowering bulbs need sustained moisture all season, just as perennials do. Water deeply every ten days unless you have a soaking rain.

FERTILIZING

All bulbs need continuing fertilization if they are to thrive and multiply.

There are two schools of thought on fertilizing spring-flowering bulbs.

In their book *Daffodils,* daffodil gurus Brent and Becky Heath recommend applying a diluted organic fertilizer to **spring-flowering** bulb plantings from the time the tips show in spring until the bulbs bloom. They suggest fertilizing again in early fall with a slow-release product (5-10-12 or 5-12-20) such as Bulb Mate.

André recommends fertilizing **spring-flowering** bulbs as soon as they finish blooming with Bulb-tone at the rate of 4 to 6 pounds to 100 square feet, and again in early September.

André recommends fertilizing established **summer-flowering** bulbs in early spring before growth begins, and again in mid-fall.

PESTS

Squirrels, chipmunks, voles, and moles truly believe you have set bulbs out just for their delight. All during the fall, squirrels are sure any bulb you plant is something they want—planters and hanging baskets not excepted. One year they tore up a heavy cardboard box of tulip bulbs I had stored on a second floor porch in DC. Only daffodils are safe; they're toxic to wildlife.

The solution is to plant bulbs in VoleBloc or PermaTill, as recommended in Planting, above.

Deer love **tulips** and **crocus** too! Spraying is no guarantee they won't eat the flowers. What does keep them away for sure is a temporary chicken-wire enclosure (see the section on Pests, Diseases, and Controls in the Appendix) or bird netting.

Did You Know?

Bulb Bouquets

Bouquets of spring bulb flowers will last up to two weeks if they are cut just as the buds begin to break. Harvest the flowers with clean, sharp shears in the cool of the evening. As you cut each stem, plunge it into a bucket of lukewarm water containing a flower preservative.

Next, to keep them straight, roll plastic around the stems just to the base of the blossoms and with the bottom end open. Set the bundles in a bucketful of fresh lukewarm water, and cure them overnight in a cool place. Just before arranging the flowers in a vase, recut the stems.

Bulbs, Corms, Rhizomes, & Tubers

Common Name (Botanical Name)	Hardiness	Type	Bloom Time	Planting Time	Planting Depth (Inches)
Amaryllis (*Hippeastrum* sp.)	Tender	Bulb	Force for indoor blooms	Fall, winter	In pot, $2/3$ covered
Autumn Crocus (*Crocus speciosus*)	Hardy	Corm	September to October	July, August	4 to 6
Autumn Daffodil (*Sternbergia lutea*)	Hardy	Bulb	September to October	Summer to late October	4 to 6
Bearded Iris (*Iris* x *germanica*)	Hardy	Rhizome	Flowers late May, early June; lasting sword-shaped foliage	Late summer, early fall	At soil surface, partly exposed
Bluebell (*Hyacinthoides non-scripta; Scilla sibirica*)	Hardy	Bulb	March and April (naturalizes easily)	Fall	4
Caladium (*Caladium bicolor*)	Tender foliage plant	Tuber	Foliage plant	Start indoors in spring	3 to 4
Calla Lily (*Zantedeschia* sp.)	Tender	Tuberous rhizome	Summer	Late spring	3 to 4
Canna (*Canna* x *generalis*)	Tender	Fleshy rhizome	All summer (some grow in water, too)	Start indoors in spring, but can be planted outdoors after the last killing frost	3 to 4
Colchicum, Meadow Saffron (*Colchicum* hybrids)	Hardy	Corm	September to October	Summer or fall	6
Crinum Lily, Spider Lily (*Crinum moorei*)	Tender	Bulb	Summer to fall	Spring	6
Crocus, Dutch Crocus (*Crocus vernus*)	Hardy	Corm	March to April	Fall	3 to 4
Crown Imperial (*Fritillaria imperialis*)	Hardy	Bulb	April	Fall	6
Daffodil (*Narcissus* sp.)	Hardy	Bulb	March, April, May	Early fall	4 to 6
Dahlia (*Dahlia* sp.)	Tender	Tuber	Blooms summer, early fall	Late spring	4 to 6 i
Dogtooth Violet (*Erythronium dens-canis*)	Hardy	Bulb	April (shade garden)	Fall	6
Flowering Onion (*Allium* sp.)	Hardy	Bulb	May to June	Fall	3 to 6 depending on species
Gladiola (*Gladiolus* x *hortulanus*)	Tender	Corm	Mid- to late summer (plant at 2-week intervals)	Spring	3 to 4
Glory of the Snow (*Chionodoxa* sp.)	Hardy	Bulb	March to April	Fall	3 to 4

Bulbs, Corms, Rhizomes, & Tubers

Common Name (*Botanical Name*)	Hardiness	Type	Bloom Time	Planting Time	Planting Depth (Inches)
Grape Hyacinth (*Muscari armeniacum*)	Hardy	Bulb	April to May	Fall	4
Greek Windflower (*Anemone blanda*)	Hardy	Rhizome	March to April	Fall	4
Hardy Cyclamen (*Cyclamen coum*)	Hardy	Corm	February to April	Fall	Just below soil surface
Hyacinth (*Hyacinthus orientalis*)	Hardy	Bulb	April	Fall	6
Italian Arum (*Arum italicum* 'Pictum')	Hardy	Tuber	Spring flower; red berries in summer	Fall; indoors in pots any time	3 to 4
Lily (*Lillium* sp. and hybrids)	Hardy	Bulb	Asiatic: late May to July; Trumpet: June and July; Oriental: July to September	Spring or fall	6
Lily-of-the-Nile (*Agapanthus* and cvs.)	Tender; 'Bressingham Blue' is hardy in Zone 6	Bulb	Late spring, summer in pots any time	Spring; indoors	6
Magic Lily, Resurrection Lily (*Lycoris squamigera*)	Hardy	Bulb	August (likes crowding)	Fall	6
Rainlily, Fairy Lily (*Zephyranthes* species)	Tender	Bulb	Summer, fall	Spring	4
Reticulated Iris (*Iris reticulata* and hybrids)	Hardy	Bulb	March to early April	Fall	4
Snowdrop (*Galanthus nivalis*)	Hardy	Bulb	February to March	Fall	4 to 6
Star Flower (*Ipheion uniflorum*)	Hardy	Bulb	April to early May	Fall	3
Summer Snowflake (*Leucojum aestivum*)	Hardy	Bulb	April	Fall	6
Tuberose (*Polianthes tuberosa*)	Tender	Rhizome	Late summer, early fall (plant at 2 week intervals)	Early June	1
Tuberous Begonia (*Begonia* x *tuberhybrida*)	Tender	Tuber	All summer in baskets or pots	Spring; indoors anytime	1 to 2
Tulip (*Tulipa* hybrids)	Hardy	Bulb	April to June	Fall	8 to 12
Winter Aconite (*Eranthis* sp.)	Hardy	Rhizome	February to March	Fall	3
Wood Hyacinth, Spanish Bluebells (*Hyacinthoides hispanicus*; *Scilla campanulata*)	Hardy	Bulb	May, June	Fall	4 to 6

JANUARY
Bulbs, Corms, Rhizomes, & Tubers

 PLANNING

A pleasant way to satisfy the hunger for spring flowers is to **tear out garden catalog pages** that show bulbs you especially like, and then to organize them into an album. Group together the spring-bloomers, summer-bloomers, fall-bloomers, and the bulbs that bloom in winter indoors. In February and in June use your album to help make decisions on which bulbs to order for the next season. When your choices have been made, place a sticky note by each plant chosen reminding you where to plant it.

John Elsley's list of plants that are first-rate companions for spring-flowering bulbs suggests where to look in your own garden for places to add **spring-flowering bulbs**. Your annuals garden log (see January, Annuals) will suggest tall hardy annual flowers that, started early indoors, can be good follow-on plants for the bulb flowers.

 PLANTING

Plant **tulip** and **daffodil** bulbs that you didn't get into the ground last fall. The bulbs may produce plants that are stunted and small, but they have a chance of growing. One thing's for sure—if you don't get the bulbs in the ground now, they're toast. They won't last until next season.

 CARE

Early this month, **check the dates and the timing chart on bulbs** potted up for forcing last fall. Move those that have finished chilling into a warmer room, and begin to water and fertilize them as you do houseplants. In two weeks or so the shoots will grow tall and initiate flower buds. Place them in good light but out of direct sun. Feed a half dose of liquid fertilizer at every watering.

 PRUNING

When all the blooms are dead on **amaryllis** and other forced bulbs, cut the flower heads off, and move the plants to a bright sunny window to grow. But do not save the **paper-whites**; discard them.

 WATERING

Keep the soil just damp in pots of bulbs being forced, as well as in those that have finished blooming and that you hope to plant outdoors later.

Don't allow the soil of pots of tender or tropical bulbs wintering in a protected place to dry out completely; they are semi-dormant.

 FERTILIZING

At every second watering of bulbs growing after blooming, add to the water a half dose of liquid fertilizer for flowering houseplants, African violet fertilizer, for example.

 PESTS

Aphids and fungus gnats can be a nuisance. Try rinsing aphids off with a kitchen sink spray or misting the plant with a horticultural soap.

Fungus gnats are tiny black gnats that hatch in potting mix and are a nuisance. Discourage them by allowing the soil to dry between waterings, and removing standing water from the plant saucers.

Discard forced bulbs you suspect of serious insect infestation, along with their soil.

A pleasant way to satisfy the hunger for spring flowers is to tear out garden catalog pages that show bulbs you especially like, and then to organize them into an album.

Did You Know?

Horticulturist John Elsley's Pick of Companion Plants for Early Spring Bulbs

If you can't find the bulb mentioned, try to match the color and the time of bloom:

Daffodils with perennials for all-season color

- **Daffodils**, with **garden mums**, in front of **daylilies**, in front of **peonies**, in front of **willowleaf sunflower**, *Helianthus salicifolius* **ornamental grasses.**

Giant snowdrop with shrubs and ground covers

- **Giant snowdrop**, *Galanthus* 'Atkinsii' and **bergenia 'Sunningdale' or 'Appleblossom'**, under **blood-twig dogwood**, *Cornus sanguinea* 'Winter Beauty', or *C. stolonifera* 'Cardinal' or red-stem *Salix* 'Erythroflexuosa'.

Good together

- **Allium** 'Purple Sensation' with **'Miss Kim' lilac;** or with **allium 'Mount Everest'** and **violets;** or with **violet-red cranesbill** *Geranium sanguineum;* or with *Iris* 'Batik'; or with **blue false indigo**, *Baptisia australis*; or with **peony 'Red Red Rose';** *Narcissus* 'Scarlet OHara' with crimson **pygmy barberry;**

- **Bluebell** *Hyacinthoides non-scripta* with white **wake-Robin** *Trillium grandiflorum* and *Rodgersia podophylla;*

- **Glory-of-the-snow** *Chionodoxa luciliae* with *Magnolia* x *loebneri* 'Merrill';

- **Grape hyacinth** *Muscari armeniacum* 'Blue Spike' with **hostas** and *Weigela* 'Wine and Roses';

- *Narcissus* 'Delibes' with **tree peony** *Paeonia suffruticosa;*

- **Giant snowdrop** and *Narcissus* 'Jet Fire' with **hellebore hybrids;**

- **Species tulip** *Tulipa saxatilis* with **bleeding heart 'Gold Heart';**

- **Tulip 'Maureen'** with **dogwood** *Cornus alba* 'Aurea';

- **Tulip 'Candy Club'** with **Solomon's-seal** *Polygonatum falcatum;*

- **Tulip 'Golden Parade'** with **'Red Jade' crabapple;**

- **Tulip 'Monte Carlo'** with **Colorado blue spruce** *Picea pungens* 'Glauca';

- **Tulips** with **American arborvitae** *Thuja occidentalis* 'Degroots Emerald Spire';

- *Tulipa tarda* with **azalea 'Staccato'.**

Shrubs that complement early spring bulbs

- **Azalea 'Tri-lights'; Cornelian cherry** *Cornus mas* 'Golden Glory' with *Scilla siberica*; **crabapple 'Louisa'; dwarf witch alder**, *Fothergilla gardenii* 'Beaver Creek'; **Eastern ninebark**, *Physocarpus opulifolius* 'Diabolo'; **Eastern redbud** *Cercis canadensis* 'Appalachian Red'; **giant arborvitae 'Deerproof'** *Thuja plicata*; *Magnolia* x *soulangiana* 'San Jose' Magnolia 'Butterflies'; and **Turkish filbert** *Corylus avellana contorta.*

FEBRUARY
Bulbs, Corms, Rhizomes, & Tubers

PLANNING

Complete your order for **summer-flowering bulbs.** Mail-order suppliers won't ship until it's time to plant. Include some of the tropicals so popular now in Mid-Atlantic gardens. The big-leaved **cannas** and **ornamental bananas** are sensational accent plants in mixed borders and in containers. The tropicals make great container plants for the patio. *Tigridia* blooms last just a day, but a tubful is a riot of color. *Amarcrinum howardii,* a recent cross between the **amaryllis** and **crinum**, bears gorgeous pink flowers. **Lily-of-the-Nile** puts up exquisite blue, white, or pink trumpets and thrives for years indoors; a mature plant is magnificent in bloom. Combine **oxalis**, **caladium**, **coleus**, **variegated canna**, and **Oriental lilies** in complementary colors in a group of containers.

This year take the **dahlia** plunge! These six-footers rival sunflowers, real show-stoppers at the back of a mixed border. Massed in the front of the bed, the smaller, bushier cactus-flowered varieties like pink **'Park Princess'** are sensational.

PLANTING

In Zone 8, late this month start new **tuberous begonias** and those saved from last year, now. Plant tubers 3 to 4 inches apart, hollow side facing up, round end down, in open trays of moist vermiculite or sphagnum peat moss or a combination of both. Keep the trays in indirect light at about 70 degrees Fahrenheit.

CARE

There's still time to force **paper-whites** (see November), and many garden centers carry them this time of year.

Bring remaining **spring-flowering bulbs** potted up last fall for forcing into a bright, warm room, and water and fertilize as you do houseplants. When they bloom, move them to bright light but not direct sun, and keep the soil barely damp.

Daffodils, hyacinths, muscari, and other little bulbs may have a second life outdoors if they are allowed to mature on a sunny windowsill. Water and fertilize as you do houseplants. When the weather is warm enough, plant them outdoors in an out-of-the-way place. If the foliage dies down before you can plant outdoors, allow the soil in the pots to dry, and plant the bulbs when the weather warms.

Check stored **cannas** and **dahlias** for disease, and remove and discard tubers showing mold or rot.

PRUNING

Deadhead **amaryllis** blooms, and grow the plants in a bright sunny window.

The **tulips** and **paper-whites** go to the compost pile. These bulbs cannot be forced again.

WATERING

Maintain some moisture in pots of bulbs that are being, or have been, forced, and which you plan to replant later. Discard **tulips** that are finished, but continue to provide a sunny sill and to water and fertilize **daffodils** and **hyacinths** that look healthy.

Don't allow the soil in pots of tender or tropical bulbs wintering in a protected place to dry out completely; they are semi-dormant.

Did You Know?

About Lilies

In late summer afternoons the perfume of the **Oriental lily 'Casa Blanca'** permeates the garden—an invitation to try these most majestic flowers.

The three major lily categories—**Asiatics, Trumpets, Orientals**—bloom in that order starting with the **Asiatics** in June/July and ending with the big **Orientals** in July/August. They have overlapping flowering periods since there are late **Asiatics** and early **Trumpets** and **Orientals**. Each bulb produces one big flowering stem.

Mail-order suppliers ship lily bulbs at planting time in spring or in early fall. The early-blooming **Asiatics** are best planted in fall. The late-blooming **Orientals** and **Trumpets** also are best planted in the fall, but may be planted in spring. Plant them as soon as possible. Container-grown lilies and lilies in bloom adapt to transplanting, but to plant a bare lily bulb that has sprouted a shoot over 2 inches long is bad news.

Give lilies a spot in full sun if your temperatures stay under 90 degrees Fahrenheit; in hotter areas, plant lilies in bright tall shade, or provide protection from direct noon and afternoon sun.

Lilies do best in slightly acid, fertile soil rich in trace elements. The **Asiatic lilies** require a pH between 5.8 and 6.8. The **Orientals** prefer pH 5.2 to 6.2, and do well with **azaleas**. The **Trumpets** are less particular. All lilies like cold feet, so mulch heavily, or underplant them with flowers such as **coreopsis** that do well in somewhat acid soil.

When the blossoms fade, pinch them off the flower stalk. When harvesting lilies, take no more than a third of the flower stalk, or it will be shorter next year. When flowering ends, cut the flower stalks to just above the leaves and allow the rest to yellow. Then cut the stalks to the ground—or leave them to mark the locations. In fall and again before growth begins in spring, fertilize the bed with Bulb-tone or Holly-tone at the rate of 4 pounds per 100 square feet. Mulch. Move or divide lilies every four years in the fall.

FERTILIZING

Monitor plantings of **spring-flowering bulbs,** and as soon as the tips show, water weekly with a diluted organic fertilizer and continue as they come into bloom.

At every second watering, add a half dose of liquid fertilizer for flowering houseplants to the soil for **amaryllis, daffodils,** and **hyancinths** still growing after blooming. Use bloom booster type fertilizers, like African violet food, which are high in phosphorus for promoting flower-bud initiation for next season.

PESTS

Get rid of aphids by spraying them with a kitchen sink spray or misting the plant with a horticultural soap. Discourage the little black fungus gnats that hover over potting mix by allowing the soil to dry between watering and removing standing water from the plant saucers.

When forced bulbs finish blooming, discard any you suspect of insect infestation, along with their soil.

MARCH
Bulbs, Corms, Rhizomes, & Tubers

 PLANNING

Now that the early **spring-flowering bulbs** are showing their true colors, consider where you'd like to see more or different colors and plants next spring. Write your ideas on sticky notes, and place them in your bulb album (see Planning, January) as reminders when preparing your order for October planting this summer.

Plan to start tender and **summer-flowering bulbs** and tropicals indoors this month; organize pots and potting mixes.

 PLANTING

When danger of frost is over and the soil is free of winter cold and moisture, start planting hardy **summer-flowering bulbs** in the garden. For soil and planting recommendations, see Planting, in the introduction to this chapter.

True bulbs are planted flat end down. Don't leave scraps of their tunic covering around because squirrels will dig. **Lilies** and a few others have no protective cover so handle with care!

Corms are rounded; plant them with the flattish bottom down. Examples are **crocosmia, poppy anemones, gladiolas.**

Rhizomes are fleshy lengths of thick, modified stem with lumpy tops—**bearded irises** for example. Plant these horizontally in the soil with the roots down.

Tubers are swollen rounded stems with growth buds, called "eyes," here and there. Think old potato. The eyes will grow roots or shoots, depending on their position in the soil. So plant them the way that seems right. **Caladiums** are an example.

Cold-tender and tropical bulbs must wait until the weather warms to go outdoors. **Dahlias** are an example. You can start them indoors early now.

 CARE

When the **tuberous begonias** (see February, Planting) begin to grow, plant them in individual 6-inch pots filled with a mix of soil, compost, and peat. Move the containers to cooler temperatures, about 65 degrees Fahrenheit. When the shoots are 4 inches tall, transplant to 8- to 10-inch baskets or azalea pans filled with sterile soilless mix. Sprinkle enough damp sphagnum peat moss over the tubers to cover them.

Transplant forced **daffodils** and other forced bulbs that look healthy to an out-of-the-way place in the garden; do not remove the foliage. If the foliage has died, allow the soil in the pots to dry, and plant the bulbs when you can.

Easter lilies, *Lilium longiflorum*, can be transplanted to a sheltered sunny spot in the garden. Don't add wood ashes or lime; they need slightly acid soil.

 PRUNING

Discard forced bulbs you suspect of insect infestation, along with their soil.

Deadhead early **daffodils, tulips,** and other large bulb flowers that have finished blooming; allow the foliage to remain. The small bulb flowers are self-cleaning.

 WATERING

Indoors. Keep the soil-less mix over **tuberous begonias** and other bulbs started indoors moist by sprinkling the surface.

Keep the soil in pots of tender or tropical bulbs wintering in a protected place moderately damp.

Outdoors. The early bulb flowers in the garden are growing full; sustained moisture is important at this time, so, if the sky doesn't do it, water slowly and deeply every ten days.

Water the bulbs whose foliage is being allowed to mature if the season is dry.

FERTILIZING

When **spring-flowering bulbs** show their tips, water with a diluted organic fertilizer.

Early this month fertilize the hardy **summer-flowering bulbs** that are out in the garden. Scratch in Bulb-tone at the rate of 4 pounds per 100 square feet. For **lilies** use Holly-tone.

At every second watering, add a half dose of liquid bulb booster or African violet fertilizer for flowering houseplants to the soil for **amaryllis** and other forced bulbs you are growing on after they've bloomed.

Did You Know?

About Dahlias

In Zones 6 and 7, gardeners start **dahlias** indoors in March or April. In Zone 8, gardeners plant dahlias right in the garden in mid-spring and have them blooming still in early November.

1 Dahlias lifted and wintered indoors should still be attached to the main stem. Separate the tubers from the stems; include with each tuber a portion of the stem with a growth bud attached. Dahlia tubers you buy are ready to plant.

2 Line a pot that has drainage holes with landscaping cloth and 2 inches of gravel. Add 2 to 4 inches of damp soil-less potting mix, or a mix of 2 parts peat moss, 1 part perlite, and 1 part vermiculite. Set the tubers on top, and cover them with 2 inches of the potting mix.

3 About four weeks later, when shoots appear, water the soil, and move the pot to a sunny spot. Keep the soil moderately damp.

4 As the shoots grow, add a few inches of soil until the soil is within 2 inches of the pot rim. When the dahlia stem is 12 inches tall, tie it to a stake.

5 Move the pots out to a protected spot when the air warms in May or June.

6 In Zone 6 and 7, dahlia tubers rot in the ground, even when mulched. So before frost gets to them, lift and store them, unwashed, in dry sand or vermiculite at temperatures between 35 and 45 degrees. In Zone 8, dahlias can survive winters in the ground if they are heavily mulched.

 PESTS

Deer love **tulips** and **crocus!** Spraying deer repellent is no guarantee against them. What does keep them away is a temporary chickenwire fence.

Get rid of aphids by spraying them with a kitchen sink sprayer or misting the plant with a horticultural soap. Discourage the little black fungus gnats that hover over potting mix by allowing the soil to dry between watering and by removing standing water from the plant saucers.

APRIL
Bulbs, Corms, Rhizomes, & Tubers

 PLANNING

Are the plants around the **spring-flowering bulbs** screening the fading foliage? If not, consider investing in good-sized seedlings of annuals and in big container-grown perennials to mask the waiting period.

 PLANTING

When all danger of frost is past, you can move the potted **summer-flowering bulbs** that wintered indoors out to the garden—**ornamental banana, canna, ginger lilies, lily-of-the-Nile** (*Agapanthus africanus*), for example. Repot them, and begin weekly watering and fertilization.

Transplanting. You can move **spring-flowering bulbs** around in the garden after the plants go out of bloom. Do it while the foliage is still green; once the foliage dies the bulbs are hard to locate.

Prepare a new planting hole by loosening the soil and adding bulb fertilizer and compost. Then dig the clump, taking care not to damage the bulbs or roots, and plop it intact into the new planting hole. Allow the foliage to ripen naturally, just as you would have had you not moved the bulbs. After six or seven weeks the foliage will have turned brown, and then you can cut it off at ground level.

The grass-like foliage of the small **fall-flowering bulbs, autumn crocus** for example, come up in spring; you can lift and transplant them in clumps any time after the foliage comes up.

Dividing. After the foliage has died down but while you can still see it is the best time to divide clumps of **spring-flowering bulbs.** Use a spading fork to lift the clumps. Gently pull the bulbs apart. Replant clusters of two and three mature bulbs, and the biggest bulbs. Plant bulblets in an out-of-the-way spot because they must grow before they'll bloom.

You can dig and divide bulbs after the foliage is gone, but best get the job done before September when they will already be rooting. If you plan to move **spring-flowering bulbs** after the foliage has died, mark their positions now.

 CARE

The **amaryllis** can be moved outdoors when the nighttime temperatures stay above 60 degrees Fahrenheit. Plant the pots up to their rims in full sun in well-drained soil. Water and fertilize them when you water other container plants.

You can remove **tulip** foliage when it has yellowed halfway down; if you hope to perennialize tulips, fertilize them now. **Darwin hybrids** and **species tulips** should be encouraged. **Tulips** that sent up foliage but failed to bloom this year we recommend you discard, or move to an out-of-the-way spot to mature.

 PRUNING

Deadhead **spring-flowering bulbs,** leaving the stems intact. Allow the foliage to ripen six to seven weeks before you remove it.

WATERING

Maintain moisture in the container plants, the **tuberous begonias** and the **summer-flowering bulbs** started indoors.

Keep the soil just damp in pots of bulbs that have finished blooming and that you hope to plant outdoors later.

Don't allow the soil of pots of tender or tropical bulbs wintering in a protected place to dry out completely; they are semi-dormant.

You can dig and divide bulbs after the foliage is gone, but best get the job done before September when they will already be rooting.

Did You Know?

About Daffodils, Narcissus, and Jonquils

Narcissus is the botanical, or genus, name; the common name **daffodil** is often used instead. **Jonquils,** a type of *N. jonquilla*, are late bloomers that bear clusters of fragrant flowers on each stem. The immense variety of daffodils, their easy ways, and their imperviousness even to deer make them spring's favorite bulb.

Plant open woodlands with big, yellow daffodils in irregular drifts of twenty, fifty, or one-hundred bulbs, and they will carpet it with gold. A dusting of wood ashes in early September is enough to keep naturalized daffs blooming.

Plant early daffs, like 8-inch **'Jack Snipe',** to edge flower beds and in rock gardens, containers, in the shelter of boulders, and along fences.

For bouquets, grow show-stoppers like 12-inch orange-cupped **'Jetfire',** and 18-inch pink-cupped **'Chinese Coral'.** Bouquets of **daffodils** are long-lasting; before combining just-cut **daffodils** with **tulips** or other flowers, place the **daffodil** stems in water overnight to detoxify.

For fragrance, in addition to **jonquils** plant **Polyanthus daffodils.** A favorite is **'Geranium'** whose crisp white petals surround frilled orange cups. The perfumed paper-whites, so easy to force, belong to this group; they're not winter hardy here. Pot up **paper-whites,** a variety of **tazetta narcissus,** in late fall, and they will bloom and perfume your house in just a few weeks (see November.)

Planting daffodils. Plant daffodils in the fall after the first hard frost. They thrive in full sun or partial shade in well-drained, slightly acid soil. Set large bulbs 8 inches deep, 3 to 6 inches apart; small bulbs 3 to 5 inches deep, 1 to 3 inches apart. Add a handful of 5-10-20 slow-release fertilizer as topdressing after planting. Deadhead the show daffs; naturalized daffs don't need it.

Perennializing daffodils. Most daffodils and jonquils perennialize. Allow the foliage to remain undisturbed until it has withered away. Binding the foliage while the leaves ripen cuts off light and oxygen the bulbs need to nourish the next year's flowers.

 FERTILIZING

Every second time you water, include a half-strength dose of soluble fertilizer to the hardy bulbs growing in containers outdoors and to pots of amaryllis. Use African violet or bloom booster fertilizer for flowering plants.

You'll have bigger and more blooms next year if you fertilize spring flowering bulbs as soon as they finish blooming with Bulb-tone at the rate of 4 to 6 pounds for each 100 square feet, and repeat the dose in early September.

 PESTS

Daffodils, **narcissus**, **jonquils** are safe from deer, but other flowering bulbs may not be. For controls, see Pests, Diseases, and Controls in the Appendix.

MAY

 ## PLANNING

Unhappy with bare spots where the **spring-flowering bulbs** have gone by? Fill in the spots with **dahlias** ready to bloom, repeat sowings of perfumed **tuberose, rain lily**, (*Zephyranthes*) **gladiola,** and other not very hardy summer flowering bulbs. If you haven't already, try **canna** and **ornamental banana** this year; their big leaves are terrific fillers for empty spots at the back of the border. All of these need to be, or can be, lifted in fall and wintered indoors. That leaves the space free for the spring-flowering bulbs to pop up next year. If you set them in the garden in pots, moving them to a frost-free place for the winter is easy.

 ## PLANTING

When the air warms, about when the **lilacs** bloom, you can plant the tender **summer-flowering bulbs** and tropicals started indoors or purchased at garden centers. Harden them off for a few days in a protected spot.

Set the plants 18 to 24 inches apart, according to mature size, in well-worked soil enriched with a slow-release, low-nitrogen fertilizer, 4-month formulation. Prepare sturdy stakes tall enough to support the upper third of the plants, like big

dahlias, that will grow up to be between 18 inches and 4 feet. Insert the stakes deep into the soil 2 inches away from the plants that need staking. Firm the plants in their holes, and water them. When the stems are 12 inches tall, tie the main stems to stakes. Tie on other branches as the plant matures.

Mid-month, start planting sets of six or eight **gladiolus** for cutting, and repeat at three-week intervals until early August.

 ## CARE

Move pots of **tuberous begonias, dahlias**, and other bulbs started indoors out now to a sheltered spot to harden off. In a week or ten days you can move them to their permanent summer location.

Move pots of **lily-of-the-Nile** and other tender bulbs and tropicals that wintered indoors in containers outdoors for a summer of R&R. Groom the plants. Repot those in small containers in fresh potting mix. Top-dress those too large to repot by adding 2 inches of compost to the container.

Stake the **lilies** growing in the garden, and mulch them to keep their feet cool; or underplant them with flowers that do well in somewhat acid soil, **coreopsis** or **lily-of-the-valley,** for example.

 ## PRUNING

Clear away yellowing leaves of the **tuberous begonias,** and deadhead the male flowers. The showy blooms are male, and most are backed by a single female flower—it isn't necessary to deadhead the female flowers.

 ## WATERING

Water potted **dahlias** often enough to maintain soil moisture, but avoid soaking them.

Keep the soil around the **tuberous begonias** evenly moist but not soaking.

Maintain the soil moisture of the **amaryllis** and the hardy bulbs growing in containers. As the season grows warmer, plants in small pots and hanging baskets may need watering every day.

FERTILIZING

At every second watering, include a half dose of fertilizer in the water for all your potted and basket plants.

As the **tulips** finish blooming, spread bulb booster around those that you hope to perennialize.

You'll have bigger and more blooms next year if you fertilize spring-flowering bulbs as soon as they finish blooming with Bulb-tone at the rate of 4 to 6 pounds for each 100 square feet, and repeat in early September.

 PESTS

Japanese beetles can wreck the foliage of **canna, dahlias,** and some other bulb flowers. Pick them off by hand. To cut down on the populations, plan to spread milky spore disease over the area and the surrounding garden in early September. For other controls, turn to Pests, Diseases, and Controls in the Appendix.

Rake or hoe weeds away with a swing-head hoe. It's a push-pull oscillating hoe that cuts through weeds and cultivates the soil without disturbing the mulch.

To deter deer, spray with a new and different deterrent, or put up a barrier to keep the deer out. See Pests in the Appendix to the book.

Did You Know?

About Caladiums

Start **caladium** tubers indoors about eight weeks before nights will be above 60 and day temperatures reach 70 degrees Fahrenheit.

1 Fill a flat with 2 to 3 inches of moist peat moss or sterile soilless potting mix.

2 Set the tubers about 8 inches apart with the knobble side up and the little straggle of roots down.

3 Keep the growing medium damp. The tubers are slow to start but do well in a grow light stand or in a sunny glassed-in porch.

4 When they sprout, transplant them to containers filled with improved soil fertilized with Plant-tone. A container 8 to 10 inches in diameter can take four to five caladiums. Cover the tubers with 2 inches of fertile soil mixed with humus or peat moss.

5 When daytime temperatures reach 70 degrees Fahrenheit and nights stay above 60, move the caladiums outdoors in their pots, or transplant them to the garden. They do best in a semi-sunny or a lightly shaded location.

6 When temperatures drop below 70 degrees in the fall, harvest the tubers, allow them to dry, and store them at temperatures between 70 and 75 degrees.

Be warned: to a deer a caladium is prime time lettuce.

JUNE
Bulbs, Corms, Rhizomes, & Tubers

 ## PLANNING

Most of the mail-order catalogs arriving discount prices on early orders for **fall- and spring-flowering bulbs.** They offer a wide selection and ship at planting time. You'll also find the most popular, and newest, varieties at full service garden centers, but the selection may be limited.

Tear out catalog pages, and add them to your bulb album (see Planning, January); then make a planting plan that will keep bulbs blooming in your garden and indoors this fall, winter, and spring.

Fall flowering bulbs. They are planted in summer or fall and bloom in September and October. Most are not much bigger than a **crocus.** Plan to plant them in drifts near paths to the house and in the front of shrub borders. **Resurrection lily,** *Amarcrinum,* and other full size late bloomers we suggest planting in containers.

Spring-flowering bulbs. The small bulb flowers open in February and March, with *Iris reticulata*, **winter aconite, snowdrops,** and **hardy cyclamen** leading the way. It's a joy to watch their progress, so plant them in drifts by house entrances.

Intermediate-size bulb flowers provide the next wave of color—**squill, oxalis,** sapphire **scillas,** luminous **species tulips,** dainty white **leucojum**—on stems 6 to 24 inches tall. Use them to fill spaces in flowering borders between perennials and where you plan to plant annuals later.

Many of the large bulb flowers bloom toward the middle and end of spring, but there are early, mid-season, and late varieties of most, including the **daffodils** and **tulips**. Order a few dozen to scatter in groups in your flower borders. Plan to plant **tulips** for cutting in the kitchen garden. Naturalized **daffodils,** which are deer proof, light up shrub borders and woodlands. For their fragrance, plant groups of **hyacinths** near entrances.

 ## PLANTING

You can plant the little fall bloomers as soon as you have them. The leaves of those already in your garden come up at this season, and then die down again in summer; before that happens, mark their positions to avoid digging them up when overplanting the area.

Continue planting sets of six or eight **gladiolus** for cutting, and repeat at three-week intervals until early August.

 ## CARE

Move **tuberous begonias, dahlias, caladiums,** and other tender bulbs to their permanent place in the garden; they need some protection from noon and late afternoon sun.

Adjust the **dahlia** stakes as the plants grow.

PRUNING

Deadhead **tuberous begonias, irises,** and the other flowering bulbs. Remove **caladium** flowers as they appear; they aren't showy and detract from the foliage.

Cut the yellowed foliage of the **spring-flowering bulbs** off at the base. If there are some you wanted to move but didn't get to, mark the spot with plant marker or a golf tee so you'll know where to dig when you have time to move them.

If spring has been wet, keep an eye out for fungal diseases.
Pick and discard infected foliage.

WATERING

Check the soil moisture of small containers of **summer-flowering bulbs,** and the **tuberous begonias,** every two days. Don't overlook pots of **amaryllis** summering in the garden.

Where the hardy **spring-flowering bulbs** have bloomed, water only if you must; they are dormant now and most prefer to be rather dry. Underground automatic sprinkling systems spell death to most bulbs unless adjusted to water deeply, and only when moisture is needed—not every day, not every other day, not even every third day.

# FERTILIZING

You'll have bigger and more blooms next year if you fertilize **spring-flowering bulbs** as soon as they finish blooming with Bulb-tone at the rate of 4 to 6 pounds for each 100 square feet, and repeat in early September.

Continue to fertilize **amaryllis** summering out in the open garden.

Did You Know?

Fall-Flowering Bulbs

A handful of fall-flowering bulbs bloom when everything else is going by except **pansies, mums,** and **flowering cabbage and kale.** Try some of our favorites:

- **Autumn Daffodil,** *Sternbergia lutea*

  Planting time: late summer for fall bloom.

- **Colchicum,** *Colchicum* species

  Planting time: late summer or early fall for mid-late fall bloom.

- **Fall Crocus,** *Crocus,* many fall-blooming species

  Planting time: summer for September or December bloom

- **Hardy Cyclamen,** *Cyclamen hederifolium*

  Planting time: July for late summer or early winter bloom.

- **Naked-lady Lily,** *Amaryllis belladona* (syn. *Brunsvigia rosea*)

  Planting time: early summer for early fall bloom

- **Oxblood Lily,** *Rhodophiala bifida*

  Planting time: early September for fall bloom.

- **Resurrection Lily, Hardy Amaryllis,** *Lycoris squamigera*

  Planting time: August for fall bloom.

# PESTS

Hand-pick **Japanese beetles** into a jar of soapy water. Try applications of neem to discourage them.

If spring has been wet, keep an eye out for **fungal diseases.** Pick and discard infected foliage. A fungicide may help control the problem. Try applications of Messenger, which is said to stimulate the plant's own defenses. For controls, turn to Pests, Diseases, and Controls in the Appendix.

To deter **deer,** spray with a new and different deterrent because they become used to what's been around for a while, or put up a barrier to keep the deer out.

JULY
Bulbs, Corms, Rhizomes, & Tubers

 PLANNING

Take advantage of the mail-order bulb suppliers' discounts for early orders. They start shipping as early as mid-August and can run out of popular varieties.

When purchasing bulbs, buy the largest ones you can find. They may cost a little more, but their performance more than makes up for the difference in price. Smaller sizes are good for naturalizing. Bargain mixes are a bargain only if they include first-rate varieties. Medium and small **hyacinth** bulbs are a good deal as the shorter flower stalks are less vulnerable to late storms.

Plan to try some of the **beautiful little bulbs that bloom in September.** The tender lavender hues of **colchicum** and **fall crocus** are very appealing in the midst of autumn's assertive reds, russets, and golds. Their leaves come up in spring and after many weeks disappear; the showy blooms rise when cool weather comes.

To make a showing with the little bulbs' flowers, order enough of each variety to plant drifts of twenty, fifty, or one hundred. For the mid-size bulbs to be effective you will need ten, twenty, or more of each. The big bulbs, the tall **Darwin tulips** for example, make a big splash planted in groups of as few as five

or ten. Order **hyacinths** in groups of three or five of one color. Choose several **tulip** varieties for cutting with bouquets.

When ordering **spring-flowering bulbs** for forcing, select large size bulbs of varieties recommended for forcing. You'll need five **daffodil** or **tulip** bulbs for each 6-inch pot, and nine for a 12-inch pot. **Hyacinths** are planted three to a 5-inch pot. **Amaryllis** are planted one to a 6-inch pot, or three to a 12-inch pot.

 PLANTING

Plant the little bulbs that bloom in the fall in a sunny spot in the shelter of a stone wall or a big rock. Most will perennialize.

Dig planting holes and beds for the small bulbs 3 to 5 inches deep. But first cover the area with 3 to 4 inches of humus, enough so that one quarter of the soil will be organic matter. Then add to the soil from the hole the following organic amendments and fertilizers.

For every 100 square feet:

Bulb-tone: 5 to 10 pounds
Rock phosphate: 5 to 10 pounds
Green sand: 5 to 10 pounds
Clay soils only : gypsum 5 to
 10 pounds
Osmocote® 8-month: 2 pounds

To foil vole and squirrels, line the bottom of the hole or the bed with 2 inches of VoleBloc™ or PermaTill®. Set the little bulbs 1 to 3 inches apart. Fill in all around them with VoleBloc or PermaTill so just the tip of the bulbs is showing. Cover with 1 inch of VoleBloc or PermaTill. Fill in with a mix that is 30 percent VoleBloc or PermaTill and improved soil.

Continue planting sets of six or eight **gladiolus** for cutting, and repeat at three-week intervals until early August.

CARE

Tie tall **dahlias** and the **lilies** to the upper third of their stakes. Stake **gladiolus** as they gain height.

Mulch around **summer-flowering bulbs** to keep their roots cool and to maintain moisture now that the year's driest season is upon us.

PRUNING

Harvest or deadhead **dahlias** and other flowering bulbs.

When harvesting **lilies**, do not take more than a third of the stem, or the stem will be smaller next year. After deadheading bulbs that have finished blooming, let

When purchasing bulbs, buy the largest ones you can find. They may cost a little more, but their performance more than makes up for the difference in price.

Did You Know?

Summer-Flowering Bulbs

Summer-flowering bulbs are superb in big pots, planters, and barrels, and great fillers for empty spots in flower beds. Plan to lift those identified here as "tender" in fall, and store them indoors for winter.

- **Amarcrinum,** x *Amarcrinum howardii*, tender
- **Caladium,** *Caladium* spp. tender
- **Canna,** *Canna* x *generalis* cvs., tender
- **Crocosmia,** *Crocosmia* spp. and hybrids, hardy
- **Flowering Onion,** *Allium giganteum*, hardy
- **Gladiola,** *Gladiolus byzantinus, G. hortulanus* semi-hardy standard and minis
- **Lilies,** *Lilium*, spp. and hybrids hardy
- **Mexican Shellflower,** *Tigridia*, tender

- **Ornamental Banana,** *Musa velutina*, tender
- **Peacock Orchid,** *Acidanthera bicolor*, tender
- **Peruvian Daffodil,** *Hymenocallis narcissiflora* syn. *Ismene calathina*, tender
- **Poppy Anemone,** *Anemone coronaria*, hardy
- **Rainlily,** *Zephyranthes*, spp., tender
- **Summer Hyacinth,** *Galtonia*, tender
- **Tuberose,** *Polianthes tuberosa*, tender
- **Wood Sorrel, Lady's Sorrel,** *Oxalis* varieties, hardy

the foliage ripen naturally. The stalks of the **lilies** and the foliage of the **Japanese irises** turns gold and bronze in late fall and can be quite beautiful.

Help flowers you harvest last longer by making an angled cut with clean shears, and at once plunging the stems into a big bucket of tepid water containing floral preservative.

WATERING

Check the soil moisture in hanging baskets and pots regularly, and water enough to keep the soil nicely damp.

Summer-flowering bulbs need sustained moisture to stay in top shape and resist the assorted pests and disease that strike about now. In July and August, regularly water deeply unless you have a soaking rain.

FERTILIZING

Add a half dose of soluble fertilizer to the water for bulbs growing in baskets and pots at every second watering.

PESTS

Keep weeds gone.

Pinch off and discard (do not compost) leaves or blossoms that show infestations or signs of disease. Spray infested plants with neem.

If **dahlias** show signs of powdery mildew, thin the interior growth to improve air-flow. Spray with André's mix: 1 tablespoon baking soda, 1 tablespoon of ultra-fine horticultural oil mixed well in a gallon of water. For other controls, turn to Pests, Diseases, and Controls in the Appendix.

To deter deer, spray with a new and different noxious spray, or put up a barrier to keep the deer out.

PLANNING

Some mail-order houses ship bulbs for fall planting as early as mid-August. **Bulbs you plan to force into bloom for winter indoors** can be planted starting in September. You must wait until after a hard frost to start planting the hardy bulbs out in the garden. Store bulbs-in-waiting in a cool cellar, a crisper, or a cool garage. **Caution:** don't store bulbs with apples. Apples, along with bananas and some other fruits and vegetables, give off ethylene gas, which initiates flower buds in **bromeliads** but ruins the blooms in flowering bulbs.

Garden centers will soon be offering shrubs and trees at end-of-season sale prices, an invitation to consider starting a border of shrubs and bulbs. **Spring-flowering bulbs** do well under tall shrubs and deciduous trees, and even in the shade of evergreens tall enough to allow sun to reach the flowers. Don't top them with more than 2 or 3 inches of mulch; more will prevent the soil from draining and that will harm the bulbs.

Turn back to January and check out horticulturist John Elsley's excellent suggestions for combinations of flowers and shrubs that do well with **spring-flowering bulbs**.

PLANTING

Late this month you can begin to **transplant established spring-flowering bulbs** marked in spring for moving. Use a pitchfork to lift them. Slowly slide the tines straight down into the soil just outside the marked position. If you feel resistance that could be a bulb, try the other side of the clump. When you have lifted a clump, ease it off the fork onto the ground. Pick through the bulbs, and replant the largest in soil fertilized with Bulb-tone in their new position. Plant the little bulblets in an out-of-the-way place to grow up.

CARE

Crocosmia doesn't need deadheading. The flowers are followed by attractive seed capsules that look good with the sword-shaped foliage.

PRUNING

Dahlias need deadheading and are good cut flowers, so don't skimp on bouquets. The crisp, almost translucent petals catch the light and in the paler shades are truly luminous. The dainty long-stemmed cactus types are beautiful massed as bedding plants, and make lovely bouquets. My favorite late summer bouquet combines **dahlias** with **basil** for the aroma, airy **cosmos** and plumes of **ornamental grasses,** with stems of **peegee hydrangeas**.

The best times to harvest **dahlias**—all flowers, really—is early morning or late evening. To give them a long vase life, re-cut the stems, and set them in 2 to 3 inches of water that is about 150 degrees Fahrenheit. Leave them there for a couple of hours, or overnight, then re-cut the stems for arranging.

When harvesting **lilies**, make the stalks you cut off less than a third of the overall height, or the plant will be smaller next year. When the blooms have faded, deadhead to where the leaves begin. The foliage of **summer-flowering bulbs,** like that of **spring-flowering bulbs,** must be allowed to ripen. Best is to leave them to fall then cut the stalks to the ground—or leave them to mark the locations if you plan to divide them later in the season.

During droughts, dahlias, lilies, crocosmia, and the other summer-flowering bulbs need watering every week to ten days, as do the annuals and perennials.

If **tall bearded iris** foliage is browning at the tips, cut the tips back to healthy tissue.

 WATERING

During droughts, **dahlias, lilies, crocosmia,** and the other summer-flowering bulbs need watering every week to ten days, as do the annuals and perennials. Watering overhead is okay.

 FERTILIZING

If you have incorporated organic or slow-release fertilizers in your soil, your bulbs shouldn't need fertilizing now.

 PESTS

Weed faithfully. We use a swing-head hoe for weeding. It's a push-pull oscillating hoe that cuts through weeds and cultivates the soil without disturbing the mulch.

Did You Know?

About Irises

The miniature **beardless irises** you see blooming in late winter and early spring are planted the fall before. Three and 4 inches tall, *Iris reticulata* is the first of the type to bloom. Charming in rock gardens and naturalized, plant these by the dozen, 2 to 3 inches apart, 2 to 3 inches deep in very well-drained soil. They do well in full or partial sun.

A second wave of **beardless irises** blooms toward mid-spring. These are the 20-inch tall **Dutch irises,** varieties of *I. hollandica*, and they also develop from bulbs planted the preceding fall. They need full sun, and are planted about 5 inches deep with 3 to 4 inches between bulbs.

In late spring and early summer the spectacular **bearded, Siberian,** and **Japanese irises** come into bloom. These are best planted and divided in spring or fall. The tall bearded (German iris hybrids) are divided in August and September.

The **bog irises** also bloom in late spring and early summer. The stately 5-foot **yellow flag,** *Iris pseudacorus*, bears bright yellow canna-like flowers. Rooted divisions are set out in early spring or fall in full or half sun in mucky, humusy soil that is moderately acid. Lovely varieties of the many-hued **Louisiana iris,** *I. hexagona,* bloom at about the same time and in the same type of soil. These irises can be divided any time after they bloom.

Mildew can be a problem. Pick off and destroy infected foliage; do not compost it. Spray infected plants with a sulfur-based fungicide recommended by your garden center, or spray with André's remedy: 1 tablespoon baking soda, 1 tablespoon of ultra-fine horticultural oil mixed well in a gallon of water.

Spider mites can be a problem now that the weather is hot and dry. Inspect plants not doing well, and if they are under attack, spray in the early morning with a miticide.

To deter deer, spray with a new and different deterrent.

SEPTEMBER

PLANNING

Working with the Planting Guide for Forcing Bulbs, plan a schedule for potting up and forcing bulbs for indoors this winter. You can start planting **hyacinths** for **forcing indoors** when outdoor nighttime temperatures fall into the 50s. Wait until closer to the holidays to pot up **amaryllis** bulbs and **paper-whites**.

PLANTING

Forcing bulbs for indoor bloom is a three-part project; pot up; chill twice (see Chilling below); move to warmth to force blooming.

Tulip and **daffodil** bulbs take a standard pot, but the others are usually planted in bulb pans, which are half pots, or else in shallow bowls, boxes, or water-proofed baskets. Before planting, soak the pots and water the soil thoroughly. To avoid the diseases that can assail forced bulbs, pot them in a mixture of one-half sterile commercial potting medium and one-half good gritty garden soil. As an added precaution, you can soak or dust the bulbs with a broad-spectrum fungicide.

Plant **hyacinths** about three to a 5-inch pot; plant **tulips** and standard **daffodils** five to a 6-inch pot, or nine to a 12-inch pot. Set **tulips** with the flat side facing out. Plant as many **muscari** and other small bulbs as there is space for. Set the bulbs just touching. Plant big bulbs so just the tip shows; cover small bulbs with potting mix.

Label the pots with the plant's name, the date, and when the bulb forcing guide indicates it likely will be time to initiate forcing.

Chilling. For the first chilling period, place the pots in the dark where temperatures are 40 to 60 degrees Fahrenheit—an unheated garage perhaps. After the first chilling period move the pots to colder temperatures—35 to 40 degrees Fahrenheit—a garden shed is likely to have the right temperature.

Water the bulbs in waiting when the soil moisture feels dry to the touch.

Forcing. As the second chilling period ends and the bulbs are showing roots and shoots, move the pots for forcing to temperatures between 50 and 60 degrees Fahrenheit and into good, indirect light. They take about two weeks to come into bloom.

Toward the end of the month you can plant **Asiatic lilies** out in the garden for next summer's bloom.

CARE

Keep bulbs that are waiting to be planted in a refrigerator crisper, away from fruit or vegetables, or in a cool garage or cellar.

Between now and when the air turns icy in October, bring in pots of **amaryllis** that summered in the garden. You can let the soil dry, or keep them growing. Either way, they need 55 degree temperatures for almost eight to ten weeks. (See Reblooming an Amaryllis in the February pages of Chapter 4, Houseplants.)

In Zone 8 when the **dahlia** tops die down, cover them with a winter mulch. In Zones 6 and 7, after the first killing frost, prepare to lift and store the tubers. Clear away the foliage, then gently lift the crowns and spread them out of direct sun to dry. Don't detach the tubers from the central stem. Don't wash them. Store them in trays of cedar chips, vermiculite, sand, or peat moss in a cool—35 to 45 degrees—area. Label each variety.

Store cold-tender and tropical bulbs at temperatures specified by the grower. For example, **caladiums** and **colocasia** need temperatures above 70 degrees; **tuberous begonias** and **crinum**, 35 to 41 degrees; **canna**, 41 to 50 degrees; **dahlia** 35 to 45 degrees.

Keep bulbs that are waiting to be planted in a refrigerator crisper, away from fruit or vegetables, or in a cool garage or cellar.

Did You Know?

Planting Guide for Forcing Bulbs

Planting Time Bulb	Container	Chilling Period 40/60 F	Chilling Period 35/40 F	Forcing Time
Sept./Oct. **Hyacinth, French, Roman**	Bowl/half pot	4–6 weeks	6–8 weeks	2 weeks at 65 F
Oct. **Crocus, Daffodil,** **Narcissus**	Half or three-quarters pot	6–8 weeks	4–8 weeks	2 weeks at 65 F
Grape Hyacinth **Muscari**	half pot	6–8 weeks	8 weeks	2 weeks at 65 F
Hyacinth, Dutch	Glass bowl, half or standard pot	6–8 weeks	6 weeks	2 weeks at 65 F
Tulips, Large	Half, three-quarters, or standard pot	6–8 weeks	6–8 weeks	2 weeks at 65 F
Oct./Nov./Dec. **Paper-whites**	Bowl and pebbles	2–3 weeks	3–4 weeks, if shoots are up skip this	2 weeks at 65 F
Tazetta Narcissus	Bowl plus pebbles	2–3 weeks	3–4 weeks	2 weeks at 65 F

 PRUNING

Cut down **lily** stalks that are fully yellow; move or divide four-year old **lilies**.

Cut off the dying foliage of **irises** and other winter-hardy bulbs.

 FERTILIZING

Spread Bulb-tone or wood ashes over established beds of **spring-flowering bulbs** at the rate of 4 to 6 pounds to 100 square feet.

 WATERING

Check the soil moisture in pots of bulbs being chilled weekly; water when the soil is dry to the touch.

Keep the soil damp in pots of tender perennials and tropicals wintering indoors; they are only semi-dormant

 PESTS

Spread milky spore disease where Japanese beetles have been evident.

OCTOBER
Bulbs, Corms, Rhizomes, & Tubers

 PLANNING

As temperatures drop into the 50s, **organize the planting of the spring-flowering bulbs.** That's about six weeks before the ground freezes hard. If you plant them while the soil's still warm, bulbs risk developing fungus or disease. Bulbs planted too late risk having insufficient root development to survive the winter.

The **daffodils** go in first, after the first hard frost. The **tulips** and other large bulbs go next, after two hard frosts. The small bulbs—**muscari, crocus**—go in after the **tulips**.

While you are waiting, set the bulbs out in groups according to where you plan to place them in the garden. Their first year, **spring-flowering bulbs** will bloom even in shade. But to come back and to bloom, they need full sun, all-day light under deciduous trees, or bright shade under a limbed-up evergreen.

Plan to plant the little bulb flowers in groups of twenty, fifty, or one hundred of each variety; mid-size bulbs in groups of ten, or twenty; big bulbs in sets of ten or fifteen; **hyacinths** in sets of three or five of each color.

For a lasting show, plant a three-tier bulb garden. Plant big bulbs on the lowest level, cover them with a few inches of soil, then plant medium bulbs, add a few inches more soil, and plant small bulbs on top.

 PLANTING

Bulbs for forcing indoors. Continue potting up the bulbs the Planting Guide for Forcing Bulbs recommends starting this month (see the September sidebar and Planting.)

Bulbs for the garden. When you are planting groups of bulbs, prepare planting beds rather than individual holes. (See Planting in the introduction to this chapter.) As a generalization, set large bulbs 4 to 6 inches apart and 8 to 10 inches deep; set bulbs under 2 inches in size about 2 inches apart in planting beds 5 to 6 inches deep.

When planting large **daffodils,** dig the holes 3 to 6 inches apart, 8 inches deep; set small **daffs** 1 to 3 inches apart, 3 to 5 inches deep.

Plant very tall **tulips** 4 to 6 inches apart, 8 inches to 10 inches deep; set the **species tulips** 3 to 4 inches apart, 4 to 5 inches deep.

Plant **hyacinths** about 3 to 4 inches apart, about 8 inches deep.

Plant **wood hyacinth** about 2 to 4 inches apart, and 5 to 6 inches deep.

To create a naturalized drift. Dig an irregularly-shaped planting bed, throw the bulbs out by the handful, and plant them where they fall.

To deter voles, moles, and squirrels, we urge you to plant all bulbs except **daffodils**, which are toxic to wildlife, with VoleBloc™ or PermaTill®.

Toward the end of the month plant **Oriental** and **trumpet lilies** in the garden for next summer's bloom.

 CARE

You can move **autumn crocus** and other **fall-flowering bulbs** after they finish blooming. Just lift the clump, and transport it to its new location.

Move or divide **lilies** that have been in place for four years or so.

When **tuberous begonias** begin to yellow, bring them indoors, let the soil dry to barely damp over five or six weeks, and then remove dead foliage and store the tubers in a cool, dry place.

 PRUNING

Cut the foliage of the **tall bearded** and **Dutch irises** down to 2 inches.

As temperatures drop into the 50s, organize the planting of the spring-flowering bulbs. That's about six weeks before the ground freezes hard.

Did You Know?

Sequence of Bloom for Spring-Flowering Bulbs

To help you find ideal places in your garden for spring-flowering bulbs, we have arranged them here in the order in which they come into bloom:

Late Winter/Early Spring

- **Early Crocus,** *Crocus* spp. and cvs.
- **Daffodils,** *Narcissus* miniatures and early varieties
- **Snowdrops,** *Galanthus*
- **Winter Aconite,** *Eranthis*
- **Squill,** *Scilla tubergeniana*
- **Dwarf Beardless Iris,** *Iris reticulata*
- **Glory-of-the-snow,** *Chionodoxa luciliae*
- **Grape Hyacinth,** *Muscari* spp. and hybrids
- **Miniature Cyclamen,** *Cyclamen coum*
- **Species Tulips,** *Tulipa saxatilis, T. tarda, T. turkestanica*
- **Striped Squill,** *Puschkinia scilloides*
- **Windflower,** *Anemone blanda*

Mid- and Late Spring

- **Daffodils,** *Narcissus* mid-season, late varieties
- **Hyacinth,** *Hyacinthus*
- **Late Crocus,** *Crocus*
- **Lily-of-the-valley,** *Convallaria majalis*
- *Fritillaria persica*
- **Silver Bells,** *Ornithogalum nutans*
- **Spanish Bluebell,** *Hyacinthoides hispanica*
- **Bluebell,** *Hyacinthoides non-scripta*
- **Summer Snowflake,** *Leucojum aestivum* 'Gravetye Giant'
- **Starflower,** *Ipheion uniflorum* 'Wisley Blue'
- **Tulips,** *Tulipa* mid-season, late varieties
- **Wood Sorrel,** *Oxalis adenophylla*

 # WATERING

Monitor the moisture in pots of bulbs being forced for indoor bloom; if the soil is dry to the touch, water it. Keep track of the chilling periods.

Maintain a little moisture in pots of tender perennials and tropicals wintering indoors.

 # FERTILIZING

Clear dying foliage and dig up weeds from established beds of **fall- and summer-flowering bulbs,** then fertilize them with Bulb-tone 4-10-6 at the rate of 5 to 10 pounds per 100 square feet. For **lilies,** spread Holly-tone at the rate of 4 pounds per 100 square feet.

 # PESTS

Clear the yard of anything that attracts deer—apples or pears, for example. Don't make pumpkins available, or ornamental bales of straw.

NOVEMBER
Bulbs, Corms, Rhizomes, & Tubers

 PLANNING

Kits of **amaryllis** bulbs are sold this time of year, along with **paper-whites**. Both take only a few weeks to force, so they can be started shortly before the holidays if you wish to have them in bloom then.

 PLANTING

Forcing freesias. These small funnel-shaped florists' flowers are so fragrant they are worth the patience and time it takes to force them into bloom indoors. The blossoms may be single or double, and the shades are subtle combinations of red, orange, yellow, and pink. Single flowered white **freesias** may be the most fragrant.

• To plant ten or twelve corms, provide an 8-inch standard pot.

• Fill the pot to within 2 inches of the rims with moist, sterile, somewhat gritty potting mix that is neutral or slightly acid—the cactus mix sold at garden centers will work.

• Arrange the corms on the soil with pointed ends up and 2 to 3 inches apart.

• Cover them with 1 inch of potting mix.

• Water thoroughly.

• Store the pots at about 55 degrees Fahrenheit for forty-five days—an unheated garage or a shed will do.

• When green shoots appear, move the pots to good light and temperatures of about 65 degrees Fahrenheit. Maintain the soil moisture, and fertilize the bulbs every two weeks with a soluble 20-20-20 fertilizer.

• Stake the stems as needed.

The flowers will appear in twelve to fourteen weeks and are long lasting.

 CARE

Cover **crocosmia** and other bulbs at the edge of their hardiness in our region with a light winter mulch.

 PRUNING

Cut down the remains of the **lilies, irises,** and other **summer-flowering bulbs.**

 WATERING

Maintain the water level of bulbs being forced in pebbles or water.

Continue to monitor the moisture in pots of bulbs being forced. Do not allow them to dry out. Plants drink their food through rootlets, and if they dry out the rootlets will die. Until the bulbs grow new roots, the bulbs go hungry as well as thirsty. Growth will be severely checked and may not resume in time for forcing.

If rain fails, water new plantings of **spring-flowering bulbs** regularly to encourage rooting.

Maintain a little moisture in pots of tender perennials and tropicals wintering indoors; they are only semi-dormant.

 FERTILIZING

If you haven't already, fertilize established beds of bulbs now. Spread Bulb-tone 4-10-6 at the rate of 5 to 10 pounds per 100 square feet. For **lilies,** spread Holly-tone at the rate of 4 pounds per 100 square feet.

 PESTS

Mulching areas planted in **spring-flowering bulbs** may discourage squirrels. But it encourages voles, so don't add mulch until the ground has frozen hard.

Did You Know?

Forcing Paper-whites, Hyacinths, and Amaryllis

Forcing paper-whites in soil. These sensationally fragrant varieties of **Tazetta narcissus** need seven to nine weeks to come into bloom. Choose bulbs not yet sprouted and plant them within four weeks. Keep paper-whites waiting to be planted in a dry warm room, about 60 degrees.

Plant the bulbs in bulb pans, six bulbs to a 6-inch pan, or twelve bulbs to a 10-inch pan. Set the bulbs up to their shoulders in gritty potting mix, and, to hold them in place, add enough gravel to cover the necks. Soak the soil in the pots, let the water drain, and set them to root in temperatures 45 to 60 degrees Fahrenheit. Water **sparingly** once a week until growth begins. See Planting, September, for further instructions.

Forcing paper-whites in pebbles. We find that sprouted paper-whites come into bloom quickly when forced in pebbles and water. Here are general instructions:

Choose a bowl that has no drainage hole and that is at about 4 or 5 inches deep. Fill it within 2 inches of the rim with marble chips, pea gravel, builder's sand, or PermaTill. Arrange the bulbs so they touch each other and are perfectly straight. Gently press the bottoms about an inch into the pebbles. Add water to just below the bottoms of the bulbs, and then add enough growing medium to cover the necks of the bulbs.

Store the containers in low light at cool temperatures, 45 to 60 degrees Fahrenheit, until they are well rooted and shoots are growing. Then move them to warmth and bright light; the warmer the room, the faster they grow—and go by.

Forcing hyacinths in water. Buy pre-chilled bulbs and "hyacinth glasses," glasses nipped in at the top so they suspend the bottom of the bulb just above the water. Fill the glass to just below the bottom of the bulb, and proceed as for forcing paper-whites in pebbles.

Forcing amaryllis. Use well-drained gritty soil and regular pots, not bulb pans. Plant these immense bulbs one to a 6-inch pot, or three to a 12-inch pot with the top third or half showing above the soil. Water the pots and the soil thoroughly, and set them in a warm room. Maintain soil moisture, and fertilize when you fertilize the houseplants. They should come into bloom in about five to six weeks at normal house temperatures. The flower stalk rises before the foliage, and the flower lasts up to two weeks.

DECEMBER
Bulbs, Corms, Rhizomes, & Tubers

 PLANNING

Catch up on entries for your garden log.

 PLANTING

Plant any remaining spring-flowering bulbs while the ground remains soft enough to dig in.

Amaryllis potted up at the beginning of this month still may come into bloom for the end of the year.

 CARE

Check **amaryllis** that dried down six to eight weeks ago for signs of growth. When a tongue of green appears, repot the bulbs in fresh fertile potting mix in the same pots, set them in bright indirect light in a warm room, and water and fertilize along with the houseplants. Wait to break off and repot offsets (baby bulbs) until the plants are in full growth in spring.

Monitor moisture in the soil of the bulbs being forced; water if the tops feel dry.

Mid-month, check the dates and the timing chart for **bulbs being forced.** Bring those that are showing roots and shoots into a warmer room and indirect light, and water and fertilize lightly when you water houseplants. When they are growing well, move them to good light, and out of direct sun. Keep the soil barely damp while they are blooming.

 PRUNING

When **amaryllis** finish blooming, cut the blossoms off, and continue to grow the plants in a bright sunny window.

 WATERING

As they come into bloom, water the soil of forced bulbs so it's slightly damp.

Keep the soil pots of tender perennials and tropicals wintering indoors damp.

 FERTILIZING

Include fertilizer when you water the **amaryllis.**

 PESTS

When the growing medium is very wet, **mold** sometimes appears on pots of bulbs being forced. Move them to a place with good air circulation and allow the soil to dry down to barely damp.

Get rid of **aphids** by spraying them with a kitchen sink spray or misting the plant with a horticultural soap. Discourage the little **black fungus gnats** that hover over potting mix by allowing the soil to dry between waterings and removing standing water from the plant saucers.

CHAPTER THREE

Herbs & Vegetables

A kitchen garden should delight the senses with its color, aroma, and superb flavors. Vegetables, herbs, and fruit grown in your own garden and harvested at the peak of perfection have a wonderful aroma and a much finer flavor than store produce.

Make your kitchen garden a source of interesting and luxury foods—the finest **sweet basils, shallots, artichokes, asparagus, 'Sungold'** and **heirloom tomatoes, Alpine strawberries, 'Little Ball'** and **golden beets, peaches, pears, cherries, grapes.** Make it beautiful, and it will be a favorite destination—even when there's weeding to be done! Most vegetables and a few of the best herbs are annuals, fine bedfellows for the beautiful annual flowers in Chapter 1.

PLANNING

The first step in designing a kitchen garden that will become a favorite destination is to **set it off handsomely.** A picket fence has charm, and chicken-wire will help keep out four-footed raiders. Make the entrance special with an antique gate, or a gated pergola supporting fragrant **climbing roses. 'New Dawn'** is perfect. Plan to train a **grape vine** over the fence, and an espaliered **pear** if there's space. Gussy it up a bit with ornate birdhouses, an antique sundial, and a water basin with a bubbler.

Make it exciting. Wake up your appetite. Grow **lemon cucumbers,** heirloom vegetables and fruits, exotic perfumed **Galia melons** from Israel, and pungent Oriental **tat-soi** greens. Pick baby **heading lettuce** and tiny **squash,** or plant a giant variety of **pumpkin** and aim for 600 pounds! Serve real **haricots verts,** true **petits pois,** without concern for the price. Grow your own **asparagus, rhubarb, strawberries,** and **artichokes.**

Make it colorful. Plant **bronze fennel,** globe and purple **basil** as well as the sweet varieties, and **variegated mint.** Plant red, not green, **romaine, Bibb, oakleaf lettuce; red scallions,** not white; yellow, purple, and orange **sweet peppers** along with red and green; scarlet, yellow, and purple **runner beans; violet broccoli** (which cooks up green).

Make it interesting. Plant summer squashes with different shapes and colors—round **'Gourmet Globe',** yellow **'Gold Rush', 'Butterstick',** and **pattypan 'Sunburst'.** Add curly **Russian kale** for texture, **arugula, radicchio,** and **mache** for fall salads. Be tempted

by little white and mauve **eggplants,** wildly colorful **hot peppers,** red new **potatoes, yellow watermelons, golden beets.**

Make it beautiful and fragrant. Plant **rhubarb,** and allow the magnificent flower heads to grow up. Edge the garden with aromatic perennial herbs—**chives, variegated thymes, colorful sages, golden oregano, fragrant English lavender.** The flowers as well as the foliage of the culinary herbs are edible. Center the beds on a little **peach, plum,** or **apricot** tree, and the air will be sweet when you arrive to plant the mid-spring crops.

Choose flowers whose colors and texture will enhance the beauty of the vegetables. Edge plain green vegetables such as **spinach** with brilliant **'Copper Sunset' mounding nasturtiums** whose flowers and foliage are edible. Grow red-stemmed **rhubarb chard** with deep red **'Empress of India' nasturtiums.** Back **bush beans** with pink or lavender **Powder Puff asters,** and edge the row with blue **ageratum** or **dwarf purple gomphrena** and **purple basil.** Plant late **tulips** in the fall,

Did You Know?

It Tastes Better Because It Is Better

To the gardener with a taste for good food, the flavor of home-grown vegetables and fruits makes growing them worthwhile. There's a reason they taste so good. The vitamin and nutritional content of fresh produce peak with the flavor. Vine-ripened, a **tomato** has three times the vitamin C of a commercial tomato because the enzymes used to ripen the tomato cause it to deteriorate once it has been harvested. **Carrots** and **apples** keep better than **sweet corn**, while **root vegetables** are fairly stable over a long period—something to remember when you are deciding which vegetables merit garden space.

and overseed the row in early spring with **leaf lettuce** and **Johnny-jump-up violas.** For fragrant summer bouquets plant aromatic **basils** with **cosmos, snapdragons,** and **dahlias.**

Intertwine snap beans with **morning glories,** and edge the row with blue **salvia,** white **cosmos Sensation Strain 'Purity',** and blue **ageratum.** Back the solid structures of the earth-hugging **lettuces, beets,** and **cabbages** with airy **bronze fennel,** tall **snapdragons, caraway,** or **cosmos.** These gardens can be prettier than flower gardens.

Caution: Don't combine edibles with poisonous plants—**larkspur, foxgloves,** and **sweet peas** are toxic.

START WITH A PLANTING PLAN

A planting plan is the first step in planning a kitchen garden. To put together herbs, vegetables, and flowers that will enhance each other, you need to partner varieties that mature at about the same time. The information you need is in garden literature and in mail-order herb, vegetable, and flower catalogs. There are early, mid-season, and late species and varieties of annual flowers. (See the Introduction to Annuals.) Match these to the cool-season, warm-season, and hot-season vegetables. (See this chapter's March sidebar, When To Plant What.)

Cool season vegetables are offered in varieties for planting in early spring, and other varieties that, planted in late summer, will mature crops in cooling fall weather; **cabbage,** for example, comes in early and in summer and late varieties. Some species of vegetables mature quickly; spring **radishes,** speed champion of pop-up vegetables, mature in twenty-six to twenty-eight days.

Warm season vegetables are available in early, mid-season, and late varieties; the tiny **cherry tomatoes,** for example, mature before the small **Early Girl** and **Early Boy tomatoes,** which mature before the **Big Boy** and long keeper types.

Hot season vegetables need a long season to mature. Examples are **shell beans** and **eggplant. Sweet potatoes** need five months to produce a crop. Some warm-season forms are available in early, usually smaller, varieties—**watermelons** and **cantaloupes,** for example, that allow frost-belt gardens to mature warm season plants.

Intensive cropping. When you know what you want to plant, the next step is to see how much of it will actually fit your space. With careful timing you can plan to get more than one crop from the same row. It's called "intensive cropping." Here are ways to do it:

1 Clear out early crops as soon as they have been harvested, and replant the rows with mid- and late season varieties.

Herbs & Vegetables

2 Combine sowings of quick-to-mature, small vegetables such as **radishes** and **lettuce,** with taller, slow-to-mature species such as **Brussels sprouts.**

3 Plant together tall and short crops that mature at about the same time, **corn** or **sunflowers,** with late-season ground-hugging **pumpkins** or **winter squash.** The rambling vines of the **pumpkins** and **winter squash** shade out weeds.

Planting Herbs and Vegetables

Since most vegetables and some important culinary herbs are annuals and must be replanted every year, the section on Starting Annuals and Biennials from Seed in the introduction to the Annuals chapter applies to vegetables. Because we are all eager for early crops, many vegetables and herbs are usually started indoors. How to start seeds early indoors appears in the January pages of that chapter.

Cool-season vegetables started indoors usually can be moved out to the garden within four weeks to six weeks. They usually are transplanted as quite young seedlings directly from the flats they were sown in.

Warm- and hot-season vegetables and herbs benefit from being grown for a few additional weeks in individual 2- to 4-inch peat pots before being moved out to the garden. In cold regions the bigger varieties of **tomato** may do best transplanted a couple of times to ever-larger containers. After transplanting vegetable and herb seedlings to larger pots, discontinue fertilizing until the appearance of two or three new leaves tells you the root system is growing again. At that stage, provide very good natural light, or grow the seedlings under continuous fluorescent light set about 3 inches above the seedlings. As the seedlings grow, raise the light to 4 to 6 inches overhead. Once the seedlings show strong growth, reduce the lights to fourteen to sixteen hours a day.

Growing Herbs and Vegetables

Here's an overview of the year in a kitchen garden:

1 In the fall or in early spring as soon as the cold and moisture have left the earth, turn the rows by hand or with a rototiller.

2 Check and adjust the soil pH and fertilize.

3 Plant cool-season vegetables starting in early spring.

4 Plant warm- and hot-season vegetables and herbs in May and June.

5 Harvest as crops mature. Replant the rows.

6 Clear the rows.

Soil. Most need well-worked, rich soil whose pH is between 6.0 and 7.0. See Soil and Fertilizing, below, and April.

Light. Most herbs and vegetables do best in full sun. To provide as much sun as possible, arrange the planting rows in your kitchen garden to run east to west. At the north end set tall plants, like staked **tomatoes, sunflowers,** and **corn** (planted in blocks to assure pollination). At the south end, set low-growing things so they won't be shaded by the taller plants. Some cool season vegetables whose enemy is heat—**lettuce, peas,** and **spinach,** for example—may last longer planted where the shade of taller plants cuts the heat of the late spring sun.

Spacing. Raised beds, or rows, about 36 inches wide are ideal as they can be worked from both sides comfortably. That gives you enough space to plant low-growing crops like **lettuce** and **beets** in the same row with flowers. When the seedlings are up, thin them out around the strongest flower seedlings. As the early vegetables are harvested, the flowers will fill in.

Big, rapid growers like **eggplants, tomatoes,** and **summer squash** need 24 to 36 inches around. To create a living mulch for these vegetables, plant spreading flowers like **edging lobelia,** *Lobelia erinus*, **alyssum, nasturtiums,** and **multiflora petunias** about 12 inches away. Where mildew is a problem avoid dense plantings, which cut down on air circulation.

Soil and Fertilizing

If you are starting a **new kitchen garden,** we recommend creating raised beds as described in the Introduction to the book under Soil Preparation and Improvement.

To support the lavish productivity of an **established kitchen garden,** every year before planting season begins you need to check and adjust the soil pH as described in the Introduction to the book.

In addition, a few weeks before planting, work into the top 6 to 8 inches of the soil a generous helping of nutrients (except for nasturtiums.) Use an organic or an eight-month formulation of a controlled-release chemical fertilizer for vegetables and annuals. (See Understanding Fertilizers in the Introduction to the book.) That will carry the plants through the whole growing season. Scratch a full dose of fertilizer into the soil around the kitchen garden perennials—**bramble fruits, asparagus,** the berry patch, **rhubarb,** and the others—in early spring before growth begins.

The long-season hot-weather crops, along with **tomatoes** benefit from a modest additional fertilization during the growing season. Prompts are given in the month-by-month pages that follow. André recommends using a water-soluble organic fertilizer, such as fish emulsion or liquid seaweed. In addition, before replanting a row that has already produced a crop, renew the fertilizer.

Planting a cover crop (see Annuals, Planting in the October pages) at the end of the growing season renews the organic content and fertility of the soil.

Watering

Seeds need consistent moisture to germinate and grow. Before sowing seeds, unless the garden is moist from recent rain, water the soil slowly and thoroughly. Use a sprinkler or a hose that lays down 1 to 2 inches of water in five to twelve hours; set a coffee tin under the watering equipment to measure the time it takes to lay down that much water, and record it in your garden log. After the seeds are planted, water the area for half an hour or so.

Maintaining soil moisture keeps root systems growing, and big root systems deliver lots of produce and withstand summer drought and heat. Your kitchen garden needs a good soaking rain every week to ten days, or enough hose water to lay down an inch or two.

In addition, water any time seedlings show signs of wilting.

Did You Know?

Flowers to Grow with Vegetables

Artichoke. Back with **bronze fennel** and *Cosmos* Sensation Strain (**'Pinkie', climbing eggplant**); edge with **purple alyssum.**

Green beans. Back with cut-and-come-again red **zinnias, ruby chard, calliopsis;** edge with dwarf white, yellow, and red **zinnias** and yellow **French marigolds.**

Shell beans. Intertwine **scarlet runner beans** with white and purple **shell beans;** edge with tall red **salvia** fronted by red **chard** and dwarf white **dahlia.**

Early cabbage. Interplant with **flowering kale;** back with tall pink and lavender **stock;** edge with blue or white **pansies** and **radishes.**

Summer and late cabbage. Back with tall **zinnias** in mixed colors; edge with pink **scent-leaf geraniums** and **mache.**

Corn. Front with magenta *Amaranthus caudatus* and multicolored '**Joseph's Coat**'; edge with white **cosmos** 'Purity' and green **chard.**

Eggplant. Interplant with **borage** and **purple basil;** edge with pink and lavender single **multiflora petunias.**

Early lettuce. Combine **several colors of lettuce;** back with **Iceland poppies;** edge with '**Pacific Giant' primroses, pansies,** and **English daisies.**

Mid-season or summer lettuce. Plant in semi-sun; back with white and pink **impatiens.**

Late lettuce. Back with **garden mums;** edge with solid-color **pansies** in matching hues.

Sweet peppers. Back with **Mexican zinnias;** edge with yellow and orange **French marigolds** and **dwarf bush basil.** Or, interplant with tall **dahlias.**

Swiss chard. Back with **red salvia** and white **cosmos 'Purity';** edge with **nasturtiums.**

Summer squash. Back with tall yellow and orange **marigolds** and blue **salvia;** edge with blue **multiflora petunias** and pink **wax begonias.**

PEST CONTROL

Integrated Pest Management, which is discussed in the Introduction to the book, is the new scientific and commercial approach to handling pests, and it includes some old fashioned controls that many gardeners swear by. Some gardeners report greater success planting tall crops when the moon is rising, and root crops when the moon is diminishing.

Organic gardeners report some success with these plant combinations:

- **Asparagus beetles**—try tomato plants nearby.

- **Aphids**—try garlic and nasturtiums nearby.

- **Beetles**—try nasturtiums nearby your radishes, beans, cucumbers, eggplant, tomatoes, and squash.

- **Colorado potato beetle**—try marigolds nearby.

- **Mexican bean beetles**—try potatoes near beans.

- **Mites**—try radishes near beans, cucumbers, eggplant, squash, and tomatoes.

- **Nematodes**—try planting marigolds nearby.

For information on common pests and diseases, and their controls, turn to the section on Pests, Diseases, and Controls in the Appendix.

Herbs & Vegetables

Herbs for the Mid-Atlantic

Common Name (*Botanical Name*)	Hardiness	Sow Indoors	Sow Outdoors	Harvest	Our Picks
Arugula (*Eruca vesicaria*)	Annual	March and August	Seedlings in April	Spring and summer	French Arugula
Basil (*Ocimum basilicum*)	Zones 9 to 10	April	Seedlings in May	Summer to early fall	'Sweet Genovese'; Holy Basil; Thai Basil; 'Purple Ruffles'
Chives (*Allium schoenoprasum*)	Zones 3 to 8	March	Seedlings in April	Summer	N/A
Cilantro (*Coriander sativum*)	Annual	April	Seedlings in May	Summer/fall	'Santo Cilantro'
Dill (*Anethum graveolens*)	Annual	April	Seedlings in May	Early summer	'Bouquet'
Lavender (*Lavandula angustifolia*)	Zones 5/6 to 10	January/ February	Seedlings in May	June	English Lavender 'Munstead'; 'Hidcote'
Mint (*Mentha spicata*)	Zones 3 to 9	N/A	Root divisions Spring/Summer/ Fall	Spring/summer	Spearmint; Applemint (*M. suavolens*); Peppermint (*M. piperita*)
Oregano/Sweet Marjoram	Zones 6 to 10	April	Seedlings in May	Summer	Common Oregano (*Origanum vulgare*); Sweet Marjoram (*O. majorana*) annual
Parsley (*Petroselinum crispum*)	Biennial	February	Seedlings in March	Summer and fall	Curly Parsley; Italian Parsley *P. crispum* 'Neapolitanum'
Rosemary (*Rosmarinus officinalis*)	Zones 7 to 9	Root cuttings, late summer	April	Summer and fall	Common Rosemary
Sage (*Salvia officinalis*)	Zones 4 to 9	March	April	Summer and fall	Common Sage
Sweet Fennel (*Foeniculum vulgare*)	Annual	March	Seedlings in May	Mid-summer	Sweet Fennel (*Foeniculum vulgare* var. *dulce*)
Tarragon (*Artemisia dracunculus*)	Zones 3 to 9	Root cuttings, summer	April	June	French Tarragon
Thyme (*Thymus* sp. & cvs.)	Zones 3/4 to 9	January/February	April	Summer	Common Thyme (*T. vulgaris*), Lemon Thyme (*T.* x *citriodorus*), Caraway Thyme (*T. herba-barona*)

Herbs & Vegetables

Vegetables for the Mid-Atlantic

Common Name	Sow Indoors*	Sow Outdoors	Approximate Time to Maturity	Our Picks
Asparagus Roots	N/A	Fall	2 years to first harvest	'Martha Washington', 'Jersey Knight'
Beans, Bush	April (in pots)	After last frost: April-August	54-58 days	'Burpee Stringless', 'Blue Lake', 'Roc D'or', (yellow wax), 'Tenderette', 'Roma', 'Royal Burgundy', Tender Green'
Beans, Green	April (in pots)	After last frost: April-August	45-75 days	'Roma II', 'Gator Green'
Beans, Bush Lima	April (in pots)	April-July	60-90 days	'Burpee Improved Bush', 'Fordhook Baby', Fordhook 242'
Beans, Pole Lima	April (in pots)	April-July	60-90 days	'Carolina Sieva', 'King of the Garden'
Beans, Pole	April (in pots)	April-June	65-100 days	'Kentucky Blue Pole', ' Blue Lake'
Beets, Early	March	April-June	50-75 days	'Cylindra', 'Detroit Dark Red', ' Red Ace Hybrid'
Beets, Late	N/A	June-August	75-100 days	'Long Season' (superb!)
Broccoli	April-May	April	50-100 days	'Green Comet', 'Goliath', 'Arcadia', 'Everest', 'Packman'
Brussels Sprouts	N/A	April-July	90-150 days	'Jade Cross' hybrid, 'Oliver'
Cabbage, Chinese	Late April	May-June	60-95 days	N/A
Cabbage, Early	Early to mid-April	April	65-100 days	'Stonehead', 'Flat Dutch', 'Savoy', 'Chieftain Savoy', 'Tendersweet', 'Early Marvel', 'Super Red'
Cabbage, Late	N/A	May-July	51-95 days	N/A
Carrots, Early	March	April and May	60-80 days	'Chantenay', 'Danver Half Long', 'Baby Sweet', 'Nantes'
Carrots, Late	N/A	May-July	60-85 days	N/A
Cauliflower, Early	February	April	50-100 days	'Chartreuse', 'Burgundy Queen', 'Snow Crown'
Cauliflower, Late	N/A	May and June	60-10 days	N/A
Celeriac	March	April and May	70-85 days	N/A
Celery	February	April and May	115-135 days	N/A
Collards	N/A	June-August	75 days	N/A
Corn, Early	N/A	Early May	60-80 days	N/A

* Use flats for sowing indoors unless otherwise specified.

Herbs & Vegetables

Vegetables for the Mid-Atlantic

Common Name	Sow Indoors*	Sow Outdoors	Approximate Time to Maturity	Our Picks
Corn Salad (mache)	N/A	April and May	45-60 days	N/A
Corn, Sweet	N/A	After last frost and every 2-3 weeks for continuous crop	65-100 days	'Kandy', 'Peaches and Cream', 'Silver Queen' (good for canning and freezing)
Cress, Upland	N/A	February-August	55 days	N/A
Cucumbers	Late March-April (in pots)	May-July	50-70 days	'Sweet Success', 'Straight Eight', 'Burpee Burpless', 'Burpless #26', 'Sweet Slice'
Eggplant	Late March-April (in pots)	May-July	65-90 days	N/A
Endive	February	April-August	65-100 days	N/A
Garlic Cloves	N/A	Zones 5-6 Oct.-Early Nov.; Zones 7-8 Nov.-Jan.	Late summer	Italian, Elephant, Softneck
Kale, Spring	Late March-April	Mid-April-May	55-65 days	N/A
Kale, Fall	N/A	July	45-60 days	N/A
Kohlrabi	Late March-April	April-July	45-60 days	N/A
Lettuce	Late March	April, May, and August	45-80 days	'Black Simpson', 'Oak Leaf', 'Butter Crunch', 'Bib', 'Romaine', 'Redsails'
Leek	February	April and May	120-150 days	N/A
Melons, Honeydew	April (in pots)	May-June (in pots)	70-100 days	'Honeypearl'
Melons, Musk	April (in pots)	May (in pots)	90-120 days	'Hales Best', 'Ambrosia', 'Athena'
Melons, Water	April (in pots)	May (in pots)	100-125 days	N/A
Mustard	February-March	March and August	35-40 days	N/A
New Zealand Spinach	April	May	70 days	(Hot weather spinach)
Okra	N/A	May and June	55-60 days	N/A
Onion Seed	February-March	Late April-May and August	70-115 days	N/A
Onion Sets	N/A	Late April-early May	60-75 days	'Candy'

* Use flats for sowing indoors unless otherwise specified.

Herbs & Vegetables

Vegetables for the Mid-Atlantic

Common Name	Sow Indoors*	Sow Outdoors	Approximate Time to Maturity	Our Picks
Parsnip	N/A	April	95-150 days	N/A
Peas (smooth), Early	N/A	March-May	50-75 days	N/A
Peas (wrinkled)	N/A	April and May	50-75 days	N/A
Peppers, Sweet and Hot	April	May	50-85 days	Sweet: 'California Wonder', 'Big Bertha', 'Better Bell', 'Sweet Banana'. Hot: 'Anaheim', 'Mucho Nacho', 'Jalapeno', 'Hungarian Hot Wax', 'Habanero'
Potatoes (sets)	N/A	April-June	60-90 days	N/A
Potatoes, Sweet	N/A	May	120 days	N/A
Pumpkin	April	May-June	90-120 days	N/A
Radish, Early	Early-April	April and September	25-50 days	'Cherry Bell' (seed again in fall)
Radish, Winter	N/A	July and August	25-50 days	N/A
Rhubarb	Perennial	April-May	Spring	'Valentine', 'Crimson Red'
Rutabaga	March	June and July	70-90 days	N/A
Salsify	N/A	April and May	125-130 days	N/A
Spinach	March	April-May	35-55 days and Sept	'Bloomsdale', 'Tyee'
Squash, Summer	April	After last frost	50-65 days	Zucchini, Scallop, Summer Crookneck
Squash, Winter	April	May-June	60-110 days	Acorn, Buttercup, Butternut, Hubbards
Sweet Potatoes	Cuttings or slips; February	May-June	100-140 days	Red and white varieties
Swiss Chard	April	April-June	50-60 days	N/A
Tomato	April	After last frost, second crop July 4th	100-120 days	'Goliath', 'Park Whopper', 'Beefmaster', 'Super Steak', 'German Johnson' (antique), 'Mr. Stripie', 'Oxheart' (antique), 'Roma', 'Italian Plum'
Turnips, Early	March-April	June	40-75 days	N/A
Turnips, Late	N/A	July-Sept	40-75 days	N/A
Turnips, Salad	N/A	April and Sept	35-45 days	N/A

* Use flats for sowing indoors unless otherwise specified.

JANUARY
Herbs & Vegetables

 PLANNING

Gather your favorite mail-order catalogs for herbs, vegetables, and annuals, and sketch a planting plan. Plan to maximize your garden's productivity by close spacing the plants and by interplanting and succession cropping.

Interplanting or intercropping describes planting two or more compatible crops in the same row at the same time, like fast-growing **radishes** with **lettuce.** Or **sweet corn** with **pumpkins** at their feet. Or **tomatoes** with **basil** all around.

Succession cropping refers to keeping a row planted with a sequence of vegetables; when the first crop is harvested, you remove it and reseed the row immediately. For example, **radishes,** followed by **lettuce,** followed by **snap bush beans,** followed by late **carrots.**

If you plan to start cool-season plants, such as **peas, onions, shallots, leeks,** and **garlic,** in the garden in mid-February, late this month cover the area with black plastic to increase the heat in the soil.

 PLANTING

Gather the equipment you will be using to start seeds indoors.

Zone 8 gardeners can sow seeds indoors now for the herbs that will need to grow pretty big before they can go outdoors to the garden, **lavender** for one. (See the Annuals chapter, January, Planting, Starting Seeds Indoors.) Some herbs are annuals, some perennial. **Parsley** is biennial. Our rule of thumb is this: for annual herbs, one plant per person in the household; for perennials, one plant or two. For **parsley,** six. Some hardy vegetables can be started indoors, too, such as **onion sets** (André strongly favors big yellow '**Candy**') and **cabbage.**

The flowers of all the culinary herbs are edible and pretty as garnishes and in bouquets, so we plant more of those we use lots of, such as **lavender** and **basil.** The herbs thrive in containers.

 CARE

If you are overwintering cold-tender herbs, such as **rosemary,** in a cold frame (see November), monitor temperatures as the days grow longer and warmer, and ventilate to keep it moderately cool inside.

 PRUNING

Harvest and groom herbs such as **parsley** you brought indoors last fall.

Remove winter-damaged limbs from the **fruit trees.**

 WATERING

Maintain the soil moisture in herbs growing indoors.

 FERTILIZING

Add five drops of houseplant fertilizer to the water for herbs growing indoors.

 PESTS

Damping off is a threat to seedlings. It's a fungal disease that attacks the seedlings at the base of their stems. It rots the stems so the plants fall over. A sterile growing medium and good drainage help avoid the condition. Applications of the fungicide Thiram (Arasan) help control the problem.

Did You Know?

Favorite Culinary Herbs

Arugula. Annual. Sow seeds indoors in late winter, outdoors in early spring; repeat in mid-summer.

Basil. Annual here. Sow seeds in mid-spring, or set seedlings out when you plant **tomatoes.** For flavor, plant **sweet basil;** for pesto, and for freezing, **'Sweet Genovese';** for cooking and to make basil oil, **East Indian** or **holy basil;** for Oriental cuisine, and basil oil, plant **Thai basil;** for color and flowers, **'Purple Ruffles';** for containers, grow topiary-like tiny **bush basils.**

Chives. Perennial. Start seeds indoors in peat pots now to late February, or sow seeds in early spring where it is to grow. Set seedlings out in early April.

Dill. Annual. Sow seeds now in peat pots, or outdoors in early spring where the plants are to grow. Use the foliage fresh, or dry and store it. Allow flower heads to go seed, then dry seeds for cooking.

Cilantro/Coriander. Annual. Sow seeds outdoors in early spring. In Zone 8, repeat in fall. The seed is the spice coriander.

Fennel. Annual. Sow seeds indoors four weeks before the last frost, or outdoors in mid-spring where it is to grow. For flavorful leaves, plant **sweet fennel,** *Foeniculum vulgare dulce;* the cultivar **'Rubrum'** is the beautiful **bronze fennel.** The vegetable is **Florence fennel,** *F. v.* var. *azoricum.*

Lavender. Perennial. Sow seeds indoors now; transplant often. When the plant is 12 inches tall, transplant to the garden. For flavor, plant **English lavender;** harvest the stems before the buds break.

Mint. Invasive perennial. Grow mint in a large container. Plant root divisions in early spring, or in late summer where winters are mild. **Spearmint,** *Mentha spicata,* is the best all-round culinary mint.

Oregano. Perennial. See **Sweet marjoram.** For flavor, plant common oregano, *Origanum vulgare;* for edging the garden, plant **golden oregano.**

Parsley. Biennial. Start seeds indoors now. Set seedlings outdoors in March. In early September sow seeds near maturing parsley plants. Choose **curly parsley** for garnishing, chopping, and floral bouquets. Plant flat **Italian parsley** for salads and cooking.

Rosemary. Tender perennial. Sow seeds indoors now. Set seedlings out in mid-spring. In Zone 6, winter rosemary indoors. For cooking, choose *Rosmarinus officinalis*; as a garden ornamental, *R. o.* 'Lockwood de Forest'.

Sage. Sow seeds indoors in March. Plant seedlings outdoors in early spring. For flavoring, plant *Salvia officinalis.* For color, plant **tricolor sage.**

Sweet Marjoram. Tender perennial. Sow seeds indoors in early spring or outdoors after the soil has warmed. A cousin to **oregano,** grow this one for use fresh.

Tarragon. Perennial. The best is **French tarragon,** *Artemisia dracunculus,* which is propagated from cuttings. For flavor, taste before you buy a plant.

Thyme. Perennial. Start seeds now. Transplant outdoors when the stem's 8 inches long. For flavor, plant **common thyme,** *Thymus vulgaris;* for display, **'Wedgewood English';** for containers, stepping stones, and in stone walls, **creeping thyme,** *T. serpyllum.* For edging, plant variegated **'Argenteus'** and **'Aureus'.**

FEBRUARY
Herbs & Vegetables

PLANNING

Prepare your **garden tools** for the season ahead. Treat all the wooden handles with applications of boiled linseed oil available where tools are sold. Oil your shears and trimmers, shovels and spading forks. Service the rototiller, or take it to be serviced, and have the blade changed if necessary.

If you plan to set vegetable seedlings out in the garden early, consider whether they will need to be covered with a **protective covering.** Various types of cones including those called "hot caps" and "walls of water" are available.

Film tenting is also sold as protective covering and to keep insects and small pests away.

Ordering seeds and plants. Check your buying plans against your inventory of seeds left over or saved last year. List what you have, will order by mail, or plan to buy at a garden center. If prices are equal, buy perennials such as **asparagus** roots (three-year-old roots for quick results), **artichokes, rhubarb, strawberries, raspberries, fruit trees,** and **onion sets** from a garden center where you can see what you are getting.

Do a web search for items not found in your mail-order catalogs. We've had good luck with it. It's also worth your while checking catalog prices against prices at online garden sites.

When your plan is final, prepare catalog orders and mail them, and prepare shopping lists for purchases to be made at garden centers.

Check your supplies of small pots suitable for transplanting seedlings started indoors. **Disinfect** pots, flats, jars, and your potting table by washing them with a solution that is 1 part bleach to 9 parts water.

You may need more potting mix for indoor plantings, and for vegetables and herbs growing in hanging baskets and other containers. Look for bagged potting mixes that include water-holding gels, and for organic liquid fertilizers.

PLANTING

Indoors. All zones can sow seeds indoors for **cabbage, chives, fennel, sage, thyme, rosemary.** (See the Annuals chapter, January, Planting, Starting Seeds Indoors.)

Outdoors. In Zone 8 the weather may encourage you to start a few of these herbs and vegetables outdoors late this month.

Elsewhere, when air temperatures are hitting 55 degrees Fahrenheit, you can begin to think of sowing cold-season crops out in the garden. **Peas** can be planted mid-February to mid-March, but cold soil may discourage quick growth. They tolerate some frost, and do well in air temperatures between 55 and 70 degrees Fahrenheit. **Potatoes** can go in St. Patrick's Day or later in April.

CARE

Indoors. When the seedlings started indoors become crowded, transplant each to an individual 3- to 4-inch pot filled with a good potting mix.

Seedlings that will be growing indoors for six weeks need good light to thrive. At this stage, an installation of grow lights burned fourteen to sixteen hours a day is especially helpful.

Repot herbs brought indoors last fall.

Outdoors. Early this month prune the **grape vines;** don't wait until later in the season as they will bleed, and that weakens the plants.

When the seedlings started indoors become crowded, transplant each to an individual 3- to 4-inch pot filled with a good potting mix.

If you planted a cover crop in your garden in the fall (see the Annuals chapter, October, Planting), turn it under when cold and moisture have left the earth. The earth is ready to be worked when a ball of earth packed between your hands crumbles easily; if it sticks together, the soil is still too wet.

PRUNING

Thin crowded seedlings. Groom potted herbs growing indoors.

WATERING

Water pots of transplanted seedlings as the soil becomes dry to the touch.

Maintain the moisture levels of the herbs you brought indoors last fall.

FERTILIZING

Indoors. Every two weeks fertilize all the seedlings that will remain indoors another six weeks or more with a soluble houseplant fertilizer at half strength.

Did You Know?

Potted Kitchen Garden

Herbs and vertical vegetables make great container plants. Tidy herbs, like **parsley, globe basil,** and **thyme** suit a windowbox and make pretty edgers for tall or short potted flowers. **Tomato** seedlings perform beautifully growing in pots, planters, and even garbage bags.

Shell beans and **eggplant** climb from a container as readily as from the soil. Small **summer squash, gourds,** or **cucumbers** can be trained to a teepee, three or four long poles tied together at the top like a Native American tent. **Melons** and even **pumpkins,** too, but the fruits will need the support of a sling made of a mesh bag or a section of pantyhose tied to the teepee when the fruits get big. Varieties with medium- to small-sized fruits carried high on the plant are more attractive for container growing than are the low-growing, heavy-fruited types.

Some of the perennial kitchen garden plants do well in big tubs and planters—**artichokes, rhubarb, strawberries, dwarf peach,** and columnar **apple** trees.

For windowbox, basket, and container plantings, we recommend a humusy commercial potting mix enriched with slow-release fertilizer. Mix a polymer such as Soil Moist into the soil, and you'll find maintaining moisture much easier. Where summers are cool, place containers in warm microclimates, in the reflected heat from a south wall, for example.

Outdoors. Zone 8: Check and amend the soil pH, and dig in organic or slow-release fertilizers. Fertilize established **asparagus** beds with a high nitrogen organic fertilizer. Fertilize other kitchen garden perennials, **fruit trees, bramble fruits,** and **berry beds.**

PESTS

Crowded seedlings in soggy soil are vulnerable to the fungus called "damping off," which rots stems near the soil surface. Discard affected plants, reduce watering, and increase light and fresh air. If the problem persists, mist the seedlings with a fungicide such as Thiram (Asaran), or with 1 tablespoon of bleach to 1 quart of water, or 4 tablespoons of bleach to a gallon of water.

PLANNING

The few perennial food plants are quite handsome. **Asparagus, red-stemmed rhubarb,** and **Jerusalem artichokes or sunchokes,** as the tuberous roots of tall, small-flowered sunflowers are often called, are decorative as well as delicious. Consider planting a few of these in front of, or alongside, the vegetable rows, and use sprawling **thyme** and **oregano,** two of the perennial herbs that are winter hardy, as edgers.

Alpine strawberries also make pretty edgers. But, if you love berries and cream, plant full-size **strawberries** in a bed of their own. Dwarf varieties of **apples** and **pears,** along with **peaches** and **nectarines,** are lovely in bloom and are used as center pieces in ornate kitchen gardens; **dwarf apples** and **pears** make handsome, productive espaliers. **Grapes** can be trained to a fence, a pergola, and as an espalier.

The **bramble fruits** need a space of their own, off to one side.

You also can grow the perennial food plants in containers. **Dwarf fruit trees** can handle cold winters as long as the containers are 18 to 36 inches square or in diameter, and lined with a double row of large bubble wrap or styrofoam. In Zone 8, **artichokes** can stand a little shade in late afternoon.

PLANTING

In Zone 8, you may be able to plant **fruit trees, bramble fruits, rhubarb, artichokes,** and **asparagus,** as the ground becomes workable.

Before transplanting vegetable and herb seedlings to the open garden, set them in a warm, sheltered spot outdoors to harden off for a few days.

When you are ready to plant:

1 Wet the seedlings thoroughly with tepid water containing fertilizer.

2 Open a generous hole in the bed.

3 Pour a little of the water into each planting hole.

4 Loosen roots that may be binding the rootball. Set each seedling upright and straight in its planting hole so the top of the rootball is just above the soil surface.

5 Fill the hole with soil, and press it down firmly around the stem.

6 Water well.

Seedlings growing together in a flat. Separate intertwined seedlings by slicing them apart with a sharp knife. Proceed as above.

Seedlings in planting pockets. Turn the flat upside down a little above the soil, and push one rootball at a time out of its pocket. Then transplant as above.

Seedlings in peat pots. Soak each peat pot thoroughly in a solution of 1 gallon of water to which you have added 1/2 teaspoon of liquid hand dishwashing detergent and liquid fertilizer. Then gently tear open the bottom third of the peat pot so the roots can tie into the earth. Set the pot and the plant upright in the planting hole, and proceed as above.

If you transplant to the open garden while frost threatens, plan to protect the seedlings with hot caps or something like Reemay®, a lightweight fabric used for the winter protection of ornamentals. You can save seedlings from an occasional night frost by covering them with newspaper, coffee cans, drycleaner's dry cleaning plastic or plastic film, old sheets, blankets, bedspreads, burlap. Don't allow the seedlings to dry out.

 CARE

In early spring remove the uppermost layer of straw on the **strawberry** plants.

Maintain the moisture for seeds and transplants—those indoors, those in a cold frame, and those in the open garden.

Leave the matted-down straw to make a clean bed for the berries to rest on.

Mulch the big perennial food plants—**asparagus, artichokes, bramble fruits,** and **fruit trees.** They benefit from annual mulching that will decompose and replenish the supply of humus in the soil.

 # PRUNING

Cut back **thyme, chives, sage, tarragon, oregano,** and other perennial herbs.

Prune the **bramble fruits.** Remove suckers (water sprouts) from the **fruit trees.**

 # WATERING

Maintain the moisture for seeds and transplants—those indoors, those in a cold frame, and those in the open garden.

Maintain the soil moisture in herbs such as **parsley** brought indoors last fall.

 # FERTILIZING

Indoors. Zones 7 and 6—Every two weeks fertilize all the seedlings that will remain indoors another six weeks or more with a soluble houseplant fertilizer at half strength.

Did You Know?

When to Plant What

Cold Season Crops: These tolerate some frost, so you can plant them outdoors even before the last anticipated frost. They will grow well when air temperatures rise to between 55 to 70 degrees Fahrenheit. Early seeding doesn't always help because the soil is cold, and seedlings can rot as they germinate, just as a too-early planting of **potatoes** rots.

The perennial herbs, seedlings of **thyme, oregano, chives,** along with **parsley** which is biennial, and the annual herbs **arugula, dill, onion sets,** and **garlic.**

Asparagus and **rhubarb,** along with **beets, broccoli, Brussels sprouts, cabbage, chicory, collards, kale, kohlrabi, leek, lettuce, peas, parsnip, radish, spinach, rutabagas, turnip greens, turnips.**

These tolerate some cold but not frost: **Artichoke, carrot, cauliflower, endive, lettuce, peas, white potato.**

Warm season crops: These are readily damaged by frost. They do well at 65 to 80 degrees Fahrenheit, but sulk or rot in cold soil: **Lavender, nasturtiums, summer savory, beans, cantaloupes, carrots, chard, corn ('Kandy' 'Peaches & Cream', 'Silver Queen'), cucumbers, muskmelon, sweet peppers, potatoes, pumpkin, squash, sweet corn, tomatoes.**

Hot weather crops: These need air temperatures at least 65 degrees Fahrenheit. They do well in temperatures above 80 degrees Fahrenheit. They require a long growing season: **Hot peppers, lima beans, shell beans, eggplant, okra, peanuts, sweet potato, watermelon.**

Outdoors. Zone 7 and 6—Check and amend the soil pH, and dig in organic or slow-release fertilizers now.

Fertilize established **asparagus** beds with a high-nitrogen organic fertilizer. Fertilize the other perennials, the **tree** and **bramble fruits** and **strawberries.**

 PESTS

Control rabbits and other pests with row covers or bird netting. A chickenwire fence is one sure way to keep rabbits out. If there are woodchucks, leave the chickenwire loose between posts; woodchucks can climb taut chickenwire.

APRIL
Herbs & Vegetables

 PLANNING

To make the most of your garden space, plan now to plant crops that will replace the cool-season vegetables.

Be prepared when temperatures reach 65 degrees Fahrenheit to set out seedlings, and sow seeds outdoors, for **nasturtiums, summer savory, beans, cantaloupes, chard, corn, cucumbers, muskmelon, potatoes, pumpkin, sweet corn, squash, rutabaga, turnips.**

Order two- or three-year-old **asparagus** roots for planting this month. A plot 20 feet square, or a row 50 to 60 feet long, will produce all five or six people could want.

 PLANTING

When the ground becomes workable, plant **fruit trees, bramble fruits, rhubarb, artichokes, asparagus,** and other perennial food plants.

When danger of frost is over, you can set out in the open garden seedlings of **artichokes, cabbage, cauliflower, chives, onion sets** (late April to early May), **fennel, sage, thyme, rosemary.** In the open garden you can sow seeds for **carrots, endive, sunflowers,** and plant white **potatoes.** Plant **broccoli** (**'Green Comet'**) and **lettuce** seedlings

or seeds now through early May. In cool Zone 6, there still is time to plant **peas.**

And this is a good time to start **asparagus.** They'll be spring's first vegetable crop for the next twenty years. Plant two-, or better yet, three-year-old crowns; you can start harvesting the second or third year after planting. André's favorites are '**Martha Washington**' and '**Jersey Knight**'.

Here's how to start asparagus:

1 Prepare deep, wide trenches 10 to 15 inches deep in rows 3 to 4 feet apart.

2 Loosen the soil in the trenches, and mix in rich composted cow manure, compost, and an organic fertilizer.

3 Set the crowns 18 inches apart in the rows, and cover them with 2 inches of soil.

4 Fill the trenches as the new shoots come up.

5 Do not harvest the first year, and harvest only a few stalks the second year. Fertilize the bed every year in spring before growth starts and when the stalks come in thin, which is also a signal to stop harvesting.

CARE

Keep weed seedlings raked up when very young, then as the good guys grow up, they'll shade out the weeds.

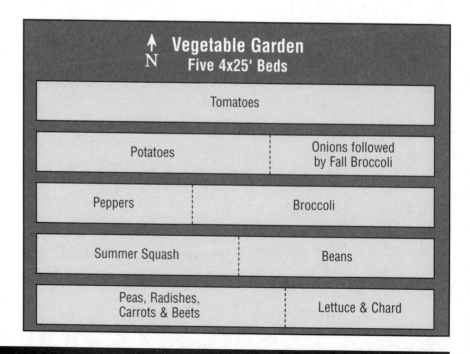

↑ N **Vegetable Garden**
Five 4x25' Beds

| Tomatoes |
Potatoes	Onions followed by Fall Broccoli
Peppers	Broccoli
Summer Squash	Beans
Peas, Radishes, Carrots & Beets	Lettuce & Chard

Keep an eye on the rows where you have sown vegetables, and when the seedlings start to come up thick and fast, thin the rows.

Did You Know?

Determining the pH for Kitchen Garden Soil

The soil elements most food plants need are readily available when the pH of the soil is between 6.0 and 7.0. The exceptions are **basil** (5.5 to 6.5), and **blueberries** (4.5 to 5.5) **dill** (5.5 to 6.7), **eggplant** and **melon,** (5.5 to 6.5), **potatoes** (4.5 to 6.0), **sorrel** (5.5 to 6.0).

Vegetable gardens produce multiple crops, and over time the soil tends to become acid, so **testing annually is important.** If your soil tests below pH 6.0, spread hydrated lime, and mix it into the soil. Try a small dose, and retest the pH a few weeks later. Applying ashes, preferably from the wood of deciduous trees, raises the soil pH and supplies water-soluble potassium as well, one of the essential nutrients.

If the soil of your vegetable garden tests above pH 6.8, apply water-soluble sulfur or iron sulfate. Ask an Agriculture Extension agent or an expert at your local garden center how. The treatment must be repeated after eight months or a year. Adding an acidic mulch such as composted sawdust, bark, leaves, pine needles, or cottonseed meal has a slow but lasting effect on pH.

The Agricultural Extension Service at your state university can provide sound advice about pH in, and the composition of, your soil. A reliable soil testing kit is sold by Cornell University; write for the Standard Kit pH 5.0 to 7.2, Cornell Nutrient Analysis Laboratories, 804 Radfield Hall, Cornell University, Ithaca, NY 14853.

 ## PRUNING

Keep an eye on the rows where you have sown vegetables, and when the seedlings start to come up thick and fast, thin the rows.

Close, dense planting shades out weeds; keep that in mind as you thin the rows.

 ## WATERING

If rain fails, be sure to water seeds and seedlings deeply.

Water vegetables and fruits growing in containers every two to three days.

 ## FERTILIZING

Weekly, include a half dose of a soluble organic fertilizer in the water for vegetables and fruits growing in containers.

 ## PESTS

Be tolerant of a small infestation of the insects that are food for the beneficials.

The buzz of a nearby bee can scare you, but they are essential to pollinate crops. Wasps are mostly parasitic and destroy countless whiteflies and aphids. Yellow jackets feed their young on many flies and caterpillars. Most lady beetles destroy aphids, mealybugs, and spider mites. There are beneficial beetles, flies that attack corn borer and cutworms, and midges that devour aphids. Other insects generally considered beneficial are dragonflies, lacewings, spiders, and beneficial mites.

To encourage these beneficials, avoid toxic sprays or dusts unless a crop is being truly harmed.

PLANNING

Kitchen garden in a container. Growing herbs, vegetables, even **dwarf fruit** trees in containers solves problems of space, light, temperature. They'll thrive as long as the soil is fertile and the moisture sustained.

Low-growing culinary herbs such as **parsley** and **arugula,** and small and miniature vegetables like **'Tom Thumb'**, a tiny heading lettuce, do well in window boxes and big pots.

Rosemary thrives in a container. Train rosemary as a topiary ball or tree now, and you'll have sensational gifts to give in December.

Legumes and squashes can be led to climb up into better light—**peas, beans,** including the beautiful **scarlet runner** and purple-stemmed **hyacinth bean, eggplant, summer squash, melons,** even **pumpkins** will grow up a teepee, a pyramid, or a trellis stuck into a big container.

Tomato varieties do well in containers. Small varieties of **cherry tomatoes** thrive in 8-inch pots and hanging baskets. The big heirloom and late keeper **tomatoes** need a 2- to 5-gallon container filled with good planting mix.

Many perennial food plants, such as dwarf and small **fruit trees, artichokes,** and **rhubarb,** and the perennial herbs do well as container plants.

 PLANTING

Sometime after the last frost, plant **tomato** seedlings. When temperatures reach 65 to 80 degrees Fahrenheit, other hot weather crops can go in, **hot** and **sweet peppers, lima beans, shell beans, eggplant, okra, peanuts, sweet potato, watermelon.**

Sowing seeds. The classic way to sow vegetable seeds is in shallow furrows (drills) created by dragging the edge of a rake or hoe handle along the planting line. Then you dribble the seeds into the drills at spaced intervals.

Small, fine seeds, such as **lettuce,** are broadcast over damp, well-worked soil. Cover them with seed starting mix, and cover that with burlap to maintain the moisture during germination.

Seeds of vining plants like **cucumbers** and **winter squash** may be sown around a supporting teepee or bramble in groups of four to six, or three to five. Or, sow them at regular intervals front and back of trellising or chickenwire. If there's to be no support, sow the seeds in hills, that is in groups, with lots of room all around for the vines to ramble away from the center.

When the seedlings are up, **thin them** to the distance suggested by seed packets, or so that they are at least 3 to 5 inches apart.

 CARE

Pinch herbs to keep them shapely. Pinch out the growing tips of **snapdragons, basil, cosmos,** and other plants with central stalks, to keep them bushing out.

 PRUNING

Harvest lettuce and other early crops as they mature.

Pluck weeds out while thinning vegetable seedlings.

 WATERING

Seeds, and seedlings, need water right after planting, and enough the first three weeks to maintain soil moisture.

 FERTILIZING

When **asparagus** spears come in thin, stop harvesting and apply a high nitrogen organic fertilizer such as dried blood or cottonseed meal.

When cool season crops are over, **peas** and **spinach** for example, pull them out and take them to the compost pile. Before replanting the rows, work an application of an organic or slow-release fertilizer into the soil.

 PESTS

Asparagus beetle maybe deterred by planting **tomatoes** nearby.

If **aphids** appear at the tips of **tomato** stems, hose them off, or pinch the tips out and put them in the garbage. Ladybugs should control them later in the season.

Cabbage worms attack crops about now, the forebears of small white moths you see flitting around. Spray the foliage with Dipel, malathion, pyrethrin, Rotenone or a Sevin insecticide.

Cutworms are the culprits when tender seedlings turn up topless. One solution is to create a collar to prevent the critters from climbing up to eat. When the crops are over, rototill the row, or by hand, turn and fluff the soil. That brings the eggs to the surface where they die.

Did You Know?

About Tomatoes

Tomatoes are warm-season vegetables that flourish when nights reach 65 degrees Fahrenheit. In summer, the blossoms fall when days are above 90 and nights above 76 degrees Fahrenheit.

Determinate tomatoes are okay without staking, reach about 3 feet and ripen a big crop in a short time. They bear all at once, not continuously. If you want to get plants in and out to make place for other plants—choose determinate.

Indeterminate tomatoes need staking or caging, and they will keep producing continuously until stopped by cold. If you want a few plants that will bear over a long season, choose indeterminate varieties.

André and Mark plant a first crop May 1 to 15, of seedlings of **'Goliath'**, **'Park Whopper'**, **Beefmaster'**, **'Mr. Stripey'**, **Supersteak'**, **'Roma'**, and the antiques **'German Johnson'**, and **'Oxheart'**. They plant a second crop July 4.

To grow your own seedlings, start the seeds for a first crop indoors in spring; or for a second crop outdoors in a cold frame, five to seven weeks before the outdoor planting date. Put them outdoors for the last ten days to harden them off.

If you are buying tomato seedlings, bypass those in small containers and already in bloom or fruiting, and choose vigorously growing healthy plants with the letters VFNA on the labels. That means they are resistant to the common insects and diseases that assail tomatoes.

Two weeks before planting time, dig an organic or timed-release 5-10-10 fertilizer into the soil along with hydrated lime to prevent blossom end rot. Mark adds a handful of gypsum for each plant to provide calcium without changing the soil pH. Set transplants so the first leaves are just above soil level; lay leggy plants in the ground horizontally with most of the stem buried and the head upright.

Mark places tomatoes 4 feet apart, with 4 to 6 feet between rows. Between plants he puts down a weed barrier, such as landscape fabric, and covers it with a layer of mulch.

When the plants start to set fruit, apply a soluble organic fertilizer.

JUNE
Herbs & Vegetables

 PLANNING

You can save space in your garden, keep it healthier and make harvesting easy by planning to stake tall flowers, and by growing vining vegetables with their heads in the air. Lead the first stems of **cucumbers, eggplant, peas, shell beans,** and small **summer squash** to a support. Surround **tomatoes** with a sturdy support system that will make the fruits easy to pick.

A fence, especially a chickenwire fence, is a great support for **peas** and **beans.** If you don't have a fence, install a **chicken-wire support** 5 feet high by 30 feet long. That's 150 square feet of climbing room for peas and beans. An east- or west-facing wall is a fine place to espalier **pears** and **apples.**

A teepee is also a suitable support for **peas** and **beans,** and it's easily made. Just gather the tops of three to five tall, sturdy bamboo supports, and tie them together. You can make a cage for **tomatoes** by twining wire around a set of four tall sturdy wooden stakes. The stylized wooden teepees sold by garden centers last for several years, as do the many and various metal frames and cages.

When installing a support, set it close to the plants; if necessary, provide green wool, raffia, or cotton string to lead stems and branches to the stake.

 PLANTING

As the weather heats up, the cool-season crops come to an end. Early **turnips** are over. **Peas** are over. **Lettuces** and **spinach** begin to "bolt"—that is, they grow tall, produce seedheads, and taste bitter. So pull them all up and compost them.

Replant the rows with seeds or seedlings of any of these not planted earlier, such as **basil, nasturtiums, summer savory, cucumbers, green bush beans, cantaloupes, chard, corn, cucumbers, muskmelon, okra, sweet peppers, potatoes, pumpkins, squash, sweet corn, tomatoes.** Replace the spinach with **New Zealand spinach,** a warm weather substitute.

 CARE

When the early **strawberries** and **raspberries** start to ripen, protect your crop from the birds by covering the bed with nylon mesh, screening, cheesecloth, or a floating row cover.

Weed patrol is essential! Any that are allowed to mature and develop roots will be taking water and nutrients from the vegetables they are invading.

 PRUNING

Continue to pull weeds, and thin vegetable seedlings.

 WATERING

Keep an eye on plantings of **corn;** they need a good deep watering when the tassels at the top are beginning to show and when the silk is beginning to show in the ear.

Peppers need to be well watered now. Maintaining moisture evenly in the **tomatoes** helps prevent blossom end rot.

Weed patrol is essential! Any that are allowed to mature and develop roots will be taking water and nutrients from the vegetables they are invading.

FERTILIZING

When the **tomato** plants start to set fruit, drench the foliage with a soluble organic fertilizer, such as fish emulsion. Water until it drips to the ground, wetting the soil beneath. The foliage absorbs nutrients quickly.

Repeat monthly until the fruits near mature size.

PESTS

Watch out for **corn borer** and **corn earworm.** Corn earworm is also the tomato fruitworm, which winters in the soil as pupae. An environmentally-friendly solution is in late fall to dig up and turn over the soil in infested areas. Genetically-engineered corn is resistant, but at this time there is a lot of controversy over genetically-engineered plants.

Planting **corn** early helps, as does planting varieties that have resistance to the pest. You can also protect the rows with floating row covers. At the feeding stage they are discouraged by products that contain Sevin insecticide.

Did You Know?

Thinning Seedlings

When you broadcast seeds, the seedlings come up too closely spaced for mature individual plants. You must thin the rows until each seedling has space enough all around to grow well. Seed packets indicate suitable spacing.

Thinnings of the root vegetables such as **turnips** and **beets,** and leafy vegetables, such as **lettuce** and **spinach,** are good raw in salads, and they add nutrients to stews, sauces, and soups. So think of thinning as early harvests of the row.

Here are some examples of our approach to thinning:

Carrots, like most root crops, don't transplant well. We broadcast the seeds over well-worked soil, and cover them a half inch deep. Germination takes several weeks. Then we thin the plants repeatedly until they stand about 3 inches apart and use the thinnings in salads, stews, and soups.

Kale thinnings are excellent greens. We scatter the seeds in a 4-inch band, then thin the seedlings several times until they are 8 to 12 inches apart.

We thin **beet** seedlings until the plants are 2 inches apart. But, you can leave some of the thinning until the extra plants are large enough to cook up as **beet greens,** which we like even better than fresh **spinach.**

Asparagus beetles strip the foliage from the stems, and that prevents the plants from storing food for next season's production. Row covers may keep them away. Or, spray with a beetle control designed specifically for food plants, such as Rotenone and neem products.

Protect **tomatoes** from tomato hornworm with Sevin when the fruit is getting to be $1/2$ inch in diameter.

JULY
Herbs & Vegetables

 ## PLANNING

To enjoy the best of your kitchen garden, **plan to harvest** each species as it reaches peak flavor. Some vegetables maturing now must be kept picked to maintain productivity—something to consider when planning your vacation.

Individual seed packets offer guidance on harvest time. Here's an overview:

Herbs. The flavor of the perennial herbs is consistent all season. But **arugula** is a cool-season herb that is sweetest harvested very young. Take no more than a third of a parsley plant at one time. If it's hot, take only tip sprigs from your herbs however full they are. In extremely hot weather the plants shut down just as they do when cold becomes extreme. To strip them is to weaken the plant.

Leafy vegetables. Long-standing summer **lettuces** and **New Zealand spinach** may need watering but not harvesting while you are on vacation. **Chard** and **kale** have the best flavor in late summer and early fall, and you can pick side leaves until frost destroys the plants.

Root crops. There are early and late varieties. Spring **beets** are best harvested when 2 to 3 inches around; winter keeper varieties can stay in the ground until twice that size, or more. **Spring planted carrots** are best harvested at 2 inches around, when the orange shoulder shows through the soil. **Winter carrots** can stay in their rows until frost threatens; the longer they stay, the better the flavor. **Parsnips** taste best harvested in spring after a winter in the garden.

Legumes, peas, and beans. They must be picked when young, or the seeds in the pods will mature and the plants will slow or stop producing.

Squash Zucchini. It tastes best harvested at about 5 inches and must be kept picked continuously to keep the plants producing. Other **summer squashes** taste best when picked young as well. The **winter squashes,** such as **butternut, Hubbard,** develop a fuller flavor when they are allowed to stay on the vine well into fall.

PLANTING

You can sow seeds now for the next round of cool weather crops. Plant late season varieties of **Brussels sprouts, cabbage, cauliflower, broccoli, chard,** and **kale.** Plant leftover seeds of cool season **lettuces, arugula,** and **mache.**

Start seeds indoors or in a cold frame now for quick-bearing **cherry tomatoes.** Transplanted to a container that can be moved to a sheltered spot later, they will furnish your own fresh tomatoes well after the regular growing season. **Sungold tomatoes** are superb in stews and sauces and delicious fresh.

 ## CARE

When the bramble fruits, especially **raspberries** and **cherries,** start to ripen, cover them with nylon mesh, cheesecloth, or a floating row cover to keep birds and deer (!) from harvesting your crop; the deer eat leaves and all.

PRUNING

For flavor, harvest **green beans, zucchini,** and **summer squashes** as they reach 5 to 6 inches long.

Harvest **fruit trees** consistently to avoid attracting deer.

Some vegetables maturing now must be kept picked to maintain productivity—something to consider when planning your vacation.

Clear the plants of maturing vegetables to keep them producing.

In cool areas, when most of the tops of the **onions** break over naturally, the crop is ready to harvest. In warm areas, you can begin harvesting when about a third of the tops break over.

 # WATERING

The water from a hose hit by July sun is as hot as hot tap water. No good for plants. So, run the hose until the water is tepid before you turn it on the garden. A vegetable garden needs at least 1 inch of water per week in summer.

Check the moisture in plant containers every three or four days; check small pots and hanging baskets every day or two.

Water your compost pile when you water the garden, and turn it weekly.

 # FERTILIZING

When the **tomato** plants start to set fruit, drench the foliage and the soil with a soluble organic fertilizer, and repeat monthly until the fruits near mature size.

Did You Know?

Holly's Basil Oil

5 packed cups fresh basil leaves, preferably Thai or Holy basil
1 quart mild olive oil

To make: Strip off the leaves, and discard the stems. Pack the leaves into a measuring cup. Heat the oil until you can just bear to dip your finger in it. Bruise the leaves between your palms, and drop them into the oil. Remove the oil from the heat; cover the pot. Let the oil return to room temperature, then reheat it as before. Turn the heat off, cover the pot, and let the leaves steep 24 hours. Reheat the oil as before, let it cool to room temperature, then strain out the leaves. Bottle the pesto, cap it, and store the oil in the refrigerator.

 # PESTS

Don't pull big weeds from bone-dry soil—the upheaval can cost soil moisture. Water first, then tug gently but firmly to get all of the roots. Shake the soil into the garden, and compost the remains.

Japanese beetles emerge this month. Spraying now with a neem product may help. Plan to treat the garden and the lawn around with milky disease spores in late summer. It begins to be effective next year.

With summer's high heat and muggy air, fruits and vegetables become more susceptible to invasions of pests and diseases just as plants are crowding their rows. Thin the plants to let in more air. Plan next year to adopt a more open planting plan.

Since many **fungal diseases** thrive in a wet garden, water only in the early morning so the rising sun will dry the foliage. Spray **tomatoes** and **cucumbers** with copper fungicide.

AUGUST
Herbs & Vegetables

 PLANNING

The best-tended kitchen gardens will show seasonal wear and tear. Wilted leaves, cracked or discolored skin, and yellowed stems are often caused by natural stresses of the growing season. Plan to keep your eye on these developments. If symptoms worsen and you can't identify or solve them, ask your full service garden center for help, or call an USDA Extension agent and apply the remedies recommended.

If you identify a symptom as a disease, before applying remedies to the plant, remove badly infected material and get it out of the garden. Put it into the garbage. Wash your hands well after handling diseased plants.

Be sure not to replant a crop that showed infection in the same spot in the garden, and don't plant any of its relatives there. (See November, Crop Rotation Equals Better Health.)

Here's another area of gardening where a kept-up **garden log** is essential. A record of when certain conditions occur, the names of the plants that exhibited the symptoms, and the methods that reduced the problem are your ally next year.

 PLANTING

Garlic cloves planted now will produce a lush harvest of fat cloves next spring.

Plant seedlings of the last of the cool-season crops for fall harvests now—**cabbage, cauliflower, broccoli**—along with **lettuce, fall radishes, spinach.**

 CARE

Weeds are maturing their seeds now. Water the garden, then tug on the weeds gently but firmly so as to get all of the roots up. Shake the soil clinging to the roots back into the garden. If you can't pull them without disturbing a nearby vegetable, cut the weeds back to the crown and put the seedheads in the trash.

 PRUNING

Keep maturing **beans** and **summer squashes** picked to keep the plants producing.

As the weather freshens at summer's end, harvest all the herbs you wish to freeze or dry for winter use. You can strip **basil** and other annual herbs, but take no more than a third of the **thyme** and other perennial herbs.

 WATERING

Check the moisture in plant containers every four days; check small pots and hanging baskets every day or two.

A vegetable garden needs at least 1 inch of water per week in summer.

Water your compost pile when you water the garden, and turn it weekly.

As the weather freshens at summer's end, harvest all the herbs you wish to freeze or dry for winter use.

 FERTILIZING

For as long as the **tomato** plants are setting fruit, every four weeks drench the foliage and the soil with a soluble organic fertilizer and continue until the fruits near mature size.

 PESTS

If mildew turns up on plant foliage, spray with André's all-natural remedy: 1 tablespoon baking soda and 1 tablespoon of ultra-fine horticultural oil mixed well in a gallon of water.

If the stems of your **cucumbers** and **summer** and **winter squash** are rotting and the leaves yellowing, the culprit is the **squash vine borer.** The moth lays her eggs at the base of the plant in early summer, and the worms eat the stalk and spread a virus that causes the stems to rot. Beneficial nematodes and *Bacillius thuringiensis* are controls.

To prevent this next year, dispose of the diseased plants now. Turn the soil, and fluff it to kill larvae. Next year, plant resistant varieties. Plant through a square of foil, and cover the row with floating row covers to keep the moths away. When the plants get too big to keep the row cover on, mist the leaves regularly with garlic spray.

Did You Know?

Too-Many-Tomatoes Brunch

Brunch for two. Cut one large **tomato** into slices half an inch thick, and spread each side lightly with crushed fresh **garlic.** In a heavy skillet over moderately high heat, melt a teaspoon of butter in a teaspoon of olive oil. Stir in a minced sprig tip of basil, then remove and discard it. Add the tomato slices, and sauté one side until slightly browned. Turn the slices, and break four eggs into the spaces around the tomato slices. Add salt and pepper, if you wish. Cover the pan, reduce the heat, and cook until the egg whites are set and glazed over. Serve at once with hot, crisp French bread and butter.

Harvesting Herbs

Herbs are most flavorful harvested in the early morning before the sun dissipates the essential oils that give them flavor. Rinse herbs only if they're muddy. You won't have to rinse the foliage if you surround your herbs with mulch. We find herb foliage stays fresh for a week or so when we seal it in a vegetable bag lined with damp paper towel, and store it in the crisper.

To encourage an herb to bush out and be more productive, early on pinch out of the tip of the main stems. Remove herb flowers as they develop— they're edible and make charming garnishes.

When the plants have filled out, you can harvest the tender tip sprigs of the youngest branches at will without harming the plant. Never strip a plant of more than a third of its foliage, or it will have trouble maintaining itself. In summer's high heat—especially in very warm summer—herbs go into semi-dormancy. During this time, you should pick herbs sparingly, as the plants are unable to replace the missing foliage and will look awful and be slow to recover.

SEPTEMBER
Herbs & Vegetables

 PLANNING

Plan to double your pleasure in your kitchen garden by planning to store and preserve your harvests. Here are fast, easy **ways to store vegetables:**

Tomatoes. When frosts threaten, pick all the ripe **tomatoes,** those turning color, and those whitening. Ripen reddish fruits on a sunny sill; wrap whitening fruits in newspaper, and store in a cool place. They will ripen over the next six weeks.

Freeze the fully ripe **tomatoes;** for cooking they're better than canned **tomatoes.** Select ripe, unblemished fruits, pop them dry into a freezer bag, and store them in the freezer. Before adding frozen **tomatoes** to a soup, a stew, or a sauce, run tepid water over the skins to make peeling easy.

Legumes and corn. Pick **snap beans** and **corn,** clean the crop, drop it into boiling water, wait two minutes, then remove and drain that portion you want to save, and freeze it. Parboil fresh **pole beans,** and freeze them; or, let the pods dry, shell the beans, dry them on screens, and store in paper bags. Or, let the vines dry, then shell the beans and store them.

Summer Squash. Pick and rinse young **squash,** slice them up, drop into boiling water, wait two minutes, remove, then drain and freeze them. Cook frozen squash the same way you cook frozen squash from the market.

Strawberries, raspberries, blueberries. Pick clean, ripe fruit, remove the stems, toss the berries with granulated sugar, spoon them into freezer bags, and freeze.

 PLANTING

Clear out crops that have peaked, turn the rows, and replant them with seedlings of cool-season crops that mature in a short time—**lettuce, arugula, mache, chard, kale.**

If your climate has less than two months growing weather ahead, plant in a cold frame, or plan to cover the rows when temperatures drop below 55 degrees at night.

Sow **parsley** seeds or seedlings; this year's crop will fade next spring.

 CARE

When temperatures fall below 65 degrees Fahrenheit, remove all the **tomato** blossoms to keep nutrients flowing to the ripening fruits.

Provide fall and winter protection for late crops. Cover the plants at night with row covers or old sheets, and they will ripen fruit for many days.

To stop Japanese beetles next year, spread milky spore disease on the soil and lawn around **raspberries** and **basil.**

Turn the compost pile weekly.

PRUNING

Keep maturing vegetables picked to keep the plants producing.

WATERING

Plants growing in containers will need watering this month every ten days if you are without rain.

Provide fall and winter protection for late crops. Cover the plants at night with row covers or old sheets, and they will ripen fruit for many days.

Did You Know?

Drying Culinary Herbs

Ideally, we would all renew our supply of herbs at the end of every season. Drying herbs is a pleasant project. Harvest the herbs in the late afternoon on a hot, dry day.

Air drying leaves:

1 Pick fresh, healthy branch tips 12 to 14 inches long. Strip the coarse lower leaves and discard. Gather the stems in loose bunches, and hang them upside down in an airy, dry, preferably dark place. When the stems are crackling dry, strip the leaves off, and discard the stems. Rub the leaves between your palms to break them up and to remove them from the tiny twigs they may be clinging to.

2 Pour the leaves into glass jars and cap tightly. After a few days, check to see whether moisture has appeared inside the glass. If yes, oven dry the herbs for two hours at 150 degrees Fahrenheit.

3 Store the herbs in small jars, and write the date and the name on the label.

Oven drying:

Spread the leaves out over paper towels, and heat them on low until crackling dry. How long depends on the herb and your oven.

Microwave drying:

Dryish herbs, like **thyme,** dry well in a microwave oven at half power. Experiment with timing when you can afford to ruin a batch or two. Drying moist herbs such as **basil** in a microwave keeps the color and the flavor. Prop several leaves on a crumpled paper towel, and microwave one or one-and-one-half minutes on High. A whole branch in our oven dries in three to four minutes.

For information on drying seeds, see the Annuals chapter, August, Harvesting and Drying Seeds.

 FERTILIZING

As long as container plants are producing, continue to fertilize at half strength at every watering.

 PESTS

If **mildew** continues to be a problem, clear the bed, rake out the remains of the plants, and dispose of it in the trash; do not compost. If the mildew is mild, spray with André's remedy: 1 tablespoon baking soda and 1 tablespoon of ultra-fine horticultural oil mixed well in a gallon of water.

PLANNING

Root vegetables and **winter squash.** They are ready to harvest this month; plan to keep them for winter eating.

Kale. Pick side leaves, rinse, bag them, and store them in the crisper. They will keep for a week or two.

Root crops. The flavor of **rutabagas** and **turnips** is improved by a light frost at maturity; **parsnips** are sweeter when they have wintered in the ground. **Beets** and **carrots** must be harvested before the ground freezes.

For short-term storage, harvest and clean the vegetables with their greens on; seal them in vegetable bags and store them in the crisper, and they will stay firm for at least a few weeks.

For long-term storage, remove the greens and layer the roots in damp sand in a spot where temperatures are between 33 to 40 degrees Fahrenheit. You also can store **beets, carrots, parsnips, rutabagas,** and **turnips** in a pit in the ground; line the bottom with clean sand, then layer in vegetables and sand, ending with a layer of sand. Cover the pit with bales of straw.

Winter squash and pumpkins. Keep maturing **winter squash** off the ground on hay or chickenwire to prevent the bot-

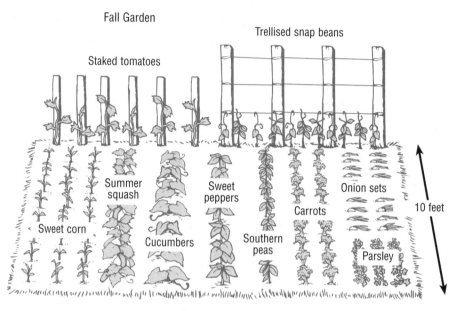

Fall Garden

Trellised snap beans

Staked tomatoes

Summer squash

Sweet peppers

Onion sets

Carrots

10 feet

Sweet corn

Cucumbers

Southern peas

Parsley

20 feet

toms from rotting. Before frosts, harvest with a 3-inch stem. Wipe the skins clean with a damp cloth, and store indoors in a cool dry place; most varieties keep for two or three months, the big blue **Hubbard squashes** up to six months.

PLANTING

Early this month is ideal for moving or dividing most of the kitchen garden perennials, and the **bramble fruits.** It also is a good time to plant **bramble fruits** and **fruit trees.**

Before frosts hit, buy a few young plants of **basil, summer savory, bay leaf, rosemary,** and **chives.** They'll do well

for a time on a sunny sill and will live for the winter in a cool Florida room.

CARE

In empty rows, plant a cover crop such as **winter rye** to improve the fertility, texture, and water-holding capacity of the soil.

Compost all the healthy vegetative material. (See Trees, October, Composting.) Now, when you have fresh organic debris from the kitchen garden, and a yard full of fallen leaves, is the perfect time to refurbish or to start the compost pile.

Now, when you have fresh organic debris from the kitchen garden, and a yard full of fallen leaves, is the perfect time to refurbish or to start the compost pile.

Did You Know?

About Strawberries

In cool regions, strawberry plants are set out in early spring as soon as the soil can be worked; in warm regions, they can be set out spring or fall.

They need a bed of their own. Soon after planting they send out runners that root new plantlets that can be used to start a new row, or to renew the original bed. The beds should be renewed every six years.

One-crop varieties bear early- or mid-season; everbearer varieties bear in late summer. A new type of everbearer described as "day neutral" produces its largest crop mid-season through fall. Plant two dozen of each for an all-season harvest.

A few weeks before planting, top a row 4 inches wide with 2 inches of compost or dried manure, and dig it in. Set the crowns at the level at which they were growing. The first season remove all the blossoms that form in spring; allow the everbearers to bloom and to set fruit from July on. Keep day neutrals clear of blossoms until mid-season and let them produce from mid-season through fall.

About six weeks after planting, strawberry plants send out runners. Remove all runners until the bed has been producing for three years. The fourth year allow them to root, and transplant them the following spring to start a new bed. The new bed will be in full production the following spring, and you can dig up the original bed.

When temperatures head towards 20 degrees Fahrenheit, cover the bed with a 6-inch straw mulch. After the ground has frozen hard, pile on a foot more of straw.

PRUNING

Empty and clear the rows of vegetables that are finished, and turn the soil by hand or with a rototiller.

FERTILIZING

Scratch a little organic fertilizer in around the kitchen garden perennials. Turn the compost pile weekly.

WATERING

If the season turns dry, water your seedlings, the cover crop if you planted one, and the kitchen garden perennials, especially any newly planted.

PESTS

Discard remaining insect or disease infected garden debris in the garbage. Do not compost it. Where infestations have been severe, turn the soil; air destroys many of the organisms there.

Basil growing indoors may be attacked by **whitefly.** Shower the plants, and especially the undersides of the leaves, every two days for ten days. If the problem persists, spray four times every seven days with Pyrethrum or neem. If the problem still persists, discard the plants before they infect other houseplants.

NOVEMBER
Herbs & Vegetables

PLANNING

If your soil is sandy, or lacking in humusy material, this is a good time to incorporate aged horse manure. There are many stables in our area, so locating a source shouldn't be difficult. Or dig in seaweed. Fall storms at sea usually leave drifts on the shore.

PLANTING

About the only thing you can plant at this point are **Egyptian onions.**

CARE

When temperatures head for 20 degrees Fahrenheit, cover **strawberries** with a 6-inch straw mulch.

PRUNING

Clear the rows of everything but **parsnips,** which are improved by wintering in the garden. Turn the soil by hand or with a rototiller.

Did You Know?

Crop Rotation Equals Better Health

You can avoid encouraging pests and diseases by rotating your crops annually. The rotation rule applies not only to individual species, but also to members of that species plant family.

These six plant families benefit from crop rotation:

- **Cabbage group.** Broccoli, Brussels sprouts, cabbage, cauliflower, Chinese cabbage, collards, kale, kohlrabi, radishes, turnips.
- **Carrot and parsley group.** Carrots, celery, coriander, dill, fennel, parsley, parsnips.
- **Cucumber group.** Cucumbers, gourds, melons, squash, pumpkins, watermelons.
- **Legumes.** Beans, peas.
- **Onion group.** Chives, onions, garlic.
- **Tomato group.** Eggplant, peppers, potatoes, tomatoes.

WATERING

Maintain the soil moisture in herbs growing indoors.

FERTILIZING

Fertilize the **fruit trees** and **bramble fruits.**

PESTS

Basil indoors may be attacked by whitefly. Shower the undersides of the leaves every two days for ten days. If the problem persists, spray four times every seven days with Pyrethrum or neem.

Clear the rows of everything but parsnips, which are improved by wintering in the garden. Turn the soil by hand or with a rototiller.

Did You Know?

Create a Cold Frame or a Hot Bed

Cold frames and hot beds give plants a head start on the seasons. A handy person can make either.

A cold frame is a bottomless box sunk into the earth and roofed over with glass or plastic. In its warmth, seeds and seedlings germinate and grow weeks before they can be started in the garden. Garden centers offer cold frames ready to assemble, and light-weight portable styles enable you to move them around to protect late and winter crops. Some are equipped with solar-powered frame openers triggered by high temperatures.

The ideal position for a cold frame is facing south on a slope that sets the cover at a 45 degree angle to the sun. That allows water and snow to slide off. The day's heat keeps the inside warm at night. When the air inside reaches 90 degrees Fahrenheit, prop the top up to vent the box, or the heat will damage the plants.

Making a cold frame:

1 Use concrete blocks, bricks, or rot-resistant boards to make a frame 5 to 6 feet long by 3 feet wide by 3 feet high.

2 Make a cover for the cold frame from a pair of old storm windows. Or, staple heavy-duty plastic film to a wooden frame that fits onto the cold frame. Hinge the cover to the frame to make airing it easy.

3 Place an outdoor thermometer inside the cold frame where you can see the temperature without opening the cover.

4 In the cold frame, place flats, boxes, or pots filled with improved soil to plant in. Each season provide new improved soil.

A hot bed is much like a cold frame, but it has some insulation and is equipped with an underground heating cable regulated by a thermostat. The heat allows you to plant earlier than in a cold frame. When the heat is off, the hot bed serves as a cold frame. In horse and buggy days, hot beds were deeper, and bottom heat was provided by the decomposition of moist layers of straw, fresh horse manure, and leaves.

Cold Frame

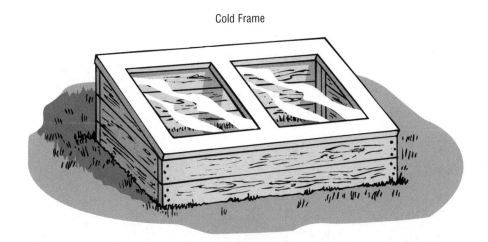

DECEMBER

 ## PLANNING

Check last year's **garden log** for ideas for the coming season, and check your album of catalog pages of garden accessories. Early this month order the things you wish to give the gardeners on your holiday list. Do family and friends a favor by telling them about the seeds, tools, and accessories you'd enjoy receiving.

Organize a seed-saver file. Each season, we usually use up at least one packet each of **beans, peas, lettuces,** and the root vegetables. But we always have left-over seeds for **basil** and other herbs, **tomatoes** and **melons,** and others we plant several varieties of. Packets of seeds of space-consuming plants like **cabbages, Brussel sprouts,** and **kale** also take a few seasons to get used up.

We organize these left-overs in a spiral binder equipped with clear plastic sleeves. We mark the year on each packet, and place all the varieties of each species in the same sleeve. When we have one, we include a catalog image of the plant, and any comments we have.

Seeds generally are considered viable for at least five years. The older the seed, the fewer will germinate. You can check out how well older seeds will do by scattering a half dozen on damp paper towel and covering them with another sheet of damp paper towel. With indoor warmth they should sprout and tell you what percentage of the seed you can expect to see germinate if you plant them.

To avoid having a lot of leftover seeds, organize a seed-sharing project among your gardening friends.

 ## PLANTING

Zone 8 may be warm enough to sow **arugula** and **mache.**

 ## CARE

As temperatures near 20 degrees Fahrenheit, cover the **strawberry** bed with a 6-inch straw mulch. When the ground has frozen hard, add a little more, but not so much you can't see some green through the straw.

 ## PRUNING

Groom **parsley** and other herbs growing indoors.

 ## WATERING

Maintain the soil moisture in herbs growing indoors.

 ## FERTILIZING

Nothing to fertilize this month.

 ## PESTS

Continue **whitefly** alert for the **basil** plants growing indoors. Showering the plants, and especially the undersides of the leaves, may lick the problem. If the problem persists, spray four times every seven days with Pyrethrum or neem. If the problem continues to persist, discard the plants before they infect other houseplants.

CHAPTER FOUR

Houseplants

For dedicated gardeners, there are not just four seasons but five—the season of the indoor garden and florist's flowers. Windowsills become greenhouses, and Ficus trees compete with the paintings and furniture for space and attention.

On a dull winter morning, a woodsy windowsill garden of **ferns** and **African violets** has more pull than a Picasso. Given good light, the **violets** will go on blooming as though still in the greenhouse, while the **ferns** double in size.

In a sunny window, many other colorful, attention-grabbing plants will bloom. The flowering star of late fall is the hybrid **cyclamen** whose foliage is patterned like silk moiré. In direct sun, a shrub-sized **gardenia** will open flower buds from spring to late winter, big-leaved **crotons** keep their bright colors, and **calamondin oranges** will fruit. Where light is lacking, walls painted white and mirrors placed where they reflect sunlight can be used to enhance nature's footcandles. You can also extend daylight with spot grow lights and fluorescents. In semi-sun the various **begonias** will bloom a little in early winter and get into high gear after the first of the year. **Chenille plant's** drooping catkins retain their color in semi-sun, and **pink polka dot plant** stays bright.

For north windows and dim corners, there are beautiful foliage plants that thrive in low light, such as **pothos,**

Did You Know?

How to Kill a Houseplant

More houseplants die from overwatering than from any other cause.

Some signs of overwatering:

1 The plant is growing poorly.

2 The **tips** of the leaves brown, the leaves curl, yellow, and wilt.

3 The leaves are limp and soft.

4 New and old leaves fall off the plant.

5 The flowers are moldy.

Some signs of underwatering:

1 The plant is growing poorly.

2 The leaves are limp and wilted.

3 The **edges** of the leaves turn brown and dry; the leaves curl, yellow, and wilt.

4 Flowers fall off, or their color fades too early.

5 The oldest leaves fall off, and then newer leaves.

Chinese evergreen, aspidistra, English ivy, philodendron, spider plant, snake plant, and **Swedish ivy.**

If the furniture refuses to yield space or light is lacking, plant hanging baskets. **Coleus, bougainvillea, donkey's-tail, bridal veil** are among the handsome basket plants for full sun.

To color up winter gardens, use the instant magic of a florist's cut flowers. Flower vials and empty herb bottles pressed into the soil of your houseplants brighten the green scene.

The secrets to keeping houseplants fresh and lovely are to keep the room as cool as possible, air the room often,

Did You Know?

Planting a Floor Garden

Single plants here and there are appealing, but as you acquire more plants (and inevitably you will!) plan to group them together in a floor garden—it will add greatly to your pleasure in the room and in the plants, and will make maintenance easier.

Here's how you might go about installing a floor garden in front of a big east- or west-facing picture window. You will need:

- A waterproof container about 8 feet (96 inches) long by 14 inches wide by 3 inches deep. (A nursery, auto body shop, or heating duct firm may be able to help you locate something like this size in plastic. A tinsmith can make one in tin or copper.)

- A sheet of treated plywood slightly narrower than the tray to protect the floor from condensation.

- Marble chips or pea gravel from the garden center—enough to fill the tray 2 inches deep; water to fill the tray 1½ inches deep.

- Four spot grow lights.

- Plants to fill the container: two *Dracaena fragrans massangeana* 5 to 6 feet tall; two *Dracaena marginata* 4 and 5 feet tall; two *Dracaena deremensis warneckei* 1½ and 2 feet tall. **Asparagus ferns** to soften the arrangement and pots of flowering plants in season—**mums, kalanchoe, cyclamen, jungle cactus, poinsettias, paperwhites**—or cut flowers in vases, branches of **forsythia** forced into early bloom, **irises.** And if you'd like it, a shallow bowl to serve as a pool with a statue at one end of it.

To create your floor garden:

1 Place the plywood on the floor next to the window, and set the tray on top.

2 Half fill the tray with the pebbles, and add enough water to place the water level a little beneath the level of the chips or pebbles.

3 Arrange the plants on the pebbles, the taller ones behind, smaller plants in front in an irregular line, and colorful flowers here and there. Use upside-down flower pots to raise small plants to desired heights.

4 Install the spot grow lights on the floor around the tray, two in front, one on either end. At dusk focus the lights on the smaller plants that get less window light.

5 Maintain the water level of the pebbles just below the surface, mist the garden every few days with water at room temperature, and air the room daily or as often as you can.

mist the plants every day or two with water at room temperature, and maintain soil moisture. That doesn't mean soggy wet soil—just slightly damp.

HOUSEPLANTS FOR HEALTH

Plants make us feel good. Where new growth, young leaves, and flower buds are present, you have a feeling of well being. Part of it is the joy of having greenery around, especially in the bare, dark months of the year. But there's more to it than that. Plants are the lungs of the planet. They produce oxygen, add moisture to the air, and filter out the toxins given off by all manner of household synthetics.

This is not wishful thinking. In the 1980s a NASA scientist, Dr. B. C. Wolverton, conducted a scientific study of the effects of various houseplants on the air indoors, and came up with the not surprising finding that houseplants are good, not only for your mood, but in a very real way for your health. His book, *How To Grow Fresh Air*, published by Penguin Books in 2003, is based on three decades of scientific studies that confirm what indoor gardeners have long known—the beneficial effect of indoor gardens on minds and bodies in homes, offices, shopping malls, hospitals.

Studies co-sponsored by Wolverton Environmental Services, Inc. and the Plants For Clean Air Council have graded popular houseplants according to their capacity to extract toxins from interiors of homes and commercial buildings.

On the whole, leafy plants like **spider plant,** and *Spathiphyllum* do the most air purifying along with **areca** and other palms. But the flowering plants we grow indoors, including **tulips, moth orchid,** and **florist's mums,** also contribute to improving the air. So when you plan an indoor garden, know it's an investment in health as well as a joy.

Did You Know?

Light Needs of Houseplants

Full sun/bright means plants are good right in or near sunlit windows, or in strong reflected light. Examples are **croton, gardenias, jade plant, miniature roses, pineapple.**

Bright indirect/medium means good in all of the above but not in full noonday sun. Examples are **aralia, fishtail** and **lady palms,** *Episcia,* **wax plant.**

Medium means diffused light, out of direct sun, or with a sheer curtain between the plant and direct sun. Plants in this group do well inside the room, 4 to 8 feet from the windowpane, or on a north-facing windowsill. This light suits a majority of houseplants, including **African violets, asparagus fern, begonias,** *Dracaena,* **ficus** and **rubber plant, Norfolk Island pine, spider plant, Swedish ivy.**

Medium to low means indirect light. These plants are okay in dull corners and even more than 8 feet from a window. The group includes *Dieffenbachia,* **English ivy** (which seems okay in any light), **parlor palm, philodendron,** *Spathiphyllum,* **snake plant.**

About Spraying Houseplants

1 Move the infected plant (see Pests) to a sink or bathtub.

2 Prepare whatever control you are using, following the directions on the container, and pour it into a mister spray bottle.

3 Spray the whole thing, including the soil, the undersides of the leaves, and the crotches between foliage and stems.

4 If the remedy says to spray "until runoff" that means keep on spraying until the liquid runs off the leaves and the stems.

5 Allow the plant to drip dry, and then place it in a spot away from other houseplants until you are sure the infestation is over.

LIGHT AND LOCATION

To be successful with houseplants, **match the plant to the light available.** Whatever your light potential, there are houseplants that can do well there. A miniature **African violet** will bloom under a desk lamp, **geraniums** on a sunny windowsill, **orchids** in a brightly lighted bathroom (for the humidity). A **miniature rose** will flower generously in a mini-greenhouse extending a

Houseplants

Did You Know?

The Fragrant Year Indoors

You can have scented flowers in bloom indoors all during the cold months. The fragrant assortment here is organized by the month in which they can be brought into bloom placed next to a south, or southwest facing window, a Florida room, or a greenhouse:

January

- *Brugmansia* 'Angel Trumpets'
- **Hyacinths, French-Roman**
- **Lemon,** *Citrus limon*
- **Orchids, Cattleya, Cymbidium, Dendrobium, Vanda**

February

- **Freesia,** *Freesia* x *kewensis* (potted in November)
- **Ginger-lily,** *Kaempferia rotunda* (potted in December)
- **Snake Plant,** *Sansevieria*

March

- *Gardenia jasminoides*
- **Japanese Pittosporum,** *Pittosporum tobira*
- **Orange,** *Citrus sinensis* 'Valencia'
- **Split-leaf Philodendron,** *Monstera deliciosa* (*Philodendron pertusum*)

April

- *Brunfelsia americana* 'Lady of the Night'
- **Glory Bower,** *Clerodendrum philipinum* 'Cashmere Bouquet'

- **Heliotrope,** *Heliotropium arborescens*
- *Mandevilla sanderi* and *M.* x *amabilis*

September

- **Jasmine,** *Jasminum sambac* 'Grand Duke of Tuscany', 'Maid of Orleans', *J. polyanthum*
- **Night-blooming Jasmine,** *Cestrum nocturnum*
- **Wax Plant,** *Hoya carnosa*

October

- **Cattleya Orchid**
- **Calamondin Orange,** *Citrofortunella mitis*
- **Willow-leaved Jasmine,** *Cestrum diurnum*

November

- **Amazon Lily,** *Eucharis amazonica* (potted in late summer)
- **Carolina Jasmine,** *Gelsemium sempervirens*
- **Sweet Olive,** *Osmanthus fragrans*

December

- **Lemon Tree,** *Citrus limon* x *Citrus sinensis*, *Citrus* x 'Improved Meyer'
- **Paper-whites** and *Narcissus*
- **Winter Spice,** *Hymenocallis speciosa*

south-facing window. Foliage plants can make do with the least light, and within a few years grow to shrub and some to tree size.

So with a small investment and much less work than it takes to maintain an outdoor garden, you can grow an indoor jungle complete with trees, shrubs, hanging vines, and flowers. It will flourish provided that you put the right plant in the right place and meet its modest needs.

Placement. The exposure—windows facing north, east, south, or west—you give a houseplant is very important. To a plant, there is a big difference in the light/heat/cold it gets from these exposures.

1 East-, northeast-, and north-facing windows are cool. That is good for most houseplants. But in the dead of winter, the air right next to a window-pane, especially where there is no double window, can get icy and

Houseplants

that can damage tender plants. Move them back at night if you are concerned.

2 West-, southwest-, and south-facing windows are bright and very hot; providing plants with protection from direct sun at noon is a good idea.

In addition, the closer the plant is to the pane, the more light/heat/cold it receives; the farther it is from the pane, the less light/heat/cold reaches it. Screens and curtains greatly reduce the amount of light that gets through to the plant.

Flowering houseplants. Miniature roses and many other flowering plants need direct sunlight for at least six hours a day so must be placed next to a window facing south, southwest, or southeast. However, **begonias, kalanchoe,** and some others get enough light from an east- or a west-facing window. **African violets** will bloom in a north-facing window that gets bounced light from snow cover or a white building—that can increase the footcandles (energy to grow on) by as much as 30 percent. In summer, direct sun in a south-facing window may be too harsh for all but **miniature roses,** but moving plants back from the window will reduce the exposure.

Foliage plants. Generally, foliage plants do well in the bright light of east- and west-facing windows. Those whose plant tags describe their light needs as minimal can make do in a north-facing window.

Light Gardens. Tiered trays under fluorescent grow lights—light gardens—will bring **African violets** into bloom in a few weeks. Spot grow lights burned after dusk during the dark months add beauty to an indoor garden and help plants whose place indoors may not provide quite enough daylight.

Additional light from incandescent bulbs increases the light received by the plants and helps during the darkest months of winter. Small plants can make do under a desk lamp providing it is on eight hours a day.

Vacations. Houseplants benefit greatly from the additional light and air they get when you summer them outdoors. **Ficus** and other indoor trees and shrubs can live with less than ideal light indoors for many months providing they have a four- or five-month vacation outdoors. My **Improved Meyer lemon trees** produce their small, exquisitely perfumed blossoms and bear so much fruit it has to be thinned in spite of winters with not nearly enough light, and all because

they summer out in the direct sun from May to the end of September.

In spring, as soon as the temperature at night stays consistently above 60 degrees Fahrenheit, you can start moving the plants to filtered light outdoors. A porch is ideal. Gradually expose **roses, geraniums, lemon trees,** and others that benefit from direct sun to brighter light before moving them into full sun.

Air, Temperature, and Humidity. The central heating and well-insulated interiors that are your best friend in winter are a houseplant's major enemy. The plants came to you from cool, humid greenhouses—how different is that from most centrally heated homes! Air conditioning dries the air, and a cold draft blowing right on a plant can harm it. Hot summer air outdoors doesn't bother houseplants much because summer air is usually humid.

Most houseplants manage in daytime temperatures between 68 and 75 degrees Fahrenheit with a drop of 7 to 10 degrees at night, and humidity between 30 and 60 percent. Winter heating above 68 degrees takes the moisture out of the air and encourages plant problems. **Miniature roses** and other hardy plants we grow indoors do best when night temperatures are

Houseplants

closer to 50. Most tropicals, on the other hand, have problems when night temperatures drop below 60. To keep the plants in tiptop shape, you might invest in a humidifier. Here are some other solutions:

- Mist the air around your plants daily with water at room temperature!!!

- If you can, open a window or a door for about ten minutes daily except when the temperature outdoors is headed for zero.

- Grow your houseplants on plant saucers or big waterproof trays filled with moist pebbles to keep moisture in the air and around the plants. The water level must be below the bottom of the pots to assure the circulation of air. A base of wet pebbles is especially helpful to plants that mustn't dry out, **gardenias**, for example, and **orchids.** A big plastic boot tray isn't pretty, but it will do.

- Group plants together in planters, and surround the pots with moist peat or sphagnum moss.

- Keep wet sponges among the potted plants.

Soil

Not all houseplants thrive in the same soil, but you do not have to be overly concerned about pH levels. The all-purpose houseplant potting soil suggested below is suitable for most plants. The problem with commercial potting mixes is they vary from company to company. So André starts with a portion of a suitable commercial potting mix then adds other ingredients. Here are his suggestions:

All-purpose houseplant potting soil. André's preferred soil for containers for foliage and most other plants growing indoors is a mix of $1/8$ your own good garden soil or bagged top soil, $1/2$ commercial soilless mix, $1/8$ compost, and $1/4$ PermaTill or perlite. Add in a modest application of Osmocote® slow-release fertilizer. To reduce watering, for pots over 12 inches in diameter add a water-holding polymer, Soil Moist for example, at the rate recommended on the package.

African violets and other moisture-loving plants. Use commercial **African violet** soil mix.

Cactuses and other succulents. These plants prefer a slightly alkaline soil pH. For **desert cactuses,** combine $1/4$ garden loam, $1/4$ peat moss, and $1/2$ coarse sand, perlite, or PermaTill. For **jungle cactuses** (Thanksgiving, Christmas, and Easter), use the all-purpose potting mix above.

Orchid potting soil. Commercial potting mixes suited to various orchids are best for gardeners new to orchid culture. For orchids commonly grown as houseplants, a pH of between 5.2 and 6.5 is suitable. Use plastic pots and a potting mix of equal parts chopped and shredded redwood bark, coarse perlite, and sphagnum moss. Humidity is very important; grow orchids on trays of moist gravel. Orchids are long-blooming and expensive; if you are interested in them, invest in a book on the subject.

Potting, Repotting, and Transplanting

Small and medium houseplants. Repotting is a constant necessity for small and medium houseplants. When you acquire a new houseplant, and when you see roots creeping out the drainage holes of a plant you already

Houseplants

Did You Know?

Propagating Houseplants

Using one of these techniques, you can multiply most houseplants. The best time is when the parent plant is growing lustily in spring and early summer. Use clean equipment, and propagate mature, healthy plants.

Root division. Houseplants that have a crown, **asparagus fern** for example, can be multiplied by root division. Lift the rootball from the pot, slice it cleanly in half, or thirds, and repot in fresh soil.

Stem cuttings. Tip cuttings of fresh green stems of vining houseplants, like **pothos** and **philodendrons,** and semi-green cuttings of single-stem plants, like **geraniums,** root easily in clean water, and in pots or trays filled with moist perlite, vermiculite, or peat-like mixes. Add 1 teaspoon of bleach per quart of water to prevent the growth of microorganisms. Keep the cuttings in indirect light. In four to six week a mass of roots will have formed at the ends of the stems. The cuttings are then ready to transplant to potting soil.

Make the cuttings 6 to 8 inches from the tip of the stem, and just behind a leaf node. Strip off the last set of leaves. Allow geranium cuttings to dry six to twenty-four hours on newspaper in a shaded place before placing them in the rooting medium.

Leaf cuttings. African violets and **Rex** and other **begonias** can be propagated by leaf cuttings.

One way to propagate an **African violet** leaf is to cut it off with 2 inches of stem, and press it to the base of the leaf in a pot containing 3 inches of moist vermiculite. Cover the cutting with a drinking glass to maintain moisture. Keep the pot in low light in a warm room. When baby leaves form at the base of the leaves, roots are developing. Wait another two weeks, and then transplant the plantlets to African violet potting soil. A **Rex begonia** leaf can be propagated by laying it on moist vermiculite. Cut off a leaf with 2 inches of stem attached. Make two shallow cuts on each vein on the underside of the leaf, and pin it with a toothpick right-side-up onto moist vermiculite or sphagnum moss. Baby leaves will develop at the cuts with tiny root systems behind. Cut the plantlets out with a scrap of leaf still attached, and grow the roots in water or one of the rooting mediums described above. When they are bigger, transplant them to a clay pot filled with potting soil. Stem cuttings of begonias will also root in a glass of water.

Air layering. This technique can be used to multiply plants and to renew plants that have grown leggy, as older **schefflera** and *Dracaena* eventually do. Notch a stem, and smear the cut with rooting hormone. Enclose the notched area in a big handful of moistened sphagnum moss. Wrap the moss in plastic, and tie it firmly to the stem top and bottom. Weekly, open the bundle, and restore lost moisture. When a mass of roots has invaded the peat moss, cut the stem off an inch below the bundle, and pot it. Now you have a new plant. Cut the trunk off at a suitable height above a bud or a pair of buds, and new growth should develop just below the cut.

Offsets. Many plants multiply by producing offsets, or plantlets. The best time to separate offsets is after the plant's resting period. Unpot the plant to separate the offset, and repot both parent and offset right after the operation.

Offsets of **amaryllis** and other bulbs are bulblets that are partially separated from the parent by the time you notice them. Free the offset by applying enough pressure to break it off, and then pot it up. **African violets** produce offsets that can be separated from the stem and potted up. The offset is a rosette of leaves that grows on the side of the main stem. Use a small sharp knife to slice all around the offset then pot it up. Damage the parent plant as little as possible. The **spider plant** and many other leafy houseplants are composed of several individual offsets. You can pull the outer offsets apart, and repot them to create new plants.

have, pull the rootball out and see if it needs repotting. If there still is soil around the rootball and in the bottom quarter or third of the pot, then the plant doesn't need repotting. A rootball totally wrapped in roots needs repotting in a container one size larger. We repot small and medium size plants when we move them outdoors for the summer. If the roots become rootbound over the summer, we repot before bringing them back indoors in September (see the September pages of this chapter.)

Large trees. Repotting large trees and shrubs is difficult and necessary only every three or four years. Other years in late winter before new growth begins, remove the top 2 inches of soil, and replace it with 2 or 3 inches of compost or fertile potting soil.

A radical facelift. If the plant is languishing, give it a more radical facelift. Tip the container on its side, and slide the rootball out. Unwind the roots binding the sides, and if there's a mat of roots on the bottom, slice it off. Add a layer of fertile soil mix to the bottom of the original container or of a container one size larger. Center the rootball inside, and remove 2 inches of the soil on the top. Pack fresh soil mix all around the sides of the tub. Add 2 inches of fresh soil to the top. Water the soil thoroughly, and include a half dose of fertilizer to the water.

CONTAINERS

The choice of containers for indoor plants is both a design and a practical consideration. When your indoor garden includes many small and medium size plants, the display will be more appealing if they are all in containers of the same color—all terracotta clay for example, or all white plastic. That unifies the plantings the way mulch unifies the plantings in a landscape. But a single big tree or shrub looks beautiful in an Italian glazed ceramic or flowered china container for pots. Every year garden centers and home furnishings shops offer ever more attractive containers and cachepots, the containers for flower pots.

Clay pots. Plants always look good in unglazed clay pots. Porous clay lets excess humidity escape, and it is the best choice for plants needing especially good drainage—**geraniums, cactuses,** and **succulents,** for example. Plants in clay pots hardly ever suffer from overwatering. Over-fertilization is easily visible by the buildup of salts on the sides. Clay pots also give weight and stability to plants. Plants in clay pots need more frequent watering, especially when outdoors. The **amaryllis** I grow in a clay pot needs watering twice as often as those growing in plastic pots.

Plastic pots. Good looking plastic pots and plastic that looks like clay or cement are available, and they make excellent homes for plants that need sustained moisture. Plastic has an added advantage; it is lightweight, so it's best for shrubs and trees that will be moved outdoors for the summer and moved indoors before freezing temperatures arrive.

Houseplants

When you are buying a cachepot for a flower pot, make it at least an inch larger all around than the pot it will house. It should not have a drainage hole, but must have a saucer. Saucers are important—condensation from the bottom of flower pots and cachepots sitting directly on wooden furniture and floors invariably damages the surface below.

Other options are to place containers on plastic saucers, or clay saucers whose interior is glazed. Cork casters are available to place under pots for an extra layer of protection to the furniture. Sturdy pot stands with wheels save the floor under indoor trees and big shrubs, and they make moving the plants easy.

WATERING

How much water your houseplants need depends on the plant, the soil mix, the heat and humidity in the air, and whether or not the plant is actively growing, as most do in late winter and spring. How often to water also is affected by the material the pot is made of.

The bottom line? You must water by feel, and to some extent by intuition, not by rote. You can minimize watering chores by placing plants in groups. That has the added advantage of increasing the humidity around them. A layer of ordinary moss or airy Spanish moss is the only mulch we use with indoor plants. It gives potted plants a nice finish and helps maintain soil moisture and the humidity in the air around the plant.

To find out whether a plant needs watering, touch the soil surface. If it is dry, press your finger into the soil, and if is still dry farther down, water. There are available a host of gadgets that help judge a plant's watering needs—but you still can't do it by rote. Over-watering is the most common cause of plant demise.

Two signs a plant needs water are that the pot feels very much lighter than usual, and the leaves hint they are going to droop and wilt.

Here are the basic rules for watering houseplants:

- Always use water that is at room temperature.

- Mist the air with water at room temperature.

- If your water is heavily chlorinated, use filtered or purified water, or let the water sit for twenty-four hours before using it on the plants.

- Water the soil and not the plants.

- Add water until it begins to seep into the saucer. An hour later check the saucer, and remove any standing water. A roasting baster, the kind with the bulb on the end, helps get it out of plant saucers.

Rehydrating a plant. Drying to the point of total wilting will ruin most houseplants. However, many are forgiving of an occasional drought. To help a plant that has wilted quickly recover:

1 Set it in the sink, and shower the foliage with lukewarm water.

2 Place the pot in a larger container partially filled with lukewarm water, and leave it there for about 45 minutes. Lift it out of the water, and allow it to drain on a drain board before returning it to its usual place.

3 Apologize, and promise you won't let it happen again.

FERTILIZING

For houseplants, use an organic fertilizer at half strength. Organic seaweed extract is an excellent choice. Follow

Houseplants

the instructions on the fertilizer package conscientiously; too much fertilizer, like too much salt, doesn't improve the broth and can result in soluble salt damage.

The rule of thumb is, in fall and early winter fertilize plants showing little or no new growth at every fourth watering. Increase that to every second watering for plants that are actively growing, and for all plants after January 15. Here's why:

- Plants from the northern (our) hemisphere start into active growth as the days grow longer after the early part of the year. So we minimize the fertilizer in fall, and resume full fertilization when there are signs of growth as days lengthen after the turn of the year.

- Houseplants from the southern hemisphere—South America and Australia—and any showing growth all year round, we fertilize at every second watering.

- **Miniature roses** and **African violets** that are blooming, **spider plants** dripping new nests of leaves, **coleus** extending its square green stems, **hibiscus** in bloom, and **lemon trees** and **citrus** may be fertilized at every second watering.

Did You Know?

About Bonsai Indoors

Most bonsais need bright light and will do best in a room where the temperature is under 68 degrees Fahrenheit. Temperatures above 68 degrees dry the air, and that's hard on everything (you, too) except desert plants.

There are two types of bonsai on the market. The most popular subject is a **juniper.** Junipers are hardy evergreens that need to be outdoors in a sheltered place in bright light ninety percent of the time. They can survive for a time on a sunny glassed-in porch or in a cold sunny room if you are faithful about watering and misting. Kept indoors ninety percent of the time, juniper bonsais won't live very long. Some merchants call them "temporary" bonsai.

The other type of plant commonly used for bonsai is a group native to semi-tropical temperatures that our year-round indoor heating systems imitate. In this group we include **aralia, fatsia,** and **ficus** that have been trimmed to look like bonsai and grown in shallow bonsai containers in gritty soil. That type of bonsai can live for a long time indoors if its watering and misting needs are met.

Take your cue from the priceless bonsai collection at the U.S. National Arboretum. Those plants live most of the year in bright light in a sheltered place either in the bonsai house or in a sheltered area behind it. Some of them are hundreds of years old.

- After severe pruning (which stimulates growth), repotting, and transplanting rooted cuttings, fertilize at every second watering.

PESTS

Plants growing indoors in optimum conditions will avoid most plant pests and diseases. But occasionally a new plant will import unwelcome guests and share them with your indoor garden. There are a few worthwhile safeguards:

1 Keep the room cool, and the air humid.

2 Groom your plants often—deadhead, remove decaying and dead foliage, and inspect the undersides of leaves and crotches of branches for signs of pests such as mealybug.

Houseplants

3 During the heating season, spray or shower your plants with room temperature water as often as practical to clean them and discourage those critters that thrive in dry still air, like spider mites.

There are several pests that commonly attack houseplants.

Red spider mites cause a yellowing of the plant that results in a rusty and sometimes silvery look to the leaf. Hosing the plant down regularly discourages spider mite activity. Insecticidal soaps, ultrafine horticultural oils, and miticides can be used.

Aphids look like tiny jade-green, brown, or tan beads on the tips of new houseplant stems. They secrete a sticky, slick substance called honeydew, which results in a black fungus (sooty mold) spreading over the plant. Aphids usually can be sprayed off with a strong jet of water from a hose. Repeat if they return. If they persist, try a horticultural soap, or products whose labels say they contain pyrethrin.

Mealybugs lay eggs that look like bits of cotton on the undersides of buds, leaves, and stems. Like aphids, they exude honeydew, and cause sooty mold. They attack **ferns, ficus, African violets, gardenias,** and many other houseplants. Spraying with horticultural soaps and ultra-fine horticultural oils controls mealybugs. You can remove them with a cotton swab dipped in alcohol.

Scale has a crawler stage, and then the insect becomes stationary, creating hard scales that resemble tiny oyster shells and occurring in great numbers. Soft scales are larger, more cup-shaped, and are especially destructive to houseplants. You can control scale by spraying with ultra-fine horticulture oils and horticultural soaps. Or, remove them one by one with a cotton swab dipped in rubbing alcohol. When a mature **fern** falls victim to scale, cleaning it up is so tedious you are better off buying a new one and discarding the old one in the trash.

Whitefly colonies erupt into clouds when the plant is touched, and then settle back. They stunt and yellow the host plant and may cause sooty mold. The most effective control is to spray four times with an insecticide, five to seven days apart. Ultra-fine horticultural oil or insecticidal soaps may be used. Pyrethrin and synthetic pyrethroids are also effective. The undersides of the leaves are where whiteflies cling, so be sure to spray there most thoroughly. Insecticidal soap can handle small infestations. For persistent infestations, use insecticides based on extract of the seeds of the tropical neem tree.

See Pests, Diseases, and Controls in the Appendix for more information.

Did You Know?

When Is a Flower a Bract?

Bracts are leaves located immediately back of the petals in a flower. In most flowers, the bracts are small or scale-like leaves, but they can be very much larger and more colorful than the flowers themselves, as is the case with **poinsettias** and **dogwoods.**

Houseplants

Common Name (*Botanical Name*)	Light	Easiest Propagation
African Violet (*Saintpaulia* sp., hybrids)	Bright indirect/medium	Leaf cuttings anytime, divide in May
Agave (*Agave* sp., hybrids)	Bright light	Division
Aloe, Medicinal (*Aloe vera* syn. *Aloe barbadensis*)	Medium to low	Pull apart the offsets in spring
Aluminum Plant (*Pilea cadierei*)	Medium	Stem cuttings late spring
Asparagus Fern (*Asparagus sprengeri*)	Medium	Divide in late spring
Begonia, Rex (*Begonia-* x *rex-cultorum*)	Bright indirect/medium	Stem cuttings in April
Boston Fern (*Nephrolepis exaltata* 'Bostoniensis')	Medium	Divide in spring
Bromeliad (*Bromeliad* sp.)	Bright indirect/medium	Pull apart offsets in spring
Calamondin, Orange or **Lime** (*Citrus mitis*)	Bright, full sun	Seeds will reproduce but not be true
Cast-iron Plant (*Aspidistra elatior*)	Medium to low	Divide large clump in late spring
Chinese Evergreen (*Aglaonema modestum*)	Medium to low	Divide large clump or take stem cuttings
Corn Plant (*Dracaena fragrans*)	Medium to low	Stem cuttings in spring
Croton, Joseph's Coat (*Codiaeum variegatum* 'Pictum')	Bright sun	Stem cuttings in summer
Crown-of-thorns (*Euphorbia milii; E. splendens*)	Bright light	Root tip cuttings
Desert Cactus (*Cactus* sp.)	Sun/bright shade	Root tip cuttings, spring or summer
Dumb Cane (*Dieffenbachia maculata*)	Medium to low	Stem cuttings, spring to fall
English Ivy (*Hedera helix* varieties)	Bright to medium	Stem cuttings, early summer
False Aralia (*Shefflera elegantissima*)	Medium light	Root cuttings, spring or summer
Gardenia (*Gardenia, jasminoides*)	Bright indirect/medium	Softwood cuttings early in season
Grape Ivy (*Cissus rhombifolia*)	Medium or low	Stem cuttings anytime
Hibiscus, Chinese (*Hibiscus rosa-sinensis*)	Bright/direct sun okay	Stem cuttings, spring or summer
Jade Plant (*Crassula argentea*)	Bright indirect	Leaf or stem cuttings in May

Houseplants

Common Name (*Botanical Name*)	Light	Easiest Propagation
Japanese Fatsia (*Fatsia japonica*)	Low	Root tip cuttings or air layer
Jasmine, Madagascar Jasmine (*Jasminum sambac*)	Sun	Root cuttings in spring or summer
Kaffir Lily (*Clivia miniata*)	Bright	Division of large clumps, offsets
Kalanchoe (*Kalanchoe* species and cultivars)	Bright light	Leaf cuttings
Moses-in-the-cradle (*Rhoeo spathacea*)	Medium	Offsets or seedlings
Mother-in-law's Tongue (*Sansevieria trifasciata*)	Bright indirect	Pull offshoots apart in spring
Norfolk Island Pine (*Araucaria heterophylla*)	Bright to moderate	Seed
Orchid, Moth (*Phalaenopsis* hybrids)	Bright indirect	Divide in June
Parlor Palm (*Chamaedorea elegans*)	Bright to medium	From seed; difficult
Peace Lily (*Spathiphyllum floribundum*)	Medium to low	Divide in February or March every two years
Peacock Plant (*Calathea makoyana*)	Low	Division; suckers; leaf cuttings
Peperomia 'Emerald Ripple' (*Peperomia caperata* 'Emerald Ripple')	Medium	Stem cuttings in spring
Philodendron (*Philodendron* sp. and hybrids)	Medium to low	Division; stem cuttings
Pothos (*Epipremnum aureum*)	Bright indirect	Stem cuttings, spring or summer
Prayer Plant (*Maranta* species)	Shade, diffused light	Division
Rubber Plant, Rubber Tree (*Ficus elastica*)	Bright indirect	Air layering
Sago Palm (*Cycas revoluta*)	High to medium light; cool temperatures	Offsets; difficult
Schefflera (*Brassaia actinophylla*)	Medium to low	Air-layer in spring
Shrimp Plant (*Justicia brandegeana*)	Medium	Tip cuttings half-ripened wood in April
Spider Plant (*Chlorophytum comosum*)	Bright indirect/medium	Separate and pot plantlets anytime
Wandering Jew (*Zebrina pendula* 'Pendulosa')	Medium light	Tip Cuttings
Wax Plant (*Hoya carnosa*)	Bright	Layering or stem cuttings

PLANNING

As you clear away the holiday trappings, **take the time to re-invent your indoor gardens.** Discard plants that aren't doing much to make space in good light for replacements. Then look over the plants that are growing well and consider which can be propagated to fill out your indoor gardens (see Propagating Houseplants in the introduction to this chapter).

 ## PLANTING

Give your out-of-bloom gift **azalea** a sunny spot on a sill since it, along with **mums** and **poinsettias,** is among those plants that test high as air purifiers. When it goes out of bloom, transplant it to a larger pot filled with all-purpose houseplant potting soil. Keep the soil moist, and when new growth appears, at every watering apply an acid-type soluble fertilizer at one quarter the recommended strength. Increase that over a four-month period until you are fertilizing at the strength recommended on the container. Forced **azaleas** are not hardy here, but if you summer it outdoors and expose it to several cool, but not freezing, fall nights before bringing it in, it may bloom again.

Find time to repot plants outgrowing their current homes. The steps are described in the section on Potting, Repotting, and Transplanting, in the introduction to this chapter.

To avoid messing up the kitchen sink, invest in a plastic potting tray with high sides and back.

 ## CARE

Move plants that are doing poorly to brighter windows, or invest in spot grow lights to extend their after-dark lighting.

Mist **gardenias, hibiscus, rosemary,** and other houseplants every day or two with water at room temperature. Air the room daily (except when it's freezing outdoors!) for ten minutes or so by opening a window or a door.

If **miniature roses** growing indoors aren't blooming, try giving them more footcandles by lighting them after dusk with spot grow lights. For more on care of **miniature roses** growing indoors, see the January pages of Chapter 7, Roses.

 ## PRUNING

Groom your plants; deadhead **roses** and **amaryllis,** remove yellowing leaves from **poinsettias,** foliage plants, **tropical hibiscus,** and other shrubs and trees wintering indoors.

Pinch out all but half a dozen or so tiny lemons developing on a **Improved Meyer lemon tree.**

 ## WATERING

Replenish the moisture in small pots every few days, medium pots every week, and big containers every ten days. Water until water runs into the saucer; remove any that remains after an hour.

Shower **miniature roses** every two weeks, and blow the plants dry with cool air from a hair dryer.

 ## FERTILIZING

Your houseplants and the **tropical hibiscus,** and other tender shrubs brought indoors last fall, are, or soon will be, growing; add a half strength dose of soluble fertilizer at every second watering. Fertilize flowering houseplants and the **miniature roses** at every second watering. For **azaleas** and **gardenias,** use a fertilizer for acid-loving plants.

Discard plants that aren't doing much to make space in good light for replacements. Then look over the plants that are growing well and consider which can be propagated to fill out your indoor gardens.

Did You Know?

After-Care of Poinsettias

1 Keep the plant in a room no warmer than 72 degrees Fahrenheit by day, no colder than 60 degrees by night. It will do best given six hours a day of natural light bright enough to read by. If its job is to brighten a dark corner in a well-heated room, give it a vacation in more ideal conditions when you can.

2 If foil is covering the pot, remove it, and set the pot on a plant saucer. That helps keep air circulating through the soil. Keep it clear of dead leaves.

3 Keep the soil damp but not moist. When the soil surface is dry to the touch, water until water dribbles out the bottom. Drain off water still standing in the pot saucer an hour after watering.

4 When the plant shows signs of new growth, apply all-purpose houseplant fertilizer at half-strength every other watering.

5 **In mid-February,** clear away fading bracts and dead leaves. Scratch up the soil surface, and add 1 or 2 inches of sterile soil mix.

6 If you have space, move the plant to a brighter location.

7 **In mid-May** when temperatures are above 60 degrees Fahrenheit at night, repot the plant, and move it outdoors to a partially shaded spot for ten days, and then to full sun for the summer. Or, plant it in the garden, pot and all.

8 **In early September,** repot the plant and move it indoors to a sunny window in a cool room.

9 To get the bracts (leaves at the top) to color up for Christmas, from the **first of October for two months give it twelve hours of uninterrupted darkness (no artificial light after dark) and twelve hours of bright daylight.** Fertilize at every other watering.

We aren't saying getting **poinsettias** to color a second season is easy! But it's fun to try.

Light and the lack of it influence fertilizing schedules for indoors plants because light governs growth. Our general take on fertilizing is in fall and early winter when there is little or no new growth, fertilize all houseplants at every fourth watering; increase that to every second watering when plants are blooming and actively growing, and for all plants after January 15.

 PESTS

Check for spider mites, mealybug, and scale; controls are suggested in the Pests section of the introduction to this chapter. To avoid problems, mist your plants with water at room temperature, air the room often, keep the temperature down, and provide humidity.

Spider mites attack **miniatures roses** growing indoors in hot, dry conditions. Rinse the plants every two weeks. Segregate infected plants. Air the room daily.

PLANNING

Visit the U.S. Botanic Garden on Capitol Hill in Washington in February, March, and the weeks before Easter. In the Garden Court off the Orangerie, you'll find a glorious indoor garden combining the many types of plants that can be grown indoors. Do it for the sheer joy of breathing plant-scented air. Visit local flower shows and garden centers; many garden centers now stage flower shows of their own, and the displays are well worth studying.

PLANTING

Many garden centers still offer **paperwhite bulbs** at this season, and you still have time to force them into bloom. For instructions, see the November pages in Chapter 2, Bulbs.

Geraniums brought indoors last fall are usually pretty leggy by now. Cut back ungainly branches to improve the structure of the plants. Branch ends that are 6 inches long root easily following the stem-cuttings procedure described under Propagating Houseplants in the introduction to this chapter.

A **geranium** that has a straight central trunk can be developed as a standard, or tree form, plant. Making A Geranium Tree Standard is described in the September pages of Chapter 1, Annuals.

CARE

Mist **gardenias, rosemary,** and other houseplants every day or two with water at room temperature. Air the room daily for ten minutes or so by opening a window or a door—except when it's freezing out.

Get rid of winter doldrums, and possible lurking plant pests, by showering small and medium plants in the sink. Shower the big plants in your shower. Use a gentle spray of lukewarm water so as not to shock the plant with a change of temperature and high pressure water. Allow the plants to drain thoroughly before moving them back.

African violets thrive with an occasional shower. Rinse the leaves clean in the sink with a gentle spray of lukewarm water. Keep the plants out of direct sun until the leaves are completely dry.

PRUNING

Deadhead and pinch back **begonias, coleus,** and **ivy** to keep the plants shapely and producing. Trim the branch tips of **tropical hibiscus** back to half their length.

Deadhead flowering plants, including **amaryllis, hyacinths, daffodils** forced into bloom; cut off the flower heads, and grow the plants in bright sunny windows.

Flowering maples bloom when warmth and light levels are at summer highs. Indoors in winter, they will bloom if you supplement the window light with spot grow lights set on a timer.

WATERING

Water **African violets** from the bottom to avoid spotting the leaves.

February is the month **ficus** and all the other houseplants look their worst. Shower them all, small and large, and cover the soil with moss, or Spanish moss, available at garden centers and florists.

Replenish the moisture in small pots every few days, medium pots every week, and big containers every ten days. Water until water runs into the saucer; remove any that remains after an hour.

FERTILIZING

By the beginning of this month, we will have almost fifty minutes more of daylight than we had at the beginning of January, so many of your plants will be growing. **Include a half dose of liquid fertilizer to the water at every second watering for all your houseplants.** For **amaryllis** and forced **spring-flowering bulbs** growing on, use a Bloom Booster fertilizer with a high phosphorus content. For flowering houseplants such as **miniature roses, cyclamen,** and **African violets,** use a liquid fertilizer for African violets. For **azaleas** and **gardenias,** use a fertilizer for acid-loving plants.

Repotting the very big trees and shrubs is difficult and necessary only every three or four years. Other years in late winter before new growth begins remove the top 2 inches of soil, and replace it with 2 or 3 inches of compost or fertile potting soil.

 PESTS

Monitor plants that have been infested by pests in the past, and renew treatments if symptoms reappear. Controls are suggested in the Pests section of the introduction to this chapter.

Did You Know?

Reblooming an Amaryllis

The amaryllis' spectacular trumpets brighten mid-winter blooms only once each season, but you can bring it back into bloom every year:

1 When the last of the trumpets fades, cut off the flower stalk(s).

2 Grow the plant on in a sunny east-, south-, or west-facing window at temperatures between 62 to 72 degrees Fahrenheit.

3 From January to August, at every other watering apply a half strength dose of bloom booster type fertilizer high in phosphorus.

4 When the outdoor temperature stays above 62 degrees Fahrenheit, put the plant outdoors in partial light.

5 Keep the soil evenly damp, and fertilize until the end of August.

6 Between the end of August and when October turns cold, bring the amaryllis indoors. You can either allow it to dry, or let it grow on a windowsill. Either way it needs to be kept at about 55 degrees for eight to ten weeks.

7 In two or three months, a tongue of green will rise in the center of the bulb. Repot the plant in the All-Purpose Potting Soil for Indoor Plants described in the introduction to this chapter. **Always pot or repot an amaryllis in a container that is no more than 1 inch larger all around than the bulb and that has a drainage hole.** Set the bulb so its top is about 1 inch below the top of the container, and fill the container with the potting mix to within 2 inches of the rim.

8 Return the plant to a sunny east-, south-, or west-facing window in a room at average house temperatures, 62 to 72 degrees Fahrenheit.

9 Moisten the soil every four or five days, and at every second watering add a half dose of a fertilizer for flowering houseplants to the water. The trumpets should unfurl in three to four weeks.

Your amaryllis may eventually send up offsets—baby bulbs—with slim new leaves. Break the babies off when you repot, and grow them like the parent plant. They will take a few years to come into bloom.

MARCH

 PLANNING

Plan to move your larger houseplants outdoors when the weather warms in mid-May. **Repotting will improve their summer performance.** To make the process easy, find the pots you will be using for plants that will need bigger containers. Before reusing old pots, clean them up:

1 Brush out the soil clinging to the sides and bottom.

2 Scrub the pots in warm soapy water.

3 Rinse away the soap, and dip each pot in a solution of 1 part bleach to 9 parts water to disinfect it.

4 Turn the pots upside down, and let them air dry.

They are now ready to be planted in.

 PLANTING

Prepare larger houseplants, trees, and shrubs too big to be repotted for the coming season of growth by top-dressing the soil.

• Use a fork to gently loosen the top 2 inches of soil. When working with a **ficus** tree, be careful not to damage the roots that are close to the soil surface.

• Replace the missing soil with compost or with all-purpose potting soil for houseplants that includes a dose of slow-release fertilizer.

 CARE

Mist your houseplants every day or two with water at room temperature. Air the room daily for ten minutes or so by opening a window or a door, but not when the outdoors is freezing.

To keep a **gardenia** growing indoors in good condition, keep it on a plant saucer filled with wet pebbles, grow it in full sun in a cool room, and air and mist the plant daily with water at room temperature. Do not let the soil run dry. At every second watering, include a soluble fertilizer for acid-loving plants.

 PRUNING

Deadhead **African violets, pentas, kalanchoe, begonias,** and other flowering houseplants.

Groom all your houseplants often, removing yellowing leaves, damaged stems, and unproductive branches. Pruning and deadheading induce fresh growth.

Cut back foliage plants that aren't producing a lot of new growth, and repot them in fresh soil.

 WATERING

Water small pots every few days, medium pots every week, and big containers every ten days. Use water at room temperature, and water until water runs into the saucer; remove any that remains in the saucer after an hour.

Mist your houseplants every day or two with water at room temperature. Air the room daily for ten minutes or so by opening a window or a door, but not when the outdoors is freezing.

FERTILIZING

Fertilize foliage plants at every second watering with soluble complete organic fertilizer. For flowering plants and **miniature roses** use African violet or Bloom Booster fertilizers. For **azaleas** and **gardenias,** at every second watering add a half dose of soluble fertilizer for acid-loving plants.

PESTS

As the weeks grow warmer, there may be unwelcome activity around your houseplants. **Watch out for aphids** clustered at the tips of new shoots and buds of **miniature roses.** Those you can rinse off in the sink. Pinch off infested shoots of larger plants. Then spray with insecticidal soap.

Did You Know?

About Jungle Cactuses

Those exotic cactuses that bear orchid-like flowers at Thanksgiving and Christmas are species of *Schlumbergera* and *Zygocactus* respectively. The varieties that bloom in spring, the **Easter cactus,** is *Rhipsalidopsis gaertneri*. All three jungle cactuses are epiphytes—plants that grow in a little humusy soil in the crotch of a tree.

All three respond to similar care:

1 Keep jungle cactuses where temperatures are about 70 degrees Fahrenheit by day, no colder than 60 degrees by night. Set the plants in sunny east- or west-facing windows, or under fluorescent lights. When the plants go out of bloom, to encourage reblooming, do not allow artificial light to strike the plant.

2 Water the plants lightly when the soil feels dry to the touch, about every four or five days. Use lukewarm water.

3 Every other year, repot one size up in March or April. Use a mix that is a third coarse sand, a third perlite, and a third all-purpose houseplant potting soil.

4 When the weather warms in May, put the plants outdoors in indirect light for the summer.

5 Water as needed to keep the soil damp, and at every second watering include a half strength dose of African violet fertilizer.

6 Towards the end of September bring the plants indoors to a cool room—65 degrees Fahrenheit by day, 60 degrees by night. For eight weeks let them rest—no artificial light, barely enough water to keep the soil from drying out, and no fertilizer.

7 At the end of eight weeks, move the pots to sunny east- or west-facing windows and water as before.

8 You can root cuttings from a mature jungle cactus taken this month just as new growth starts. Break off branch ends that include three or four of the claw-like segments. Let them dry three or four days. Press the ends into dampened cactus potting mix in an 8-inch pot. They'll be rooted in six weeks and can be individually potted.

APRIL
Houseplants

 ## PLANNING

The garden centers are filling up with plants for outdoor gardens, and many discount their larger houseplants this time of year rather than store them for the next six months. So, if you are in the market for a wonderful big **palm**, a braided **ficus,** a shrub-size **jade plant,** this is a good time to shop around.

And, while you are there, check out the **blue lily of the Nile,** *Agapanthus africanus*, and the **Kaffir lily,** *Clivia miniata.* These both can live for years indoors and grow into big elegant plants with beautiful flowers in spring and early summer.

The **blue lily of the Nile** is an imposing flower from Southeast Africa. Late spring to early fall a dense cluster of beautiful blue, white, or pink funnel-shaped flowers appears on a 3- to 5-foot stalk that stands well above a mound of strap-shaped leaves. It is highly regarded as a tub plant for terraces, steps, patios, or near outdoor pools.

The **Kaffir lily** is from South Africa. It develops a fan of sword-shaped evergreen leaves topped in spring (indoors) or summer (outdoors) by big long-lasting showy amaryllis-like flower heads in brilliant orange-red or salmon. In cool regions it blooms in spring or early summer indoors, and may rebloom outdoors later.

 ## PLANTING

Repot small or medium size houseplants a few at a time this month to ready them for the move outdoors. It will be time to move them outdoors as soon as the weather stays above 60 degrees at night.

 ## CARE

Continue to mist your indoor plants every day or two with water at room temperature. Air the room daily for ten minutes or so by opening a window or a door, unless it's freezing outdoors.

PRUNING

Continue to deadhead the flowering plants. Keep pinching back the growing tips of **ivy, geraniums, pothos,** and other vining plants to keep them bushy and beautiful.

Some taller plants, and especially **Chinese evergreen, dieffenbachia,** and **dracaena** when mature end up with a naked trunk under awkward tufts of leaves. The same is true of **avocados.** To remedy this, cut the trunk back to about 8 inches from the pot. That will force new leaves to emerge, and the plant will be beautiful again. A **Norfolk Island pine** that has hit the ceiling has to be air layered to get a fresh start; topped, it won't regrow.

Removing Plant from Container

Repotting Plant

If you suspect spider mites are at work, shake the leaf over a piece of white paper. Specks that move are spider mites.

Did You Know?

About African Violets

African violets are favorites of ours not only because they are beautiful and easy to grow, but also because they bloom for months on end.

1 Light is ideal in winter in any bright window, but west- and south-facing windows are too hot in summer. They flower best spring and fall when the day length is twelve to fourteen hours. African violets also flower well placed 9 inches below fluorescent grow lights burned twelve hours a day.

2 Temperatures are just right between 60 and 80 degrees Fahrenheit. A cool-vapor humidifier helps, and as with all houseplants, we recommend you air the room daily for five to ten minutes when the temperature outside isn't freezing.

3 Humidity is necessary. These plants do well grouped on trays filled with pebbles and half filled with water.

4 Use commercial African violet soil. For best flowering, keep the plants slightly potbound.

5 Use plastic containers for these moisture-loving plants.

6 Apply water at room temperature often enough to keep the soil evenly moist. Water from the bottom to avoid spotting the leaves; partially fill the plant saucer, and an hour later empty what remains.

7 To encourage blooming, add a half strength dose of African violet Bloom Booster fertilizer every second time you water.

8 African violets can be propagated by leaf cuttings and offsets, described under Propagating Houseplants in the introduction to this chapter.

 WATERING

Replenish the moisture in small pots every few days, medium pots every week, and big containers every ten days. Water until water runs into the saucer; remove any that remains after an hour.

 FERTILIZING

Include a half-strength dose of soluble fertilizer at every second watering. For azaleas and gardenias, use a fertilizer for acid-loving plants.

 PESTS

If you suspect spider mites are at work, shake the leaf over a piece of white paper. Specks that move are spider mites. A simple way to control spider mites on small plants is to turn the plants upside down in a basin of soapy lukewarm water. Follow by spraying with insecticidal soap.

Check for mealybug and scale; controls are suggested in the Pests section of the introduction to this chapter. To avoid problems, mist your plants and air the room often, keep temperatures down, and provide humidity.

PLANNING

Houseplants benefit enormously from summer out in the fresh air and sunlight. Before you start to move your plants outdoors for their summer vacation, locate places that will give them the light they need—and not more. With longer days, the sun rises higher above the horizon, resulting in more intense light. A sunburn can ruin plant foliage.

 PLANTING

It's a good idea to repot your plants before putting them outdoors. Most of them, that is. Don't repot your **amaryllis;** harden the plant off outdoors in indirect light for a week, and then set the plant pot up to its rim in the garden in full sun in well-drained soil.

Remove the flowering stems of **orchids** as soon as they finish blooming, and repot any that are crowding their containers. They can summer outdoors on a lightly shaded patio safe from high wind, or a bright airy porch, or attach them to tree branches protected from wind and safe from a lot of hot direct sun.

African violets can summer outdoors in indirect light on an airy porch, but you will have to watch the moisture in those pots closely. African violets should not be allowed to dry out, and that can happen very quickly on a warm breezy day because they usually are growing in small pots. If you can, group several pots on a tray filled with pebbles and water, and check the water level in the tray and the moisture level in the pots daily.

Repot **miniature roses** in fresh soil, and put them outdoors in bright light but not broiling noon sun.

 CARE

When nighttime temperatures stay steady at 60 degrees Fahrenheit and above, start moving your houseplants outdoors. Place them in indirect light in a sheltered spot for the first week. Like you, houseplants sunburn when exposed too long too early to direct sun. Gradually move them into brighter light.

Don't be alarmed if some drop leaves their first week or two outdoors. The change of light has that effect on some, notably **ficus.**

 PRUNING

Deadhead flowering plants, and groom them, that is, remove yellowing foliage and ungainly and damaged stems. Keep the soil clear of decaying vegetation.

 WATERING

Maintain the soil moisture of the houseplants and **amaryllis** outdoors. As the season grows warmer, plants outdoors in small pots and hanging baskets will need watering every day.

 FERTILIZING

Include a half dose of fertilizer in the water every second watering for all houseplants. For **azaleas** and **gardenias,** use a fertilizer for acid-loving plants.

When nighttime temperatures stay steady at 60 degrees Fahrenheit and above, start moving your houseplants outdoors. Place them in indirect light in a sheltered spot for the first week.

Did You Know?

Shrubs for Indoors

Shrubs of different heights bring grace to a house tree that may look lost when standing alone. Use upended pots to raise young plants higher if you need to. Young plants acclimate more easily than mature plants to the dry and warm environment of a heated house, and they are far less costly than mature shrubs, and most grow up quickly.

Here are easy plants that start out shrub size:

Calamondin orange (*Citrofortunella mitis*) is a dwarf citrus that bears small white flowers followed by bitter, bright orange fruit good for making marmalade.

Dracaena (*Dracaena deremensis* 'Warneckei') is a tall, single-trunked plant with leathery leaves rather like corn.

Dumbcane (*Dieffenbachia* species) are fast-growing shrubs with long thin leaves variegated yellow, white, or chartreuse.

European fan palm (*Chamaerops humilis*) is a beautiful bushy palm that sometimes grows as a clump, sometimes with a single trunk topped by fronds.

False aralia (*Dizygotheca elegantissima*) is an airy, lacy-leaved, tree-like shrub.

Fiddleleaf fig (*Ficus lyrata*) has bold wavy deeply quilted leathery leaves that are a waxy green with yellow veins.

Gardenia (*Gardenia* hybrids) are shiny-leaved shrubs that bear beautiful creamy-white perfumed flowers.

India Rubber Plant (*Ficus elastica*) has big, rubbery leaves, and eventually grows to tree size.

Jade Plant (*Crassula argentea*) a handsome succulent, has a tree-like structure and bears airy, pale pink flower heads.

Japanese Pittosporum (*Pittosporum tobira*) develops rosettes of bright green leaves at the end of long stems.

Lady Palm (*Rhapis excelsa*) and species are miniature palms with broad leaves.

Neanthe Bella Palm (*Chamaedorea elegans* 'Bella') is a slim, elegant dwarf of the big parlor palm.

Sago Palm (*Cycas revoluta*) has stiff fronds that grow all the way up the stem like a fern. Not a "true" palm—an ancient plant of the Cycadaceae family.

Screw Pine (*Pandanus veitchii*) starts as a rosette of sword-shaped green and white striped leaves and grows to tree size.

Cut- or Split-leaved Philodendron (*Philodendron selloum*) is a vining plant that has deep-cut leaves up to 2 feet wide. It is sold staked to a bark-covered half log.

PESTS

In the fresh air, houseplants are less susceptible to the insects that trouble them indoors. Nonetheless, watch out for mealybug and aphids. Controls are recommended under Pests in the introduction to this chapter and in the Appendix.

Squirrels are curious creatures that often dig in plant pots. If they are a persistent problem, spray the soil with a commercial repellent.

PLANNING

Plan to fill out your houseplant collection by starting your own **avocado** and **citrus** trees. Children enjoy the magic. The trees also make fine holiday presents.

Avocado tree. Avocado seeds or pits will root and produce a fine house tree, although I have yet to hear of one ripening fruit.

1 Clean the pit under running warm water.

2 Push three toothpicks into the seed at equal distances from each other around the circumference of the seed, mid-way between the pointed tip and the base, and use the toothpicks to suspend the seed at the top of a narrow glass or jar.

3 Fill the container with water until a half-inch of the base of the avocado seed is immersed.

4 Set the glass in a dark closet, and maintain the water level.

5 When the seed has developed a good set of roots, a sprout will grow from the top. When the sprout opens leaves, move the glass to bright indirect light on a windowsill.

6 When the sprout is 8 inches tall, cut it back to 4 inches.

7 When the sprout again reaches 8 inches, plant it in moist all-purpose potting soil with the top third of the seed uncovered.

8 Grow the seedling in bright indirect light, and pinch it back often to encourage it to bush out. Keep the soil evenly damp, and include a half dose of all-purpose fertilizer at every second watering.

9 In May move the container to bright indirect light outdoors.

10 In mid-September move the plant back to its indoor home. Maintain the soil moisture, and fertilize at half strength at every second watering.

Lemon tree. Seeds of the various citrus fruits, lemon, lime, orange, and grapefruit will germinate, and in a few years grow into a very respectable little tree that may bear fruit if summered outdoors.

1 Choose six big whole seeds, and let them dry for a day or two.

2 Plant the seeds in moist, all-purpose houseplant potting mix with about an inch of soil over the top.

3 Cover the pot with a glass saucer or plastic film to help maintain the moisture. Keep the pot in a dark closet.

4 Water often enough to maintain the soil moisture.

5 When the seeds germinate, remove the cover, and move the pot to bright indirect light.

6 Keep the soil evenly damp, and include a half dose of all-purpose fertilizer at every second watering.

7 One-by-one, remove and discard the weakest seedlings until only the two sturdiest remain.

8 When the two seedlings are crowding each other, discard one (unless you have time and space for two trees), and repot the other in a pot one size larger.

9 Grow the tree(s) in a south-facing window. Maintain moisture, and continue to fertilize as before.

10 In mid-May, move the container to bright indirect light outdoors.

11 In mid-September, move the plant back to its indoor home. If it fails to flower, keep it pot bound for two or three years.

 PLANTING

Plant young **tropical hibiscus** in the garden for summer color, and then pot it up and bring indoors in September. It will eventually grow into a handsome flowering tree blooming almost non-stop.

Check the soil moisture of mid-size containers of houseplants summering outdoors every two days, and maintain soil moisture.

CARE

If you see sunburn—browned patches—on houseplants moved outdoors, move the plants to more shaded situations.

Move **miniature roses** grown as houseplants to a spot that gets six to eight hours of morning sun.

PRUNING

Deadhead **begonias,** and pinch back **coleus** and vining plants. Pinch back **flowering maple** to encourage bushiness. Deadhead **hibiscus, miniature roses,** and other flowering houseplants.

Pinch out all but half a dozen or so tiny lemons developing on a **Improved Meyer lemon tree.**

WATERING

Check the soil moisture of mid-size containers of houseplants summering outdoors every two days, and maintain soil moisture. Don't overlook pots of **amaryllis** summering in the garden.

Maintain the soil moisture for houseplants summering indoors.

Did You Know?

Trees for Indoors

A full-size tree is a handsome ornament, and costly. But, with patience, a young plant will take only a few years to grow up to indoor tree size.

Areca Palm, *Chrysalidocarpus lutescens*, the butterfly palm, is a graceful palm.

Bamboo Palm, *Chamaedorea erumpens*, looks like a bamboo and is the most enduring palm.

Clustered Fishtail Palm, *Caryota mitis,* has leaves that look like fishtails.

Dracaena marginata and *D. fragrans massangeana* look like corn plants and grow into big, tall, enduring house trees.

Lemon Tree, *Citrus limon* x *Citrus sinensis* Improved Meyer variety, is a beautiful little lemon tree with perfumed flowers and real lemons.

Norfolk Island pine, *Araucaria excelsa*, is a slim evergreen that reaches the ceiling.

Polyscias balfouriana and *P. filicifolia* are evergreens with bold, rounded leathery leaves.

Queensland Umbrella Tree, *Schefflera actinophylla,* has big, beautiful leaves and a handsome structure.

Weeping Fig, *Ficus benjamina,* has leaves like a birch, a slim woody trunk, and a graceful habit.

Yucca elephantipes is a rosette of sword-like leaves when young, and then it grows into a trunk topped with rosettes of leaves.

FERTILIZING

Add a half strength dose of soluble fertilizer at every second watering for houseplants and outdoor **tropical hibiscus** and other tender shrubs. For **azaleas** and **gardenias,** use a fertilizer for acid-loving plants. Continue to use African violet fertilizer for flowering houseplants.

PESTS

Check young shoots frequently, and spray away aphids clinging there. Watch out for scale on **spider plant, orchids, gardenias,** and houseplants with woody trunks. For controls, see the section on Pests in the introduction to this chapter and in the Appendix.

PLANNING

Before your vacation, arrange to have the container plantings watered. Ease the chore by grouping the containers in a semi-shaded spot and providing each with a saucer. Investigate automatic watering systems.

Your houseplants are lush right now, so this is a good time to take cuttings to create holiday gifts. You will find instructions in the section on Propagating Houseplants in the introduction to this chapter.

They will eventually need containers. In July and August, garden markets generally have sales on containers and other hard goods. Some quite beautiful imported pieces sell for modest prices, so check them out with a view to finding attractive homes for your new plants.

PLANTING

Multiply your holdings by rooting stem cuttings taken when you pinched back **begonias, ivy, pothos, philodendrons,** and other vining houseplants.

Pineapple is plentiful at this season. Rooting the top of a **pineapple** is an interesting project, and one that children enjoy. The **pineapple** we eat is *Ananas comosus*, a handsome **bromeliad** that can be grown as a houseplant. Here's how to root it:

1 Cut off the top of a fresh, ripe **pineapple** including a half-inch of the fruit below the top.

2 Tip it on its side, and air dry it for forty-eight hours.

3 Place it upright on barely moist sand or vermiculite with the fruit portion buried in the rooting medium.

4 Set the plant in a bright northeast or northwest-facing window.

5 Keep the growing medium barely moist until the top starts to grow, and then provide a little more water.

6 When it is growing well, transplant it to a standard cactus potting mix.

CARE

Houseplants that remain indoors benefit from the cool created by air conditioning, but may be harmed if the air blows directly on them.

PRUNING

A ficus tree needs pruning annually. It's best to do it outdoors because the cuts ooze a sticky white sap—the **ficus** is related to the **rubber tree.** Prune out dried twigs and new sprouts developing at the base and along the main trunk, and remove branches crossing others. Then step back and consider what else can be done to thin out the crown.

Continue to deadhead flowering houseplants, and to pinch back **coleus, ivy, pothos,** and the other vining houseplants.

WATERING

Maintain the soil moisture of the houseplants in pots outdoors, and **amaryllis** and **tropical hibiscus** growing in the garden. As the season grows warmer, plants that are living outdoors in small pots and hanging baskets may need watering every day.

On very hot days, cool and moisten the air around the houseplants outdoors with a gentle spray from the hose.

Houseplants left indoors for summer usually benefit from a shower now and then as well.

Before your vacation, arrange to have the container plantings watered. Ease the chore by grouping the containers in a semi-shaded spot and providing each with a saucer.

 FERTILIZING

Add a half strength dose of soluble fertilizer at every second watering for houseplants and the **tropical hibiscus** and other tender shrubs summering outdoors. For **azaleas** and **gardenias,** use a fertilizer for acid-loving plants. Continue to use African violet fertilizer for flowering houseplants.

 PESTS

Aphids may be a problem. Check young shoots frequently, and spray away aphids clinging there.

Watch out for scale on **spider plants, orchids, gardenias,** and plants with woody trunks.

Pest controls are recommended in the section on Pests in the introduction to this chapter and in the Appendix.

Did You Know?

Rosemary Christmas Tree

Rosemary has a sweet-pungent aroma that is addictive. The foliage is evergreen, and with care, the plant can live indoors at least half the year. A rosemary Christmas tree makes a superb holiday present. Here's André's method for turning a young rosemary plant into a mini Christmas tree in about a year:

1 Select a young plant about 6 to 8 inches tall that has a straight central stem and evenly-placed branchlets thick with needles all around.

2 Repot the plant in a mix of half-and-half gritty cactus soil and all-purpose potting soil.

3 Tie the central stem to a stake to keep it growing straight.

4 Grow it in full sun in the garden in summer, and move it indoors when the thermometer heads for 55 degrees. Place it in a sunny south-facing window.

5 Year-round pinch the branch tips back by half to encourage a pyramidal shape like that of Christmas tree, and to stimulate bushy new growth.

6 Maintain soil moisture. Every four weeks add a half strength dose of a complete fertilizer to the water.

7 When the plant is indoors, mist it and air the room daily.

AUGUST
Houseplants

PLANNING

Take the time to order spring-flowering bulbs for winter forcing. You'll find step-by-step instructions and timing for forcing bulbs in the September pages of Chapter 2, Bulbs. A few dozen spring-flowering bulbs potted up this fall will provide fragrant flowers for many weeks this winter. Wrapped in white tissue paper and tied with red bows, bulbs about to burst into bloom make much appreciated holiday gifts.

Here's an overview of the forcing process:

1 To avoid the diseases than can assail indoor bulbs, pot them in a mix of half sterile commercial potting medium and half good gritty garden soil.

2 Follow the instructions for planting and forcing bulbs for indoor bloom in the September and October pages of Chapter 2, Bulbs, particularly those instructions relative to temperatures for the various steps in forcing.

3 Crowd the bulbs in their containers so they touch; that helps keep them upright. I've measured the height of forced **paper-whites** and found some over 36 inches tall—once they reach that height I tie them loosely to a stake set in the center of the pot.

4 Bring them into flower in bright light in cool rooms. In temperatures below 72 degrees Fahrenheit, the flowers last longer.

PLANTING

Begin now to prepare the in-ground plants that you will move indoors in fall—**basil, thyme, rosemary, coleus, browallia, geraniums, heliotrope, lantana, impatiens, pentas, kalanchoe, wax begonias** are some that can winter over in an indoor garden. **New Guinea impatiens** may do well indoors if you can keep it in temperatures above 65 degrees Fahrenheit.

Well-grown, these all make fine holiday gifts.

1 Cut the tops and branches back to 4 to 6 inches.

2 Dig up the plants, and pot each one in a container about an inch larger all around than the rootball.

3 Water and fertilize the plants.

4 Place them in a sheltered spot in indirect light to recover from the shock of transplanting. That will also prepare them for the lower light levels they will have when they are brought indoors.

CARE

If your **hibiscus** drops flower buds, it's probably because they are too numerous for the amount of leaves processing nourishment. It happens—not to worry! This is nature's way of protecting itself from over-production.

Whiteflies flock to houseplants summering outdoors in warm airless corners on a porch or veranda. Spray the plants often with a hose on the gentle cycle to help control populations.

 ## PRUNING

If you plan to bring a potted bougainvillea standard or hanging basket indoors for the winter, reduce fertilization now, keep the plant on the dry side, and prune back the wild growth until about September 1. In early fall, bring it indoors to a bright, cool room—about 55 degrees Fahrenheit. The shoots that develop as the days get shorter and temperatures fall will flower all winter and into the following summer. In its native tropics, **bougainvillea** blossoms appear when day lengths are twelve hours or less.

 ## WATERING

Maintain the soil moisture of the houseplants in pots outdoors, and **amaryllis** and **tropical hibiscus** in the garden. As the season grows warmer, those plants that are growing in small pots and hanging baskets will need watering every day.

On very hot days, cool and moisten the air around the houseplants outdoors by showering the area with a gentle spray from the hose.

Houseplants left indoors for summer benefit from a shower now and then as well.

 ## FERTILIZING

Add a half strength dose of soluble fertilizer at every second watering for houseplants and the **tropical hibiscus** and other tender shrubs summering outdoors. For **azaleas** and **gardenias,** use a fertilizer for acid-loving plants. Continue to use African violet fertilizer for flowering houseplants.

 ## PESTS

Whiteflies flock to houseplants summering outdoors in warm airless corners on a porch or veranda. Spray the plants often with a hose on the gentle cycle to help control populations. Move plants you suspect of being infected to a breezy spot in the garden.

SEPTEMBER

PLANNING

When night temperatures drop to 60 degrees Fahrenheit, begin to bring in all but the hardiest houseplants. Take cuttings of **coleus, begonias, geraniums** if you do not have enough indoor space for the plants themselves.

• Before moving plants indoors, rinse them squeaky clean with a hose, and spray each with an insecticidal soap at least once. Twice is better. Indoor warmth helps the bugs to breed! Spray plants that have been trouble in the past with a product containing Sevin insecticide, pyrethrin, or malathion, and a fungicide such as Daconil.

• Repot in fresh soil your plants growing in small containers—young plants, new plants, and plants that are rootbound.

• Plants finicky about changes in light should come indoors now even if they can take colder temperatures. **Ficus** often responds to sudden changes in light by dropping leaves—sometimes almost all its leaves—and sulking. Bring **ficus** indoors now while a lot of daylight still is reaching its indoor habitat.

• Your tropical plants—the big beautiful **tropical hibiscus,** for example—can stay outdoors a few more weeks, until early October. Bring **mandevilla** in to bright light. Don't prune it. Mist it often, but keep the soil on the dry side.

• Plants that need as much sun as possible—**miniature roses, gardenias, geraniums,** and **jasmine,** for example—can stay outdoors in cities in Zone 7 and 8 until mid-October. In the suburbs, frost comes sooner.

• **Geraniums** can winter over in a sunny window and be grown like other houseplants. They also will winter over dormant in any place where temperatures are 55 degrees Fahrenheit or so; water the soil of semi-dormant geraniums once a month, just enough to keep the canes from drying out.

• **Amaryllis** can take quite a bit of cold. When you move them indoors they need to dry down for a dormant period, so they do not need repotting now. See February for follow-on care.

• In early September, repot **poinsettias** you hope to rebloom, and move them indoors to a sunny window in a cool room.

• Gift **azaleas** need two to three weeks of cool nights outdoors (not colder than 40 degrees Fahrenheit) before coming in.

• Toward the end of September bring **jungle cactuses** indoors to a cool room—65 to 70 degrees Fahrenheit by day, 60 degrees by night. For eight weeks let them rest—no artificial light, barely enough water to keep the soil from drying out, and no fertilizer. See March for follow on care.

PLANTING

Potted up, many **tender perennials** make happy houseplants. **Basil, browallia, coleus, geraniums,** and **scented geraniums, impatiens, kalanchoe, pentas, wax begonias** are some that do well indoors. See August for information on preparations for moving plants indoors.

Potted up now, and in October **hyacinths, daffodils, paper-whites** can be brought into flower this winter indoors. See September pages in Bulbs, Chapter 2.

CARE

Mist **gardenias, hibiscus, rosemary,** and other plants moved indoors every day or two with water at room temperature. Air the room daily for ten minutes or so by opening a window or a door, unless it's freezing outdoors.

Bud and leaf drop is common when you bring plants indoors, because you have

When night temperatures drop to 60 degrees Fahrenheit, begin to bring in all but the hardiest houseplants.

Did You Know?

Repotting Houseplants

1 A pot one size larger than the original container is best for most, but keep **amaryllis** and the **desert** and **jungle cactuses** slightly pot bound.

2 To keep the soil from dribbling through the drainage hole, cover the bottom of the pot with a square of fiberglass window screening, Reemay, or landscape fabric.

3 Add enough soil so that the crown of the plant will be 1 inch below the rim level for small plants, and 2 inches for large plants. Then the water won't overflow when you water.

4 If the rootball is encased in roots, make shallow slashes on all four sides, and remove the roots matting the bottom.

5 Set the plant straight on the soil, and spoon soil in around the sides. Press it down with a wooden dowel, and continue adding soil and pressing it down until the sides are level with the crown and 1 to 2 inches below the pot rim.

6 Groom the plant; remove fading flowers and leaves, prune back ungainly branches, and spray the foliage.

7 Water well with water containing a mild dose of starter solution.

8 Set the plant in filtered light for a day or two to recover, and then return it to appropriate light.

---

changed its location, light intensity, and environment. Too bad, but not to worry!

thin the tiny lemons and leave no more than one or two fruits per branch.

for acid-loving plants. Continue to use African violet fertilizer for flowering houseplants.

 ## PRUNING

Stems of tender perennials you cut back for a move indoors can be rooted in water. Group them in bouquets in a large glass bowl to save space and maintenance. Add a teaspoon of bleach to every quart of water.

Thin the fruit on your lemon tree! A **Improved Meyer lemon** typically creates a lemon for each flower, and it produces flowers all year. Based indoors it can't support that much fruit, so be sure to

 ## WATERING

Water indoor plants when the soil feels dry, and houseplants remaining outdoors when needed.

 ## FERTILIZING

Add a half strength dose of soluble fertilizer at every fourth watering for houseplants and the **tropical hibiscus** and other tender shrubs moved indoors. For **azaleas** and **gardenias,** use a fertilizer

 ## PESTS

Keep a close watch on plants brought indoors, and at the first sign of spider mites, mealybug, scale, or other problems common to indoors plants, apply the controls recommended in the Pests section of the introduction to this chapter.

To ward off problems, mist your plants and air the room daily or as often as practical, and keep temperatures as low as is comfortable.

OCTOBER
Houseplants

PLANNING

Assess the health and happiness of your houseplants, and then visit garden centers for fresh ideas for indoor gardens and new plant material.

PLANTING

With the gift-giving season ahead in mind, take stock of your houseplant assets. Plants potted up and cuttings taken in August and September make fine presents for family, friends, and co-workers. Houseplants are very acceptable casual gifts for office friends. You still have time to propagate many types of houseplants; see Propagating Houseplants in the introduction to this chapter.

Here are some suggestions:

• Plant cuttings, offsets, and plants you have propagated in new terracotta pots, and move them to bright light or a light garden if you have one; a cool room is best for getting them into top shape for giving.

• Bulbs being forced—decide which will be far enough along in the forcing process to make worthwhile gifts in December. If some need a little hurry-up, move them to warmth a little sooner than scheduled. Scout for attractive inexpensive baskets to hold containers that are less appealing than you would wish for a gift.

• Fresh or rooted cuttings of desirable plants grouped several to a small attractive vase, make a welcome gift.

CARE

Mist your houseplants and the plants you brought indoors in September daily with water at room temperature to help them to acclimate to the changed environment. Air the room daily for ten minutes or so by opening a window or a door.

You can encourage continued blooming in **miniature roses** by growing them under fluorescent lights and fertilizing at every other watering with a half strength dose of African violet or Bloom Booster fertilizers.

Bring in your **amaryllis** about mid-month when the air turns icy. See the February pages of this chapter for information on reblooming an amaryllis.

To get a **poinsettia** to rebloom (color up), from the first of October give it twelve hours of darkness **(absolutely no artificial light after dark, not even two or three minutes)** and twelve hours of bright daylight.

PRUNING

Deadhead your flowering plants. Pinch out flowers forming on **coleus.**

Impatiens can live through the winter in a cool, sunny window and can be beautiful if it stays free of whitefly and aphids. When the plants get leggy, cut back the longer stems. You can root 6- to 8-inch cuttings in a jarful of water; keep a few inches of water in the bottom, and every month or so add a drop or two of liquid fertilizer. In late winter, pot the cuttings that have the strongest roots. When the weather warms, transplant them to the garden.

With the gift-giving season ahead in mind, take stock of your houseplant assets. Plants potted up and cuttings taken in August and September make fine presents for family, friends, and co-workers.

Did You Know?

About Gardenias

The gardenia is a beautiful evergreen shrub whose flowers have a gloriously rich perfume. Buy a young plant in fall, and it will have doubled in size by spring.

Here's how to grow it:

1 Give a gardenia full sun, and a cool room—68 (or as close to that as you can get) degrees Fahrenheit is ideal. Flower buds will open and continue to form if there's adequate sun.

2 Never let the soil dry out! Constant, even moisture is important. Grow the plant on a saucer filled with pebbles and half-filled with water. A shower and a good soaking every ten days or so in room-temperature water for half an hour will keep the foliage crisp.

3 Fertilize at every second watering with a half dose of acid type fertilizer. Discontinue fertilizing when new buds appear, and mist the buds lightly every day with water at room temperature.

4 Watch for tiny webs indicating spider mites are setting up housekeeping. If they appear, shower the plant more often, and spray with insecticidal soap.

5 When heavy flowering dies down, clean out imperfect leaves and branches, shear the plant back lightly, and add an inch or two of fresh soil to the container. New growth in gardenias usually begins in March.

6 Repot the plant in April, and move it outdoors in April or May.

7 In October, bring it back indoors.

 WATERING

Check pots of **miniature roses** often, and keep the soil moderately damp. Rinse them every two weeks to discourage spider mites.

 FERTILIZING

Add a half strength dose of soluble fertilizer at every fourth watering for houseplants and **bougainvillea, mandevilla, tropical hibiscus,** and other tender shrubs brought indoors. For **azaleas** and **gardenias,** use a fertilizer for acid-loving plants. Continue to use African violet fertilizer for flowering houseplants.

 PESTS

Check for spider mites, mealybug, and scale; controls are suggested in the Pests section of the introduction to this chapter. To avoid problems, mist your plants, air the room often, keep the temperature down, and provide humidity.

PLANNING

Visits to the houseplant displays at garden centers will provide fresh ideas for indoor gardens and new plant material. Buy young plants, and grow them up.

 PLANTING

Creating a terrarium for shade-loving plants is an interesting indoor garden project. Here's how to do it:

1 Glass cases for terrarium gardens are available at garden centers, by mail-order, and online. Or use a fish tank or a round bowl about 12 to 14 inches across. To keep the moisture in, you will need a pane of clear plexiglass or glass to cover the top.

2 Buy the following plants in the smallest pot size you can find, probably a 3-inch pot: **maidenhair fern; aluminum plant; selaginella;** one miniature flowering plant, such as *Begonia bowera* or *B. hydrocotilifolia*; and one **creeping fig**—*Ficus pumila* or *F. radicans*.

3 Line the bottom of the container with marble chips 1 inch deep, and top them with a thin layer of charcoal chips to keep the soil fresh.

4 Scoop into the bowl 2 to 3 cups of moist sterile commercial terrarium soil (African violet potting soil will do). Shape the soil into a miniature terrain with hills and valleys. Add tiny statues, rocks, and other ornaments that suggest landscape scenes.

5 Set the tallest plants in their places first, and add enough soil to cover their roots. Then tuck the roots of the little **begonia** and the **creeping fig** into the soil.

6 Dribble in just enough water to settle the roots.

7 Cover the top. When the inside fogs over, as it will, take the cover off for an hour or so; do this more than once if needed. When the excess moisture is gone, the misting will stop. Mist monthly with water at room temperature. It should not need watering for months.

8 Keep the terrarium in dim light for ten days, and then gradually move it into brighter light in a west- or east-facing window.

9 Fertilize once a year with a quarter dose of an all-purpose fertilizer.

 CARE

To get a **poinsettia** to color up for Christmas give it two months with twelve hours of darkness (no artificial light after dark) and twelve hours of bright daylight—which may require turning grow lights or fluorescents on the plant at dusk. Fertilize at every other watering.

Mist **gardenias, hibiscus, rosemary,** and other houseplants every day or two with water at room temperature. Air their space daily for ten minutes or so by opening a window or a door.

If **miniature roses** aren't flowering, light them with spot grow lights after dusk and occasionally place them under fluorescents in a light garden.

If your thermostat is set higher than 68 degrees Fahrenheit, install a humidifier. Or set out vases filled with water, pans of water on radiators, or jars of water among your plants. Mist the plants often.

 PRUNING

Deadhead **miniature roses, begonias, coleus,** and other flowering houseplants. Groom the foliage plants.

WATERING

You can tell without poking a finger into the soil whether the plant is dry. The leaves look less perky—one step away from wilting. When you pick up the pot, it will be far lighter than you remember.

You can tell without poking a finger into the soil whether the plant is dry. The leaves look less perky—one step away from wilting.

Did You Know?

About Desert Cactuses

Some as are big as trees, others the size of a pincushion, and most are very prickly. They all can store enough water to carry on through the severe droughts of their native habitat. However, to flourish in an indoor garden, desert cactuses do need watering, and not just when it rains in West Texas.

Here are their requirements:

1 Light is best in a south-facing window, the most sun you can give the plant.

2 House temperatures of 60 to 80 degrees Fahrenheit will suit most desert cactuses. But they can do quite well in an unheated room or sun room where temperatures go as low as 38 to 45 degrees Fahrenheit. Some need a cold period to set flowers; growers instructions will say so.

3 For soil, use commercial cactus potting soil, which is a very well-drained grainy mix, or make your own with the recipe in the introduction to this chapter.

4 Water desert cactus when the soil feels dry. Let the water run out of the saucer, and after an hour empty what remains. Shower the plants occasionally during the dry winter months indoors.

5 Spring and summer only, fertilize at every third or fourth watering using a half strength dose of an all purpose plant food.

6 Summer the plants outdoors in full sun.

7 Bring them back indoors before temperatures fall below 60 degrees Fahrenheit. Many can take much more cold, but bringing them all in together is the easy, safe way to handle them in fall.

When a plant runs dry, the soil shrinks away from the sides of the container, and the water may run down the interior sides of the pot and not into the soil. The surface doesn't drain as quickly as usual either. Have the patience to add water a little at a time until the soil accepts the water in a normal way. When the plant has rehydrated, see whether the plant is rootbound. If yes, repot it in fresh soil in a larger container.

 FERTILIZING

Add a half strength dose of soluble fertilizer at every fourth watering for houseplants and the **tropical hibiscus** and other tender shrubs brought indoors. For **azaleas** and **gardenias,** use a fertilizer for acid-loving plants. Continue to use African violet fertilizer for flowering houseplants.

 PESTS

Check for spider mites, mealybug, and scale; controls are suggested in the Pests section of the introduction to this chapter and in the Appendix. To avoid problems, mist your plants with water at room temperature, and air the room often, keep temperatures down, and provide humidity.

DECEMBER
Houseplants

PLANNING

Make a **Norfolk Island pine**, a **ficus**, a **podocarpus** or any one of the house trees recommended in the June pages of this chapter into your Christmas tree.

PLANTING

The choice and early care of a **poinsettia** have everything to do with how well the plant will last. Choose a **poinsettia** with tightly clustered flowers, and whose foliage is crisp and green all the way down to the soil. Protect the plant from cold winds while you are getting it home. Unwrap it, and remove the foil wrapping, or cut away the bottom of the foil so water can drain. Keep it at about 72 degrees Fahrenheit during the day and 60 degrees at night. Provide six hours a day of natural light bright enough to read by. You can move it into the room for the evening, but get it back in its window in the morning. Keep the soil moist, but don't let water stand in the saucer.

CARE

Mist **gardenias, rosemary,** and other houseplants every day or two with water at room temperature. Air the room daily for ten minutes or so by opening a window or a door unless it's too cold.

If your **hibiscus** stops blooming, it's going into dormancy, probably from lack of sun, and perhaps from lack of warmth as well. Water it only enough to keep the soil from drying out. Don't fertilize. The plant will drop lots of leaves, but it should live.

African violets flower best in spring and fall when the day length is twelve to fourteen hours. This time of year, place them 9 inches below grow lights, and burn the lights twelve hours a day. The leaves will subside, and won't be as green, but they'll flower in eight to ten weeks.

PRUNING

Deadhead flowering plants.

WATERING

Monitor the soil moisture in houseplants as conscientiously as you do during dry spells outdoors. Shower **miniature roses** every two weeks.

FERTILIZING

Add a half strength dose of soluble fertilizer at every fourth watering for houseplants and the **tropical hibiscus** and other tender shrubs brought indoors. For

azaleas and **gardenias,** use a fertilizer for acid-loving plants. Continue to use African violet fertilizer for flowering houseplants.

PESTS

Check for spider mites, mealybug, and scale. Controls are suggested in the Pests section of the introduction to this chapter and in the Appendix. To avoid problems, mist your plants with water at room temperature, and air the room daily if it's not too cold outside.

Growing tropical hibiscus indoors means you may be challenged by whitefly and soft scale. They like to raise families on a grand scale on the undersides of the leaves. Insecticidal soap controls them if you catch them early. The sticky yellow cards that nurseries use handle only minor infestations, but they do show you how fast the group is multiplying. If you have a showerhead with a flexible extension, turn each leaf upside down and hose it at full pressure with lukewarm water. Leave the plant in the shower to dry, and then spray insecticidal soap all over the tops and the undersides of the leaves, and in the nodes where branches and leaves meet.

CHAPTER FIVE

Lawns

A lawn is a highly visible part of your house. It can be a joy or a curse, depending on how you treat it.

There are four types of lawns: The **lawn lover's lawn** looks like the sod lawns you see in spring flower shows. Flawless. Fiercely defended nine months of the year against growth, weeds, wilts, pests, diseases, and droughts, it gives meaning and purpose to its caregiver's life.

The nature lover's lawn is a flowering meadow with a brush cut. Carpeted in spring with golden dandelions, blue violets, purple jewelweed, bright crabgrass and jointgrass, ajuga, ivy, and other ground covers, here wildlife abounds—voles run, moles mound, birds enjoy a rich supply of grubs that will metamorphose into multihued Japanese and other beetles. In summer the wild flowers will self-sow then brown out leaving bare patches that save on mowing and watering.

The environmentalist's lawn is a work in progress—turfgrass being replaced with ground covers, and there are motels for birds that will eat the grubs that feed the moles that fight the voles that dig the lawn that no longer surrounds the house that Jack built.

The good gardener's lawn is a hybrid of 1, 2, and 3. It's a beautiful lawn maintained by fertilizing adequately, mowing knowledgeably, watering wisely.

FERTILIZING AND FERTILIZERS

A well-maintained lawn creates oxygen, removes pollutants from the air, traps dust and dirt, stops erosion, makes a fine playground, and enhances your home and the whole neighborhood. Like teenagers, turf grasses grow fast and need unchecked access to food, drink, and air to do well. The type of fertilizer you use decrees how often you need to fertilize.

Organic fertilizers. Organics release their nutrients slowly; two applications a year are enough. A Cornell University study found that using organic fertilizers may suppress some diseases, including brown patch, snow mold, dollar spot, and red thread. With organic fertilizers, herbicides, pesticides, and fungicides are usually applied separately.

Chemical fertilizers. Quick-release, balanced chemical fertilizers green the lawn overnight and are soon depleted, so you need to apply them four or five times a year. "Fertilizer-plus" products that include pre-emergent or post-emergent herbicides can be used to control crabgrass and broadleaf weeds. Insect and disease controls are usually applied separately.

Herbicides, pesticides, and fungicides are applied only when needed. Granular products applied with a drop-spreader are safest for the garden.

SOIL PREPARATION AND IMPROVEMENT

Soil pH. The condition of your soil impacts the lawn's access to the nutrients you spend real money and scarce time providing. If the pH of the soil is between pH 6.0 and 7.0 it should do well. The ideal pH for turfgrass is 6.5. Heavily cropped soils—like lawn soils—eventually become acid and have a lower pH reading. However, do not lime by rote to raise the pH. Some of our soils are naturally alkaline, and there the pH may need to be lowered, not raised. Check the pH of your soil annually, but adjust it only when adjustment is needed.

Lawns

Sandy soil whose pH has been corrected is good for two years, clay soil for three. A pH check can be made any month. We recommend February before the first fertilization. (See February.)

Aeration (Coring). Running feet, foot traffic, heavy mowing equipment, bikes, cars, and loaded wheelbarrows all pack (compact) the top 2 or 3 inches of the soil into a dense layer. Compacted soil has no space for water or air, nor does it have growing room for roots. The solution is to aerate the soil by cutting out core plugs of sod so that water, air, and fertilizer can get down to where they are needed.

If the lawn is well used and beginning to bald or show a thatch buildup, aerate. If all is well, every two or three years, aerate to keep it that way. You can do it by hand, and you also can rent power equipment to aerate and dethatch. (See April and May.)

Thatch and dethatching. Grass clippings landing on the lawn are decomposed by the microorganisms there, and that adds nutrients to the soil. That layer of clippings is called thatch, and it's a good thing as long as the clippings are less than $1/4$ inch deep. However, if the lawn gets too much fast-acting high-nitrogen fertilizer and water, it may grow quickly and the clippings may fall so thick and so fast the microorganisms can't keep up; that's when a layer of thatch a couple of inches deep accumulates, which is harmful. A lawn that feels spongy when you walk on it probably has thatch building to unhealthy levels. You can fix it by aerating and dethatching. You can also prevent thatch buildup. (See May.)

WATERING

Grass is programmed to thrive on a good soaking every week to ten days. Soak it more often, as nature does when we have a wet spring, and it will grow, use up the nutrients in the soil, and need mowing almost twice as fast. Water the lawn frequently and shallowly—every one to three days—and the roots will grow near the surface of the soil, which warms and dries out when the weather does, a bad place for roots to be. Excess water speeds up the rate of growth, which depletes the fertilizer and increases the need for water. That makes the grass vulnerable to drought, and more susceptible to the myriad pests and diseases lawns are heir to.

The watering program in the July pages below is easy on your time, effort, pocketbook, and lawn. Only your patience will suffer.

REPAIR AND RESTORATION

The rule of thumb is that if seventy percent of a lawn needs fixing, then you need a new lawn. If thirty percent or less is in trouble, it can be patched or restored.

Unhappily, it's a fact that on packed dirt only dandelions, crabgrass, and their associates grow readily. For lawn patching or restoration to succeed, you must mix humus and fertilizers into the soil before you seed or sod the area.

Repair. You can repair a small area with sod, new or stripped from somewhere else in the lawn, or by seeding the area. Lawn patching products include mulch and nutrients and are easy to apply.

Restoration. This involves sowing seed into an existing lawn after vigorously cultivating the ground with rented power equipment. (See August.)

Starting a new lawn. To seed or to sod, that is the question. It is not nobler to seed, just less costly. Sodding is faster, but the soil needs the same deep preparation and patient watering until it is established. Sod won't keep weeds out forever, and sod varieties are limited.

Seeding saves money. The bigger the lawn, the greater the savings. To seed

Lawns

1000 square feet costs about $10, not including the humus, fertilizer, and other soil amendments the soil will need to get a good start. If you seed, you can choose from among the varieties of grasses in our turfgrass table.

Sod if you enjoy making magic. It's the way to have an instant lawn. The cost for a 1000 square foot area is about $200, if you do the work yourself. Your choice of grasses will be limited.

Timing for a new lawn. Cool-season grasses peak in spring, go semi-dormant in mid-summer and peak again in fall.

They're best started around Labor Day. Early spring is second best. Most seeds germinate when daytime temperatures are 68 to 95 degrees Fahrenheit.

Zoysia, a warm-season grass preferred by some in Zone 8, peaks in warm weather and is best planted in mid-summer. (See September and November.)

MOWING

In our area mowing may begin as early as late March, goes weekly in May, slows with August heat and drought, slows for real in October, and ends in November. The rule of thumb is to mow every five to seven days during the peak season, and as needed at other times.

Good mowing equipment and knowledgeable mowing practices improve the beauty and the health of your lawn. In the long run that saves you time, effort, annoyance, and the cost of repairing what has gone wrong. Keep the mower blades sharpened, cut the grass high, and don't let the mowing get away from you. Don't over-fertilize. Water wisely. Mow at the right height for the grass and the season. (See Mowing, May.)

The table of grasses for the Mid-Atlantic includes the mowing heights of each grass recommended.

About mowers. Buy the best equipment you can afford and the right size. That will make it easier and help you to keep up without feeling burdened. There are many sizes and types of mowers, but only two ways of cutting—reel or rotary. The reel mower does a better job but is slower. The rotary mower does a fine job and is faster. The most important thing to know about a mower is that it must be sharpened throughout the mowing season. Dull blades tear and damage the grass blades, and that shows up in the appearance of the lawn and the health of the grass plants. (See December.)

LEAVES AND YOUR LAWN

If there's just a scattering of leaves on your lawn, they'll dry and crumble into bits the microorganisms in the soil will reduce to nutrients. The residue will blow away with winter winds and weather. But, matted accumulations of leaves rob the grass of the sunlight it needs as growth continues through fall. The grass grows as long as the soil is warm, and it will remain warm in our region at least through November, and in Zone 8, even later.

Crunch the leaves under the lawn mower, rake and bag them, or grind them, and distribute the bits over the garden with a blower-vacuum. (See October.)

COOL SEASON AND WARM SEASON GRASSES

For the Mid-Atlantic states in Zones 5, 6, and 7, André recommends cool season grasses. Even in Zone 8, tall **fescues** give you a greener lawn many more months than **zoysia**. Zoysia is a great grass for summer, drought tolerant, and good looking, but it goes dormant and turns golden below 63 degrees Fahrenheit. To keep it green, some dye it green for winter, which makes it look like plastic turf, or it is overseeded with annual rye, and that's a chore.

Lawns

Beware of too-good-to-be-true sales of grass seed.

CONTROLLING WEEDS, PESTS, AND DISEASES

Weeds, pests, and diseases attack lawns made vulnerable by lack of fertilizer and poor garden practices. There are ways to control them.

Cultural practices. Feed, mow, and water your lawn properly.

Biological methods. Apply agents such as beneficial nematodes, bacteria, and other organisms. A biological control becoming more available is endophytes—fungi bred to live within grasses and stop insect pests.

Chemical controls. Pre-emergent and post-emergent herbicides, and pesticides and fungicides—some natural, some man-made—are used to control weeds, pests, and diseases. Those now on the market are considered environmentally sound. Once again we caution you to apply these only if really needed.

For an overview of how and when to do what, turn to the March pages.

WEEDS

All post-emergent liquid weed killers work best when the dose called for on the label is combined with 1 teaspoon of liquid dish detergent to each gallon of water.

Annual bluegrass. Prevent by applications of pre-emergent controls such as Betasan and Banlan made in early August and repeated one month later. There is no good post-emergent treatment.

Broadleaf weed seeds. These weeds, including dandelions, can be controlled by applications of a **pre-emergent** broadleaf weed killer when the forsythia petals drop. Repeat in September and October.

Broadleaf weed plants. If a variety of weeds leaf out in May and June, apply a **post-emergent** broad-spectrum herbicide.

Chickweed, bindweed, ground ivy, violets, sorrel, and clover plants. Kill these weeds by applications in April and May of a post-emergent control such as 2,4-D+TurflonD; Dicamba 2,4-D+BanvelD; or Gordon's Trimec Broadleaf Herbicide. Repeat in September and October.

Crabgrass seeds. When the forsythia petals drop in late March or April, control by applying pre-emergent weed killers such as Betasan, Tupersan, Balan, Dacthal, Team, or Sidriron.

Dandelion, plantain, and other broadleaf weed plants. Control them by individual applications in April and May of 2,4-D and 2,4-D combinations.

Ground ivy. Control by applying a post-emergent control such as Gordon's Trimec Broadleaf Herbicide or 2,4-D+TurflonD any time it appears.

Nutgrass. Apply a pre-emergent control such as Manage or Pennant when the forsythia petals drop in late March or April, and repeat one month later.

Controlling Weeds

Lawns

When nutgrass first becomes visible in spring, and again ten days later, apply a post-emergent control such as Basagran, DSMA, MSMA, or Bentazon.

Wild onion (garlic). Apply a post-emergent control such as 2,4-D+ Dicamba (Banvel D) or 2,4-D+TurflonD in early spring when the onions first emerge, and repeat two weeks later.

Pests

From November through March pests and diseases are on vacation. They're with you April through October.

Grubs. To control the larvae that become rose chafer or Asiatic beetle, in May and June, and again in August and September, apply biological controls such as beneficial nematodes; for the grubs of Japanese beetles, use milky spore disease. Or apply chemical controls such as Merit or Marathon.

Ants. Use Permethrin.

Chinch bugs. Apply Sevin, Permethrin, or Baygon in April and May, and again in August and September.

Cutworms. Use beneficial nematodes, Sevin, or Safer soap in spring.

Japanese beetles. Apply neem, rotenone, or Sevin.

Sod webworms. In late June and again in late August and early September, apply Bt, Sevin, Permethrin, or Baygon.

Diseases

To control a variety of diseases at one time, apply a broad-spectrum fungicide, or better yet a broad-spectrum systemic fungicide. Some André recommends are Daconil, Mancozeb, Chipco, Clearys 3336, and Bayleton.

Make the applications when the disease appears and twice a month in May, June, July, and August.

Fusarium blight (now called necrotic ring spot), copper spot, and dollar spot. They show up as a circle of dead grass with some green tufts in the middle. The disease will likely run its course. The controls are fungicidal copper or sulfur, Bayleton, or Cleary 3336.

Helminthosporum leaf spot and melting out. These diseases cause brown and black spots on the leaves, and the grass dies in irregular patches. Treat with a fungicide labeled for use on turf and melting out diseases, such as Fore or Heritage, every two weeks from the first appearance of the problem until it is gone.

Powdery mildew. It looks as though the leaves have been powdered. Powdery mildew turns up in shady spots, so try to get more light to the area. Or control with applications of fungicidal copper or sulfur, or a systemic fungicide such as Bayleton or Banner Maxx applied twice a month from June through September.

Red thread and pink patch. Patches of grass turn light tan to pink, and pink threads bind the blades. From the time it appears, treat the lawn with a contact fungicide twice, seven to ten days apart.

Rust-infected leaves. These leaves are spotted yellow, orange, or brown. Rust is common in new lawns with a high percentage of ryegrass. It generally fades as other grass varieties take over from the rye. Control with applications twice a month of sulfur, mancozeb, or manzate, or a systemic fungicide such as Bayleton and Banner Maxx, from the time it appears—usually May through September.

Snow mold. This is most prevalent in the cooler zones of our region and causes small to large gray or white matted patches of grass. Rake the lawn in early spring, and avoid overuse of nitrogen fertilizers.

Lawns

Types of Grass	Shade Tolerance	Problems	Start As	Sow	Mowing Height
Fine Fescues: chewings, creeping red, hard fescue	Excellent	Does not recover quickly from damage. Tends to lie flat and cause uneven mowing.	Seed in spring or fall	3 to 4 pounds per 1,000 square feet	2 to 2$\frac{3}{4}$ inches
Tall Fescue	Good	Older versions (Kentucky 31) tend to clump. Vulnerable to pythium, brown patch diseases, cutworms, sod, webworms, billbugs.	Seed spring or fall; sod spring, early summer, or fall	Seed 6 to 10 pounds per 1,000 square feet	2$\frac{1}{4}$ to 3$\frac{1}{2}$ inches
Kentucky Bluegrass	Full sun best, also light shade	Heavy feeder, needs lots of water. Vulnerable to powdery mildew, fungal diseases, chinch bugs, cutworms, grubs, sod webworms.	Seed or sod, spring or fall	Seed 1 to 2 pounds per 1,000 square feet	2 to 2$\frac{3}{4}$ inches
Perennial Ryegrass	Some varieties tolerate some shade	Suffers in extreme heat—may get pythium. Vulnerable to brown patch, red thread, rust, snow mold, dollar spot.	Seed or sod in spring, early summer, or fall	Seed 4 to 5 pounds per 1,000 square feet	2 to 2$\frac{1}{2}$ inches
Zoysia	Good	Is brown 6 to 8 months of the year in Zones 5 to 7. Chronic heavy thatch buildup.	Plugs or sod in spring	Plugs or sod	2 inches

JANUARY
Lawns

 PLANNING

If your lawn mower was serviced when mowing ended last year, great! If not, see December for suggestions.

 PLANTING

Zone 7 can sow cool-season grasses even this early. Seed sown on frozen ground or a thin layer of snow will survive until moisture and warmth encourage germination.

 CARE

Walking on frozen grass damages it.

Shovel walk and driveways before applying snowmelt salts. Otherwise you risk damaging the lawn.

 MOWING

None needed.

 WATERING

If the lawn reaches under overhanging eaves and the season has been dry, that area may need water.

Did You Know?

Fertilizing and Fertilizers

Save $$ by leaving grass clippings on the lawn. Reduced to their elemental forms by microorganisms in the soil, clippings can lower the amount of fertilizer needed by as much as thirty percent. Clippings from a 1,000 square foot lawn contribute 1/2 to 2 pounds of nitrogen depending on how much the lawn was fertilized.

Insect and disease controls are applied separately. (See March for timing.) Avoid fertilizing cool-season grasses (**zoysia** is okay) when temperatures are over 90 degrees.

When to fertilize:

Organic fertilizers. Organic fertilizers are applied twice a year. They can be applied in any season without danger of burning. Organics do not include herbicides, pesticides, or fungicides; these are applied separately and only when needed. The first fertilization is best made as grass starts into growth in early spring. For Zones 6 and 7 that's usually late February to April; for Zone 8 organic fertilizers can be applied as early as January. The second fertilization is best applied in September to October. The third fertilization is optional, and can be made December or January.

Chemical fertilizers. Chemical fertilizers are applied four to five times a year. Formulations are available that include pre-emergent or post-emergent controls for crabgrass and broadleaf weeds. For a new lawn, choose a fertilizer with an NPK of 1-1-1, or 1-2-2. For an established lawn, choose a fertilizer whose NPK ratio is 3-1-2 or 4-1-2. The first fertilization is best made as grass starts into growth in early spring. For Zones 6 and 7 that's usually February to March; for warm Zone 8 a chemical fertilizer may be applied as early as January. The second fertilization is April to June; the third is made June to August; the fourth is August or September. The fifth fertilization is optional and can be made October or November.

 FERTILIZING

An extra fertilization this month will benefit a lawn that hasn't been growing well. A light coat of granular fertilizer can be applied over a few inches of snow.

 PESTS

In Zone 6, snow mold is possible. Just rake the patches clear, and avoid over-use of nitrogen fertilizers in the future.

FEBRUARY

Lawns

 PLANNING

If your lawn mower needs servicing, take it to the dealer now because this is the dealer's quiet season. Keeping the blades sharp is essential to giving the lawn a good cut, one that will be good for the lawn and good for the viewer.

 PLANTING

You can overseed thin areas in late winter or early spring. It's okay to sow seed on a few inches of snow. For suggestions on how to repair damage—where a tree limb has fallen or a delivery truck has gouged the turf—and how to overseed a lawn, see August.

 CARE

Check the pH of your lawn soil, and adjust it if needed.

If your lawn has developed low spots, top-dress it with improved soil now, and overseed it. (See September.)

 MOWING

Mowing is not likely to be needed unless the weather has been warm in Zone 8.

Did You Know?

Soil pH and Lime

To keep your soil in top condition for growing grass, check and adjust the pH annually.

The ideal pH for turfgrass is pH 6.5. Some gardeners lime their lawns every year, but you shouldn't lime by rote. Some soils in our region are naturally alkaline, and there the pH needs to be lowered, not raised.

The pH can be adjusted any time the lawn isn't in full growth, but checking in February gives you time to correct the pH before the grass-growing season begins. A sandy soil whose pH has been corrected is good for two years; a clay soil is good for three years. But we recommend you check the pH every year. Kits for analyzing pH are sold at garden centers and by mail-order suppliers, as are products used for adjusting the soil pH.

- To raise the pH by 1 pH point, apply Dolomitic limestone:

  Sandy soil—50 pounds per 1000 square feet
  Clay soil—100 pounds per 1000 square feet

- To lower the pH by 1 pH point, apply elemental sulfur (water-soluble garden sulfur).

  Sandy soil—50 pounds per 1000 square feet
  Clay soil—100 pounds per 1000 square feet

Other acidifiers are aluminum sulfate and iron sulfate; they act faster but do not last as long in the soil as elemental sulfur.

 WATERING

Water areas that have just been seeded or sodded.

 FERTILIZING

The first application of an organic fertilizer can be made between now and April.

The first application of a chemical fertilizer can be made this month or next.

 PESTS

If wild onion (garlic) was a problem last spring, plan to apply a post-emergent control such as 2,4-D+Dicamba (Banvel D) or 2,4-D+TurflonD at first appearance.

MARCH
Lawns

PLANNING

If you haven't already, get the lawn mower and trimmer into good condition, and sharpen the blades. Check supplies for your mower and trimmer.

PLANTING

Overseed areas where the grass is skimpy.

CARE

Check and adjust the soil pH. Aerate if you haven't in the last two years. Check and correct thatch build-up. Use a grass rake to fluff the soil, and discard debris.

MOWING

Begin to mow when the grass tops the height our turfgrass table recommends.

WATERING

Water lawn areas snow or rain can't reach.

FERTILIZING

The first application of an organic fertilizer can be made this month or next.

Did You Know?

Herbicides, Pesticides, and Fungicides

Herbicides. The best defense against weeds is a thriving lawn cut high. If a few weeds do appear, pull them by hand before they set seed. If lots of weeds appear, apply a **post-emergent** broad-spectrum herbicide. If crabgrass is a problem, apply a **pre-emergent** crabgrass killer. If broad-leaved weeds such as violets and dandelions are also a problem, use a broad-spectrum **pre-emergent** herbicide that kills weeds as well as crabgrass. Crabgrass germinates in late March or April, about the time forsythia petals fall and dandelions fluff out their seedheads. If the lawn is infested with a particular weed, apply a product specific to that weed as and when the label directs.

Pesticides. All lawns are home to insects, most of them beneficial. Biological and chemical controls are available if insects are numerous, but don't overdo; pesticides also kill beneficial insects. To get rid of harmful insects, you can use a combination of a chemical fertilizer plus a pesticide. If you are using an organic fertilizer, apply a broad-spectrum pesticide (insecticide) June to August. To control a specific insect infestation—Japanese beetles, for example—apply a control specific to the insect **when and how the label directs.**

Fungicides. Fungi cause lawn diseases. Most feed on dead vegetation, recycling it as soil nutrients. A few bad-guy fungi feed on live plants. Symptoms and controls are described in this chapter's introduction.

The best defense is a healthy lawn—fertilize adequately, mow correctly, water wisely, and keep your soil in good condition by adjusting the pH as needed by aerating (coring, plugging) every two or three years and by avoiding thatch buildup. Treat problems immediately.

The first application of a chemical fertilizer should be made by the end of this month. (See January.)

PESTS

If you've had crabgrass, when the forsythia petals fall, apply a pre-emergent broadleaf weed killer. If dandelions and other broadleaf weeds turn up as well, use a control that deals with both. If wild onion (garlic) pops up, apply a post-emergent control such as 2,4-D+Dicamba (Banvel D) or 2,4-D+ TurflonD, and repeat two weeks later. For other controls, turn back to the Pests and Diseases section in the introduction to this chapter.

APRIL
Lawns

 PLANNING

Evaluate the weed and pest populations in your lawn, and work out a plan to keep them under control. Get together last year's herbicides and pesticides. Figure out what you'll need, and acquire it now while garden centers are fully stocked.

 PLANTING

Repair areas in the lawn that have been damaged by falling branches, snow-blowing equipment, and so on. (See August.)

 CARE

If you haven't checked the pH, do it now.

Before mowing begins, rake away debris and fluff up the grass.

 MOWING

Mowing begins in earnest this month. Keep the blades sharpened; a clean cut is a healthy cut. Set your mower at the height recommended in our turfgrass table for your type of grass. If you don't know what type you are growing, set the mower at 2½ inches.

 **Did You Know?**

About Aeration (Coring)

To solve compaction, avoid thatch buildup, and condition the soil, aerate every two or three years. Aerating equipment punches 2- to 3-inch deep holes in the soil, and lets fertilizer, air, and water penetrate. Aerators that are "corers" have hollow tines, and these are more effective than aerators with solid tines.

To aerate 1,000 square feet or less you can use a manual aerator. It looks like a spading fork, but the tines are hollow tubes. For a larger area, you need a drum-mounted aerator, or to hire a firm that is equipped to do the job.

The best time to aerate is when the grass isn't actively growing, early spring or fall. The day before, lightly water the grass so the tines will enter the soil easily. Before using the aerator, make a light application of fertilizer. Be thorough, and make two passes at right angles to each other with the aerator. Spread grass seed over the aerated area at the rate recommended on the bag. Water slowly and gently.

 WATERING

Water enough to keep the surface of newly sodded or seeded areas moist.

 FERTILIZING

The first application of an organic fertilizer should have been made by the end of this month.

If your first application of a chemical fertilizer was made at the end of February, the second can be made between now and June.

PESTS

If crabgrass or nutgrass have been problems, when the forsythia petals drop, apply a pre-emergent control; if they do leaf out, apply a post-emergent control. This month and next, watch for chickweed, bindweed, ground ivy, violets, sorrel, clover plants, dandelions, plantain, and other broadleaf weed plants. If there are only a few, pull them by hand. If there are many, kill them before they go to seed. If you spot chinch bugs, apply controls this month and next, and again in August and September.

Controls for each of these problems are suggested in the chapter introduction.

MAY
Lawns

PLANNING

If you want to reduce the amount of water you use on the lawn, consider replacing outlying areas with a drought-tolerant ground cover.

PLANTING

You can seed or oversow areas of the lawn this month. (See August.)

CARE

May is a fine time to aerate and dethatch.

In Zone 8, if you suspect grubs, check late this month. Cut out and remove a square foot of turf 8 inches deep. If you find three or four grub larvae in the top 6 inches, apply a grub control. Check again in mid-August or early September.

MOWING

Mow often enough so you never have to cut off more than a third of the grass to maintain the height recommended. Keep the mower blades sharpened.

Did You Know?

Thatch and Dethatching

Grass clippings left on the lawn are returned to an elemental state by microorganisms in the soil and recycled as nutrients. A 1/4-inch layer of clippings is good; more is not. Clippings build when overdoses of pesticides kill the soil microorganisms, and when soluble high-nitrogen (N2) fertilizers and excessive watering push grass growth. Your lawn could need dethatching if it feels spongy to walk on.

- Look before you leap. Cut out a pie-shaped plug of turf that includes dirt with the roots. If the spongy layer between the grass and the soil measures more than 1/2 inch, dethatch.

- The best time to dethatch a cool-season grass is in early fall; dethatch **zoysia** in early spring.

- A convex rake with short knife-like blades in place of tines can be used to dethatch a small lawn. For a big dethatching job, a gas-powered vertical mower and power rake attachment is needed. If the thatch is thick, make two passes at right angles to each other.

WATERING

Water newly sodded or seeded areas.

FERTILIZING

Organic fertilizer. If the first application hasn't been made yet, do it now.

Chemical fertilizer. If your first application was in February, repeat now. If you made it in March, wait until May or June to repeat. If weeds are a problem, use a fertilizer that includes a post-emergent herbicide.

PESTS

If **dandelions, plantain, chickweed, bindweed, ground ivy, violets, sorrel, clover plants, or other broadleaf weeds** appear, apply post-emergent controls before they go to seed.

Apply controls this month for the larvae that become chinch bugs, rose chafer, Asiatic, Japanese, and other beetles.

Rust may appear in new lawns with a high percentage of ryegrass. If rust shows up, spray immediately.

JUNE
Lawns

 PLANNING

The lawn's period of major growth is over till the weather cools in September; time to assess your mowing equipment and perhaps take advantage of sales to upgrade.

 PLANTING

Sod installed now will do well as long as it is watered daily until it begins to root and grow again.

 CARE

In Zones 6 and 7, if you suspect grubs in an area, check early this month. Cut out and remove a square foot of turf 8 inches deep. If you find three or four grub larvae in the top 6 inches, apply a grub control. Check again in mid-August or early September.

 MOWING

Check the mowing height of equipment, and make sure it is at the height recommended for your type of turfgrass on the table in the introduction to the chapter.

Keep the mower blades sharpened.

 WATERING

Keep the soil for newly planted seed or sod moist by watering every day or two.

 FERTILIZING

Organic fertilizer. If the first application hasn't been made yet, do it now. Organics can be applied any time, but grass grows rapidly in spring and needs to have the nutrients replenished.

Chemical fertilizer. If you haven't made the second application, make it now. If your second fertilization was in April, you can make the third application between now and August.

If weeds are a problem, use a fertilizer that includes a post-emergent herbicide. If insects are a problem, look for fertilizer-plus products that include a broad-spectrum pesticide.

 PESTS

If you see broadleaf weeds in the lawn, apply a **post-emergent** broad-spectrum herbicide.

If you've had problems with rose chafer, Asiatic beetle, Japanese beetle, or other white grubs, apply controls now.

Watch out for sod webworms; initiate controls immediately.

Powdery mildew can appear about now. It occurs most often in shaded areas of the lawn. Initiate controls now, and continue throughout the summer.

If you've had problems with rose chafer, Asiatic beetle, Japanese beetle, or other white grubs, apply controls now.

Did You Know?

How to Avoid Thatch Buildup

• Remove less than 1 inch of grass blade when you mow. Use a mulching mower to double-cut the clippings, which makes it easier for the microorganisms in the soil to break them down.

• Avoid excessive dosing with pesticides that kill the soil microorganisms.

• Avoid soluble high-nitrogen (N2) fertilizers and excessive watering.

• Aerate every two or three years. Aeration helps avoid a big thatch buildup although it isn't enough alone to solve one.

• Beneficial insects speed the breakdown of thatch, so be conservative in your use of pesticides.

Mowing: The Six Commandments

Good mowing practices help to keep the lawn beautiful and healthy.

1 Mow when the lawn is dry.

2 Keep the mower blades sharpened throughout the cutting season.

3 Cut the grass high. For the ideal height for your grass, turn back to the turfgrass table. Grass mowed higher than 2 inches develop extensive roots, reducing the need for water and nutrients. A Virginia study showed:

• Cut grass 1 inch high: 43.1 weeds per 100 square feet (a plot 10 by 10 feet).

• Cut grass 2 inches high: 2.5 weeds per 100 square feet.

• Cut grass 3 inches high: .2 weeds per 100 square foot.

4 Mow often enough so you never have to cut off more than a third of the grass to maintain the height recommended in the turfgrass table. If your mower is set at 2½ inches, mow when the grass is 3½ inches high.

5 Use a mulching mower to make it easy for soil organisms to recycle clippings.

6 Vary your cutting pattern; that's easier on the grass.

JULY
Lawns

PLANNING

As summer reveals the pests and diseases that love your lawn best, plan fall and spring strategies for reducing their numbers.

PLANTING

You can repair with sod now, but wait until late September for any serious seeding project.

CARE

The little moths hovering over the grass are laying the eggs of sod web-worms—soon to become larvae. If you applied a control in June, the moths are a prompt that you must repeat in late August and in September.

MOWING

When you will be away for more than a week, arrange to have the lawn mowed. The growth rate of cool-season grasses is slowing, but if on your return you have to cut more than a week's worth of growth, the lawn will suffer.

Keep the mower blades sharpened.

Did You Know?

How to Water Your Lawn

Lawns need water every week. When you water, imitate a slow soaking rain. Then it will go deep, and the roots will grow down away from the heat and drought at the surface.

- When you water, lay down $1^1/2$ inches **slowly and gently.**

- Purchase a sprinkler that delivers the water slowly, avoiding wasteful runoff. Or, put down $3/4$ of an inch of water, wait an hour, and then repeat.

- Between 5 am and 10 am is the most efficient time to water. But water any time your lawn retains footprints or grass blades curl inward. Where soil is thin—over rock outcroppings, for example—the grass dries out first and turns a bluish color, signaling that the lawn needs water.

- Watering systems deliver water at highly individual rates. To time how long it takes for your system to deliver $1^1/2$ inches of water, do this: With a waterproof marker, draw horizontal lines $1^1/2$ inches up from the bottom of the interior of five empty 1-pound coffee tins. Arrange the tins in a straight line out from the sprinkler to just inside its farthest reach. Turn it on, mark the time, and run the sprinkler half an hour. Check the water levels in the cans. Check at 15-minute intervals until the water reaches the $1^1/2$ inch marker lines. Compare the amounts of water in the cans. If some have less than others, overlap the areas the sprinkler reaches. Average the amounts and the time. Record the timing in your garden log. You think you'll remember but likely you won't.

WATERING

The lawn needs a good soaking every week, especially in very hot weather.

FERTILIZING

Chemical fertilizer. If you haven't applied your third fertilization yet, do it this month or next.

PESTS

Look out for fusarium blight (now called necrotic ring spot), copper spot, and dollar spot; helminthosporum leaf spot and melting out diseases; powdery mildew; red thread and pink patch; and rust-infected leaves. As soon as you have identified a disease, apply the controls recommended in the chapter introduction. Repeat twice this month and next.

AUGUST
Lawns

 PLANNING

When a high tide threatens a coastal lawn, flood it until the soil is so saturated it can't absorb much of the salt water.

 PLANTING

August is considered a good month for repairing and overseeding problem spots.

 CARE

Grub damage becomes obvious during dry periods; apply grub controls.

 MOWING

Mowing high is especially important during the hot dry months.

 WATERING

Grass that is consistently and deeply watered has deep roots and will be just fine in spite of the heat and drought.

Did You Know?

Repair and Restoration: Patching

1 Level the sod and soil in the damaged area.

2 Cut away jagged pieces of sod.

3 Top with 3 to 4 inches of humus or topsoil. For each 10-by-10-foot area, add: Espoma Organic Lawn Food 5-3-5—5 to 10 pounds; Rock phosphate—5 to 10 pounds; Green sand—5 to 10 pounds; for clay soils—gypsum 5 to 10 pounds.

4 Mix this into the soil. For seeding or using a patching product, tamp it level with the lawn. For sod, tamp it down $1/2$ to $3/4$ inch below grade.

5 Sow seed, spread the patching product, or install sod, using, if possible, turfgrass matching the existing grass.

6 Fertilize the entire lawn lightly.

7 If you have seeded, cover it with straw so that only thirty to fifty percent of the soil is visible.

8 Water slowly and often to keep the soil moist until the seeds have (nearly) all germinated. When the grass is an inch high, reduce watering to every four or five days. After the first mowing, water deeply every seven days unless it rains.

9 Mow when the grass is $1/3$-inch taller than its optimum height. For seeded lawn, avoid the riding mower until the soil is firm underfoot. For sodded lawn, use the riding mower after two or three weeks.

 FERTILIZING

Chemical fertilizer. If you haven't applied your third fertilization yet, do it now.

 PESTS

Repeat controls for chinch bugs, rose chafer, and Asiatic or Japanese beetles. Apply pre-emergent controls for annual bluegrass. Treat again for sod webworms.

SEPTEMBER
Lawns

 PLANNING

Mid-fall is the best time to aerate because the grass isn't actively growing.

 PLANTING

Labor Day is the beginning of the best season for repair, renovation, and starting a new lawn.

 CARE

The best time to dethatch a cool-season grass is in early fall; dethatch **zoysia** in early spring.

 MOWING

Keep the mower blades sharpened.

 WATERING

Water if you have more than seven or eight days without rain, especially newly seeded or sodded areas.

 FERTILIZING

Organic fertilizer. The second fertilization can be made this month or next.

Did You Know?

Repair and Restoration: Renovation

If thirty percent or less of the lawn is poor, patch. If seventy percent needs fixing, renovate. Mow the lawn as low as possible, then renovate by:

Option 1
If the soil isn't compacted, rent a slit seeder, which drops seed onto the soil after slicing it. Use half the seeds to plant in one direction, and then go over the area again in the other direction dropping the remaining seeds.

Option 2
- Cultivate compacted soil with a power rake to slice through thatch and into the soil so the seeds can touch the earth.

- Use a hollow tine core aerator to bring soil to the surface.

- Go over it again with the power rake to smooth out the cores and prepare for seeding.

- Distribute seed evenly with a mechanical spreader, preferably drop style. Make two passes at right angles to each other.

After the lawn has been seeded, follow steps 6 through 9, for Patching Your Lawn (see August).

Chemical fertilizer. If you have not yet made the fourth application, do it now.

 PESTS

For annual bluegrass, make the second application of a **pre-emergent** weed killer now, and repeat in October. For chickweed, bindweed, ground ivy, violets, sorrel, clover, and other broadleaf weeds, apply a **post-emergent** weed killer now.

Controls for sod webworm, rose chafer, Asiatic or Japanese beetles must be applied in September. Repeat the spring treatments for chinch bugs this month and next.

Start or continue treatments for powdery mildew and rust, fusarium blight, helminthosporum disease, red thread, and dollar spot.

Water if you have more than seven or eight days without rain, especially newly seeded or sodded areas.

Did You Know?

Starting a New Lawn: Seed or Sod

September is the best month to sow seed for cool-season grasses; early spring is second. The best time to start **zoysia**, a warm-season grass, is in mid-summer.

Seed

1 Spray the area with RoundUp to kill existing weed seeds. Wait seven to ten days, and then repeat.

2 Wait seven to ten more days, check the pH, adjust it if needed, and add the amendments and fertilizers described in the section on Repair and Renovation in the August pages.

3 Rototill all this into the soil.

4 Sow the seed evenly using a mechanical spreader, preferably drop style. Make two passes, at right angles to each other using half the seed allotted each pass.

5 Rake the seed into the top few inches of the soil.

6 Rent a lawn roller, and roll the seeded area.

7 Apply a straw mulch, thin enough so only thirty to fifty percent of the soil shows.

8 Water and mow. (See Repair and Restoration on the August and September pages.)

9 Fertilize following the annual schedule given in this chapter.

Sod

1 Prepare the soil as for seeding; see steps 1, 2, 3, above.

2 Lay the sod in a staggered brick pattern so that the seam on one row of sod falls in the center of the previous row. Butt the edges firmly together, and, standing on a board laid over the previous row, tamp the seams firmly in place with the back of a rake.

3 Water enough to wet 4 to 6 inches of the underlying soil. For the next month, water deeply every four to five days unless you have rain.

4 Mow when the grass is a third taller than its optimum height. Use a hand mower rather than a riding mower for the first season.

Sod Placement

5 Fertilize following the annual schedule given in this chapter.

OCTOBER
Lawns

 PLANNING

A healthy lawn is its own best defense against the weeds, pests, and diseases that cause deterioration. **Use your experience with the lawn this year to plan a lawn care schedule that will build on current successes.**

 PLANTING

The soil still has warmth, and the air is cooling, a happy time for cool-season grasses. You can still seed or sod, repair, overseed, or renovate early this month.

 CARE

The best time to dethatch a cool-season grass is in early fall; dethatch **zoysia** in early spring.

The best time to aerate is when the grass isn't growing, early spring or mid-fall. Now, while you are still expecting lots of fall rain, is a good time.

 MOWING

Grass growth is slowing. Mow only when the grass is a third taller than the cutting height we recommend for your type of plant. Keep the mower blades sharpened.

Did You Know?

Leaves and Your Lawn

Leaves are assets. Not one should leave your property. However, matted leaves rob the grass of the sunlight it needs as it continues to grow through fall. Grass grows when the soil is warm, and it will remain warm in our region at least through November, and in Zone 8, even later.

- As long as you can still see the grass blades through the fallen leaves, you can shred them with a mower, and leave them on the lawn to decompose into nutrients. To crumble, they must be mowed when dry.

- If or when the leaf layer is such that you can see just a little of the grass, mow, rake up the mess, spread it over annual beds and the kitchen garden, and dig it into the top 6 inches; that's next spring's supply of humus!

- When the leaf layer is about 4 inches deep, suck the leaves up in a blower-vacuum, and blow the residue over the surrounding lawn. Or, bag the ground leaves, and store them to use next spring as mulch.

- If the leaves get deeper than 4 inches, gather them into leaf bags, and put them on your compost pile. (See October in Chapter 9, Trees.)

 WATERING

October should be wet, but if it isn't, water. For new lawns, follow the watering schedule recommended in the September pages.

 FERTILIZING

Organic fertilizer. If you didn't make the second fertilization last month, do it now.

Chemical fertilizer. An optional fifth fertilization can be made this month to give the lawn a boost through winter.

 PESTS

To be effective, a September application of **pre-emergent** broadleaf weed killer to control annual bluegrass and/or broadleaf weeds must be repeated in October. That goes for controls for chickweed, bindweed, ground ivy, violets, sorrel, and clover plants.

Repeat the September treatment for chinch bugs this month.

For controls, turn back to the Pests and Diseases section in the introduction.

NOVEMBER
Lawns

PLANNING

If you are in snow country, lay in a supply of sand, kitty litter (the old-fashioned, non-clumping kind), or environmentally friendly de-icing products that will enable you to have skid-proof paths and walks without harming the surrounding lawn.

PLANTING

It's too late to seed or sod this year except in warm Zone 8; there you could take a chance on the weather holding and repair a small area.

CARE

Inventory your supply of herbicides, pesticides, and fungicides, and put them away for the winter in a safe place.

Seal herbicides, pesticides, and fungicides in their original containers. It is unwise to transfer them to unmarked containers, and in some states illegal. Store all three in a locked cupboard where they will be safe from the curiosity of children and pets.

Store granular formulations of all kinds, including fertilizers, in a cool, dry location to keep them in good condition for next year. Store liquid formulations away from direct sun and where temperatures do not go down to freezing. They may deteriorate.

MOWING

The only thing left to mow should be small drifts of leaves; let the wind blow the chaff away. **Zoysia** lawns overseeded with rye grass will need mowing all winter.

WATERING

Keep areas recently seeded or sodded watered if November runs dry.

FERTILIZING

Fertilizing is over for the year.

PESTS

Weeds, pests, and disease should be hibernating; you're on vacation!

DECEMBER
Lawns

 PLANNING

The giving time is near; draw up a lawn wish list.

 PLANTING

Planting season is over. If you must repair a gash, use sod.

 CARE

If you have a gas powered lawn mower, run it until the tank is dry. Drain and replace the oil. Clean the air filter. Oil the spark plugs. Clean and store the engine. Rinse the spreader. Oil the wheels and put it away.

Shovel snow away before spreading de-icing products, and you will use less. Use snowmelt products safe for concrete and safe for grass and plants. Even better, use sand or non-clumping kitty litter.

 MOWING

Zoysia lawns overseeded with rye grass may need mowing all winter.

About Lawn Mowers

A lawn that is more than a half-acre calls for a gas or electric powered mower. The blades have to be of good enough quality to hold an edge because dull blades harm the grass. Electric mowers are lighter and quiet, but suited only to smaller lawns; the farther you drag the cord, the lower the voltage, the slower the mower. Battery powered electric mowers are heavier, but not limited by the length of the cord. Riding mowers make sense if the lawn is over an acre. If you have several acres to maintain, make it a tractor mower that can till, scoop snow, and pull large loads.

Reel mower. A reel mower cuts with a scissor-like action and does the best job when the blades are sharp, and set at the height right for the grass. Otherwise it tears and mashes the leaves and causes the tips to brown. This is a good choice for a lawn that is level and cut regularly. The cost and maintenance may be higher than a rotary mower.

Rotary mower. A flat circular blade rotating very quickly lops off the grass. The machine is easily maneuvered and does a fine job if the blades are sharpened regularly. If the blades aren't sharp, the lawn next day may look scorched or singed. Also, the whirling blades can be dangerous, so allow only adults wearing closed-toe shoes to operate it.

Mulching mower. A mower built for mulching has four blades rather than two, and recuts the grass as it moves, leaving behind very fine clippings that decompose and feed the lawn. It also grinds dry leaves finely in the fall. To work most efficiently, it must move slowly, and the turf must be dry.

 WATERING

Hose season is over. Drain and store the hose before freezing weather.

 FERTILIZING

Organic fertilizer. An optional third application can be made this month or next if you find your lawn can use extra help.

PESTS

They're waiting for spring. Happy holidays!

CHAPTER SIX

Perennials

To have a beautiful perennial garden, buy good stock, and put the right plant in the right place.

Some need light, some shade. A few do best in well-drained soil, but there are also bog lovers. Most need slightly acid soil—some prefer slightly alkaline soil. Some take more cold than others. Information is widely available in mail-order catalogs and in books like our new books on perennials and in the *Gardener's Guide to the Mid-Atlantic*.

The most beautiful perennial gardens include:

1 Flowers that bloom in each season—spring, summer, and early fall.

2 Foliage plants for color and for diversity.

3 A few small evergreens to anchor the composition and keep it green in winter.

4 Perennials with large distinctive leaves.

5 Tall sculptural perennials, including ornamental grasses (see Chapter 10) and ferns that add structure to the composition.

6 Tropicals for accent.

To be everything you want it to be, choose perennials that:

1 Survive the extremes of winter and summer temperatures in your garden.

2 Will do well in the light your garden can give them.

3 Will peak when they will do most for your garden design.

4 Will be resistant to pests and diseases.

What all the perennials have in common is similar and quite simple maintenance requirements:

1 Before growth begins in late winter and early spring, clean up the beds. Fertilize and refurbish the soil. Repeat in fall.

2 Don't let the soil go dry, and keep a year-round mulch to protect plant roots.

3 Deadhead and groom the plants during the growing season, and every few years divide the crowns, to keep plants producing and healthy.

4 Control the problems described in the section on pests and diseases.

COLD AND HEAT HARDINESS

A perennial's rating for cold and heat tolerance is the first consideration when you are making choices. Check it carefully; don't assume all varieties or cultivars of the same species have the same tolerance for cold and heat because tolerance differs.

Also, whether the flowers are single or double and a variety that blooms early, mid-season, or late should be taken into consideration in relation to cold and heat tolerance. Single early varieties have time to develop fully before heat strikes, and that's useful information for gardeners in the Tidewater and warm areas of Virginia interested in growing perennials hardy further north.

Take **peonies,** for example. They are rated okay for Zones 3 to 8. They bloom early because they like it cool, and indeed must have a chilling period at below 40 degrees Fahrenheit to flower. All varieties of peonies—early, mid-season, and late, single and double—bloom fully in spring in our Zone 6 (and north). In Zone 7, the early and mid-season varieties bloom but fade

Perennials

quickly when the weather heats up. In Zone 8, only peony varieties advertised as early and mid-season are likely to have time to open fully before heat spoils them. Late peonies and the big semi-doubles and doubles often don't make it.

At the other extreme, heat tolerance is so meaningful for daylilies that they are grouped into categories for north and for south. There are many more rebloomers listed among **daylilies** and **tall bearded iris** for the south than for the north. Rebloomers usually flower a second time in late summer or fall, though some rebloom immediately after the initial flowering period, prolonging the display.

If late spring frost is common in your area, choose late-blooming varieties of spring-flowering species. To foil frosts that come early in fall, choose early-blooming varieties of perennials that bloom in late summer.

To sum up: before buying a perennial for your garden, make sure it tolerates the cold and heat in your area, and consider how its form, single or double, and its season of peak bloom will improve your plan.

LIGHT

Most flowering perennials need full sun to flower completely unless they are described as plants for semi-shade or shade. In Zone 6, plants growing in full sun may be able to stand colder temperatures. In warm Zones 7 and 8, protection at noon—a trellis, the dappled shade of tall trees—may be needed.

Full sun means at least six hours of direct, full sun, especially the strong sun between 10 am and 4 pm.

Light or bright shade calls for four to six hours of direct—preferably morning—sun or bright dappled light all day.

Semi-shade can be two to three hours of direct—preferably morning—sun a day or bright dappled shade all day, such as the high shade of a tall tree.

A southern exposure provides the most light and in general is warmer, and that's good in Zone 6. **A western exposure** gets more afternoon sun than gardens facing east. That's not good in the warmer reaches of Zone 8 as the afternoon sun tends to be hotter. **An eastern exposure** gets the rising and noon sun, and that's best everywhere, especially in Zone 8. **A northern exposure** is cooler and doesn't dry out as quickly since it receives the least direct sunlight—not our first choice.

If you are in Zones 7 and 8, early morning sun is more beneficial than hot late afternoon sun for shade plants. In the Tidewater and the warmest spots in Zone 7, Washington, DC, for example,

shade-tolerant varieties benefit from protection at noon. The shade provided by lathing, a tall hedge, or a vine arbor will keep a shade plant safe. The plants can stand more noon sun when they are growing in humusy moist soil, and when you maintain a 2- to 3-inch layer of mulch over the roots in summer.

WHEN WILL IT BLOOM/COLOR/PEAK?

Most perennials come into bloom for the first time their second season and grow fuller each year thereafter until they reach a point where they need dividing (see below).

A few perennials will bloom the first year from seed you sow directly in the garden, but most start to flower only the second year. To be sure of a nice show of flowers the first season, buy a **big container-grown** root division or second-year seedling. Generally speaking, the larger the crown (and container and price) the fuller will be the floral display that year. If the perennial that you are interested in blooms in early or mid-spring—**columbine,** for example—you'll get more flowers the first spring if you set out a container-grown specimen in early fall than if you plant it in early spring.

Some catalogs ship perennials in spring "bare root," with planting instructions—**astilbes,** for instance. In

Perennials

my experience, these often flower fully only in the second season.

But when you need lots of a particular perennial—**catmint** for edging a big bed, for example—seeds are the way to go. But while annuals usually germinate within twenty days, most perennial seeds need more time. You can start seeds in flats indoors or in a cold frame. Perennials can also be started from seed sown in the garden, either in spring two weeks after the last frost date, or in summer up to two months before the first frost date. When fall sowing is recommended on a seed packet, it means those seeds will benefit from a chilling period. They can be sown in October and November and will germinate in the spring. The process, called "stratification," is described under Planting in the November pages of this chapter.

Planting

Soil for Perennials. The "good garden loam" perennials thrive in is more often created than inherited. Humus, the spongy remains of decomposed leaves, peat moss, and other organics, holds moisture and nutrients. Humus is the great modifier of both sandy and clay soils, but it's not a permanent fixture. As plants grow, they deplete the organic content of the soil, and it loses its capacity to hold moisture and nutrients.

The solution to assorted soil problems, including poor drainage, is to grow perennials in raised beds and in soil that has been improved and enriched with organic additives as recommended in the Introduction to the book. You will find information about adjusting soil pH, additives for soil, and creating raised beds under Soil Preparation and Improvement.

In addition to starting with the right soil, it is essential to follow an annual and continuing fertilization and maintenance program for the soil.

Planting Procedures and Techniques. Whether you are planting in the soft soil of a new raised bed, or preparing a planting hole in an established perennial border, make the hole three times the diameter of the rootball, and twice as deep.

If you are preparing a planting hole in an established bed, test and amend the soil pH as described in the Introduction's information for preparing a raised bed, and then mix in 3 to 4 inches of humus, enough so that a quarter of the soil is organic matter. Mix in a slow-release organic fertilizer, half fill the hole with the amended soil, and tamp it down firmly.

Free the plant from matted roots circling the rootball. If you can't untangle them, make four shallow vertical slashes in the root mass and slice off the bottom half inch. Dip the rootball in a bucket containing starter solution. Half fill the hole with improved soil. Set the plant a little high in the hole. Fill the hole with improved soil, and tamp firmly. Water slowly and deeply, and then apply a 2- to 3-inch layer of mulch starting 3 inches from the crown.

The spacing for perennials depends on what size the mature plant will be. Front of the border plants under a foot tall need 12 to 18 inches all around. Intermediate sizes 1 to 1½ feet tall—which is most perennials—need 18 to 24 inches between plants. Larger plants need be set about 3 feet apart. **Hostas** and **daylilies** need 24 to 30 inches. **Peonies** need 3 to 4 feet. Cool climate gardeners find that close planting shades out weeds. Where warm, muggy summers encourage diseases, it's better to space each plant so it has plenty of air all around.

Fertilizing and Fertilizers

Fertilizing. To sustain growth and satisfying bloom, your perennials need a continuous supply of nutrients. The fertilization schedule for established beds begins in late winter or early spring. After that how often you fertilize depends on the type of fertilizer you are using.

Perennials

But before that first annual fertilization, check the pH of the soil. Soil-testing kits are generally available in gardening stores as are the products you need to adjust the pH. To raise the pH of soils whose pH is too low, we mix in 5 to 10 pounds of limestone per 100 square feet of garden bed. To lower pH that is too high, we apply elemental fertilizer sulfur (water-soluble garden sulfur) at the rate of 5 to 10 pounds per 100 square feet. Other acidifiers are aluminum sulfate and iron sulfate; they act faster but do not last as long in the soil.

In addition to an annual check of the pH, André recommends an annual application of Rich Earth humate. And, every three to five years, add applications of phosphate, green sand, and gypsum, the granular soil additives he recommends when you are preparing a new planting bed. Just measure the products into a bucket, and with your fingers scratch them into the soil surface a quarter inch deep.

Generally speaking, the first application of fertilizer is before growth begins in spring, and the last application is as growth slows at the end of the growing season. When plants slow down in high heat, don't try to force growth by pruning, watering, or fertilizing with chemical fertilizers. Shutting down is the plants' way to protect themselves from extremes of weather.

The growing season slows in Zones 6 and 7 early September to early October. In Zone 8, Richmond and the Tidewater areas of Virginia, the last fertilization can be between the end of September and mid-October.

Fertilizers. If you are using **organic fertilizers,** you will need to fertilize the first time about four to six weeks before growth is due to begin in spring, and then again toward the end of the growing season.

If you are using **time- or controlled-release chemical fertilizers** then you will need to fertilize just before the plants start to grow and to repeat according to the formulation inscribed on the fertilizer container. If you use a nine-month formula, that should carry you through the whole growing season.

If you are using only **chemical fertilizers,** such as 5-10-5, which are quickly available to the plants, then you will need to fertilize just before growth begins in spring, and repeat every six weeks from then until the end of the growing season.

PRUNING, SHEARING, AND DEADHEADING

You can improve the performance, and the health of some perennials, by selective pruning, shearing, and deadheading. Our suggestions on when to do it and which plants to do it to appear in the month-by-month pages that follow.

Pruning or shearing some perennials early in their growth cycles keeps the plants compact and encourages later and more, though usually smaller, blooms.

Removing fading and dead blooms—deadheading—from branching perennials stops the development of seeds, and stimulates the production of flowers. Starting in June, André goes through his six acres of gardens with hand-held head shears and deadheads spent flowers. It takes him about an hour to do the whole garden. There usually is not a lot to deadhead at any one time.

Shearing is the way to deadhead plants with very small flowers—**creeping phlox, miniature pinks, baby's-breath,** for example. For those of us who are less expert than André at wielding shears, the quick and easy way to deadhead larger blooms is by pinching them out. Just place your thumbnail and forefinger in back of the bracts—the small scale-like leaves behind the petals—and squeeze the flower head off. When the flower stems are too thick to pinch out, snip them off with small pruning shears sold for the purpose, or with nail scissors.

Perennials

Pruning and shearing also helps the health of plants attacked by leafminer and mildew. Cut the diseased stems back to the ground, and dispose of the foliage in the garbage. The new foliage should grow in clean.

WATERING AND MULCHING

Watering. Sustained soil moisture makes the nutrients in the soil available as well as water, and is essential to the growth and health of all the herbaceous perennials. Your zone and the condition of your soil will determine how often you need to water. Common sense—and the soil—will tell you that sandy soils need more frequent watering than clay soils. However, if you let clay soil bake dry, it will take forever to get it moist again. The soil in windy situations dries out more quickly.

André's rule of thumb for newly-planted perennials is to put down 1½ inches of water right after planting. Established flower beds need 1½ inches of gentle rain every ten days to two weeks; if the sky fails, run your sprinkler or irrigation system long enough to lay down 1½ inches of water. Set an empty 1-pound coffee tin under your sprinkler, and record how long it takes to accumulate 1½ inches of water so you'll know for the future.

Winter moisture leaves the earth in March in Zones 6 and 7, earlier in the Tidewater. From late winter on there's usually enough rain to keep gardens growing through June. Summer storms drench our gardens in July, but the unrelenting summer heat in Zones 7 and 8 often causes perennials to wilt at mid-day, and some stop growing. Though that doesn't necessarily mean they are out of water, André recommends overhead watering any time your perennials are wilting. Late July and August is drought season in the Mid-Atlantic, and you will probably need to water two or three times before the fall rains arrive in September.

Even in the muggiest Mid-Atlantic regions, overhead watering is fine as long as you water deeply. However, there's less waste when you water before the sun reaches the garden in the early morning, and in late afternoon or early evening. Most commercial nurseryowners, general gardeners, and farmers use overhead watering systems. During very hot, dry periods, watering during the day is a good idea because it lowers leaf temperatures and reduces transpiration and stress on the plants. Evening watering is fine, contrary to popular opinion; dew naturally wets foliage every clear night anyway.

André does not recommend electrically-timed mechanical watering systems that ignore the weather

and water too often and shallowly. However, they can do a good job if they are set up with the correct low-gallon nozzles, and timed to run long enough to water and gently and deeply every week or ten days.

One of the most important preparations for winter is a deep and thorough watering before the soil freezes; if the sky doesn't provide the rain, you will have to.

Mulching. André recommends keeping a 2- to 3-inch layer of mulch around perennials. A mulch deeper than 3 inches can bury the crown and kill some perennials. (See Mulching in the Introduction to the book.) Start the mulch a few inches from the crown, and spread it out over an area wider than the plant's diameter. That is enough to minimize the loss of soil moisture—saving water and the time applying it—and to moderate soil temperatures.

We replenish mulch after the late winter/early spring fertilization; again before the high heat of summer; and a third time in fall to slow the freezing of the ground, and to keep moisture around the roots that continue to grow until the ground grows cold.

The need for a **winter mulch** depends on the severity of your climate, the hardiness of the plants, and on the exposure of the beds. In Zone 6, the

175

Perennials

main purpose of winter mulch is to keep the perennials from heaving out of the ground as the ground freezes and thaws in winter and early spring. In Zones 7 and 8, a winter mulch can save perennials that are borderline hardy during especially severe winters. Apply a winter mulch only after the ground has frozen hard, and remove it when you first spot signs of active growth in the plants.

As a winter mulch, we recommend airy organics such as straw or pine boughs. Tent the plants so thinly you can still see some of the plant and the soil through the mulch. For coastal dwellers, marsh hay and salt hay from the shore are excellent winter mulches as they are weed free, and they can be saved, covered, in a pile from year to year.

For year-round use we recommend organic mulches such as shredded bark and pine needles (which can be piled a little deeper) because they add humus and nutrients to the soil as they decompose.

Winter Care

When summer is over, we like to leave in place healthy seed-bearing perennials with woody upright structures, like **black-eyed Susans.** They're interesting in the winter, and they provide

seeds for the birds. Some self-sow and will refurnish your bed.

In the late fall, clear away dead foliage; cut it off, rather than pull it off because that may damage the crown beneath. Look before you leap; be careful not to damage burgeoning stems.

To repeat a recommendation given above, it is most important that perennials facing winter receive a deep and thorough watering before the soil freezes.

Dividing Perennials

You can help your perennials to stay healthy and productive by dividing and replanting them every few years. Division forces the crowns to grow new roots, and replanting provides an opportunity for you to refurbish the soil.

A plant signals when it's time to divide by producing fewer and smaller blooms, and by growing crowded and leggy. In our long growing season, many perennials benefit from division every four to five years.

You can divide in early spring before growth begins, but the best time of year for most perennials is toward the end of the growing season—late summer, and early fall. The soil is still warm enough then to keep existing roots growing while new roots are develop-

ing. Once the ground gets cold in late fall, planting divisions—especially of **irises** and **daylilies**—makes them susceptible to heaving.

In Zone 6, André recommends dividing most perennials September 1 to September 15. In Zone 7, divide between September 1 and mid-October. In the warm Tidewater and Richmond areas of Virginia, the soil doesn't cool until after Thanksgiving, so gardeners can wait to divide until as late as November 1.

There's more than one way to divide a crown. For the gardener who wants to multiply his/her supply, the most profitable way is to lift the whole crown with a spading fork, divide it, amend and fertilize the soil, and replant the pieces. While waiting to replant, keep the divisions moist and out of the sun. This method is best for perennials that have very hard crowns.

For the method that is easiest on the gardener: with a shovel, chop through the center of the crown and dig up one half. Amend and fertilize the soil around the section that is to remain where it is; it will grow on in lively fashion. Divide and replant the other section in improved soil. We recommend this method for **peonies** and other perennials slow to recover from being moved. This method allows for reproduction without interrupting the blooming cycle of the garden.

Perennials

PESTS AND DISEASES

Insects and Diseases. Pests, such as aphids, caterpillars, beetles, and mealybugs, and diseases, such as powdery mildew, root and stem rot, rust disease, and spider mites, can afflict perennials. See Pests, Diseases, and Controls in the Appendix for complete information.

Resistance in Perennials. Many beautiful perennials that aren't commonly challenged by pests or diseases aren't necessarily labeled as resistant. In fact, when a variety is labeled as resistant, chances are that species may have problems. Choose pest and disease-resistant varieties when available. Those recommended on our plant lists are among the best.

Follow the healthy garden practices we recommend, and you will have few of the common problems that bother perennials—mildew, rust, aphids to name a few. When you spot problems, apply the controls we recommend at once. If the problem persists, try controlling it by cutting back and disposing of the foliage, and spraying the crown with one of the controls we recommend. If it still persists, remove the plant and destroy it.

Weeds. Get rid of weeds to eliminate competition for water and nutrients, to keep the air moving in the garden, to avoid the pests and diseases inherent to some perennials, and to keep the garden looking beautiful.

Especially with a perennial bed, preventing weeds from getting a start is essential. Allow a weed to go to seed, and it will produce legions in no time. Once weeds mature seeds in the middle of a crown, getting rid of them is a real pain. So get rid of every last one early in the life of a new bed, and early every year in an established bed. When they are young, you can easily rake them up. By the time they're 6 inches high you'll need a hoe. Use a swing-head hoe with a push-pull oscillating action that cuts through weeds and cultivates the soil without disturbing the mulch.

Maintaining a mulch cover is your ally in minimizing weeds. Dense planting shades out weeds when the plants fill out in summer, especially in **hosta** gardens.

Don't pull big weeds by the roots from bone dry soil—the upheaval can cost moisture. Water the garden first, and then tug on the weeds gently but firmly so as to get all of the roots up.

Compost healthy looking weeds.

Deer and Rodents. Deer love the perennials as much as we do. They prefer cultivated to wild flowers—**daylilies** and **phlox** for example—adore **tulips,** relish **lilies, white mums, 'Autumn Joy' sedum. Hostas** are deer candy, and so is **shrub althea** when it blooms in late summer. So far they are snubbing **ornamental grasses, ferns,** and perennials with dainty foliage and tiny flowers, **baby's-breath** for example.

The variety of deterrents on the market tend to keep deer away only until the deer realize these smelly sprays and flashing lights are not hazardous to their health. Dogs, electric fences, and deer fences also work . . . to a point. Your best bet is to change the deterrent regularly to keep the deer on their toes.

To keep rabbits, woodchucks, and other rodents away from your flower beds, try chemical fungicide formulations such as Thiram (Arasan) and hot pepper wax.

If you see signs of vole activity, bait the main runway with a rodenticide. See the April pages for more information about voles.

See Pests, Diseases, and Controls in the Appendix for complete information.

Perennials

Did You Know?

Basics for a Perennial Border

Here are fourteen easy-care summer-blooming perennials whose performance you can count on:

Front of the border

1 **Catmint,** *Nepeta* x *faassenii* 'Blue Wonder', for its mint-scented foliage and repeating blue blooms.

2 **Cheddar pinks** and other low-growing *Dianthus* species and hybrids, for their sweet, clove-scented mini carnations and grassy foliage.

3 Small and sprawling *Campanula* species and hybrids in blue-lavender or white.

Backed by

4 *Astilbe chinensis* 'Sprite', which is just 12 inches tall and has soft pink flower heads and ferny foliage.

5 Deep gold **black-eyed Susan** *Rudbeckia fulgida* var. *sullivanti* 'Goldsturm'.

6 Semi-evergreen *Sedum spectabile* 'Autumn Joy' for its succulent foliage and flower heads that change from early jade green to pink to rose to late rosy-rust.

Middle of the border

7 Silky flower heads of the many types and colors of **phlox,** but especially *Phlox paniculata* 'David' with its scented white flowers and mildew resistant foliage.

8 **Yarrow,** *Achillea millifolium*, for its ferny, pungent odor, foliage, and lasting flower heads in lovely subtle shades.

9 **Dwarf daylilies,** especially *Hemerocallis* 'Stella de Oro' hybrids, for their multiple blooms and cascading foliage.

10 Shrub-like *Salvia* x *sylvestris* 'May Night' for its deep blue spikes; the rosy pink variation is 'Rose Wine'.

Back of the border

11 Tall mid-border spikes of the lovely **pink hollyhock mallow,** *Malva alcea* var. *fastigiata,* and white *M. moschata* 'Alba'.

12 **Globe thistle** *Echinops ritro* 'Taplow Blue', for its beautiful, deeply cut foliage and perfectly round steel blue spiky flower heads.

13 Tall, substantial **daylilies,** *Hemerocallis* hybrids, for their magnificent trumpet-shaped flowers and cascading foliage.

14 Six-foot *Rudbeckia* 'Autumn Sun' ('Herbstonne') for its showy, sunny yellow flower heads with swept back petals.

Perennials

Common Name (*Botanical Name*)	Hardiness Zones	Bloom Time	Light	Height (Inches)
Adam's Needle (*Yucca filamentosa* 'Bright Edge')	5 to 9	Summer	Full sun	5 feet
Aster, New York Aster, New England Aster (*Aster* species and cultivars)	Most 4 to 8	August through October	Most need sun; some tolerate part shade	1 to 6 feet
Astilbe (*Astilbe* x *arendsii* and cvs.)	4 to 8	Summer	Part sun	14 to 36
Baby's-breath (*Gypsophila paniculata*)	3 to 8	June to August	Full sun	3 to 4 feet
Balloon Flower, Japanese Bellflower (*Platycodon grandiflorus* var. *mariesii*)	3 to 8	Early summer	Full sun to early fall	1 to 2 feet
Barrenwort (*Epimedium* spp. cultivars)	5 to 8	Spring	Bright shade	12 to 15
Beebalm (*Monarda* sp. and hybrids)	4 to 8	Late June through August	Sun to part shade	2 to 4 feet
Bellflower (*Campanula* sp. and hybrids)	3 to 8	Late May, early June	Sun to part shade	4 to 36
Black-eyed Susan (*Rudbeckia fulgida* 'Goldsturm')	Most 3 to 9	July through September	Sun	2 to 3 feet
Blazing Star, Spike Gayfeather (*Liatris spicata*)	Most 4 to 9	July and August	Sun	2 to 3 feet
Bleeding Heart (*Dicentra eximia*)	Most 3 to 8	April and May	Sun to part shade, shade in summer	12 to 18
Blue False Indigo, Wild Blue Indigo (*Baptisia australis*)	3 to 8	Spring	Sun	24 to 30
Bluestar (*Amsonia hubrechtii*)	6 to 9	Spring	Sun	12 to 36
Brunnera, False Forget-me-not (*Brunnera macrophylla*)	4 to 7	Spring	Sun to part shade	12 to 16
Butterfly Weed (*Asclepias tuberosa*)	3 or 4 to 9	Spring, summer	Sun to part sun	24 to 30
Candytuft (*Iberis sempervirens*)	3 to 9	Late May	Sun	8 to 12
Catmint (*Nepeta faassenii*)	3 to 9	Spring, some repeat if deadheaded	Sun to part sun	12 to 15
Chrysanthemum, Garden Mum (*Chrysanthemum* x *morifolium*)	3 to 7	August to November	Sun	1 to 3 feet
Columbine (*Aquilegia* sp. and hybrids)	3 to 8	May	Sun to part shade	1 to 3 feet
Coral Bells (*Heuchera* sp. and hybrids)	Most 3 to 8	May and June	Sun to part shade	2 feet
Cranesbill, Hardy Geranium (*Geranium* sp. and hybrids)	Most 4 to 8	May to July	Sun to part shade, or shade	6 to 24
Crocosmia (*Crocosmia* sp. and hybrids)	5 to 8	Late summer	Sun	18 to 36

Perennials

Common Name (Botanical Name)	Hardiness Zones	Bloom Time	Light	Height (Inches)
Daylily (*Hemerocallis* hybrid)	Most 4 to 9	June through September	Sun for best bloom, tolerates bright shade	1 to 4 feet
Foamflower (*Tiarella* species and cultivars)	3 to 8	Spring	Bright shade	8
Foxglove (*Digitalis* sp. and hybrids)	4 to 8	Spring to early summer	Sun to part shade	2 to 4 feet
Globe Thistle (*Echinops ritro* 'Taplow Blue')	3 to 7	Summer to early fall	Sun to part sun	2 to 4 feet
Goldenrod (*Solidago* sp. and hybrids)	4 to 9	Mid-summer to fall	Sun to part shade	2 to 4 feet
Hardy Begonia (*Begonia grandis*)	6 to 9	Late summer and fall	Part to full shade	18 to 24
Heliopsis (*Heliopsis helianthoides* hybrids)	3 to 9	Summer, fall	Sun	3 to 4 feet
Hellebore, Lenten Rose (*Helleborus orientalis*)	6 to 8	March to April	Part shade to shade	15 to 20
Hosta, Plantain Lily (*Hosta* sp. and hybrids)	3 to 8	July to September	Part shade to shade	6 to 36
Japanese Anemone (*Anemone hupehensis* var. *japonica*)	5 to 8	Summer and early fall	Sun to part shade	2 to 3 feet
Lady's Mantle (*Alchemilla mollis*)	3 to 7	Spring and early summer	Sun to part shade, or shade	1 foot
Lamb's Ear (*Stachys byzantina*)	4 to 8	All season silver-gray foliage	Sun, part shade	12
Lavender, Common Lavender (*Lavandula angustifolia*)	6 to 9	Late spring and summer	Full sun	10 to 24
Lily (*Lilium* sp. and hybrids)	4 to 8	Early to late summer, depending on species	Sun	30 to 40
Lobelia (*Lobelia* sp. and hybrids)	Most 4 to 8	Summer and fall	Part shade, sun in moist soil	2 to 4 feet
Lungwort, Bethlehem Sage (*Pulmonaria* spp. and hybrids)	4 to 8	Early to mid-spring	Part to full shade	12
Marsh Rose Mallow (*Hibiscus moscheutos*)	5 to 9	Mid-summer	Sun to bright shade	3 to 6 feet
Meadow Rue (*Thalictrum aquilegifolium*)	5 to 8	Spring	Sun	3 to 4 feet
Mist Flower, Hardy Ageratum (*Eupatorium coelestinum*)	6 to 10	Late summer, summer, early fall	Sun	24 to 36
Monkshood (*Aconitum* species)	3 to 7	Late summer and fall	Sun	2 to 3 feet
Oriental Poppy (*Papaver orientalis* and cultivars)	2 to 7	Spring, early summer	Sun	24 to 36
Peony (*Paeonia* sp. and hybrids)	4 to 8	Late May to June	Sun to part shade	2 to 3 feet

Perennials

Common Name (Botanical Name)	Hardiness Zones	Bloom Time	Light	Height (Inches)
Penstemon (*Penstemon digitalis*)	4 to 8	Summer	Sun	20 to 30
Phlox, Garden Phlox, Summer Phlox (*Phlox paniculata*)	4 to 8	July and August	Full sun	2 to 40
Pinks, Cottage Pink (*Dianthus plumarius*)	4 to 8	June and July	Sun	12 to 18
Plumbago (*Cerastostigma plumbaginoides*)	5 to 8	Late summer, fall	Sun to bright shade	10 to 14
Primrose (*Primula* x *polyantha*)	3 to 8	April to May	Part shade	6 to 12
Purple Coneflower (*Echinacea purpurea* and cultivars)	3 to 9	July to August	Sun	2 to 4 feet
Red Hot Poker Plant (*Kniphofia uvaria* and cultivars)summer	6 to 9	Late spring, early summer	Sun	18 to 36
Russian Sage (*Perovskia atriplicifolia*)	5 to 9	Summer and early fall	Full sun	To 36
Salvia (*Salvia nemerosa* 'May Night')	5 to 8	Late spring, early summer	Sun	18 to 24
Scabiosa (*Scabiosa columbaria*)	3 to 9	Mid-spring to fall	Sun, in warm regions some noon shade	12 to 18
Shasta Daisy (*Chrysanthemum* x *superbum*)	4 to 8	June and July	Sun to part shade	1 to 3 feet
Stonecrop (*Sedum* 'Autumn Joy')	3 to 8	August to October	Sun to part shade	24
Siberian Iris (*Iris sibirica* and cultivars)	3 to 8	Late spring and early summer	Sun to part sun	24 to 40
Spotted Dead Nettle (*Lamium maculatum* cultivars)	3 to 8	Spring flowers, colorful foliage	Sun to bright shade	12 to 15
Sweet Violets (*Viola odorata* and cultivars)	6 to 8	Spring	Sun or shade	6 to 10
Solomon's Seal, Variegated Japanese (*Polygonatum odoratum* 'Variegatum')	3 to 9	Spring	Shade	2 to 3 feet
Southernwood, Silver King Artemesia (*Artemesia ludoviciana* var. *albula*)	3 to 9	Late summer	Sun	18 to 24
Tickseed (*Coreopsis* group)	3 to 9	Summer	Sun	1 to 2 feet
Veronica, Speedwell (*Veronica* sp. and hybrids)	4 to 8	June and July	Sun	1 to 3 feet
Spurge (*Euphorbia epithymoides, E. dulcis, E. griffithii*)	5 to 9	Spring	Sun	15 to 18
Stoke's Aster (*Stokesia laevis* hybrids)	4 or 5 to 9	Summer, late summer	Sun	12 to 14
Yarrow (*Achillea* sp. and hybrids)	3 to 10	June to August	Full sun	1 to 4 feet

PLANNING

If you haven't yet grown **daylilies,** make a New Year's resolution to explore their potential this year. One of André's favorites, daylilies bloom July through August in the gardens surrounding the Viette home in the Shenandoah Valley, and thousands more flower in the trial fields below the Viette nursery. Large-flowered daylilies typically open one to three blossoms per stem every day; the **miniatures** open three to seven blossoms per stem every day. Daylilies thrive in clay, loam, or sandy soils, and tolerate heat, wind, cold, and seashore conditions.

Here's how to grow daylilies:

- **Planting season:** The best planting time is spring. Soak tuberous roots for two to six hours before planting; plant container-grown daylilies any time, but early spring is best.

- **Light:** Daylilies bloom most fully in full sun but do well in bright shade. In Zone 8, afternoon shade is beneficial.

- **Planting:** Prepare beds or planting holes in improved soil (see Soil Preparation and Improvement in the Introduction to the book). For fertilizer, use Plant-tone.

- **Bare root:** Fan the roots out in the planting hole, and set the crown so it is about 1 inch below the soil surface.

- **Container-grown:** Set the crown so it is about an inch above the surface of the surrounding soil.

- **Spacing**: 24 inches apart for minis, 36 inches apart for large daylilies.

- **Watering:** Water gently and thoroughly after planting. The first season, water weekly unless it rains. Water established daylilies when needed.

- **Mulch:** Spread pine needles, pine bark, or hardwood bark 2 to 3 inches deep starting 3 inches from the crown.

- **Fertilizing:** Fertilize in early spring and in fall as recommended under Fertilizing and Fertilizers in the introduction to this chapter.

PLANTING

Start seeds of fast-sprouting perennials indoors. It's a two-part project. First you sow the seeds and encourage them to germinate; then you transplant the seedlings and grow them into sturdy plants ready for their date with the garden. (See Starting Seeds Indoors under Planting in the January pages of Annuals.) Seed packets tell you whether the seeds can be started early indoors, and when.

Outdoors. This month or in early February sow seeds outdoors of perennials that need to be stratified (chilled) in order to germinate. The November pages explain stratification.

CARE

If you are without snow cover, make the rounds of your perennial beds to see if there are crowns that have been heaved. If yes, gently heel them in, and cover them with a **winter mulch** of evergreen boughs to keep the ground cold until winter ends. If there has been heaving, cover the crowns of **mums, veronica,** and other perennials whose basal foliage is showing.

Use only snowmelt products that don't harm plants, turf, and concrete.

PRUNING

Prune back ornamental grasses that are looking weather-beaten. Use shears to cut the low-growing grasses and new plantings of the big grasses back to within a few inches of the crown. When a big grass begins to mature, simplify the annual haircut by roping the leaves together with sisal twine. Tie them all the way to the top so that they end up looking like a telephone pole. Then saw the top off a few inches above the crown. If you use a chain saw (as you must when a big grass reaches full size), take care not to catch the twine in the teeth!

WATERING

Indoors. Water often enough to sustain moisture in big containers of tropical (cold tender) perennials stored indoors for the winter.

Outdoors. Water the soil of containers of hardy perennials wintering outdoors if there's neither snow nor rain. Add just enough to keep the soil from drying out.

FERTILIZING

No fertilizing this month.

PESTS

Damping off is a threat to seedlings started indoors, (described under Pests in the January pages of Annuals).

It's a fungal disease that attacks the seedlings at the base of their stems. It rots the stems so the plants fall over. A sterile growing medium and good drainage help avoid the condition. The fungicide Thiram (Arasan) is a good preventative against damping off.

Did You Know?

Soil and Water for Containers

André's recipe for soil for perennials to be grown in containers is:

$\frac{1}{4}$ good garden soil or bagged top soil
$\frac{3}{8}$ commercial soilless mix
$\frac{1}{4}$ compost
$\frac{1}{8}$ PermaTill or perlite

Add a modest application of Osmocote® slow-release fertilizer. To reduce watering chores, mix in a water-holding polymer, Soil Moist, for example. Line the bottom of the container with gravel or a piece of landscape fabric to keep the soil in.

Throughout July and August, check the soil moisture daily in small pots and baskets. On hot windy summer days, check the soil moisture in big containers every few days. When you water containers, pour it on until you see water dripping from the bottom.

You can minimize watering chores by planting in containers equipped with built-in water reservoirs or water rings that let the plant soak up the water from the bottom.

Frequent watering soon leaches the nutrients from the soil of small containers. To compensate, include a half dose of a water-soluble fertilizer every second time you water during the growing season.

Naturalize and Perennialize

The two words are not synonymous. "Naturalize" applies to a garden plant that becomes a wildflower of the region. **Annual phlox** has naturalized on the Outer Banks of North Carolina and is considered a wildflower of the region. It is not however, a native wildflower of the region. It has "naturalized."

Since there is no rule without exception, we confess the term "naturalize" is used by the industry about bulbs that "perennialize"—those that come back for four years or more. However, the term "perennialize" is correctly applied to plants that come back year after year but do not go wild.

FEBRUARY
Perennials

 PLANNING

While the cold keeps you housebound, **look through your garden catalogs for summer-flowering bulbs, tender tropicals, aromatic herbs, dwarf evergreens, and flowering trees** that can add to your pleasure in your gardens. Study your garden through the windows, and decide what to order now. It's time.

 PLANTING

Indoors. When seedlings started indoors become crowded, transplant each to an individual 3- to 4-inch pot filled with a sterile commercial potting mix. Give seedlings that will be growing indoors six weeks the best light available. An installation of grow lights burned fourteen to sixteen hours a day is helpful.

Outdoors. Early this month sow seeds outdoors of perennials that need to be stratified—chilled—in order to germinate. The November pages explain stratification.

The planting depth for seeds is usually given on the seed packet. The rule of thumb is to sow seeds at a depth about three times the seed's diameter, not its length.

The easy way to sow fine seeds evenly is to "broadcast" them, that is, sprinkle them over the bed. Cover them lightly with finely milled sphagnum moss or vermiculite. When the seedlings are up, thin them to the distance suggested by seed packets, or so that they are at least 3 to 5 inches apart.

Larger seeds are sown in "hills," groups of four to six, or three to five, equidistant from each other. Flowers for edging paths or the fronts of flower beds are usually sown in "drills," dribbled at spaced intervals along a shallow furrow. The easy way to make a furrow is to drag the edge of a rake or a hoe handle along the planting line.

 CARE

Early this month, **replenish winter mulch** of perennials that may have been heaved during freeze and thaw cycles. Protect perennials that retain green foliage during winter with evergreen boughs—for example, **garden mums, candytuft, Oriental poppies, basket-of-gold.**

Start cleaning up the perennial beds; discard, don't compost the debris, in case it harbors diseases and pests.

After the late winter fertilization described below, add enough fresh mulch to maintain a 2- to 3-inch layer. This organic blanket will stabilize soil temperature.

Check stored dahlias, and discard tubers showing mold or rot.

Use only snowmelt products that don't harm plants, turf, and concrete.

Unless the winter is exceptionally warm, it is still too early to plant dormant bare root perennials you may receive from eager beaver mail-order sources. Keep the plants in their packaging in a dark, cool, but frost-free place. You can plant in early March in Zone 8 and the Tidewater, mid-March n Richmond and Zone 7, and the end of March in Zone 6.

 PRUNING

Cut off battered **hellebore** foliage to make space for new growth and flowering. Be careful not to cut off new growth, which may already be showing.

Cut back the **ornamental grasses** before growth begins. When a big grass begins to mature, simplify the annual haircut by using sisal twine to rope the leaves together all the way to the top so that it ends up looking like a telephone pole. Then saw the top off a few inches above the crown. You can use a chain saw if you take care not to catch the twine in the teeth!

WATERING

Water transplanted seedlings started indoors when the soil is dry to the touch.

Maintain the soil moisture in containers of tropical perennials stored indoors. Water hardy perennials in containers wintering outdoors if you lack snow and rain.

 # FERTILIZING

Indoors. Do not fertilize transplanted seedlings until the appearance of two or three new leaves tells you the root system is growing again.

Every two weeks fertilize all the seedlings that will remain indoors another six weeks or more with a soluble houseplant fertilizer at half strength.

Outdoors. After your perennial beds have been cleaned up, prepare the soil for the season ahead:

- Check and adjust the soil pH.

- Apply Rich Earth humate.

- If you are using organic fertilizers, apply them four to six weeks before growth begins.

- If you are using chemical fertilizers, apply them just before growth begins.

- If you are using time-release fertilizers, wait just before growth begins apply an eight-month formulation.

Container gardens of hardy perennials. Top dress the soil by scratching in an inch or two of humus and fresh potting soil that includes a nine-month formulation of a slow-release fertilizer.

Did You Know?

Love Language of the Flowers

For the Victorians, floral valentines spoke volumes because each flower has meaning in the Language of the Flowers. The Language was invented by Persian courtiers, and its influence is present whenever a lover sends roses to a sweetheart.

- **Anemone**—abandoned
- **Bachelor's Button**—single and blessed
- **Bluebell**—faithfulness
- **Blue salvia**—thinking of you
- **Carnation** white—love
- **Carnation** red—alas for my poor heart
- **Forget-me-not**—love that is true
- **Hyacinth** white—beauty
- **Jonquil**—desiring a return of affection
- **Lily-of-the-valley**—happiness returns
- **Pansy**—my thoughts are with you
- **Peach blossom**—I am captive
- **Pink single**—love that is pure
- **Rose**—love
- **Rose** yellow—jealousy
- **Tulip**—love

PESTS

Indoors. Seedlings started indoors that are crowded, lack good drainage and air, may show symptoms of damping off, which rots stems near the soil surface. Discard affected plants, reduce watering, and increase light and fresh air. If the problem persists, mist the seedlings with a fungicide, such as Thiram (Arasan.)

Outdoors. When the forsythias come into bloom, apply a pre-emergent weed killer to the beds of perennials.

MARCH
Perennials

PLANNING

Take advantage of sales this month of fertilizers and other soil additives. But be cautious—these may be leftovers. If the price is a steal, make sure the bag is unbroken. Moisture that gets into bags of coco hulls encourages mildew.

The first of the plants you've ordered will arrive soon; go to the garden and reserve the space meant for them. Take along a set of row markers on which you have written the names of the plants you will be setting out. Outline planting bays reserved for annuals, and plant row markers indicating the flowers you plant to put there.

Clean the birdhouses. Put out new ones. If mosquitoes are a problem, consider installing houses for purple martins and also for bats.

PLANTING

In Zone 8, gardeners can start dahlia tubers right in the garden any time in mid-spring. They can survive winters in the ground if they are heavily mulched.

In Zone 6 and 7 we start dahlias indoors in March or April, set them out in the garden in May or June, and lift and store them indoors in September or October.

Dahlia tubers sold in spring are ready to plant. The tubers of dahlias lifted from the garden last fall and wintered indoors must be separated from the stem before planting. With each tuber be sure to include a portion of the stem that has a growth bud attached. For information on starting dahlia tubers indoors, see March in the chapter on Bulbs.

Store dormant bare root perennials received from too-eager mail-order suppliers in their packaging in a dark, cool but frost-free place until time to plant; that is early in March for Zone 8 and the Tidewater, mid-March for Richmond and Zone 7, and the end of March for Zone 6 gardeners.

CARE

As new growth appears in your perennial borders, finish clearing away dead plant material and complete the fertilization of the beds. See Fertilizing in the February pages of this chapter.

PRUNING

Indoors. Pinch out the growing tips of seedlings that are becoming leggy.

Outdoors. Hellebores in a woodsy setting will multiply if you let them go to seed.

Cut back **Russian sage** leaving just 6 to 12 inches of woody stem. Pinch out the tips of the new growth when it emerges to encourage bushier growth.

WATERING

Indoors. Continue watering seedlings planted indoors in January. Water the soil in containers of tropical perennials wintering indoors. Add just enough to keep the soil from drying out.

Outdoors. If there's not much rain, water hardy perennials wintering in containers outdoors.

As new growth appears in your perennial borders, finish clearing away dead plant material and complete the fertilization of the beds.

FERTILIZING

When to fertilize depends on the type of fertilizer you are using. The section on Understanding Fertilizers in the Introduction to the book explains how and when to use the various categories of fertilizer.

If you did not fertilize the garden last month, do it now. See Fertilizing in the February pages. Be sure to fertilize the soil of containers of tender and hardy perennials by scratching in an inch or two of humus and fresh potting soil that includes a nine-month formulation of a slow-release fertilizer.

Most **ornamental grasses** need annual fertilization. The time for it is when signs of new growth appear. Apply a slow-release organic fertilizer such as Holly-tone Espoma Organic lawn food.

PESTS

If your **peonies** were affected by botrytis last year—ugly blackened patches on the stews and foliage—spray emerging peony tips with Mancozeb or Manzate, fungicides.

Did You Know?

About Astilbes

Astilbes are among the loveliest—and most useful—of all shade-loving perennials. In late spring and early summer the plants raise graceful plumes in mostly pastel shades. The deeply-cut fernlike foliage is green or bronzed, attractive both before and after flowering.

Astilbes are excellent fillers for the middle or back of the border and perfect for edging a woodland path, a stream, or a pond. You can achieve a lasting show by planting early, mid-season, and late bloomers. For instance: plant the white early-blooming favorite **'Deutschland,'** red **'Fanal',** and pink **'Europa'** with mid-season **'Ostrich Plume'** (**'Straussenfedder'),** and late bloomers such as the lilac **'Superba'** and little **'Pumila'.**

'Pumila', a variety of *A. chinensis*, spreads by underground runners. The others spread by clump enlargement, and in time make large, dense mats. Catalogs ship bare-root astilbe crowns in early spring. Follow their planting instructions, and be patient. For a quick show, set out container-grown astilbes from early spring to late summer. Astilbe grows best in light shade in well-drained, rich, moist humusy soil. Summer drought and winter wetness are their worst enemies. Except for voles, which love them. For vole controls, see April in this chapter.

Slugs and snails haven't surfaced yet, but if winter has been warm and moist, they may be preparing an unwelcome appearance. Diatomaceous earth, a natural control, works in dry soil but isn't effective on moist soil. Instead, do them in with iron phosphate (Sluggo), slug and snail bait, and traps. You can make your own slug trap by pouring a little beer in shallow aluminum plates or empty tuna fish cans.

Deer sometimes graze the tender young leaves of **daylilies.** If you've run into this in the past, spray the foliage as it emerges with Deer-Off or some other evil-smelling liquid to keep them away while the plants grow up. If that has failed other years, lay chickenwire loosely over the tops. You can remove it when the tender leaves begin grow up and get tough.

APRIL
Perennials

PLANNING

Use your garden log to record dates your perennials bloomed to help plan your garden next year.

PLANTING

Indoors. Transplant seedlings started indoors that are outgrowing their containers to larger pots.

Outdoors. Plant as soon as possible your mail-order deliveries of bare root and container perennials. Here's how:

1 Remove the wrapping, and clear away the moist packing materials. Soak the roots as directed by the supplier.

2 Dig a roomy planting hole large enough to accommodate the roots spread out to their fullest extent.

3 Improve the soil from the hole with the amendments recommended in the introduction to the book under Soil Preparation and Improvement.

4 Build a firm cone of soil in the center of the hole. Make it high enough to place the crown of the plant a half inch or so higher than the level of the surrounding ground.

5 Center the roots over the cone, and spread them out into the hole.

6 Half fill the hole with improved soil, and tamp it down. Fill the rest of the way, and tamp that down.

7 Create a saucer around the crown.

8 Water the planting slowly, gently, and thoroughly.

9 Apply mulch 2 to 3 inches deep starting 2 to 3 inches or so from the crown of the plant.

CARE

You can divide four- to six-year old perennials that are losing productivity before spring growth begins. Fast-growing perennials—**asters,** *Eupatorium, Helianthus, Heliopsis, Monarda*—are likely candidates. For how-to information, turn back to the section titled Dividing in the introduction to this chapter.

In late April, lift and divide the roots of last year's **garden mums.** Discard the old centers, and plant the young roots in new places. You'll get a better show than you will if you leave them in same place for years on end.

When temperatures reach 60 degrees Fahrenheit, move containers of tropical perennials outdoors for the summer. Move containers of hardy perennials wintering in protected spots to their summer locations.

PRUNING

Indoors. Pinch out the tips of leggy seedlings growing indoors.

Outdoors. Experiment with pinching back by half an inch or so branching perennials to encourage shorter, bushier growth, and more (though smaller) flowers. Perennials that benefit from this include **pink turtlehead,** *Veronica spicata,* and **'Autumn Joy' sedum.**

Remove old tired-looking stems from the **hellebores,** but allow the flowers to remain as the seeds will drop to the ground and germinate; in May, look for seedlings at the base of the plants, and transplant them to a humusy semi-shaded site.

WATERING

Outdoors. Seeds and seedlings in the garden, and perennials in containers, need rain often enough to maintain soil moisture. If spring runs dry, or if you see signs of wilting, water deeply.

Seeds and seedlings in the garden, and perennials in containers, need rain often enough to maintain soil moisture. If spring runs dry, or if you see signs of wilting, water deeply.

Did You Know?

About Moles and Voles

You think "moles" when you see tunnels heaving the lawn, and blame them when perennials disappear and bulbs move around. But they are innocent. Moles eat bugs, grubs, and worms only. The culprits are voles, *Nicrotus* species. Often called pine and meadow mice, these small rodents are reddish-brown to gray, 2 to 4 inches long, and have short tails, blunt faces, tiny eyes and ears. They live in extensive tunnel systems usually less than a foot deep with entrances an inch or two across.

Protecting the plant is easier than getting rid of voles. They dislike tunneling through coarse material. André keeps them away by planting with VoleBloc or PermaTill, which are bits of non-toxic, light, long-lasting aggregates like pea gravel with jagged edges. The stuff promotes rooting.

Established plantings: Dig a 4-inch wide, 12-inch deep moat around the drip line of perennials under attack, and fill it with VoleBloc, and mulch with VoleBloc.

New plantings: Prepare a planting hole 2 inches deeper than the rootball(s), and layer in 2 inches of VoleBloc. Set the rootball in place, and backfill with VoleBloc. Mulch with more VoleBloc.

If vole damage appears in winter:

- Bait the main area around the plants with a rodenticide.
- Pull the mulch apart, spray the crown lightly with a repellent, and put the mulch back in place.

 FERTILIZING

If you are using only chemical fertilizers which are quickly available, such as 5-10-5, then you will need to fertilize garden and container plants every six weeks from beginning to end of the growing season.

 PESTS

Hoe and rake weeds away now, particularly around perennials towards the back of the border where they won't be as easy to spot when the garden fills out.

Weed **lily-of-the-valley** beds when the flowers are in full bloom—that way you get to breathe in their exquisite perfume.

Watch out for aphids on the growing tips of **mums, coreopsis, sedum,** and **verbena.** Blow them off with a strong spray from the garden hose. Or remove the infested tips, and discard them.

The ants that crawl over **peony** buds are harmless; let them be.

When the **hostas** break ground, watch out for slugs and snails (see Pests, March). If traces of leafminers appear on **columbine** foliage, remove and discard the leaves. If the condition persists, when the plants finish blooming, cut the foliage to the ground. It will regrow free of miners and be beautiful all summer. If leafminers are a continuing problem, replace your plants with *Aquilegia canadensis,* which is more resistant.

Blackened patches on **peonies** is Botrytis, a fungal disease. Immediately remove and destroy every affected part of the plant, and apply Mancozeb or Manzate, a fungicide. Make a note in your garden log for next March to spray peony tips when they first appear.

MAY
Perennials

 PLANNING

In our long growing season, **many perennials benefit from division every four to five years.** The signal it's time to divide is fewer and smaller blooms, a crown that is crowded, and stems that are leggy.

You can divide perennials that need help any time before growth begins in the spring. But for most, the best time of year for dividing is toward the end of the growing season, late summer and early fall. Keep an eye on the productivity of the older perennials in your garden, and plan to divide those that need it this fall.

 PLANTING

Try to get all your new perennials into the ground before the heat starts. For how-to information, turn to the section on Planting Procedures in the Introduction.

Replace perennials that aren't performing with big container-grown plants that will bloom this year.

Set **tropicals** growing in containers outdoors now, and transplant **dahlias** started indoors to the garden.

Move seedlings of perennials started indoors out to a sheltered corner to harden them off in preparation for planting them in the open garden.

As the spring-flowering bulbs in your perennial borders go out of bloom, replant the area with big seedlings of colorful annuals and aromatic herbs.

 CARE

Prepare sturdy stakes tall enough to support the upper third of your taller tall plants, **delphiniums,** for example, and the big **dahlias,** that will grow to end up between 18 inches and 4 feet. Insert the stakes deep into the soil 2 inches away from the crowns. Firm the plants in their holes, and water them. When the stems are 12 inches tall, tie the main stems to stakes. Tie on other branches as the plant grows up.

 PRUNING

Thin the seedlings of perennials sown out in the garden.

As the new growth of **cheddar pinks** and **creeping phlox** reaches a height of 4 to 6 inches, shear it back by an inch or so to encourage bushiness.

This doesn't work to **evergreen candytuft;** shear the plant immediately after blooming to encourage bushiness.

When the new shoots of common **phlox** are 8 to 10 inches high, remove all but four or five stems; this will result in bigger and better flowers, and, more important, will keep air circulating through the stems and help prevent powdery mildew.

 WATERING

This month begin bi-weekly checks of the moisture in large plant containers; check the moisture level in small pots and hanging baskets every day or two.

Maintain the moisture in newly planted seeds and seedlings. Unchecked growth is essential to the development of root systems so they'll be strong enough to bloom and withstand summer heat. If you do not have a good soaking rain every week to ten days, water planted beds gently and slowly long enough to lay down 1 or 2 inches.

Water seedlings that show signs of wilting.

Unchecked growth is essential to the development of root systems. If you do not have a good soaking rain every week to ten days, water planted beds gently and slowly long enough to lay down 1 or 2 inches.

 FERTILIZING

If you are using only chemical fertilizers, such as 5-10-5, which are quickly available to the plants, then you will need to fertilize garden and container plants every six weeks from beginning to end of the growing season.

 PESTS

Weeds are flourishing; scuffle and rake or hoe them away, every last one. Get those in the middle and back of the border before they disappear begin a screen of foliage.

Use the hose to blow away aphids, and to deter spider mites and whiteflies, which are especially fond of **coneflowers, daylilies, mums,** and **phlox.**

Early spraying with fungicidal formulations of copper will help to save susceptible perennials from **blackspot, powdery mildew, rusts, and bacterial diseases such as bacterial leaf spots and wilt.**

Did You Know?

Perennials in Containers

You can outwit limitations imposed by light, wind, and some pests by planting in containers. Deer bait like the beautiful, perfumed '**Casa Blanca' lily** is safer in pots on your terrace than in the open garden.

Light. Set planters too big to move where they will receive some sun on all sides over the course of a day. Turn often those small enough to move easily so all sides receive some direct sun; that keeps the plant upright and growing evenly. Plant saucers and containers equipped with casters make it easy to move a container garden around to take advantage of the shifting light.

Containers. Hardy perennials can survive Zones 6 and 7 winters outdoors in containers as long as they are in enough soil to buffer the cold. In these zones the minimum size is 14 to 16 inches wide and deep. In warmer zones the containers can be somewhat smaller. Grow perennials not quite hardy enough for your climate in big tubs, and move them for the winter to a frost-free shed or garage. **Tropical perennials** and **dahlias** for example, winter successfully in big containers in an unheated greenhouse or a garage attached to the house.

Insulation. Wrap the interior of containers that will remain outdoors for the winter with a double row of large bubble wrap before filling them with soil. You can also pack bags of leaves around them to keep the cold out.

Scribbled tracings on **columbine** foliage is a sign of leafminer; when the flowers have finished blooming, cut the foliage to the ground. It will regrow healthy and make a lovely green filler all summer.

If the weather has been rainy, check your **hostas** and other shaded plantings for chewed leaf edges and shiny mucous trails—signs of slugs and snails. March describes controls.

JUNE
Perennials

 ## PLANNING

Plan to sow seeds of perennials if you need quantities of edgers and ground covers like **candytuft** and **catmint,** for example, and garden staples like **shasta daisies, coneflowers,** and **coreopsis.** The seeds will be easiest to coddle sown in trays or flats kept indoors or in a cold frame. When the seedlings are 2 to 3 inches high, transplant them to an empty row in your kitchen garden, or to a sheltered spot in the flower beds. When the weather cools in September, transplant the seedlings to permanent homes in the garden.

 ## PLANTING

Plant fillers—**annuals, herbs, tender summer-flowering bulbs**—where the passing of spring-flowering bulbs leaves gaps in the flower beds. You can move bulbs whose foliage hasn't finished ripening to an out-of-the-way spot if you need their space. Wait until the flowers have faded, and then cut off the flower heads but keep the leaves. Dig the root systems carefully to avoid damaging the roots, and move the whole clump to the desired location. Allow the foliage to ripen naturally, just as it would have in its original spot.

 ## CARE

Every few weeks adjust the ties on the tall flowers you have staked.

To keep roots cool and weeds down, renew the mulch on flower beds. André uses fine grade hammermill bark and also recommends pine and hardwood bark, West Coast fir bark, cedar bark, and cypress. Coconut hulls are pretty, but they aren't best where mold is a problem. Compost and leaf mold (decomposed leaves) are beneficial mulches, but weeds and roots grow into them, and they decompose quickly in heat.

 ## PRUNING

Deadhead faded flowers at least twice a month. Removing dead blooms prevents a plant from developing seeds, and that stimulates the production of new flowers. Starting in June, André goes through his six acres of flower gardens with hand-held head shears and de-heads spent flowers and is through in about an hour. There's not a lot to dead-head at any one time.

Shear to the ground plants showing the irregular serpentine tracings of leafminers. **Columbine** is very susceptible. The new foliage should grow in clean.

To keep the plants compact and improve flowering, around June 1 (and repeat July 1) prune back **garden mums** by a third, along with **asters, baby's-breath, 'Snow Bank'** *Boltonia,* **bee balm,** *Eupatorium, Helianthus, Heliopsis,* **scabiosa.**

Shear back *Artemisia, Amsonia,* and *Baptisia* by half when they reach half their mature height. That will keep them from flopping later in the summer.

Deadhead **catmint** and other repeat bloomers to encourage a second round of flowers.

Trim back stems and shoots of perennials crowding their neighbors to maintain the definition between individual groups of perennials

 ## WATERING

Every day, check and adjust the soil moisture in small pots and baskets. On hot windy summer days, check the soil moisture in big containers of perennials, and water as needed to keep the soil nicely damp.

Deadhead faded flowers at least twice a month. Removing dead blooms prevents a plant from developing seeds, and that stimulates the production of new flowers.

If June has little rain, water the garden slowly and deeply every week to ten days. Apply 1½ inches of water as measured in a 1-pound coffee tin or rain gauge.

Maintain moisture in new plantings. Water plants wilting at noon or in late afternoon.

FERTILIZING

Every two weeks add a half dose of fertilizer to the water for small containers. Add compost or potting soil to large containers of perennials whose soil level seems to be shrinking.

If you are using only chemical fertilizers, such as 5-10-5, which are quickly available to the plants, then you will need to fertilize garden plants every six weeks from beginning to end of the growing season.

Did You Know?

Staking

Most tall perennials that are spaced properly and fertilized organically don't need staking. Weak growth is often the result of force-feeding with non-organic fertilizers. Wide spacing improves the plants' access to light and air, and that strengthens them. However, **delphiniums, lilies,** the tallest **dahlias,** and some other very big perennials usually do need staking.

When you set a new plant that needs staking—or when an established plant that will be very tall starts to grow—insert a stake as tall as the plant will be into the soil as close as you can get to the crown. Tie the main stem loosely to the stake with soft green wool raffia, cotton string, wool yarn, or strips of pantyhose. As the plant grows tie the main stem and branches on higher up.

PESTS

Watch out for aphids and mites.

Handpick Japanese beetles—they're sluggish in the cool of early morning. Drop them into soapy water, and flush them down a drain. If they multiply, spray the plants with neem, which will discourage feeding by adults. **Try placing Japanese beetle traps far from the plantings** you wish to protect, not among them. Insecticides containing neem, rotenone, or Sevin insecticide are controls.

Protect *Phlox, Monarda, Veronica,* and other plants that have shown signs of powdery mildew in the past with a mixture of 1 tablespoon baking soda, and 1 tablespoon of ultra-fine horticultural oil combined in a gallon of water.

JULY
Perennials

 PLANNING

Before your vacation, arrange to have the container plantings of perennials watered. Ease the chore by grouping the containers in a semi-shaded spot and providing each with a saucer. Investigate automatic watering systems.

 PLANTING

In Zone 8, there is still time this month to start seeds of perennials outdoors. Though most perennials need two to three years to bloom from seed, some bloom in less than a year. Some that tend to come into bloom sooner are the large-flowered **tickseed** varieties *Coreopsis grandiflora* **'Goldfink'** and **'Early Sunrise'; purple coneflower, shasta daisies, speedwell,** *Veronica spicata,* **oxeye daisy,** *Heliopsis helianthoides,* **violet sage,** *Salvia* x *superba,* and **yarrow.**

 CARE

Tie tall **dahlias** and **lilies** to the upper third of their stakes.

Replenish the mulch in the perennial beds to keep their roots cool and to maintain moisture now that the year's driest season is upon us.

Take care to check, and when needed, water seeds started indoors or in a cold frame earlier. These baby plants need your attention in July and August.

 PRUNING

Deadhead daily if you enjoy it, but anyway every two weeks, except for perennials whose seed pods you are planning to let develop.

Groom the garden, and trim back stems and shoots of perennials invading their neighbors.

To keep the plants compact and improve flowering, July 1, prune back once again by a third the **asters, baby's-breath, 'Snow Bank'** *Boltonia,* **beebalm,** *Eupatorium,* **garden mums,** *Helianthus, Heliopsis, Scabiosa.*

 WATERING

Every day, check and adjust the soil moisture in small pots and baskets. On hot windy summer days, check the soil moisture in big containers of perennials, and water as needed to keep the soil nicely damp.

If July has little rain, water the garden slowly and deeply every week to ten days. Apply 1½ inches of water measured in a 1-pound coffee tin or rain gauge.

 FERTILIZING

If you are using only chemical fertilizers, such as 5-10-5, which are quickly available to the plants, then you will need to fertilize the garden every six weeks from beginning to end of the growing season.

Frequent watering quickly leaches the nutrients from the soil in small containers, so you must fertilize to compensate. Include a half dose of a water-soluble fertilizer every second time you water.

Deadhead daily if you enjoy it, but anyway every two weeks, except for perennials whose seed pods you are planning to let develop.

Did You Know?

Pruning and Reblooming

Deadheading—removing faded and dead blooms—encourages almost all flowering perennials to bloom on. To keep the plant shapely, cut off the stem of the spent bloom just above the next node on the stem. That's where the next flowering stem will arise.

Cutting back the stems of some perennials all the way down to the crown after the first flush of bloom is the way to encourage reblooming. Some that respond to this treatment are: **Catmint,** *Campanula carpatica, Centranthus, Echinops, Chrysanthemum* **'May Queen'** and cultivars of the **shasta daisies, daylilies** that are rebloomers, **delphiniums,** *Salvia nemerosa, Scabiosa, Stokesia, Tradescantia, Verbena, Veronica,* **yarrow.**

Shearing tall fall-blooming perennials by half their height June 1 and again July 1, or no later than eight weeks before their scheduled bloom time, results in more attractive plants and better blooms. Some that benefit from this treatment are **asters, boltonia, chrysopsis, helianthus, heliopsis mums, Russian sage** *Salvia grandiflora, Saponaria officinalis.*

Shearing spring bloomers soon after they finish blooming keeps them from getting leggy and promotes fuller bloom next season. Some that benefit from this treatment are **arabis, candytuft, creeping phlox,** and **sweet alyssum.**

Deadheading and Pruning

 PESTS

Continue to control infestations of Japanese beetles, aphids, mites, and whiteflies.

Keep an eye on **asters,** *Monarda, Phlox,* **dahlias,** and other flowers susceptible to **powdery mildew.** It often starts on the older, denser foliage at the base of the plant where there is less air. If you see a smoky film forming, thin the interior growth to improve air flow. Spray all the foliage of that plant and other susceptible and nearby plants with 1 tablespoon baking soda, and 1 tablespoon of ultra-fine horticultural oil mixed well in a gallon of water. When the affected plants finish blooming, cut them back to the ground to promote clean healthy new growth. Destroy the prunings. Spray the clump and the surrounding soil with a fungicide for mildew.

Control rust by avoiding overhead watering, and dispose of infected foliage and twigs, applying an anti-transpirant every other week, or spraying with a horticultural oil, Mancozeb, manzate, or sulfur of copper.

For other controls, turn to Pests, Diseases, and Controls in the Appendix.

AUGUST
Perennials

 ## PLANNING

This month and next many garden centers keep cash coming in by staging sales that are very advantageous. They sell not only good-sized perennials at sale prices, but also many put hard goods on sale. So this is the moment to consider stocking up on flower holders, pots, and cachepots, as well as mulch, compost, wood chips for paths, tiles, and stones for hardscaping and so on.

Catch up on your garden log. Record the effect of staking taller plants and the result of cutting back **asters, boltonia,** and others that bloom in late summer and fall.

Evaluate the light reaching the flower beds. If some flowers are flopping forward, they may be short of light. Tree branches may have grown out and be casting shade on flower beds once in full sun. You can prune culprits now, the sooner the better. It takes full sun for most flowers to bloom up to their potential.

 ## PLANTING

In spite of the heat and drought, **container-grown perennials** can be planted successfully this month as long as you water them every week or so, and hose them down gently if they show signs of wilting on especially hot days.

 ## CARE

Check and adjust the stakes supporting **boltonia,** the big **dahlias, lilies, Japanese anemones,** and other very tall flowers. Tie on straggling branches, and add stakes as needed to make sure the plants can handle the full weight of the plant in bloom.

 ## PRUNING

Dahlias need deadheading and are excellent vase flowers.

Continue to deadhead and shear spent blooms of **phlox, perennial salvia, scabiosa, purple coneflower,** and other summer-flowering perennials.

Remove dead, damaged, diseased, and insect-infested stems wherever they occur.

Shear **silvermound artemisia** to keep it from collapsing in hot weather.

 ## WATERING

Every day, check and adjust the soil moisture in small pots and baskets. On hot windy summer days, check the soil moisture in big containers of perennials, and water as needed to keep the soil nicely damp.

 ## FERTILIZING

If you are using only chemical fertilizers, such as 5-10-5, which are quickly available to the plants, then you will need to fertilize garden and container plants every six weeks from beginning to end of the growing season.

Include a half dose of a water-soluble fertilizer every second time you water small containers.

Evaluate the light reaching the flower beds. If some flowers are flopping forward, they may be short of light.

Did You Know?

About Watering Perennial Beds

Climates and microclimates and the weather patterns from year to year affect the size, color, and health of perennials, their bloom time, their hardiness, and their seasonal performance. Understanding how heat and humidity affect your perennials helps you to water correctly.

- The hotter and drier the air, and the windier the weather, the more water your plants need. Don't water by rote; water when the soil feels dry.

- The sandier the soil, the more often your garden will need watering. You can offset sandy soil by incorporating plenty of humus in the soil before planting new plants.

The windier the exposure, the sooner container and plants and garden soil will dry out.

- The higher the heat, the drier the air will be, and the more likely you are to encounter spider mites infesting your plantings. Overhead watering humidifies the air and can help. Perennials growing in moist humusy soil and mulched 2 to 3 inches deep can stand considerably more heat, sun, and drought than plants without mulch.

- The wetter the season, the higher the humidity and the more likely the soil is to become waterlogged, especially in beds that don't drain well. Humidity encourages mildew, rust, and other negative conditions.

The first line of defense against disease in areas of high heat and humidity is to plant perennials advertised as disease resistant. Equally important is to provide your plants with very well-drained soil, a must for most perennials. Uncrowded, well-spaced plants have better drainage and good air circulation. The solution to finding the right spot where you want to put your perennials is to create a raised bed as described in the Introduction.

 PESTS

High humidity and heat encourages powdery mildew. Avoid overhead watering. Cut down to the ground plants that have finished blooming, clear all fallen foliage, discard the mulch under the plants, and replace it with fresh mulch.

Apply sulfur, ultrafine horticultural oil, copper fungicide, Immunox, or Bayleton to those afflicted plants that are not yet finished blooming. Make a note in your garden log next season to move the affected plants farther apart to increase air circulation. Or, if the infestation was very bad, in early spring replace the

affected plants with mildew-resistant varieties.

Check for fungal leaf spot, and apply a fungicide if needed. If you see continuing signs of mites, hose the plant down regularly and spray with insecticidal soaps or ultrafine horticultural oils.

SEPTEMBER
Perennials

 ## PLANNING

This is an excellent month to plan— and start—new flower beds. Now to mid-October is ideal for planting.

The solution to assorted soil problems, including poor drainage, is to plant in raised beds whose soil that has been improved and enriched with organic additives. See Soil Preparation and Improvement and Starting a Raised Bed in the Introduction to the book.

 ## PLANTING

When rain and cool air arrive, transplant the seedlings started earlier to a nursery row, or to permanent places in the flower beds.

In Zone 6, September 1 to 15 you can divide and transplant perennials. In Zone 7, September 1 to mid-October is fine for dividing. In the warm Tidewater, the soil cools after Thanksgiving, so gardeners can divide as late as November 1. See Dividing Perennials in the introduction to this chapter.

 ## CARE

In Zones 6 and 7, after the first killing frost, prepare to lift and store **dahlia** tubers. Clear away the foliage, and then with a spading fork gently lift the crowns, and spread them out of direct sun to dry. Do not detach the tubers from the central stem. Store them in trays of cedar chips, vermiculite, sand, or peat moss in a cool dry area. Label each variety. Dig and store **canna, calla lilies, glads** in a frost-free location.

In Zone 6, when temperatures head for 60 degrees Fahrenheit, move **tropical perennials** growing in containers to a frost-free shed or garage.

Clean up, and bring indoors to good light and a cool room potted perennials that winter indoors—**geraniums, impatiens, lantana, mandevilla.** (For detailed information, turn to Houseplants, Planning on the September pages.) Keep the soil nicely damp throughout the winter.

Dividing Perennials

Move big containers of hardy perennials to sheltered locations for the winter. You can also pack bags of leaves around them to keep the cold out.

 ## PRUNING

Continue to deadhead, and shear spent blooms.

 ## WATERING

September rains should keep the garden well watered, but check, and when needed, water small pots and baskets. There should be enough rain this month for the garden and containers of hardy perennials.

Include a half dose of a water-soluble fertilizer every second time you water small containers.

 ## FERTILIZING

If you are using organic blend fertilizers, such as Holly-tone or Plant-tone, then you will need to fertilize the last time a few weeks before the end of the growing season. The growing season slows in Zones 6 and 7 early September to early October. In Zone 8, Richmond and the Tidewater areas of Virginia, the

The solution to assorted soil problems, including poor drainage, is to plant in raised beds with soil that has been improved and enriched with organic additives.

last fertilization can be between the end of September and mid-October.

If you are using only **chemical fertilizers**, such as 5-10-5, which are quickly available to the plants, then the last fertilization for garden and container plants will be six weeks before the end of the growing season.

If you are using **time-release fertilizers** in large containers and the garden, earlier applications should carry the plants through the end of the growing season.

 PESTS

I'm a firm believer in **radical weeding** this month. Edge the flower beds to keep grass from creeping in. Then scratch up the soil around clumps of perennials, and get all the weeds out. That has the added virtue of opening up the soil so fall rains can give the plants a deep watering.

If **hostas** show signs of slug or snail damage, set out traps.

Remove, and discard infected every scrap of foliage and mulch from under plants that have been attacked by insects or diseases.

Did You Know?

About Oriental Poppies

A spangle of these brilliant, beautiful blossoms lifts the spring/early summer garden from beautiful to extraordinary. Blossoms 5 to 10 inches across unfold crinkled silky petals in vibrant colors edged and splotched at the base in contrasting colors. The wiry stems bend to a whisper of wind, but withstand storms of amazing proportions. These gorgeous flowers last as cut flowers if you sear the bottom of the stem before putting it into water. The big fuzzy seedpods are great dried.

André specializes in Oriental poppies, and here are his recommendations for growing them:

1 Set out sturdy container-grown plants in early spring.

2 Plant in full sun, or bright shade. In Zone 8 they succeed under tall trees.

3 Soil with a pH 6.0 to 7.5, that is well-drained, deeply-dug, light, somewhat sandy, and humusy is ideal.

4 Set the crown about 1½ inch below the soil level, and space the plants 2 to 3 feet apart.

5 Water gently and thoroughly after planting

6 Mulch 2 to 3 inches deep starting 3 inches from the crown.

7 Maintain moisture during the growing and flowering period, but don't water when the plants go dormant in the summer. Keep the bed on the dry side.

8 Remove the big, decorative seedheads, but allow the foliage to yellow and brown before removing it.

9 When the foliage begins to regrow in the fall, fertilize with Holly-tone, 4 pounds per 100 square feet. The fleshy taproot is difficult to transplant, but Oriental poppies rarely need dividing.

PLANNING

Now that the foliage in the perennial beds is dying or has died down, **you can evaluate the plant combinations.** There's time ahead to make all things new for next year. Consider making places for colorful foliage plants and ornamental grasses. Some for up front, some for behind, but not directly behind, those up front, and some for farther back.

The silver-gray fuzz of **lamb's-ears** lightens the front of a border. Clumps of **dwarf bamboo,** *Pleioblastus fortunei*, add variety to the texture of middle rows. Variegated foliage appears light green, or gray green, at a distance. To change the texture at the back of the border, plant **verbascum,** a tall candelabra of a plant with felted, gray foliage. In shady areas, make room for colorful **hosta** varieties. The yellow-lime-green hostas are luminous, and some bluish hostas have wonderfully textured ribbed or quilted leaves.

Replace poor performers with sturdier look-alikes. **Delphiniums,** for example, that aren't doing all that well, can be replaced with **hardy agapanthus 'Bressingham Blue'** or with dwarf **balloon-flower,** *Platycodon grandiflorus* var. *mariesii* and *Aconitum,* which bear beautiful blue flowers that take more heat than

the **delphiniums.** Seed sprinkled over a well-worked planting area might still have time to germinate this fall if the temperatures stay above freezing, and make enough growth to flower next year.

 PLANTING

In Zone 7, you can divide and transplant perennials until mid-month.

In the warm Tidewater and Richmond areas of Virginia, the soil doesn't cool until after Thanksgiving, so gardeners can divide perennials up to November 1. See Dividing Perennials in the introduction to this chapter.

 CARE

In Zone 8, move hardy perennials in containers to a sheltered corner for the winter.

In Zones 6 and 7, move **tropical perennials** that are still out in the open to a frost-free shed or garage.

Clear dead leaves from the flower beds, and compost them. They may shelter pests and diseases.

Continue to root out weeds that appear in the flower beds. Dandelion seeds germinate well in compost and must be rooted out, not just chopped off at the surface because they grow from root cuttings.

 PRUNING

Cut **peonies** and **lantana** to the ground before the first frost.

 WATERING

Outdoors. The most important preparation for winter is a **deep and thorough watering** of all new, established, in-ground, and container perennials before the soil freezes. If the sky doesn't do it, then you must compensate.

Indoors. Water the soil in big containers of tropical perennials stored indoors. Add enough to keep the soil from drying out.

 FERTILIZING

In Zones 6 and 7, the growing season slows between early September and early October. In Zone 8, Richmond and the Tidewater areas of Virginia, the growing season slows between the end of September and mid-October.

If you are using fertilizers that are organic blends such as Holly-tone or Plant-tone, you should fertilize for the last time four to six weeks before the end of the growing season.

If you are using only chemical fertilizers, such as 5-10-5, which are quickly avail-

There's time ahead to make all things new for next year. Consider making places for colorful foliage plants and ornamental grasses.

Did You Know?

For Winter Interest

In winter, ornamental grasses dance with the wind, woolly betonies stand tall above fallen leaves and evergreen edgers and ground covers rimmed with ice catch the sun and sparkle—if you have planted for winter interest. Here are a few of many perennials that stand out when storms of falling leaves give way to ice-blue skies and crisp winter air.

Blue False Indigo, Wild Blue Indigo, *Baptisia australis*, maintains its seed pods and leaves in winter.

Blue Oat Grass, *Helictotrichon sempervirens*, is a small grass whose gray-blue leaves last year round.

Boltonia, *Boltonia asteroides* 'Snow Bank', has rich brown stalks and leaves in winter.

Carpet Bugle, *Ajuga reptans* 'Burgundy Glow', maintains its variegated foliage—white, pink, rose, and green.

Chinese Chives, Garlic Chives, Oriental Garlic, *Allium tuberosum*, keeps its white seedheads till spring.

Coreopsis verticillata 'Moonbeam' retains its stems in winter, an interesting, dark feathery texture in the garden.

Edging Candytuft, *Iberis sempervirens*, remains dark green most winters.

Hellebore, *Helleborus* species and cultivars, keeps its evergreen deeply divided foliage in winter.

Japanese Anemone, *Anemone* x *hybrida*, and *A. hupehensis* var. *japonica*. The lean, branching stems are covered in winter with seedheads like cotton balls.

Lilyturf, *Liriope* cultivars, is evergreen until late winter.

Russian Sage, *Perovskia atriplicifolia*, is like a huge white bird's nest all winter.

Sage, *Salvia officinalis*, the best-known culinary sage, retains its purple gray foliage.

Siberian Iris, *Iris sibirica*, has tall flowering stems that develop attractive seedpods. The grassy foliage turns rusty brown in fall.

Silver Grass, *Miscanthus sinensis*, can soar to 6 or 8 feet, and in winter is all fine foliage and flower tassels, lovely with snow at its feet.

Spiraea, Perennial Spiraea, *Astilbe* species and varieties, keep their rich brown flower stalks in winter, and are particularly handsome in the snow.

Woolly Betony, Lamb's Ears, *Stachys byzantina*, has big, semi-evergreen, gray leaves that remain in fall and winter.

Sedums 'Autumn Joy' and 'Vera Jameson', *Sedum spectabile*, retain their seedheads all winter. A new crown forms at the base preparing for next year.

---

able to the plants, then the last fertilization should be just before the end of the growing season.

If you are using time-release fertilizers, a spring application of a nine-month formulation should carry the plants through the end of the growing season—no fertilizer need be added at this time.

 PESTS

Outdoors. Apply or change whatever deer deterrents you are using. The section on Pests, Diseases, and Controls in the Appendix explains why.

If vole runs appear around shrubs, bait the main runway with a rodenticide.

Indoors. Check **tropical perennials** moved indoors for whiteflies and spider mites. If you find problems, apply the controls recommended in the Pests section in the Appendix.

NOVEMBER
Perennials

 ## PLANNING

This gray month, take the time to enlarge your horticultural knowledge. Here's the way horticulturists talk about flowers and explanations of what the words represent:

Anatomy of a Flower. Buds are enclosed in **sepals;** together they make up the **calyx.**

Petals develop next. **Calyx** and **petals** make up the **corolla;** and sometimes these come together and make a **tube** or **cup,** as with daffodils. Sepals and petals make up the **perianth. Bracts** are the leaves immediately behind the petals; they are small or scale-like leaves in most flowers, but very much larger than the flowers themselves in poinsettias.

Organs are inside the petals: The male organ is made up of **stamens,** and each stamen includes a **filament** (stalk); tipped with an **anther;** anthers form **pollen.**

Female organs are the seed-bearing **carpels;** when they fuse together in a blossom, the organ is called a **pistil.** Pistils may have three parts: an **ovary** in which seeds are formed, a slender **style,** which ends in a **stigma.** The stigma usually is either rough or sticky to hold the pollen that falls on it.

That's what fertilizes the seed.

 ## PLANTING

Some seeds are programmed to withhold germination in the fall when they can be killed by winter frosts. They will germinate only after being exposed for a specific time period in the garden—typically four to eight weeks—to winter cold and moisture. Seed packets designate these seeds as needing "stratification" to germinate and tell you for how long. You can sow the seeds now in the garden, and they will germinate in the spring.

For more control of the stratification process, you can start them in containers. Here's how that works:

1 Sow the seeds in pots or trays, as described in Starting Seedlings Indoors under Planting in the January pages of Annuals. Label and date the containers. Cover them with plastic film (plastic bags from the drycleaners for example) to keep the moisture from evaporating.

2 Keep the containers for the stratification period designated on the seed packet in an unheated garage, a shed, porch, or cold frame where they will be exposed to cold temperatures of less than 40 degrees Fahrenheit, but safe from snow, rain, and wind.

3 When the temperature climbs to between 45 and 60 degrees Fahren-

heit, the seeds will begin to germinate—each species in its own time framer. Once the seedlings pop, remove the plastic, and begin the care program for seedlings described in Starting Seedlings Indoors.

Plan to have enough large containers for each seedling so you can grow them on until outdoors planting weather arrives in May or so.

 ## CARE

In Zone 8, protect perennials that are borderline hardy with a **winter mulch** of pine boughs or straw on newly-planted and evergreen perennials.

In the warm Tidewater and Richmond areas of Virginia, the soil doesn't cool until after Thanksgiving, so gardeners can divide as late as November 1. See Dividing in the introduction to this chapter.

 ## PRUNING

If you would like your **garden mums** to perennialize, let the old stems stand as insulation for the new growth emerging at the base of the plants.

Let perennials attractive in winter remain. Even old flower stalks can be

The beds are bare now, and dandelions and other weeds that have taken root are easy to spot and uproot.

Did You Know?

Best-of-the-Best Perennials

The Perennial Plant Association (PPA) is a professional trade association dedicated to improving the industry. André Viette has served as president. Each year the PPA chooses a Plant Of The Year rated according to multiseasonal interest and low maintenance. Here are recent choices. To keep up with Plant of the Year choices to come, check out www.Perennialplant.org.

- **Astilbe,** *Astilbe chinensis* 'Sprite' 1994
- **Coral Bells,** *Heuchera* 'Palace Purple' 1991
- **Coneflower,** *Rudbeckia fulgida* var. *sullivantii* 'Goldsturm' 1999
- **Coreopsis,** *Coreopsis* 'Moonbeam' 1992
- **Creeping Phlox,** *Phlox stolonifera* 1990
- **Feather Reed Grass,** *Calamagrostis acutiflora* 'Karl Foerster' 2001
- **Japanese Painted Fern,** *Athyrium nipponicum* 'Pictum' 2004

- **Penstemon,** *Penstemon* 'Husker Red' 1996
- **Perennial Salvia,** *Salvia nemerosa* 'May Night' 1997
- **Phlox,** *Phlox* 'David' 2002
- **Purple Coneflower,** *Echinacea* 'Magnus' 1998
- **Russian Sage,** *Perovskia atriplicifolia* 1995
- **Scabiosa,** *Scabiosa columbaria* 'Butterfly Blue' 2000
- **Shasta Daisy,** *Leucanthemum* 'Becky' 2003
- **Veronica,** *Veronica* 'Sunny Border Blue 1993

interesting. Seed-bearers feed the birds, and color their architectural branches rust, or rich brown or, in the rain, sooty black. *Sedum* **'Autumn Joy'**, **Siberian iris** in its rusty winter brown, the **coreopsis** bramble, and the dry, leaves of *Allium tuberosum*, give the garden form while the earth rests.

 WATERING

If the season is dry, water container and garden plants often enough to keep the soil from drying out. Before the first anticipated hard freeze, water thoroughly.

FERTILIZING

Fertilizer is not needed now because the growing season is over.

 PESTS

If you see signs of vole activity, bait the main runway with a rodenticide. See also the April pages of this chapter.

The beds are bare now, and dandelions and other weeds that have taken root are easy to spot and uproot.

DECEMBER
Perennials

 PLANNING

Tools that make gardening easier become companions of sorts. You get attached. **Good tools are expensive and make welcome gifts.** Here's a handful—arranged in order of importance to us—that we use all the time when we work in the flower beds:

• A tool every seasoned gardener (and farmer) carries, but no one thinks of as a tool, is a little knife, a pocket knife, or a folding pruning knife, for digging up dandelions, cutting twine, impulse pruning—a thousand little jobs. It should be a size that is very comfortable in your palm, opens and closes easily, and is so well made it will last a lifetime.

• A pair of tiny shears for deadheading and harvesting flowers. Fiskars, manufacturers known for their line of pruning tools, make the little shears, and you can find the same type in shops with fabrics and sewing materials.

• For planting, the two most basic tools are a hand cultivator and a garden trowel. The fat-bellied type of trowel is the most versatile: the narrow variety incised with inches is mainly for planting bulbs. Painted trowels tend to peel. Cast aluminum is homely but light and durable; choose models whose handles are sheathed in plastic so they won't blacken your palms.

• The broad flat tines of a spading fork are the gardener's best friend when it comes to dividing perennials, loosening soil, and lifting perennials. (I am small, and I find tools designed for women easier to handle.)

• A shovel gets less use than a spading fork, but you'll need it to dig planting holes and move dirt and gravel.

• A hand rake (as opposed to a long-handled rake) for cleaning up flower beds.

• A swing-head scuffle hoe for weeding. It's a push-pull oscillating hoe with a double-edged blade that cuts through weeds on the forward and backward swing and cultivates the soil without disturbing the mulch.

 PLANTING

Seeds that need stratification can be planted this month. See Planting, in the November pages.

 CARE

Use only snowmelt products that don't harm plants, turf, and concrete.

 PRUNING

Cut back perennials that have turned to mush due to frost, and discard them. Let plants with seeds of interest to birds remain—the **coneflowers** and *Heliopsis* for example.

 WATERING

Maintain soil moisture in containers stored indoors, and also in containers of hardy perennials outdoors if there's neither snow nor rain. The roots need just enough moisture to keep the roots from drying out.

 FERTILIZING

Fertilizer is not needed now because the growing season is over.

PESTS

Before mulching your plants for the winter, remove fallen leaves and any remaining weeds.

CHAPTER SEVEN

Roses

In full bloom a rose bush rewards you with the heart-stopping beauty of its flowers. The very best have a rich perfume that makes everything else go right out of your head.

True, like other great beauties, roses can be demanding, although some are more demanding than others. Pruning is a must; fertilizing too. But when a rose's growing requirements are satisfied, it will perform in your garden beyond all expectations. You'll feel really triumphant! The right rose in the right place can do wonders for your life. Roses are easier than you think, and they thrive in the Mid-Atlantic.

COLD HARDINESS

A superb rose garden begins with plants that can stand your winters. The hardiness rating of a rose needs to be questioned. Some rose lovers are willing to take a chance on roses whose hardiness isn't certain. That's okay with a banana plant, but to throw out a rose that stopped you in your tracks one wonderful spring morning is a sadness. In general you can expect the **species roses,** a rose we haven't changed in any way, and many once-blooming **old garden roses,** to be very cold-hardy. These roses are growing on their own roots, and the roots are hardy. Of the repeat bloomers, **rugosas** are very hardy, and many **David**

Did You Know?

About Roses

The rose is America's beloved favorite national flower. Since André and Mark first began teaching classes on roses at Blue Ridge Community College, Weyers Cave, Virginia, interest in roses has shifted. Gardeners still fall in love with, and exhibit, the unforgettable **hybrid teas**. But now landscaping roses that are easier to place and to manage, and **miniature roses** are very popular. The romantic **old garden roses** also have a strong following.

The American Rose Society, All-America Rose Selections, and World Federation of Rose Societies are constantly reorganizing rose classifications—both the grading and the titles—to make understanding and remembering roses easier. The groupings on these pages are an attempt to reconcile old and new rose classifications.

Roses That Climb (CL)

Climbers (pillar roses) and **ramblers** have long canes that can be trained to grow up or sideways, and they occur in all rose categories. **Climbing roses,** and the **floribundas,** are the roses most often trained as **"standard" or "tree" roses. Climbers** are very tall roses with stiff canes. Most bear large flowers singly or in clusters. **Ramblers** bear clusters of small flowers and bloom in spring and early summer. The initials CL after a rose's name stand for "climber." For example: CFL—Climbing Floribunda; CHT—Climbing Hybrid Tea; and LCL—Large Flowered Climber.

Austins and other bush roses are, too. **Miniatures** and modern roses growing on their own roots are usually hardy in our region.

Hybrid teas and other desirable roses are "budded," a form of grafting, onto cold hardy roots not their own; there are various reasons for this, such as improved vigor, cold hardiness, and disease resistance. If the top of a budded rose dies, the understock (or hardy root) will put forth its own canes, and

Did You Know?

Large-Flowered Roses

The roses that bear show-time flowers are the modern **hybrid teas** (HT) and **grandifloras** (GR). Modern varieties bear generously in spring, throw out a few flowers in summer, and bloom well from September until severe cold. **Hybrid teas** like the famous **'Peace'** rose produce large, exquisite, high-centered double or semi-double flowers each on its own long stem. Many are very fragrant. **Grandifloras,** for example **'Queen Elizabeth',** bear bouquets of large, full-petaled flowers on long stems. The roses are upright, leggy, and 3 to 6 feet tall. Rather ungainly, they're usually given a bed of their own interplanted with bushy plants like **lavender** or **blue salvia** to mask their legginess.

Cluster-Flowered Roses

This group includes **modern bush roses (Meidilands), polyanthas (POL), English (E)** and **David Austin** roses, and the **floribundas** (FL). These are roses that bear flowers in clusters and bloom all season and are known for easy maintenance.

The **modern bush roses,** including the peachy pink AARS 1987 winner **'Bonica'** and others in the **Meidiland** family, are hybrid everblooming roses known for easy maintenance. They grow on their own roots, need little pruning and can be shaped with hedge shears.

The **English** and **David Austin** roses bear full roses 2½ to 5 inches in diameter. The bushes may be 3 but more often are 4 to 5 feet tall, compact, and easily managed.

The **polyanthas** are 2 to 3 feet tall, and bear clusters of charming little flowers under 2 inches across.

The **floribundas** (many-flowered) are large-flowered **polyanthas** 3 to 5 feet tall that bear big trusses or sprays of 2- to 5-inch roses, some shaped like hybrid teas. A favorite for hedges is **'Betty Prior',** a vivid pink with emerald foliage.

Compact and Patio Roses

These roses are compact, larger than **miniatures,** smaller than **floribundas.** They produce clusters of blossoms freely from early summer until fall. The roses are between 2 and 4 feet tall and wide-spreading. They're planted in flower beds, patio containers, as low hedges.

André's Remedy for Rose Problems

From Cornell University came this control for mildew that may also help with blackspot and some other rose problems: Apply a spray made by combining 1 tablespoon baking soda and 1 tablespoon of ultra-fine horticultural oil in a gallon of water.

these will not produce the desirable roses budded onto the roots. The label "own-root" on a rose is an indication that the rose was grown from a cutting and provides assurance that, if the top suffers in severe winters, the canes will grow back and eventually produce roses as before. Some very beautiful roses are budded, and we do plant them, but when winter hardiness is in doubt, we provide winter protection. You'll find suggestions in Winter Care for Roses, later in this introduction.

Roses

DESIGNING WITH ROSES

Roses are the quintessential flowering bushes. There's a right type of rose for every place in your garden—roses for a glorious one-time spring display; roses that fill their corner of the yard with flowers all season long; compact bushes to tuck in with the perennials; wide-spreading earth-bound roses for ground cover; climbers, miniatures for baskets, and indoors; roses whose perfume is unforgettable. They're all beautiful. For more on the uses and placement of the various categories of roses, turn to Planning on the January pages.

PLANTING

The humidity present spring and fall is kinder to new roses, but they'll succeed planted even in hot dry summer months if given adequate care. For a rose to bloom up to its potential, it must be placed where it has full sun, air all around it, well-drained top quality soil to grow in, and adequate fertilizer and water.

Roses are sold **bare root, container-grown,** and **in plantable containers.**

- Bare-root roses are available when it's time to plant them, early spring before growth begins. Follow exactly the suppliers' planting instructions.

Did You Know?

Miniature Roses

Miniature roses are exquisite little upright or trailing bushes that bear tiny roses in many colors and various forms. Some have fragrance. They flower freely all season, are quite disease-resistant and easy to grow, succeed indoors, and are great in containers.

The average miniature is about 12 inches high, and 6 to 18 inches across. The large miniatures (macro-minis) reach 2 feet; a few small minis (micro-minis), such as **'Elfin Gold'** and **'Tiny Flame'**, are only 6 inches high and bear dime-sized flowers. Miniature roses that grow upright are excellent edgers for flower beds and rose gardens. Those with trailing branches are used as basket and container plants.

Heirloom, Rugosa, and Species Roses

Old garden roses ("heirloom roses") were in culture before 1867. These are for collectors and time travelers. Many are fragrant species used then and now in perfumery. Most flower for about four weeks in early or mid-spring; a few repeat bloom.

The modern **rugosa** roses are tall stiff bushes that bear single or double flowers in spring with occasional repeats. The very spiny upright canes make fine hedges and seashore windbreaks. Many **rugosas** develop big colorful rose hips. Two famous for their flowers are silvery pink **'Frau Dagmar Hastrup'** and the lovely white **'Blanc Double de Coubert'**.

Species roses are roses as they evolved in nature, the original roses from which all modern roses were developed. These come true from seed. Some sprawl, and some are upright.

- Container-grown roses are available throughout the season, and you can plant them late February/early March through to December 1.

- Roses in plantable containers are easy to plant, but they are available only in spring and early summer.

Light. The right place for a rose is one that receives at least six hours of direct sun, and eight is better in cold areas. In warm regions, they can handle more shade. Morning light is valuable because it dries the leaves, and helps prevent disease. Shade tolerant roses, like the **floribunda 'Gruss an Aachen',** will bloom in partial light but may perform better in full. When talking roses, shade means bright, filtered shade.

Roses

Did You Know?

ARS and AARS Ratings

Two major influences on the U.S. world of roses are the non-profit American Rose Society (ARS) and All-America Rose Selections (AARS). The ratings given roses are national ratings based on how roses do nation-wide. Some do better or worse regionally than the national rating. Local rose societies and growers will know.

The ARS is an association of rosarians who rate rose introductions on a scale of 1 (worst) to 10 (best). The ratings average individual ratings given by beginners as well as experienced rose growers. They are printed yearly in the "Handbook for Selecting Roses" available from the ARS. The highest rating given even the enduringly popular roses, **'New Dawn'**, **'Double Delight'**, **'Iceberg'**, **'The Fairy'**, and **'Bonica'**, reach no higher than 8.7.

The rose gardens near ARS headquarters in Shreveport, Louisiana, are open to the public during the growing season. Their web site can help you locate local rose societies. You'll find their address in the Appendix.

The AARS is a non-profit association of rose growers and rose producers that introduces and promotes roses judged exceptional in their trial programs. They are headquartered in Chicago. The roses judged go through a two-year field trial. The AARS seal of approval has influenced rosarians since 1938.

Pruning Cuts for Roses

Where you cut—whether pruning, deadheading, or harvesting flowers—shapes the bush's future. Roses tend to send a strong lateral (sideways) cane (branch-stem) out from the node just below a cut. You can keep the center of the bush open by **making all cuts about ¼ inch** above an outward facing bud or leaf cluster. **Use sharp bypass shears.**

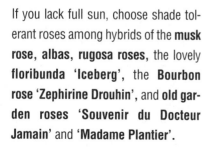
Cutting Roses

- Always cut at a diagonal, a 45-degree angle. Make the top of the cut the side the bud or leafset is on.

- When deadheading or harvesting roses, make the cut just above the first five- or seven-segment leaf below the flower or an outward facing bud. If this would cause too much of the cane to be removed, make the cut at a three-segment leaf instead.

- The first year, cut back to the first three- or five-segment leafset. In following years, cut far enough down to get to a five-segment or seven-segment leafset or bud that is facing outward. This will open up the plant.

If you lack full sun, choose shade tolerant roses among hybrids of the **musk rose, albas, rugosa roses,** the lovely floribunda **'Iceberg'**, the **Bourbon rose 'Zephirine Drouhin'**, and **old garden roses 'Souvenir du Docteur Jamain'** and **'Madame Plantier'**.

Don't plant **minis** outdoors where the summer growth of taller plants will take away their sunshine.

Miniature roses growing indoors need all the light you can give them. If they are not getting enough light, try adding spot flood grow lights. And give them an occasional vacation under fluorescent lights in a light garden.

Soil. The ideal soil for roses has good drainage, lots of water-holding humus, and is loose enough for good root growth.

Roses

The pH of soil is a very important factor with roses. They prefer a slightly acid soil with a pH factor of 5.8 to 6.8. To raise the pH, mix in 5 to 10 pounds of limestone per 100 square feet of garden bed. If the pH is too high, lower it with an application of elemental fertilizer sulfur (water-soluble garden sulfur) at the rate of 5 to 10 pounds per 100 square feet. Aluminum sulfate or iron sulfate are acidifiers that act faster but do not last as long in the soil.

The hole for a bush rose needs to be at least 24 inches deep. If your soil is less than wonderful or if you have difficulty digging deeply enough, create a **raised bed** for roses. For instructions on preparing a **new planting hole** or **bed** for roses, turn to March.

Spacing. In addition to full sun, roses need air. Be sure to give your roses enough space all around for good air circulation. The rule of thumb is: **compact roses** need to be 2 to 4 feet apart. **Climbing** and **heirloom roses** need 5 to 10 feet between them. **Miniature roses** do well with just 18 to 24 inches all around.

FERTILIZING

Roses are heavy feeders, and the soil they grow in needs regular attention. The first chore of the year is to renew the soil—early spring, late February, or early March, is about right. Here's the drill:

1 Check, and adjust the soil pH.

2 Apply Rich Earth humate.

3 Fertilize:

• If you are using an organic fertilizer, apply it four to six weeks **before** growth begins;

• If you are using a chemical fertilizer, apply it **just before** growth begins;

• If you are using a time-release fertilizer, **just before** growth begins apply an eight-month formulation.

4 Renew the mulch. This organic blanket will stabilize soil temperature and renew the humus content of the soil.

5 Every three to five years enrich the soil by applying rock phosphate, green sand, and gypsum, the granular soil additives used in preparing a bed for roses (See March.) Measure it all into a pail, and spread the stuff over the planted area. Rain will do the rest.

Did You Know?

Rose Collection for Beginners

Climbers

• Fragrant blush-pink **'New Dawn'** and **'White Dawn'**.

Flowering Carpet Rose

• Low-growing wide spreading white **'Jeeper's Creepers'**.

Hedge Roses

• Sprawling bramble with clusters of small shell pink flowers **'The Fairy'** and vibrant pink **'Betty Prior'**.

Hybrid Tea Rose

• Very fragrant red and cream blend **'Double Delight'** and coral-red **'Fragrant Cloud'**.

Miniature Rose

• Yellow **'Rise 'N Shine'**.

Roses

FERTILIZERS FOR ROSES

Roses need three primary nutrients—nitrogen for foliar growth, phosphorus for healthy roots and flower development, and potassium to maintain vigor. You can provide these essential ingredients using organic, chemical, or a timed-release (slow-release) chemicals.

In the Introduction to the book in the section titled Understanding Fertilizers there's a complete explanation of these three types of fertilizer. **When you use them** depends on the type of fertilizer you are using.

Organic blend fertilizers. Every six weeks spread Rose-tone, Plant-tone, or your favorite organic fertilizer blend over the inside perimeter of the watering basin at the rate of 10 pounds per 100 square feet.

1 Make the first application four to six weeks before growth begins;

2 Second application six weeks later, in early summer;

3 Third application six weeks later, in mid-summer;

4 Last application between early September and early October for Zones 6 and 7, and by mid-October in Zone 8.

Chemical water-soluble fertilizers. If you are using chemical fertilizers, apply these every six weeks beginning just before the roses come into bloom and ending with a final application between early September and early October in Zones 6 and 7. In Zone 8, Richmond and the Tidewater areas of Virginia, make it between the end of September and mid-October.

Time-release fertilizer. Just before growth begins, apply an eight-month formulation.

Roses that have been producing masses of blooms benefit from an occasional foliar feeding with a solution containing a liquid fertilizer. You'll find soluble organics such as fish emulsion, liquid seaweed, compost, and manure teas available at garden centers, as well as water-soluble chemical fertilizers.

PRUNING, DEADHEADING, AND HARVESTING

Roses bloom more fully when they are pruned and deadheaded.

Pruning. Roses must be pruned annually to remain shapely and stay healthy and productive. The best time is late in their dormant period before the buds begin to swell and new leaves appear—March and April. But late is better than not at all. The exception to the spring-pruning rule is one-time bloomers. They are pruned after they have finished blooming because they bear their flowers on the previous year's growth.

Prune to remove any cane thinner than a pencil and all damaged, weak, and non-productive canes. That allows the plant's energy to go into flower production and larger, healthier canes. **Hybrid teas** and **exhibition roses** are pruned hard when the goal is to encourage a few large blooms. The **cluster-flower roses** and **compact roses** are pruned lightly to encourage growth and maintain their shape. For detailed information on when and how to prune the various categories of roses, turn to February.

Deadheading and harvesting. Removing spent blooms encourages the bushes to produce. Harvesting roses for bouquets is a form of deadheading—so indulge!! If you don't, blooms that were pollinated may begin to form seed pods (hips), which takes away energy needed for growth and flower production. **Miniatures,** small **polyanthas, species,** and **carpet roses,** generally do not need deadheading.

Roses

Deadheading and pruning is over about October 1. Let the last roses on **hybrid teas** produce hips. That causes the plant to undergo chemical changes that slow growth, inhibit blooming, and generally prepare for dormancy by focusing on "hardening" the canes. The formation of hips tells the plant that it's done its job and can now rest.

Watering and Mulching

Watering. Roses need large root systems to support all that foliage and flower production. They need lots of nutrients. They get nutrients either from their leaves through foliar feeding, or through their roots. The only medium for transporting nutrients is water. Ergo, they need sustained soil moisture—you must not let the root systems run dry.

Frequent, light watering causes roots to form very near the soil surface, making the plant more susceptible to drought, heat damage, and freezing— not what you want! What roses need— what all plants need—is deep watering because that encourages the roots to grow deep into the soil. A deep root system survives dry spells and winter freezes. By "deep watering" we mean a slow, gentle, and thorough watering with a sprinkler, a soaker hose, a bubbler, or by hand. You need to put down

$1^{1}/_{2}$ inches of water measured in a 1-pound coffee can. Or, slowly pour on two to three 5-gallon bucketfuls of water.

Sustained moisture all around a newly planted rose helps it to survive transplant shock and to reach out into the surrounding soil. Water deeply after planting, then every week for the next eight weeks, pour two or three 5-gallon bucketfuls of water around the roots unless you have a soaking rain.

In good soil in average summer weather, new and established roses need 1 to $1^{1}/_{2}$ inches of water each week, by rain or by you. During a hot summer, each established bush needs a 5-gallon bucketful of water each week. Roses growing in sandy soil need more frequent watering than roses in clay soil. One of the most important winter preparations is a deep and thorough watering before the ground freezes.

André favors installing a drip irrigation system or soaker hoses for roses. These two methods release water directly to the plant roots and not to the foliage, which helps avoid some diseases, and you don't waste water in runoff.

Mulch. Mulch is a great timesaver! It helps to conserve soil moisture, minimize weeds, and moderate soil temperatures. Organic mulches of

compost, bark, or leaf mold are the best because as they decompose, the nutrients and humus are added to the soil.

After planting or transplanting a rose, spread mulch 2 to 3 inches deep starting 3 inches from the main stem and out to a point wider than the plant's diameter. Replenish the mulch in later winter after fertilizing, in early summer, and in late fall.

Winter Care for Roses

To help roses harden off and mature for winter, stop the use of high nitrogen chemical fertilizers about six weeks before the first frost. Instead, make the last fertilization a slow-release, organic product such as Espoma Rose-tone or Plant-tone. It will work slowly over winter without promoting top growth that can be harmed by fall frosts.

When cold weather threatens, stop deadheading and allow the flowers to go to seed and form rose hips. The formation of hips encourages the plant to slow growth and blooming, and harden the canes in preparation for dormancy. When the bush is bare of leaves, to prevent disease and fungus from overwintering, remove every scrap of leaves and other debris on the ground. Spray the bush with dormant oil to kill insects and diseases on the bush and on the ground. Water the plant thoroughly before the ground freezes hard.

PESTS

Weeds. When weeds, including grass and dandelions, get going under roses they can be painful to remove. So rake weedlings out early. If you must hand weed, wear leather gauntlets. Keep earth covered with 2 to 3 inches of mulch to keep new weed seeds from sprouting.

Deer love roses. Deer are a great problem, even in such urban areas as Richmond, Virginia. "Bambi" eats rosebuds, tips of rose canes, and somehow nibbles leaves without being deterred by the thorns. Sprays containing very bitter Bitrex may keep deer away if they're not starving. The only sure protection is to screen the roses with chicken wire. It isn't noticeable at a distance. For controls, turn to Pests, Diseases, and Controls in the Appendix to the book.

Voles. Voles (short-tailed pine or meadow mice) are most active October to March. They can girdle roots and canes of roses under mulch. To control them:

- Bait the main area around the roses with a rodenticide.

- If you expect more winter weather, pull the mulch apart, spray the stem and the lower branches lightly with a repellent, and put it back in place. If winter is almost over, don't replace the mulch.

- To protect new and established plantings, see About Moles and Voles, in the April pages of Chapter 6, Perennials.

INSECTS AND DISEASES

The first line of defense is to plant pest- and disease-resistant roses, to give your roses lots of air all around, to fertilize, and to water well. **When you encounter an infestation, treat it, and immediately remove every scrap of infected vegetation from the plant and the ground.**

Blackspot and powdery mildew. These two fungi are the bane of rose growers. Blackspot causes black spots about $1/16$ to $1/2$ inch in diameter on the leaves and sometimes the stems. The infected leaves later turn yellow around the spots and fall off. Blackspot can defoliate a bush. It is promoted by wet foliage, splashing water, and warm temperatures.

Powdery mildew covers buds, stems, and leaves with a white-gray powdery substance. High humidity increases the severity of powdery mildew.

Unlike blackspot, wet conditions actually inhibit the development of powdery mildew. It cannot reproduce in water. It thrives during high humidity but forms on dry leaves. Warm dry days and cool dry nights are ideal for powdery mildew.

You may succeed in warding off these two diseases if you:

- Spray with a combination of $1\frac{1}{2}$ tablespoons of baking soda and either 2 tablespoons of horticultural oil or a few drops of dishwashing liquid in 1 gallon of water. The first application is made before foliage appears. It must be reapplied after rain.

- Use watering systems that don't wet the leaves. Use drip watering, soaker hoses, or just soak the ground with a light stream from a garden hose. If you water overhead, do it in the morning so the leaves dry off before evening; do it no more than three or four times a month.

- Remove leaves close to the ground (the first 6 to 8 inches), which are likely to be wetted. Mulch well to minimize water splashing onto the leaves.

- Remove all diseased leaves from the plant or ground immediately to prevent spreading the disease. Prune infected canes all the way back to healthy tissue in late winter.

Roses

• Prune to open the center of the bush to allow sunlight and air to reach all the plant. Roses planted too close to each other or a wall may not get enough airflow.

• Remove the old mulch in early spring of plants that had a lot of blackspot the previous year. Allow the area to dry, and spread clean new mulch.

• Keep the plant well watered. A weak or stressed plant is more susceptible to disease.

• Apply chemical fungicides can prevent blackspot and mildew. Spray every seven to fourteen days—especially the undersides of the leaves. **Follow the label directions exactly.** Too much fungicide can cause leaf burn. Water the plants well before spraying. Early morning and early evening are the best times to spray. Avoid spraying under windy conditions. Read the product label.

Remember: Using a single fungicide over and over may cause the fungus to become resistant. Alternate between two fungicides, Triforine (Funginex) and Daconil for example, to keep resistant fungi from building up. Fungicides generally can prevent blackspot, but do not cure an existing case of blackspot.

Japanese beetles. These green and maroon insects devour flowers and foliage. Some controls:

• Apply a grub control such as Milky Spore Disease to the soil under the roses and to the surrounding lawn and garden.

• Place Japanese beetle traps far away from the roses.

• Knock the beetles off into soapy water in very early morning when they are sluggish.

• Loose native parasitic wasps and flies.

• Apply insecticides containing neem, rotenone, or Sevin insecticide.

Aphids. Aphids look like tiny jade beads clustered on the bud tips and on new stems. To control them:

• Rinse them off with a strong spray from the hose.

• Pinch out and discard branch tips.

• Release ladybugs, a natural predator of aphids. Water the area well, and release the ladybugs around sunset to discourage them from leaving.

• Spray with insecticidal soap.

• Apply Permethrin or Pyrethrum three times at seven-day intervals. Be sure to spray leaf undersides.

Spider mites. Piercing, sucking pests, they cause a pale stippling of the leaves, and build tiny webs in the interior. The leaves yellow and get a rusty look. Controls include:

• Rinse the plants every few days for two or three weeks until the leaves recover their color.

• Spray with an insecticidal soap as recommended by the manufacturer until the problem is ended.

• Apply Permethrin or horticultural soaps three times at seven-day intervals. Be sure to spray the undersides of the leaves.

Leaf cutter bees. These busy bees cut semi-circle shaped holes in the leaves of roses. They pose no real threat to rose health, but they drive exhibitors crazy.

Viral diseases. Symptoms are a mottling or mosaic discoloration of the leaf or ring spots. In most cases removing the infected plant is the only control. Another suggestion is to buy roses from growers who are committed to producing resistant plants. These growers, including Jackson & Perkins, make cuttings from "indexed" blocks of mother plants. An "indexed" block is a group of plants that have been tested and have a high likelihood of not being infected with a virus.

For additional information on all of these problems, turn to Pests, Diseases, and Controls in the Appendix.

Roses

Large Flowering Bush Roses: Hybrid Tea Roses and Grandifloras

Name	American Rose Society Rating	Color
'Chrysler Imperial' R	7.7	Deep red classic flower form.
'Double Delight' R	8.6	Creamy white and red bi-color.
'First Prize' R	8.3	Silvery pink.
'Fragrant Cloud'	-	Full-bodied coral-orange.
'Garden Party' R	8.0	Creamy white blooms with a touch of pink.
'Peace' R	8.0	Bright yellow and pink bicolor.
'Perfumed Delight' R	7.5	Deep rose pink.
'Queen Elizabeth' R	7.7	Clear pink.
'Royal Highness' R	7.7	Pink flowers.
'Tiffany' R	7.8	Soft pink double blooms.
'Tropicana' R		Strong coral-orange.

Cluster-Flowered Bush Roses: Floribundas and Polyanthas

Name	American Rose Society Rating	Color
'Betty Boop' R	8.1	Clusters of brilliant scarlet-orange blooms.
'China Doll'	8.1	Small double ruffled flowers.
'Europeana' R	8.7	Clusters of dark-crimson flowers.
'Iceberg'	8.8	White.
'Sentimental' R	7.7	Shocking burgundy-red with swirls of creamy white all over the petals.
'The Fairy'	8.7	Large clusters of small, ruffled double pink flowers. (Polyantha)
'Betty Prior'	8.2	Deep pink single blooms.

Climbing Roses, Including Climbing Teas and Large-Flowered Climbers

Name	American Rose Society Rating	Color
'Altissimo'	8.5	Lipstick red saucer.
'Blaze Improved'	7.2	Intense red flowers.
'Don Juan'	8.2	Deep red flowers.
'Fourth of July'	8.0	Bright red rose with white stripes.
'Climbing Iceberg'	8.6	White.
'New Dawn'	8.6	Large pale pink blooms.
'Sally Holmes'	8.9	Clusters of white blooms with a blush of apricot in the buds.

Roses

Shrub Roses, Including Hybrid Rugosas

Name	American Rose Society Rating	Color
'Bonica' R	8.4	Many small ruffled pink flowers.
'Carefree Beauty' R	8.7	Large pink flowers.
'Carefree Delight' R	8.2	Pink with white centers.
'Carefree Wonder' R	8.0	Bright pink and white blooms with cream on the reverse side.
'Father Hugo's Rose'	8.5	Sprays of pale yellow flowers in spring.
'Hansa'	8.4	Double deep pink blooms.
'Knockout' R	8.4	Deep cherry red.
'Pink Grootendorst'	7.8	Medium pink blooms.
'Pink Meidiland'	8.6	Single pink blooms with a white eye.
'Sea Foam'	8.1	Creamy white double rose.

Old Garden Roses

Name	American Rose Society Rating	Color
'Blush Noisette'	-	Dainty, loose, light pink double blooms.
China Rose Mutabilis (*Rosa* x *mutabilis*)	-	Stunning scarlet, pink, and yellow single rose. The flowers change color, opening yellow, turning pink, deepening to red.
'Duchess of Portland'	-	Semi-double light crimson.
'Semiplena' (*Rosa alba*)	-	Large clusters of semi-double white blooms.
Cabbage Rose (*Rosa centifolia*)	-	Huge double medium pink to pink-purple blooms.
'Chapeau de Napoleon' (*Rosa centifolia*)	-	The crested moss rose, a brighter pink color than a true *R. centifolia*.
'Celsiana' (*Rosa damascena*)	-	Pale pink semi-double blooms.
Apothecary Rose, Red Rose of Lancanster (*Rosa gallica* 'Officinalis')	-	Light crimson.
True Musk Rose (*Rosa moschata*)	-	Creamy white single blooms.

*R indicates an All-America Rose Selection winner

PLANNING

Take this respite from the garden to learn more about roses. Mail-order catalogs from the rose specialists named in the Appendix are great teachers. Make an album of catalog pages of roses you would like to try. Go out to the garden and scout likely places to plant them.

Roses that climb (CL) need 5 to 10 feet between plants. Train them to climb or ramble, and the canes will cover split rail fences, stone walls, pillars, posts, pergolas, or arches. A large flowered **climber** trained to a trellis makes a beautiful backdrop for a rose garden. **Ramblers** and **miniature climbers** are excellent basket and container plants.

Large-flowered bush roses need 3 to 4 feet between plants. These roses are all about big, breathtakingly beautiful flowers, ideal for exhibition and for collectors. The group includes **modern hybrid tea (HT)** and **grandiflora (GR)** roses. The plants are large, upright, leggy, and need a bed of their own. In formal gardens **hybrid tea roses** are set off, parterre style, in geometric shaped beds edged with low hedges of clipped **boxwood** or **lavender cotton,** *Santolina chamaecyparissus.*

Cluster-flower bush roses need 2 to 3 feet between plants. Medium size, these easily managed roses bear clusters of flowers all season. They're excellent in big perennial borders, and grouped in transitional spaces. Some can be pruned just with hedge shears. The **floribundas** (many-flowered) are planted in Europe along the roads and in parks. The **modern bush roses,** including the peachy pink AARS 1987 winner **'Bonica'** and other **Meidilands,** are hybrid everbloomers growing on their own roots. Smaller **polyanthas** like the rambling, fragrant seashell pink **'The Fairy',** make pretty, low, carefree hedges. The **English** and **David Austin** roses are graceful plants that bear very pretty flowers in the style of old garden roses, but with more modern disease resistance built in.

Compact and patio roses need 2 to 4 feet or more. Compact, 2 to 4 feet tall, somewhere between **miniatures** and **floribundas,** they bloom freely all season. They are planted in perennial borders, for hedges, as ground covers, as edgers, and as fillers for rose beds. The **flower carpet** group has a 5-foot spread.

Miniature roses need 18 to 24 inches between plants. The enchanting **minis** bloom all season, are winter hardy, disease-resistant, and are easy to grow indoors, too. The upright forms are 12 inches high and 6 to 18 inches across, and make pretty edgers. Those with trailing branches are lovely basket and container plants.

Heirloom, rugosa, and species roses need 5 to 6 feet or more between plants. Heirloom roses are **old garden roses,** a passport to time travel. Many are exceptionally fragrant. Most bloom once for about four weeks in early or mid-spring, on canes 3 to 6 feet long. The modern trouble-free **rugosa roses** are tall stiff bushes with spiny upright canes, perfect for tall hedges, as windbreaks, keep-outs to intruders. Deer don't trouble them, and they are excellent at the seashore.

Some rose species are excellent subjects for a naturalized garden. The magenta-pink **Virginia rose** (*Rosa virginiana*) is extremely cold hardy, and has brilliant autumn foliage.

PLANTING

Lay out a new rose bed now, and you will be ready to start digging it when cold and moisture have left the earth next month.

CARE

Indoors. If **miniatures** growing indoors aren't blooming, add spot grow lights for the evening.

Make an album of catalog pages of roses you would like to try. Go out to the garden and scout likely places to plant them.

Did You Know?

Growing Miniature Roses Indoors

Miniature roses that do well indoors are available from florists and garden markets. Some favorites are **'Rise 'n Shine'**, **'Little Jackie'**, **'Red Beauty'**, and **'Starina'**. To grow a mini indoors:

- Repot it in a clay pot lined with pebbles or PermaTill, and filled with a potting mix that includes a water-holding polymer.
- Grow it on a south-facing windowsill, under grow lights, or in a window greenhouse.
- Keep the plant cool at night.
- Water the soil, **not the leaves,** when the surface feels dry to the touch.
- Fertilize at every watering with a half dose of a water-soluble fertilizer.
- Deadhead back to the first five-leaflet set.
- Prune out crowded and crossing stems to keep the center open.
- Remove infected foliage and stems at once.
- Shower every two weeks.
- In May move the plant outdoors to a semi-sunny spot for a summer vacation.

Outdoors. Check and adjust the winter mulch and other forms of protection for in-ground roses.

 PRUNING

Deadhead **miniature roses** indoors; remove crossing and crowded stems to keep the center open.

 WATERING

Indoors. Keep the soil moderately moist for **miniatures.** Shower them every two weeks. Every other time you water, moisten only the soil, not the leaves.

Maintain moderate soil moisture for tender roses wintering in containers indoors, and for containers of hardy roses sheltered in a cold garage or shed.

Outdoors. If winter has been dry, water the roses out in the garden.

 FERTILIZING

Fertilize **miniature roses** growing indoors at every watering with a half dose of a water-soluble plant food for flowering plants, African violet, or some other bloom booster.

 PESTS

Indoors. If spider mites attack **miniatures,** rinse the plants every two weeks. Air the room daily. Segregate infected plants. See also Pests in the introduction to this chapter.

Outdoors. If vole runs appear around the roses, treat the area with a rodenticide.

FEBRUARY
Roses

 ## PLANNING

When ordering new roses make sure they withstand your winters. Be wary of roses that have no hardiness rating; growers don't always know how new roses will perform. It's also a good idea to be skeptical of winter ratings based on experience in the United Kingdom—plants perform differently there.

Species roses, and many once-blooming **old garden (heirloom) roses** are very cold-hardy. Of the repeat bloomers, **rugosas** are very hardy, and many **David Austins** and **modern bush roses** are okay. **Miniatures** and **modern bush roses** growing on their own roots are usually hardy. If the tops suffer, canes will grow back and bloom. This isn't applicable to roses that bloom just once. They flower in spring only on the last year's canes—no old canes, no flowers. Many yellow and lavender roses are especially tender.

Hybrids teas and other budded roses. Labels identifying propagation as "own-root" and the rootstock as hardy in your area are fine. Their hardiness depends on natural resistance to cold. Killed to the ground, shoots from the rootstock will regenerate and bloom "true" to the parent variety.

Protecting roses against winter weather is an added safeguard against loss and a necessity for roses not growing on their own roots. In warm Zone 8, tender roses may winter over without protection.

 ## PLANTING

In Zone 8 the soil may have warmed enough to plant and to transplant.

 ## CARE

When the annual fertilization is complete, add enough fresh mulch to maintain a 2- to 3-inch layer starting about 3 inches from the central stems.

 ## PRUNING

Indoors. Continue to deadhead and groom the **minis.**

Outdoors. Look your roses over now, and evaluate the when and how of the pruning job ahead.

If you want to slow the growth and promote flowering in some roses, root prune them. The best time for it is early spring before growth begins. With a spade sever the roots in a circle all around the bush to where the roots are about the size of your little finger. If you encounter roots you need a saw to cut, you are too close. If the roots are web fine, you are too far out.

 ## WATERING

Indoors. Keep the soil moderately moist, not the leaves, for **miniatures.** Maintain soil moisture for containers of hardy roses sheltering in a garage or shed.

Outdoors. If winter has been dry, water the roses out in the garden.

 ## FERTILIZING

Late this month, or in early March, about four to six weeks before your roses start to grow:

- Check and adjust the soil pH.

- Fertilize with an organic fertilizer (see Fertilizing Roses in the introduction to this chapter).

- Apply Rich Earth humate.

 ## PESTS

Remove the mulch under roses troubled by **blackspot** last year. Allow the area to dry, then spread new mulch.

Smother overwintering insect eggs with an ultrafine (dormant) horticultural oil spray. There are temperature limits for effectiveness, so read the label.

If vole runs appear around the roses, bait the main runway with a rodenticide.

Did You Know?

About Pruning Roses

Wear thick leather gloves, and use sharp, clean pruning shears for small canes, and a small pruning saw for large canes.

- Pruning begins: Zone 8: end of February; Zone 7: mid-March; Zone 6: mid-April.

Basics

- Place pruning cuts so the center of the bush remains open for maximum air circulation.

- Make cuts 1/4 inch above an outward-facing bud or leafset. Cut at a 45-degree angle with the high side on the side the bud or leafset is on—the outward facing side.

- Squeeze a drop of white glue over the cut ends of larger canes to keep borers out.

- Scrub the woody surface of the bud union with a brass wire brush (sold by hardware stores) to clear dead tissue and stimulate growth.

Pruning Established Roses

- **All roses.** Before or as the buds swell, remove dead canes, growth skinnier than a pencil, and canes crossing the center that are growing in the wrong direction and crowding others. Cut winter-damaged canes back to healthy green wood. Leave enough stem above the bud union for new growth to develop.

- **All roses.** Saw off old woody canes as close to the bud union as possible.

- **All budded roses.** Remove suckers growing from below the bud union of **hybrid teas, grandifloras,** and other budded roses—or they will take over.

- **Hybrid teas and grandifloras.** Cut **hybrid teas** back to six well-placed canes and **grandifloras** back to eight canes. Reduce the canes a third, to 14 to 18 inches long.

- **Floribundas and polyanthas.** Cut three-year old canes off at the bud union. Cut two-year old stems back by half. Cut back new canes by a third, or to just below where they bloomed last year.

- **Modern bush roses, 'Bonica' and the Meidiland family.** Trim branch tips back to shape the plant.

- **Cluster-flower bush roses, heirloom, and species roses.** Prune lightly to shape the plant.

- **Miniatures.** Remove all but the best four or five canes, and cut those back by a third.

- **Climbers.** For the first two years, prune to remove unproductive canes. After that, prune out the oldest canes leaving five or six healthy canes, and shorten their side shoots by two-thirds.

- **One-time bloomers.** Prune shortly **after** they have flowered.

- **Carpet roses.** Prune the canes back to 6 inches.

- **Rugosa roses.** Cut unproductive older canes back to the ground.

MARCH
Roses

 PLANNING

When winter moisture and cold leaves the soil, you can start planting new roses.

 PLANTING

Preparing a rose for planting:

- **Bare root.** Keep the rose in its package in a dark, cool place until planting time. The roots need to be soaked in tepid water before planting—usually six to twelve hours.

- **Container-grown.** Make shallow slits in the container sides, and peel the pieces away. If roots wrap the rootball, make four shallow vertical cuts in the sides of the rootball, and slice off the bottom 2 inches.

- **Roses in plantable containers.** Open the top, and maintain the soil moisture until you are ready to plant. Follow the package planting directions.

 CARE

When the forsythias start to bloom, remove the winter mulch and other protective materials from the roses—but don't get ahead of the weather.

Adjust the leads and supports for climbers.

Return containers that sheltered in a garage or shed to the garden, fertilize, and prune them.

 PRUNING

Indoors. Deadhead **miniature roses.**

Outdoors. Roses are best pruned before the buds swell (see February); keep an eye on their progress.

 WATERING

Indoors. Maintain the soil moisture of **miniature roses.**

Outdoors. Keep the soil in containers of roses sheltering in a garage or shed moderately damp. Water hardy roses outdoors in containers and in the ground if you run into a dry spell.

 FERTILIZING

Prepare **established rose beds** for fertilization:

- Check and adjust the soil pH.

- Apply Rich Earth humate.

- Every three to five years enrich the soil by applying phosphate, green sand, and gypsum.

Turn ahead to Fertilizing in the April pages where the timing for various types of fertilizers is explained.

 PESTS

Remove old mulch under plants that had blackspot last year. Allow the area to dry, then spread new mulch.

Apply an ultrafine (dormant) horticultural oil spray **to smother overwintering insect eggs.** There are temperature limits for effectiveness, so read the label.

If vole runs appear around the roses, bait the main runway with a rodenticide.

Did You Know?

New Planting Hole

1 Outline a hole at least 20 inches wide. Dig a hole twice as deep as the rootball.

2 Test the pH of the soil. Bring to the site the products needed to adjust the pH, along with the fertilizers and amendments recommended for a new 100 square foot bed, below. If the area you are planting measures only 10 square feet, combine one-tenth of the amount of each supplement given for a bed over 100 square feet.

3 As you dig, every 4 or 5 inches mix a portion of the fertilizer and amendments into the soil from the hole. The soil by the side of the hole is now "improved" and ready for the next step.

4 Pack in enough improved soil to place the graft (bud union—a thickened node at the base of the stem) at the right depth. The **right depth** depends on your plant-hardiness zone. In Zone 6, budded roses do best planted so the graft lies 1 to 2 inches below the soil surface. In Zone 7, the bud union can be at soil level. In Zone 8, the bud union may be slightly above the ground.

5 **Bare root rose.** Firm a cone in the center of the mound, drape the roots over it, and spread them out in the hole. **Container rose.** Settle the rootball on packed improved soil so the stem is straight. **Plantable container.** Make sure the container sits straight in the hole.

6 Backfill with improved soil. Pack it firmly over the roots, or around the rootball, or the plantable container. Shape the soil around the crown into a wide saucer (water basin), and create a rim around it that will keep rain or hose water from running off. Water the soil slowly, gently, and thoroughly with a sprinkler, a soaker hose, a bubbler, or by hand. You need to put down $1^1/_2$ inches of water. Or, slowly and gently pour on 10 to 15 gallons of water from a bucket. Mulch 2 to 3 inches deep starting 3 inches from the main stem.

New Bed for Roses

Any airy, sunny, well-drained site soil can be made into a fine bed for roses. Start three to four weeks early so soil amendments will settle in before you plant.

1 Choose a site with full sun—six hours, eight in cold areas. Farther south, roses can take more shade.

2 Lay out the bed. Check and adjust the pH. Thoroughly water the turf.

3 Spray with RoundUp® Weed and Grass Killer. The turf will be completely dead in about two weeks. Or, remove the turf (and compost it).

4 Cover the bed with 3 to 5 inches of organic material— any combination of decomposed bark, compost, partially decomposed leaves, sphagnum peat moss, black peat humus, well-rotted animal manure.

5 For every 100 square feet of garden bed, spread on these long-lasting organic fertilizers and amendments:

> Rich Earth humate: 1 pound; Rose- or Plant-tone: 5 to 10 pounds; Rock phosphate: 5 to 10 pounds; Green sand: 5 to 10 pounds; Clay soils: gypsum 5 to 10 pounds; Osmocote® eight-month: 2 pounds

6 With a rear-tine rototiller, which you can rent from a garden center, mix all this as deeply as the rototiller will go. Rake the bed smooth, and discard rocks, lumps, and bumps.

APRIL
Roses

 PLANNING

Keeping a record of which bush did what and when will be helpful next year when you are preparing to amend the soil and prune your roses.

 PLANTING

Brighten your porch, patio, or steps with roses planted in containers. The **miniatures** thrive in moss lined baskets, planters, and clay or cement containers. **Compact** and **patio cluster-flowering** varieties and **tree roses** bloom non-stop in a container.

 CARE

If you did not prepare the soil in established rose beds with an annual fertilization last month, do it now:

- Check and adjust the pH.

- Spread an application of Rich Earth humate.

- Every three to five years enrich the soil by applying phosphate, green sand, and gypsum.

 PRUNING

Indoors. Continue to deadhead **miniature roses.**

Outdoors. If you have not yet pruned your roses, do so now. The rule is to prune before the buds break. But late is better than not at all. See the February pages for recommended timing. **The exception to the early spring pruning rule** are one-time bloomers. Prune this type **after** blooming as they bear their flowers on the previous year's growth.

Prune first-year plants only lightly to allow them to concentrate on establishing a strong root system.

 WATERING

Indoors. Keep the soil for miniatures moderately moist. Wet the soil, not the leaves.

Outdoors. Maintain soil moisture for **tender roses** sheltering in a garage or shed, and in **hardy roses** outdoors in containers and in the ground. Roses are growing now and must have $1^1/_2$ inches of water every week—that's 2 to 3 five-gallon bucketfuls.

 FERTILIZING

Before growth begins, fertilize the soil around in-ground and container roses. How far in advance depends on the type of fertilizer you are using. **Mark the date in your garden log, and note on your calendar when the next application is due.**

- **Organic fertilizers.** Early this month, or four to six weeks before growth begins, apply to every 100 square feet of bed:

  Rose-tone or Plant-tone: 5 to 10 pounds
  Rock phosphate: 5 to 10 pounds
  Green sand: 5 to 10 pounds
  Clay soils only: gypsum 5 to 10 pounds
  Osmocote® eight-month: 2 pounds

The next application is due in early summer, about six weeks from now, and every six weeks until September 15.

- **Timed-release fertilizers.** Four to six weeks before growth begins, apply an eight-month formulation.

Supplement this with foliage feedings of water-soluble organic or fast-acting liquid fertilizers if the roses fail to bloom up to expectation or show a lack of vigor.

Brighten your porch, patio, or steps with roses planted in containers. The miniatures thrive in moss lined baskets, planters, and clay or cement containers.

Did You Know?

Growing Roses in Containers

Smaller roses do well in containers. **Miniatures, rose trees,** smaller **Meidilands, floribundas,** some **hybrid teas** are all candidates.

- **Light.** Provide at least six hours of sun each day. Turn the pot often to keep the bush growing evenly all around. A movable container makes it easy to take advantage of shifting light. Garden centers offer plant saucers and containers equipped with casters.

- **Container size.** For a **miniature rose,** a 6-inch pot that's 5 inches deep is sufficient. For **standard roses,** provide a tub that is at least 18 inches in diameter and 14 inches deep. Save watering time by planting in a container with a built-in water reservoir or water ring that lets the plant soak up the water from the bottom.

- **Preparation.** Soak porous containers—clay, wood—before adding soil, or they will take moisture from the soil you put into them. For winter protection, wrap the interior with a double row of large bubble wrap or Styrofoam™.

- **Planting.** Line the bottom with PermaTill®, then fill with this mix: 1/4 good garden soil or bagged top soil, 1/4 commercial soilless mix, 1/4 compost, and 1/4 sand, or 1/8 perlite and 1/8 PermaTill. Add a modest application of Osmocote® slow-release fertilizer and a water-holding polymer such as Soil Moist to help maintain moisture. Soak the growing medium before you plant.

- **Watering.** After planting, water well and maintain soil moisture thereafter.

- **Fertilizing.** Liquid feed every two weeks with a half strength dose of a good rose or container plant fertilizer.

- **Winter care.** Before freezing cold temperatures, store the container in a detached, unheated garage, shed, or cool basement. A rose needs to be cold enough to go dormant but must not freeze. Water lightly once a month.

- **Chemical water-soluble complete fertilizer.** Make a first application just before growth begins. The next applications are due in six weeks, and every six weeks ending September 15.

 PESTS

Weeds are popping. Rake them away.

Spray with an anti-desiccant spray or André's remedy for **blackspot and mildew.** If you have had serious infestations, start spraying with a rose fungicide.

Aphids cluster on rosebuds and cane tips. Spray them off every morning with a hose, or spray with neem or insecticidal soap.

Deer are up, hungry, and enjoy tender new shoots and rose foliage. For controls see Pests, Diseases, and Controls in the Appendix to the book.

MAY
Roses

 PLANNING

Other gardener's roses, like someone else's grass, always look better. That's usually because we see them from a distance.

But to get a notion of how stunning roses can be, **visit some of the public rose gardens** in our area because roses are in full bloom. Bring a notebook, and write down the names of those you must have—then look for them a garden centers. They're brimming with roses this time of year, all in top condition.

 PLANTING

May is a fine month for planting new roses.

Fill gaps in the rose bed with leafy annuals—**salvias, wave petunias, sun coleus.**

 CARE

Repot **miniature roses** growing indoors in fresh soil, and put them outdoors in bright light, but not in direct sunlight, to prepare them for summer outdoors.

 PRUNING

Prune one-time bloomers when they finish blooming. See February pages for recommended timing.

To keep roses looking good and producing flowers, **deadhead religiously**—that is, remove spent blooms. Deadheading is especially important with large-flowered roses, the **hybrid teas,** and **grandifloras. Miniature roses** and the small **polyanthas** and **species roses** generally do not need deadheading.

To deadhead, make the cut a 45-degree diagonal just above the next five- or seven-segment leaf down the stem. The first year cut back to the first three- or five-segment leafset. In following years, cut far enough down to get to a five-segment or seven-segment leafset or bud that is facing outward. This will open up the plant.

 WATERING

As the weather warms, begin daily checks of the moisture in the soil of roses growing in small pots and baskets. Water enough to keep the soil from drying out.

From late spring to mid-autumn, roses growing in big tubs may need watering every four to six days, or weekly. The larger the container, the less often it will need watering.

Make sure in-ground roses receive $1\frac{1}{2}$ inches of water every week—that's two or three 5-gallon bucketfuls.

 FERTILIZING

Liquid feed roses growing in containers every two weeks with a half strength dose of a good rose or container plant fertilizer.

For in-ground roses, six weeks after your first application of organic blend fertilizers or chemical water-soluble fertilizer, repeat the application. The usual timing is early summer, but it depends on when you make the first application

Supplement this with foliage feedings of water-soluble organic or chemical liquid fertilizers if the roses fail to bloom up to expectation or show a lack of vigor.

To keep roses looking good and producing flowers, deadhead religiously—that is, remove spent blooms.

 PESTS

Use a hoe to root out weeds creeping into the mulch under the roses.

If blackspot or powdery mildew appear, remove, and discard (do not compost!!) every leaf and spoiled blossom on the plant and petals on the ground. Prune out diseased canes. Apply a rose fungicide according to the label directions.

Aphids

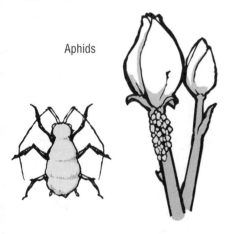

Aphids cluster on rosebuds and cane tips. Use a strong spray of water to blow them away in the early morning. If they persist, spray with neem or insecticidal soap.

Did You Know?

Harvesting Roses

- Harvest roses early, before the sun gets to them.

- Take to the garden a 5-gallon plastic bucket filled with lukewarm water containing floral preservative, clean sharp pruning shears, and thick gauntlets.

- Choose stems whose buds haven't fully opened.

- The first year make the cut just above the first three- or five-segment leafset. In following years cut far enough down to get to a five-segment or seven-segment leafset or bud that is facing outward.

- Immediately plunge the cut stem into the water bucket, remove the foliage that will be below the water line, and condition the roses in fresh water overnight in a cool place.

- Scour the bucket and vases with a dilute bleach solution ($\frac{1}{2}$ teaspoon of bleach per gallon of water) each time they are used.

At the first spell of hot, dry weather **watch out for spider mites.** Three applications of Permethrin or Pyrethrum at five to seven day intervals will help you to control these pests. Be sure to spray the undersides of the leaves.

Roses that are wilting, yellowing, and seem stunted may be troubled by nematodes. The control is applications of ground crab shells.

Deer nibble the tender new wood and leaves on roses and eat the flowers and the buds; the Pests, Diseases, and Controls section in the Appendix has suggestions for controlling them.

JUNE
Roses

PLANNING

The roses that didn't sell this spring may be on sale now—or soon. Be tempted but be wise. Check out the rootball, and go for plants whose leaves are shiny, green, plentiful, no yellowing, no stippling, and no little spider webs.

PLANTING

If you haven't tried **miniature roses** yet, see what's on sale at the garden markets this month. The minis bloom freely and will almost surely come back better than ever next year. The little blossoms are somewhat reserved about sharing their scent, but it's there. **'Starina'**, **'Jennifer'**, **'Pacesetter'**, and **'Party Girl'** are among scented minis, and some say **'Rise 'n Shine'**, which bears beautiful little yellow flowers shaped like a hybrid tea, is perfumed.

Many **miniatures** are hybrids of **'Minima',** a selection of the **China rose** (*Rosa chinensis*). One of the wonderful characteristics the **China rose** imparted to modern roses is summer-long bloom. Pot yours up in September, and bring it indoors, and it will bloom all winter.

CARE

Top up the mulch around the roses before heat gets intense.

Attach the new growth of the climbers and ramblers to their supports.

PRUNING

Check budded roses, and remove new canes coming from the rootstock below the bud union.

Deadhead **hybrid teas**, **grandifloras**, and other show-time roses.

Prune one-time bloomers as soon as possible after they finish blooming. See February for likely timing.

WATERING

Growing in good soil, new and established roses need 1 to 1$\frac{1}{2}$ inches of water each week, from the sky or your watering system. Or, slowly pour two or three 5-gallon bucketfuls of water around and in the water basin.

Miniature roses growing in small pots and baskets probably need water daily. Check the roses growing in big containers every couple of days, and water when the soil feels dry a few inches down. Water until the water runs out the bottom.

FERTILIZING

Liquid feed roses growing in containers every two weeks with a half strength dose of a good rose or container plant fertilizer.

The second application of organic blend fertilizer or chemical water-soluble fertilizer was due six weeks after the early spring application. Do it now if you haven't done it yet.

PESTS

Deer nibble roses, buds, and leaves; deterrent sprays may not keep them away. See the section on Pests, Diseases, and Controls in the Appendix.

Continue to root out weeds, and look out for aphids, spider mites, thrips, blackspot, and powdery mildew. If you have already sprayed without effect, switch to another control.

Japanese beetles get busy now. This rather handsome metallic green and coppery maroon insect wrecks the flowers and chews the leaves and stems as well. In early morning knock them into soapy water, and destroy them. If there are wild grape vines on your property, root them out; they are an attractive host plant for the Japanese beetle. Grub-proof the lawn and gardens now, and there should be fewer Japanese beetles next year. But that won't stop them from flying in. **Beetle traps are effective, only if they are placed far away from the roses.** If Japanese beetles become a real problem, apply insecticides containing neem, rotenone, or Sevin.

Did You Know?

Rooting Cuttings to Multiply Your Roses

Propagating roses by softwood cuttings is a fascinating project, and a thrill when you succeed. Some easy to propagate from softwood and semi-softwood cuttings are **old roses, English roses,** and **miniatures.** Take cuttings from the ends of new canes that are green to semi-green and whose flowers have lost almost all their petals.

1 Set a 2-gallon baggie upright, and pack the bottom with 6 inches of sterile potting mix well-moistened with water containing 1 teaspoon of soluble rose food for every 4 quarts.

2 Shake about 2 inches of rooting hormone powder Number 3, or Roottone, into a small glass.

3 Take the cutting in early morning. From the blossom end, count down four leafsets to a five-leafset, and cut the stem off about an inch below.

4 Working in the shade, cut the top off about a half-inch above the top leafset. Remove the leaves from the bottom 2 inches. Mist the foliage. Score the bottom inch or so of the stem vertically. Dip the wounded end in the rooting powder, and knock off the excess.

5 Bury the cut end upright in the middle of the potting mix deep enough to cover the wounds. Press the soil up around the stem.

6 Mist the cutting, blow the baggy full of air, and zip it closed.

7 Place the baggy in bright, indirect light.

8 Sometime between two and six weeks there should begin to be roots showing along the bottom of the baggy.

9 When top growth begins, acclimate the cutting to the air in the room. Each day for the next two weeks unzip the baggie a little more, and leave it open a little longer. Start with four hours the first day.

10 Fill a pot as big as the baggy to within 4 inches of the top with half potting soil and half peat. Set the baggie on top, and slit the bottom. Gently firm the soil up around the roots.

11 In about a week move the pot outside, and week by week expose it to increasingly stronger light. Maintain the soil moisture. In September, transplant the plant to the garden, and cover it with an open mulch of hay or evergreen boughs.

JULY
Roses

PLANNING

This month and next, visit public gardens, and gardens noted for roses—and smell the roses. Note the names of those that are really fragrant, and plan to try them. For the perfumed roses to be truly fragrant, I find they need to grow in full sun—eight hours.

PLANTING

You can **plant container roses now**—at home and even at the shore. If Japanese beetles are ruining your roses, try one they don't pay much mind to, the **rugosa rose.** *Rosa rugosa* is a tall (5 feet or more) native of China, Russia, Japan, and Korea, that does so well at the sea it is used to create wind breaks in very exposed positions.

Yes, it's tall and thorny, but modern cultivars bear clove-scented single or double flowers that are quite lovely, and the rose hips are spectacular. Most bloom for quite a while in spring, and some repeat bloom.

The roses are very cold hardy, and resist not only the Japanese beetle, but also many other pests. The only pruning needed is the removal in early spring of older canes to encourage vigorous new growth.

One of the most beautiful is **'Frau Dagmar Hastrup',** which bears light pink roses and is so dense it can be pruned repeatedly without much diminishing the production of flowers. The flowers of **'Therese Bugnet'** are large, flat, slightly fragrant deep pink and repeat some. Almost thornless **'Linda Campbell'** produces large clusters of crimson flowers with six to seven flushes of blooms.

When preparing containers for a seashore garden, use commercial potting soil rather than the sandy soil of the area. The humidity in the air reduces the need to water, but check the soil moisture often anyway.

CARE

Heat is here. Check and replenish the mulch under the roses.

PRUNING

Harvest—and deadhead—**hybrid teas** and **grandifloras.** The everblooming roses that bear clusters of small flowers generally do not need deadheading, but if they aren't producing as expected, groom and deadhead them, and apply a liquid fertilizer.

WATERING

This month and next **check the soil moisture daily in small pots and baskets.** They may need a good soaking almost every day. Roses growing in big containers in hot windy places may need watering every three to five days now. Water until you see water dripping from the bottom of the container.

Make sure in-ground roses receive 1½ inches of water every week—that's two to three 5-gallon bucketfuls.

Keep roses that suffered from powdery mildew well watered. Unlike blackspot, wet conditions actually inhibit the development of powdery mildew. It cannot reproduce in water. While it thrives in high humidity, it forms on dry leaves. Warm dry days and cool dry nights are ideal for powdery mildew. A weak or stressed plant is more susceptible to disease.

If blackspot is a problem on the same plant, water the roots and avoid wetting the foliage.

FERTILIZING

Liquid feed roses growing in containers every two weeks with a half strength dose of a good rose or container plant fertilizer.

This month and next check the soil moisture daily in small pots and baskets. They may need a good soaking almost every day.

The third application of organic blend fertilizer or chemical water-soluble fertilizer is due six weeks after the second application, in mid-summer.

If roses fertilized with a timed-release chemical fertilizer are failing to bloom as expected, or look peaked, supplement it with foliar feedings of water-soluble organic or fast-acting liquid fertilizers.

Roses that have been in bloom all season and are slowing production or that aren't growing vigorously, may respond to foliage feedings of water-soluble organic or fast-acting liquid fertilizers

PESTS

Weed! Don't let them get going!

Mites attack roses stressed by hot weather and drought. Make them miserable with vigorous hosing of the leaves, and especially the undersides of the leaves, every day or two for a week. If there are signs of webs on twigs and leaf stems, apply neem or an insecticidal soap.

If caterpillars become numerous, spray with a biological control such as *Bacillus thuringiensis*. Other controls are Sevin or malathion insecticide, pyrethrin, or rotenone.

If Japanese beetles persist, spray their bodies with a Pyrethrum product. It's a contact sport.

The **rose midge larvae** causes deformed buds and dead branch tips. Prune off, and destroy infested buds and tips. Spray with neem every five days as directed.

Deer may be eating your roses and their foliage; see Pests, Diseases, and Controls in the Appendix of the book.

PLANNING

Late afternoons in August the scent of perfumed roses is heady because the fragrant oils have been volatilized by a whole day of hot sun. Once upon a time oils drawn from the scented florals were our only source of fragrance. The roses that scented the old potpourris are still available. **It's fun on a lazy fragrant summer evening to dream of planting a garden of roses for making potpourris.** You would interplant the roses with **English lavender,** *Lavandula officinalis,* whose lasting scent when dried make it a "must" in recipes for dry perfumes.

The scented **Bourbon roses** in general, and the very fragrant pink **'La Reine Victoria'** in particular, would be good candidates. Many of the cabbage roses, *Rosa centifolia,* are sweetly fragrant, including the cultivar **'Fantin Latour'.** The damask roses are fragrant, including the beautiful white **'Madame Hardy'.** If you have room for only one rose for potpourri, choose the rose grown commercially for its scent, *Rosa gallica* **'Officinalis',** the **Apothecary Rose.** This rose is unique in that the petals are more fragrant after drying.

 ## PLANTING

If roses go on sale and you haven't the inclination to plant your purchases in August's high heat, buy them anyway, and grow them in their containers until September brings cooler and better weather for planting. **Miniature roses** are safe in their original container as long as you keep it watered. The larger roses will do better while waiting if they are repotted in a larger container.

 ## CARE

If the foliage of the **hybrid teas** is wilting in temperatures over 90 degrees Fahrenheit, help them recover by misting the leaves with a mild solution of liquid seaweed. Apply it in early morning before the sun starts to climb.

 ## PRUNING

Deadhead the **hybrid teas** and the **grandifloras**.

Remove suckers growing up from under the bud union of your hybrid roses, along with any diseased or damaged canes.

 ## WATERING

This month and next check the soil moisture daily in small pots and baskets. They may need a good soaking almost every day. Roses growing in big containers in hot windy places may need watering every third or fifth day. Water until it is dripping from the bottom of the container.

Make sure in ground roses receive $1\frac{1}{2}$ inches of water every week—that's two to three five-gallon bucketfuls.

Keep roses attacked by powdery mildew well watered. Wet conditions actually inhibit the development of powdery mildew. If blackspot is a problem in the same plant, water roots, and avoid wetting the foliage.

 ## FERTILIZING

Liquid feed roses growing in containers with a water-soluble fertilizer every two weeks.

The third application of organic blend fertilizer or chemical water-soluble fertilizer was due six weeks after the second application, in mid-summer. If you haven't done it yet, do it now. If the roses look as though they need a quick pick-up, spray a liquid fertilizer on the foliage.

If roses fertilized with a timed-release chemical fertilizer are failing to bloom as expected or look peaked, supplement it with foliar feedings of water-soluble organic or fast-acting liquid fertilizers.

 ## PESTS

Roses weakened or stressed by hot dry weather are especially vulnerable to mites, aphids, and Japanese beetles.

Control rust by avoiding overhead watering, and dispose of infected foliage and twigs, applying an anti-transpirant every other week, or spraying with a horticultural oil.

Control powdery mildew by applying an anti-transpirant, and by maintaining good air circulation.

Control blackspot by removing fallen leaves, pruning out diseased twigs, and avoiding wetting the foliage.

Viral diseases may strike now. There's no remedy. Symptoms are a mottling or mosaic discoloration of the leaf or ring spots. In most cases removing the infected plant is the only control.

Continue weed patrol.

Deer may be eating your roses and their leaves; see Pests, Diseases, and Controls in the Appendix.

Did You Know?

English Rose Potpourri

The ancient recipe that follows is from my book *Potpourris and Other Fragrant Delights*, which was published here and in Europe some years ago. Gum storax is from the resin of the tree *Styrax officinalis*, and it is the "benjamin" mentioned in the old stillroom potpourris recipes. Gum benzoin and oil of benzoin are substitutes and are offered by several on-line suppliers.

3 cups dried petals of a fragrant rose
2 cups dried lavender buds
1 cup lemon verbena leaves
1 tablespoon ground allspice
1 tablespoon fresh-ground cinnamon
1 tablespoon fresh-ground cloves
1/4 ounce or more gum benzoin, gum styrax, or oil of styrax

Combine all the dry ingredients, then add in the gum benzoin, gum styrax, or oil of styrax, mixing as you go until the scent seems satisfyingly strong. Seal the container, and set it to cure in a dark, dry place, shaking the contents every day. Put the potpourri into a decorative container that has a close-fitting lid.

Uncap the container when you wish to scent a room, but keep it well covered at all other times.

SEPTEMBER
Roses

 ## PLANNING

Time to begin thinking about winter protection for your roses. You will not need to do much to protect the **old garden roses, miniatures, rugosas, species roses,** and other roses growing on their own roots.

Budded roses are less certain to survive winter without help. The first line of defense for those roses is to plant the bud union at the proper depth as described in the March pages. Check bud unions now of budded plants, and, if need be, dig and replant the roses this month. The Care section of the November pages have detailed instructions on winter care of budded roses.

 ## PLANTING

As the weather cools, repot the **miniature roses,** rinse and spray them with insecticidal soap, and bring them indoors to a sunny sill.

September is a fine month for planting as well as transplanting roses, so take advantage of end-of-season sales to complete your rose collection.

 ## CARE

To help roses harden off and mature for winter, stop the use of high nitrogen fertilizers about six weeks before the first frost.

If you did not **check and adjust the pH of the soil in your rose beds** in March or April, you can do it now. Roses prefer a slightly acid soil, pH 5.8 to 6.8. To raise the pH use 5 to 10 pounds of limestone per 100 square feet of garden bed. If the pH is too high, lower it with an application of elemental fertilizer sulfur, (water-soluble garden sulfur) at the rate of 5 to 10 pounds per 100 square feet. Aluminum sulfate or iron sulfate are acidifiers that act faster but do not last as long in the soil.

 ## PRUNING

Let the last blossoms on **hybrid teas** develop into rose hips. It causes the plant to undergo chemical changes that slow growth, inhibit blooming, and generally prepare for dormancy by hardening the canes. The formation of hips tells the plant that it's done its job and can now prepare to rest.

 ## WATERING

Indoors. Keep the soil for **miniatures** moderately moist. Moisten the soil, not the leaves. Shower them every two weeks.

Outdoors. Continue to check soil moisture daily in roses growing outdoors in small containers. Water big containers every week or so unless you've had a soaking rain.

Make sure in-ground roses receive $1\frac{1}{2}$ inches of water every week—that's two to three 5-gallon bucketfuls. If you are using a watering system or a hose, measure the amount in a 1-pound coffee tin, or use a rain gauge, available from garden centers and catalog suppliers. The plants must be well watered before the ground begins to freeze.

 ## FERTILIZING

If you are using organic or water-soluble chemical fertilizers, the last application in Zones 6 and 7 should be made between early September and early October. In Zone 8, Richmond and the Tidewater areas of Virginia, make it between the end of September and mid-October. If you are using a timed-release fertilizer

If you did not check and adjust the pH of the soil in your rose beds in March or April, you can do it now.

Did You Know?

About Hedge Roses

A rose hedge is a pleasure and an effective barrier. The height you want to achieve indicates the variety to plant.

Low borders. Miniature roses make pretty borders for rose gardens, and they bloom all season. **'China Doll'** tops out at about 18 inches, and covers itself with clusters of 1½-inch light pink, semi-double blooms.

Low hedges. The rose advertised as the "living fence" hedge is **'The Fairy'**, a **polyantha** under 30 inches that blooms all season. 'The Fairy' and other polyanthas grow into brambly hedges covered with clusters of roses under 2 inches.

Medium hedges. The vigorous **floribundas,** which are cluster-flowered bush roses that bloom all season, make fine hedges 4 to 5 feet tall. Our favorite is **'Betty Prior',** whose vivid pink flowers and emerald green foliage stay beautiful all summer. The **Meidiland group** of roses develops into wide-spreading naturalized hedges that bloom all season with little care. **'Bonica',** an upright 4- to 5-foot bush, bears 3-inch fully double shell pink flowers set off by rich deep green glossy leaves.

Tall hedges. The **rugosa roses** grow into tall, very thorny hedges that withstand strong winds and sea spray. The only pruning they need is the removal in early spring of older canes to encourage vigorous new growth. The flowers of the modern cultivars are quite beautiful, and many produce spectacular rose hips.

and applied an eight-month formulation in early spring, it will carry the roses all the way through October.

PESTS

Continue to check your roses for signs of aphids and spider mites.

Powdery mildew remains a threat. Remove and destroy the leaves on the plants affected, and replace the mulch beneath with fresh mulch.

Rake away, and destroy mulch under roses that have had blackspot, mildew, and other problems. Let the soil air and dry, then apply fresh mulch.

Root out weeds and grasses that have crept into the mulch under big roses.

Deer may be eating someone else's apples instead of your roses, but don't count on it.

OCTOBER

Roses

 PLANNING

If your winter temperatures will fall to 10 degrees Fahrenheit or lower, be prepared to cover **hybrid teas, floribundas, grandifloras,** and other budded roses. (See the Care section of the November pages.) Late fall before the ground freezes is about the right timing.

Be wary of covering roses before the temperature falls to 28 degrees Fahrenheit as that may keep the rose from hardening properly and will slow the onset of dormancy, leaving it vulnerable to frost. Cover the rose too late, however, and it may be damaged by the cold.

 PLANTING

This month, apply potassium to the soil to help winterize your roses.

When tree leaves start to change color is an excellent moment to plant new roses, and to start digging and transplanting roses. In Zone 8, you can plant roses throughout October, November, and into early December. In Zone 7, you can still plant roses in October and November. In Zone 6, you can plant roses in October and into the very beginning of November.

 CARE

Begin to prepare climbers, roses growing in containers, and tree roses for winter:

Climbing Roses. Climbers exposed to high winds will do better with protection in winter. Spray the canes with a rose fungicide or dormant oil, and use an anti-desiccant, such as Wilt-Pruf®, to help them withstand winter dryness. Clear fallen leaves and mulch from the soil beneath the climber, and apply new mulch about a foot deep.

Untie the canes from the trellis or fence. Wrap them with an insulation material (such as you use to keep pipes from freezing), and then retie them in place. If the stems are very flexible, you may find it easier to just lay them along the ground, and cover them with a foot of soil or mulch.

Container Roses. In Zone 6, as temperatures plunge toward 28 degrees, move roses growing in containers to an unheated garage or shed. First, remove the leaves, cut the canes back to 36 inches, tie them together to make the container easy to move, and clear the mulch away from the soil surface. Add new mulch, move the containers to their winter quarters, then water the container thoroughly.

Standard or Tree Roses. Prepare tree roses **growing in containers** for winter as recommended for container roses, above. Before temperatures reach 28 degrees Fahrenheit, move them to an unheated garage or shed.

A tree rose **growing in the ground** needs winter protection. Remove the leaves, clear away old mulch, and replace it with new mulch. Tie the canes together loosely. Enclose the plant in salt hay wrapped in burlap, translucent white plastic, or roofing paper, and tie the bundle together with a cord to keep everything in place.

In Zone 6, a tree rose growing in an exposed location may need more help. Cut free one side of the roots, then tip the entire tree rose over into a trench. Cover it with a foot of soil topped by mulch.

 PRUNING

As the weather cools, stop deadheading, and allow the roses to form rose hips. That encourages the plant to slow growth and blooming, and harden the canes, all in preparation for dormancy.

WATERING

Indoors. Check pots of **miniatures** every day or two, and keep the soil moderately damp. Rinse them every two weeks to discourage spider mites.

Outdoors. One of the most important winter preparations for all roses is a final deep and thorough watering before the ground freezes.

Renew the mulch; that protects the ground from freezing, which keeps moisture available for roots.

 # FERTILIZING

Fertilizing is over for now.

 # PESTS

When the roses have lost their leaves, prevent disease and fungus from over-wintering by removing fallen leaves, old mulch, and weeds under the roses. Spray with dormant oil to kill bacteria on the bush and on the ground.

Did You Know?

Rose Hip Jam

When you plan to make rose hip jam, avoid spraying the roses whose hips you want to use with anything bad for your health. The **rugosa roses** produce the biggest and most colorful rose hips, and generally are pest- and disease-resistant, so their hips are good candidates for jam making. Wait until after the first frost to pick the hips, and choose the biggest.

This recipe was given to me by my friend, the late Sally Erath.

Frances Chrystie's Rose Hip Jam

4 cups rose hips
1 cup water
Sugar (as needed, see below)

Place the rose hips and the water in a large pot over medium heat. Cover, and simmer about 30 minutes, until the fruit is very tender. Force the pulp through a fine sieve.

Measure the pulp then return it to the pot. For each cup of fruit pulp, stir in 1 cup of sugar. Simmer for 10 to 15 minutes, or more until the mixture is thick. Remove the pot from the heat, and skim off the foam. Pour the jam into jelly glasses cleaned and dried in your dishwasher. Fill the glasses to within $1/2$ inch of the rim, and seal with melted paraffin.

Store in the fridge.

If vole runs appear around your roses, bait the main runway with a rodenticide.

If you've been troubled by rodents in winters past, wait until after a hard frost, then mound VoleBloc or PermaTill all around the main stem of each rose bush, and cover that with a winter mulch.

PLANNING

Now that the leafy season is over and the garden bare, evaluate the setting you've given your roses, and consider which might do and look better moved to another spot.

PLANTING

You can still plant and transplant roses if the weather stays comfortable.

CARE

Winter protection for roses is meant to keep the canes from drying in bitter winds, to avoid cold damage to the canes and bud union, and damage to the crown when alternate thawing and freezing cycles cause the soil to heave it.

In the Tidewater region of Virginia, established roses require little winter protection other than a winter mulch.

In Zones 6 and 7 for their first winter, protect newly planted roses and the **miniatures,** even those rated winter hardy in your area. As the temperature heads toward 28 degrees Fahrenheit:

1 Cut the canes back to 36 inches, and tie them together with string. These canes will be trimmed back further in the spring to remove portions winterkilled.

2 Spray the canes with an anti-desiccant.

3 The "thaw/heave" cycles that can occur when warm spells hit can heave the crown from the ground. Mulch will prevent the ground from thawing. So:

• Cover the crown or the bed at least a foot deep with tree leaves. Do not use rose leaves as they may harbor disease. Oak leaves are best as they are more resistant to rot and seem to drain better.

• Or, cover the bed with straw.

• Or, spread a mound a foot deep of soil from another part of the garden over the base of the plant. Bark, fresh compost, or shredded leaves can be used instead of soil.

4 Along with any one of the above, in Zones 6 and 5 and in sites exposed to stiff wind, protect the canes:

• Wrap the whole plant in burlap or Reemay®.

• Or, encase the plant in a cage of wire and straw.

• Or, wrap the plant in straw covered with burlap and tied with rope.

• Use rose cones made of Styrofoam™ as protection. You need to trim and defoliate the rose first, then mound the crown with 12 inches of soil and mulch. Tie up the canes, place the protective cone over them, and set a weight on the cone to keep it from blowing away.

PRUNING

Cut back long canes of big roses that look as though they could be whipped around by wind. Save other pruning of long canes for late winter and early spring as branch tips generally have some winter die back, and you'll have to prune them then anyway.

WATERING

Indoors. Keep the soil for **miniatures** moderately moist. Shower them every two weeks, but the other times you water them, wet the soil, not the leaves.

Outdoors. A major danger to roses in winter is lack of water before the plant is completely dormant. One of the most important winter preparations is a deep and thorough watering before the ground freezes.

Maintain moderate soil moisture for hardy roses in containers, and for containers of hardy roses sheltering in a cold garage or shed.

FERTILIZING

To encourage blooming, fertilize **miniature roses** growing indoors under grow lights with a light application of African violet or another of the liquid bloom booster fertilizers.

Did You Know?

About 'The Fairy'

A question André is often asked on the radio is the name of a little pink rose that's used as a hedge. It's sure to be 'The Fairy', a low-growing polyanthus hybrid rambler or hedge rose that's just the right shade of seashell pink because you never tire of it. The flowers last well when you cut them for bouquets, and there's a little fragrance.

'The Fairy' was first produced in 1932, but it wasn't until the Conard-Pyle Company introduced it in 1941 that it began to appear in our gardens. It's one of just a handful of roses from that period that is disease resistant and always spectacular. 'The Fairy' never needs spraying, even for blackspot, and it produces flowers in dense clusters and sprays from early summer until freezing weather shuts it down.

The original polyanthus roses came from natural crosses of the **China Rose** (*Rosa chinensis*) and a dwarf sport of *Rosa multiflora*, Baby Rose, which is the understock for rose cultivars like 'The Fairy' and other roses described as "living hedges." The modern hybrids are low—less than 30 inches high—and flower freely throughout the season.

PESTS

Indoors. Spider mites are a threat to **miniatures roses.** Pale, fine stippling on leaves is the give-away. Spray affected plants in a kitchen sink every day or two for a couple of weeks. If that doesn't work, spray with insecticidal soap. Air the room every day.

Outdoors. To prevent disease spores from infecting new growth when it comes along in the spring, strip off the leaves, and pick up all fallen leaves under your roses. Remove the mulch below diseased plants, and replace it with fresh.

If vole runs appear around your roses, bait the main runway with a rodenticide.

DECEMBER
Roses

 PLANNING

Bring your garden log up to date.

 PLANTING

A raised bed for roses solves drainage problems and gives the roses a very good start. Get the project under way three to four weeks before you plan to plant. In our area, you can plant roses from late February to December 1.

See Starting a Raised Bed in the Introduction to the book for complete details.

 CARE

If **miniature roses** growing indoors aren't flowering, increase the light by adding grow lights after dusk and putting them under fluorescents in a light garden.

 PRUNING

Deadhead **miniature roses** indoors.

 WATERING

Indoors. Keep the soil moderately moist for **miniatures** growing indoors.

Outdoors. Don't let the containers of hardy roses sheltering in a cold garage or shed dry out.

If December is short of snow or rain, water the roses overwintering in the open garden.

 FERTILIZING

To encourage blooming, fertilize **miniature roses** that are growing indoors under grow lights with a light application of African violet or another bloom booster fertilizer.

Did You Know?

Gifts for the Rose Gardener

Grooming and pruning roses are essential to their health and beauty. Here's a set of tool rose growers love to give—and to receive:

1 For pruning and cleaning up—a set of bypass pruners; the scissor type, not the anvil type which crush the stems.

2 For removal of large woody canes at the graft—a pruning saw small enough to access the graft area so the cut can be made flush with the main stem.

3 For cutting canes $1/2$ inch diameter or greater—lopping shears with 18-inch handles.

4 To scrub loose bark away from the bud union—a brass wire brush about 2 inches wide by 3 inches deep. Hardware stores sell them.

5 To seal pruning cuts on canes greater than $1/4$ inch diameter to prevent cane borers from entering—clear nail polish or white glue.

6 To save hands and arms from scratches—long leather gauntlets.

 PESTS

Indoors. Dry air invites spider mites to adopt **miniature roses;** air the room every day. When you water container roses, water the soil, not the foliage.

Outdoors. If vole runs appear around the roses, bait the main runway with a rodenticide.

CHAPTER EIGHT

Shrubs

Shrubs give the most pleasure for the least maintenance. What do established shrubs really need? Annual fertilization. Watering during droughts. Mulch. Winter care. Regular maintenance of this type, and its timing, is easy to understand and provide.

More complex is the annual pruning that enhances a shrub's structure and its production of flowers and foliage. Pruning takes thought because **when** and **how** differs with each shrub group. As does the plant's "habit," the natural form a well-grown shrub will have when it matures **if well pruned.**

Guides to pruning the various categories of shrubs that appear on the pages for March and for May will help you to sort it out.

For the rest, you will find that shrubs that are pest- and disease-resistant, and are given a good start are worth many times over your investment in money and time.

Design. The growth "habit" of shrubs and hedge plants you choose to add or subtract have a tremendous impact on the traffic flow and the design of your garden. Like other structures—trees, fences, hedges, furniture, statuary— shrubs are the "bones" that anchor the garden design. Shrubs may be arched **(forsythia)**, rounded **(barberries),** upright (*Kerria japonica* 'Peniflora'), or columnar (**dwarf Alberta spruce,** *Picea glauca* 'Conica').

Did You Know?

When Is a Shrub a Shrub?

A forester's definition of a shrub is a multi-trunked woody perennial plant reaching not more than 10 to 20 feet at maturity. Some woody plants can be trained either as trees or shrubs, **crapemyrtles,** for example, and **shrub althaea, lilacs, witchhazels, shadblow, smokebush.** Yes, **lilacs,** though so often they are trained to a single stalk so they look like small trees.

The most interesting shrub borders include a variety of tall and small flowering, foliage and berry plants, evergreen and deciduous types, and a variety of shapes and colors.

PLANTING

How a shrub is packaged has everything to do with when it can be planted. Shrubs are sold bare root, container grown, and balled and burlapped—B&B. The very best planting seasons are early spring, and fall from the time the leaves start to turn through October, November, to December 1 or so. Evergreens are best planted or moved late August, September, and into October.

Bare-root shrubs. In early spring before growth begins, mail-order suppliers ship some shrubs bare root. Ascertain the size of a mail-order purchase before deciding it's a bargain. Follow the shipper's instructions for planting exactly.

Container-grown shrubs. In the Mid-Atlantic, you can plant container-grown shrubs from early spring—late February and March—through summer and fall until December 1. Buying locally allows you to select shrubs whose flower and foliage color, and structure, are exactly what you expect.

Balled-and-burlapped shrubs. You can plant B&B shrubs from early spring until December 1. Evergreens are best moved August, September,

Shrubs

Did You Know?

About Hedges

A well-kept hedge adds structure to a garden design. A hedge also makes a handsome frame for a flower bed, a shrubbery border, a garden room, paths. You can use a hedge to lead the eye to, or from, features in the landscape, dampen noise, and block blown leaves and debris. A prickly hedge can discourage (some) unwelcome visitors. A tall hedge can create a privacy screen, mask neighboring walls, mark distant property boundaries, and break the force of the wind.

To help you decide whether a hedge is for you, here's some advice from seasoned hedge keepers:

- Be sure you will have enough time available to keep your hedge trimmed. Hedges trimmed with hand pruners have a more natural look . . . and that takes time.

- Don't site a hedge on your property line using shrubs whose branches will reach into the neighbor's space. The neighbor has the legal right to remove branches and roots that invade his/her space.

- Choose species suited to the light and ground space available for the whole length of the hedge.

- Buy young shrubs, 3 feet or less. They are less expensive and adapt quickly.

- If the hedge will run through both tall shade and real shade, choose species that succeed in either light. Among candidates are most hollies, including **American, Foster's,** and **Japanese holly,** and **longstalk holly,** *Ilex pedunculosa,* **Canadian hemlock,** and **'Otto Lukyen' laurel,** *Prunus laurocerasus.* In the shadiest area plant the shrubs closer together.

For more about hedges, see Planting in September.

---

and into October. In summer, avoid buying B&B shrubs dug in spring that have been sitting for months in the open air with their bare rootball naked to the wind and sun. B&B shrubs dug in spring and "heeled in," that is protected by mounds of mulch or soil, stay in good condition. We recommend pay-ing extra to have large B&B shrubs planted and guaranteed by the supplier.

Light and spacing. Many shrubs got their start in light shade under tall trees in a forest or at its edge. So most can do with less than a full day of sunlight. **Azaleas, rhododendrons,** and **garde-nias** do very well in the filtered light of tall trees.

Space shrubs at distances that allow plenty of space for the lateral develop-ment of branches. To calculate the best spacing for two or more young shrubs, add together the widths given on the plant tags, and divide by two. To occupy the bed while young shrubs fill out, plant shade-tolerant hostas or ferns, and annuals such as impatiens, pentas, and caladiums. Avoid airless corners.

Soil. The information on Soil Prepa-ration and Improvement and pH given in the Introduction to the book apply to shrubs. With shrubs, suitable pH varies widely. For **azaleas,** it's between pH 4.5 and 6.0; for **boxwood,** pH 6.0 to 7.0; for **dwarf burning bush** (*Euonymus alatus* 'Compactus'), the pH is 6.0 to 7.5. You can grow a small shrub successfully in soil whose pH is not perfect because its roots are mod-est. A big shrub needs lots of growing room and will have an edge if it is growing in soil whose natural compo-sition and pH are compatible.

Digging the hole. Make the planting hole three times as wide and twice as deep as the rootball. Loosen the sides of the hole, and blend the soil taken from the hole with the organic amend-ments described in Soil Preparation and Improvement in the Introduction. Half fill the bottom of the hole with

Shrubs

improved soil, and tamp it down to make a firm base for the roots.

Set the shrub so the crown will be an inch above ground level. Half fill the hole once more with improved soil. Tamp it down firmly. Finish filling the hole with improved soil, and tamp it down firmly. Shape the soil around the crown into a wide saucer.

Water the soil slowly, gently, and thoroughly with a sprinkler, a soaker hose, a bubbler, or by hand. You need to put down 1½ inches of water (see Watering, below). Or, slowly pour on 10 to 15 gallons of water from a bucket.

Mulch newly planted shrubs 2 to 3 inches deep starting 3 inches from the main stem. Replenish the mulch as needed to keep it 2 to 3 inches deep.

Growing shrubs in containers. You can grow a shrub in a container outdoors indefinitely—a hardy shrub, that is—providing the container is large enough to insulate the roots from winter cold. (See April, Growing Shrubs in Containers.)

Transplanting shrubs. Spring and fall through November are the best seasons to move shrubs. Evergreen shrubs can be transplanted spring and fall through October. You will find information on moving large established shrubs under Planting, in the February pages. Move flowering shrubs well before, or after they have bloomed.

FERTILIZING AND MULCHING

Fertilizing. A new shrub in improved soil rich in lasting organic fertilizers doesn't need fertilizing until the following year. The first annual application of fertilizer should be made before growth begins in spring. The last application should be as growth slows toward the end of the growing season. The number of applications in between depends **entirely** on the type of fertilizer you are using. (See Understanding Fertilizers in the Introduction to the book.) The growing season in Zones 6 and 7, comes to an end between early September and early October. In Zone 8, Richmond and the Tidewater areas of Virginia, the last fertilization can be between the end of September and mid-October.

Mulching. Mulch shrubs 3 to 4 inches deep (no more!) after planting, starting 3 inches from the central stem(s), and top it off three times a year; first, after the early spring fertilization; again before summer heat arrives; and third, in fall. (See Mulching, in the introduction to Chapter 9, Trees.) Winter mulches are discussed under Mulching in the Introduction to the book.

WATERING

Once established, most shrubs will require less extra watering than perennials; when the weather isn't supporting growth, they adapt by slowing down unless forced by shallow watering and inappropriate fertilizing to grow. Always water slowly and gently, and try to pour on 1½ inches. Set a 1-pound coffee can or other container under the sprinkler or the hose, and record how long it took to put 1½ inches in the can—then you'll know.

Newly planted and transplanted shrubs need sustained moisture—for the first eight weeks, two or three 5-gallon bucketfuls of water around the roots weekly throughout spring unless you have sustained soaking rains. In summer, every week or ten days, unless you have a soaking rain, slowly and gently lay down 1½ inches of water. In fall, even after cold sets in, shrub roots continue to develop so water often enough to prevent the soil from drying out. One of the most important winter preparations is a deep and thorough watering before the ground freezes.

PRUNING

You can reduce the amount of pruning your shrubs will need by selecting dwarf and slow-growing varieties. Most important when choosing shrubs

Shrubs

Did You Know?

Shrubs for Flower Arrangements

- **Butterfly Bush,** *Buddleia* x *weyeriana* 'Honeycomb'
- **Bigleaf Hydrangea,** *Hydrangea macrophylla* 'Amethyst'
- **Drooping Leucothe,** *Leucothoe fontanesiana*
- **Highbush Cranberry,** *Viburnum trilobum* 'Compactum'
- **Lilac,** *Syringa vulgaris* 'Beauty of Moscow'

for hedges. But even dwarfs grow, albeit slowly, so even they may need some pruning to maintain their size. See the introduction to the Trees chapter for the proper ways to prune.

We prune shrubs at different seasons and with a variety of purposes:

To rejuvenate. Prune drastically in late winter **while still dormant** to rejuvenate leggy shrubs. Take away no more than a third or a quarter of the branches in one season. Make the cut about a foot from the ground. Repeat the process the next two years until the pruning project is complete.

To encourage flowering. Prune shrubs that flower on the current season's wood—**butterfly bush** and **vitex** for example—well **before growth begins** to encourage the production of many new flowering shoots. Prune shrubs that bloom on last year's wood—**azaleas** for example—when they **finish blooming,** because they

soon start initiating flower buds for the next season.

To stimulate fullness. Prune shrubs when they are **growing actively** to encourage more, bushier growth. Fresh, young shoots that are cut back by half immediately begin to grow lateral shoots.

To encourage branching. To encourage more foliage in broadleaf evergreens that branch—**azaleas** and **abelias,** for example—prune succulent new shoots while they are **growing actively** back by half. **Rhododendrons** are different; cut just above a whorl.

To limit growth. Prune leafy plants **after the season's growth** to reduce the leaf surfaces, which limits the sugar synthesized and sent to the roots, and that limits next year's growth.

To top a plant. Top a shrub or a hedge **after the season's growth** has been completed to maintain the current height.

PEST CONTROL

Weeds. In naked earth weeds sprout from April to October. Mulch helps keeps them out, and the few that do get started are easy to hand pull.

Critters. Bears harvest the berries of the handsome **highbush blueberry,** *Vaccinium corymbosum*, which we plant for its autumn color. Deer graze **rhododendrons, arborvitae, hydrangeas, shrub althea,** and many other favorite shrubs. Rabbits can girdle stems especially above the snow line. For solutions to these and other pests, see Pests, Diseases, and Controls in the Appendix.

Insects and diseases. Choose shrubs that are disease resistant, and be willing to accept a normal quota of insect damage. See Integrated Pest Management in the Introduction to the book.

Good garden practices help keep problems away—air, space, light, good soil, water as needed. Avoid planting shrubs in airless corners. Whitefly and spider mites love hot, airless spots and will spoil the leaves even if they don't do permanent damage. Neem based products control these two; spray the plants two or three times at intervals of ten days or so. See Pests, Diseases, and Controls in the Appendix for more information.

Shrubs

Common Name (*Botanical Name*)	Hardiness Zones	Light	Blooom Period	Blooms on Old or New Wood	Type
Andromeda, Japanese Andromeda (*Pieris japonica*)	6 to 8	Sun to part sun	—	—	Evergreen
Aucuba, Gold-dust Tree (*Aucuba japonica*)	6 to 8	Part shade or shade	—	—	Evergreen
Azalea, Deciduous (*Rhododendron* sp. and hybrids)	4 to 8 (Native)	—	Early, mid-, late spring	Old wood	Deciduous
Barberry, Japanese Barberry (*Berberis thunbergii* 'Atropurpurea')	4 to 8	—	Mid-spring	Old wood	Deciduous
Beautyberry, Purple Beautyberry (*Callicarpa dichotoma*)	5 to 8	—	Berries in fall	New wood	Deciduous
Beautybush (*Kolkwitzia amabilis*)	6 to 9	—	May/June	Old wood	Deciduous
Blueberry (*Vaccinium corymbosum*)	3 to 7 (Native)	—	May	Old wood	Deciduous
Blue-spirea, Bluebeard (*Caryopteris* x *clandonensis*)	5/6 to 9	—	Mid-summer	New wood	Deciduous
Boxwood, Box (*Buxus sempervirens* sp. and hybrids)	5 to 8	Sun to part sun	—	—	Evergreen
Butterfly Bush (*Buddleia davidii*)	5 to 9	—	Late summer to frost	New wood	Deciduous
Bush Cinquefoil, Shrubby Cinquefoil (*Potentilla fruticosa* cultivars)	2/3 to 7	—	June through early frost	New wood	Deciduous
Camellia, Japanese Camellia (*Camellia japonica* sp. and hybrids)	6/7 to 9	Part sun to part shade	—	—	Evergreen
Canadian Hemlock (*Tsuga canadensis*)	4 to 7	Sun to part shade	—	—	Evergreen
Cherrylaurel (*Prunus laurocerasus* 'Otto Luyken')	6 to 8	Sun to part shade	—	—	Evergreen
Cotoneaster, Rockspray Cotoneaster (*Cotoneaster horizontalis*)	4 to 8	Sun to part shade	—	—	Evergreen
Daphne 'Carol Mackie' (*Daphne* x *burkwoodii* 'Carol Mackie')	4 to 8	—	Mid-spring	Old wood	Deciduous
Deutzia (*Deutzia gracilis* 'Nikko')	5 to 8	—	May	Old wood	Deciduous
Dwarf Burning Bush (*Euonymus alatus* 'Compactus')	4 to 8	—	Fall foliage	Old wood	Deciduous

Shrubs

Common Name (*Botanical Name*)	Hardiness Zones	Light	Blooom Period	Blooms on Old or New Wood	Type
Dwarf Hinoki False Cypress (*Chamaecyparis obtusa* 'Nana Gracilis' Dwarf)	4 to 8	Sun to part sun	—	—	Evergreen
Dwarf Mugo Pine (*Pinus mugo* var. *pumilo*)	4 to 7	Sun to part sun	—	—	Evergreen
Evergreen Azalea (*Rhododendron* hybrids)	5 to 9	Part sun to part shade	—	—	Evergreen
Firethorn (*Pyracantha coccinea* cultivars)	6 to 8	Sun or part sun	—	—	Evergreen
Flowering Quince, Japanese Quince (*Chaenomeles speciosa*)	5 to 8	—	Early spring	Old wood	Deciduous
Forsythia (*Forsythia* x *intermedia*)	5 to 8	—	Early spring	Old wood	Deciduous
Fothergilla (*Fothergilla gardenii*)	5 to 9 (Native)	—	Spring	Old wood	Deciduous
Glossy Abelia (*Abelia* x *grandiflora*)	6 to 9	—	Summer through frost	New wood	Deciduous
Holly (*Ilex crenata* 'Convexa')	5 to 8	Sun to part sun	—	—	Evergreen
Hydrangea 'Annabelle' (*Hydrangea arborescens* 'Annabelle')	5 to 9	—	Summer	New wood or old	Deciduous
Japanese Kerria (*Kerria japonica* 'Pleniflora')	4 to 9	—	Early to mid-spring	Old wood and some new wood	Deciduous
Japanese Maple (*Acer palmatum* 'Bloodgood')	4 to 9	—	Foliage plant	Not relevant	Deciduous
Juniper (*Juniperus* sp. and hybrids)	3 or 5 to 9	Sun	—	—	Evergreen
Lilac (*Syringa* species and hybrids)	4 to 8	—	Early and mid-spring	Old wood	Deciduous
Mockorange (*Philadelpbus coronarius* hybrids)	4 to 8 (Native)	—	Mid-spring	Old wood	Deciduous
Mountain Laurel (*Kalmia latifolia*)	4 to 8	Part sun to part shade	—	—	Evergreen
Nandina, Heavenly Bamboo (*Nandina domestica* 'Moyers Red')	6 to 9	Sun to part shade	—	—	Evergreen

Shrubs

Common Name (*Botanical Name*)	Hardiness Zones	Light	Blooom Period	Blooms on Old or New Wood	Type
Oakleaf Hydrangea (*Hydrangea quercifolia*)	5 to 9	—	Late spring, summer	Old wood	Deciduous
Oregon Grape Holly (*Mahonia aquifolium*)	5 to 8	Part sun to part shade	—	—	Evergreen
Privet (*Ligustrum vulgare*)	3 to 8	Sun to part sun	—	—	Evergreen
Rhododendron (*Rhododendron* sp. and cultivars)	4 to 8	Part sun to part shade	—	—	Evergreen
Rose of Sharon (*Hibiscus syriacus*)	5 to 8	—	Summer and early fall	New wood	Deciduous
Scotch Broom (*Cytisus scoparius*)	5/6 to 10	—	May and June	Old wood	Deciduous
Shadblow, Serviceberry (*Amelanchier* sp.)	3 to 8 (Native)	—	Very early spring	Old wood	Deciduous
Smokebush (*Cotinus coggygria* cultivars)	5 to 8	—	Early summer	Old wood	Deciduous
Spicebush (*Lindera benzoin*)	4 to 8	—	Mid-April	Old wood	Deciduous
Spirea (*Spiraea* sp. and cvs.)	Zones 3 to 9	—	Summer	Old or new wood according to species	Deciduous
Summersweet, Sweetpepper Bush (*Clethra alnifolia* sp. and hybrids)	4 to 9 (Native)	—	Summer	Old wood	Deciduous
Viburnum (*Viburnum* sp. and hybrids)	5 to 8	—	Early and mid spring	Old wood	Deciduous
Virginia Sweetspire (*Itea virginica* 'Henry's Garnet')	5 to 9 (Native)	—	Spring to mid-summer	Old wood	Deciduous
Weigela (*Weigela florida*)	5 to 8	—	Mid- and late spring	Old and some new wood	Deciduous
Winterberry Holly (*Ilex verticillata*)	3 to 8/9 (Native)	—	Fall and winter berries	New wood	Deciduous
Yew, English-Japanese Yew (*Taxus* x *media*)	5 to 7	Sun	—	—	Evergreen
Yucca (*Yucca,* sp. and hybrids)	5 to 9	Sun	—	—	Evergreen

JANUARY
Shrubs

 PLANNING

In winter your garden reveals its "bones," the naked woody structures that anchor the landscape. Take the garden catalogs arriving now to a comfortable chair by a window, and consider what a few new shrubs, or a hedge, could do for your view. You can start planting new shrubs as early as March, but we recommend waiting to plant a new hedge until fall.

Flowering shrubs. For flowers early to late spring and four-season greenery consider varieties of flowering broad-leaved evergreens—**mountain laurels, rhododendrons, azaleas.** Evergreen **azalea** foliage adds shades of plum and maroon to the fall scene, and some are flecked with gold. **Kaempferi azaleas,** including **'Armstrong's Fall'** and **'Indian Summer'**, rebloom in September, just as **nandina's** lipstick red berries begin to shine.

Shrubs for fragrance. In their season of bloom, shrubs that bear fragrant flowers become garden destinations. **Winter daphne,** *Daphne odora* 'Aureo-marginata', scents the garden early on, followed by the perfumed **viburnums.** You can count on **mock oranges** for late spring perfume, and in November the tiny blooms of **sweet holly olive**

(*Osmanthus heterophyllus*) fill the air around with a haunting fragrance.

Evergreen shrubs for perennial beds. If you haven't included shrubby evergreens in your flower beds, plan to try a few this year. The lively green anchors the beds off season. We use the dark little **mugo pines** that way. A trio of small, clipped ball-shaped **boxwoods** among the perennials adds greenery and a smile. Small, columnar evergreens like **dwarf Alberta spruce,** *Picea glauca* 'Conica', are sensational in a large flowering border. **Alberta spruce** is attacked by spider mites, so make a note to keep it sprayed periodically with horticultural soaps.

Evergreen shrubs for hedges and edging. The **junipers** (*Juniperus* spp. and cultivars), the indestructible **yews** (*Taxus*), the handsome **Meserve hybrid hollies** (*Ilex* x *meserveae*) **'Blue Boy'** and **'Blue Princess'**, and **dwarf variegated hollies** make handsome hedges, great edging for paths and driveways, and foundation plants.

Deciduous shrubs for seasonal change. Flowers and foliage that changes with the seasons is the domain of the leaf-losing shrubs. In early fall the **dwarf winged spindle tree,** *Euonymus alata* 'Compacta', is a blaze of pink-scarlet. *Spiraea* and the silver-backed leaves of **wil-**

lowleaf cotoneaster (*Cotoneaster salicifolius* 'Autumn Fire') turn purplish when the weather is cold. Yellow **Japanese barberry** (*Berberis thunbergii* 'Aurea') and golden **Scotch heather** (*Calluna vulgaris*) brighten dark corners. Cultivars of the exquisite **Japanese maple** (*Acer palmatum*) rival the crimson of the **swamp maple.** The beautiful cultivar **'Osakazuki'** is yellow to light green in the summer and turns a stunning fluorescent red in fall.

Berried shrubs for winter interest. The bright berries of both evergreen and leaf-losing **hollies, barberries,** and other berried shrubs cheer winter's gray skies. **Oregon grape** (*Mahonia aquifolium*), *Nandina domestica,* and **sweet box** *Sarcococca hookeriana* var. *humilis* add dabs of shiny red to the seasonal mix. Bright blue/black or white berries follow the flowers in many species.

PLANTING

Give your out-of-bloom gift **azalea** a sunny spot on a sill since it, along with **mums** and **poinsettias,** is among plants that test high as air purifiers. When blooming is over, transplant the **azalea** to a larger pot filled with mixture that is one-fourth garden soil and three-fourths peat moss. Keep the soil moist, and when new growth appears, at every watering apply an acid-type fertilizer at one quarter the recommended strength. Increase that over a four-month period until you are fertilizing at the strength recommended on the container. Forced azaleas are not usually hardy here, but if you summer it outdoors and expose it to several cool, but not freezing, fall nights before bringing it in, it may bloom again.

CARE

Free evergreen branches burdened by snow or ice. Use a broom to brush away accumulations of snow and ice that might harm hedges.

Renew the anti-desiccant spray on **camellias** and other **broadleaf evergreen shrubs** growing in exposed positions. If they are suffering, wrap them in Reemay.

PRUNING

Remove branches damaged by heavy snow fall and winter storms.

WATERING

Indoors. Water shrubs wintering inside as needed.

Did You Know?

About Shrubby Needled Evergreens and Conifers

The shrub-size needled evergreens and conifers are dwarf or slow-growing species and varieties of the familiar evergreen trees. Some are perfect for keeping green alive year round in shrubbery borders and flower beds. Others make fine dense hedges, wind breaks, and edgers for paths and driveways.

Among small evergreens we use to anchor beds of perennials are the dark, chunky little **Mugo pine** *Pinus mugo,* 'Globosa' and similar **dwarf blue spruces;** narrow columnar **dwarf Alberta spruce,** *Picea glauca* 'Conica'; pyramidal *Picea pungens* 'Fat Albert', a **dwarf Colorado blue spruce;** and shrubby *Chamaecyparis obtusa,* **Hinoki falsecypress** and the **dwarf golden Sawara falsecypress** *Chamaecyparis pisifera*, both members of the *Chamaecyparis* clan.

To furnish neglected corners, and for low and mid-height screening, consider some of the sprawling **dwarf junipers** *Juniperus* cultivars; **dwarf falsecypresses,** *Chamaecyparis* spp. and cultivars; and upright little **yews,** *Taxus* spp. and cvs. like 'Pygmaea'.

Outdoors. Without snow cover or rain, the soil may run dry around shrubs growing next to foundations and under overhangs, and shrubs in containers that are under arbors and similar shelters. During the January thaw, give them a slow, thorough watering.

FERTILIZING

Tropical hibiscus, potted **gardenias,** and other tender shrubs brought indoors last fall are beginning to grow again; add a half strength dose of water-soluble fertilizer at every second watering.

PESTS

Indoors. Monitor **tropical hibiscus** and shrubs growing indoors for signs of spider mite, whitefly, and other problems. See Pests, Diseases, and Controls in the Appendix for controls.

Outdoors. Repair and/or renew deer deterrents and sprays. Check and adjust burlap covers and chickenwire cages protecting shrubs.

If vole runs appear around shrubs, bait the main runway with a rodenticide.

FEBRUARY

PLANNING

When the buds on branches of shrubs that flower in early spring are swelling, harvest a few to force into bloom indoors.

Place your catalog orders for shrubs now.

PLANTING

In Zone 8, the soil may have warmed enough to do some transplanting. Small shrubs can be moved any time before growth begins. Moving very large shrubs is a two-year project. Known as **root pruning,** the process also slows growth by depriving the plant of nutrient intake.

Year 1. Before growth begins, sever the roots in a circle all around the trunk of the shrub to stimulate root growth within the circle.

Year 2. This time next year, tie the branches together at the top. Dig a trench outside the root-pruned circle, lift the rootball onto a big piece of burlap, and tie the burlap up around the trunk. Very gently transport the plant to its new location. Prepare the soil, and plant the shrub as described in Planting in the introduction to this chapter, and then free the branches and prune out damaged twigs.

CARE

Clear snow, dead branches, and winter debris from the shrubbery, especially the **boxwoods.**

After the late winter fertilization (see Fertilizing below), add enough fresh material to maintain a 2- to 3-inch layer of mulch starting about 3 inches from the central stems.

PRUNING

Thin **forsythias, quince,** and other spring-flowering shrubs well before they bloom, and use the branches for forcing into bloom indoors.

You can prune summer-flowering shrubs February, March, or April.

Prune out evergreen branches damaged by winter storms.

To rejuvenate the **hollies,** prune heavily in late winter to early spring. You can cut the plants down to about a foot from the ground.

WATERING

Indoors. Water shrubs as needed.

Outdoors. The soil is usually still wet from winter rain and snow, so no water-

ing should be needed this month, except for new transplants. Throughout spring, unless you have a soaking rain, pour two or three 5-gallon bucketfuls of water around the roots once a week throughout spring.

FERTILIZING

Indoors. Fertilize **tropical hibiscus** and other tender shrubs brought indoors last fall at every second watering.

Outdoors. Check and adjust the soil pH in the beds of shrubs, especially any that aren't performing well, including **azaleas, rhododendrons,** and other acid-loving plants. To raise or lower the pH, see Soil Preparation and Improvement in the Introduction to the book.

Fertilize the beds late this month or early next month. The section on Understanding Fertilizers in the Introduction to the book explains how and when to use the various types of fertilizer.

Halve the amount of fertilizer for mature hedges; do not overstimulate when you no longer have a lot of room for growth.

 PESTS

Indoors. Watch shrubs growing indoors for signs of whitefly, spider mites, and

When the buds on branches of shrubs that flower in early spring are swelling, harvest a few to force into bloom indoors.

Did You Know?

Forcing Flowering Branches

In late winter, branches of spring flowering shrubs (and trees) can be forced into bloom indoors. The time to harvest the branches is when the buds begin to swell. The warmer the zone, the earlier the forcing date.

Harvest branches 2 to 3 feet long and heavily studded with buds. Monitor the water levels in the containers—it may need topping twice a week.

Cold method. Press the cut ends into snow or icy cold water, and let them rest two days in a cool, dark place. Fill tall vases with cool water, recut the branch ends, and arrange the branches in the vases. Set them in the sun next to a window.

Warm method. Bring the cut branches indoors, and place them in tall containers in water at bath temperature—90 to 110 degrees Fahrenheit. Tent the containers and the branches with plastic, and set them in a dim, warm room. The warmth and humidity will encourage the scales covering the flower buds to expand, and activate dormant buds.

Here are a few of our favorites:

• *Chaenomeles,* **Japanese Quince, Flowering Quince;** cut February to mid-March; force for two to five weeks; bloom period, four to seven days.

• *Cornus florida,* **Dogwood;** cut Mid-March; force for two to four weeks; bloom period, seven to ten days.

• **Forsythia;** cut February to mid-March; force for one to three weeks; bloom period, seven days.

• *Malus,* **Apple, Crabapple;** cut Mid-March; force for two to three weeks; bloom period, seven days.

• *Prunus calleryana,* **Flowering Pear;** cut late January to mid-March; force for two to five weeks; bloom period, seven to fourteen days.

• *Prunus persica,* **Flowering Peach;** cut early February; force for four to five weeks; bloom period, seven days.

• *Prunus serrulata,* **Japanese Flowering Cherry;** cut late January to mid-March; force for two to four weeks; bloom period, seven to fourteen days.

• *Prunus triloba,* **Flowering Plum;** cut late January to February; force for three to four weeks; bloom period, ten days.

• *Salix* species, **Pussy Willow;** cut February; force for one to two weeks; bloom period, indefinitely if allowed to dry. (Remove the bud scales, and when they reach the fuzzy bud stage, remove the branches from the water.)

• *Syringa,* **Lilac;** cut early March; bloom period, four to six weeks; bloom period, three to seven days.

---

other pests. If you find problems, look up controls in the Pests, Diseases, and Controls section in the Appendix.

Outdoors. Check and adjust burlap covers and chickenwire cages protecting shrubs from deer.

As the ground thaws, voles get lively, they can damage young shrub roots. If vole runs appear, bait the main runway with a rodenticide.

To keep rabbits, woodchucks, and other rodents away from shrubs, try chemical fungicide formulations such as Thiram (Arasan) and hot pepper wax.

Before buds on plants suspected of insect infestation break, spray them with horticultural oil. The oil smothers insects and their eggs.

PLANNING

March is a great month to plant the shrubs you'd like to add to the garden.

Begin to plan the pruning of shrub borders and hedges.

 ## PLANTING

As soon as winter cold leaves the ground, you can start planting new shrubs. Use Tree-tone, Holly-tone, or Plant-tone as fertilizers.

Container-grown shrub. To free the shrub, tip the pot on its side, and roll it around. If it's too large for that, slit the sides of the container, and peel off the pieces. If roots wrap the rootball, make four shallow vertical cuts in the sides of the rootball, and slice off the bottom 2 inches.

Bare-root shrub. Keep the shrub in its packaging in a dark, cool place until you are ready to plant. Soak the roots in tepid water six to twelve hours before planting.

B&B shrub. Handle the rootball gently, and as little as possible. Avoid disturbing the burlap, twine, or wire basket as you put the rootball into the planting hole. After the rootball is in the hole, cut the twine around the trunk, and cut off or push the ends of the burlap into the hole.

If the cover is plastic, cut away as much as possible, and poke holes in what remains.

Follow these steps for planting:

1 Dig a planting hole three times as wide and twice as deep as the rootball; after planting, the crown of the shrub should be about an inch above the soil line.

2 Mix into the soil from the hole the amendments recommended under Soil Preparation and Improvement in the Introduction to the book.

3 Half fill the bottom of the hole with the improved soil, and tamp it down. Make a firm mound in the center of the hole, and drape the plant roots over and around the mound.

 ## CARE

Indoors. To keep a **gardenia** indoors in good condition, put the pot on a saucer of moist pebbles, grow it in a sunny window, and air and mist the plant daily. When you water, add a half dose of water-soluble fertilizer for acid-loving plants.

Outdoors. Remove covers from protected shrubs. March winds can blow hard enough to disturb the mulch applied last month after fertilizing the beds; top it off if necessary.

 ## PRUNING

Shear hedges. The pruning guide for deciduous shrubs on this month's pages and the May guide for evergreens will help you to determine when to clip shrubs and hedges.

In mid-March, shear damaged (and browning or whitened) **boxwood** branches back to live growth. To regenerate a multi-stemmed deciduous shrub that is overgrown, before it begins to grow, take out a third or a quarter of the branches. Make the cut about a foot from the ground.

Deadhead and prune back flowering shrubs that bloom on the current season's wood now before the buds break. Cut **butterfly bush,** *Buddleia,* back to 6 to 12 inches from the ground to force new growth. To encourage flowering and maintain a shrubby height and form in **shrub althea (rose-of-Sharon)** and **crapemyrtle,** prune older branches back to a strong outward facing bud.

You can prune summer-flowering shrubs this month and in April.

 ## WATERING

Indoors. Water shrubs wintering inside as needed.

To regenerate a multi-stemmed deciduous shrub that is overgrown, before it begins to grow, take out a third or a quarter of the branches.

Outdoors. Maintain the soil moisture in new and transplanted shrubs. Pour two or three 5-gallon bucketfuls of water around the roots once a week throughout spring.

FERTILIZING

Indoors. Continue to fertilize **tropical hibiscus, gardenias,** and other tender shrubs at every second watering.

Indoors and outdoors. Before growth begins, top-dress the soil of shrubs growing in containers indoors and outdoors. Tip the containers on their sides, and gently remove the top 2 inches of soil. Replace it with a fertile potting mix that includes Holly-tone. Renew the mulch.

Outdoors. Fertilize beds not fertilized last month. Avoid fertilizing flowering shrubs shortly before blooming. That stimulates growth at a time when you want the plants to direct their energy into flowering. **If you've missed the right moment for fertilizing, wait to fertilize until after they have bloomed.**

Did You Know?

Pruning Guide for Deciduous Shrubs

Dead or damaged wood. Prune any time between late winter and early autumn.

Flowering shrubs that bloom on new wood. Prune in late winter or early spring, well before growth begins.

Flowering plants that bloom on old wood. Prune right after they bloom to avoid removing next year's flower buds that develop on new growth.

To encourage dense branching. Prune during active growth; cut back by half succulent stems beginning to grow lateral shoots.

To control height. Prune after new growth has fully developed. Cut into the old wood.

To slow or dwarf growth. Prune after the season's new growth is complete.

PESTS

Indoors. Watch shrubs growing indoors for signs of whitefly, spider mites, and other problems. If you find problems, look up controls in the Pests, Diseases, and Controls section in the Appendix.

Outdoors. Before the buds begin to swell, apply a dormant horticultural oil spray to insect-infested shrubs. These dense oils smother the insects and their eggs.

In deer country, apply a new and different spray to vulnerable shrubs (**rhododendrons, arborvitae,** and other broadleaf evergreens), and replace old deterrents with new deterrents. (See Pests, Diseases, and Controls in the Appendix.) If deer are very audacious, surround small treasured shrubs with temporary chickenwire screens; for larger plantings, try unobtrusive bird netting.

Voles are active in March. If you see vole runs, bait the main runway with a rodenticide.

APRIL
Shrubs

PLANNING

Considering adding shrubs with colorful foliage and/or bark to brighten your shrubbery border. Some of our favorites are **golden privet**, *Ligustrum* x *vicaryi*, and **variegated gold-dust tree**, *Aucuba japonica* 'Variegata'. At a distance the foliage of **variegated bigleaf hydrangea**, *Hydrangea macrophylla* 'Variegata', and *Weigela florida* 'Variegata', and 'Wine & Roses' are a lovely soft jade.

PLANTING

You can transplant container-grown and B&B shrubs all the months ahead until about December 1. Evergreen shrubs may do best August through October. But right now the new stock at your garden center is likely to be in top condition. Before buying a container-grown shrub, tip it partly out of the pot, and make sure the rootball isn't heavily rootbound.

CARE

Indoors. Repot **azaleas, gardenias, citrus,** and other tender shrubs outgrowing their containers, and as soon as the weather stays above 60 degrees at night, move them outdoors for summer R&R. Place them in bright indirect light.

Outdoors. Don't be alarmed if **crapemyrtles** and some other late shrubs don't come to life when you expect them to. Wait until June before deciding they didn't survive winter.

PRUNING

As flowers fade on shrubs that bloom on the previous year's wood, prune back branches that are compromising the natural form of the shrub, and older non-productive wood.

Prune **azaleas** when they finish blooming to a shape suggesting a layered cloud; don't just shear off the branch tips.

WATERING

For a shrub's first season, unless there's a soaking rain, throughout spring slowly and gently pour two or three 5-gallon bucketfuls of water around the roots once a week.

Water shrubs growing in containers as needed.

FERTILIZING

Outdoors. Mophead and **lacecap hydrangeas** may be cream through rose to dark blue. The color depends not only on the variety, but also on the soil pH. Acidity makes aluminum in the soil more available, and that's what keeps the flowers blue. A pH of 5.0 to 5.5 results in a soft blue color. To maintain pink, the soil must be in the pH range of 6.0 to 6.5 or slightly higher. Test the soil now. If the pH needs adjusting, see Soil Preparation and Improvement in the Introduction to the book. The time to adjust the pH is before new growth begins to emerge.

If you are using chemical fertilizers, you should be fertilizing every six weeks or so. Check the section on Understanding Fertilizers in the Introduction to the book for timing.

At every second watering, add a half dose of a water-soluble fertilizer to the water for shrubs growing in containers.

PESTS

Outdoors. Continue preventive measures to protect your garden from deer.

At every second watering, add a half dose of a soluble fertilizer to the water for shrubs growing in containers.

Did You Know?

Growing Shrubs in Containers

You can grow almost any shrub successfully in a container as long as it has good drainage and is big enough to hold enough soil to protect the roots from winter cold. Casters on the bottom of the larger containers make moving easier.

Container. For a small shrub, a container 14 to 16 inches in height and diameter is enough. Start a young larger shrub, like **Japanese maple,** in an 18- to 20-inch tub, and plan to move it to a 30-inch tub.

Insulation can keep containers from cracking in winter's cold. Wrap the interior of containers that will remain outdoors for the winter with a double row of large bubble wrap or Styrofoam before filling them with soil. You can provide added winter protection by packing bags of leaves around the containers in fall.

Soil. The ideal container soil is a fertile semi-soilless mix. André's recipe is: 1 part good topsoil, 1 part horticultural perlite, and 2 parts coarse peat moss. For every 7 inches of planter height, add $1/3$ cup slow-release fertilizer, and 1 cup dehydrated cow manure. Adding a soil polymer, such as Soil Moist, can reduce watering by as much as 50 percent. Soak the growing medium before you plant. After planting, water until water runs out the bottom. Apply and maintain a 2- or 3-inch layer of mulch.

Watering. From late spring to mid-autumn, plan to water weekly or bi-weekly. The larger the container, the less often you will have to water it. Containers with built-in water reservoirs, or with water rings that let the plant soak up the water from the bottom, help to keep the soil moist.

Fertilizing. Once a month during the growing season, add a water-soluble fertilizer, seaweed or manure tea, to the water.

In late winter before growth begins, top-dress the soil. Tip the container on its side, and gently remove the top 2 inches of soil. Replace it with fresh fertile potting mix that includes Holly-tone slow release fertilizer, and renew the mulch.

Aphids, whiteflies, and spider mites are gearing up to get you down. **Azaleas** growing in full sun are especially susceptible to spider mites and lacebugs. Three applications of Permethrin or *Pyrethrum* at three to four day intervals will help you to control these pests. Be sure to spray the undersides of the leaves.

Scale is a problem with hollies and camellias. Spray with summer weight horticultural oils or neem.

Rake up weeds as they raise their little green heads to avoid dealing with mature weeds later.

Late this month gypsy moths may appear. Spray with a biological control such as *Bacillus thuringiensis.* Other controls are Sevin or malathion insecticide, pyrethrin, or rotenone.

PLANNING

Spring gardens are peaking in the Mid-Atlantic, a wonderful time to visit public and private gardens. **Check out the azalea collection at the U.S. National Arboretum in Washington, and note the names of some you would like to see in your shrubbery border.**

When the weather keeps you out of the garden, visit your full-service garden centers looking for must-haves and bargains.

Investigate the many **viburnums.** Some of these big handsome shrubs bear flowers that are spicily perfumed, and many have colorful foliage and fruits in fall. Some bloom with the flowering cherries, some as late as the end of June. The earlier types bear large rounded flower heads and are called "snowball" or "semi-snowball" varieties. **'Mohawk'** and **'Cayuga'** are two of several superb fragrant disease-resistant cultivars introduced by the late great plant hybridizer, Dr. Donald R. Egolf of the National Arboretum. "Double-file viburnums" bloom later, and they perch rows of pure white flowers all along the tops of their branches; Dr. Egolf's **'Shasta'** is a superb example.

 PLANTING

May is a fine month for planting new shrubs and transplanting shrubs that have finished blooming.

Fill gaps left by the passing of the spring-flowering bulbs by planting big seedlings of flowering annuals, along with young tropical shrubs and tender shrubs from last year that you wintered indoors.

 CARE

Indoors. Move indoor shrubs that still are indoors outside to bright indirect light for their summer vacation.

Outdoors. To keep summer's downpours from eroding the soil around your shrubs, and to protect their roots from the coming heat, replenish the mulch. Make it 2 to 3 inches deep starting 3 inches from the main stem.

 PRUNING

Prune shrubs that bloomed on last year's wood when the flowers are finished.

Deadhead **rhododendrons** very carefully; pinch out the dead blossoms, taking care not to damage the tiny emerging leaf buds right behind them.

As **azaleas** finish blooming, clip or prune 2 to 3 inches off the branch tips that have flowered.

To lower an **azalea** or a **rhododendron** that is getting too tall, take a third of the oldest branches back to 12 inches. Aim at creating a layered look.

Prune **forsythia** by taking older branches right back to the ground. If you leave a stump, new branches will develop there in a direction that crosses other branches.

Cut a few central stems of **nandina** bushes right to the ground.

Scorched lower branches of evergreen shrubs may be from salt damage that occurred when streets or sidewalks were de-iced; drench the soil to leach out the remaining salts, and cut out the damaged branches.

Dog urine also can turn a shrub lower branches yellow, especially **boxwoods.** Drench the soil, and fence the area, and spray the plants with dog and cat deterrent.

 WATERING

If watering, or April rains, have eroded the soil on sloping shrub borders, shovel it back up the slope, and re-establish

When the weather keeps you out of the garden, visit your full service garden centers looking for must-haves and bargains.

Did You Know?

Pruning Guide for Evergreens

Winter and snow damage is best pruned before growth begins.

Dead or damaged wood on evergreen conifers can be removed at any time.

Flowering broadleaf evergreens that bloom on new wood, like **abelia,** should be pruned in late winter or early spring before growth begins.

Flowering broadleaf evergreens that bloom on old wood—azaleas and **rhododendrons** for example—should be pruned immediately after they bloom and before they initiate new growth to avoid cutting off buds being initiated for the following season.

To slow or dwarf a broadleaf evergreen, after its main spurt of growth, remove up to a third. You can cut the main stem (leader) back to the first side shoots, but don't take off more than has grown the last year or two.

To encourage dense branching in evergreens whose growth is initiated by candles (new, candlelike growth), cut the candles back by half when growth is complete. Prune the tips of **yews, junipers,** and **hemlocks** lightly any time during the growing season.

To establish a shape, prune evergreen shrubs and hedges when they are three to five years old.

For holiday greens, prune lightly in December.

saucers around the plants to catch and hold the rain.

For a shrub's first season, unless there's a soaking rain, throughout spring slowly and gently pour two or three 5-gallon bucketfuls of water around the roots every week.

FERTILIZING

Twice a month add a water-soluble fertilizer, or dilute seaweed or manure tea, to the water for shrubs growing outdoors in containers, and to the annuals and tender and tropical shrubs summering in the shrubbery border.

How often the in-ground shrubs need fertilizing depends on the type of fertilizer you are using; for that information, turn to section on Understanding Fertilizers in the Introduction to the book.

PESTS

Early this month **gypsy moths** may appear. Spray with a biological control such as *Bacillus thuringiensis.* Other controls are Sevin or malathion insecticide, pyrethrin, or rotenone.

Apply or change whatever deer deterrents you are using. See the section on Pests, Diseases, and Controls in the Appendix.

Mugo pines and other needled evergreen shrubs that show denuded branch may be under attack by pine sawfly larvae. Spray the affected plants with Bt (*Bacillus thuringiensis*).

Keep the beds weed free.

JUNE
Shrubs

 ## PLANNING

When the color of a shrub's blossoms matter, buy it from a local garden center when you can see the plant in bloom. Buying locally will also provide an opportunity to:

- Select the very best cultivars for your area.

- Check the undersides of the leaves, and the crotch of the branches for signs of insect infestation.

- Check the condition of the rootball. It's okay if a few roots circle the rootball and there's a thin mat of roots at the bottom; much more than that will need removal, however, and the plant will need time to recover.

- Get good cultural advice.

 ## PLANTING

Transplant **azaleas** that have finished blooming.

If shrubbery borders look bare, plant seedlings of **flowering maples,** *Abutilon*, and **tropical hibiscus.** In September you can pot them up, and winter them indoors as houseplants.

 ## CARE

If wands of willowy **butterfly bush** get flattened by rain and wind, stake them. They can be pruned and shaped throughout the summer.

Make sure the mulch around hedges and shrubbery is a full 3 inches deep—no more—before heat arrives.

 ## PRUNING

Finish deadheading late-blooming **rhododendrons** and **azaleas.** Deadhead **tropical hibiscus, flowering maples,** and other tender shrubs.

To let light and air into the interior of old clipped **boxwoods,** remove older inside branches.

After the first flush of new growth in **evergreen hedges,** trim the top and sides to keep the height down and the greenery full. Keep the top narrower than the bottom so light can reach the lower branches, or they will lose their leaves.

Cut the succulent new shoots on **deciduous hedges** in half.

Prune elongated **boxwood** shoots after new growth is complete to keep them trim and beautiful.

 ## WATERING

A newly-planted shrub needs a good soaking every week to ten days in summer. If it doesn't rain, slowly and gently pour two or three 5-gallon bucketfuls of water around the roots.

Every few days check the soil moisture in shrubs growing in containers, and water as often as necessary to keep it nicely damp.

 ## FERTILIZING

New growth is emerging in the **mophead** and **lacecap hydrangeas**—time to adjust the color toward pink or blue by increasing or decreasing the soil acidity. A pH of 5.0 to 5.5 results in a soft blue color. For pink keep the soil pH 6.0 to 6.5 or slightly higher. To adjust the pH, see Soil Preparation and Improvement in the Introduction to the book.

How often the in-ground shrubs need fertilizing depends on the type of fertilizer you are using; for information, turn to section on Understanding Fertilizers in the Introduction to the book.

At every second watering, add a half dose of a water-soluble fertilizer to the water for shrubs growing in containers.

When the color of a shrub's blossoms matter, buy it from a local garden center when you can see the plant in bloom.

Did You Know?

Rooting Cuttings to Multiply Your Shrubs

Azaleas, winterberry, magnolias, nandina, osmanthus, coniferous evergreens, and many other shrubs can be rooted from semi-hardwood cuttings taken June and July. New green growth that is just turning brown and hardening is what is meant by "semi-hardwood." Snap a twig, and if the bark clings to the branch, it's likely semi-hardwood.

Here's how it works:

1 Prepare a rooting box about the size of a seed flat and 5 to 6 inches deep. It must have drainage. Fill the box with 4 inches of a moist mix of half and half peat and perlite or coarse sand. With a pencil, make twelve equidistant planting holes.

2 Cover the bottom of a saucer with rooting hormone powder Number 3, or Root-tone.

3 In early morning, cut a dozen semi-hardened branch ends 4 to 8 inches long at a point about 1 inch below a leaf cluster. Remove the leaves from the bottom 3 inches. Mist the foliage.

4 Working in shade, remove a strip of bark 1/2 to 1 inch long on the side of each cutting close to the cut end. Lightly coat the cut ends and the wounds in the rooting powder.

5 Insert the cut ends 2 to 3 inches in the rooting box, deep enough to cover the wounds. Press the soil up around the cuttings.

6 Water well, and enclose the box in clear plastic. Use hoops made of wire coat hangers to support the plastic, and punch a few tiny holes in the plastic for ventilation.

7 Place the box in a shaded, sheltered location. Check the soil moisture every five days; the cuttings mustn't dry out.

8 In about six weeks, test the cuttings to see if they are rooted. Very gently tug on a couple of the cuttings; when you meet real resistance, they are rooted.

9 Transplant the rooted cuttings to pots filled with half potting soil and half peat.

10 Gradually expose the pots to increasingly strong light while keeping the soil moist. In September, transplant them to the garden, and protect them with a light mulch of hay or open evergreen boughs.

 PESTS

Repair and/or renew deer deterrents and sprays.

Check **rhododendrons** and **azaleas** for lacebug damage. The leaf surfaces will be dull, speckled, pale, and the undersides will show specks of insect excrement. Spray the foliage at intervals with horticultural oil or insecticidal soap.

Whitefly and spider mite damage shows up as spotted and blanched leaves. Remove dead or severely infected twigs, and spray with neem at intervals until the infestation is gone. See Pests, Diseases, and Controls in the Appendix.

Keep the beds clear of weeds. If they mature and go to seed, there will be an army to rout later.

JULY
Shrubs

PLANNING

Keep abreast of research on natural controls and improved shrub varieties. Find time for a trip to the U.S. National Arboretum in DC to learn more about the many improved and disease-resistant varieties of popular shrubs introduced in recent decades by scientists working there.

Many new mildew-free **crapemyrtles,** superior **viburnums** like the doublefile beauty called **'Shasta',** and hardy **hibiscus (shrub althea, rose-of-Sharon)** were selected and introduced by the late great Dr. Donald R. Egolf. **Euonymus** specimens at the National Arboretum are now free of scale insects, a pest that can make growing these beautiful evergreen shrubs a never-ending battle. Scales on the insect's back literally protect them from insecticides, but USDA scientists found predator beetles in Korea that attack and control the pest at the Arboretum without the aid of insecticides.

PLANTING

When planting shrubs in containers at the seashore, use commercial potting soil rather than the sandy soil of the area. The humidity in the air reduces the need to water, but check the soil moisture often anyway.

You can continue to plant container-grown shrubs this month. B&B shrubs, too, but don't buy B&B shrubs whose rootballs have been sitting unmulched and baking at a garden center since they were dug in early spring.

CARE

After heavy summer storms, check, and if needed, replenish the mulch around shrubs.

To prevent plant damage from coastal storms, spray the upper and lower sides of the leaves with anti-desiccants.

PRUNING

Groom and prune back the spring-flowering shrubs and hedges.

Continue to deadhead **tropical hibiscus, flowering maples,** and other shrubs that bloom all summer.

Toward the middle of the month, you can take a half inch off leggy shoots of older **azalea** shoots; do not prune new growth—that's where next year's flowers will be.

WATERING

Shrubs growing in big containers are likely to need watering every four to seven days, the smaller containers more often. Containers with built-in water reservoirs, or with water rings that let the plant soak up the water from the bottom, minimize watering chores.

Late July is drought season, and you will probably need to water the garden two or three times before the fall rains arrive in September. **If you go ten days without rain, water slowly, and deeply, especially newly planted shrubs. Shrubs slow their growth to adapt to high heat unless forced by shallow watering and inappropriate fertilizing to grow when the weather isn't supporting growth.**

Before going on vacation, group shrubs growing in containers in light shade, make sure each one has a generous saucer, and water them thoroughly.

FERTILIZING

At every second watering add a half dose of a water-soluble fertilizer, liquid seaweed, or a manure tea to the water for shrubs growing in containers.

How often the in-ground shrubs need fertilizing depends on the type of fertilizer you are using; for information, turn to the section on Understanding Fertilizers in the Introduction to the book. If you are using chemical fertilizers, you should be fertilizing every six weeks or so.

 PESTS

Continue preventive measures to protect your garden from deer.

When you see the first Japanese beetles, go after them. **Japanese beetle traps are effective, provided they are placed far away from the plantings you are trying to protect, not among them.** In the cool or early morning, knock the beetles off into a jar of sudsy water. Do not install pheromone traps that attract beetles from everywhere. Spray serious infestations with *Pyrethrum*.

Whitefly, mealybugs, scale, spider mites, and aphids multiply in hot, airless spots and will spoil the leaves even if they don't do permanent damage. Spray infestations two or three times with some form of neem, *Pyrethrum,* or horticultural soaps—they won't harm the environment. You can also use horticultural oils. See the section Appendix on Pests, Diseases, and Controls.

Continue to weed shrub beds.

Did You Know?

Shrubs at the Shore

These plants tolerate salt spray and sandy situations at the shore and inland, too. Most require well-drained soil.

- **Adam's-needle,** *Yucca filamentosa.* Big, dramatic evergreen rosette of sword-like leaves that sends up 6-foot flower spikes.

- **Bayberry,** *Myrica pennsylvanica.* For Zone 6 and north. Beautiful big shrub with gray-green, semi-evergreen leaves that are aromatic when crushed.

- **Beach Plum,** *Prunus maritime.* Round bush that bears clusters of white blooms followed by purplish fruit.

- **Fragrant Elaeagnus,** *Elaeagnus pungens.* Tall evergreen shrub that bears fragrant white flowers in September and October.

- **Hydrangea,** *Hydrangea* species and varieties. Deciduous shrubs with huge flower heads in mid- and late summer.

- **Inkberry,** *Ilex glabra.* Black-berried, usually evergreen, shrub to 3 feet high. **'Leucocarpa'** has white fruit.

- **Japanese Rose, Rugosa rose,** *Rosa rugosa.* Tall rugged bush that bears handsome roses and brilliant fruit.

- **Juniper, Creeping Juniper,** *Juniperus horizontalis*; **Shore juniper,** *J. conferta.* Spreading gray-green evergreen foliage and blue berries.

- **Lavender Cotton,** *Santolina* species and varieties. Gray-leaved, low, evergreen shrubs with aromatic leaves and inconspicuous flowers.

- **Scotch Broom,** *Cytisus scoparius.* The arching stems bear pea-like flowers in spring or summer.

- **Tamarisk, Salt Cedar,** *Tamarix ramosissima.* For Zone 7 and north. Tall shrubs with delicate leaves and feathery clusters of flowers in late summer.

- **Vicary Golden Privet,** *Ligustrum* x *vicaryi.* Small-leaved evergreen for tall hedges.

AUGUST
Shrubs

PLANNING

If you are interested in adding a hedge to your yard, lay it out, and order the plants now, so you can start planting when the weather turns cool in early September.

Formal hedges are clipped and follow symmetrical lines—straight with squared corners, a circle, an oval, a triangle. Hedges facing each other left and right are common. Shearable evergreens like **boxwood** and **privet,** or naturally columnar evergreens like **dwarf Alberta spruce,** *Picea glauca* 'Conica' are used.

Informal hedge plants have a loose habit and follow lines that curve and lead off at an angle. Choose open, asymmetrical shrubs like **forsythia** and *Juniper chinensis* **Hetzii.** Or plant a mix with compatible needs, for example, **Mugo pines, potentillas,** and **'Crimson Pygmy' barberry.**

Texture. For a close-up hedge, choose fine-textured *Pyracantha* and **Korean box.** For a distant hedge, choose coarse foliage, like the **Meserve hollies** and **holly olive.**

To slow growth and keep an informal hedge attractive, trim it at least once a year. Trim a clipped hedge at least twice a year. Hand shears are better than hedge shears for informal and natural styles.

PLANTING

Fall is considered by André as the best planting season in our area. You can plant this month, but if you wait until the leaves start to turn in October, the plants will benefit. Evergreen shrubs do well moved August through October.

CARE

If the harvest from your **highbush blueberries** is shrinking, blame birds or bears. You may be able to save remaining berries by covering the bushes with bird netting. Console yourself with the thought of the vibrant color highbush blueberry foliage brings to the garden later in the season.

PRUNING

Give hedges their final trimming for the year.

WATERING

You will probably need to water all the shrub beds two or three times before the fall rains arrive in September. The ideal is to put down 1 1/2 inches of water at each session. To find out how long your watering system takes to deliver that much water, mark 1 1/2 inches on the inside of an empty 1-pound coffee tin or other container, and set it where it will catch the water.

Overhead watering is fine as long as you water deeply. There's less waste if you water before the sun reaches the garden in the early morning or late afternoon or evening. In hot dry periods, daytime overhead watering lowers leaf temperatures and reduces stress. Evening watering is fine since dew naturally wets foliage every clear night anyway.

André doesn't recommend electrically-timed mechanical watering systems that ignore the weather and water too often and shallowly. But he does believe they can do a good job if they are set up with the correct low-pressure nozzles, and timed to run long enough and to water and gently and deeply every week or ten days in periods of drought.

Continue to water shrubs in containers as needed.

FERTILIZING

If shrubs fertilized with a timed-release chemical fertilizer are failing to bloom as expected, or look peaked, supplement with foliar feedings of water-soluble organic or fast-acting liquid fertilizers.

If shrubs fertilized with a timed-release chemical fertilizer are failing to bloom as expected, or look peaked, supplement with foliar feedings of water-soluble organic or fast-acting liquid fertilizers.

Did You Know?

Shrubs for Hedges

- **Barberry, Japanese Barberry 'Crimson Pigmy',** *Berberis thunbergii*; **Yellow Japanese Barberry,** *B. t.* 'Aurea'; **Evergreen Barberry,** *B. linearifolia, B. verruculosa*
- **Boxwood, English box,** *Buxus sempervirens,* 'Suffruticosa', and 'Arborescens'; **Dwarf Little Leaf Box,** *B. microphylla* 'Compacta' and 'Kingsville Dwarf'; **Edging Box,** *B. s.* 'Suffruticosa'; **Korean Littleleaf box,** *B. microphylla* var. 'Koreana'
- **Common Buckthorn,** *Rhamnus cathartica*
- **Canadian Hemlock,** *Tsuga canadensis*
- **Cripp's Golden Hinoki Falsecypress,** *Chamaecyparis obtusa* 'Cripsii'
- **Dwarf Alberta Spruce,** *Picea glauca* 'Conica'
- **Dwarf Chinese Juniper,** *Juniperus chinensis* 'Mas,' 'Spartan'; **Golden Juniper, Dwarf Colorado Blue Spruce,** *Picea pungens* 'Glauca' and 'Fat Albert'; *P. p.* 'Glauca Montgomery'
- **Dwarf Winged Spindle Tree,** *Euonymus alata* 'Compactus'
- **Firethorn,** *Pyracantha coccinea*
- **Forsythia,** *Forsythia* x *intermedia* 'Spectabilis'
- **Fragrant/Sweet Olive,** *Osmanthus fragrans* 'Aurantiacus'; **Holly Olive, Hardy Sweet Olive,** *O. heterophyllus*
- **Germander,** *Teucrium chamaedrys*
- **Glossy Abelia,** *Abelia* x *grandiflora* cultivars
- **Holly,** including the **Meserve hybrids 'Blue Boy'** and **'Blue Princess'; Foster hybrid hollies,** *Ilex attenuata* 'Fosteri #2'; **Japanese Holly,** *Ilex crenata; I. c.* 'Convexa'; *I. c.* 'Helleri'; *I. c.* 'Microphylla'
- **Leyland Cypress,** *Cupressocyparis leylandii* (classed as a tree but shearable)
- **Myrtle,** *Myrtus communis*
- **Nandina, Heavenly Bamboo,** *Nandina domestica* 'Umpqua Warrior'
- **Oleander, Rose-bay,** *Nerium oleander* cultivars
- **Photinia, Fraser's Photinia** or **Red Tip,** *Photinia* x *fraseri*
- **Potentilla, Shrubby Cinquefoil,** *Potentilla fruticosa*
- **Privet, Amur Privet,** *Ligustrum amurense*; *L.* x *ibolium*; **California Privet,** *Ligustrum ovalifolium*; **Wax-leaf/Japanese Privet,** *Ligustrum japonicum* (*Texanum*)
- **Pyramidal American Arborvitae,** *Thuja occidentalis* 'Emerald' (Classed as a tree.)
- **Roses, Polyantha/Floribunda/Rugosa,** *Rosa* species and varieties
- **Santolina, Lavender Cotton,** *Santolina* species and varieties
- **Sawara falsecypress,** *Chamaecyparis pisifera* 'Boulevard'; *C. p.* 'Filifera Aurea'
- **Wintercreeper Euonymus,** *Euonymus fortunei* 'Gracilis'
- **Yew, English Yew,** *Taxus baccata* 'Fastigiata'; **Dwarf Japanese Yew,** *T. cuspidata* 'Nana'; **Upright Japanese Yew,** *T. c.* 'Capitata'; **Hick's Japanese Yew,** *T.* x *media* 'Hicksii'

If you are using chemical fertilizers, fertilize every six weeks or so.

 PESTS

Change deer deterrents and sprays around in the garden.

If your berries are harvested before you can get to them, there may be a bear in the vicinity. If, in addition, bear sightings are reported, it's probably not a good idea to put out bird feeders this winter.

Clear the beds of all weeds; don't let them grow up and go to seed!

September

 ## PLANNING

If you've been wanting to do something positive for the environment, plant a rain garden this fall to handle runoff from severe storms and to preserve water.

A rain garden is sited where the runoff from concrete surfaces goes, or where building gutters empty. It is designed to take flooding. The center is slightly lower than the soil level so water can pool there. The plants use up the runoff so it goes into the soil of the rain garden and doesn't all go into the water table, sewers, or streams. Runoff water often carries pesticides, herbicides, heavy metals, and other toxins.

Rain garden plants are bio-remediators—their roots and foliage tie up toxins. Some excellent plants for a rain garden are **birches, ornamental grasses, coneflowers, rudbeckia, weigela, baptisia, coreopsis.** Other plants include **river birch, North Lights series azaleas, red-osier dogwood, asters, astilbe, campanula, hostas, salvia, Siberian iris, Joe-Pye weed, red milkweed, switchgrass.**

 ## PLANTING

Late plant sales and perfect planting weather combine to make this a fine time to install a hedge.

Laying out the bed. Make the width of the bed equal to the height of the shrubs at maturity. For a 1- to 2-foot high hedge, make the bed 18 inches wide; for a hedge 3 feet tall, make it 3 feet wide; for a hedge 15 feet tall, make it 15 feet wide. Columnar plants need less space. For a double hedge, measure the width of the bed starting with the outside plant on either side.

Planting. Prepare a trench 12 to 18 inches deep, and improve the soil. Set low-growing shrubs 18 inches apart for a single row. For a double row set them zig-zag 12 inches apart; to keep out intruders, weave chickenwire between the shrubs. Crowded shrubs can be moved later to replace failed plants. Finish the bed with 3 inches of mulch.

Fertilizing. Encourage growth the first two years by fertilizing in late winter, again after the main spurt of growth, and again in fall. As the hedge matures, fertilize at half strength when you feed other shrubs.

 ## CARE

In Zones 7 and 6, pot up, and move **tropical hibiscus, flowering maple,** and other tender shrubs indoors when the thermometer hits 60 degrees Fahrenheit. Hose them down, and then spray them with insecticidal soap before the move.

Toward the end of the month in Zone 6, move hardy shrubs growing in containers to sheltered locations for the winter.

 ## PRUNING

Deadhead fall-flowering shrubs.

 ## WATERING

Indoors. Water shrubs moved indoors for the winter as needed.

Outdoors. Even after cold sets in, the soil stays warm, and roots continue to develop, so water both established and new shrubs sufficiently to keep the soil from drying out.

Pour two or three 5-gallon bucketfuls of water around the roots of newly planted shrubs once a week throughout fall unless you have good, soaking rains.

Late plant sales and perfect planting weather combine to make this a fine time to install a hedge.

FERTILIZING

Indoors. Add a half strength dose of fertilizer to shrubs indoors at every fourth watering.

Outdoors. The last fertilization of in-ground shrubs is toward the end of the growing season. If you are using organic or water-soluble chemical fertilizers, the last application in Zones 6 and 7 should be made between early September and early October. In Zone 8, Richmond and the Tidewater areas of Virginia, make it between the end of September and mid-October. If you are using a timed-release fertilizer and applied an eight-month formulation in early spring, it will carry plants all the way through October.

Did You Know?

Preserving Leaves and Berries

Branches of evergreen leaves. Broadleaf evergreen foliage—*Magnolia grandiflora,* **holly, euonymus**—are preserved by splitting and mashing the branch ends and immersing them in a solution that is ⅔ drugstore glycerin and ⅓ water, warmed to 80 degrees Fahrenheit. Leave them there until the color of the leaves changes—some darken, some lighten—then air-dry them.

Trailing stems. Ivy and other trailing stems can be preserved by laying them for 6 or more days in a solution of half glycerin and half water.

Berry branches. Stems of berries can be preserved by dipping them in a solution of half-and-half wood alcohol and clear shellac, and then hanging them upside down over newspapers to drip dry.

Baby's-breath. This airy plant air-dries quickly. It also can be preserved by leaving the stems overnight in a solution of 1 part glycerin to 2 parts water, and then hanging them upside down in loose bunches.

PESTS

Indoors. Check shrubs for whitefly and spider mites. You will find controls in the Pests, Diseases, and Controls section in the Appendix.

Outdoors. Change whatever deer deterrents you are using. If there are bears in your area, don't stock a bird feeder.

Continue to search for and destroy weeds.

OCTOBER
Shrubs

 PLANNING

Visit nearby public gardens and learn more about the shrubs that blaze into color in the fall. Foliage in the **azalea** collection at the U.S. National Arboretum will be showing streaks of plum, maroon, and gold. While you are there, look for the **witchhazel 'Diane'**, *Viburnum* 'Cayuga', and ask about other National Arboretum introductions whose fall foliage is exceptionally rich.

The reddest leaves at your garden center are likely to belong to the *Euonymus* called **burning bush,** or the **dwarf winged spindletree.** The most fluorescent yellow foliage will be on little **Japanese maples 'Osakazuki'** and **'Sangokaku',** whose bark becomes brilliant coral-red in winter. **Willowleaf cotoneaster 'Autumn Fire'** has purplish leaves and scarlet fruits. The **fothergillas** turn brilliant yellow and orange-red. **Chokeberry 'Brilliantissima',** a cultivar of *Aronia arbutifolia,* **'William Penn'**

barberry, the **American smoke tree, chittamwood, sweetspire,** and some of the **sumacs** are others with exceptional autumn color.

The colorful stems of shrubby **red- and yellow-twig dogwood** brighten the scene in winter, especially when there's snow on the ground.

 PLANTING

When the leaves start to change color is a good time to dig and transplant shrubs. Excellent months for planting are October, November, and into early December. **Evergreen shrubs** may do better planted this month rather than next.

Plant open spaces in the shrubbery border with spring-flowering bulbs. For ideas, turn to the October pages of Chapter 2, Bulbs, Corms, Rhizomes, and Tubers.

 CARE

Zone 8, move hardy shrubs growing in containers to a sheltered corner for the winter.

Zone 6 and 7, move shrubs that are borderline hardy and still out in the open to a frost-free shed or garage.

 PRUNING

From now until next spring the only pruning you should do is to remove diseased or dead wood.

 WATERING

Indoors. Water indoor shrubs as needed.

Outdoors. Unless you have good soaking rains, pour two or three 5-gallon bucketfuls of water around the roots of newly planted shrubs once every week this fall.

The most important preparation for winter is a deep and thorough watering of all shrubs, new, established, in-ground and in containers, before the soil freezes; if the sky doesn't provide the rain, you will have to.

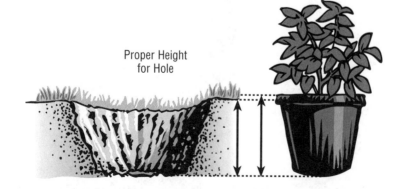

Proper Height for Hole

The most important preparation for winter is a deep and thorough watering of all shrubs, new, established, in-ground and in containers, before the soil freezes; if the sky doesn't provide the rain, you will have to.

FERTILIZING

Indoors. Add a half dose of fertilizer to the water for shrubs growing indoors at every fourth watering.

Outdoors. In Zones 6 and 7, the time for the last application of fertilizer is between early September and early October.

In Zone 8, Richmond and the Tidewater areas of Virginia, the last fertilization can be between the end of September and mid-October.

PESTS

Indoors. Watch shrubs moved indoors for signs of whitefly and spider mites. If you find problems, look up controls in the Pests, Diseases, and Controls section in the Appendix.

Outdoors. Apply or change whatever deer deterrents you are using.

If vole runs appear around shrubs, bait the main runway with a rodenticide.

Did You Know?

About Boxwoods

Deer are smart enough to avoid boxwood, which is toxic to animals. That's one more plus for this slow-growing, small-leaved evergreen shrub whose refined foliage and tolerance for shearing and reshaping have made it an outstanding subject for hedging, edging, and topiary treatment since the days of classical Greece.

In the Mid-Atlantic, some long-lived slow-growing **English box,** *Buxus sempervirens*, dates back to Colonial times. Unclipped, its natural shape is billowing and somewhat pyramidal, and it grows to 15 to 20 feet.

Six-foot **'Vardar Valley'** tolerates cold, and drought. Columnar **'Graham Blandy,'** and 5-foot gray-green-silver **'Elegantissima'** are excellent accent plants. Five-foot **'Green Mountain'** stands repeated shearing and holds its rich green color in winter. For warm dry climates the 3- to 6-foot **littleleaf boxwood** cultivar **'Morris Midget'** is a popular choice.

A container-grown boxwood transplants easily in fall or spring. In well-drained humusy soil, pH around 6.0, it thrives in sun or light shade. Boxwoods don't tolerate salt or wet feet, but once established, they can stand some drought. Fertilizing every two or three years is enough for slow-growing **English box.**

In mid-March shear damaged, browning, or whitened boxwood branches back to live growth. Prune elongated shoots in late spring after new growth is complete to keep the plants trim, bushy, and beautiful.

Save the clipping of overgrown boxwoods until December, and use the branches to make holiday roping and topiary trees.

NOVEMBER
Shrubs

 ## PLANNING

To enjoy the beauty that is unique to the garden in November, learn to appreciate the wonderful structures nature bares when the foliage falls. The twiggy forms of naked shrubs, **barberries** for example, are quite beautiful in winter. Deciduous **hollies** like the National Arboretum introduction **'Sparkleberry'**, *Pyracantha,* many of the **viburnums,** and other berried shrubs are colorful assets, and attract birds. **Oregon grape,** *Nandina,* and **sweet box** (*Sarcococca hookeriana* var. *humilis*) add scraps of color to the seasonal mix. In some species blue, black, or white berries follow the flowers, and add winter interest.

The tiny white blooms of evergreen *Osmanthus* spread a sweet subtle perfume in the cool November air, almost miraculous at this season. **Aucuba** and other needled evergreens, **crapemyrtle** bark, **oakleaf hydrangea's** towering stems, **southern magnolia** leaves, the **viburnums, Virginia sweetspire**— nature's fall parade rivals spring if you take the time to stop and to really see, feel, smell, breathe in the seasonal changes.

 ## PLANTING

In Zone 8, when the outdoor temperatures head for 60 degrees Fahrenheit, pot up **tropical hibiscus, flowering maples,** and other tender shrubs growing in the open garden to containers, spray them with insecticidal soap, and move them indoors.

November, into early December, it is still okay to plant deciduous shrubs that are either container grown or balled and burlapped. The air is cold, but the earth still has warmth.

 ## CARE

Winter protection for shrubs is applied to keep the foliage from drying in bitter winds, and to avoid damage to the crown especially of newly planted shrubs when alternate thawing and freezing cycles cause the soil to heave it. Apply an anti-desiccant spray to the foliage of **camellias** and other **broad-leaved evergreen** shrubs growing in exposed positions, or wrap them in Reemay or burlap.

 ## PRUNING

Even in Zone 8, it's too late to prune shrubs now; pruning will encourage new growth that won't have time to harden before winter.

 ## WATERING

Indoors. Water shrubs as needed.

Outdoors. A major danger to newly planted shrubs in winter is lack of water before the plant is completely dormant. **One of the most important preparations for winter is a deep and thorough watering of your shrubs before the ground freezes.** If the sky doesn't do it, then you must.

Maintain moderate soil moisture for hardy shrubs and those that are less hardy and sheltering in a cold garage or shed.

Did You Know?

About Shrubs That Bear Berries

The shrubs that produce berries are colorful late-season and winter assets. To make sure you will have the show of berries you hope for, before buying a plant for its berries, ask your supplier about the pollinating needs of the species. For some species of berry-producing shrubs you will need to make sure a male pollinator is nearby in order to guarantee a showy crop of berries.

Most plants have male and female flower parts in the same flower, and they self-pollinate—don't need outside help to produce berries. Other species include both male and female flowers separately on the same plant. These don't require pollinators either; just a little shaking by the wind will do the trick.

But some important berry-producing shrubs are not unisex; they develop as either female or male plants. They're referred to as "dioecious" shrubs. Among popular shrubs that are dioecious are **aucuba, bayberries, fringe tree, hollies, skimmia,** and **yews.** The female of these species must have a suitable male pollinator within pollinating reach to produce a heavy crop of berries. Female plants generally produce the showiest fruit, and they also litter most.

As a rule of thumb, you can provide one male shrub and expect it to cross-pollinate two to ten females or more, depending on species and location. In a neighborhood with many gardens, you may not need to provide a male pollinator. Your garden center or nursery supplier will be able to advise you.

 FERTILIZING

Indoors. At every fourth watering, add a half dose of water-soluble fertilizer to the water for **tropical hibiscus, flowering maple,** and other shrubs moved indoors for the cold months.

Outdoors. Fertilizing is over for the shrub garden this year.

 PESTS

Indoors. Watch shrubs moved indoors for signs of whitefly and spider mites. If you find problems, apply the controls recommended in the section on Pests, Diseases, and Controls in the Appendix.

Outdoors. In deer country, wrap **rhododendrons** and other susceptible **evergreens** in chickenwire cages. Change whatever deer deterrents you are using.

If vole runs appear around shrubs, bait the main runway with a rodenticide.

DECEMBER
Shrubs

 PLANNING

Browse your catalogs for holiday giving—to yourself and others.

If you worry lots about pests and diseases, ask Santa for a Brunton Macro-Scope—a microscope that focuses from infinity down to 18 inches, and lets you see insects at a distance of 6 feet! (www.closetoinfinity.com)

Gifts that gardeners deeply appreciate and never have too many of are superior pruning tools. Inexpensive pruning tools don't cut well and don't last. Good pruning tools cost more, but with care they last a lifetime. A gardener with lots of shrubbery needs four basic pruning tools:

1 The tool that goes where the gardener goes is a pair of **bypass pruning shears.** Really good shears snap through twigs and small branches as effortlessly as a hot knife cuts butter.

2 Long-handled **lopping shears** are bypass shears long enough to reach the interior of large shrubs.

3 To cut through main stems and larger branches, you need a little **pull saw.** Half handle and half short blade with multifaceted teeth, it makes a deep cut as you pull back.

4 For anyone who owns a hedge, scissor-like **hand-held hedge shears** are essential. If the hedge is a long one and meant to be trimmed, then electric shears or gas are almost essential.

A good pruning tool is a treasure, to be cleaned and wiped with an oily rag after each use. After pruning diseased plants, disinfect tools by dipping them in a solution of 1 part bleach to 9 parts water.

 PLANTING

You can still plant deciduous shrubs the first days of this month. In Zone 8, some winters are mild enough to plant all winter long.

 CARE

After storms, check and adjust the protective covering on shrubs.

With a broom, as soon as possible after a heavy snowfall, free **evergreen** shrubs that are weighed down. Use only snow-melt products that don't harm plants, turf, and concrete.

 PRUNING

Prune overgrown **boxwoods** and **evergreens** lightly to obtain material for making roping, swags, topiary trees, and wreaths for the holidays.

 WATERING

Indoors. Water shrubs indoors as needed.

Indoors/Outdoors. Maintain the soil moisture on shrubs growing indoors, and new shrubs outdoors as well if the season runs dry. Make sure the shrubs are watered thoroughly and deeply before the ground freezes.

 FERTILIZING

Indoors. Don't fertilize shrubs indoors until you see new growth.

Outdoors. Fertilizing is over for the year.

 PESTS

Indoors. Watch shrubs growing indoors for signs of whitefly and spider mites. If you find problems, apply the controls recommended in the Pests, Diseases, and Controls section of the Appendix.

Outdoors. The scent-carrying oils in evil-smelling deer deterrents don't volatilize in cold air. If you see a lot of deer, wrap **rhododendrons** and other endangered shrubs in chickenwire cages for the winter.

If vole runs appear around shrubs, bait the main runway with a rodenticide.

CHAPTER NINE

Trees

A well-grown tree is a gardener's pride and joy, a property's defining element, an asset of great majesty and beauty in every season.

MATURE TREES

A healthy mature tree needs little attention. Most trees will be fertilized as you fertilize the surrounding lawns and gardens. Mature trees do need watering in periods of deep drought—two or three weeks without rain—and pruning now and then to remove misplaced or damaged limbs. Maybe a treatment for tent caterpillars or webworms. But that's about it.

Established trees that aren't doing well can be brought back to good health in a few seasons. Crowding and loss of light, compacted soil, lack of nutrients and water are the history you may have to overcome. The recommendations in the month-by-month pages ahead will help you to get them back into good shape.

CHOOSING NEW TREES

When you are adding a new tree to your property, look for a species that will add variety to existing plantings, make the tree line and the longer views more interesting, and enhance your pleasure in the garden. Habit, color, and texture are a tree's most obvious aspects. Habit refers to the way a species grows, the structure or silhouette the trunk and branching develop naturally. Color and texture are the effects of foliage, flowers, berries, and bark. If the garden is small, double your pleasure in a new tree by choosing species that have several assets. The **Foster hollies,** for example, are evergreen, have a handsome silhouette, interestingly textured evergreen foliage, bright berries, and few enemies.

Habit and size. A tree is the largest plant in the garden, so its silhouette as it matures should be your first consideration when you are choosing a new tree. What it will become makes an important difference, not only to your yard but to the surrounding landscape. Each species has a recognizable volume and sculptural structure—spreading, pyramidal, oval, vase-shaped, round, columnar, clumping, weeping. When adding—or deleting—trees, aim for a variety of silhouettes. Variety makes a landscape more interesting.

Consider how the tree's shadows when fully grown will enhance, or not, your own and neighboring yards. Avoid trees that will grow so big they dwarf your house or neighboring houses and cut off the light.

Evergreen and deciduous. The next question to settle when looking for a new tree is whether an evergreen or a deciduous species will do the most for your view.

You can count on evergreens to block unwanted views with a highly textured wall of green foliage winter, spring, summer, fall. If you want a really solid green presence, consider a broad-leaved evergreen—the **hollies** thrive here and come in many sizes and shapes. The majestic evergreen **magnolias** have beautiful leaves in addition to extraordinary flowers. Conifers that have flat scale-like leaves—**American arborvitae** and the fast-growing **Leyland cypress** for example—also present a substantial silhouette. The needled evergreens—**hemlock, pine, and spruce**—have an airier presence.

Trees

Did You Know?

When Is a Tree a Tree?

The forester's definition of a tree is a woody plant having a single main trunk, and reaching not less than 10 to 20 feet at maturity. Some tall shrubs can be trained to a tree-like single trunk, **lilacs** and **crapemyrtles,** for example.

A deciduous tree's great asset is that it does lose its foliage annually. You can count on deciduous trees to change your garden view beginning with spring's tender greens and throughout the year. Many deciduous trees are famous for flaming fall finales—**'Autumn Glory' maple,** for one. In winter the bare branches and twigs of the deciduous trees frame the sky and the clouds scudding by, and their bark presents arresting textures—the silky gray kid of the **American beech,** for example, and the chalky white of **river birch.**

Both evergreen and deciduous trees shade the house and protect it fom the sweep of winter wind, thereby saving on the costs of cooling and heating.

Flowering trees. All trees flower. In early spring the red **maples** wrap their twigs in tiny garnet velvet leaf buds, and the **willows** drip golden catkins. But a real flowering tree in bloom is a sky-high pastel bouquet. There are lots of species to choose from. Your property, if big enough, can host a flowery parade from March when the **ornamental cherries** bloom until mid-fall when the last fragrant blossom falls from the little **Franklin tree,** *Franklinia alatamaha*. Double your pleasure by selecting flowering trees that bear colorful fruits. The **flowering crabapples** and **dogwoods** are two whose flowers are followed by plentiful fruits that attract birds. Or opt for fragrance, and plant a scented **flowering apple,** or **Yoshino cherry** *Prunus* x *yedoensis* 'Akebono,' **Chinese witch-hazel,** *Hamamelis mollis.*

PLANTING

Making healthy choices. Success with a new tree begins with a healthy choice—check on the pest and disease resistance of varieties before making final decisions.

Location. Site large trees where they will reach full sun as they mature. Many small flowering trees are understory plants that developed in the partial shade of a forest, and they will thrive in partial light. If you are trying a tree that is at the edge of its cold hardiness zone in your yard, such as a **dogwood** or a **redbud,** place it in a spot that provides shelter from the north wind. Don't plant a tree, large or small, in an airless corner, or close to a wall or overhang.

Space trees at distances from each other that allow plenty of space for the lateral development of branches. Columnar trees can be set more closely than pyramidal trees. Large shade trees are best set 75 feet apart. The absolute minimum for a street tree is 8 feet in every direction, and 12 feet is better. Staggered plantings achieve greater density in less space.

Don't plant tall trees near electric or phone lines, and avoid proximity to pipes and septic systems.

Before placing a large tree in the vicinity of a garden, consider not only how the shade under the branches will affect the plants, but how the shade the mature tree will cast at various times of the day and the year will affect the garden design. Don't plant so close to a sidewalk or patio that the big roots that develop near the trunk will heave the paving.

Trees

When to plant. In our area, you can plant trees from March through the end of November. When the leaves start to change color is the beginning of an excellent planting season—October, November, and even into early December in mild years. Choose early spring for planting balled-and-burlapped (B&B) trees considered difficult to transplant, **Florida dogwoods** and **magnolias,** for example.

It is okay to plant container-grown and B&B trees in summer, providing the rootballs haven't been baking on the tarmac at a garden center since early spring. B&B trees whose rootballs have been "heeled in," and protected by mounds of mulch or earth, stay in good condition even in summer.

Bare-root trees. In early spring before growth begins, mail-order suppliers ship young trees bare root. Before placing your order, ask about the size and age of the sapling so you know what you are getting. The tree will be shipped at the right planting season. Follow the shipper's instructions for planting exactly.

Container-grown and B&B trees. Container-grown and balled-and-burlapped trees can be planted from early spring, through summer and all fall up to December 1. Big trees are now being grown in 10-, 15-, and even 50-gallon containers. B&B trees dug in spring and protected in the months since by mounds of mulch or soil stay in good condition. B&B packaging is usually reserved for very large trees. Container and B&B trees are more costly than bare-root trees.

You can save on costs by choosing young trees. Young trees knit into their new environments quickly; trees 7 to 8 feet tall soon overtake the growth of 15-foot trees set out at the same time. If you are buying a large, expensive specimen, we recommend buying from a full service nursery or garden center and paying extra to have it planted and for a warranty in case of loss.

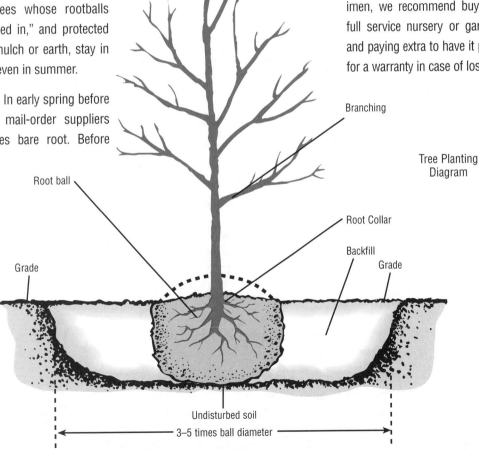

Branching

Tree Planting Diagram

Root Collar

Root ball

Backfill

Grade

Grade

Undisturbed soil

3–5 times ball diameter

271

Trees

Soil and pH. Within a year or two, a new tree will send roots out well beyond the amended soil of its planting hole, so your greatest successes will be with species growing in native soil whose pH matches their pH needs. However, amending the pH of the planting hole helps them get started and is especially useful for hard-to-transplant specimens like the **sweetbay magnolia, American hornbeam,** and **sour gum.** You will find information on modifying pH and amending soil in the section on Soil Preparation and Improvement in the Introduction to the book.

Digging the hole:

1 Make the planting hole for a tree three times as wide and twice as deep as the rootball.

2 Loosen the sides of the hole, and blend the soil taken from the hole with the organic amendments described in Soil Preparation and Improvement in the Introduction to the book.

3 Half fill the bottom of the hole with improved soil, and tamp it down **very firmly** to make a solid base. Instructions for planting bare-root trees may call for the creation of a cone in the center of the hole over which the roots are to be spread.

4 Plant the tree in the hole so the trunk is 1 to 2 inches above the level of the surrounding earth. The weight of a container or B&B tree on unsettled soil will cause it to sink some after planting.

5 Half fill the hole once more with improved soil. Tamp it down firmly. Finish filling the hole with improved soil, and tamp it down firmly. Shape the soil around the crown into a wide saucer.

6 Water the soil slowly, gently, and thoroughly with a sprinkler, a soaker hose, a bubbler, or by hand. You need to put down 1$\frac{1}{2}$ inches of water. (See Watering, later in this introduction.) Or, slowly pour on two or three 5-gallon bucketfuls of water.

7 Mulch newly planted trees 3 to 4 inches deep starting 3 inches from the trunk out to the edge of the saucer. Replenish the mulch as needed to keep it 3 to 4 inches deep.

Ground covers such as **pachysandra, ivy, myrtle, hostas,** drought-tolerant **rudbeckias**, and small flowering **bulbs** may be planted outside the water basin (saucer) around a tree when it is first set out. The ground covers will move in around the trunk and become a living mulch that keeps weeds out and spares you hand trimming lawn grasses. In Europe, garden flowers are also planted around trees. The flowers compete for water and nutrients, so fertilizing and watering such plantings are essential for their success.

STAKING AND PROTECTING THE TRUNK

It isn't essential to stake a young tree unless the stem or trunk shows a tendency to lean or to grow at an odd angle. Remove the stake when the tree is growing straight and true.

In cold Zone 6, a burlap windbreak is helpful the first winter after you plant. You can either wrap the tree loosely in burlap or place a burlap screen between the tree and the sweep of wind. Where wildlife is active, wrapping a tree trunk with a protective tape or a plastic casing may keep the critters from chewing through the bark; remove the wrap in spring when growth starts. If your concern is the injury winter sun can inflict on a young trunk, paint it with whitewash, which is calcium carbonate with resins in it, or envelop it in a tree wrap.

FERTILIZING

Established trees surrounded by lawn or growing in a shrub border receive all the nutrients they need when you fertil-

Trees

ize the ground around. Groves of trees benefit from an annual fertilization with an organic lawn food high in nitrogen, for example, Espoma organic lawn food 18-8-6. Woodland trees get their nutrients from the decomposition of their fallen leaves.

New trees growing in improved soil rich in organic fertilizers will benefit from fertilization twice a year for the next eight or ten years.

The first annual application of fertilizer should be made before growth begins in spring. For **flowering and fruit trees,** use Holly-tone or Plant-tone. In the following years, in late winter or early spring apply fertilizer from the drip line (the outer ring of leaves on the tree) outward to a distance that equals the height of the tree, plus half again its height. The last application should be as growth slows toward the end of the growing season. **The number of applications in between depends entirely on the type of fertilizer you are using.** (See Understanding Fertilizers in the Introduction to the book.) The growing season in Zones 6 and 7 comes to an end between early September and early October. In Zone 8, Richmond and the Tidewater areas of Virginia, the last fertilization can be between the end of September and mid-October.

Compost the leaves you rake up in the fall. The nutrients they contain should go to enriching your soil, not clogging a landfill! (See Composting, in the October pages.)

MULCHING AND WEEDING

Spread a 3- to 4-inch deep mulch around the trunks of newly planted trees, and maintain the mulch levels for the first two or three seasons. That is enough to keep weeds out and to maintain soil moisture and temperatures. If you mulch 5 and 6 inches deep or and more, it keeps the ground so wet the roots lack oxygen, and the soil stays frozen late into spring. Top your mulch off at 3 to 4 inches in spring after fertilizing, again before summer heat to keep the roots cool, and once more before winter cold sets in; the last application helps maintain moisture in the ground, which retains its warmth for some time after the air turns freezing cold.

Start the mulch 3 inches from the trunk, and spread it to the outer edge of the saucer. Piling mulch right up against the trunk prevents it from drying out after rain and may harm the bark. Deep mulch right against the trunk also makes a cozy home for field mice that may girdle the tree—eat through the outer layer of the trunk, and that can kill a young tree.

If and when lawn grasses or ground covers move in around to the trunk, they will act as a living mulch, and you can stop mulching.

Keep the mulch free of weeds.

WATERING

Newly planted and transplanted trees need sustained moisture. For the first eight weeks, pour two or three 5-gallon bucketfuls of water around the roots once a week. The first summer, water every week or ten days, unless you have a soaking rain. Slowly and gently lay down $1\frac{1}{2}$ inches of water. Set a 1-pound coffee can or other container under the sprinkler or the hose, and record how long it took to put $1\frac{1}{2}$ inches in the can—then you'll know.

When the weather isn't supporting growth, young trees adapt by slowing down unless forced to grow by shallow watering and inappropriate fertilizing. In fall, even after cold sets in, roots continue to develop, so water often enough to prevent the soil from drying out.

After the first year or two, most trees require watering only in times of severe drought.

Trees

Did You Know?

Pruning Ground Rules

New trees may need some shaping, and they will shape up best if you follow the supplier's instructions for pruning after planting and for pruning the next two or three years.

- Prune dead or damaged wood any time. It is easier to identify damaged limbs before the leaves fall. After the leaves go, it is more difficult to tell dead wood from dormant wood.

- Prune trees that need regular shaping while the tree is still dormant, just after the coldest part of the season.

- Prune a summer flowering tree that blooms on **current growth** before growth begins.

- Prune a spring flowering tree that blooms on **last year's wood** after the flowers fade.

- Don't get carried away, and don't be timid. Focus on supporting the tree's natural outline, its growth "habit." Never prune away more than 20 percent at one time.

PRUNING DECIDUOUS TREES

Damaged wood can be pruned at any season.

Flowering trees when mature are too big to make deadheading—removing faded flowers—practical, and it isn't really necessary. But we do recommend clearing away dead flowers and foliage from trees that live part of the year indoors—**flowering maples** and **hibiscus,** for example.

New deciduous trees benefit from periodic light pruning. Remove any branches growing into the center of the tree, or that cross or crowd other branches. Never remove more than 25 percent of a tree's growth at one time; "dehorning" causes "water sprout" growth. Water sprouts shoot straight up at a 90-degree angle from the branch, which must be removed to maintain the tree's own natural shape.

You can prune shade trees in summer, fall, and early and late winter. The best time to prune trees is when the tree is dormant, just after the coldest part of the season. If sap starts to flow, never mind. It will stop when the tree leafs out. Light pruning and thinning in summer will not promote unwanted growth in trees, and you can see what you're doing. However, heavy pruning and even dehorning in summer can stimulate new unwelcome growth. Prune a spring flowering tree that blooms on last year's wood after the flowers fade. Prune a summer flowering tree that blooms on current growth shortly before growth begins.

PESTS AND DISEASES

Good garden practices help keep problems away. In naked earth, weeds sprout from April to October. Mulch helps keeps them out, and the few that do get started are easy to hand pull. Make sure each tree, old or new, has air and light all around.

Insects and diseases. Choose trees that are disease resistant, and be willing to accept a normal quota of insect damage. See Integrated Pest Management in the Introduction to the book and the section in the Appendix on Pests, Diseases, and Controls for more information.

Be realistic when faced with insect infestations or diseases. You can spray young and small trees, but if full size trees have problems, we recommend you get professional help from a tree company or a full service garden center or nursery.

Trees

Common Name (*Botanical Name*)	Hardiness Zones	Height	Type/ Bloom Time
American Arborvitae (*Halesia tetraptera*)	3 to 7 (Native)	40 to 60 feet	Evergreen —
American Beech (*Fagus grandifolia*)	3 to 8 (Native)	50 to 70 feet	Deciduous —
Birch (*Betula* sp. and hybrids)	2 to 6/7	30 to 40 feet	Deciduous —
Blue Atlas Cedar (*Cedrus atlantica* 'Glauca')	6 to 9	40 to 50 feet	Evergreen —
Carolina Hemlock (*Tsuga caroliniana*)	4 to 7	45 to 65 feet	Evergreen —
Carolina Silverbell (*Halesia tetraptera*)	4 to 8	40 to 50 feet	Deciduous/flowering Early spring
Catalpa, Northern (*Catalpa bignonioides*)	5 to 7 (Native)	30 to 40 feet	Deciduous —
Chaste-tree (*Vitex agnus-castus*)	6/7 to 8/9	12 to 15 feet	Deciduous/flowering Summer
Colorado Blue Spruce (*Picea pungens* 'Glauca')	2/3 to 7/8	30 to 50	Evergreen —
Crapemyrtle (*Lagerstroemia indica* and cultivars)	6 to 10	15 to 30 feet	Deciduous/flowering Mid-July
Dawn Redwood (*Metasequoia glyptostroboides*)	6 to 8	70 to 100	Evergreen —
Eastern Redbud (*Cercis canadensis*)	4 to 9	20 to 30 feet	Deciduous/flowering Early spring
European Hornbeam (*Carpinus betulus* 'Fastigiata').	4 to 7	30 to 40	Deciduous —
Florida Dogwood (*Cornus florida* cultivars)	5 to 8	20 to 30 feet	Deciduous/flowering Early May
Flowering Cherry Group (*Prunus* spp. and hybrids)	5 to 8	20 to 30 feet	Deciduous/flowering Early spring
Flowering Crabapple (*Malus* and hybrids)	4 to 8	15 to 30 feet	Deciduous/flowering Spring
Flowering Pear, Callery Pear (*Pyrus calleryana*)	4/5 to 8	35 to 40 feet	Deciduous/flowering Early spring
Franklin Tree, Ben Franklin Tree (*Franklinia alatamaha*)	5 to 8	15 to 25 feet	Deciduous/flowering Summer
Ginkgo, Maidenhair (*Ginkgo biloba*)	4 to 9	30 to 50 feet	Deciduous —
Golden Hinoki Cypress 'Crippsii' (*Chamaecyparis obtusa* 'Crippsii')	5 to 8	8 to 30 feet	Evergreen —
Hawthorn (*Crataegus viridis* 'Winter King')	5 to 7	25 to 30 feet	Deciduous/flowering May

Trees

Common Name (Botanical Name)	Hardiness Zones	Height	Type/ Bloom Time
Holly, American Holly (*Ilex opaca*)	5 to 9	40 to 50 feet	Evergreen —
Honeylocust (*Gleditsia triacanthos* var. *inermis* 'Shade Master')	3 to 7 (Native)	About 70 feet	Deciduous —
Japanese Pagoda Tree, Chinese Scholar-tree (*Sophora japonica* 'Regent')	4 to 7	40 to 50	Deciduous —
Japanese Snowbell (*Styrax japonicus*)	6 to 8	15 to 20 feet	Deciduous/flowering Late spring
Katsura Tree (*Cercidiphyllum japonicum*)	4 to 8	40 to 60 feet	Deciduous —
Kentucky Coffee Tree (*Gymnocladus dioicus*)	4 to 8	50 to 60 feet	Deciduous —
Lacebark Pine (*Pinus bungeana*)	4/5 to 8	30 to 50 feet	Evergreen —
Lawson's Falsecypress (*Chamaecyparis lawsoniana*)	5 to 7	40 to 60	Evergreen —
Leyland Cypress (x *Cupressocyparis leylandii*)	5 to 10	60 to 70	Evergreen —
Linden, Littleleaf (*Tilia cordata*)	4 to 8 (Native)	60 to 70	Deciduous —
Magnolia (*Magnolia* sp. and hybrids)	4 to 9 (Some native)	25 to 50 feet	Evergreen —
Maple, Japanese (*Acer palmatum*)	4 to 9	15 to 25 feet	Deciduous —
Maple, Swamp Maple (*Acer rubrum*)	4 to 9 (Native)	40 to 50 feet	Deciduous —
Oak (*Quercus* sp. and hybrids)	4/5 to 8 (Native)	40 to 60 feet	Deciduous —
Pine, Eastern White Pine (*Pinus strobus*)	3 to 7 (Native)	50 to 80 feet	Evergreen —
Planetree (*Platanus* x *acerifolia*)	5 to 8	70 to 100 feet	Deciduous —
Red Horse Chestnut (*Aesculus* x *carnea* 'Briotii')	4 to 7	45 to 60 feet	Deciduous —
Sour Gum, Black Tupelo (*Nyssa sylvatica*)	4 to 9	30 to 50 feet	Deciduous —
Sourwood (*Oxydendrum arboreum*)	5 to 9 (Native)	25 to 30 feet	Deciduous —
Stewartia, Japanese Stewartia, Wild Olive (*Stewartia pseudocamellia*)	Zones 4 to 8	20 to 30 feet	Deciduous/flowering Summer to early fall
Sugar Maple (*Acer saccharum*)	3 to 8 (Native)	50 to 70 feet	Deciduous —

Trees

Common Name (*Botanical Name*)	Hardiness Zones	Height	Type/ Bloom Time
Sweetgum, American Sweetgum (*Liquidambar styraciflua*)	5 to 9 (Native)	50 to 60 feet	Deciduous —
Tuliptree, Tulip Poplar (*Liriodendron tulipifera*)	4 to 9 (Native)	70 to 90 feet	Deciduous —
Umbrella Pine, **Japanese Umbrella Pine** (*Sciadopitys verticillata*)	5 to 8	20 to 30 feet	Evergreen
White Fir (*Abies concolor*)	3 to 7/8	30 to 50 feet	Evergreen —
White Fringe Tree (*Chionanthus virginicus*)	3/4 to 9	12 to 18 feet	Deciduous/flowering Mid-spring
Witchhazel (*Hamamelis* x *intermedia* hybrids)	5 to 8	15 to 20 feet	Deciduous/flowering Late winter/spring
Yellowwood (*Cladrastris kentukea*)	4 to 8 (Native)	30 to 50 feet	Deciduous —
Zelkova, Japanese Zelkova (*Zelkova serrata*)	5 to 8	60 to 70 feet	Deciduous —

Did You Know?

About Pruning Cuts

When you remove a large limb, follow the three-cut pruning method to avoid stripping bark from the trunk:

1 About a foot out from the trunk, cut from the bottom of the branch upward about a third of the way through the limb.

2 A couple of inches out, or beyond the first cut, cut from the top of the branch down. The branch will break away cleanly.

3 Find the collar or ring at the base of the limb where it springs from the trunk. Taking care not to damage the ring, remove the stub. From the collar, an attractive, healthy covering for the wounded area can develop.

Limb Removal

Current wisdom says "no" to painting or tarring these cuts. That said, André prefers to paint with orange shellac large wounds caused by removing big branches; the alcohol in the shellac disinfects, and the cuts are sealed.

PLANNING

Sit down with your mail-order catalogs by a window overlooking your garden, and dream about trees. **January winds bring a big sky, and the possibility of a new vision for your landscape.**

Adding a tree makes a big difference to the overall design. Balanced plantings create a sense of security and well-being. Pairs of same-size shrubs or trees lining a walk or a driveway express balance, and are perfect for a formal dwelling. You can add a dynamic to balanced plantings by duplicating a silhouette without duplicating the plants that create it. Combining the arresting silhouettes of the symmetrical evergreen **incense cedar** and the stylized **Serbian spruce** with the sprawl of wide-spreading pyramidal **maples** and clumping **birches** adds interest to the view.

PLANTING

A live **Christmas tree** (see December) can begin to deteriorate after ten days indoors in a heated house. As soon as possible move the tree outdoors. If you have not prepared a planting hole (see Planting, November and December), place the tree in a sheltered spot, and cover it with 14 to 18 inches of leaves kept in place by evergreen boughs. As soon as you can, dig a hole, plant the tree, and then mulch the area (see Planting in the introduction to this chapter).

Repotting larger indoor trees is difficult and necessary only every three or four years. Other years in late winter before new growth begins, remove the top 2 inches of soil, and replace it with 2 or 3 inches of compost or fertile potting soil.

CARE

Established trees. Use a broom to brush away accumulations of snow and ice on the lower branches of the evergreens.

New Trees. Renew the anti-desiccant spray—a coating that keeps leaves from losing moisture—on evergreen trees, especially broadleaf evergreens in exposed positions. Check and adjust the burlap protecting new trees.

PRUNING

Outdoors. Prune away winter and snow damage before growth begins. Cut down old and injured trees. Cut the wood of deciduous trees into logs the size of your fireplace, and stack them to dry. Evergreen wood is soft and bad for your chimney, so make it into chips to top paths, or compost it.

Indoors. Remove dead flowers from **flowering maple** and **hibiscus,** as well as yellowing leaves and twigs crowding the crowns of indoors trees, *Ficus,* for example. Pinch out all but half a dozen or so of the tiny lemons developing on a **Improved Meyer lemon** tree.

WATERING

Outdoors. Trees growing outdoors in containers under overhangs and other shelters don't benefit from snow fall and may need watering.

If you have planted a live **Christmas tree**, water it as you do other new trees.

Indoors. Maintain the soil moisture of the indoor trees, for example, **citrus,** *Ficus,* **tropical hibiscus, flowering maples, palms.** Mist and air the room daily or often.

FERTILIZING

When you see new growth in indoor trees, begin adding a half-strength dose of fertilizer at every second watering.

Adding a tree makes a big difference to the overall design of your garden.

Did You Know?

Pruning Evergreen Trees

Pruning woody plants stimulates growth, so avoid heavy pruning in summer when the plant is preparing to go dormant.

Dead or damaged wood on evergreen conifers can be removed at any time.

Winter and snow damage is best pruned before active growth.

To encourage dense branching in evergreens with candle-like new growth, cut the candles back by half. Prune the tips of hemlock branches lightly any time during the growing season. Prune yews and junipers lightly or heavily any time during growth.

To establish a shape, prune evergreens (sparingly) when they are three to five years old.

To slow or dwarf a broadleaf evergreen tree—**hollies,** for example—when growth ends, cut back no more than 20 percent of the new growth. You can reduce the main stem back to the first side shoots, but don't remove more than has grown the last year or two.

To have holiday greens, save some pruning of new growth on **hemlocks, hollies, spruce, cedars** until December.

Winter Care of Indoor Trees

For trees that live indoors in winter, a bright, airy, cool room is best. Daytime temperatures should be between 68 and 75 degrees Fahrenheit with a drop of 7 to 10 degrees at night, and humidity between 30 and 60 percent. Temperatures higher than 68 degrees take the humidity from the air.

Air the room daily for about ten minutes unless it's freezing outside, and mist the plants with water at room temperature. If the room is warm, run a humidifier, keep wet sponges around, and grow the plants on saucers filled with wet pebbles. Keep the soil evenly damp, not soaking wet. When there's new growth, include a half-strength dose of houseplant fertilizer at every second watering.

Supplement inadequate window light with spot grow lights. Check for insects often. For controls, see Pests, Diseases, and Controls in the Appendix. Every few weeks remove yellowing or damaged foliage, dead flowers, branches that cross, and those that are becoming ungainly. When repotting, use the houseplant soils recommended under Soil in Chapter 4, Houseplants.

 PESTS

Voles are most active October to March. If you see vole runs, bait the main runway with a rodenticide.

Deer go for the tips of reachable branches of **arborvitae, cedars, yews,** and other evergreens. Spraying may deter them, but wrapping them with burlap or chickenwire is a surer safeguard. Deer also nibble bark; check the wraps on newly planted trees.

Apply dormant horticultural oils to small trees before growth begins to smother insects that have wintered over.

FEBRUARY
Trees

 PLANNING

Place catalog orders for trees now. Buy only resistant cultivars of trees that we've noted as susceptible to problems.

 PLANTING

Bare-root deciduous trees can be planted about a month before the last freeze; mail-order suppliers ship them dormant at your planting time. Here's a general view of how to plant them:

1 Soak the roots as instructed by the supplier.

2 Dig a planting hole twice as wide and deep as the roots.

3 Loosen the sides of the hole, and blend the soil from the hole with the organic amendments described in Soil Preparation and Improvement in the Introduction to the book.

4 Half fill the bottom of the hole with improved soil, and tamp it down **very firmly** to make a solid base. In the center of the hole build a cone. Gently separate the roots of the tree, and arrange them over the cone. Set the tree so the crown is 1 inch above the level of the surrounding earth.

5 Half fill the hole with improved soil, and tamp it down. Fill the hole with improved soil, and tamp it down firmly. Shape the soil around the crown into a wide saucer.

6 Slowly pour on ten to fifteen gallons of water.

7 Mulch newly planted trees 3 to 4 inches deep from 3 inches out from the trunk to the edge of the saucer.

 CARE

Established trees. Remove snow weighing down **evergreen** limbs and damaged and dead branches.

New trees. After fertilizing (see Fertilizing below), top off the mulch to keep it 3 to 4 inches deep starting about 3 inches from the trunk.

Check the stakes and ties of newly planted trees. If the ties are damaging the bark, loosen them a little. If the tree is growing straight and true, remove the stakes.

If cycles of thawing and freezing have heaved roots, press them back into place, and replenish the mulch to insulate the soil.

If you have planted a live **Christmas tree,** check and maintain the soil moisture.

 PRUNING

Prune **spring flowering trees** well before they bloom.

This month and next prune **summer-flowering trees.** Clear out underbrush, saplings, and weed trees crowding desirable trees in woodlands and groves. You can use a string trimmer to level small growth. Use **bypass pruning shears**—powerful shears with a scissor-like action—to take down saplings. Then remove diseased and dead trees and trees crowding others. Prune out big branches that could fall on driveways and paths in a storm. Remove from deciduous trees any limbs spoiling the symmetry of the structure.

Remove dead and damaged limbs from **mature deciduous trees,** and all that cross others or crowd the center of the tree. If the soil beneath appears compacted, loosen it with a hoe—take care not to damage roots near the surface. Then fertilize and water generously.

Root-pruning of deciduous and evergreen trees to check growth and prompt flowering can be undertaken now before growth begins. Use a spade to sever the roots in a circle around the trunk. Go out to where the roots are about the size of your little finger. If your spade encounters roots you need a saw to cut, you are too close; if the roots are web-fine, you are too far out. Water well, and fertilize after root pruning.

 WATERING

Outdoors. Check the soil under **broadleaf evergreen trees;** the foliage continues to lose water through transpiration during the winter, and if snow or rain has been scarce or if the soil under the mulch is dryish, water.

If there's no snow and no rain, water all your new outdoor plantings thoroughly.

Indoors. Water trees growing indoors, **citrus,** *Ficus,* **tropical hibiscus, palms.** Mist and air them daily or often.

 FERTILIZING

Add a half-strength dose to the water for trees growing indoors every second time you water.

Fertilize **newly planted trees** the first two or three years. When the buds begin to break, scratch in an application of Holly-tone for acid-loving trees, and Plant-tone for the others. **Established trees** in lawns, shrub, and flower borders should be okay with the fertilizer applied to the surrounding lawn and beds.

Did You Know?

Outstanding Flowering Trees

Callery Pear, *Pyrus calleryana* 'Aristocrat', 'Chanticleer', 'White House'

Common Smoke Tree, *Cotinus coggygria*

Crapemyrtle, *Lagerstroemia indica* and hybrids

Chinese Dogwood, *Cornus florida* hybrids, *C. kousa, C.* x *rutgersensis* Stellar Series

Eastern Redbud, *Cercis canadensis*

Flowering Cherry Group, *Prunus sargentii* species and hybrids

Flowering Crabapple, *Malus* hybrids

Franklin Tree, *Franklinia alatamaha*

Japanese Snowbell, *Styrax japonicus*

Japanese Stewartia, *Stewartia pseudocamellia*

Southern Magnolia, *Magnolia grandiflora* 'Little Gem', 'St. Mary's', 'Lennei', *M. stellata* 'Waterlily'

White Fringe Tree, *Chionanthus virginicus*

Witch-hazel, *Hamamelis* x *intermedia* hybrids

 PESTS

Voles can damage young tree roots. Bait the main runway with a rodenticide.

To keep rabbits, woodchucks, and other rodents away from new trees, try chemical repellents and fungicide formulations such as Thiram (Arasan) and hot pepper wax.

Deer are definitely up and hungry. Spray evergreen foliage that is munching-height with deer repellents. Check and adjust burlap covers and chicken-wire cages.

Before the buds open on trees suspected of insect infestation, spray them with horticultural oil. The oil smothers insects and their eggs.

PLANNING

If you want to plant a **street tree,** get municipal permission and their recommendations for trees that tolerate urban conditions. If it's up to you, choose trees that stay under 20 to 30 feet, or narrow understory trees—examples are the **American hornbeam** and **columnar flowering pear 'Capital'.** The **London plane tree 'Columbia',** which was introduced by the National Arboretum, is a fine shade tree for wide streets. Water and fertilize the tree until it is well-established, and then water during droughts.

You can pave around a tree to within 2 feet of the trunk if the paving is set in sand and gravel.

 PLANTING

It's spring planting—and transplanting—time when winter cold and wet leave the ground. Pack a ball of earth between your hands, and if it crumbles easily, it's ready to be worked.

Detailed instructions for planting appear in the introduction to this chapter. To prepare a tree for planting:

Container-grown tree. To free the rootball, tip the container on its side and roll it around. If it is too large for that, slit the sides of the container, and peel the pieces away. If roots wrap the rootball, make four shallow vertical cuts in the sides of the rootball, and slice off the bottom 2 inches.

Bare-root tree. Leave the tree in its packaging in a cool dark place until you are ready to plant. Soak the roots in tepid water as directed by the planting instructions, or six to twelve hours before planting.

 CARE

New trees. Remove trunk covers from protected trees. If a tree that was staked is growing straight and not being heaved, remove the stakes. After fertilizing, renew the mulch.

Trees in containers. Before growth begins, top-dress the soil. Remove the top 2 inches of soil, and replace it with soil enriched with Holly-tone. Renew the mulch.

 PRUNING

Outdoors. You can prune summer-flowering trees this month and in April. Harvest branches from flowering trees that can be forced into bloom indoors, **flowering cherry trees, crabapples,** and **dogwoods,** for example. (See Forcing Flowering Branches into Bloom Indoors in the February pages of Chapter 8, Shrubs.) If sap starts to flow, never mind. It will stop when the tree leafs out.

The ends of **hemlock** branches can be lightly pruned throughout the growing season. Prune **yews** and **junipers** any time during the growth cycle.

Prune newly-planted trees lightly the first few years to control the development of the scaffold (the limb structure). Remove branches heading into the center of the tree or crossing others.

Never take away more than 20 to 25 percent of a tree's growth; this is called "dehorning," and it causes "water sprout" growth. To learn how to prune your own trees, study the trunk and branch structures of well-grown trees in arboreta and public gardens.

Indoors. Continue to deadhead and groom trees growing indoors.

 WATERING

Outdoors. For new and transplanted trees, including a live **Christmas tree,** pour two or three 5-gallon bucketsful of water around the roots once a week throughout spring unless you have a soaking rain.

Regular check the soil moisture of hardy trees growing outdoors in containers, and water enough to maintain soil moisture.

Indoors. Continue to maintain the soil moisture of the trees growing indoors, **citrus,** *Ficus,* **tropical hibiscus, palms;** mist the trees, and air the room often.

 # FERTILIZING

Indoors. Add fertilizer at half-strength dose to the water every second time you water. Mist often with water at room temperature.

Established trees. If, in its third or fourth season, or later, a tree isn't growing well, fertilize.

Stunted growth and leaves that are uncharacteristically red or dark green may signal a shortage of phosphate. Applying a fertilizer with a higher ratio of phosphate should improve matters. **Weak stems and a susceptibility to disease might be caused by a shortage of potash;** fertilizer with a higher ratio of phosphorus and potash would help.

Did You Know?

Pruning Deciduous Trees

- **Winter damage.** Prune any time.

- **Damaged branches.** Prune them before the leaves fall—they're easier to spot.

- **In fall.** Prune lightly in fall when the plant is preparing to go dormant.

- **Flowering trees that bloom on new wood.** Prune them before growth begins in late winter or early spring.

- **Flowering trees that bloom on old wood.** Prune immediately after they bloom to avoid cutting off branches where buds are being initiated for the following season.

- **To control height.** Prune after the season's new growth has fully developed.

- **To slow or dwarf growth.** Prune in summer when the plant has stopped growing.

 # PESTS

If you see vole activity, bait the main runway with a rodenticide.

If you didn't spray with a dormant horticultural oil last month, do it now. These botanical oils sprayed on the egg and immature stages of insects smother them.

If you spot the **webs of bagworms or tent caterpillars,** in the cool of the evening scoop the tents out with a stick and destroy them. The other way is to spray with a biological control such as *Bacillus thuringiensis.* Other controls are Sevin or malathion insecticide, pyrethrin, or rotenone.

To keep deer away from evergreens and newly planted trees, spray with a repellent they haven't smelled recently. Circle small trees, whose bark the deer are damaging, with chickenwire; for larger trees, use unobtrusive bird netting.

 PLANNING

Need more colorful trees? Check out the yellow, and yellow-green evergreens. Cripps golden Hinoki cypress *Chamaecyperis obtusa* 'Crippsii' is fast-growing and has rich golden yellow foliage. Some of the new **Japanese maple** cultivars are breathtaking when sun shines through the leaves. **Variegated hollies** and **beeches** are quite beautiful. Enter the names of trees that catch your fancy in your garden log, and plan to buy them at a local nursery late in the season when you can see the summer color and maybe buy at a bargain price.

PLANTING

You can transplant newly planted container-grown trees the first two years without trauma.

Small well-established trees can be moved successfully if you plan ahead.

Year 1. Before growth begins, sever the roots in a circle all around the trunk to stimulate root growth within the circle.

Year 2. The following year tie the branches together at the top. Dig a trench outside the root-pruned circle, lift the rootball onto a big piece of burlap, and tie the burlap around the rootball. Very gently drag the plant to its new location. Prepare the soil, and plant the tree as described in the introduction to this chapter. Free the branches, and prune out damaged twigs.

 CARE

Established and new trees. Mow with care around the trunks of trees young or old. If the mower consistently gets too close, keep it away by surrounding the trunk with a ring of mulch 3 inches deep. A 3-inch deep mulch starting 3 inches from the trunk keeps the roots cool and weeds down—and replenishes the organic material in the soil beneath.

Container tree. Root pruning every two or three years keeps a tree growing well, and dwarfs it without impairing its form. **The best time for root pruning is late winter before growth.** A small tub can be tipped onto its side, and the rootball slipped out. Disentangle roots binding the bottom of the rootball, and cut away roots growing straight down the outside of the rootball. Next, add a layer of fertile soil mix to the bottom of the tub, and center the rootball inside.

If the tub is too big for this operation, then slide a hand-pruning saw inside the container, and sever an inch of the roots growing around the outside of the rootball. Remove the top inch or two of the soil covering the rootball. Push soil mix down into the sides of the tub, and add 2 or 3 inches to the top of the rootball, and then renew the mulch 3 inches deep. Water the container thoroughly.

 PRUNING

The ends of **hemlock** branches can be lightly pruned throughout the growing season. Prune **yews** and **junipers** lightly or heavily any time during their growth season.

Remove "water sprout" growth from tree limbs, and suckers from around the base of the fruit and other trees and on tree trunks and branches.

Did You Know?

Growing Trees in Containers

Small hardy trees succeed in containers big enough to allow for growth and insulation. For insulation, wrap the interior with a double row of large bubble wrap or Styrofoam before you add soil. Bags of dry leaves placed around the containers for winter add extra protection.

A young tree can stand winters in a container 14 to 16 inches in height and circumference even in Zones 6 and 7. A larger tree would need a 14- or a 16-inch tub and eventually one 30 inches high and 24 inches in circumference.

Soil. André lines the bottom of these large containers with 4 to 5 inches of PermaTill® for drainage. It's lighter than gravel. The ideal container soil is a fertile semi-soilless mix. André's recipe is: one part good topsoil, one part horticultural perlite (or half-and-half perlite and PermaTill®), and two parts coarse peat moss. For every 7 inches of planter height, add 1/3 cup slow-release fertilizer, and 1 cup dehydrated cow manure. Adding a soil polymer, such as Soil Moist, can reduce watering by as much as 50 percent.

Water and mulch. Before planting, soak the tub until water runs out of the bottom. After planting, top-dress the soil with 2 or 3 inches of mulch.

 ## WATERING

Water the soil in containers of trees growing indoors, and those you have moved outdoors. Always use water at room temperature.

Water hardy trees growing outdoors in containers when the soil feels dry. You will need to water less if you included water-holding polymers in the container soil.

For new and transplanted in-ground trees, including a **Christmas tree**, pour two or three 5-gallon bucketfuls of water around the roots once a week throughout spring unless there's a good rain.

 ## FERTILIZING

Indoors. At every second watering, add a half-strength dose of fertilizer to trees growing indoors—**citrus,** *Ficus,* **palms,** and others.

Outdoors. Frequent watering leaches nutrients from the soil in containers, so start monthly applications of a water-soluble organic fertilizer, seaweed or manure tea, for example.

In-ground trees growing in lawns and flower and shrub borders will get all the fertilizer they need when you fertilize the surrounding lawns and borders.

 ## PESTS

Continue protecting your trees from the deer.

Scale may turn up on your **hollies.** Spray with summer-weight horticultural oils or neem.

Rake up weeds.

Late this month tent caterpillars emerge. Spray trees with signs of infestations with a biological control such as *Bacillus thuringiensis.* Other controls are Sevin or malathion insecticide, pyrethrin, or rotenone.

Pick off the cone shaped nests of bagworms and destroy them.

PLANNING

To furnish your yard with song—and to keep insects down—look for places to plant a few trees that meet the needs of birds. They nest in the branches of evergreens like **Canadian hemlock,** *Tsuga canadensis,* and **white pine,** *Pinus strobus.* They eat the fruit of **American holly,** *Ilex opaca,* and **red cedar,** *Juniperus virginiana.* The tiny fruits of the flowering, or ornamental, fruit trees are staples for birds—beautiful cultivars like the **crabapple** *Malus* 'Narragansett', and the **Florida** and *Cornus kousa* **dogwoods** and **weeping cherries.** Many native trees bear fruits birds love— **chokecherry** *Prunus pennsylvanica,* and **wild red cherry,** *P. virginiana,* and **American hornbeam,** *Carpinus caroliniana,* a lovely shade tree.

 PLANTING

This is a fine month to plant new trees.

Crapemyrtles are slow to start up, so if new plants seem to have died, wait until late next month before deciding you must replace them.

 CARE

Indoors. When nighttime temperatures stay steady at 60 degrees Fahrenheit and above, start moving your indoor trees—**citrus,** *Ficus,* **tropical hibiscus, palms**—outdoors for a summer vacation. Summered out in the bright light on a porch or under a tall tree, they'll survive less favorable winter conditions indoors.

Place them in indirect light in a sheltered spot for the first week. Like you, houseplants sunburn when exposed too long too early to direct sun. Gradually move them into brighter light. Don't be alarmed if some drop leaves their first week or two outdoors. The change of light has that effect on some, notably *Ficus*.

Outdoors. Renew the mulch under newly-planted trees before summer heat arrives.

 PRUNING

Prune to encourage dense branching to the ground in **pines, firs, spruces,** and **other evergreens** whose growth is initiated by candles (new candlelike growths at the ends of branches); cut the candles back by half when they appear at the branch tips. The ends of **hemlock** branches can be lightly pruned throughout the growing season. Prune **yews** and **junipers** any time during their growth season.

Prune and shape up **crapemyrtles** you wish to grow as trees before they bloom. Remove dried flower clusters. To encourage a canopy to form, remove the branches a third of the way up the trunk. Remove branches rubbing across others and any growing into the center of the canopy. Prune unbranched limbs back to an outward facing bud.

Check the fruit trees for an oversupply of tiny fruits. In the next several weeks thin **apples, pears,** and **peaches** so that the fruits are no closer than 4 to 6 inches.

 WATERING

Keep track of how often the soil in containers of the indoor trees moved outdoors needs watering, and plan a regular watering schedule.

Water outdoor trees growing in containers every two weeks, or when the soil seems dry.

Did You Know?

Change the Grade

Sometimes new landscaping or building plans require changing the grade of the land around an established tree. It can be done without killing the tree, if you avoid destroying the roots from at least half the distance from the trunk to the outer edge of the drip line. That means you must maintain the existing grade that far out from the tree trunk.

If you are **lowering the grade**, shore up the soil around the tree by building a retaining wall.

If you are **raising the grade**, arrange to channel downpours so as avoid having water collect over the roots. Do not cover the roots with more than a few extra inches of soil. **Dogwoods** and **live oaks** are especially sensitive. If the change of grade is severe, surround the trunk and roots with a retaining wall, fill it with rocks, and cover them with chickenwire to keep the well from filling up.

For newly planted and transplanted in-ground trees, pour two or three 5-gallon bucketfuls of water around the roots once a week throughout spring unless you have rain.

 ## FERTILIZING

Since frequent watering leaches nutrients from the soil, once a month give all the trees growing in containers a light application of a water-soluble organic fertilizer, seaweed or manure tea, for example.

 ## PESTS

Deer sightings may subside now that the woods are full of browsing material. Even so, continue to discourage them from visits to your yard looking for treats.

Woolly adelgid attack **Canadian hemlock** and can do severe damage. Spraying twice a year with horticultural oil is the preferred control. These lightweight botanical oils also control **aphids, cankerworms, leafhoppers, leaf rollers, mealybugs, mites, psylids, scale, tent caterpillars, and webworms.**

Caution: Spraying with horticultural oils can temporarily remove the blue in blue hostas and Colorado blue spruce. Never spray during droughts, and always water deeply before applying.

Rake up weeds.

Late this month gypsy moths emerge. Spray trees with signs of infestations with a biological control such as *Bacillus thuringiensis*. Other controls are Sevin or malathion insecticide, pyrethrin, or rotenone.

Continue to look for and destroy the nests of bagworms.

JUNE
Trees

PLANNING

You can grow small ornamental trees in the limited space afforded by a rooftop, a balcony, or a deck by planting them in containers. The best subjects are small flowering trees, and dwarf, semi-dwarf, small, columnar, weeping, and slow growing forms.

Choose trees well within your cold hardiness range; the soil is more likely to freeze in pots than in the ground. Be aware that containers on rooftops are generally receiving more bottom heat than those on wooden decks or cement patios—not good in Zone 8 summers, but helpful in Zone 6.

Containers on rooftops must be raised three inches from the roofing material. Resting directly on the rooftop, a heavy container full of damp soil can create considerable damage to the ceiling below.

Use lightweight soil mixes to keep down the weight of pots that will require seasonal moving. André adds PermaTill®, an aggregate lighter than gravel, to soil mixes for very large containers. When you have to move a container, do it before watering.

Planters made of redwood are good for several years. Plastics hold moisture longer, and are okay if they have drainage holes. Clay containers are beautiful, and allow the plants to breathe, but they dry out more quickly especially in high, windy places.

PLANTING

You can plant even big container-grown trees—and entire landscaping projects—this month as long as you follow the watering practices recommended.

Many species of trees can be propagated from cuttings taken at certain times of the year. Softwood (new wood) cuttings of some **hollies** and **red maples** taken in June and July root fairly easily. **Witchhazels** root from softwood cuttings taken from trees three to five years old. **Juniper** cuttings taken during the winter will root. "Softwood" means new green branch tips whose bark has not yet begun to harden.

If you are interested in trying, turn to the section on Rooting Cuttings To Multiply Your Shrubs in the June pages of Chapter 8, Shrubs.

CARE

New Trees. Make sure the mulch around new plantings is a full 3 inches deep before heat arrives.

PRUNING

As seasonal growth comes to an end, you can prune trees whose growth you want to slow or dwarf. Reducing the leaf surface reduces the sugar synthesized and translocated to the roots and limits next year's growth in the tree.

Remove yellowing leaves and twigs beginning to crowd the crown of indoors trees, *Ficus*, for example. Pinch out all but half a dozen or so tiny lemons developing on a **Improved Meyer lemon** tree.

As seasonal growth comes to an end, you can prune trees whose growth you want to slow or dwarf.

Did You Know?

Small Trees for Containers

- **American Hornbeam,** *Carpinus caroliniana* (syn. *americana*) 'Fastigiata'
- **American Smoke Tree, Chittamwood,** *Cotinus obovatus*
- **Amur Maple,** *Acer ginnala* 'Flame'
- **Flowering Autumn Cherry,** *Prunus subhirtella* 'Autumnalis Rosea'
- **Flowering Weeping Cherry,** *P. s.* 'Pendula'; **Double Flowering Weeping Cherry,** *P. s.* 'Pendula Plena Rosea'
- **Carolina Silverbell, Wild Olive,** *Halesia carolina*
- **Chinese Dogwood,** *Cornus kousa* var. *chinensis*
- **Crapemyrtle,** *Lagerstroemia indica* x *fauriei* cvs.
- **English Hawthorn,** *Crataegus laevigata* (syn. *oxyacantha*)
- **English Holly, White-edged,** *Ilex aquifolium* 'Argenteo marginata'
- **Flowering Cherry,** *Prunus serrulata* 'Kwanzan', 'Shirotae'
- **Flowering Cherry,** *Prunus yedoensis* 'Akebono'
- **Flowering Weeping Cherry,** *Prunus subhirtella* var. *pendula*
- **Fragrant Snowbell,** *Styrax obassia*
- **Japanese Flowering Crabapple,** *Malus floribunda*
- **Japanese Maple,** *Acer palmatum* 'Atropurpureum'; **Moon Maple,** *A. japonicum* and other cvs.
- **Japanese Snowbell,** *Styrax japonicus*
- **Japanese Tree Lilac,** *Syringa reticulata* (syn. *amurensis* var. *japonica*)
- **Redbud, Eastern Redbud,** *Cercis canadensis*
- **Sargent Cherry,** *Prunus sargentii*
- **Smoke Tree,** *Cotinus coggygria* cvs.
- **Sourwood, Sorrel Tree,** *Oxydendrum arboreum*
- **Trident Maple,** *Acer buergeranum*
- **Washington Thorn,** *Crataegus phaenopyrum*
- **Southern Black Haw,** *Viburnum rufidulum*
- **Varnish Tree, Golden-rain Tree,** *Koelreuteria paniculata*

 WATERING

Maintain the soil moisture of the indoor trees moved outdoors for the season—**citrus,** *Ficus*, **palms.**

Water trees growing in containers once or twice every week or so, or when the soil seems dry. Since frequent watering leaches nutrients from the soil, once a month during the growing season, give the plants a light application of a water-soluble organic fertilizer—seaweed or manure tea, for example.

Pour two or three 5-gallon bucketfuls of water around new trees every week or ten days, unless you have a soaking rain.

 FERTILIZING

Add a half-strength dose to the water for container trees and indoor trees growing outdoors at every second watering.

 PESTS

Early June is spray time for bagworms. Use *Bt*, Sevin, Neem, Permethrin, which is also effective against whitefly. If you spot bagworm tents, remove and destroy them now. Apply fungicidal formulations of copper to control powdery mildew, rusts, and bacterial diseases such as fire blight, bacterial leaf spots, and wilt.

PLANNING

In seashore gardens so close to the water they are within reach of salt spray, high tides, and brine-laden wind, plant only trees that tolerate salt. In coastal gardens that are out of the reach of salt water or salt spray, you can plant trees that do well in light, sandy soil.

At the shore, evergreens are the best plants for windbreaks. Your choices are varied; broadleaved evergreens such as **American holly,** and **privet,** needled evergreens such as **Austrian black pine, hemlock,** and the **junipers.** The fast-growing evergreen **Leyland cypress,** x *Cupressocyparis leylandii,* is an excellent choice for windbreak, hedges, and screening. The bluish-green foliage is feathery and graceful, and the scaly reddish brown bark is handsome. **'Naylor's Blue',** which has soft grayish-blue foliage accents, and **'Castlewellan',** whose new growth is yellow, are colorful cultivars.

PLANTING

When filling containers for a seashore garden, use commercial potting soil rather than the sandy soil of the area. The humidity in the air reduces the need to water, but check the soil moisture often anyway.

To prevent plant damage from coastal storms, spray the upper and lower sides of the leaves with anti-desiccant; that coats them with a barrier against salt wind and spray.

You can plant container-grown trees this month and balled-and-burlapped shrubs, too. Don't buy B&B shrubs if they've been sitting unmulched and baking at a garden center since they were dug in early spring.

CARE

To help trees at the seashore recover from exposure to heavy spray and high winds after a storm, spray the foliage thoroughly with a hose to wash off as much salt as possible.

If a dangerously high tide is expected, it may be helpful to flood a stand of trees with sprinklers until the soil is so saturated it can't absorb much of the sea water that comes in. The damage will be reduced if the ground is wet when the salt water comes in.

PRUNING

Prune dead wood on evergreen conifers at any time.

Remove water sprouts and suckers from around the base, the trunks, and the branches of flowering fruit trees. The flowering cherries usually need repeated attention.

Study the shade enveloping your gardens. Where you are losing too much light to tree branches, mark limbs that can be removed to thin the canopy, and consider whether removing a few lower branches will help; late winter is a good time to remove them.

Use a string trimmer to keep down undergrowth in woodlands and groves. Leave the debris in place, and it will decompose and nourish the trees growing there.

WATERING

Maintain the soil moisture of the indoor tree moved outdoors for the season— **citrus,** *Ficus,* **palms.**

Water outdoor trees growing in containers every two weeks or when the soil seems dry. Since frequent watering leaches nutrients from the soil, once a

Where you are losing too much light to tree branches, mark limbs that can be removed to thin the canopy, and consider whether removing a few lower branches will help; late winter is a good time to remove them.

month during the growing season, give the plants a light application of a water-soluble organic fertilizer—seaweed or manure tea, for example.

Established trees. They need watering in times of severe drought—more than two or three weeks without rain.

New trees. Water every week or ten days, unless you have a soaking rain. Slowly and gently lay down 1½ inches of water. Set a 1-pound coffee can under the sprinkler or the hose, and record how long it took to put 1½ inches in the can—then you'll know.

FERTILIZING

At every second watering, add a half-strength dose of fertilizer to the water for indoor trees growing outdoors for the summer.

In-ground trees get all the fertilizer they need when you fertilize the surrounding lawns and beds.

PESTS

Troops of **Japanese beetles** are at full strength right now. The creature is a beautiful metallic green and coppery maroon, and it chews the leaves and

stems of many ornamentals. The grub stage is devastating to lawns and gardens, and while grub-proofing reduces the populations in your yard, it does not control the beetles that fly in.

Japanese beetle traps are effective, providing they are placed **far away** from the plantings you are trying to protect, not among them. If the infestation is minor, beetles can be picked off by hand. Insecticides containing neem, rotenone, or Sevin insecticide

help control this and other bad guy beetles.

Neem is an effective control for **whitefly, mites, and bagworms.** If you spot bagworm tents, remove and destroy them now. Apply fungicidal formulations of copper to control powdery mildew, rust, and bacterial diseases such as fire blight, bacterial leafspot and wilt.

PLANNING

A tree's winter assets are its silhouette against the sky, its bark, and its fruit. The symmetrical winter silhouettes of the **incense cedar,** the **white oak,** the stylish **Serbian spruce,** are arresting. The gnarly form of the **California sycamore** is high drama. The bark of most trees becomes more rugged and interesting with the years, and some species shed their bark in beautiful patterns. The peeling bark of **paperbark maple,** *Acer griseum*, reveals variations on its rich cinnamon color. The chalky white bark of the **lacebark pine** rivals the beauty of the **paper birch.**

 PLANTING

You can plant container-grown trees this month. B&B trees, too, but don't buy

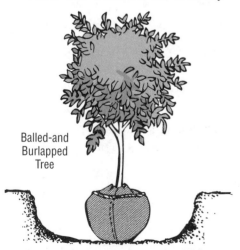

Balled-and
Burlapped
Tree

B&B shrubs if they have been sitting unmulched and baking at a garden center since they were dug in early spring.

Evergreen trees do well moved August through October.

 CARE

Don't leave orchard fruit lying on the ground. It attracts raccoons, skunks, possums, and yellow jackets. Not to mention deer.

 PRUNING

Begin to prepare indoor trees summering outdoors for their return to winter quarters—**citrus, tropical hibiscus, flowering maples,** and the others. Deadhead, clear away yellowing foliage, and prune out branches that are crossing or crowding the crown.

 WATERING

Maintain the soil moisture of the indoor trees moved outdoors for the season—**citrus,** *Ficus*, **palms.**

Water outdoor trees growing in containers every week or when the soil seems dry. Since frequent watering leaches nutrients from the soil, once a month

during the growing season give the plants a light application of a water-soluble organic fertilizer, seaweed or manure tea, for example.

New trees. Water every week or ten days, unless you have a soaking rain.

Established trees. They need watering in times of severe drought—more than two or three weeks without rain.

 FERTILIZING

Mid-month, stop fertilizing established outdoor trees growing in containers. Do continue to fertilize indoor trees summering outdoors at every second watering.

To make room for the leaves the trees will begin to shed next month, use up, or store, finished compost. Composting can happen in just one summer in our warm, humid regions if you have been keeping the pile watered and turned. (See Composting in this chapter's October pages.)

 PESTS

Bagworms and tent caterpillars are usually very active right now. If you spot bagworm tents, remove and destroy them now. You can also spray with a

Did You Know?

Trees with Colorful Fall Foliage

- **American Smoke Tree, Chittamwood,** *Cotinus obovatus*
- **American Sweet Gum,** *Liquidambar styraciflua*
- **Amur Maple,** *Acer ginnala*
- **Black Gum, Sour Gum,** *Nyssa sylvatica*
- **Bradford Pear,** *Pyrus calleryana* 'Chanticleer', 'Aristocrat'
- **Chinese Dogwood,** *Cornus florida* hybrids; *C. kousa*, *C.* x *rutgersensis* Stellar Series
- **Golden Larch,** *Pseudolarix amabile*
- **Japanese Stewartia,** *Stewartia pseudocamellia*
- **Japanese Zelkova,** *Zelkova serrata*
- **Katsura Tree,** *Cercidiphylium japonicum*
- **Maidenhair Tree,** *Ginkgo biloba*
- **Mountain Ash, Korean Mountain Ash,** *Sorbus alnifolia*
- **Northern Red Oak,** *Quercus rubra*
- **Pistachio,** *Pistacia chinensis*
- **Red Maple, Swamp Maple,** *Acer rubrum* 'October Glory', 'Red Sunset'
- **Sassafras,** *Sassafras albidum*
- **Scarlet Oak,** *Quercus coccinea* 'Superba'
- **Sourwood, Sorrel Tree,** *Oxydendrum arboreum*
- **Sugar Maple,** *Acer saccharum* 'Bonfire,' 'Green Mountain'
- **Sweet Gum,** *Liquidambar styraciflua*
- **Tatarian Maple,** *Acer tataricum*
- **Tulip Tree,** *Liriodendron tulipifera*
- **Washington Hawthorn,** *Crataegus phaenopyrum*
- **Witchhazel,** *Hamamelis* x *intermedia* 'Diane'

Trees with Exceptional Bark

- **American Beech,** *Fagus grandiflora*
- **American Sweet Gum,** *Liquidambar styraciflua*
- **American Sycamore,** *Platanus occidentalis*
- **American Yellowwood,** *Cladrastis lutea*
- **Asian White Birch,** *Betula platyphylla*
- **Beech,** *Fagus*
- **Chinese Elm, Lacebark Elm,** *Ulmus parviflora*
- **Crapemyrtle,** *Lagerstroemia indica*
- **Dove Tree, Handkerchief Tree,** *Davidia involucrata*
- **Franklin Tree,** *Franklinia alatamaha*
- **Hawthorn,** *Crataegus viridis* 'Winter King'
- **Japanese Larch,** *Larix kaempferi*
- **Japanese Stewartia,** *Stewartia pseudocamellia*
- **Korean Stewartia,** *Stewartia koreana*
- **Lacebark Pine,** *Pinus bungeana*
- **London Planetree,** *Platanus* x *acerifolia*
- **Paperbark Cherry,** *Prunus serrula*
- **Paperbark Maple,** *Acer griseum*
- **River Birch,** *Betula* 'Heritage'
- **Sargent Cherry,** *Prunus sargentii*
- **Shagbark Hickory,** *Carya ovata*
- **Stewartia,** *Stewartia*
- **Whitebarked Himalayan Birch,** *Betula utilis jacquemontii*

biological control such as *Bacillus thuringiensis (Bt)*. Other controls are Sevin or malathion insecticide, pyrethrin, or rotenone.

Powdery mildew and rust turn up on susceptible plants. Sulfur controls both, as do fungicidal formulations of copper, which also control bacterial diseases such as fire blight, bacterial leafspot, and wilt.

SEPTEMBER
Trees

PLANNING

Check out the changing color of the trees in your neighborhood and at public gardens, where the names of those you admire are sure to be available. Then look in your own garden for a spot just asking for a little red, coral, or yellow in the fall. **Fall is one of the best planting seasons, and it's on its way.**

Consider investing in a few trees that are especially beautiful in fall and winter to brighten corners that appear dull at this season. The **spruces** are gorgeous when they are outlined by snow, so plant one where you will see it from indoors. Even in a small garden you can find space for at least one deciduous specimen that has beautiful bark—the **river birch 'Heritage'**, for example. Planted where it will shelter a big rock, a stand of grass that turns gold in fall, **ferns,** a few brilliant early **tulips** and **narcissus**, it will be a year-round destination.

PLANTING

When the leaves start to change color is the beginning of an excellent planting season for trees. Plant sales and pleasant September weather combine to make this a fine time to install a hedge. You'll find suggestions for planting hedges under Planting in the September pages of Chapter 8, Shrubs.

If you've been wanting a too-expensive tree, a good-sized **Japanese maple** for example—take advantage of the seasonally discounted prices offered now. If you are buying a balled-and-burlapped tree, choose one that has just been dug rather than a tree that was dug in spring. Avoid B&B trees that have been unmulched and baking on the nursery lot all summer long.

CARE

In Zone 6, get ready to move outdoor trees growing in containers in exposed locations to more protected spots for the winter.

Before the end of the month move the indoor trees back inside for the winter. But first, hose them down, let them dry, and then spray the foliage lightly, top and undersides, with a horticultural soap. (See Planning in the September pages of Chapter 4, Houseplants.)

You may need to wrap new trees as a protection from deer rubbing, critter nibbling, and sunscald this fall and winter. Plan to remove it come spring as wrappings eventually constrict the trunks and can cause cracking.

An easy way to prevent winter sun from injuring the bark of young trees is to paint the trunks with white wash—calcium carbonate with resins in it.

As the leaves begin to fall, gather and save them for the compost pile. (See Composting in this chapter's October pages.) Dry leaves, along with grass clippings, are a major source of organic material for the compost pile.

PRUNING

Early this month, before preparing the indoor trees vacationing outdoors for their move back inside—*Ficus*, **citrus, palms**—groom them. Remove yellowing foliage and branches that are crossing so that the interior has air and light. Pinch off all but half a dozen or so tiny lemons developing on a **Improved Meyer lemon** tree.

Clear away spent flowers on late blooming flowering trees.

WATERING

Pour two or three 5-gallon bucketfuls of water around the roots of newly-planted trees once every two weeks throughout fall. The earth remains warm even after leaves fall and the air cools, so roots continue to develop.

Check the soil moisture of the indoor trees you moved back indoors for the winter. Dry air indoors soon sucks the moisture out of the soil.

Indoors. Maintain the soil moisture for indoor trees, mist them, and air the room often.

FERTILIZING

In Zone 8, the last fertilization can be between the end of September and mid-October. In Zones 6 and 7, the time for the last application is between early September and early October.

Include mature trees that are doing poorly when you fertilize.

Did You Know?

Trees Used as Hedges

These are some beautiful trees that can be pruned to maintain a desired hedge height.

- **American Arborvitae,** *Thuja occidentalis* cvs.
- **American Hornbeam,** *Carpinus caroliniana*
- **American Incense Cedar,** *Calocedrus decurrens*
- **Canadian Hemlock,** *Tsuga canadensis* 'Bennett', 'Jeddeloh', 'Jervis'
- **Crapemyrtle,** *Lagerstroemia indica* cvs.
- **European Beech,** *Fagus sylvatica*
- **European Hornbeam,** *Caarpinus betulus*
- **European Smoke Tree,** *Cotinus coggygria*
- **Foster Holly #2,** *Ilex attenuata*
- **Hinoki False Cypress,** *Chamaecyparis obtusa*
- **Japanese Cedar,** *Cryptomeria japonica* 'Yoshino'
- **Juniper,** *Juniperus* spp.
- **Leyland Cypress,** x *Cupressocyparis leylandii*
- **Oleander, Rose-bay,** *Nerium oleander*
- **Pine,** *Pinus* spp.
- **Privet,** *Ligustrum* spp.
- **Upright Atlas Cedar,** *Cedrus atlantica* 'Fastigiata'
- **Washington Thorn,** *Crataegus phaenopyrum*

 PESTS

Fall tent caterpillars can be controlled by *Bacillus thuringiensis* (Bt). Other controls are Sevin or malathion insecticide, pyrethrin, or rotenone.

Treat the indoor **trees, citrus,** *Ficus,* **palms,** that have been summering outdoors for insects before moving them back inside for the winter.

Change whatever deer deterrents you are using. If bears have been reported in your area, do not put out bird feeders; they attract bears. See the section on Pests, Diseases, and Controls in the Appendix of the book.

Continue to search out and rake up weeds.

If you see signs of vole activity, bait the main runway with a rodenticide.

OCTOBER

Trees

PLANNING

If there's no place in your yard for a compost pile, consider installing one of the many composters offered at garden centers and by mail-order. Or, compost in a black leaf bag; layer in it dry leaves, green weeds, chopped vegetable or fruit peelings, and then poke holes all over the outside. Wet the interior thoroughly, close the bag, and set it in a warm, out-of-the-way place to do its thing. Shake the bag, and turn it upside down often to speed the process.

PLANTING

When the leaves start to change color you can dig and transplant trees. Now through November into early December is the perfect time for planting trees. The air is cold, but the earth still has warmth.

CARE

Before adding leaves to an existing compost pile, gather the humus collected there, and use it or store it for use next year.

Save the fallen leaves, and heap them in an out of the way place for composting, for insulation, or grind them to use as mulch. If you have only a few leaves, suck them up in a vacuum-blower, and blow the residue out over the lawn or the flower borders.

PRUNING

You can prune out dead or diseased tree limbs, but delay any major pruning until later.

WATERING

Indoors. Maintain the soil moisture of the indoor trees, mist them often, and air the room daily if you can.

Outdoors. Water newly planted trees and hardy trees in containers every week or ten days if the season runs dry.

FERTILIZING

In Zone 8, the last fertilization can be between the end of September and mid-October. In Zones 6 and 7, the time for the last application is between early September and early October. See Understanding Fertilizers in the Introduction to the book.

PESTS

Check trees for signs of scale, aphids, mealybug infestations, and control with ultrafine horticultural oil, horticultural soap, neem products, or Permethrin.

Voles are most active October to March. If you see vole activity, bait the main runway with a rodenticide.

Change whatever deer deterrents you are using; they disregard deterrents they become accustomed to. See the section on Pests, Diseases, and Controls in the Appendix. If bears have been reported in your area, do not put out—or do remove—bird feeders.

In Zone 8, continue to rake away weeds.

Change whatever deer deterrents you are using; they disregard deterrents they become accustomed to.

Did You Know?

Composting

Dead leaves become an asset when you use them to make compost, the soil-like substance remaining when nature reduces organic material to humus.

Compost is called "black gold" because a 1-inch layer mixed into the soil every month releases its nutrients as the plants grow. Compost also replaces the organic content lost to healthy plant growth. It improves drainage, soil structure, aeration; sustains the microbial activity essential to healthy soil; encourages big root systems; buffers soil temperatures; and reduces the need for watering—100 pounds of humus holds 195 pounds of water.

Along with dry leaves, the other materials used in building a compost pile are grass clippings, chopped vegetable and fruit peels, healthy weeds, and plant debris. **Never compost disease and insect-infested plant materials.**

Your compost pile will deliver finished (ready to use) compost sooner if you break up the leaves with a blower/vacuum or a leaf shredder before putting them on the pile. Or, run a mulching mower over them. Or, pile them into a garbage can, and churn them with a string trimmer.

Here's the basic approach to building a compost pile:

1 Heap dry leaves in an out-of-sight place with access to a hose. Outline a base for the compost pile that is about 4 feet wide by 4 feet long. As the ingredients become available, build onto this base a 4 foot high pile of layers of any of the following four combinations of organic materials:

3 parts dry leaves (Carbon)
- 3 parts fresh grass clippings (Nitrogen)

2 parts dry leaves (Carbon)
- 2 parts straw or wood shavings (Carbon)
- 1 part manure (Nitrogen)
- 1 part fresh grass clippings (Nitrogen)
- 1 part fresh garden weeds/harvested plants (Nitrogen)
- 1 part kitchen food scraps (Nitrogen)

6 parts dry leaves (Carbon)
- 3 parts kitchen scraps (Nitrogen) (no meat or fish)
- 3 parts fresh grass clippings (Nitrogen)

3 parts dry leaves (Carbon)
- 1 part fresh garden weeds/harvested plants (Nitrogen)
- 1 part fresh grass clippings (Nitrogen)
- 1 part kitchen food scraps (Nitrogen)

2 As you build the pile, sprinkle over each layer about an inch of garden soil and/or compost to encourage microbial activity. Or, sprinkle on a microbial activator to speed up decomposition. Compost starter, activators, and/or inoculants hasten the composting. To make a compost rich in nitrogen, add dustings of bone meal for the phosphorus and calcium it contains, blood meal, or a high nitrogen garden fertilizer. To make it high in potassium, calcium, and carbon, and to reduce acidity, dust fireplace ashes onto the layers. If you wish to help reduce soil compaction and enhance aeration, dust on gypsum, which also adds calcium and sulfur.

3 Keep the pile moist, and turn it weekly, or as often as you can, with a pitchfork to hasten decomposition. Depending on the season, your climate, and how often you turn it, the pile will become compost in a few months (warm regions), or in year or two (cooler areas).

NOVEMBER
Trees

 PLANNING

Hollies are very successful here and a joy at holiday time when the spiky leaves are ornamented by the bright red berries that tell us the holidays are just around the corner. Try one; you'll enjoy harvesting your own holly branches to make Christmas swags and holiday arrangements.

The most durable holly tree is the 40- to 50-foot pyramidal **American holly,** *Ilex opaca*, which is hardy in Zones 5 through 9 and tolerates urban pollution. The bright red berries mature in October and persist through winter. André's favorite varieties are 'Merry Christmas', 'George Hart', 'Xanthocarpa', and 'Old Heavy Berry'. Other fine tree hollies are **longstalk holly,** *I. pedunculosa,* and **English holly,** *I. aquifolium.* Slender 25-foot **'Foster's Holly #2'**, a pyramidal tree 15 to 25 feet high with small toothed leaves and masses of tiny red berries, does well even in cities

American and **Foster's holly** make a handsome pair. **Hollies** are dioecious (see About Shrubs That Bear Berries in the November pages of Chapter 8, Shrubs). That means that most females require a male pollinator to fruit well.

 PLANTING

November and into early December is a still a good time to plant trees.

If you are planning to have a live Christmas tree, choose a permanent home suited to the tree's mature width and height, and dig the planting hole now. Improve the soil from the hole (see with Soil Preparation and Improvement in the Introduction to the book), and put it back in the hole. Cover the area with 12 to 18 inches of leaves held down by evergreen boughs to keep them from blowing.

 CARE

Apply an anti-desiccant spray to the foliage of newly-planted **hollies** growing in exposed positions, or wrap them in Reemay or burlap.

In snow country, move hardy trees growing in containers to a sheltered corner out of the wind for the winter, or store them in a garage or shed.

 PRUNING

Don't be concerned for their health when evergreens show some yellow in the interior of the branches—pines, arborvitae, juniper, and **yews** among them. It's most likely normal. The plants we call evergreens lose some of their older leaves at more or less regular intervals, but they look green all year because, except for the **golden larches,** they don't drop them all at the same time. Every plant must renew its foliage as part of its life cycle. Some **pine** species lose needles every fifteen to eighteen months, some **hollies** drop their leaves at four-year intervals. So when yellow shows up in an evergreen, chances are that it is a normal part of a cycle and not a problem.

 WATERING

The earth remains warm even after leaves fall and the air cools, so roots continue to develop. That's why watering is recommended when fall runs dry.

Maintain the soil moisture of the indoor tree—**citrus,** *Ficus,* **palms**—mist them often, and air the room daily if you can.

Water outdoor trees growing in containers every two weeks or when the soil seems dry. Water thoroughly before the ground freezes so the plants don't go into winter dry.

 # FERTILIZING

Do not fertilize trees at this season, indoors or out.

 # PESTS

Deer will eat holly leaves when they are starving, and young trees are especially susceptible. See the section on Pests, Diseases, and Controls in the Appendix the book.

Bait vole runs approaching trees with a rodenticide.

Did You Know?

Pollarding and Pleaching

Europe's pollarded trees and pleached allées are the result of severe pruning. The process is lengthy, labor intensive, and interesting, and the results are elegant.

Pollarding is a form of pruning where the branches of a tree are cut back every year or so almost to the main trunk. The result is that you get branches that are long, thin, and flexible, and a tree whose crown is ball-shaped. In Europe, **willows** were commonly pollarded to produce whips used in basket-making.

Pleaching is a system of shearing trees (or tall shrubs) that are closely planted alongside a broad garden path or walk—**lindens, maples, sycamores** are often used. Set side-by-side, the branches are encouraged to grow together overhead. Shearing trains the top growth into a thin hedge overhead. Because a pleached allée takes forever to achieve and is time-consuming to maintain, you're likely to see this only in public gardens and arboreta. There's a pleached allée in one of the lower garden rooms at Dumbarton Oaks in DC.

DECEMBER
Trees

 PLANNING

Cut Christmas trees. The **Douglas fir** and the **balsam fir (**Abies balsamea) stay fresh longest, so they are popular. **Balsam fir** looks like **spruce,** the traditional evergreen with short, stiff needles. **Live Christmas trees.** André recommends the **Colorado blue spruce,** Picea pungens glauca and its varieties 'Hoopsii' and 'Thompsonii'. An 8-foot ceiling can't take a tree taller than 7 feet. Before buying, give the plant a health check. Is the rootball moist? Do needles drop when you shake it?

 PLANTING

If you're planning on a **live Christmas tree**, prepare a planting hole for it (see November Planting).

 CARE

Cut tree. Remove the lower branches to make room for the tree holder, and cut at least 1 inch off the bottom so it can more easily take up the water, which should contain Christmas tree preservative. Keep the tree in a shaded location. Before bringing the tree indoors, to keep the needles fresh longer, spray the tree with an anti-transpirant like biodegradable Wilt-Pruf. One application before you decorate the tree should last. After the holidays, take the branches for winter mulch, and move the tree to be recycled as mulch or wood chips.

Live tree. Keep a live tree indoors no more than two weeks. Before it comes in, keep it outdoors in a sheltered spot with good light; spray needles with an anti-desiccant to help prevent drying out, water the soil well, and let it drain. If it's a B&B tree, place it in a leak-proof tub. Stand the tree far from radiators, fireplaces, and other heat sources. Keep the temperature under 65 degrees Fahrenheit if, or when, possible. Don't fertilize, and water only if the soil feels dry. Air the room, and mist the air around the tree—not the tree itself because of the ornaments and the lights—daily. If you cannot plant your live tree when you move it outdoors, place it in a sheltered spot with good light, and heap leaves, or bags filled with leaves, 14 to 18 inches deep all around the rootball.

New trees outdoors. Spray an anti-desiccant on young evergreens in exposed positions. Protect them from bitter winds by erecting a burlap screen.

 PRUNING

Lightly harvest mature evergreens with cones and berries to use in holiday decorations—**pines, fir, hollies.**

 WATERING

Cut Christmas tree. Keep the stand filled with water containing floral preservative; fresh **fir** trees drink lots; **pine** trees drink some; **spruce** don't take up much water at all.

Maintain the soil moisture of the indoors trees—**citrus,** Ficus, **palms,** and mist them and air the room often. If there's no snow or rain, water all new outdoor plantings thoroughly.

 FERTILIZING

Make a New Year's resolution to stick to non-polluting fertilizers and biodegradable controls. Decades of nursery experience have convinced André and Mark that trees that are inherently healthy, planted in suitable climate, in soil properly prepared (see Understanding Fertilizers in the introduction to the book), and given all the water they need the first years, are strengthened by normal stresses.

 PESTS

Trees growing indoors come under attack from mealybugs and spider mites. Frequent showers, and spraying with horticultural soaps discourages them.

Chapter Ten

Vines, Ground Covers, & Ornamental Grasses

Vines, ground covers, and ornamental grasses solve landscaping problems by speedily greening barren areas with low-maintenance plants. Because they're speedy, all three types of plants also tend to be weedy—so some maintenance is necessary.

Vines

The lush vertical accent a vine creates is invaluable when you want to soften a bare corner, dress up a balcony, clothe a naked wall, or hide an eyesore without taking up a lot of space on the ground. For the amount of foliage it produces, a vine requires relatively little watering. Most vines will grow up, down, or sideways, according to how you train the leading stems, and the supports you provide.

Caution. Even cultivated vines can be as invasive as weed vines—so plant even the vines we recommend only where they won't escape and invade native plants.

Perennial vines. Generally deep-rooted, the **perennial vines** grow vigorously and thrive for years rooted in a modest planting hole or a large planter or tub. Which is better—evergreen or deciduous? An evergreen vine—**ivy** or **euonymus** (*Euonymus fortunei* var. *radicans* for example)—is a good choice when you want year-round greening and screening. A deciduous vine is a better choice when you want summer screening coupled with access to sun in winter—**clematis** for the sake of its extraordinary flowers, or **Dutchman's pipe** for screening a porch or a pergola for outdoor dining.

Cold-hardiness in your area has to be there in a perennial vine. The top of it will be up in the wind, so you want to make sure it will withstand the coldest winters your region can throw at it. If a vine's cold-hardiness is doubtful, place it where it will have the protection of a north-facing wall at its back.

While a perennial vine's major contribution is its foliage, some maximize your investment. **Wisteria** and **sweet autumn clematis** produce masses of blooms and add a sweet fragrance to the garden. **Climbing hydrangea** produces flowers, and the foliage takes on a nice color in fall. (One of the most beautiful of all vines, the climbing hydrangea takes its time growing, unlike most vines.)

The beautiful leaves of **woodbine,** *Ampelopsis henryana*, turn purplish-red with the coming of the cold, and it ripens blue berries. That particular woodbine is okay environmentally, while its cousin the **Virginia creeper,** which turns such a glorious scarlet in fall, is so invasive we can't recommend it.

Annual Vines. The annual vines grow at the speed of light and produce beautiful flowers. Some have fragrance, such as **sweet peas,** for example. The lovely **hyacinth bean** is somewhat scented, and its handsome purple beans are edible.

Annual vines are also used to create an instant effect, and because of their speedy growth, they give you a quick opportunity to see whether a vine is the right answer to a given situation. They're often used for summer screening, and they're also good choices to clothe walls and fences that will need repainting periodically. Most annual vines need only light support. Many are easily grown from seed planted in spring. Where the growing season is short, the annual vines are usually started indoors early or purchased as seedlings.

Tropical and semi-tropical vines. In late spring pretty **mandevilla** and **bougainvillea** are sold in big pots already blooming. They're great accent plants for patios and porches. Both are perennial in warm climates, so they can live through winter in a greenhouse or a bright window as houseplants. In Zones 6 and 7, they are not likely to survive wintering in their pots in a shed or garage unless some heat is provided.

TRAINING, PLANTING, AND MAINTENANCE

Training. Vines need supports. How a vine climbs—the plant parts it uses to hold itself to advancing positions—dictates the type of support it needs. When you are choosing a vine, that's an important consideration. **Carolina jessamine** climbs by twining itself around its support. **Chinese trumpet vine** uses aerial rootlets to attach itself to its next position. **Clematis** holds on with twisting leaf-stalks (petioles).

Vines also require pruning in spring, summer, autumn, and winter. You prune a new vine lightly the first year or two to direct its growth and develop a graceful framework. Then you prune it annually to control growth and encourage flowering. So another important consideration when you are choosing a vine is how you will prune it when it gets up on whatever you want it to climb.

Caution: Don't plant a vine where it can get into shutters, gutters, windows, attic, or other areas of your house. Vines get into things. It's their nature. They grow over things. That's their nature. Don't plant a vine near trees or large shrubs; if you fail to keep a vine pruned, it will smother everything within reach.

Planting. Vines are sold bare root and also as container-grown plants. Because a vine makes considerable growth in a single season, the most practical time to plant one is early spring before growth gets underway, or in fall after the plant has become dormant and been cut back.

Bare-root vines. In early spring before growth begins, mail-order suppliers ship some vines bare root. Follow the shipper's instructions for planting and providing a training support.

Container vines. You can plant container-grown vines from early spring—late February and March—through summer and fall until December 1.

Transplanting vines. You can transplant a vine planted a year or two ago fairly easily. Before you dig it up, cut the stems back to within 2 or 3 feet from the crown, and tie them together. Then proceed as described for moving established shrubs under Planting, in the February pages of Shrubs, chapter 8. If the vine is a flowering plant, move it shortly after it bloomed to avoid cutting off next year's blooms.

You can grow a vine in a container outdoors indefinitely—a hardy vine, that is—providing the container is large enough to insulate the roots from winter cold. Follow the instructions for preparing soil and containers in the April pages of Chapter 8, Shrubs.

Vines, Ground Covers, & Ornamental Grasses

Pruning. Vines need a regular schedule of pruning to lead the branches in the direction you want them to grow, and to contain their usually exuberant growth. Those vines that flower on last year's growth—spring bloomers usually—should be pruned as soon as they finish blooming, late spring or early summer. Flowering vines that bloom on new wood are pruned before they begin to grow, late winter or early spring; they usually bloom late in the season. See About Pruning Vines in the February pages.

WATERING, MULCHING, AND FERTILIZING

Watering. When you finish planting a vine, water the soil slowly, gently, and thoroughly with a sprinkler, a soaker hose, a bubbler, or by hand. You need to put down 1½ inches of water. Or, slowly pour on 5 to 10 gallons of water from a bucket.

During the vine's first season, slowly and gently pour two or three bucketfuls of water around the roots every week or ten days unless there's a soaking rain. If the vine is sheltered from rain, in summer hose it down now and then—but don't hose it when it is coming into, or already in, bloom as that may bruise flowers that are open, or make them soggy.

Mulching. Mulch your vine 3 to 4 inches deep (no more!) after planting, starting 3 inches from the central stem(s). Top up the mulch three times a year; first after the early spring fertilization, again before summer heat arrives, and finally in fall. Mulches and winter mulches are discussed under Mulching in the Introduction to the book.

Fertilizing. A new vine planted in improved soil you have enriched with lasting organic fertilizers doesn't need fertilizing until the following year.

The first annual application of fertilizer should be made before growth begins in spring. The last application should be as growth slows toward the end of the growing season. **The number of applications in between depends entirely on the type of fertilizer you are using.** (See Understanding Fertilizers in the Introduction to the book.) The growing season in Zones 6 and 7 comes to an end between early September and early October. In Zone 8, Richmond and the Tidewater areas of Virginia, the last fertilization can be between the end of September and mid-October.

GROUND COVERS

Ground covers are low-maintenance plants used to carpet the earth where lawn turf and ornamental plants are impractical or undesirable. Any fast-growing plant that spreads and grows without much attention can be used as ground cover—**daylilies** in the sun, **hostas** in shade. Many vines also fit the job description. But the plants specifically designated as ground covers spread rapidly and grow so thickly they keep out weeds even when they die down in winter; an example is that the foliage of **lily-of-the-valley** vanishes in the fall, but the rhizomes remain so densely packed few weeds can get in.

If you like a garden that has a serene look, use just one type of plant as ground cover. Like a turf lawn, it will unify the various elements in view—shrub borders, flower beds, specimen plantings, and trees. Combining several compatible ground covers adds extra texture to the garden, makes it more interesting and exciting. Using several also is a safeguard should one type of plant fail. For a richly varied carpet plant drifts of small winter-flowering bulbs in sunny places here and there, overplanted with aromatic **Greek oregano, thyme,** and **ajuga.** In areas that have part sun, plant **myrtle** (*Vinca minor*) or **pachysandra.** In the dappled shade under trees, the luminous foliage of **lamium** is lovely.

Caution: The plants designated as ground covers, like weeds, spread rapidly.

The toughest evergreen ground covers are **ajuga, pachysandra, myrtle** (*Vinca minor*), and **ivy.** All four can be walked on some and can be used as replacement for a lawn. **Ajuga** and **myrtle** bear sweet little flowers in early spring. **Ivy** can take a few years to get going, but once started spreads irresistibly. All four are seen by environmentalists as a potential threat to native plants so use them responsibly. Don't plant a ground cover where it might invade stands of native plants or woodlands.

PLANTING AND MAINTENANCE

We recommend starting a ground cover with rooted cuttings. Starting with seed is likely to prove frustrating—patches may fail to germinate, and very young seedlings are easily destroyed by dry hot wind and weather. Before you spend money, though, ask your friends and acquaintances if they'd like to thin their ground covers.

To get a ground cover off to a fast, successful start, provide a well-prepared bed and humusy fertile soil. Dig the whole area to be planted, and improve the soil just as completely and carefully as you do a bed for perennials. If you are installing an invasive ground cover such as **ivy, vinca,** or **ajuga,** plan to edge it with a 6-inch metal barrier to prevent it from overrunning neighboring plantings.

Planting through a mulch cover will minimize weeding chores, which can be burdensome in the season or two the ground cover will need to thicken enough to keep invaders out.

The first season of growth, a newly installed ground cover will need watering any time the perennial bed needs watering, weekly or every ten days unless you have a soaking rain. Water the soil slowly, gently, and thoroughly with a sprinkler, a soaker hose, a bubbler, or by hand. In the following years it should need watering only if the leaf tips are wilting; then water thoroughly as you would a perennial bed.

An occasional pruning keeps a ground cover neater and stimulates branching and new growth—**pachysandra, plumbago** (*Ceratostigma plumbaginoides*), and **ivy** when fully mature will benefit from shearing every few years.

In fall, clear ground covers of fallen leaves only if they have matted down. Leaves that slip through the foliage decompose on the ground, and that nourishes the soil.

You fertilize a bed of ground covers twice a year, just as you do perennials. (See Fertilizing and Fertilizers in the introduction to Chapter 6, Perennials.)

Like perennials, grasses don't fill out until the second season. But once they are flourishing, you can divide them to make new plants to fill gaps or enlarge the beds.

Vines, Ground Covers, & Ornamental Grasses

ORNAMENTAL GRASSES

The ornamental grasses come in all sizes. The big and medium tall grasses make excellent ground covers for transitional areas—from lawn to woodland, garden to shore, yard to road. The very tall grasses—6 feet and up—can be used to create screening and to enhance bare walls. **Northern sea oats,** a medium-tall, narrow, upright woodland grass is an excellent ground cover, especially lovely growing on a slope where the seedheads are backlit in early morning or late afternoon. **Silver grass** is a large landscaping grass to use boldly, in big spaces. Blue fescue is a small grass used to add texture and color to flower beds.

Medium and small grasses are used more and more in perennial beds. On hot summer days the foliage sways and whispers in the slightest breeze, and the airy dancing flower heads (inflorescences) are beautiful late in the season when so many flowers are over. The seedheads and drying foliage remain beautiful fall and winter, anchoring the garden's fourth season.

DESIGNING WITH GRASSES

The use of grasses of all sizes is beautifully illustrated in the two-acre Friendship Garden at the U.S. National Arboretum in DC. Plantings combining naturalized flowering perennials, bulbs, trees, and shrubs flow together and are dominated and unified by a variety of ornamental grasses. The heights, mixtures, and widths of the flower beds vary to avoid any formal sense. Medium-size grasses are islands with curved borders. There are no straight lines in pathways. The garden includes lots of fruiting and berrying plants, a design that promotes a healthy ecological balance encouraging to birds and beneficial insects. (See the October pages of this chapter.)

Wolfgang Oehme, co-designer with Jim van Sweden of the National Arboretum Friendship Garden, advises gardeners to plant ornamental grasses densely. He believes that several should be planted together rather than just one. They will have better impact and make a small space look larger.

To choose ornamental grasses for a perennial border, refer to the sidebar on the December page.

Size. The size of an ornamental grass is judged by the end-of-season height and width of the foliage. To add variety to the front of a flower border, choose grasses that stay under 2 feet, like the little **sedges** (*Carex* species), **mosquito grass** (*Bouteloua gracilis*), and **Japanese blood grass,** *Imperata cylindrica* 'Red Baron', **blue sheep's fescue,** *Festuca amethystina* var. *superba.*

Grasses 2 to 5 feet tall are ideal for the middle and back of a flowering border and can be used as a transitional ground cover. Some we like are the arching **silver grasses (***Miscanthus sacchariflorus* and company), bold plants with broad, grassy, gracefully arching leaves. We also favor **switchgrass,** *Panicum virgatum* and the **pennisetums,** whose graceful arching foliage is topped at the end of the summer by flower spikelets that have conspicuous bottle-brush bristles.

After that the sizes go on up to the very, very invasive *Phragmites australis,* an enormous reed 19 feet tall that grows wild in wetlands, brackish or fresh, everywhere. The fluffy tannish seedheads swaying in the wind on rigid golden stalks are tempting, but you're best off avoiding it. Instead, where a very tall grass is needed, plant **ravenna grass**, *Erianthus ravennae* (Zones 6 to 9) a magnificent architectural plant 9 to 12 feet tall with broad, arching silvery leaves.

Form and texture. Almost as important as the size of the plant are its form and texture. **Chinese silver grass** is very erect, **maiden grass** arches, while the foliage of the **pennisetums** fountains. The texture of the leaves and their color impacts the garden design—fine, coarse, bold, bluish, greenish, reddish, gold, striped, variegated. We like contrast, so we recommend combining both upright and fountaining forms, fine and coarse-textured grasses, green and variegated forms.

Think all this through before you fall in love with the seedheads, the "flowers" of the ornamental grasses. They are almost all irresistible!

Finally, when planning a grass garden, we recommend grouping several plants of a few varieties rather than setting out a few plants of many varieties.

PLANTING, LIGHT, AND MAINTENANCE

Like the perennial flowers, ornamental grasses begin to fill out the second year. They can be started from seed in spring, but the seedlings will take two years to gain any size. Planting root divisions is far more satisfactory.

Container-grown grasses. These grasses can be planted any time in the growing season. Because of the size they acquire during the growing season, tall species are best planted in early or mid-spring.

Bare-root grasses. In early spring, mail-order suppliers ship some ornamental grasses bare root, and these plants must be soaked thoroughly before planting; follow the shipper's instructions to the letter.

Soil. Most of the ornamental grasses thrive in the fertile humusy soil best for most perennials. Most need a well-drained site, but some can handle, and a few need, moist soil. You will find information about adjusting soil pH, additives for soil, and creating raised beds in the Introduction to the book under Soil Preparation and Improvement. Set the crowns $1/2$ to 1 inch higher than the soil surface. Don't "drown" the grasses in mulch—2 to 3 inches of mulch is enough.

Maintenance. In the grass garden at the National Arboretum, the plants are allowed to develop throughout the year without pruning, staking, spraying, or deadheading. Seedheads ripen and stand through fall and winter. In late winter or early spring, as new foliage begins to emerge they are cut back to within a few inches of the ground, mulched, and fertilized.

Most ornamental grasses need annual fertilization. The time for it is when signs of new growth appear. Apply a slow-release organic fertilizer such as Holly-tone or Espoma Organic Lawn Food. In prolonged droughts, water slowly and deeply.

Once installed, ornamental grasses are not expected to require division for at least five to ten years.

PESTS AND DISEASES

The vines, ground covers, and grasses we recommend are vigorous plants with no particular pest or disease problems.

Did You Know?

Ground Covers for Problem Sites

Lawn substitute. Four ground covers are commonly used as substitutes for turf lawns. They are evergreen and can be walked on occasionally without being damaged.

English ivy, (*Hedera helix*). An evergreen with tough glossy dark-green leaves on woody vines. Lots of interesting variegated types.

Vinca, Periwinkle (*Vinca minor*). Small, dainty, shiny dark green leaves on slim trailing stems 2 to 3 feet long. Lavender-blue flowers in early spring.

Pachysandra, Japanese Spurge (*Pachysandra terminalis*). Low-growing, wide-spreading, formal ground cover. Short green-white flower spikes in early spring.

Wintergreen, Checkerberry (*Gaultheria procumbens*). Evergreen shrubby ground-hugging mat with aromatic foliage and bright berries.

Under trees. Tree shade and root competition are hard on turf grass. These ground covers do well under trees.

Bugleweed, *Ajuga reptans.* Semi-evergreen rosettes of leaves and flowering spikes in blue or white in spring.

Hosta. Small colorful hostas like 8-inch **'Gold Edger'**; 3-inch **'Venusta'**; 7-inch *H. helemoides*; 15-inch **Purple & Gold.**

Lilyturf, (*Liriope muscari*). Grass-like, and 12 to 18 inches high. Flowering spikes in blue, purple, lavender, or white in late summer.

Spotted Deadnettle, (*Lamium maculatum*). Semi-evergreen, low-growing, silver-white-green variegated foliage lightens the shadows. Pink or white florets in May and June.

Barrenwort, (*Epimedium* sp.). Deciduous, heart-shaped green foliage carpets the earth and turns reddish or gold in the fall. Dainty spurred yellow, pink, white, red florets in early to mid-spring.

Golden Moneywort, (*Lysimachia nummularia* 'Aurea'). Deciduous, lime-green, low-growing, and spreads rapidly in moist soil. In early summer, it bears masses of small cup-shaped yellow flowers.

Lily-of-the-valley, (*Convallaria majalis*). Deciduous, lovely 6- to 8-inch high ground cover ideal for open woodlands. The flowers are exquisitely fragrant.

Vines, Ground Covers, & Ornamental Grasses

Perennial Vines

Common Name (Botanical Name)	Hardiness Zones	Light	Height (Feet)	Climbing Method
Boston Ivy (*Parthenocissus tricuspidata*)	4 to 8	Sun	50 plus	Clinging
Carolina Jessamine (*Gelsemium sempervirens*)	6 to 9	Sun to part shade	10 to 20	Twining
Chinese Trumpet Creeper (*Campsis grandiflora*)	6 to 9	Sun	15 to 20	Clinging
Clematis (*Clematis* sp. and cultivars)	3 to 9	Sun, bright shade; shade for roots	5 to 20	Twisting petioles
Climbing Hydrangea (*Hydrangea petiolaris*)	5 to 9	Part shade to shade	Over 60 feet	Clinging
Confederate Jasmine (*Trachelospermum jasminoides*)	8 to 10	Sun to part-shade	10 to 15	Twining
Coral Honeysuckle (*Lonicera sempervirens*)	6 to 9	Sun to shade	30 to 50	Clinging
Cross Vine (*Bignonia capreolata*)	5 to 9	Sun to shade	8 to 12	Twining
English Ivy (*Hedera helix*)	5 to 9	Sun, part shade, shade	To 90	Clinging
'Goldflame' Honeysuckle (*Lonicera x heckrottii*)	4 to 8	Sun to part shade	10 to 20	Twining
Hardy Kiwi (*Actinidia kolomikta*)	4 to 8	Sun to part sun	To 30	Twining
Japanese Hydrangea Vine (*Schizophragma hydrangeoides*)	5 to 7/8	Sun to part shade	20 to 30	Clinging
Jasmine, Poet's Jasmine (*Jasminum officinale*)	8 to 10	Sun to part sun	10 to 15	Twining
Virginia Creeper (*Parthenocissus quinquefolia*)	3 to 9	Sun to part shade	30 plus	Clinging
Wisteria (*Wisteria* sp.)	5 to 8	Sun	25 to 30	Twining

Annual Vines

Common Name (Botanical Name)	Hardiness Zones	Light	Height (Feet)	Climbing Method
Black-eyed Susan Vine (*Thunbergia alata*)	10	Morning sun, afternoon shade	6 to 8	Twining
Cypress Vine (*Ipomoea quamoclit*)	6 to 11	Sun to shade	10 to 20	Twining
Glory Bush (*Tibouchina urvilleana*)	9 to 10	Sun to part sun	5 to 10	Must be tied to a support

Vines, Ground Covers, & Ornamental Grasses

Common Name (*Botanical Name*)	Hardiness Zones	Light	Height (Feet)	Climbing Method
Hyacinth Bean (*Dolichos lablab*)	9 to 11	Sun	15 to 20	Twining
Madagascar Jasmine (*Stephanotis floribunda*)	Tropical	Sun	15	Twining
Mandevilla (*Mandevilla* x *amabilis*)	Tropical	Sun; will tolerate some afternoon shade	8 to 10	Twining
Moon Vine (*Ipomoea alba*)	8 to 10	Sun	10	Twining
Morning Glory (*Ipomoea purpurea*)	7 to 10	Sun	10	Twining
Sweet Pea (*Lathyrus odoratus*)	6 to 8	Sun to part shade	To 6	Clinging

Perennial Ground Covers

Common Name (*Botanical Name*)	Hardiness Zones	Light	Height	Type
Astilbe (*Astilbe chinensis* 'Pumila')	4 to 8	Part sun	12 inches	Deciduous
Barren Strawberry (*Waldsteinia ternata*)	4 to 7	Sun to shade	6 inches	Deciduous
Barrenwort (*Epimedium* sp.)	5 to 8/9	Shade	6 to 12 inches	Deciduous
Bearberry Cotoneaster (*Cotoneaster dammeri*)	5 to 8	Sun to part sun	To 12 inches	Evergreen
Bearberry, Kinnikinick (*Arctostaphylos uva-ursi*)	2 to 8	Sun to part shade	6 to 12 inches	Broadleaved evergreen
Beech Fern (*Thelypteris hexagonoptera*)	3 to 9	Shade	10 to 24 inches	Deciduous fern
Bellflower (*Campanula poscharskyana*)	3 to 7	Sun; shade in the afternoon	8 to 12 inches	Semi-evergreen
Bergenia (*Bergenia cordifolia* cvs.)	3 to 8	Sun to part shade	8 to 12 inches	Perennial
Bouncing Bet (*Saponaria officinalis* 'Rosea Plena')	2 to 8	Sun	24 to 36 inches	Deciduous
Bugleweed (*Ajuga reptans* cvs.)	4 to 9	Part sun/part shade	4 to 8 inches	Semi-evergreen
Christmas Fern (*Polystichum acrostichoides*)	3 to 8	Part shade	24 inches	Evergreen
Cinnamon Fern (*Osmunda cinnamomea*)	3 to 8	Bright shade	To 5 feet	Deciduous
Creeping Juniper (*Juniperus horizontalis* sp. and hybrids)	3 to 9	Sun	4 to 6 inches	Evergreen

Perennial Ground Covers

Common Name (*Botanical Name*)	Hardiness Zones	Light	Height	Type
Creeping Phlox (*Phlox stolonifera*)	3 to 8	Part shade to part sun	5 to 12 inches	Deciduous
Dwarf Mondo Grass (*Ophiopogon planiscapus* 'Arabicus')	6 to 10	Shade	10 inches	Evergreen
Foamflower (*Tiarella cordifolia* and hybrids)	3 to 8	Bright shade	6 to 12 inches	Semi-evergreen
Ginger (*Asarum europaeum*)	4 to 7	Part shade	6 to 8 inches	Evergreen
Golden Moneywort (*Lysimachia nummularia* 'Aurea')	3 to 8	Sun to part sun to shade	1 to 2 inches	Deciduous
Japanese Painted Fern (*Athyrium nipponicum* 'Pictum')	3 to 8	Dappled light	12 to 18 inches	Deciduous
Japanese Shield Fern (*Dryopteris erythrosora*)	5 to 9	Bright shade	24 to 36 inches	Deciduous
Japanese Spurge (*Pachysandra terminalis*)	4 to 8	Bright shade	8 to 10 inches	Evergreen
Lamb's-ear (*Stachys byzantina*)	5 to 7	Sun to part sun	6 to 12 inches	Deciduous
Leadwort (*Ceratostigma plumbaginoides*)	5 to 9	Part sun	6 to 12 inches	Deciduous
Lenten Rose (*Helleborus orientalis*)	4 to 8	Sun to part sun	12 to 18 inches	Evergreen
Lily-of-the-valley (*Convallaria majalis*)	2 to 7	Part shade	6 to 8 inches	Deciduous
Lilyturf (*Liriope muscari* cvs.)	5 to 9/10	Part sun to part shade	12 to 18 inches	Deciduous
Mondo Grass (*Ophiopogon japonicus*)	7 to 10	Part shade	8 to 12 inches	Semi-evergreen or evergreen
Ostrich Fern (*Matteuccia pennsylvanica*)	3/4 to 8	Sun to part shade	3 to 5 feet	Deciduous
Rock Polypody, American Wall Fern (*Polypodium virginianum*)	3 to 8	Part shade	12 inches	Evergreen
Snow-in-summer (*Cerastium tomentosum*)	3 to 10	Sun	6 to 12 inches	Evergreen
Spotted Deadnettle (*Lamium maculatum*)	4 to 8	Part shade	8 to 12 inches	Semi-evergreen
Sweet Woodruff (*Galium odoratum*)	4 to 8	Dappled light	6 to 8 inches	Deciduous
Two-row Stonecrop (*Sedum spurium* 'John Creech' and cvs.)	3 to 8	Sun	2 to 6 inches	Evergreen

Vines, Ground Covers, & Ornamental Grasses

Common Name (Botanical Name)	Hardiness Zones	Light	Height	Type
Variegated Solomon's-seal (*Polygonatum odoratum* 'Variegatum')	4 to 8	Shade	To 36 inches	Deciduous
Vinca, Periwinkle (*Vinca minor*)	4 to 9	Sun, part shade, shade	3 to 6 inches	Evergreen
Wintergreen, Checkerberry (*Gaultheria procumbens*)	3 to 7	Part shade	3 to 5 inches	Evergreen

Ornamental Grasses

Common Name (Botanical Name)	Hardiness Zones	Light	Height
Blue Fescue (*Festuca cinerea*)	4 to 8	Full sun	8 to 12 inches
Blue Oat Grass, Avena Grass (*Helictotrichon sempervirens*)	4 to 8	Full sun	2 to 3 feet
Blue Switchgrass (*Panicum virgatum* 'Heavy Metal')	5 to 9	Full sun	4 feet
Compact Pampas Grass (*Cortaderia selloana* 'Pumila')	6 to 10	Full sun	4 to 6 feet
Feather Reed Grass (*Calamagrostis* x *acutiflora* 'Karl Foerster')	6 to 9	Full sun	4 to 5 feet
Fountain Grass (*Pennisetum alopecuroides* 'Little Bunny')	5 to 9	Sun	3 feet
Hakonechloa, Golden, Variegated (*Hakonechloa macra* 'Aureola')	6 to 9	Part shade	2 feet
Little Bluestem (*Schizachyrium scoparium*)	3 to 4	Full sun	2 to 3 feet
Moor Grass (*Molinia caerulea*)	4 to 9	Full to part sun	3 to 8 feet
Northern Sea Oats (*Chasmanthium latifolium*)	5 to 9	Sun to part sun	3 to 5 feet
Ravenna Grass, Plume Grass (*Erianthus ravennae*)	6 to 9	Full sun	9 to 12 feet
Red Baron Blood Grass (*Imperata cylindrica* 'Red Baron')	5 to 9	Full sun to part shade	1 foot
Silver Grass, Chinese Silver Grass, Japanese Silver Grass, Eulalia (*Miscanthus sinensis* sp. and cvs.)	6 to 9	Sun	6 to 8 feet
Switchgrass (*Panicum virgatum*)	3 to 8	Full to part sun	4 to 6 feet

PLANNING

Take your garden catalogs to a window with a view of the garden—and consider whether plantings of vines, ground covers, and ornamental grasses can solve problems and make some tired old things new.

Vines. Imagine a vine blooming on a garage corner, the garden shed, hiding a tree stump, covering an unsightly structure. Trial the idea by plant a fast-growing annual climber. The three best are the purple-podded, scented **hyacinth bean** whose beautiful beans are edible; white-flowered **moonvine;** and **morning glory,** *Ipomea tricolor* **'Heavenly Blue'.**

Ground covers. If drought plagues your lawn—or your lawn plagues you—consider replacing outlying portions of the grass with a ground cover.

Ornamental Grasses. Dream a grass garden. Low-growing species add a texture and movement to the front of flower beds. Mid-height grasses are the natural transition plant to a woodland or water, and, in combination with native wildflowers, make a beautiful flowering meadow. The recommended ratio for a sunny meadow garden is one-third flowers to two-thirds ornamental grasses for sunny places; one-third grasses and two-thirds flowers for shade. Grasses 6 feet and up can replace a high-maintenance espalier fronting a masonry wall by growing into a low-maintenance screen.

 PLANTING

Outdoors. This month or in early February, sow seeds outdoors of vines that need to be stratified (chilled) in order to germinate. This way you can multiply **trumpet vine,** which also can be sown in fall.

The Planting section of the November pages of Chapter 6, Perennials, describes stratification.

 CARE

Winter winds are going to keep blowing for weeks, so check and adjust the ties and supports of mature vines. Tie down branches whipping in the wind. Free branchlets burdened by snow or ice, including any lower branches buried in snow.

 PRUNING

Ornamental grasses. In Zone 8 check established cool season grasses for signs of new growth. If the tips of new shoots are visible, cut the old stalks back to within a few inches of the crown.

 WATERING

If the winter has been short of snow or rain, check the soil moisture of vines growing under overhanging structures. If the ground is dry and not frozen, water.

Water vines wintering in containers in a shed or garage often enough to keep the soil slightly damp.

If the winter has been short of snow or rain, check the soil moisture of vines growing under overhanging structures.

Did You Know?

Barbering Ornamental Grasses

Allowing the grasses to stand through winter adds to your pleasure in the view, but you can cut them down any time they lose their looks. Late in the season the stalks flop over providing some winter protection for the new shoots—not so nice looking. But you must give them an annual haircut *before* those new shoots get much growth, or you will be in danger of trimming the newbies with the golden oldies.

The best time to barber is just as new growth begins, so knowing when to check for growth is helpful.

The low-growing grasses and new plantings of the big grasses can be trimmed with hand shears. When a big grass matures, simplify the annual haircut by roping the leaves together with sisal twine. Tie them all the way to the top so they end up looking like a telephone pole. Then saw the top off a few inches above the crown. If you use a chain saw, take care not to catch the twine in the teeth!

Cool Season. The cool-season grasses shoot up in late January or February unless the winter is exceptionally cold. So check now to see if they are ready for the barber.

These grasses are a good choice when you are looking for plants that will be highly visible—the main show—starting early in the growing season.

Warm Season. The warm-season grasses begin to grow later—March or April. That's when you want to check their progress, shears in hand.

A warm-season grass is a good choice when you are combining grasses and flowers. Early spring-flowering bulbs come into bloom after the grass's annual haircut and make the garden pretty while the grass is growing up. As the grass grows it will hide the ripening of the bulb foliage.

 ## FERTILIZING

It's too early to fertilize.

 ## PESTS

Repair and/or renew deer deterrents on vines. Check and adjust burlap covers and chickenwire cages.

Spray **euonymus** with a dormant oil to keep scale away.

If vole runs appear near vines, bait the main runway with a rodenticide.

FEBRUARY

PLANNING

Place your order for mail-order catalog plants now.

You want to be ready to start planting in early March in Zone 8 and the Tidewater, mid-March in Richmond and Zone 7, and the end of March in Zone 6.

The ground around the ornamental grasses always seems bare before the grasses get their growth, but it doesn't have to be. Plan in June to order lots of the small early bulbs to plant around the grasses. In early fall, overplant the area with some of the big showy flowers recommended in To Plant with Ornamental Grasses on the September pages of this chapter.

 PLANTING

Indoors. Start seeds of **annual vines** late this month or next. **Morning glory, moonflower,** and **hyacinth bean** can be started eight to ten weeks before the outdoor air warms to 60 degrees Fahrenheit. They and many of the perennial vines grow readily from seed.

If you plan to plant lots of ornamental grasses, consider starting your own from seed. See Starting Seeds Indoors under Planting in the January pages of Chapter 1, Annuals.

Outdoors. This is the last month you can sow seeds outdoors of annual vines that need to be stratified (chilled) in order to germinate. Planting in the November pages in Chapter 6, Perennials, explains stratification.

If you plan to move a vine, root prune it now to prepare it for the change. A vine that has been in the ground a year or two can be moved any time before growth begins. Moving a mature vine is a two-year project. See the February pages of Chapter 8, Shrubs, under Planting.

CARE

As winter relents, start cleaning up the ground covers; a light raking will do, just enough to get rid of soggy patches of leaves, twigs, and such. Discard, don't compost the debris; it may be incubating pests and diseases.

Early in the month check new plantings of ground covers, vines, and ornamental grasses for signs of heaving. Gently press the crowns back into the ground. Replenish the mulch to stabilize soil temperatures.

PRUNING

Ornamental grasses. Cool-season grasses are likely to have started growing. As soon as you see new growth, cut the old stalks back to within a few inches of the crown.

In late winter or early spring, prune weak stems of big-flowered **clematis** like **'Dutchess of Edinburgh',** and the **Jackmanii group** back to a healthy stem. Take dead stems back to the ground. Prune the remaining stems back to a pair of strong buds.

WATERING

Indoors. Water transplanted seedlings started indoors when the soil is dry to the touch. Water vines wintering in containers in a shed or garage often enough to keep the soil slightly damp.

Outdoors. If the winter has been short of snow or rain, check the soil moisture of vines growing under overhanging structures, and water if it is dry.

FERTILIZING

Indoors. Fertilize transplanted seedlings when the appearance of two or three new leaves indicates the root system is growing again.

Every two weeks, fertilize all the seedlings that will remain indoors another six weeks or more with a soluble houseplant fertilizer at half strength.

Outdoors. Vines, ground covers, and ornamental grasses produce a lot of foliage and need regular fertilization. It can begin in Zone 8 towards the end of this month. See fertilization, in the March pages of this chapter.

 PESTS

Indoors. Seedlings started indoors that are crowded and lack good drainage and air may show symptoms of damping off. It rots stems near the soil surface. Discard affected plants, reduce watering, and increase light and fresh air. If the problem reappears, mist the seedlings with a fungicide such as Thiram (Arasan).

Before buds on vines suspected of insect infestation break open into flowers, spray them with horticultural oil. The oil smothers insects and their eggs.

To keep rabbits, woodchucks, and other rodents away from shrubs, try chemical fungicide formulations such as Thiram (Arasan) and hot pepper wax.

Did You Know?

About Pruning Vines

All vines need pruning to develop a strong beautiful framework and to enhance production. But the rules vary with the vine. **Wisteria** needs pruning two or three times a year; **clematis** varieties have individual pruning requirements.

Here are some of the guidelines:

- Prune a newly-planted vine lightly for a year or two to direct its growth so that it develops a graceful framework.

- Prune all vines to remove dead, extraneous, or weak wood now and then throughout the growing season.

- Prune large, fast-growing rampant vines like **trumpetcreeper** and **sweet autumn clematis** severely in spring and again as needed. When depends on the plant.

- In late winter and spring, prune flowering vines that bloom on new wood. These typically bloom late in the season. Any time just after the coldest part of the season and before growth begins is good. Cut back shoots that bloomed last year to a strong bud or buds near the base of the shoot, leaving the framework of the vine intact.

- In late spring and early summer, prune flowering vines that bloom on wood produced last year right after the flowers fade. These mostly bloom in spring. Cut branchlets that have flowered back to strong replacement shoots or buds; they will carry the next year's flowers. That gives the plant time to mature the wood that will flower the following year.

- In summer, prune vines grown for their foliage—like **ivy** and **Virginia creeper**—right after the major thrust of seasonal growth. It's best to avoid pruning vines in fall. The wounds heal more slowly, and pruning may stimulate growth, which could come too late to harden off before the first frosts.

MARCH
Vines, Ground Covers, & Ornamental Grasses

PLANNING

Vines hold moisture, so make sure the lumber you acquire to make a support for a vine is pressure-treated; untreated wood rots in the presence of constant moisture.

PLANTING

In Zone 8 and the Tidewater, gardeners can start planting in early March; in Richmond and Zone 7, in mid-March; in Zone 6, at the end of March.

Ready string supports for **sweet peas,** and plant the seeds. They can take a lot of cold. We grow them in the kitchen garden.

Planting vines. A vine is a shrub with a boarding-house reach—so think shrub, and look in Chapter 8, Shrubs, for basic how-to information.

- Site the planting hole within reach of the support it will climb, but allow room for the roots to mature without crowding the wall, pole, or whatever.

- Keep an air space of 3 inches or more between vine foliage and a house wall. Vines need air circulation all around; moisture can cause damage to and through even masonry walls.

- If it's destined to climb a wall that will need maintenance, train a vine on a hinged trellis (that can be lowered for access to the wall) or a framework of wires attached to nails driven into the wall. You must leave 3 inches of space between the vine and the wall for air circulation. That keeps the vine healthy, and saves the wall (inside and out) from the moisture damage.

- For walls and fences that need regular painting, choose annual vines. **Dutchman's pipe's** big, heart-shaped leaves create a dense screen in a single season.

- Avoid planting vines within reach of trees, large shrubs, windows, or shutters.

- After planting, lead or tie the longest stems to the support with an soft, unobtrusive twine.

CARE

Indoors. Pinch out the growing tips of seedlings that are becoming leggy.

Outdoors. After the late winter fertilization described below, top the mulch off to maintain a 2- to 3-inch layer.

PRUNING

Ornamental grasses. Check warm season grasses for new growth. If it's happening, cut the grasses back to a few inches above the crown.

Ground covers. Some ground covers benefit from shearing in early spring before growth begins, among them **liriope, mondo grass, plumbago.**

Vines. Early this month prune back vines that flower on shoots that will grow this year. Remove crowded shoots of **sweet autumn clematis** and **trumpet vine** (*Campsis radicans*); they bloom on new wood late in the growing season.

WATERING

Indoors. Continue watering seedlings started indoors. Water vines wintering in containers in a shed or garage often enough to keep the soil slightly damp.

Outdoors. Water new plantings if it does not rain for more than a week or ten days.

FERTILIZING

Indoors. Fertilize transplanted seedlings when two or three new leaves appear. Every two weeks fertilize seedlings that will remain indoors another six weeks

Check warm season grasses for new growth. If it's happening, cut the grasses back to a few inches above the crown.

Did You Know?

About Clematis

Clematis species and hybrids have a lot of give. The vines are deciduous and climb by attaching leaf petioles (stalks) to their supports. Once established, clematis species expand at a rate of 5 to 10 feet in a single season and will cover other vegetation, walls, trellises, posts, fences, and arbors. The big beautiful flowers of the clematis hybrids are especially lovely planted with **climbing roses.**

Site. Clematis vines need to have their heads in the sun, but the roots need to be in cool, moist earth. If the roots aren't in shade, mulch heavily. A site with protection from strong winds is best; avoid hot, dry, airless sites. **Soils.** A pH between 6.5 and 7.5 is best, but clematis tolerates somewhat acid soils. **Support.** Provide a structure of twine or wire for support; use twine or wire to lead the vines to a fence, a tree, or other support. **Pruning.** Pruning affects the way clematis blooms, and the timing is important. When you buy a clematis, ask for pruning instructions.

To have masses of small fragrant flowers in spring, prune clematis that blooms on new wood—for example, **anemone clematis,** *C. montana* hybrids rosy-red **'Rubens'** and white **'Alba'**—immediately after flowering. This reduces the bulk and size of the plant and controls its growth.

To have spectacular flowers in the summertime, in late winter or early spring prune back large-flowered hybrids like **'Dutchess of Edinburgh',** a double white; **'Henryi',** a large single white; **'Jackmanii Superba',** dark purple; and **'Nellie Moser',** a mauve pink. These bloom on old and new wood. Prune weak stems back to a healthy stem. Take dead stems back to the ground. Prune the remaining stems back to a pair of strong buds.

To keep its growth in check, in early spring remove congested shoots of **sweet autumn clematis,** *C. terniflora* (formerly *C. maximowicziana*), a rampant vine that bears a froth of tiny, fragrant, whitish flowers on new wood.

---

with a water-soluble houseplant fertilizer at half strength.

Outdoors. Spring clean ground covers, vines, and ornamental grasses:

1 Check and adjust the soil pH.

2 Apply Rich Earth humate and fertilize:

- If you are using organic fertilizers, apply them four to six weeks before growth begins.

- If you are using chemical fertilizers, apply them just before growth begins.

- If you are using time-release fertilizers, wait just before growth begins apply an eight month formulation.

 PESTS

Indoors. Damping off is a fungus that rots stems of young seedlings near the soil surface. Discard affected plants, reduce watering, and increase light and fresh air circulation. If the problem persists, mist the seedlings with a fungicide, such as Thiram (Arasan).

Outdoors. About the time the **forsythia** petals fall, treat the ground covers with a pre-emergent weed killer whose label says it won't harm perennials, annuals, shrubs, and so on. It will kill seeds and control established weeds.

In deer country, apply a new and different spray to vines they come to browse.

Voles are very active eating plants October to March. If you see vole runs, bait the main runway with a rodenticide. See Pests, Diseases, and Controls in the Appendix.

APRIL

 ## PLANNING

Record in your garden log the dates the flowering vines bloomed as a prompt for next year's pruning dates.

 ## PLANTING

Indoors. Transplant seedlings started indoors that are outgrowing their containers to larger pots.

Outdoors. Now until mid-May is an excellent planting times for vines, ground covers, and ornamental grasses.

 ## CARE

Mulch the ground under **sweet peas** to keep the earth cool and so prolong their flowering.

 ## PRUNING

Indoors. Pinch out the tips of leggy seedlings, and transplant the bigger ones to larger pots if the weather is still too cold for transplanting out to the garden.

In Zone 6, warm season grasses should be showing new growth now, so plan for their annual haircut.

Liriope should be cut back to just above the ground about now to keep it full and enhance blooming.

Hand prune winter-damaged leaves of **barrenwort** (*Epimedium*) and **lamium.** Cut back wandering strands of vinca.

Prune **wisteria, Carolina jessamine,** and other spring-flowering vines soon after the flowers fade.

 ## WATERING

Indoors. Continue to water seedlings. Water vines wintering in containers in a shed or garage often enough to keep the soil slightly damp.

Outdoors. New plantings need rain often enough to maintain soil moisture.

 ## FERTILIZING

If you are using chemical fertilizers which are quickly available, such as 5-10-5, fertilize vines, ground covers, and ornamental grasses every six weeks from beginning to end of the growing season. How often you need to fertilize depends on the type of fertilizer you are using; it's explained in Planting A Ground Cover.

 ## PESTS

Hoe and rake weeds away now. Weed beds of **lily-of-the-valley** when the flowers are in full bloom—that way you get to breathe in their exquisite perfume.

Check **clematis** hybrids for signs of whiteflies, spider mites, and scale, and apply the controls recommended in the Pests, Diseases, and Controls section of the Appendix.

Continue preventive measures to protect your garden from deer.

Cats and dogs investigate new plantings; ground covers are particularly vulnerable. Dog urine is high in nitrogen and burns. Squirrels dig up new plantings because they are sure you have hidden nuts in the hole. Try animal deterrents to keep them away.

If cats are the main problem, apply diatomaceous earth. It's dusty, and cats are fastidious and hate dust on their paws. It doesn't bother dogs, but some of the animal deterrents offered by garden centers do.

The more environmentally sensitive we become, the more we are going to allow wildlife to share our gardens. The more information we can share on how to get along with our furred and feathered friends, the more pleasure we'll have in them and our gardens.

Pinch out the tips of leggy seedlings, and transplant the bigger ones to larger pots if the weather is still too cold for transplanting out to the garden.

Did You Know?

Planting a Ground Cover

A new ground cover takes off and fills out most rapidly when you start with rooted cuttings and plant in fertile, improved soil.

1 If you will be replacing turf, in early spring or in fall when the soil is dry, spray the bed with Round-Up®, or remove the top layer.

2 Cover the area with the amendments recommended in the Introduction to the book under Soil Preparation and Improvement, and add 2 or 3 inches of compost, decomposed leaves, or peat moss.

3 Rototill all this 8 inches deep and three times over a two-week period. If you are installing an invasive ground cover such as **ivy** or **ajuga,** bury a 6-inch metal barrier along the border to keep it from overrunning neighboring plantings.

4 To keep weeds out, plant through a cover of 3 inches of mulch. If even minimum weeding will be difficult, plant instead through a porous landscape fabric; push the edges of the fabric sheet into the ground, and weight them with rocks, or heel them in. Make rows of X-shaped slits in the fabric, and insert the plants through the slits with a trowel. Landscape fabric slows the rooting of the above-ground branches, so plant densely.

5 Working in even rows and starting at the widest end, scoop out a row of evenly spaced planting pockets 8 to 14 inches apart. If you are planting on a slope, dig the holes so the slope side is lower to keep water from escaping down the slope. Set the cuttings in the hole, and firm them into place.

6 Position the second row of plants zig-zag between those of the row above. Row three repeats row one; row four repeats row two.

7 Put down 1½ inches of water right after planting. Set an empty 1-pound coffee tin or other container under your sprinkler and record how long it takes to accumulate 1½ inches of water so you'll know for the future. Newly-planted ground covers need 1½ inches of gentle rain every ten days to two weeks; if the sky fails, run your sprinkler or the irrigation system long enough to lay down 1½ inches of water.

8 Keep the mulch topped up until the ground cover has grown dense enough to keep weeds from growing. Meanwhile, keep the bed weeded. Very especially do not allow weeds to grow up and go to seed the first year or two; getting rid of them will be daunting. Plan on at least two years for the plants to grow enough to keep weeds down.

9 Plan to fertilize the bed just as you do perennials—twice a year if you are using organic fertilizers. The first application is before growth begins in spring and the last application is as growth slows at the end of the growing season.

If you're using organic blends, such as Holly-tone or Plant-tone, fertilize six weeks before growth begins in spring, and then again toward the end of the growing season.

For time- or controlled-release chemical fertilizers apply just before the plants start to grow, and repeat according to the formulation. A nine-month formulation should carry you through the whole growing season.

MAY

PLANNING

Keep a record of the year you plant ornamental grasses. They will benefit from dividing every five to ten years.

If you are looking for a great accent plant for your garden, patio, or porch, look over some of the beautiful tropical/semi-tropical vines—like **glory bush,** *Tibouchina urvilleana,* **mandevilla,** and **bougainvillea**—offered in late spring already blooming in big pots.

PLANTING

Early this month, move seedlings started indoors to a protected shaded spot outdoors to harden off for a week or so, and then transplant them to the garden.

If you would like to add fragrance to the garden without having, or giving up, a lot of garden space, plant a fragrant vine. Here are some of our favorites:

Moonflower, *Ipomoea alba.* A tender perennial with huge leaves, it opens fragrant pure white flowers up to 6 inches across toward evening and closes them about noon the next day. It climbs by twining stems and needs strong support, such as a sturdy fence or pergola.

Sweet Pea, *Lathyrus odoratus.* A sweetly scented annual, in cool spring weather it bears masses of small blooms that range from purple to pale lavender, ruby red, pale pink, white, and bicolors. It climbs by climbing tendrils and needs either a set of training strings or wires—or to be allowed to clamber over rocks and walls.

Carolina Yellow Jessamine, *Gelsemium sempervirens.* A perennial, it's a fast-growing woodland vine with dainty foliage that in late winter covers itself with small fragrant, golden flowers. The plant climbs by twining around anything handy, including fencing, porches, or trellises. Sun or shade.

Anemone Clematis, *Clematis montana* hybrids like rosy-red **'Rubens',** and white **'Alba'.** Perennials, they bear masses of have small fragrant flowers in spring.

Japanese Wisteria, *Wisteria floribunda* 'Longissima Alba'. This perennial bears long, drooping clusters of lightly scented, pastel-colored single or double blooms. It climbs by wrapping strong, slim stalks around anything handy.

Sweet Autumn Clematis, *Clematis terniflora.* This perennial blankets itself with tiny, sweetly-scented flowers in September and October. **Clematis** climbs by attaching leaf petioles (stalks) to the support provided.

CARE

Vines are growing vigorously now. **When you go to the garden, carry twine with you, and tie up new shoots in the direction you want them to follow.**

Early this month move **tropical and semi-tropical vines** that have wintered in a shed or garage back to their spot outdoors. Remove the top 2 inches of soil in the pot, and replace it with compost and a slow-release fertilizer in an eight-month formulation.

PRUNING

Prune **anemone clematis,** *Clematis montana* hybrids immediately after flowering to reduce the bulk and size of the plant and to control its direction.

Check the new shoots on all vines; cut back to the main framework all shoots not headed in the direction you intend.

Root out seedlings of ground covers that are stepping out of bounds. If you need new plants, pot up the rogues and coddle them until they are growing lustily, then transplant them to bare spots.

Pruned—deadhead and pinch back—vines that have finished blooming.

Keep **sweet pea** flowers picked to keep the plants producing.

Early this month, move seedlings started indoors to a protected shaded spot outdoors to harden off for a week or so, and then transplant them to the garden.

Did You Know?

About Vines and Their Supports

How a vine attaches itself to its support is stated in the table of plants in this chapter. How it climbs tells you what type of support it will need. That tells you whether a vine is suited to the job you have planned for it. There are variations, but here's the general idea:

Twining stems. For vines that climb by twining stems, **Carolina jessamine,** for example, suitable supports are narrow—a slim post, a pipe, wires, or strings.

Tendrils (twisting petioles). Vines that climb by twisting tendrils—**clematis,** for example—require a structure of wires, or wire mesh to climb on.

Clinging aerial rootlets. Vines that climb by aerial rootlets that secrete an adhesive glue, like **English ivy,** need only a rugged surface, such as a brick or stucco wall, or a rough, unpainted fence, for support.

However they climb, vines that eventually will be very heavy—like **climbing hydrangea, bittersweet, trumpet vine,** and **wisteria**—need supports built of heavy timbers, or even a dead tree, to hold them up.

Vines hold a lot of moisture. It is essential that the lumber you buy to create their support be pressure-treated.

 WATERING

Maintain the moisture in beds planted in seeds and seedlings. Water is essential to the unchecked growth that will develop root systems strong enough to bloom and withstand summer heat. If you do not have a good soaking rain every week to ten days, water planted beds gently and slowly long enough to lay down 1½ or 2 inches.

Check the moisture level in soil of vines growing in containers even if it rains; their foliage keeps the rain from the soil beneath.

 FERTILIZING

If you are using only chemical fertilizers, such as 5-10-5, which are quickly available to the plants, then you will need to fertilize garden and container plants every six weeks.

Scratch in organic or time-release fertilizers if you haven't done it yet.

 PESTS

Weeds are flourishing; use a scuffle hoe or rake to get rid of them.

Apply or change whatever deer deterrents you are using. See the section on Pests in the Appendix to the book.

Early spraying with fungicidal formulations of copper will help to save susceptible plants from blackspot, powdery mildew, rusts, and bacterial diseases such as bacterial leaf spots and wilt.

Depending on your zone, gypsy moths may begin to appear. The Pests section in the May pages of the Trees chapter describes controls.

JUNE
Vines, Ground Covers, & Ornamental Grasses

 ## PLANNING

Good sized container-grown vines, ornamental grasses, and ground covers may be on sale this month, so if you are in the market for new plants, make a point of visiting the garden centers.

 ## PLANTING

If you are thinking of planting a large transitional area in ornamental grasses, consider starting seeds now for transplanting in September or early October. (If the grasses you are interested in are named varieties—**blue switchgrass 'Heavy Metal'** for example, not just the original blue switchgrass species—then it's best to plant divisions, as cultivars do not reliably come true from seeds.)

Coddling the seeds and monitoring the germination will be easy if you start them in trays or flats kept indoors or in a cold frame. When the seedlings are 2 or 3 inches high, transplant them to an empty row in your kitchen garden, or to a sheltered spot in the flower beds. When the rains return in September, transplant the seedlings to permanent homes in the garden.

 ## CARE

As new vines grow, every few weeks tie the new shoots to their supports.

Top up the mulch around your vines. Make sure the roots of the **clematis** vines have enough mulch to stay cool. The heads can be in sun, but the roots need to be cool. André uses fine grade hammermill bark and also recommends pine and hardwood bark, West Coast fir bark, cedar bark, and cypress. Compost and leafmold (decomposed leaves) are beneficial mulches, but weeds and roots grow into them, and they decompose quickly in heat.

 ## PRUNING

As the blooms fade, lightly prune stems and shoots of vines that have finished blooming.

Sweet pea vines are likely to be yellowing—pull the roots up, and compost them. The vines add nitrogen to the soil—as do all legumes. A leafy annual vine, **Dutchman's pipe** for example, would be a good follow-on plant for sweet peas, or seedlings of large **marigolds.** If you grow sweet peas in the kitchen garden, a good follow-on crop would be a leafy vegetable such as **kale.**

Run control patrol on established ground covers, and root out and pot up or discard stragglers headed for far pastures.

 ## WATERING

Keep track of the soil moisture of seedlings and newly planted ground covers. Unchecked growth is the name of the growing game, and that requires sustained moisture. If June has little rain, water the garden slowly and deeply every week to ten days. Apply $1\frac{1}{2}$ inches of water measured in a 1-pound coffee tin or rain gauge.

Check the moisture level in vines growing in containers even if it rains; their foliage keeps the rain from the soil beneath.

 ## FERTILIZING

If you are using only chemical fertilizers, such as 5-10-5, you need to fertilize every six weeks. If you have already applied an organic fertilizer, you won't need to repeat until fall.

PESTS

Renew deer deterrents and sprays.

Check vines for lacebug damage. The leaf surfaces will be dull, speckled, pale, and the undersides will show specks of insect excrement. Spray the foliage with horticultural oil or insecticidal soap as directed on the package.

Whitefly and spider mite damage shows up as spotted and blanched leaves. Remove dead or severely infected shoots, and spray with neem at the intervals indicated on the package until the infestation is gone. See Pests, Diseases, and Controls in the Appendix.

Watch out for aphids, and mites.

Handpick Japanese beetles—they're sluggish in the cool of early morning. Drop them into soapy water, and flush them down a drain. If they multiply, spray the plants with neem, which will discourage feeding by adults. Try placing Japanese beetle traps far from the plantings you wish to protect, not among them. Insecticides containing neem, rotenone, or Sevin insecticide are controls.

Did You Know?

About Pruning Ground Covers

It isn't necessary to prune ground covers every year. But when a ground cover like **pachysandra** or **plumbago** matures, it gets straggly and loses its thick full look. When that happens, renew it by pruning to stimulate new growth and branching. Do not remove more than a third of the top growth at one time.

- Use hand shears to thin ground covers like **pachysandra, ivy, vinca, euonymus.**
- Use head shears to shear **euonymus, juniper, liriope, ophiopogon.**
- Use a string trimmer to cut back **tall meadow plants.**
- Use a hedge trimmer to trim **ferns** when the growing season is over.
- Use a lawn mower if you can raise it sufficiently, at least 2 to 3 inches off the ground—to trim renew old patches of **ivy** and **pachysandra** in early spring.
- In early spring, prune ground covers that bloom in summer or fall, for example, **leadwort,** *Ceratostigma.*
- Deadhead **ajuga,** and prune back **myrtle** and other spring-blooming ground covers immediately after they have bloomed.

Keep the beds clear of weeds. **Weeds that mature and go to seed will be followed by an army of offspring.**

Slugs and snails are good climbers. Diatomaceous earth, a natural control, works in dry soil but isn't effective on moist soil. Instead, do them in with iron phosphate (Sluggo), slug and snail bait, and traps. You can make your own slug trap by pouring a little beer in shallow aluminum plates or empty tuna fish cans.

JULY
Vines, Ground Covers, & Ornamental Grasses

 PLANNING

Assess your ground covers, vines, and ornamental grasses, and tell your garden log what you plan to put there next year.

Check garden centers for bargain plants that could meet your needs, and go through the garden catalogs for ideas for companion plants for vines and ornamental grasses that can be planted in September and October.

 PLANTING

Set tall containers planted in colorful summer-flowering bulbs—lilies, for example, or dahlias—among beds of ornamental grasses to improve the view while waiting for the grasses to come into their summer/fall glory period.

 CARE

Prune, and retie new shoots of **clematis, trumpet creeper,** and other vines to keep the plants growing in directions that will improve the framework.

 PRUNING

Wisteria needs pruning two or three times a year to keep its exuberant growth in bounds and to make it produce a sumptuous show of flowers. The time to do it is soon after the blooms begin to fade. Prune both to establish the framework of the vine, and to encourage flowering. Cut the long lateral (side) branches back to about two or three buds. You will need to prune again in fall.

Many vines, including **wisteria** and **trumpet vine** can be multiplied by rooting cuttings taken this month. Rooting cuttings is described in the June pages of Chapter 8, Shrubs.

 WATERING

Vines that are sheltered from rain benefit from being hosed down now and then in summer—but don't hose a vine when it is coming into, or is already in, bloom, as that may bruise flowers that are open, or make them soggy.

Check the moisture level in vines growing in containers even if it rains; their foliage keeps the rain from the soil beneath.

Ornamental grasses once established are pretty well drought-tolerant. They only need watering in prolonged droughts. You can tell they need water because the edges of the leaves curl up. Water slowly and deeply, making sure you're laying down at least an inch and a half of water.

 FERTILIZING

If you are using only chemical fertilizers, such as 5-10-5, you will need to fertilize every six weeks.

If you have already applied an organic fertilizer, you won't need to repeat until fall.

 PESTS

Continue preventive measures to protect your garden from deer.

Continue Japanese beetle patrol and control.

Assess your ground covers, vines, and ornamental grasses, and tell your garden log what you plan to put there next year.

Did You Know?

Spring-Flowering Bulbs Are Great Companion Plants

Many of the spring-flowering bulbs offered at good prices in the bulbs catalogs you receive this time of year are excellent companion plants for ornamental grasses and low-growing ground covers. The small early bulbs carpet the earth with color while the grasses are still dormant. The larger bulbs bloom above ground covers such as **pachysandra, myrtle, ivy, and ajuga.** They also show up well against the emerging growth of the grasses, which later masks their ripening foliage.

These small spring bulb flowers are very effective planted in front of the taller ornamental grasses—they appear in about this order:

- **Early Crocus,** *Crocus* spp. and cvs.
- **Daffodils,** *Narcissus* miniatures and early varieties
- **Snowdrops,** *Galanthus*
- **Winter Aconite,** *Eranthis*
- **Squill,** *Scilla tubergeniana*
- **Glory-of-the-snow,** *Chinodoxa luciliae*

- **Bluebell,** *Hyacinthoides non-scripta*
- **Grape Hyacinth,** *Muscari* spp. and hybrids
- **Botanical/Species tulips**
- *Tulipa turkestanica*
- **Giant Snowflake, Summer Snowflake,** *Leucojum aestivum*

These large flowering bulbs are attractive planted here and there among ground covers, and add early color to beds of ornamental grasses:

- **Yellow daffodils**
- **Lily-flowered tulips**
- **Red Parrot tulips**
- **Fosteriana tulips 'White Emperor', 'Orange Emperor', 'Red Emperor'**

- *Tulipa greigii* 'Sweet Lady', 'Goldwest', 'Oriental Splendour'
- **Foxtail Lily,** Eremurus stenophyllus
- **Giant Onion,** Allium giganteum
- **Indian Lily,** Camassia quamash

Whitefly, mealybugs, scale, spider mites, and aphids multiply in hot, airless spots and will spoil the leaves even if they don't do permanent damage. Spray infestations two or three times with some form of neem, *Pyrethrum,* or horticultural soaps—they won't harm the environment. You can also use horticultural oils. See the section in the Appendix of the book on Pests, Diseases, and Controls.

Rust loves **lily-of-the-valley.** Control rust by avoiding overhead watering and by cutting out and disposing of infected foliage. Twice a month spray with a horticultural oil, Mancozeb, manzate, sulfur or copper.

Continue weed patrol and control of ground covers and other plantings.

AUGUST

 ## PLANNING

Spend some time in the early morning or late afternoon asking your plants for progress reports.

Summer heat and drought reveal the vulnerabilities of plants, sites, and your annual soil maintenance program. Young vines whose leaves are showing crisped edges here and there may need more consistent watering. Patches of ground cover that are wilting when others do not may need more mulch or more humus added to the soil when you fertilize and refurbish the soil early next year.

Patches of **pachysandra** that are dying may be getting too much sun in winter when the leaves fall, or suffering from volutella leaf and stem blight. Consider replacing problem patches of **Japanese pachysandra,** *Pachysandra terminalis* with **Allegheny pachysandra,** *P. procumbens.* It is native to the Southeast, and more tolerant of heat.

 ## PLANTING

In spite of the heat and drought, **container-grown vines, ground covers, and the smaller ornamental grasses** can be planted successfully this month as long as you water them every week or so, and hose them down with a gentle spray if they wilt on hot days.

 ## CARE

After summer thunderstorms, check the vines, and make sure they are securely fastened to their supports.

 ## PRUNING

By now, aggressive vines like **autumn clematis, Carolina jessamine, trumpet creeper,** and **wisteria** will have made a lot of new growth; prune to thin excess growth and to keep the main stems developing the framework.

 ## WATERING

Now and then hose down vines that are sheltered from rain. Check the moisture level in vines growing in containers even if it rains; their foliage keeps the rain from the soil beneath.

This month is usually dry, so expect to replace the missing rain by watering ground covers, vines, and ornamental grasses two or three times this month, every week to ten days. The ideal is to put down $1\frac{1}{2}$ inches of water at each session.

Overhead watering is fine as long as you water deeply. There's less waste if you water before the sun reaches the garden in the early morning or late afternoon or evening. In hot dry periods, daytime overhead watering lowers leaf temperatures and reduces stress. Don't water more than three or four times in a month.

André doesn't recommend electrically-timed mechanical watering systems that ignore the weather and water too often and shallowly. But he does believe they can do a good job if they are set up with the correct low-pressure nozzles, and timed to run long enough and to water gently and deeply every week or ten days in periods of drought.

 ## FERTILIZING

If you are using chemical fertilizers, you should be fertilizing every six weeks or so.

If you have already applied an organic fertilizer, you won't need to repeat until fall.

This month is usually dry so expect to replace the missing rain by watering ground covers, vines, and ornamental grasses two or three times this month, every week to ten days.

Did You Know?

Spacing for Ground Covers

To know how many plants you will need to plant an area in a ground cover, divide the square footage of the bed by the amount of space each plant will need.

To figure out how many plants you will need, start by measuring the area to be planted. Outline the bed with marking paint or a hose, and then measure the length and the width. Multiply the length by the width, and that gives you the square footage. To get the approximate size of a free-form shape, outline the area with a hose, and then shape the hose into a square or a rectangle that encompasses the area, measure, and multiply the length by the width.

Then divide the spacing required for the plant you have chosen into the square footage of the area to be planted. The answer is the number of plants you will need.

Some growers' tags indicate how many plants to set out per square yard; Blooms of Bressingham tags recommend for the **barren strawberry 'Red Ruby Strawberry'** three to four plants per square yard. A square yard is 9 square feet. Dividing 9 (square feet) by four (plants) yields 2.2—one plant for every 2.2 square feet.

Most plant tags recommend you allow a certain distance between plants. Typical spacing for crowns of **Japanese painted fern** is 24 inches apart; for **lavender 'Munstead'**, 15 inches; for **Dusty Miller,** 8 inches apart. The number of inches "apart" means "all around." To get the square inches needed for one **Dusty Miller** plant, multiply 8 times 8, which gives you 64 square inches. Divide 64 into the square footage of the area multiplied by 12, the number of inches in a foot. That tells you how many plants you will need.

Small ground covers that spread are planted one to four per square foot—four for upright plants like **pachysandra;** one to two for vining plants like **vinca**—two plants if it is rooted in a small pot, one if it is rooted in a large pot.

Closely spaced, these ground covers fill in the area in about a year and a half. More widely spaced, the plants will need two years to fill in.

If vines fertilized with a timed-release chemical fertilizer are failing to grow as expected, supplement it with foliar feedings of water-soluble organic or fast-acting liquid fertilizers.

PESTS

Change deer deterrents and sprays around in the garden.

Clear the ground covers and other beds of all weeds; don't let them grow up and go to seed!

High humidity and heat encourages powdery mildew. Avoid overhead watering, and apply sulfur, ultrafine horticultural oil, copper fungicide, Immunox, or Bayleton.

Check for fungal leaf spot, and apply a fungicide if needed. If you see continuing signs of mites, hose the plant down regularly, and spray with insecticidal soaps, or ultrafine horticultural oils.

SEPTEMBER

PLANNING

Consider reducing the amount of hand trimming around deciduous trees by planting a no-maintenance all-season ground cover like **ajuga, lamium,** or **vinca**—plants that take shade in summer and sun in winter. Next month is ideal for the project:

1 To avoid disturbing tree and shrub feeder roots located in the top 12 inches of the soil, remove the turf by hand, or kill it with RoundUp®.

2 Starting 4 to 5 inches from the trunk, add 4 to 5 inches of topsoil, and top that with 2 to 3 inches of humus—compost, partially decomposed leaves or seaweed, or other decomposed organic material.

3 Over every 100 square feet (an area 10 by 10 feet) spread the following—available at any garden center.

Holly-tone: 4 to 7 pounds
Superphosphate: 3 to 5 pounds
Green sand: 5 to 10 pounds
Clay soils only: gypsum 5 to
  10 pounds
Osmocote® four-month: 2 pounds
Rich Earth Humate: 1 pound

4 Fork all this into the bed by hand.

5 Rake the bed smooth, and plant your ground cover. Mulch 2 to 3 inches deep.

6 Water slowly and gently to put down about 1 1/2 inches of water.

7 Water every week to ten days if you run into a dry spell.

8 In the following years, fertilize an evergreen ground cover with lawn fertilizer when you fertilize the lawn. Fertilize a flowering ground cover twice annually with Holly-tone.

PLANTING

September begins an excellent planting season.

The best planting, dividing, and transplanting dates for Zone 6 are September 1 to 15; for Zone 7, September 1 to mid-October. In the warm Tidewater, the soil cools after Thanksgiving, so gardeners can plant, divide, and transplant as late as November 1.

CARE

When temperatures head below 60 degrees Fahrenheit, move winter tender and tropical vines to a greenhouse, or try them as houseplants. Or, move them to a frost-free shed or garage.

PRUNING

You can divide to multiply established stands of **blue fescue, blue oat grass,** and **feather reed grass** and many other grasses and ground covers this month.

Wisteria benefits from pruning two or three times a year. Give it its second trim now or in October. Cut the laterals back again leaving only two or three buds to each shoot.

WATERING

If your vines are sheltered from rain, even when rainfall is plentiful make sure the soil doesn't dry out.

FERTILIZING

If you are using organic blends, such as Holly-tone or Plant-tone, then you will need to fertilize the last time about six weeks before the end of the growing season.

The growing season slows in Zones 6 and 7 early September to early October. In Zone 8, Richmond and the Tidewater areas of Virginia, the last fertilization can be between the end of September and mid-October.

When temperatures head below 60 degrees Fahrenheit, move winter tender and tropical vines to a greenhouse, or try them as houseplants.

Did You Know?

To Plant with Ornamental Grasses

Ornamental grasses can stand alone as specimen plants. But to achieve a naturalistic effect, plan to include foliage, bark, and stem plants—that's the way nature designs her wild gardens.

For structure and contrast, include small- and medium-sized deciduous trees such as:

- **Chinese Dogwoods,** *Cornus kousa* var. *chinensis*
- **Crapemyrtle**
- **Franklin Tree,** *Franklinia alatamaha*
- **Fringe Tree,** *Chionanthus retusus*
- **Serviceberry, Shadblow,** *Amelanchier* species
- **Witchhazel,** *Hamamelis* x *intermedia* hybrids

For change and as foils to the dramatic effects of dried seedheads and grasses in the winter landscape, include shrubs and some evergreens:

- **Azalea,** *Rhododendron* evergreen hybrids
- **Cotoneaster,** *Cotoneaster* hybrids
- **Fountain Buddleia,** *Buddleia alternifolia*
- **Rhododendron,** *Rhododendron* species and cultivars
- **Rugosa Rose,** *Rosa rugosa* 'Sir Thomas Lipton'
- **Siebold Viburnum,** *Viburnum sieboldii*
- **Winterberry,** *Ilex verticillata* 'Sparkleberry'

For contrast with the grasses' buff and tan, sea green and green, gold and pale gold colors, plant bright, carefree perennials:

- **Asters,** *Aster* species and cultivars
- **Astilbe,** *Astilbe* x *arendsii*
- **'Autumn Joy' Stonecrop,** *Sedum spectabile*
- **Black-eyed Susan,** *Rudbeckia fulgida* var. *sullivantii* 'Goldsturm'
- **Catmint,** *Nepeta* x *faassenii*
- **Daylilies,** *Hemerocallis* hybrids
- **Joe-Pye Weed,** *Eupatorium purpureum*
- **Fern-leaved Yarrow,** *Achillea filipendula* 'Coronation Gold'
- **Purple Coneflower,** *Echinacea purpurea* and cultivars
- **Russian Sage,** *Perovskia atriplicifolia*
- **Tickseed,** *Coreopsis verticillata* 'Golden Showers'
- **Yellow Loosestrife,** *Lysimachia punctata*

If you are using only chemical fertilizers, such as 5-10-5, the last fertilization for garden and container plants will be six weeks before the end of the growing season.

If you are using time-release fertilizers, earlier applications should carry the plants through the end of the growing season.

 PESTS

Change the deer deterrents you are using.

Give new ground covers a radical weeding. Check and remove ground covers creeping outside their boundaries.

Weed around vines and ornamental grasses, scratching up the soil so fall rains can give the plants a deep watering.

OCTOBER
Vines, Ground Covers, & Ornamental Grasses

 PLANNING

The Friendship Garden at the U.S. National Arboretum peaks this month. A brilliant example of a grass garden suitable for the average ranch home, it covers a one-third acre front yard.

The plants develop throughout the year without pruning, staking, spraying, or deadheading. In late winter, they are cut back to the ground, mulched, and fertilized as growth begins. Watering is by underground or surface irrigation system. Seedheads ripen and stand through fall and winter. Fruiting and berrying plants promote a healthy ecological balance that encourages birds and does not exclude insects. A majority of insects are beneficial.

Color, texture, and unfolding growth are present in all four seasons. In spring, naturalized flowering bulbs carpet spaces between the cut-back ornamental grasses. **Tulips** in exotic forms with **narcissus** and **species iris** work wonderfully well here. In summer, easy-care flowering perennials like **black-eyed Susan** and **Russian sage** bloom along the walks and among the half-grown grasses.

From early summer to fall, the dominant grasses lift tall, light-catching inflorescences to the wind. The tallest grasses and a few **hollies** shield the gift shop from the road. Smaller species grow closer to the building. A few well-placed trees and flowering or fruiting shrubs mimic a meadow's variety. Additional seasonal color comes from big tubs of annuals, vegetables, and herbs.

In fall, sweeps of **sedum** turn russet-pink-coral, then fade to brown, and the fruiting trees color red and orange. With cold weather, ornamental grasses come into their own—rustling, tossing in the wind, and eventually binding snow at their feet.

Through all its seasons, the broad paths and comfortable stopping places invite meditation. For the birds there are banquets of seeds, insects, worms, as well as nesting spaces and materials in this garden where chemical controls are never needed.

 PLANTING

Continue to plant **spring-flowering bulbs** and big, low-maintenance showy **perennials** with the ornamental grasses.

 CARE

In fall, clear your ground cover of fallen leaves with a leaf blower.

 PRUNING

Limit pruning to dead or diseased material.

 WATERING

Check vines sheltered from rain, and keep the soil moderately damp. The roots are still growing even if the air is cold, and water is essential.

FERTILIZING

In Zones 6 and 7, the growing season slows between early September and early October. In Zone 8, Richmond and the Tidewater areas of Virginia, the growing season slows between the end of September and mid-October.

If you are using fertilizers that are organic blends such as Holly-tone or Plant-tone, you can fertilize for the last time about six weeks before the end of the growing season.

If you are using only chemical fertilizers, such as 5-10-5, the last fertilization should be four to six weeks before the end of the growing season.

If you are using time-release fertilizers, a spring application of a nine-month formulation should carry the plants through the end of the growing season—no fertilizer need be added at this time.

 PESTS

Apply or change whatever deer deterrents you are using. See the section on Pests, Diseases, and Controls in the Appendix.

If vole runs appear around shrubs, bait the main runway with a rodenticide. André's winter baiting station is a pair of paper cups scented with apple juice, with a dose of the bait in the bottom, set under a half tire. Another way is to nestle the baited cups in straw held down by plywood and topped with a brick or a big stone.

Did You Know?

Ground Covers: Thinking Outside the Box

If you are considering planting a slope with a ground cover, think outside the box. Consider, for example, **forsythia.** Most species and varieties are upright and fountaining, but *Forsythia* x *intermedia* **'Arnold Dwarf'** roots where it touches, can withstand drought, and needs only periodic trimming. A lovely complement for a **forsythia hill** is naturalized bulbs—**daffodils, narcissus,** and **lemon yellow daylilies.**

Another attractive ground cover good for steep grades is the ground-hugging **memorial rose,** *Rosa wichuriana.* The white flowers, which are typical of wild roses, are succeeded by modest reddish fruits. The branches trail and root when they touch moist soil, producing thick mats of glossy foliage that is evergreen in mild regions.

A new series of ground cover roses won Gold Medals in 1996 from rose societies in Australia, Britain, and America. These bloom continuously, are immune to pests and diseases, and do not need deadheading. The plants are 2 to $2^{1}/_{2}$ feet tall by 4 feet across. The star is **Flower Carpet Rose,** whose blooms are lavender pink and spicily perfumed. **Jeeper's Creepers** is a white variety, and **Baby Blanket** is a light pink.

November

PLANNING

Gather the seedheads of the most beautiful grasses before the wind gets to them. Tie them loosely in bunches, and hang them to dry upside down in a dark, dry, warm place.

To keep feathery grasses from shedding, spray them with hair spray or a spray varnish.

Snip off the heads of **oat grass,** and bind them with florist's wire to make "ornaments" for holidays trees and decorations. Make a wreath from strands of **clematis,** by pruning away small shoots, and twining the stem into a circle.

PLANTING

Sow seeds that will benefit from stratification in the garden.

It's late to be planting container plants in Zones 6 and 7. If you have unplanted containers of vines, ground covers, or grasses, water them thoroughly, and sink the pots up to the tops of their rims in empty rows in the kitchen garden or elsewhere. With a winter mulch of evergreen boughs they should still be good to go in late winter when the ground dries enough for planting.

CARE

Rake matted leaves away from the ground cover.

PRUNING

Run control patrol on ground covers like **ajuga** and **vinca,** and use an edger to root out escapees. Pot offsets and plantlets for later use.

WATERING

Before the first anticipated hard freeze, water all your vines, ground covers, and ornamental grasses slowly, deeply, and thoroughly.

FERTILIZING

There is no fertilization this month.

PESTS

In deer country, wrap susceptible evergreen vines with Reemay, or if they have been attacked in the past, circle them with bird netting or chickenwire cages. Change whatever deer deterrents you are using. See the section on Pests, Diseases, and Controls in the Appendix to the book.

Dig up any young dandelion sprouting in new ground cover beds or around vines or ornamental grasses; they are still small enough to pull if you are careful. Any scrap of root left will consider itself a cutting and start a new plant, so dig carefully.

If vole runs appear around shrubs, bait the main runway with a rodenticide. See Pests, Diseases, and Controls in the Appendix.

Before the first anticipated hard freeze, water all your vines, ground covers, and ornamental grasses slowly, deeply, and thoroughly.

Did You Know?

Multiply By Dividing

Now that the season is over, consider what you want for next year. If you need more, plan to multiply your plants.

Vines
Cuttings. Many vines, including **wisteria** and **trumpet vine,** can be multiplied by rooting cuttings. The process is described in the June pages of Chapter 8, Shrubs.

Stratification. Annual vines and some perennial vines will grow from seed. Some need stratification (chilling) to germinate. Seeds of **trumpet vine** sown in the fall will germinate some months later. Planting in the November pages in Chapter 6, Perennials, describes the process of stratification. Seeds to be stratified this time of year are sown out in the garden.

Ground Covers
Some ground covers can be started from seed, including common **myrtle** (*Vinca minor*) and **plumbago.** When seeds are available, starting the plants yourself from seed is the most cost-efficient way, but remember that named varieties may not come true from seed, as we explained in the Planting section of this chapter's June pages.

Most ground covers root easily from cuttings or root division. Those that multiply by means of above-ground runners like **ajuga** and **vinca** you can divide by simply cutting the plantlet from the parent and pulling it up.

Ivy is easy; you can divide a densely-rooted clump in spring, but rooting cuttings taken in late summer or fall is easier. **Lamium** cuttings root easily in spring; divisions of the plant root easily in spring or early fall. Rampant growers like **creeping Jenny** (*Lysimachia nummularia*) can be grown from cuttings taken in spring or divisions planted in fall. **Pachysandra** will root from cuttings almost all year round. Division is best in early spring before the plants start to grow or in early fall. Dig it by the shovelful including the dirt it is growing in.

Ferns are usually propagated by root division in spring. Plants that clump, like **liriope,** are multiplied by dividing a mature crown; use a spading fork to lift and gently break the clump apart, or use a spade to cut the clump apart.

Ornamental Grasses
You can buy seeds for some ornamental grass species (not hybrids or cultivars), including **blue fescue,** *Miscanthus sinnensis* and the **pennisetums.** To get a head start, sow the seeds indoors early next year. Starting Seeds Indoors under Planting in the January pages of Chapter 1, Annuals explains the process.

Like perennials, the ornamental grasses don't fill out until the second season, so if you are a hurry-up-and-grow gardener, you will be happier planting root divisions. André Viette and other nurserymen ship grasses bare root in spring, and potted rooted divisions spring, summer, and fall.

The grasses are not likely to need division for at least five to ten years. However, once a grass has filled out, you can divide the crown every year. Use a spading fork to lift and gently break the clump apart, or use a spade to cut the clump apart. The important thing is to be sure that each division has at least one growing point.

Most grasses are best divided in spring, before new growth begins, including **Japanese blood grass, fountain grass, Chinese silver grass,** and **switchgrass.** The smaller grasses can be divided in spring but also in fall, including **blue fescue, blue oat grass,** and **feather reed grass.**

DECEMBER
Vines, Ground Covers, & Ornamental Grasses

PLANNING

If you find turf grass high-maintenance, or have a problem with the grass under trees, consider a ground cover.

PLANTING

If the weather remains mild, and soil temperatures are warm, you can still plant deciduous vines the first days of this month.

In Zone 8, some winters are mild enough to plant all winter long.

CARE

Use evergreen boughs to provide winter protection for **European ginger,** the **hellebores,** and other ground covers that suffer in cold weather. A discarded Christmas tree provides greens to cover them.

PRUNING

Prune **wisteria** laterals back again leaving only two or three buds to each shoot.

Did You Know?

What You Need to Know Before Buying Ornamental Grasses

- Height and width at maturity
- Form—upright or fountaining
- Texture—fine or coarse
- Color—solid green, variegated, or striped
- Drainage—most need a well-drained site, but a few are excellent choices for moist spots
- Light—full sun for nearly all
- Cold hardiness—almost all the popular ornamental grasses survive winters in the Mid-Atlantic, so for most cold hardiness isn't crucial. One beautiful grass not likely to winter over in Zones 6 and 7 is tall **pampas grass,** whose plume-panicles are luminous. The compact variety, *Cortaderia selloana* 'Pumila' does winter over here.

WATERING

Keep the soil for tropical and semi-tropical vines wintering indoors moderately damp.

FERTILIZING

Nothing to fertilize this month.

PESTS

The scent-carrying oils in deer deterrents don't volatilize in cold air. If you are concerned, wrap clinging **hydrangea** and other still-green vines in Reemay for the winter.

If vole runs appear around shrubs, bait the main runway with a rodenticide.

CHAPTER ELEVEN

Water and Bog Plants

A water garden is a living biological organism that exhibits an exquisite beauty and intelligence . . . if you take the time to get to know the components and their life cycles.

WATER GARDENING

Water, the flowers and fish, the **submerged plants** that help to clean and oxygenate the water, and the snails that graze on the dark green algae fuzzing the sides of the pond—each element plays a vital role and the whole makes a healthy, delightful garden ornament that is at least as easy to maintain as a small flower bed. A balanced complement of **aquatic plants** and livestock, with or without a pump and filtering system, makes it a garden, and keeps the water fresh and clear.

Water garden containers. A water garden consists of a container, water, plants, and fish. It can be as small as a wall fountain, as simple as a Chinese water pot, or a half-barrel out on your patio. Preformed plexiglass liners in sizes up to about 10 by 10 feet are used to contain smaller in-ground ponds. Larger and free-form in-ground ponds are waterproofed by relatively inexpensive flexible rubber liners or some form of cement or gunnite.

Fountains, streams, and waterfalls. To enjoy sparkle and splash, you will need to add a pump that pushes the water through a bubbler or a fountainhead. Upgrading the pump and adding a filter to the system improves aeration. To return the water to the pond via a stream or a waterfall you will need a more powerful pump.

Recirculating bog gardens. An interesting and environmentally friendly way to filter the water and return it to the pond is via a recirculating liner-proofed garden of bog plants and a pebble-lined stream.

You can have a beautiful pond without pump or filter. The magic formula given in the April pages is a combination of plants and fish that does a pretty good job of keeping the pond's biosystem in balance. Richard Koogle, Director of Operations at Lilypons Water Gardens®, recommends including in pond care the use of a supplemental bacterial product that controls algae by speeding the decomposition of waste from fish and plants. This is especially important if you are not using a pump or filter.

An in-ground water garden comes together in three basic steps:

1 You prepare the physical container, the excavation for the pond and other features you have decided on—recirculating bog garden, streambed, waterfall. You waterproof the system and add water. If you are using a recirculating pump and a filter, they go in next.

Water Plants in a Pond

Water and Bog Plants

Did You Know?

Bog Gardens

A recirculating bog garden will improve your water garden's filtering system. It's a shallow pond waterproofed with a flexible liner and planted with **bog plants.** A streambed that leads the water back to the pond is part of it. The plants rooted in gravelly muck at the bottom take up nutrients that feed on undesirable algae; that helps to keep the water clear and fresh.

Typically, a bog garden and streambed are about 12 inches deep. The bottom is a planting bed consisting of about 4 inches of coarse gravel topped by 4 inches of pea gravel or sand. You plant the roots and ball of soil around the **bog plants** directly in the gravel at a depth that gives them about $1/2$ to 1 inch of water overhead.

Avoid invasive bog plants like **cattails** and **saggitaria** which take over unless diligently weeded out. Go instead with **irises, papyrus,** and **dwarf bamboo,** *Dulichium arundinaceum,* a low-growing, feathery bamboo-like plant that stays less than 15 to 18 inches tall and is not overly invasive.

2 You set containers of water garden plants under the water in the pond. Some may need to be raised on platforms, which can be pots, bricks, or stones. Plants for a recirculating bog garden are rooted in the gravelly mix at the bottom of the bog.

3 You release fish, snails, and other livestock to help control pests and unwanted algae—and for the pleasure of learning more about them.

Planting

Like land plants, water garden plants respond to fertilizing and have active and dormant seasons. Some are hardy, surviving **frost belt** winters; others are tropical and need winter protection in the frost belt. The containers for pond plants have no drainage holes.

There are three groups, 1. **submerged or oxygenating** plants, 2. **aquatics,** and 3. **bog plants.**

1 The **submerged plants** (also called oxygenating plants) are leafy stems that grow up from containers at the bottom of the pond. They're there to take up nutrients that otherwise fuel algae growth that makes water murky, and to add oxygen to the water.

2 The **aquatics** are **large-leaved floating plants,** and **small-leaved floating plants.** The stars are the **water lilies** and the **lotus.** They bear exotic blossoms and spread out big beautiful leaves that provide the fish with cool shade and a refuge from predators.

The **small-leaved floating plants** are mainly for contrast. They trace delicate green patterns between the **lily** pads and the **lotus** leaves. Some bear tiny flowers. The prettiest are perhaps white and yellow **snowflake,** the sweetly fragrant species of *Nymphoides* whose flowers are $3/4$ of an inch across and centered by yellow stamens. They flower abundantly spring through fall. Another popular little floater is **Australian water clover,** *Marsilea mutica,* a dainty little plant that looks just like its nickname, **four-leaf clover.**

3 The **bog plants,** also known as marginal plants because they are placed at the margins of a water garden, are upright forms that thrive in partially submerged containers or in a bog's mucky soil or gravel. Some are narrow-leaved, like water-loving varieties of **irises,** and others are broad-leaved, like **elephant's-ear.** These linears provide contrast with the flat, floating forms of the aquatics.

Water and Bog Plants

Bog plants can also be planted in a naturally wet spot. But before planting in any area big enough to be considered a wetland, consult the local environmental authorities.

CARE

Here's a quick look at year-round maintenance for a water garden:

Spring. Clear organic debris from the pond, the bog area, stream, or waterfall. Groom and fertilize the plants. In the **frost belt** start the pump; in frost-free regions it would have been on through winter. Add a supplemental bacterial product to speed the decomposition of waste from fish and plants, especially if you are not using a pump and filter. Resume feeding the fish. Clean the filter as needed. Maintain the water level.

Spring/Summer. Clean the filter. Remove fading foliage and blooms. Feed the fish. Every thirty days add a pellet to kill mosquito larvae. Anytime plants and livestock are in the pond, it is necessary to keep up the water level. Wind and hot dry weather can evaporate so much pond water you might think the liner is leaking, especially if it is running over a waterfall and over a bog garden and/or streambed.

Fall. Keep the pond clear of leaves and dead plant material. Clean the pump. In

Did You Know?

About Water Lilies

Water lilies are the stars of the water garden. They come into bloom and fade away over a period of three to four days. There are two types:

Hardy water lilies are perennial in the Mid-Atlantic. Set out after the chill of very early spring but before growth gets under way, hardy water lilies may produce blooms the first summer, but they need two to three years to reach their peak. The flowers are open only during the day.

Tropical water lilies bloom where temperatures stay above 80 degrees Fahrenheit for three to four weeks. In Zone 8, they begin to bloom in May. In Zone 6, in June. They open the year they are planted. To keep them for another year, collect and store the tubers in a frost-free location for the winter (see October, Planting). There are day- and night-blooming varieties. Day bloomers are sweetly fragrant; night bloomers are headily scented, open as the stars come out, and stay open until late morning. They're likely to continue to bloom after the hardy water lilies have shut down for the season.

One of a pond owner's few chores is removing yellowing foliage; a lily pruner makes the job easy. Removing closed four-day old blossoms seems to speed the rate at which water lilies present new flower buds.

the **frost belt,** shut the pond down for winter. If the pond is small and less than thirty inches deep, fish may be safer indoors in a fish tank for the winter. Empty and clean the pond, then refill it. Maintain the water level.

Still in the **frost belt,** if the pool is large, discard or bring indoors for the winter the frost-tender **tropical water lilies** and tender pond **bog plants.** In **frost-free regions,** you can keep the pump and filter working through the winter.

Winter. If ice threatens a pond where fish and plants will winter, put a de-icer to work.

PESTS

If predators are plentiful in your area, make the sides of the pond excavation vertical. That makes fishing harder. You might also place a few cinder blocks in the pond to give the fish hiding places.

Water and Bog Plants

Water Plants

Common Name (*Botanical Name*)	Hardiness Zones	Light	Type
Anacharis (*Egeria densa*)	6 to 10	Sun	Submerged/oxygenating plant.
Australian Water Clover (*Marsilea mutica*)	6 to 11	Sun to part sun	Aquatic with floating leaves.
Coontail (*Ceratophyllum demersum*)	4 to 10	Sun to part sun	Submerged/oxygenating plant.
Dwarf Saggitaria (*Sagittaria subulata*)	5 to 11	Sun	Submerged/oxygenating plant.
Floating Fern (*Ceratopteris pteridoides*)	6/7 to 11	Sun to part sun	Aquatic with floating leaves.
Lotus (*Nelumbo* sp. and hybrids)	4 to 11	Sun	Aquatic with floating leaves.
Myriophyllum (*Myriophyllum* species)	4 to 11, according to species	Sun to part shade	Submerged/oxygenating plant.
Parrot's-feather (*Myriophyllum aquaticum*)	6 to 10	Sun to part shade	Aquatic with floating leaves.
Snowflake, Floating-heart (*Nymphoides* species)	5/6 to 11	Sun to part sun	Aquatic with floating leaves.
Water lilies, Hardy (*Nymphaea* cvs.)	3 to 10	Sun	Aquatic with floating leaves.
Washington Grass (*Cabomba caroliniana*)	6 to 11	Sun to part sun	Submerged/oxygenating plant.
Water Lilies, Tropical (*Nymphaea* sp. and cvs.)	10 to 11	Sun to part shade	Aquatic with floating leaves.
Wild Celery (*Valisneria americana*)	4 to 11	Afternoon sun	Submerged/oxygenating plant.

Water and Bog Plants

Bog Plants

Common Name (*Botanical Name*)	Hardiness Zones	Light	Height
Arrowhead (*Sagittaria* sp. and cvs.)	Varies with species	Sun to part sun	2 to 4 feet
Canna (*Canna* sp.)	7 to 10	Sun	6 feet plus
Dwarf Bamboo (*Dulichium arundinaceum*)	6 to 11	Sun to part sun	15 to 18 inches
Dwarf Papyrus (*Cyperus haspan*)	9 to 11	Sun to part shade	30 inches
Elephant's-ear (*Colocasia* species and hybrids)	8 to 11	Any light	5 feet
Golden Club (*Orontium aquaticum*)	6 to 10	Sun to shade	18 inches
Horsetail (*Equisetum hyemale*)	3 to 11	Sun to shade	Up to 4 feet
Iris (*Iris* sp. and hybrids)	4 to 8/9	Sun to part shade	Up to 4 feet
Lizard's Tail (*Saururus cernuus*)	4 to 9	Sun to part shade	Up to 24 inches
Narrow-leaved Cattail (*Typha angustifolia*)	2 to 11	Sun to part sun	To 4 feet
Pickerel Rush (*Pontederia cordata*)	3 to 11	Sun	24 to 36 inches tall
Spike Rush (*Eleocharis montevidensis*)	6 to 9	Sun to part sun	To 12 inches
Sweet Flag, Calamus (*Acorus calamus*)	4 to 11	Sun to part sun	30 to 36 inches
Water Arum (*Peltandra virginica*)	5 to 9	Sun to part sun	2 to 3 feet
White Bullrush (*Scirpus albescens*)	5 to 11	Sun to part sun	4 to 6 feet

PLANNING

January is a fine time to plan a water garden. Study your garden from indoors to determine where you'd like to see a pond, keeping in mind a water garden's need for light, good drainage, and so on.

Potential locations. On flat land, a pond in the curve of a flower border is quite lovely. A stone wall or a fence can be an appealing backdrop. A sloping yard invites an installation of small ponds spilling into each other and makes it easy to establish a recirculating bog garden and a stream. If you are home mostly in the evening, or wish to grow the fragrant **night-blooming tropical water lilies,** look for a spot where the pond surface will reflect sunsets and moonrises.

If the yard is tiny, you might pave it and install a fountain splashing water back into a basin. For a deck, the water garden could be a Chinese water pot with a miniature **water lily** surrounded by potted plants or a wall fountain planted with a single small floating-leaved plant.

Light, power, water, maintenance. Light influences the blooming of **aquatics.** For **water lilies** and **lotus** to bloom fully, they must receive at least six hours of direct sun daily. Small tub and wall fountains need shade at noon to avoid

overheating. If your pond is to be aerated by a sun-powered fountain, the site must be in full sun.

If you plan to have an electrically-run pump to move water, the pond must be close enough to a power source and also within reach of a hose. For low maintenance, avoid sites that collect blown debris and leaves.

If your pond is to be an in-ground installation, make sure the site isn't home to buried electrical, gas, or water lines.

Drainage. Good drainage is necessary. Do not site a pond where puddles collect during wet periods because it may be heaved when the water table rises—with spring thaw and after big storms.

Where a site is lower than the surrounding land, be prepared to grade the area to avoid run-off water that will bring mud, grass, and weeds into the pond and contaminate it with residues from chemically-treated trees and grounds, roofing, spouting (fresh copper in particular), and petroleum from driveways.

Or, be prepared to create diversion channels to conduct the runoff away from the pond.

Land level matters. Site your pond on ground that is or can be leveled. A rock ledge can be a problem, but if it juts well above ground you may be able to use it as the base for a waterfall (see December).

Protection from predators. When choosing a site, avoid places popular with predators, notably raccoons. Scrambling for fish, they'll upset the plantings, not to mention the fish. They love *escargots naturel;* they pick the meat out, and leave the shells in a row on the edge.

PLANTING

You have time now to carefully study water garden plants and equipment in water garden catalogs. An **album of aquatic plants and materials**—liners, pumps, bubblers, fountains, and other accessories—comes in handy when choosing plantings for the pond. Make one up from catalog pages, and take it when you are shopping for pond materials at local garden centers.

CARE

Established pond. Rake dead leaves and other debris away from the edges of the pond to avoid having anything blow into the water.

You have time now to carefully study water garden plants and equipment in water garden catalogs.

Did You Know?

About Filters

A water garden that includes a pump usually—but not necessarily—has some sort of filtering device. Some small pumps handle solids without the help of a filter. Others you can encase in a home-made mesh basket to keep out larger bits of debris.

You need a filter if you are returning water to the pond via a fine spray nozzle and for larger ponds. How frequently the filter will need cleaning should be a consideration when you are choosing one. There are three main types:

1 **Mechanical filters.** For a small pond (say under 5 by 8 feet and holding 300 gallons of water), a small, inexpensive combination pump-and-filter is sufficient. These filters slip off and on easily for cleaning, likely to be a daily occurrence in hot weather. For ponds twice that size, a popular filtering system consists of a small pump connected by tubing to a velcro-fastened filter. This type likely needs cleaning every one to five days.

Pumps for large ponds (say 16 by 26 feet and holding 4,000 gallons of water) usually push the water through large filters outside the pond and may return it via a waterfall, a streambed, or/and a recirculating bog garden. These filters are likely to need maintenance every two to seven days.

2 **Biological filters.** A biological filter needs cleaning only a few times a month. The filter is a large or small gravel-filled cylinder installed outside the pond and screened by a waterfall, plantings, or decorative fencing. Filtering is done by bacteria that colonize layers of gravel. Though not inexpensive, costs balance out as biological filters are powered by inexpensive pumps and use less electricity.

3 **Recirculating bog garden.** The most effective filtering system for a large pond is one that pumps the water to a biological filter outside the pond and returns the water via a shallow recirculating bog garden and streambed or waterfall.

Break ice forming on the surface of the pond—gases from the pond must have an escape route.

 PRUNING

Established pond. Check on and maintain the moisture of the **tropical water lilies** and **bog plants** wintering indoors. Discard plants showing signs of rot.

 WATERING

Established pond. In warm areas, ponds kept active throughout the cold season may need additions of water as the weather turns mild.

 FERTILIZING

There is no fertilizing to do during this season.

 PESTS

If you see signs of scale or whitefly on the **tender aquatics** you brought indoors for the winter, rinse the stems and foliage at weekly intervals until the condition clears.

PLANNING

When the weather permits, visit sites you like for your water garden and try to visualize a shape that will be just right.

If your architecture and landscaping are formal, then consider a symmetrical shape form—an oval, a circle, a triangle, a square, or a rectangle. Plan to include a pump and to return the water to the pond through classical statuary—the human form or stylized metal frogs, for example. A tall stream of water also makes a formal statement.

If your architecture is casual and the landscaping naturalized, then consider an asymmetrical or a free-form pond design. In nature there's hardly a perfect curve or a straight line anywhere. Returning the water via a pump tumbling over piled-up rocks, a stream, or a bog garden would enhance the natural look.

In-ground ponds. When you have settled on a shape for your water garden, the next decision is size. The surface area and depth govern the number of gallons a pond will hold. That influences the size of the pump and filter and the number of plants and fish you can have.

Calculating the size of the pond. The pond size many find about right aesthetically and for maintenance is between 10 by 10 feet and 10 by 15 feet. Outline the shape you have chosen on the site with a hose or a string. Then measure the length and the width. Multiply the length by the width and that gives you the square footage of the surface. With that number you can figure out how many gallons it will hold (see Calculating Pond Measurements), and the number of gallons it holds influences many other choices.

To get the approximate size of a kidney-shaped or a free-form pond, outline it with a hose, then shape the hose into a square, a rectangle, or a combination of these shapes that encompasses the area, and measure the length and the width.

The usual pond depth is between 18 and 30 inches. Anything deeper may be classified as a pool and local regulations may require that you fence it. Bog gardens and streambeds are about a foot deep.

In Zone 6, fish are considered safe to overwinter in a pond 24 inches deep. In a large pond, the depth can be as little as 18 inches. In Zone 7, the fish are okay for winter in a pond 18 inches deep. In Zone 8, the fish stay all year, even in a small pond 18 inches deep.

Most pumps for in-ground ponds push or pull the water through a cleansing filtering system (see January). The number of gallons of water in the pond dictates the size of the filtering system and the power of the pump, and the number of gallons is determined by surface size. The farther and higher the water has to be pushed by the pump, the more powerful the pump needs to be. And, the more powerful the pump, the more it costs to buy and to operate.

Calculate the size and depth of your pond and the gallons it will hold, and your supplier will help you to choose suitable equipment.

PLANTING

Take cuttings or divide **tender bog plants** overwintering indoors.

CARE

In warm regions where the pump may have been running all winter, take it out and clean it.

The usual pond depth is between 18 and 30 inches. Anything deeper may be classified as a pool and local regulations may require that you fence it.

PRUNING

Established pond. Plants overwintering in the pond may be showing winter damage. Clear away damaged and dead foliage.

WATERING

Established pond. Continue to monitor the moisture in pond plants stored indoors last fall and replenish it if needed.

FERTILIZING

Established pond. When pond plants wintering indoors show signs of growth, fertilize them at half strength.

PESTS

Continue to check tender **aquatics** wintering indoors for signs of scale or whitefly. The remedy is to rinse the stems and foliage at weekly intervals until the condition clears.

Did You Know?

About Recirculating Pumps

The sound and movement of a water garden is created by a pump. The pump returns the water via a bubbler or a fountain and that aerates it. Or, the pump returns the water via a filter, a waterfall or streambed, and/or a recirculating bog garden.

The larger the pond and the farther the water has to be pushed, the more powerful the pump needs to be, and the more costly it will be to buy and to operate.

Small floating fountains powered by the sun are the easiest to install and maintain, ideal for small water features like wall fountains and tubs. They rest on islands of wiring encased in watertight containers. Sun power turns them on and sends up sprays or showers 8 to 24 inches high, depending on the strength of the unit. The largest solar fountains can move 60 gallons an hour!

The downside to this free energy and beauty is that when the sun doesn't shine, sun-powered pumps don't perform. You can't count on a sun-powered floating fountain to make magic in the moonlight.

Calculating Pond Measurements

To Calculate the Square Footage of the Pond Surface

• **Rectangle** length x width = square feet of surface

• **Circle** 3.14 x {$\frac{1}{2}$ the diameter x $\frac{1}{2}$ the diameter} = square feet of surface

To Calculate the Cubic Feet of Water in a Pond

• **Rectangle** length x width x depth = cubic feet

• **Circle** 3.14 x {$\frac{1}{2}$ the diameter x $\frac{1}{2}$ the diameter} x depth = cubic feet.

To Calculate the Gallons a Pond Holds

There are 7.5 gallons of water per cubic foot, so the number of cubic feet multiplied by 7.5 gallons = the number of gallons in the pond

PLANNING

You can install a good-sized in-ground pond in one weekend with just one helper. And if you have four or five strong backs and pairs of willing hands, you can do it in one day. **This month invite likely helpers to a mid-May pond installation picnic.** Plan to have the equipment delivered before the date chosen.

If you are planning to enhance your pond with a stream, a waterfall, or a flowing bog garden, prepare these elements before you buy the equipment.

Electrical source. To accommodate the line from the pump to its source of electricity, dig a trench 12 inches deep from the pond edge to the outlet. It must be at least 6 feet from the edge of the pond.

Have a licensed electrician install a weatherproof outlet for the pump. Any standard three-prong household electrical outlet will do, but it must have a ground fault circuit interrupter.

The electrical circuit must have reserve amp capacity beyond what is needed for the operation of the pump. This is especially important with pumps using more than 8 amps. Overload can cause the circuit breaker to turn off the current.

Equipment. Water garden kits simplify installation. Otherwise, for the day of the installation, plan to have on hand: the pond liner, pump and filter, and tubing to take the water from the pump to its point of return—bubbler, fountain, bog garden, waterfall, stream. If the liner is flexible rubber, it will need an underlay (old carpeting will do) and coarse builder's sand to level the liner. If you plan to edge the pond with flat coping stones, be sure to provide the stones and mortar to cement them in place; in the frost belt, you'll also need metal reinforcing strips or wire for the cement. Before you order the equipment, outline the pond on the site and take final measurements to make sure there will be no problems when the great day comes.

Preformed pond. With a string and stakes, outline the pond, **adding 2 inches all around** to allow for the sand that will buffer the liner. At either end, dig holes to make sure there are no hidden obstructions.

Flexible liner. At the site, outline the pond with string and stakes. For a rectangular or a square pond, use a carpenter's square to get the angles just right; for a circular pond, use a string tied to a central stake to outline the circle.

To determine the **width** of the liner, measure the outline at the widest point then add twice the depth to allow for the sides, **plus** 2 feet more to cover the edges of the ground around the pond. To determine the **length,** measure the maximum length, then add twice the depth, **plus** 2 feet more.

 PLANTING

Established pond. As the weather permits, clean up any flower beds around the water garden and plant hardy perennials.

Prepare for planting the **tropical water lilies** you overwintered. See Planting in the October pages for details.

 CARE

Established pond—frost belt. Clean the water garden pump and turn it on. Fertilize the soil in the containers of the perennials in the pond, and return them to their places in the water.

If you are not using a pump and filter, as the weather warms add a supplemental bacterial product to speed the decomposition of waste from fish and plants and to prevent the growth of detrimental algae.

 # PRUNING

If you are not using a pump and filter, as the weather warms **add a supplemental bacterial product to speed the decomposition of waste** from fish and plants and to prevent the growth of detrimental algae. Read the container directions and make a mental note about the timing of additional doses.

 # WATERING

Continue to monitor moisture in **bog plants** wintering indoors and the water levels over the **tropical water lily** tubers.

 # FERTILIZING

As the fish become active (when water temperature exceeds 44 degrees Fahrenheit), resume feeding them.

 # PESTS

Wild creatures are getting restless; keep an eye out for raccoons in a fishy mood.

Did You Know?

About Pond Liners

You can create a water garden in any almost container that is watertight and non-toxic, from a wall fountain to a half barrel to as large as you please.

The smallest container that is a suitable home for plants and fish is a round or oval kettle about 3 feet in diameter by 18 inches deep. That's enough to accommodate a couple of snails, two or three goldfish, one pretty little **water lily**—such as **'Dauben'** or the white pygmy **'Ermine'**—and the lovely **bog plant** we call **sweet flag.** A small electric pump and a bubbler would add a musical dimension and aerate the water.

Next in size are in-ground ponds waterproofed by preformed fiberglass pond liners that start at about 4 by 6 feet. They accommodate enough livestock and vegetation to keep a pond in balance; the snails, the fish, **submerged plants,** and a pair of **water lilies** like white **'Gonnere'** and **'Albida',** along with a small floating-leaved plant, and one or two marginal or **bog plants.**

The most popular water garden is an in-ground pond waterproofed by a sheet of flexible rubber about 10 by 10 feet. It accommodates snails, fish, five **water lilies,** one space-eating **lotus,** a few small-leaved floaters, and a few marginals.

Larger ponds, free-form ponds, bog gardens, and streams are all waterproofed with flexible rubber liners or fish grade PVC (polyvinyl chloride) rubber. Black pond liners give the pond a natural look; black reflects the sky and shows off the flowers and the fish.

APRIL

PLANNING

Mail-order suppliers deliver **aquatics** at about the right moment to plant them in your area; they must be stored in a cool shady place and kept wet. Most except **lotus** will hold for at least two weeks.

The formula in the sidebar gives the proportions of living elements needed to keep a pond in balance. A 10-by-10-foot pond with 100 square feet of surface (see February) can have sixty to seventy percent floating cover. A 20-by-50-foot pond is more beautiful with only a third of its surface covered.

This "magic formula" for stocking a pond and keeping it in balance was developed by Charles Thomas, former President of Lilypons Water Gardens, Buckeystown, Maryland. You can substitute a **lotus** for one large **water lily.**

PLANTING

Suppliers sell **aquatics** and **bog plants** already planted in pans or pails; catalogs often ship them bare root packed in moist materials. Plant hardy **aquatics** any time after the pond water is warm enough to work in comfortably, about 55

degrees Fahrenheit. Plant **tropical water lilies** after the pond water stays above 69 degrees Fahrenheit (see July, The Magnificent Lotus).

Plant the rhizomes and tubers in pans 6 to 8 inches deep that hold 9 to 20 or more quarts of soil, the larger the better. Extra growing room encourages multiple crowns and more flowers. Heavy garden soil, which garden centers sell bagged, is good for **aquatic plants.** Keep it free of peat, manures, vermiculite, and anything light that floats. Avoid commercial mixes. Optimum pH is 6.5 to 7.5. Push a fertilizer tablet for **aquatics** into the soil of each container.

Set tubers and rhizomes so the growing tips are just above the soil; set plants with crowns so the crown is an inch below the soil level. To keep the soil in place, cover it completely with $1/2$ inches of rinsed gravel $1/2$ to $3/4$ inches in diameter. Soak the planted containers, and keep them in bright shade and wet, until you are ready to place them in the pond. Be sure to pack the garden soil tightly into the container, so that once the potting is completed and the container has been topped with gravel it is brim full. Otherwise, when you submerge the container and the air in it is displaced with

water, you'll end up with a pot half full of soil, which isn't enough for the plants to perform to their greatest potential.

CARE

Established pond. Check the pH of the water, and if needed, adjust it to between pH 6.5 to 7.5, as recommended in the introduction to this chapter.

Lift and clean the filter, pump, and air pump, and return them to the pond.

Don't be alarmed if the pond water gets murky as air temperatures rise. Pond plants and critters will soon become active, and the water will clear.

PRUNING

Established pond. Lift out the **hardy perennials** and groom them. Check **aquatics** and **bog plants** that have been in their containers for two or three years and if they are crowded, divide them. Plants growing in large tubs can wait twice as long to be divided.

Prune and groom the **submerged plants** and repot them.

Don't be alarmed if the pond water gets murky as air temperatures rise. Pond plants and critters will soon become active, and the water will clear.

Did You Know?

Containers for Aquatic Plants

Aquatics and **bog plants** for a water garden (but not those for a flowing bog recirculating system) grow in soil in pans, pails, and tubs placed in the pond. The container sizes are measured in inches and quarts. Containers for **aquatics** do not have holes for drainage. When you are planting **bog plants** for the pond in containers for **aquatics,** make one or two nail holes in the bottoms.

Formula for Every 1 to 2 Square Feet of Pond Surface

- 1 bunch (6 stems) **submerged/oxygenating plants**

- 1 black Japanese snail

- 2 inches of fish for fish up to 6 inches long

- $1/10$ of a small, or medium-size, **water lily** (that is, 1 lily per 10 to 20 square feet)

- $1/3$ of a **marginal** or a small, floating-leaved plant (that is, 1 bog or marginal plant or 1 small-leaved floater for every 3 to 6 square feet)

- Here's a "for instance" for planting and stocking a pond about 10 by 10 feet, that is, 100 square feet of surface:

- 50 to 100 bunches of **submerged/oxygenating** plants

- 50 to 100 black Japanese snails

- 100 to 200 inches of fish in assorted sizes **up to 6 inches long**

- 5 to 10 **water lilies**

- 18 to 33 marginal and/or floating-leaved plants, 3 each of each variety chosen

 # WATERING

Established pond. When the water level falls below normal, **top the pond.** When adding tap water that includes chlorine, chloramine, or chlorine dioxide, follow label directions on a neutralizing agent to get rid of these elements.

 # FERTILIZING

Established pond. Push a bar of aquatic fertilizer into the soil in each container. Use a nitrogen-phosphate-potash formulation (NPK) of 10-14-8.

As fish become active, resume feeding them. If your water garden does not have a pump and filter, add a supplemental bacterial product to speed the decomposition of waste from fish and plants.

 # PESTS

Established pond. With spring warmth, insects become active. Moving water and hungry fish discourage insect development, and so do frogs. Add tadpoles if you foresee insect problems.

PLANNING

Before your pond installation party, review the pond equipment you have ordered, and lay out digging tools, a crowbar for rocks, shears, a tarp for the excavated soil, a 2-by-4-inch board the width of the pond, a carpenter's level, a tape measure, and cement blocks, bricks, slate, or treated wood to help level the edges.

Installation. The installation procedure goes about like this:

1 Digging the Pond:

Preformed pond. Following the outline created earlier (see March), excavate a hole that will fit the preformed liner.

Flexible liner. Following the outline created earlier (see March), dig a hole 15 to 30 inches deep and in the center create a trough 1 inch deep and 18 inches across. If the soil is firm, slope the sides at a 75 degree angle; if it crumbles, slope the sides at a 45 degree angle.

2 Leveling the excavation:

Flexible liner and preformed pond: Center a 2-by-4-inch board across the hole and check the level of the rims, then make them even. Flatten high spots. Use sand to raise spots that are low by less than 2 inches. To raise areas more than 2 inches low, use cement blocks, bricks, slate, or treated wood covered with sand.

3 Creating a pond rim:

Preformed pond and flexible liner. To prepare for the edging that will be installed later, cut the sod around the pond into strips 10 inches wide and 12 to 15 inches long. Without detaching the strips from the lawn, roll them up gently away from the pond.

4 Placing the liner:

Preformed pond. Line the bottom of the excavation with an inch of sand. Place the pond so the rim is just above ground level. Check and adjust the level of the rim to within 1/4 inch.

Flexible liner. Line the bottom of the excavation with an inch of sand, then cover the sand with the underlayment. Open the liner, and gently spread it over the underlayment. If you find the liner heavy, fold it in fourths and unfold it from inside the excavation. Smooth the liner, pushing the excess up over the rim of pond.

5 Filling the pond:

Preformed pond. Begin filling the pond, and as the water level rises, pack sand (or soil) behind the sides of the form. Keep the pressure inside and outside similar by adding sand or soil at a rate matching the rise of the water level so the form doesn't buckle.

Liner pond. Fill the pond to within 1 inch of the top. Cut the surplus liner off leaving an overlap of 6 to 12 **extra** inches all around. Smooth the overlap over the dirt around the pond, and nail it firmly in place using 4- to 6-inch spike nails (no other kind).

6 Edging the pond:

If you'd like to edge the pond with sod, scratch up and fertilize the soil you stripped of sod in Step 3, then roll the grass strips back and firm them in place.

If you plan to edge the pond with coping stones (stones used for the flat topmost layer of a stone wall), cut off and discard the sod strips. To protect the liner, place the coping stones so they extend 1 to 2 inches over the rim of the pond. Use mortar to keep them in place. In the **frost belt,** use metal reinforcing rods or wire inside a 2- to 3-inch mortar base. Use as little mortar as possible so the stone looks natural. Check the level of the stones often as you work.

After the mortar has dried, clean the stones with a stiff brush and a mixture of 1 part ordinary vinegar to 1 part water or muriatic acid and water, and

Did You Know?

About Submerged/Oxygenating Plants

Submerged plants are included among pond plantings to gobble the nutrients feeding undesirable algae and to add oxygen. Four available from most suppliers are: **Anacharis** (*Elodea canadensis* var. *gigantea*); **dwarf saggitaria** (*Sagittaria subulata*); *Myriophyllum* species; **Washington Grass** (*Cabomba caroliniana*).

The plants are usually sold in bunches of six stems about 6 inches long. Growing in sand-filled pans set on the pond bottom, they quickly develop stems 2 to 3 feet long. Allow 6 square inches of container surface for every bunch of submerged plants, and use a separate container for each variety. To plant, take off the rubber bands, and gently press the ends of each bunch 2 inches into the sand. Add sand to within an inch of the rim, and top that with rinsed gravel. Water the containers to displace trapped air. Never fertilize—their job is to take nutrients from the water.

Koi and goldfish over 6 inches can nibble the submerged plants to death. Cover the pans with plastic mesh domes; the plants grow through the mesh and the fish graze without harming the roots. You can make your own dome using a plastic mesh sold by aquatics suppliers.

rinse thoroughly. Drain the pond, and refill it with fresh water.

 PLANTING

Instructions for planting and stocking the pond are given in June, Planting.

CARE

Established pond. Clear the filter as often as suggested by the manufacturer.

PRUNING

You can help keep the pond healthy if you **promptly remove yellowing and** **dying vegetation**, as well as spent blooms.

 WATERING

Restore the level of the pond water any time it shows a measurable dip.

 FERTILIZING

As long as the water temperature remains under 75 degrees Fahrenheit, fertilize **lotus** and **water lilies** monthly.

Take care not to get lawn chemicals and clippings into the pond when you are fertilizing and mowing.

 PESTS

If you do not have a pump and filter to help keep an excess of algae from developing, apply a supplemental bacterial product to speed the decomposition of waste from fish and plants.

Fish should be enough to keep insects to a minimum. If not, add tadpoles. **Pesticides and herbicides aren't recommended** around ponds.

Control grass and weeds growing into the pond from the edging.

Add a pellet to kill mosquito larvae.

JUNE
Water and Bog Plants

PLANNING

The beauty of your water garden depends in part on its setting. Here are some suggestions:

Pot, tub, or barrel water garden. Surround the container with potted plants of different heights.

Formal pond. Plant **boxwood, roses,** or **Japanese maples** in the background of a pond that is symmetrical, oval, circle, triangle, square, or a long narrow rectangle. Repeat the dominant color of the pond flowers in the plantings around it.

Naturalized pond. Use native plants found near water in the setting—**reeds, native shrubs, dogwoods,** and, in shaded areas, **ferns, green mosses, Solomon's-seal.**

Free-form pond. Use Japanese-style garden ornaments with a kidney-shaped or free-form water garden—a **dwarf ornamental cherry, dwarf azaleas, Siberian irises, quilted hostas, ferns, mosses,** and **forest flowers.**

PLANTING

Before placing fish and other wildlife in a new pond, allow the water a couple of weeks to de-chlorinate and warm.

The plants can go into the pond any time after it is filled. **Aquatics** need a specific amount of water overhead, and the amount is indicated in mail-order catalogs and on plant tags. Some can rest on the bottom of the pond, while others will need to be raised on platforms that can be made of stones, clean bricks, and weathered cement blocks. Avoid new cement blocks because they raise the water pH. When wet, plant containers can be heavy, so slide and float them to their destinations.

The **submerged plants** are set out first, at a depth of 1 to 2 feet. Next, set out the **large floating-leaved plants.** Allow several feet between **water lily** and **lotus** containers. Place the **small floaters** next. Group the pond **bog plants** on the far side of the pond 1 to 2 feet apart.

Plant the plants for a recirculating bog garden in the gravel on the bottom, with a ball of soil around the roots and about $1/2$ to 1 inch of water overhead.

CARE

Clear the filter as often as necessary to keep the pump free. If the filter becomes clogged, the water flowing back to the pond will slow or stop.

If you do not have a pump and filter, add a supplemental bacterial product to speed the decomposition of waste from fish and plants.

Keep fertilizer carts and lawn mowers far from the pond rim to avoid getting chemicals and grass clippings into the water.

New pond. If you have mortared the coping stones around the pond rim, check the pH of the water, which may be affected by runoff from the mortar. If the pH is way up, particularly after the first couple of rains, adjust it as directed in the introduction to this chapter.

PRUNING

Remove yellowing leaves and dead flowers, leaving nothing to decay.

If strands of the **submerged plants** elongate and become puny, raise the containers to positions where they receive more direct sunlight. When they're 8 inches tall and growing well, you can cut them back or divide them and make more plants. Just break off the top 5 or 6 inches, press the ends into a container filled with sand, and place it in the pond.

If strands of the submerged plants elongate and become puny, raise the containers to positions where they receive more direct sunlight.

Did You Know?

Adjusting the Water pH

Livestock will do best in water with a pH between 6.5 and 7.5. Before putting fish or livestock into a new or recently dechlorinated pond, use a pH tester to take the pH readings for three days running. Mornings, the water is nearest neutral. If the pH is too high, use a pH reducer such as AlkaMinus to lower it. If it is too low, use AlkaPlus to raise it. You also can raise pH with baking soda; for each 100 gallons of water add one teaspoonful of soda each day until the water test is satisfactory.

Most water gardeners don't have pH problems, but to be on the safe side check it now and then. An excess of fish and fish food create more ammonia than plants absorb, which can raise the pH of the water up to and over 8.0. The solution is to correct the condition and to cut back on fish and fish food. If the fish become lethargic but show no sign of disease, that can be a sign the pH is off.

A Caution About Submerged/Oxygenating Plants

Two beautiful but **extremely invasive plants** that rob algae of nutrients are illegal where they survive winters—**water hyacinth,** and **water lettuce.** They multiply rapidly in climates where they live through the winter, get into the waterways, and clog them.

Federal statute forbids the shipment of **water hyacinth** in interstate commerce.

Harvesting Water Lilies

Water lilies last three or four days as cut flowers if they're picked early the first day they open. To pick a **water lily,** plunge your arm down the stem and pinch off a foot of the plant.

Arrange **hardy water lilies** in water that reaches within an inch of the base of the flower; set **tropical water lilies** so the water is within 3 inches of the base of the flower.

To stop water lilies from closing at night, drop hot wax onto the base of each flower petal. The wax will keep the petals from closing when bedtime comes.

WATERING

Maintain the water level of the pond.

FERTILIZING

When the water temperature is over 75 degrees Fahrenheit, fertilize **lotus** and **water lilies** twice monthly. Fertilize the pond **bog plants** monthly, if they are not growing well. Do not fertilize the plants in the recirculating bog system or the **submerged plants;** their job is to starve out the nutrients that feed unwanted algae.

PESTS

Weed around and between the coping stones.

Add a pellet that kills mosquito larvae. Avoid pesticides and herbicides around the pond.

JULY
Water and Bog Plants

 PLANNING

Ask your aquatics supplier to recommend a biological or microbial product to suppress **algae** that turn the water a murky green or green-brown. These products control algae by speeding up the decomposition of the fish and plant waste on which unwanted algae feed.

Algae can be beneficial, but some are not. **The three main algae** are a good-guy, moss-like clinging algae, and two other not-good guys—a floating surface type and a drifter. The good-guy clinging algae mosses the stones and the sides of the pond with beautiful deep-green filaments, and fuzzes plant stems and snail shells. Welcome it. You can control the unwanted floating type by raising the water level and pushing it off the surface with a broom. Biological products keep them all in check.

 PLANTING

The sun changes positions throughout the year, and it can happen that your pond ends up with more shade at certain times than you anticipated. **Shade may be the culprit** if **water lilies** and **lotus are failing to bloom up to expectation.** You can solve the problem by replacing sun-lovers with water lilies that bloom with 4 to 6 hours of direct sun. Among them are the very popular hardy **water lilies 'Charlene Strawn',** which is yellow, **'Virginia',** a white, and red **'James Brydon'.**

A few **tropical water lilies** also bloom with less sun. Along them are: **'Albert Greenberg',** a rose-tinged gold that does well in any pond over 4 feet and blooms longer than other tropicals; **'Director George Moore',** a compact tropical with magnificent deep blue flowers; and **'Panama Pacific',** blue tinged with red, which grows small or large according to the space available.

Several tropical **bog plants** also succeed in partial sun, including **elephant's-ear** and **taro,** species of *Colocasia,* and several species of **papyrus,** *Cyperus,* including **umbrella plant.** These are all tender perennials in our region.

 CARE

Clear the filter. If you do not have a pump and filter, add a supplemental bacterial product to speed the decomposition of waste from fish and plants.

When thunderstorms come close, turn off the pond pump to avoid attracting lightning.

Pinch off yellowing leaves and dead flowers as they occur. **Water lilies** are continually putting out new leaves and stretching them outward as more arise. As they fade, get rid of them.

 PRUNING

Deadhead the flowering plants, and immediately remove yellowing and decaying vegetation.

 WATERING

Now that the high heat of summer is here, **check and adjust the water level** of your pond daily, especially when the day is hot, dry, and windy.

If your water is heavily chlorinated, and you are adding as much as 10 percent to the volume of the pond—if it's down as much as 2 inches, for instance—add a 10 percent solution of a de-chlorinator when you top it.

Lawn sprinklers have little effect on pond water unless their spray drips into the pond from foliage that's been treated with herbicides or pesticides. You want to avoid that.

FERTILIZING

When the water temperature rises above 75 degrees Fahrenheit, fertilize the **water lilies** and the **lotus** twice monthly.

PESTS

Add a pellet that kills mosquito larvae.

Get rid of grass and weeds growing into the pond from the edging, but avoid pesticides and herbicides near the pond.

Did You Know?

The Magnificent Lotus

The **lotus** is an extraordinary plant. The large pointed bud rises above the water on a stem 2 to 6 feet tall, and unfolds an enormous perfumed blossom. Colors are lush shades and combinations of white, pink, red, yellow, and cream. For three days the lotus blossom opens mornings before the **water lilies,** and closes at tea time. The third day the petals fall, leaving the seedpod that is sought after for dried arrangements. It looks like the spout of a watering can, or ET, the movie character.

Mail-order suppliers ship lotus tubers bare root the few weeks in spring when the rootstock is in tuber form. Later the tubers send out runners and atrophy, which makes planting impossible. They can be planted as soon as the water temperature is in the 40s or above.

Use pans 16 to 24 inches in diameter, 9 to 10 inches deep, for standard lotus; miniatures make do with half to two-thirds this size. Set the tubers 2 inches under the soil with the top half inch of the growing tip above the soil (see April, Planting). Place the pans in the pond with 2 to 3 inches of water overhead; they bloom sooner in shallow water.

Two or three weeks after being planted, a lotus sends up a first set of floating leaves. They look like lily pads without the notch. A second set of leaves rises and opens high above the water. The leaves of miniature lotus are 6 to 16 inches across, and the stems are 2 to 3 feet tall; standard lotus leaves can be 2 feet wide, and the stem the height of a tall person—6 feet.

PLANNING

Goldfish usually live ten to fifteen years unless they encounter a predator. When you go on vacation, you won't have to plan to have the fish and other pond creatures to be fed in your absence. In a balanced pond (see the April sidebar), the fish feed on the **submerged plants,** on the moss-like algae on the sides of the pond, and on the insects and larvae you do want to be rid of. Your pond might be clearer when you come back because you haven't been feeding the fish.

PLANTING

Now that your pond plants are maturing, keep an eye out for those that can be, or need to be, divided.

You can plant or transplant container-grown and rooted hardy **water lilies,** and many **bog plants,** from early spring until a few weeks prior to the first killing frost. Water lilies that are moved while blooming just sulk a bit.

Water lilies need dividing when they become crowded. The blossoms of **water lilies** like '**Virginia**' and '**Charlene Strawn**' usually stand an inch or two above the water; when their pads also are held high (and the rhizomes are 12 or more inches under water), that's a sign the plants will need dividing next spring before growth begins.

Lotus tubers are shipped bare root in spring in plastic bags containing moist materials. They're almost as easy to grow as **water lilies,** but they can be transplanted only during the few weeks in spring when the rootstock is in tuber form. When the rootstock puts out runners, the tubers atrophy, and transplanting is virtually impossible.

Irises can be divided any time after they bloom, including **Japanese irises,** such as *Iris kaempferi, I. laevigata* '**Variegata,**' the big **yellow flag,** *I. pseudacorus* and the **Louisiana hybrid irises.**

CARE

When thunderstorms threaten, turn off the pump.

Clean the filter consistently. It's apt to clog more often this time of the year. If you do not have a pump and filter, add a supplemental bacterial product to speed the decomposition of waste from fish and plants.

Monitor the pond as the trees begin to shed their first leaves, and remove leaves and debris from the pond daily.

PRUNING

The submerged plants may need pruning and division. **If you are losing the open water to the summer growth of small- and large-leaved floating plants, cut it back enough** to keep about a third of the water surface clear.

Deadhead consistently, and remove yellowing and decaying foliage.

WATERING

When the water level of the pond falls below its normal height, top the pond. If you are adding more than an inch of tap water to the pond—water that includes chlorine, chloramine, or chlorine dioxide—**add a de-chlorinating chemical** according to the label directions for neutralizing these elements.

When the water level of the pond falls below its normal height, top the pond.

Did You Know?

Attracting Wildlife

In a city, a pond 2 feet by 3 feet is enough to attract songbirds, butterflies, and dragonflies, though it's minimal space for frogs.

In less urban settings, a secluded pond 10 by 10 feet and up attracts small animals such as deer, fox, raccoons, possums, and uplands game birds. In wild mountain terrain, a large pond will draw in all sorts of native animals.

Site your pond where you can watch nervous visitors and not be seen. Stock the pond with native minnows and small goldfish rather than showy koi, which attract predators, especially raccoons. If you want showy fish, do without a filter that keeps the water clear. Or, add a black dye (see November), which is used to limit visibility and make the water look deep and inviting; there are no bad side effects.

Make the area safe for birds. If there are cats around, provide a high observation post 6 to 8 feet from the pond for the birds. It can be a tree, or shrubbery that screens them from hawks. Birds like a clear a path to the water—a high-up branch far away, then one closer and lower, then a landing site at the pond, a broad stone for example. Plant berried shrubs, and let **pines** and **hemlocks** grow tall to provide nesting places, materials, and safe perches.

 FERTILIZING

Fertilize **water lilies** and **lotus** in ponds in Zones 7 and 8 early this month.

Hardy plants rooted in a recirculating bog should be taking all the nutrients they can use from the water. However, some may be more aggressive than others; cut these back, and push a half-strength dose of fertilizer into the soil of the containers of less successful plants.

In Zone 6, **aquatics** will be shutting down soon and should not be fertilized after August 1.

 PESTS

Add a pellet that kills mosquito larvae.

If your **aquatic plants** begin to have a chewed look at the edges, look for little brown snails, and remove them by hand.

Pull out grass and weeds growing into the pond from the edging.

If night raiders are visiting your pond, cover it with screens at night. Or, install a grid of broad mesh fencing that the fish can dive through to evade marauders. Less colorful fish attract fewer predators.

PLANNING

In our region, **fall is an important planting season.** Make time now to evaluate the effect of the plants in your water garden and around the pond. Consider additions that will increase your pleasure in your pond. For inspiration, study the album of **aquatic plants** you made from the pages of mail-order catalogs back in January.

 PLANTING

You can divide **spring-blooming hardy bog perennials** successfully any time during the next few weeks.

In the beds that create the setting around your pond, hardy perennials can be divided up to a month before the ground is expected to freeze and in early spring before new growth begins. The rule of thumb for **autumn-flowering** perennials is to divide them in early spring, before any sign of growth appears.

Most perennials benefit from division. If you want more plants to fill out or enlarge the beds, check out those that been in the ground two years—if they are growing well it's okay to divide them.

The next four to six week are first rate for planting and transplanting trees and shrubs. Consider adding an evergreen to the setting for your pond. **Gold-dust tree,** *Aucuba japonica*, gets tall enough here to make a handsome backdrop. The **weeping hemlock** is a dark evergreen that stays low for years. For fun, add three baby **boxwoods** pruned to globe shape.

Deciduous trees and shrubs add structure and a more open look to a pond setting. A **Sargent crabapple** (6 to 10 feet high) in bloom beside a pond is lovely. For summer bloom, plant a miniature **crapemyrtle** such as **'Chickasaw';** for late summer bloom plant the hardy hibiscus **'White Chiffon'.** You can keep the **crapemyrtles** and **shrub althea** at shrub height by trimming them back before growth begins in early spring.

 CARE

Continue to keep the pond filter clear. If you do not have a pump and filter, add a supplemental bacterial product to speed the decomposition of waste from fish and plants.

Remove leaves that fall into the water at once. If there are deciduous trees near the pond, when the first leaves begin to fall, cover the surface with bird netting. Keep the netting in place until all the leaves have fallen and been cleared away.

Fish in Zone 6 and cool Zone 7. When the water temperature falls below 55 degrees Fahrenheit, any tubs, half-barrels, and water gardens less than 30 inches deep are likely to become too cold for the fish. You have two solutions; set the fish free in a large pond, a stream, or a lake; or bring them indoors to a fish tank for the winter. In any case, stop feeding them (see October).

PRUNING

Continue to deadhead flowering pond plants, and clear away yellowing and dead foliage as soon as you spot it. Rotting foliage may incubate pests and diseases over the winter months.

Keep an eye on the annuals and discard them when they are played out.

In our region, fall is an important planting season. Make time now to evaluate the effect of the plants in your water garden and around the pond.

Did You Know?

Attracting Butterflies and Hummingbirds

It takes just a few nectar-bearing plants in the pond area to attract butterflies and hummingbirds, and fall is a good time to plant those that are hardy perennials.

Butterflies fly down to showy plantings of brilliant blooms—purple, yellow, orange, and red. They hover over flowers that have flat-topped or short, open-mouthed tubular blossoms that make landing platforms. Single rather than double flowered types make gathering nectar easier for them.

The number one attraction for butterflies is the **butterfly bush,** *Buddleia davidii.* It bears graceful flower spikes on new wood, so if it doesn't die to the ground in your climate, before growth begins in early spring, cut it back. Other butterfly magnets are **butterfly weed,** *Asclepias tuberosa,* a sweetly scented perennial, and *Lantana camara,* which is grown as an annual in our cooler regions. **Passion flower,** *Passiflora,* a flowering tropical vine, is popular with these beautiful flying acrobats.

Hummingbirds spend their days looking for the food necessary to fuel their amazing energy output. Their primary diet is nectar, rounded out with tiny insects. They rely on sight, not scent, to locate nectar, and go to many of the flowers that attract butterflies. Some that do well in part sun are **pentas, impatiens, red cardinal flower,** and **beebalm.**

 ## WATERING

Keep track of the water level in your pond, and bring it back to normal as often as it falls.

 ## FERTILIZING

Monitor the changing water temperature—when it falls below 75 degrees Fahrenheit, stop fertilizing the plants.

 ## PESTS

Where fall is warm, if mosquitoes are a concern, add a mosquito larvae control pellet.

As the foliage in the pond collapses with the cold, colorful fish become more obvious to predators. The bird netting recommended in the Care section of this month to keep leaves out of the pond also affords some protection for the fish and snails.

OCTOBER
Water and Bog Plants

 PLANNING

In **frost-free regions,** a water garden in a sheltered spot can likely go right on all winter without missing a beat—pump, fish, plants, and all, although there will be fewer flowers.

In the **frost belt** as the thermometer plummets, the foliage and flowers of the pond plants begin to subside, a signal the season is over. Now you must evaluate what to discard and what to keep. If the growth of the small floating-leaved plants is invasive, discard a few. At the end of the season, many pond owners discard the less costly cold-tender **pond bog plants,** saving limited indoor winter storage space for the most valuable.

If your **tropical water lilies** grew from tubers you saved last year, decide now whether their performance this year makes saving them worth the effort.

 PLANTING

When nights are below 65 degrees Fahrenheit, **bring the most valuable tender pond bog plants indoors to save them** for next year. They thrive set in pans filled with an inch of wet pea gravel in a big south-facing window. Keep the soil moist. During the darkest months of the year, supplement the daylight with fluorescent light.

In the **frost belt** when the **tropical water lilies** stop blooming many owners discard them and start fresh next year. But it's possible to collect and save the tubers. Here's how:

1 A week or so after a killing frost, lift the rootstock, and gently wash off as much soil as you can.

2 Pick off one or more tubers, air dry them for two days, and then remove the remaining soil.

3 Store them in jars of distilled water, in a cool closet at about 55 degrees Fahrenheit.

4 In late winter, two months before the pond water temperature will warm to 70 degrees Fahrenheit, bring the tubers out and set them to sprout in a pan of water in a sunny window.

5 When the pond temperature reaches a constant 69 degrees Fahrenheit, replant the tubers and return them to the pond. They should bloom two to three months later.

 CARE

To keep falling leaves from getting into the pond, cover it with bird netting. It's black and not very visible.

A biological filter (see January) needs a thorough cleaning at the end of the growing season.

Discard played-out annuals. Cut back the **submerged/oxygenating plants.** Clear away fading vegetation. Dying organic matter in the pond will decay producing toxic levels of methane gases that harm the fish and the hardy perennials staying on for winter.

In the **frost belt**, slide the cold-hardy **water lily** and the **pond bog plant** containers to the deepest spot in the pond for the winter. The water will be warmest there.

 PRUNING

Keep any plants still in the pond clear of decaying foliage and spent flowers. Cut back the **submerged plants.**

When nights are below 65 degrees Fahrenheit, bring the most valuable tender pond bog plants indoors to save them for next year.

Did You Know?

Feeding the Fish

Fish gobble larvae and insects and nibble plants, so it's not necessary to feed them. But they're fun to feed. Once they know you they will come as you approach and make their interest in food obvious.

The fish in a well-balanced pond may not need feeding, but fish that aren't fed remain wild. They will hide when you are there, by vanishing behind submerged plants or under lily pads. Feeding creates a relationship fairly rapidly with the goldfish and koi—golden orfe are less responsive.

To make friends with your fish, the first days they are in a pond, let them find their own food. Then, at a time of day you can come regularly to the pond, relax next to the water and lean over the pond for a minute or so. Then gently drop a pinch of fish flakes onto the water. The first few times you drop in food they'll wait till you are gone to come up for it. But eventually they'll come when you are there and even be at the surface before you feed them.

Feed fish only as much as they eat in five minutes. Extra fish food and waste loads the water with more nutrients than the plants can absorb. The result is a green growth called algae bloom that uses up nitrogen then dies, consuming oxygen faster than the water can absorb it from the air. Lacking oxygen, the fish die. The bigger fish die first. Smaller fish tolerate water with low oxygen content longer.

Fish eat more in hot weather and again in the fall as they stoke up for winter dormancy. When the water temperature drops to 55 degrees Fahrenheit, their body processes slow as they become dormant and they can no longer digest the food.

WATERING

Maintain the water level of the pond for the sake of the fish and the plants overwintering there.

FERTILIZING

There is no fertilizing to do at this season.

PESTS

When raccoons and other little mammals are getting ready to nap for winter they become very interested in food.

With the vegetation fading or gone from the pond, the fish are more visible. If you see a lot of critter activity, cover the pond with bird netting to discourage fishing expeditions.

NOVEMBER
Water and Bog Plants

PLANNING

As winter approaches, plan to find time to prepare the pond for the cold season. If the pump is not hard-wired into its electrical source, unplug it and lift it. Clean it and store it indoors. If it can't be unplugged, take the pump out of the pond, flush it with clean water, and return it to the pond. In warm regions, you can turn it back on.

In the **frost belt** the pump must not go on in winter. Here's why: in summer the coolest water is at the bottom of the pond, but in winter the warmest water is in the bottom and that's where fish gather. If the pump goes on, the bottom will get cooler and the fish will suffer.

A large pond **benefits from cleaning** every two or three years. Small pond and water features need annual cleaning. Plan to begin after the pond plants have subsided and all the tree leaves have been cleared away.

1 Begin by filling a large container with pond water as a temporary home for the pond livestock. Use the pump and a hose to spill the water out over nearby garden plants; it's rich in nutrients.

2 When the water is almost gone, net the fish, snails, and other livestock and place them in their temporary home. Cover it to keep the fish from jumping out.

3 Slide the plant containers from the water, and cover them with moist newspaper.

4 Use a plastic scoop to remove the organic waste from the pond bottom. Use a hose and sponges to clear algae and clean the sides.

5 Refill the pond. If the water includes chlorine, use a de-chlorinating agent to prepare the water for the return of the critters.

6 Gradually blend enough of the fresh pond water into the fish container to bring its temperature down so the fish will have acclimated to the new temperature in the pond before you return them to it.

7 Clean and groom the plants. If you are in a **frost-free region** fertilize the pond plants and return them to their accustomed places.

8 If you are in the **frost belt** slide the winter-hardy plants to the deepest spot in the pond and submerge them.

PLANTING

In the **frost belt,** hardy **water lilies** stored in water **below ice level** can live through winter. If the winter is hard and the pond isn't deep enough to escape ice even its lowest point, move the **water lilies** in their pans to a frost-free garage or a root cellar. Cover each with damp newspaper, and wrap it in a plastic bag. Check the rhizomes now and then—don't let them dry out.

CARE

If you have covered the pond with bird netting to keep falling leaves out, you can remove it as soon as they all have fallen and been removed. But keep the netting on if the pond is attracting the attention of wild visitors like raccoons and herons.

In the **frost belt** if fish are going to winter in your pond, stop feeding them when the thermometer drops to 45 degrees Fahrenheit. They will go dormant and can winter safely in the deepest part of ponds 30 inches deep. If they are disturbed, they'll swim a bit, then go back to their rest.

As winter approaches, plan to find time to prepare the pond for the cold season.

Did You Know?

Frogs in the Pond

Frogs are a water garden's very good friend and charming ornament. In the tadpole stage, they do a fine job of clearing up leftover fish food and undesirable algae. Those that make it to froghood are a huge help with mosquito control.

Frogs sleep winter buried in mud around the edges of your pond. If your water garden includes a recirculating bog garden, they likely will winter in the gravelly muck at the bottom.

The only trouble with frogs is you get fond of them, and they are independent creatures that may not stay, especially when rainy weather invites them to venture abroad. But if they are happy in your pond, they will make babies and in time may provide a frog chorus that will add greatly to your evening pleasure.

Black Water Is Beautiful

A black dye sold by water garden suppliers is the magic that gives a velvety black look to the water gardens in many public gardens, including the National Aquatic Gardens at the U.S. National Arboretum in Washington, DC. The inky surfaces mirror the sky, mask the algae, and the **water lilies** stand out beautifully while the fish seem to float in and out of a mysterious deep.

The vegetable-based dye doesn't kill the algae, but it does hide it.

The label on the dye container tells how much to use. The proportions don't change with regional temperature or the contents of the water. After you've used the dye a few times, you'll know how much you want to put in. It's safe for pets and wildlife that may come there to drink.

 PRUNING

In warm regions where water garden plants may remain active over the winter, it is necessary to continue to deadhead the few flowers that bloom and to remove decaying foliage. In the **frost belt** groom bog plants wintering indoors.

 WATERING

Any time the water level of the pond falls below its normal height, top it.

 FERTILIZING

There's no fertilizing to do at this season.

 PESTS

Raccoons spend winter in a den, sleeping but not hibernating. Be aware that in warm periods they're up and about, and they're good fishermen.

December
Water and Bog Plants

 PLANNING

Now, with the gift-giving season near, is a fine time to plan ways to make your water garden more interesting next year.

If you put together an album of catalog pages showing garden equipment such as liners, pumps, bubblers, fountains, and other accessories, look through it for inspiration. Santa may be pleased to know of your interest.

Adding a waterfall. If you're considering changing the configuration of the pond, perhaps by adding a waterfall, this is a good time to start it.

 PLANTING

In warm regions where there is still a month before the first frosts are expected, there's time to divide hardy **water lilies** and pond **bog plants.**

 CARE

In **frost-free regions,** keep the pump and filter in place and working through the winter. At the coolest moment in winter, give the biological filter a thorough cleaning.

In the **frost belt,** if your pond is likely to develop a thin coat of ice now and then and you are keeping fish and plants there for the winter, plan to cover the pond until the danger of frost is past.

You can offset frosts by covering the pond with a couple of 2-by-4 boards with a tarp or canvas over them. If you don't think that will be enough to stop the surface from freezing, cover the tarp with a 3-inch layer of leaves held in place with netting. Secure the edges with rocks so the arrangement can withstand winter winds. Allow a small open space on the down side of the prevailing winds for ventilation. **Don't seal the pond.** Gases from the pond must have an escape route, and fresh air must be available.

Where it is likely **ice** will cover the pond surface for more than three or four consecutive days, install a floating de-icer. A little ice isn't bad, but ice that covers the surface for days on end keeps the pond from breathing. The surface of the water takes from the atmosphere the oxygen your pond creatures need and disperses gases released by organic decay and carbon dioxide wastes built up by animal life. The exchange can't take place while ice covers the surface.

A de-icer is a simple heating element attached to a flotation device. The best de-icers are equipped with thermostats so they turn themselves on only when warmth is needed. The most popular are rated at 1500 watts. Float the de-icer only during the weeks or months that it is needed and always in conjunction with a ground fault circuit interrupter.

 PRUNING

In warm regions, continue to deadhead and clear dying foliage from lilies and bog plants throughout the winter.

 WATERING

Keep track of the water level in your pond, and bring it back to normal as often as necessary.

 FERTILIZING

There's no fertilizing to do at this season.

 PESTS

Raccoons and other intrepid fishermen are the only likely pests this time of the year.

Mid-Atlantic gardens, like gardens everywhere, can host problems. In this section, we give you an overview of some of the pests you might encounter and how to control them.

COMMON INSECT PESTS AND CONTROLS

Many factors play a role in how light or heavy your insect problems will be.

1 The presence of natural parasites and predators cuts down on pests and diseases.

2 Dry or wet seasons encourage certain problems.

3 Very cold winters can reduce insect populations.

By choosing pest- and disease-resistant plants that thrive in our climate, and by being faithful to the healthy garden practices we recommend, you can avoid many of the most common problems in the Mid-Atlantic—spider mites, whitefly, Japanese beetles, blackspot, mildew, rust, and nematodes.

What you can't avoid, try to control. Identify the problem and apply controls early in the developmental cycle, not late. The development stage of each species is affected greatly by warm early seasons and cool late seasons. Just as the growth of the plant on which an insect or disease preys is delayed or stimulated by the weather, so is the insect affected.

Keep an eye on plants that hosted problems in previous years. The colder the zone and the season, the later the infestation will come. Blackspot, mildew, mites, whitefly, Japanese beetles will appear earlier in gardens in Zone 8 of Tidewater Virginia than in

yards in Zones 6 and 7. Gardeners in the warmer climates may face more broods of insects per year.

Various controls are appropriate for certain stages in the development of various pests and diseases. Here's an outline:

• With aphids, leafhoppers, earwigs, thrips, crickets, grasshoppers, scale, and similar insects, the metamorphosis to adulthood is simple: All stages of larvae and adults are similar to each other and all feed on the host plant. The egg hatches and there is a series of nymphs, which shed their skin (molting), getting larger each time until the final adult stage. A little cricket molts and molts, and becomes a large adult cricket. You use the same control from beginning to end of the cycle.

• For other creatures, metamorphosis requires an egg stage, a larval stage, a pupal stage (resting stage), and then there is a miraculous transformation into a very different adult.

• With some insects such as beetles, the grub stage feeds on the roots of plants, and the adult beetle feeds on the leaves, stems, and flowers of the host plant.

• In the case of moths and butterflies, nectar feeds only the adult butterfly. For the larval stage—the caterpillar—most butterfly species must locate a specific host plant because the caterpillar would die rather than eat anything else. After mating, a female butterfly flutters slowly near plants, touching down and tasting them through organs on her front legs. When she finds a plant acceptable for her kind, she will deposit one or more eggs, and

then wander off looking for other host plants.

Here is a list of common insect pests and their controls:

Aphids. Aphids attack a wide range of plants. Small, pear-shaped insects, they have piercing, sucking mouthparts, and in some cases can transmit diseases. The symptoms of aphid damage are the stunting and deformation of leaves and stems. Aphids produce enormous amounts of a sugary, sticky, honey-like substance called honeydew. A black fungus quickly spreads on the honeydew and slows down photosynthesis. This fungus is called sooty mold. *Controls: Aphids usually can be sprayed off with a strong jet of water from a hose. Repeat if they return. If they persist, try a soap-based insecticide or products with malathion or pyrethrin. Some biological controls are green lacewings, lady beetles, and aphid lions. Some natural controls are applying rubbing alcohol with cotton swabs, horticultural soap, and ultrafine horticultural oil.*

Beetles. Beetles and weevils belong to a group called *Coleoptera.* Weevils, or curculios, are beetles that have jaws at the end of long snouts. Some have a larval stage that feeds on plants. An example is the black vine weevil, which is most destructive to garden plants. Many other species of beetles, including the June beetle and the rose chafer, affect garden plants. The Japanese beetle, a metallic green and coppery maroon insect, is one of the most destructive pests east of the Mississippi. They chew the leaves and stems of some 200 species of perennials, ruin roses, basil, and other favorites, completely devouring those they like. The grub stage is devastating to lawns and gardens. Grub-proofing lawns and gardens reduces the population already existing in your yard, but does not control those beetles that fly in. *Controls: Japanese beetle traps are effective, providing they are placed far away from the plantings you are trying to protect, not among them. If the infestation is minor, beetles can be picked off by hand. Insecticides containing, neem, rotenone, or Sevin insecticide control many of the negative beetles.*

Bugs. This is a term sometimes used loosely to describe all insects. True bugs belong to the *Hemiptera* family and do their damage by piercing and sucking. Examples are squash bugs, stink bugs, and the tarnished plant bug. *Controls: Products containing Sevin insecticide, or are best, along with Pyrethrin or malathion. These are most effective when the bugs are in an early stage of development.*

Caterpillars. Caterpillars are the immature stage of moths and butterflies. Their mouthparts chew holes in the leaves, stems, and flowers of most everything. Caterpillars may be smooth or fuzzy, and range in size from very small to the huge tomato hornworm. They include leaf rollers and tent makers. Also in this group are other destructive pests such as the gypsy moth and tent caterpillar. *Controls: One of the best ways to get rid of a minor infestation is to pick the critters off by hand. The other way is to spray with a biological control such as Bacillus thuringiensis. Other controls are Sevin or malathion insecticide, Pyrethrin, or rotenone.*

Leafminers. Leafminers can be the larval stage of small flies, moths, and beetles. Over seven hundred kinds of leafminers affect plants in North America. There can be as many as four life cycles in warmer climatic zones. Leafminers burrow between the upper and lower epidermis of the leaf, making irregular serpentine tunnels. *Controls: Spray with a product containing malathion or Pyrethrin. Sprays must be applied before the larvae hatch out and enter the leaf. Once inside, the only effective control is a leaf systemic insecticide. An alternative is to cut off the affected foliage; columbine and some plants affected by leafminers generally grow back healthy.*

Mealybugs. Mealybugs are one-eighth of an inch long and have a mealy, waxy covering. They lay eggs on the undersides of leaves and affect stems, roots, and foliage. Like aphids, they exude honeydew. The presence of sooty mold is an indicator that mealybugs, aphids, or soft scale are present. Mealybugs affect a wide range of hosts, including ferns, ficus, and African violets. *Controls: Lady beetles are a predator control and are available from biological companies. Spraying with horticultural soaps and ultra-fine horticultural oils controls mealybugs.*

Scales. Soft and hard scales have piercing, sucking mouthparts. The crawler stage is mobile. After that the insect becomes stationary. Hard scales resemble tiny oyster shells and occur in great numbers. Soft scales are larger, more cup-shaped, and are especially destructive to houseplants. *Controls: Ultra-fine horticulture oils and horticultural soaps are effective controls.*

Whiteflies. These tiny whiteflies erupt into clouds of insects when the plant is touched, and then settle back. Their piercing, sucking mouthparts stunt and yellow the host plant. Sooty mold may follow. *Controls: The most effective control is to spray four times with an insecticide, five to seven days apart. Ultra-fine horticultural oil or insecticidal soaps may be used. Pyrethrin and malathion are also effective. The undersides are where whiteflies cling, so be sure to spray there most thoroughly. Insecticidal soap can handle small infestations. For persistent infestations, use insecticides based on seeds of the neem tree.*

BOTANICAL AND NATURAL CONTROLS FOR COMMON INSECT PESTS AND DISEASES

Copper. Use fungicidal formulations. *Use to control: Blackspot, peach leaf curl, powdery mildew, rusts, and bacterial diseases such as fire blight, bacterial leaf spots, and wilt.*

Crab Shells. Crab shells (Chitin) is the crushed shells of crabs, crab meal. A source of nitrogen must be provided, such as dried blood or cottonseed meal. *Use to control: Harmful nematodes. Apply crab meal at the rate of 5 pounds per 100 square feet.*

Diatomaceous earth. This is a powdery substance mined from fossilized silica shells that are the remains of an algae. Physical contact destroys soft-bodied insects. Rain and high humidity may render it less ineffective. *Use to control: Ants, aphids, caterpillars, cockroaches, leafhoppers, slugs, snails, and thrips.*

Horticultural oils. These are botanical oils sprayed on the egg and immature stages of insects to smother them. *Use to control: Woolly adelgids (which do so much damage to Canadian*

Pests, Diseases, & Controls

hemlocks), aphids, cankerworms, leafhoppers, leaf rollers, mealybugs, mites, psylids, scale, tent caterpillars, webworms. **Note:** *Spraying with horticultural oils can temporarily remove the blue in blue hostas and Colorado blue spruce. Never spray during droughts, and always water deeply before applying.*

Horticultural soaps. This control dates back to the late 1800s. *Use to control: Soft bodied insects such as aphids, fruit flies, fungus gnats, lacebugs, leafhoppers, mealybugs, phyllids, scale, scale crawlers, spittle bug, thrips, whiteflies.* **Note:** *Water deeply before using. Do not use on plants under stress, especially drought. Do not use plants you have just set out, nor on delicate plants such as ferns and lantana.*

Neem. These products are derivatives of various parts of the neem tree, *Azadirachta indica*. Neem is a broad-spectrum repellent, growth regulator, feeding inhibitor, contact insect poison, and is partial systemic. The most effective formulation is made from the extract of the neem seed. It also controls certain diseases. *Use to control: Aphids, leafminers, gypsy moths, loopers, mealybugs, thrips, mites, crickets, mosquitoes, face flies, flea beetles.*

Pyrethrin. This is an extract of the flowers of *Chrysanthemum cinerariifolium*. *Use to control: Many piercing, sucking and chewing insects, such as ants, aphids, beetles, cockroaches, coddling moths, grasshoppers, Japanese beetles, leafhoppers, leafminers, loopers, Mexican bean and potato beetles, spider mites, stink bugs, ticks, thrips, weevils, whiteflies.*

Rotenone. Rotenone is a very old botanical pesticide, first used in the mid-1800s. It is prepared from the roots of the tropical plant *Lonchocarpus. Use to control: Aphids, beetles, caterpillars, Colorado potato beetle, thrips.*

Ryania. This is a powdered extract from the roots and stems of the South American shrub, *Ryania speciosa. Use to control: Caterpillars, corn earworms, European corn borer, leaf beetles, thrip.*

Sabadilla. Sabadilla is made from the grinding of the seeds of the Sabadilla plant. *Use to control: True bugs, caterpillars, Mexican bean beetle, thrips.*

Sulfur. This is a mined mineral. *Use to control: Blackspot, leaf spot, mites, powdery mildew, rusts, and other plant diseases.*

Ultra-fine horticultural oils. These are dense refined oils, some based on petroleum and others on vegetables such as cottonseed and soybeans. Sprayed on, they smother insects in the egg and immature stages, and they control certain diseases. *Use to control: Blackspot, mildew, and certain insects including adelgids, aphids, leafhoppers, mealybugs, mites, scale.* **Note**: *A Cornell University control for mildew is to spray with a solution consisting of 1 tablespoon of ultrafine oil and 1 tablespoon of baking soda (soda bicarbonate) dissolved in 1 gallon of water.*

CHEMICAL CONTROLS FOR COMMON INSECT PESTS AND DISEASES

Carbaryl (Sevin). *Use to control: Beetles, caterpillars, Japanese beetles, mealybug, thrip.*

Mancozeb, manzate. *Use to control: Fungal diseases (especially rust on asters and hollyhocks), anthracnose, botrytis blight.*

Sevin (see Carbaryl).

Malathion. *Use to control: Aphids, beetles, leafhopper, leafminer, mealybug, spider mites, thrips, whitefly.*

Parzate (see Mancozeb, Manzate).

Permethrin. *Use to control: A wide range of insects, including whitefly.*

COMMON NON-INSECT PESTS AND CONTROLS

Nematodes. Nematodes are microscopic worm-like creatures. Some feed on roots, others feed on foliage. Endoparasitic nematodes enter the root, causing galls. An example is root-knot nematode. Others are cyst nematodes, such as the golden nematode of potatoes. There are ectoparasitic forms that feed on the outside of the roots. Symptoms are a yellowing and stunting of the plant, lack of vigor, and wilting during hot weather. *Controls: Growing orange French marigolds for three months and tilling into the soil before planting has been effective. Also effective is the application of ground crab shells, which are commercially available.*

Spider mites. Spider mites are more closely related to spiders than to insects. So tiny you need a magnifying glass to see them, spider mites can attack all parts of a plant but are most prevalent under the leaf. These piercing, sucking pests cause a yellowing of the plant, and finally result in a rusty and sometimes silvery look to the leaf. For a positive identification shake the plant onto a white pad, and if little dots move on the paper, you have spider mites. Roses, indoor plants in hot dry conditions, and evergreens in dry airless corners, are especially susceptible. *Control: Hosing the plant down regularly discourages spider mite activity. Insecticidal soaps, ultrafine horticultural oils, and miticides can be used.*

Slugs and snails. These plant pests feed on lush foliage, leaving holes in the leaf. Irregular shiny, slimy trails are a telltale sign. Complete defoliation can occur on some lush-leaved annuals and perennials, hostas, for example. *Control: Diatomaceous earth, iron phosphate (Sluggo), slug and snail bait, beer in shallow aluminum plates or tuna fish cans, or commercially available traps.*

COMMON DISEASES AND CONTROLS

Bacterial disease. Bacteria is not a fungus, and although the symptoms may be similar, in order to control the causative agent, you must use a bacteriacide such as copper fungicide. *Controls: Copper fungicide, Kocide 101, Agri-Strep.*

Botrytis grey mold (Botrytis Blight). Symptoms are a grayish-to-brown powdery covering on buds, leaves, and stems. This disease affects many perennials, including peonies. *Controls: Sulfur, Daconil 2728.*

Foliar diseases. Symptoms are leaf spots and blight on perennials that can be bacterial or fungal in origin. *Controls: Sulfur, copper fungicides, Daconil, Mancozeb, Immunox.*

Leaf spots. Most gardeners encounter this as blackspot. Leaf spots can be caused by a bacterial or fungal agent. Examples are blackspot of roses and leaf spot on tall bearded iris. *Controls: Copper fungicide, Daconil, horticultural oil, Immunox, sulfur.*

Powdery mildew. This fungus covers buds, stems, and leaves with a white-gray powdery substance. High humidity increases the severity of powdery mildew. If you water often with underground sprinkling systems you may find this disease difficult to control. Powdery mildew is commonly found on asters, monarda, and phlox. *Controls: If it appears in your garden, when buying new plants, go for those advertised as mildew resistant. Roses, phlox, lilacs, and many other garden favorites are susceptible. Wide spacing for good air circulation and air movement helps. Apply sulfur, ultrafine horticultural oil, copper fungicide, Immunox, Bayleton.*

Root and stem rot. Symptoms are the wilting and rapid death of the plant. The crown or rhizome of the plant may be wet or slimy. The cause may be bacterial or fungal. *Controls: For fungal causes, use Terrachlor or Mancozeb. For bacterial causes, use copper fungicides, Kocide 101, Agri-Strep.*

Rust disease. This form of fungus may be a single or double host disease. The first indication is yellow or pale spots on the upper surface of the leaf, with powdery orange spores visible on the bottom of the leaf. Asters, chrysanthemums, lily-of-the-valley, and hollyhocks are many common hosts. *Controls: Any fungicidal control labeled for rust. Also, sulfur, copper fungicide, Daconil, Immunox, Mancozeb.*

Viral diseases. These diseases are not fungal or bacterial in origin, but in fact are particles of protein and genetic material, so small that an electron microscope is needed to see the virus. Piercing sucking insects commonly spread viral diseases. Viral diseases may be difficult to diagnose and there is no known control. Symptoms are a mottling or mosaic discoloration of the leaf or ring spots. *Control: No known control except removing the infected plant.*

COMMON ANIMAL PESTS AND CONTROLS

Deer. The most destructive of all the wild creatures that visit our gardens is the deer. New repellents for deer come on the market every season, but at this writing we know of none that has proven to be a *permanent* deterrent.

When deer really want what you've got, they come on in and get it in spite of flashing lights, jets of water, ultra sound devices, evil smelling egg and protein sprays, predator odors, bitter Bitrex, hot pepper wax, garlic, and systemic repellants. Deer-Off® can be used on fruits and vegetables as well as flowers, trees, and shrubs. Tested by Rutgers University, it lasted for up to three months. Some nurseries successfully protect clients' plants with their own deterrent sprays and may sell you their version. Some gardeners have luck by hanging old pantyhose containing human or canine hair around the property. However, most deterrents of this type fail to keep deer away once they get used to it. Here are approaches that have some effect:

• *Don't invite deer by planting Class A fatal attractions:* Apple or pear trees. If you have fruit trees, be sure to harvest the fruits daily before the deer get to them. Arborvitae, rhododendrons, and broadleaved evergreens are winter favorites, along with shrub althea and hydrangeas. Hostas and other big, lush leaved plants, phlox, 'Autumn Joy', and other Sedum spectabile varieties, tomatoes, peas, beans, and other leafy vegetables, are summer favorites. Roses, raspberries, and other members of the *Rosa* family—deer relish them all.

• *Protect small endangered plantings,* beds of hostas and daylilies for example, by screening them with enclosures of deer fencing or chickenwire supported by wooden or metal stakes. Deer generally avoid small, enclosed spaces that could be traps. Protect large plantings with bird netting.

• *Enclose your property or gardens with a single strand of electric wire 30 inches high* with a stake every 20 feet and baited with peanut butter can be effective. Close the peanut butter into a square of tinfoil, and crimp it on to the wire every 20 feet. The deer nibble the peanut butter and, without being really hurt, learn to avoid the fence.

• *Enclose your property with a deer fence 8 to 10 feet high* supported by a post every 40 feet. This high tensile steel fencing is unobtrusive.

• *Train a dog* to run deer off your property without leaving it.

• *Discourage visits by positioning a variety of alarming and distasteful smells* where deer customarily enter your grounds, and change the smells often. For example, hang at the height of a deer's nose tubes of crushed garlic, or predator urine, or Irish Spring or lavender soap, or human hair dampened with odorous

lotions. Place a different scent at each entry point. And, *this is crucial,* change each deterrent every four to six weeks while the weather is warm enough to volatilize scents.

• *For winter, wrap rhododendrons, arborvitae, and other species that deer love in burlap or chickenwire.*

• *Choose new plants from those on the list of deer-resistant plants* at André and Mark Viette's site, www.inthegardenradio.com.

Moles and Voles. You think "moles" when you see tunnels heaving the lawn, and blame them when perennials disappear and bulbs move around. But they are innocent. Moles eat bugs, grubs, and worms only. The culprits are voles, *Nicrotus* species. Often called pine and meadow mice, these small rodents are reddish-brown to gray, 2 to 4 inches long, and have short tails, blunt faces, tiny eyes and ears. They live in extensive tunnel systems usually less than a foot deep with entrances an inch or two across.

Protecting the plant is easier than getting rid of voles. They dislike tunneling through coarse material. André keeps them away by planting with VoleBloc or PermaTill, which are bits of nontoxic, light, long-lasting aggregates like pea gravel with jagged edges. The stuff promotes rooting.

Established plantings: Dig a 4-inch wide, 12-inch deep moat around the drip line of perennials under attack, and fill it with VoleBloc, and mulch with VoleBloc.

New plantings: Prepare a planting hole 2 inches deeper than the rootball(s), and layer in 2 inches of VoleBloc. Set the rootball in place, and backfill with VoleBloc. Mulch with more VoleBloc.

If vole damage appears in winter, bait the main area around the plants with a rodenticide, and pull the mulch apart, spray the crown lightly with a repellent, and put the mulch back in place.

Bears. Where bears may be a problem, they may come to bird and hummingbird feeders. They harvest berries and sometimes your pets. If there are bear sightings near you, take in bird feeders and other attractions.

Birds. Our feathered friends are beautiful, lovable, inspiring, and useful in that they eat insects, some good and some bad. They also eat berries and fruit, your kind as well as theirs; seeds you give them and seeds you don't; and sunflowers.

• A bird mesh cover is the almost only way to protect fruit birds want to eat.

• Cover ponds with bird netting to keep the fish safe from herons and other expert fishermen.

Rabbits, woodchucks, raccoons, and other rodents.

• Try chemical fungicide formulations such as Thiram (Arasan) and hot pepper wax.

• Fence gardens with 6 feet high chickenwire that starts 24 inches underground. If you have woodchucks to deal with, leave the chickenwire loose and floppy, not stiff enough to climb. Keeping raccoons out of the vegetable garden requires enclosing your garden overhead as well; keeping them from fishing in your water garden may require covering the pond with netting.

Public Gardens & Resources

ROSE GARDENS

Delaware
Hagley Museum and Library
298 Buck Road East
P. O. Box 3630
Wilmington, Delaware 19807
Phone: 302 658 2400

District of Columbia
Dumbarton Oaks
1703 32nd Street NW
Washington, D. C. 20052
Phone: 202 339 6401

The George Washington University
2033 G Street NW and 730 21st Street
Washington, D. C. 20052
Phone: 202 994 4949

United States Botanic Garden
245 First Street SW
Washington, D. C. 20052
Phone: 202 225 8333

Maryland
**Brookside Botanical Gardens
    Rose Garden**
1500 Glenallen Avenue
Wheaton, Maryland 20902
Phone: 301 495 2503

Ladew Topiary Gardens
3535 Jarrettsville Pike
Monkton, Maryland 21111
Phone: 410 557 9466

**Maryland Rose Society Heritage
Rose Garden**
The Clyburn Arboretum
4915 Greenspring Avenue
Baltimore, Maryland 21209
Phone: 410 396 0180

William Paca Garden
1 Martin Street
Annapolis, Maryland 21401
Phone: 410 263 5553

Virginia
Bon Air Memorial Rose Garden
Bon Air Park
850 North Lexington Street
Arlington, Virginia 22205
Phone: 703 228 6525

Confederate Cemetery
401 Taylor Street
Lynchburg, Virginia 24501
Phone: 434 847 1465

**Norfolk Botanical Garden
Bicentennial Rose Garden**
6700 Azalea Garden Road
Norfolk, Virginia 23519-5337

**River Farm—American
Horticulture Society**
7931 E. Boulevard Drive
Alexandria, Virginia 22308
Phone: 703 768 5700 or
    1 800 777 7931

Woodlawn Plantation
9000 Richland Highway,
Alexandria, VA 22309
Phone: 703 780 4000

PUBLIC GARDENS

Delaware
**Hagley Museum's E. I. Du Pont
Restored Garden**
298 Buck Road East
P. O. Box 3630
Wilmington, Delaware 19807
Phone: 302 658 2400

**Mount Cuba Center for the Study of
Piedmont Flora**
Barley Hill Road
Greenville, DE 19807
Phone: 302 239 4244

Nemours Mansion and Gardens
1600 Rockland Road
Wilmington, DE 19803
Phone: 302 651 6912

District of Columbia
Bishop's Garden
Washington National Cathedral
Massachusetts & Wisconsin
    Avenues, NW
Washington, DC 20016
Phone: 202 537 2937

Dumbarton Oaks
1703 32nd Street
Washington, DC 20007
Phone: 202 339 6401

Hillwood Museum & Gardens
4155 Linnean Avenue, NW
Washington, DC 20008
Phone: 1 877 HILLWOOD

**United States Botanic Garden
and Conservatory**
245 First Street SW
Washington, DC 20024
Phone: 202 225 8333

United States National Arboretum
3501 New York Avenue, NE
Washington, DC 20002
Phone: 202 245 2726

The George Washington University
2033 G Street and 730 21st
    Street NW
Washington, D. C. 20052
Phone: 202 994 4949

Maryland
**Clyburn Wildflower Preserve and
Garden Center**
4915 Greenspring Avenue
Baltimore, MD 21209
Phone: 410 396 0180

Brookside Gardens
1500 Glenallan Avenue
Wheaton, MD 20920
Phone: 301 949 8230

Ladew Topiary Gardens
3535 Jarretsville Pike
Monkton, MD 21111
Phone: 410 557 9570

McCrillis Gardens
6910 Greentree Road
Bethesda, MD 20817
Phone: 301 365 5728

William Paca Garden
186 Prince George Street
Annapolis, MD 21401
Phone: 410 263 5553

Virginia
André Viette Farm & Nursery
994 Long Headow Road
P O Box 1109
Fishersville, VA 22939
Phone: 800 575 5538
www.inthegardenradio.com

Public Gardens & Resources

Ashcroft Hall
4305 Sulgrave Road
Richmond, VA 23221
Phone: 804 353 4241

Colonial Williamsburg Foundation
PO Box C, Horticulture Department
Williamsburg, VA 23187
Phone: 804 229 1000

Community Arboretum at Virginia Western Community College
Colonial Avenue
Roanoke, VA 24014
www.vw.vccs.edu/arboretum

Green Spring Gardens Park
4603 Green Spring Road
Alexandria, VA 22312
Phone: 703 642 5173

Gunston Hall
10708 Gunston Road
Lorton, VA 22079
Phone: 703 550 9220

Kenmore
1201 Washington Avenue
Fredericksburg, VA 22401
Phone: 540 373 3381

Lewis Ginter Botanical Garden
1800 Lakeside Avenue
Richmond, VA 23228-4700
Phone: 804 262 9887

Maymont
1700 Hampton Street
Richmond, VA 23220
Phone: 804 358 7166

Monticello
Thomas Jefferson Foundation
PO VA 53
Charlottesville, VA 22902
Phone: 804 984 9822

Montpelier Gardens
James Madison's Home
11407 Constitution Highway
Montpelier Station, VA 22957
Phone: 540 672 2728

Mount Vernon Estate & Gardens
South End of George Washington
    Memorial Parkway
Mount Vernon, VA 22121
Phone: 703 780 2000

Norfolk Botanical Garden
Airport Road off of Azalea Garden Rd
Norfolk, VA 23518
Phone: 804 441 5830

Oatlands Plantation
200850 Oatlands Plantation Ln. US 15
Leesburg, VA 20175
Phone: 703 777 3174

River Farm
American Horticultural Society
7931 East Boulevard Drive
Alexandria, VA 22308
Phone: 703 768 5700

Virginia House
4301 Sulgrave Road
Richmond, VA 23221
Phone: 804 353 4251

Rose Organizations
American Rose Society
P. O. Box 30000
Shreveport, Louisiana 71130-0030
Phone: 318-938-5402
For local rose societies
web site: www.ars.org
E-mail: ara@ara-hq.org

District Rose Societies
Colonial District
Delaware, Maryland, Virginia,
    Washington, D. C.
Nita Bowen
2703 Pony Farm Court
Oakton, VA 22124

Mail-Order Sources for Natural Controls For Pests and Diseases

Earlee, Inc.
2002 Highway 62
Jeffersin, IN 47130
Phone: 812 282 9134

Gardens Alive!
5100 Schenley Place
Lawrenceburg, IN 47025
Phone: 513 656 1482

Natural Gardening Company
217 San Anselmo Avenue
San Anselmo, CA 94960
Phone: 707 766 9303

Nature's Control
PO Box 35
Medford, OR 97501
Phone: 503 899 8318

Peaceful Valley Farm Supply
PO Box 2209
Grass Valley, CA 95945
Phone: 916 272 4769

Safer, Inc.
9959 Valley View Road
Eden Prairie, MN 55344
Phone: 800 423 7544

Nurseries with Good Plant Selections
Behnke Nurseries
11300 Baltimore Avenue
Beltsville, MD 20705
Phone: 301 937 1100

Homestead Gardens
Route 214
743 West Central Avenue
Davidsonville, MD 21035
Phone: 800 300 5631

Merrifield Garden Center
12100 Lee Highway
Fairfax, VA 22030
Phone: 703 968 9600

Merrifield Garden Center
8132 Lee Highway
Merrifield, VA 22116
Phone: 703 560 6222

Mail-Order Sources for Perennials, Daylilies, Peonies, Irises, Hostas, and Grasses

André Viette Farm & Nursery
994 Long Headow Road
P O Box 1109
Fishersville, VA 22939
Phone: 800 575 5538

Bluestone Perennials
7211 Middle Ridge Road
Madison, OH 44057
Phone: 800 852 5243

Borbeleta Gardens
15974 Canby Avenue
Faribault, MN 55021
Phone: 507 334 2807

Public Gardens & Resources

Caprice Farm Nursery
10944 Mill Greek Road SE
Aumsville, OR 97325
Phone: 503 749 1397

Kuk's Forest Nursery
10174 Barr Road
Brecksville, OH 44141-3302
Phone: 216 546 2675

Kurt Bluemel Inc.
22740 Greene Lane
Baldwin, MD 21013
Phone: 800 248 7584

Mellinger's Inc.
2310 W South Range Road
North Lima, OH 44452-9731
Phone: 800 321 7444

Milaeger's Gardens
4838 Douglas Avenue
Racine, WI 53402-2498
Phone: 800 669 1229

Plant Delights Nursery Inc.
9241 Sauls Road
Raleigh, NC 27603
Phone: 919 772 4794

Prairie Nursery—Wild Flowers
P O Box 306
Westfield, WI 53964
Phone: 800 476 9453

Roslyn Nursery
21 1 Burrs Lane
Dix Hills, NY 11746
Phone: 516 643 9347

The Fragrant Path
P O Box 328
Fort Calhoun, NE 68023
Send $2 for a catalogue

Thomas Jefferson Center for Historic Plants
RD Box 316
Charlottesville, VA 22092
Phone: 800 247 7333

K. Van Bourgondien & Sons
245 Route 109, RD. Box 1 000
Babylon, NY 11702-9004
Phone: 800 552 9916

White Flower Farm
P O Box 50
Litchfield, CT 06759-0050
Phone: 800 503 9624

Mail-Order Sources
for Flowers, Annuals, Perennials, Wildflowers, Vegetables, Herbs, Rare and Antique Seeds

W. Atlee Burpee & Co.
300 Park Avenue
Warminster, PA 18991
Phone: 800 888 1447

Franklin Hill Garden Seeds
2430 Rochester Road
Sewickley, PA 15143-8667
Phone: 412 367 6202

Gurney's Seed & Nursery Co
110 Capital Street
Yankton, SD 57079
Phone: 605 665 1930

Harris Seeds
60 Saginaw Drive
RO. Box 22960
Rochester, NY 14692-2960
Phone: 716 442 0410

Johnny's Selected Seeds
955 Benton Avenue
Winslow, ME 04901-2601
Phone: 207 861 3900

Nichols Garden Nursery
1190 N. Pacific Highway
Albany, OR 97321
Phone: 541 928 9280

Park Seed
1 Parkton Avenue
Greenwood, SC 29647
Phone: 800 845 3369

Pinetree Garden Seeds
P O Box 300
New Gloucester, ME 04260
Phone: 207 926 3400

Primrose Path
921 Scottsdale-Dawson Road
Scottsdale, PA 15683

Seeds of Change Heirloom Seeds
P O Box 15700
Santa Fe, NM 87506
Phone: 888 762 7333

Seeds of Distinction
P O Box 86
Toronto, Canada M9C 4V2
Phone: 416 255 3060

Select Seeds
180 Stickney Hill Road
Union, CT 06076
Phone: 860 684 9310

Seymour's Selected Seeds
PO Box 1346
Sussex, VA 23884-0346
Phone: 803 663 3084

Shepherd's Garden Seeds
30 Irene Street
Torrington, CT 06790
Phone: 800 482 3638

R H Shumway Seedsman
P O Box 1
Graniteville, SC 29829
Phone: 803 663 9771

Southern Exposure Seed Exchange
PO Box 460
Mineral, VA 23117
Phone: 540 894 9480

Stokes Seeds Inc.
P O Box 548
Buffalo, NY 14240
Phone: 800 263 7233

Thompson & Morgan Inc.
P O Box 1308
Jackson, NJ 08527
Phone: 800 274 7333

Wildseed Farms
P O Box 3000
Fredericksburg, TX 78624
Phone: 800 848 0078

Mail-Order Sources for Tender
Perennials, Annuals, Tropicals, Houseplants, Bromeliads, Bougainvilleas, Cactus, Orchids, Pineapples, Begonias, Gesneriads, and African Violets

Banana Tree, Inc.
715 Northampton Street
Easton, PA 18042
Phone: 610 253 9589

Davidson-Wilson Greenhouse, Inc.
RR2, Box 168
Crawfordsville, IN 47933
Phone: 317 364 0556

Public Gardens & Resources

Glasshouse Works
Church Street
Stewart, OH 45778
Phone: 614 662 2142

Going Bananas
24401 SW 197 Avenue
Homestead, FL 33031
Phone: 305 247 0397

Good Scents
RR2, P O Box 168
Crawfordsville, IN 47933
Phone: 765 364 0556

Kartuz Greenhouse
P O Box 790
Vista, CA 92085
Phone: 760 941 3613

Lauray of Salisbury
493 Undermountain Road, RT 41
Salisbury, CT 06068
Phone: 860 435 2263

Logee's Greenhouse, Ltd
141 North Street
Danielson, CT 06239
Phone: 860 774 8038

Lyndon Lyon Greenhouse, Inc.
P O Box 249
Dolgeville, NY 13329
Phone: 315 429 8291

Stokes Tropicals
P O Box 9868
New Iberia, LA 70562
Phone: 800 624 9706

Sunshine State Tropcials
6329 Alaska Avenue
New Port Richey, FL 34653
Phone: 813 841 9618

Mail-Order Sources for Roses

Chamblee's Rose Nursery
10926 US Highway 69 North
Tyler, TX 75706-8742
Phone: 800 256 7673

David Austin Roses Limited
15059 Highway 64 West
Tyler, TX 75704
Phone: 800 328 8893

Edmund's Roses
6235 SW Kahle Road
Wilsonville, OR 97070-9727
Phone: 888 481 7673

Hardy Roses for the North
Box 2048
Grand Forks, BC Canada VOH 1HO
Phone: 604 442 8442

Heirloom Old Garden Roses
24062 NE Riverside Drive
St Paul, OR 97137
Phone: 503 538 1576

High Country Roses
P O Box 148
Jensen, UT 84035-0148
Phone: 800 552 2082

Historical Roses
1657 W Jackson Street
Painesville, OH 44077
Phone: 216 357 7270

Jackson & Perkins Co.
1 Rose Lane
Medford, OR 97501-0702
Phone: 800 292 4769

Lowe's Own-Root Roses
6 Sheffield Road
Nashua, NH 03062
Phone: 603 888 2214

Meilland Star Roses
P O Box 249
Cutler, CA 93615
Phone: 800 457 1859

Nor'East Minature Roses, Inc.
P O Box 307
Rowley, MA 01969-0607
Phone: 800 426 6485

The Antique Roses Emporium
9300 Lueckemeyer Road
Brenham, TX 77833
Phone: 800 441 0002

Mail-Order Sources for Trees, Shrubs, and Evergreens

Arborvillage Farm Nursery
15604 County Road CC
Holt, MO 64048
Phone: 516 643 9347

Arrowhead Nursery
5030 Watia Road
Bryson City, NC 28713
Phone: 440 466 2881

Camellia Forest Nursery
125 Carolina Forest Road
Chapel Hill, NC 27516
Phone: 919 968 0504

Collector's Nursery
16804 NE 102nd Avenue
Battle Ground, WA 98604
Phone: 706 356 8947

Fairweather Gardens
P O Box 330
Greenwich, NJ 08323
Phone: 800 548 0111

Forest Farm
990 Tetherow Road
Williams, OE 97544
Phone: 503 543 7474

Foxborough Nursery Inc.
3611 Miller Road
Street, MD 21154
Phone: 360 574 3832

Girard Nurseries
P O Box 428
Geneva, OH 44041
Phone: 919 967 5529

Greer Gardens
1280 Goodpasture Island Road
Eugene, OR 97401
Phone: 609 451 6261

Porterhowse Farms
41370 SE Thomas Road
Sandy, OR 97055
Phone: 409 826 6363

Roslyn Nursery
211 Burrs Lane
Dix Hills, NY 11746
Phone: 541 846 7269

Wayside Gardens
1 Garden Lane
Hodges, SC 29695
Phone: 800 845 1124

Mail-Order Sources for Water Plants and Ponds

Lilypons Water Gardens
6800 Lilypons Road
Buckeystown, MD 21717
Phone: 800 999 5459

Gilberg Farms
2172 Highway O
Robertsville, MO 63072
Phone: 636 451 2530

Springdale Water Gardens
P O Box 546
Greenville, VA 24440-0546
Phone: 800 420 5459

Bibliography

A Garden of Herbs, Eleanor Sinclair Rohde

A-Z of Annuals, Biennials & Bulbs, Reader's Digest

The American Horticultural Society A - Z Encyclopedia of Garden Plants, Christopher Bricknell and Judith D. Zuk

The American Horticultural Society Flower Finder, Jacqueline Hériteau and André Viette

America's Garden Book, Brooklyn Botanic Garden, Howard S. Irwin

André Viette Gardening Guide, Viette Staff

Annuals 1001 Gardening Questions Answered, Editors of GardenWay Publishing

Annuals & Bedding Plants, Nigel Colborn, Trafalgar Square Publishing

Annuals for the Connoisseur, A-Z Horticulture

Annuals, Sunset Publishing Corp.

Armitage's Manual of Annuals, Biennials, and Half-Hardy Perennials, Allan M. Armitage

Botanica, R. G. Turner, Jr.

The Brooklyn Botanical Garden: America's Landscaping Book, Louise and James Bush Brown and Howard Erwin

The Brooklyn Botanical Garden Illustrated Encyclopedia of Horticulture Volumes A-Z, Thomas H. Everett

Burpee, America Gardening Series, Annuals, Suzanne Fruitig Bales

Cathey Wilkinson Barash's Edible Flowers, Cathey Wilkinson Barash

Check List of Pyracantha Cultivars, Donald R. Egolf and Ann O. Andrick

The Complete Guide to Texas Lawn Care, Dr. William E. Knoop

Conifers for Your Garden, Adrian Bloom

Designing with Perennials, Pamela J. Harper

Discovering Annuals, Graham Rice, Timber Press

Diseases of Annuals and Perennials, A. R. Chase, Margery L. Daughtrey, Gary W. Simone

Eastern Butterflies, Peterson Field Guides

Easy Care Ground Covers, Donald Wyman

Encyclopedia of Organic Gardening, J. I. Rodale and Staff

The Exotic Garden, Designing with Tropical Plants in Almost Any Climate, Richard R. Iverson

Eyewitness Handbook, Herbs, Lesley Bremness

Eyewitness Handbook, Ornamental Grasses, Mary Hockenberry Meyer

Fern Growers Manual, Barbara Hoshizaki

Ferns And Fern Allies of Shenandoah National Park, Peter F. Mazeo

Ferns of Eastern Central States, Jesse M. Shaner

Ferns to Know And Grow, Gordon Foster

Field Guide to Ferns and Other Pteridophytes of Georgia, James Bruce and Lloyd Snyder

Field Guide to North American Trees, revised (Grolier)

For Your Garden Ornamental Grasses, Rick Darke

The Gardener's Guide to Growing Hardy Geraniums, Trevor Bath and Joy Jones

The Gardener's Guide to Growing Hellebores, Graham Rice and Elizabeth Strangman

The Gardener's Illustrated Encyclopedia of Trees and Shrubs, 2000 Varieties, Brian Davis

Gardening with Climbers, Christopher Grey-Wilson, Victoria Matthews

Gardening with Grasses, Michael King, Piet Oudolf

Gardening with Herbs for Flavor and Fragrance, Helen Morgenthau Fox

Gardening with Perennials Month by Month, Joseph Hudak

Garlic, Onions & Other Alliums, Ellen Spector Platt, Stackpole Books

Genus Hosta, W. George Schmid

Glorious Gardens, Jacqueline Hériteau

Good Housekeeping Illustrated Encyclopedia of Gardening, Hearst Publishing

Growing and Decorating with Grasses, Peter Loewer

Hardy Geraniums, Peter F. Yeo

The Hearst Garden, Annuals, Ted Marston, Editor

Heirloom Flowers, Tovah Martin and Diane Whealy

The Herb Society of America Encyclopedia of Herbs and Their Uses, Deni Brown

Herbaceous Perennial Plants, Allan M. Armitage

Herbaceous Perennials' Diseases and Insect Pests, Margery L. Daughtrey and Morey Semel

Herbaceous Perennials, Volume 2, Leo Jellito, Wilhelm Schacht

Herbs And Things, Jeanne Rose's Herbal

Herbs, Their Culture and Uses, Rosetta E. Clarkson

Hollies: The Genus Index, Fred C. Galle

Hortus Third, Staff of L. H. Bailey Hortorium, Cornell University

The Hosta Book, Paul Aden

Illustrated Encyclopedia of Conifers, Two Volumes, D. M. van Gelderen and J. R. P. van Hoey Smith

Illustrated Encyclopedia Houseplant Identifier, Peter McHoy

Indoor Greenhouse Plants, Volumes 1 & 2, Roger Phillips, Martyn Rix

Index Hortensis, Volume 1 Perennials, including Ground Covers and Ferns, Piers Threhane

Index of Common Garden Plants, Mark Griffiths, RHS

Japanese Iris, Currier McEwen

Jekka's Culinary Herbs, Jekka McVicar

Landscape Plants of the Southeast, R. Gordon Halfacre, Anne R. Shawcroft

Landscape Plants: Their Identification, Culture and Use, Ferrell M. Bridwell

Lawns: Your Guide to a Beautiful Lawn, Nick Christians with Ashton Ritchie

Manual of Cultivated Conifers, P. Den Ouden, Dr. B. K. Boom

The Manual of Woody Landscape Plants, Michael A. Dirr

Michigan Gardener's Guide, Tim Boland, Laura Coit, Marty Hair, Cool Springs Press

Mid-Atlantic Gardener's Guide, André and Mark Viette with Jacqueline Hériteau, Cool Springs Press

Morning Glories and Moonflowers, Anne Halpin

Naamlijist Van Vaste Planten, vander Laar, Fortgens, Hoffman and Jong

National Gardening Association Dictionary of Horticulture, The Philip Lief Group, Inc.

The National Arboretum Book of Outstanding Garden Plants, Jacqueline Hériteau, H. M. Cathey, and the Staff of the National Arboretum

The New York Botanical Garden Illustrated Encyclopedia of Horticulture, Thomas H. Everitt, Volume 10

North Carolina Gardener's Guide, Toby Bost, Cool Springs Press

Ornamental Grass Gardening, Reinardt, Reinardt, and Moskowitz

Ornamental Grasses: The Amber Wave, Carol Ottesen

Ortho's Complete Guide to Vegetables, Jacqueline Hériteau

Pennsylvania Gardener's Guide, Liz Ball, Cool Springs Press

Peonies, Allan Rogers

Perennial Garden Plants, Graham Stuart Thomas

Perennial Ground Covers, David S. MacKenzie, Timber Press

Perennials for American Gardens, Ruth Rogers Clausen and Nicolas Ekstrom

Plants and Their Names, A Concise Dictionary, Roger Hyam and Richard Pankhurst

The Plant Finders Guide to Tender Perennials, Ian Cooke

Plants That Merit Attention, Volume 1, Trees, Janet M. Poor

Poppies, Christopher Grey-Wilson

The Pruning of Trees, Shrubs and Conifers, George E. Brown

Rhododendrons of the World, David G. Leach

Rodale's All-New Encyclopedia of Organic Gardening, Rodale Press

Rose Gardening, Elvin McDonald, Meredith Books

Shrubs and Vines for American Gardens, Donald Wyman

Siberian Iris, Currier McEwen

Southern Living, Annuals and Perennials, Lois Trigg Chaplin, Editor

Tender Perennials, Ian Coors

Tennessee Gardener's Guide, Judy Lowe, Cool Springs Press

Thyme on My Hands, Eric Grissel

Timber Press Dictionary of Plant Names, Allen J. Coombes

The Time-Life Complete Gardener: Perennials, André Viette, Stephen Still

The TriState Gardener's Guide, Ralph Snodsmith

Tropical Flowering Plants, Kristen Albrecht Llamas

Tropical Gardening, Fairchild Tropical Garden

Tropicals, Gordon Covetright

The Vegetable Gardener's Bible, Edward C. Smith, Storey Books

Virginia Ferns & Fern Allies, A. B. Massey

Water Gardens, Charles Thomas and Jacqueline Hériteau

The Well-Tended Perennial Garden, Planting & Pruning Techniques, Tracy DiSabato-Aust

Wyman's Gardening Encyclopedia, Donald Wyman

The Year in Trees, Timber Press

André Viette

Radio host of the weekly three-hour live nationwide call-in radio program "In the Garden," aired every Saturday from 8 to 11 am, a distinguished horticulturist, author, and lecturer, André owns the Viette Farm and Nursery in Fishersville, Virginia, (website: inthegardenradio.com) and is the former owner of the famous Martin Viette Nursery in Long Island, New York. A graduate of the Floriculture School of Cornell University, New York, instructor in horticulture at the Blue Ridge Community College, noted breeder of daylilies, and Past President of the Perennial Plant Association of America, André was honored in 2001 with the PPA Award of Merit for his contribution to the perennial plant industry. He holds the Garden Club of America 1999 Medal of Honor for his outstanding contribution to horticulture, and numerous other awards including Conservation Farmer of the Year. He has served on the Advisory Council of the National Arboretum, the Board of the American Horticultural Society, and is presently on the Board of the Lewis Ginter Botanical Garden and the Edith J. Carrier Arboretum. André is the recipient of the 2004 Liberty Hyde Bailey Award, the highest honor given by the American Horticultural Society.

Mark Viette

Nurseryman, lecturer, and contributor to horticultural journals, horticultural instructor at the Blue Ridge Community College, Mark Viette is alternate host as well as president and general manager of Viette Communications, which produces and distributes the national weekly radio call show, "In The Garden With André Viette." Mark is also director of marketing and sales for the André Viette Farm and Nursery. He holds a BS degree in horticulture from Virginia Tech and has completed five plant-finding trips to Europe and South America in search of exotic perennials to introduce to American home gardens.

Jacqueline Hériteau

Jacqueline (Jacqui) is the author of many noteworthy garden books, including *The National Arboretum Book of Outstanding Garden Plants* and the *Virginia Gardener's Guide*. With André, she co-authored *The American Horticultural Society Flower Finder* and the *Mid-Atlantic Gardener's Guide*. She is a Fellow of the Garden Writers Association of America and her contribution to gardening literature won her the 1990 Communicator of the Year Award from the American Nursery & Landscape Association. Jacqui's most recent book is the *New England Gardener's Guide*, (Cool Springs Press, 2003) co-authored with her daughter Holly Hunter Stonehill.